CHILD LABOUR

A Socio-Legal Perspective

CHILD LABOUR

A Socio-Legal Perspective

V. K. DEWAN

Senior Advocate

Foreword by

VARSHA CHANDRA

Advocate, Delhi High Court

PENTAGON PRESS

CHILD LABOUR: A SOCIO-LEGAL PERSPECTIVE

First Indian Edition: 2009

ISBN 978-81-8274-360-1

Published in India by

PENTAGON PRESS
206, Peacock Lane, Shahpur Jat, New Delhi-110049
Phones: 011-64706243, 26491568
Telefax: 011-26490600
email: rajan@pentagon-press.com
website: www.pentagon-press.com

Printed at New Elegant Printers, New Delhi

CONTENTS

FOREWORD

It gives me great pleasure to write a foreword of the book titled "*Child Labour: A Socio-Legal Perspective*". The editor, Shri V.K. Dewan has provided many new insights to the subject. The most unique feature of this book is that the author has tried to deal with a complex topic pertaining to "Child Labour" by assimilating the international laws along with national laws and various campaigns held for the resolution of the problems of Child Labour globally.

The editor has tried to be comprehensive while dealing with the subject area Child Labour: A Socio-Legal Perspective some related Act have also been added, for greater elaboration of the Indian situation. The editor has taken great pains to arrange the different heading in a systematic order and make it reader firendly. I am really touched with his sincere attempt to cover such as important issue. I am sure that the book will prove a boon to the society especially to the Bar, the Bench and the NGOs, who have been working on the issue of child labour. The public at large will also a benefit from it to a great extent. I congratulate the editor for his efforts.

VARSHA CHANDRA
Advocate, Delhi High Court

PREFACE

This publication titled "Child Labour: A Socio-Legal Perspective" provides readers with a complete overview of the issue both in Indian and global context. It reflects briefly on the contemporary trends in global child labour problem. A comparative analysis of global child labour scenario is presented. Major international child labour laws and related human rights laws to child labour are discussed in detail. A Report on proposed Convention and recommendation prepared by the Committee on Child Labour is dealt. This Encyclopedia also provides readers with selected national laws on child labour and the action plans and programmes being followed for the elimination of child labour problem in India. India's child labour rules and related initiatives are analyzed critically vis-à-vis various attempts being made towards elimination of child labour globally.

About 250 million children between the ages of five and fourteen work in developing countries—at least 120 million on a full time basis. Sixty-one percent of these are in Asia, 32 percent in Africa, and 7 percent in Latin America. Most working children in rural areas are found in agriculture; many children work as domestic labourers; urban children work in trade and services, with fewer in manufacturing and construction. Child labour ranges from four-year-olds tied to rug looms to keep them from running away, to seventeen-year-olds helping out on the family farm. In some cases, a child's work can be helpful to him or her and to the family; working and earning can be a positive experience in a child's growing up. This depends largely on the age of the child, the conditions in which the child works, and whether work prevents the child from going to school. For instance, children making silk thread in India dip their hands into boiling water that burns and blisters them, breath smoke and fumes from machinery, handle dead worms that cause infections, and guide twisting threads that cut their fingers. Denied an education and a normal childhood, some children are confined and beaten, reduced to slavery. Some are denied freedom of movement—the right to leave the workplace and go home to their families. Some are abducted and forced to work. The human rights abuses in these practices are clear and acute. Of nearly 250 million children engaged in child labour around the world, the vast majorities—70 percent, or some 170 million—are working in agriculture. Child agricultural workers frequently work for long hours in scorching heat, haul heavy loads of produce, are exposed to toxic pesticides, and suffer high rates of injury from sharp knives and other dangerous tools. Their work is grueling and harsh, violating their rights to health, education, and protection from work that is hazardous or exploitative. According to the ILO's new report on child labour, the number of children working in agriculture is nearly ten times that of children involved in factory work such as garment manufacturing, carpet-weaving, or soccer-ball stitching. Yet despite their numbers and the difficult nature of their work, children working in agriculture have received little attention compared to child labour in manufacturing for export or children involved in commercial sexual exploitation. Similarly, child domestic workers are nearly invisible among child labourers. They work alone in individual households, hidden from public scrutiny, their lives controlled by their employers. Child domestic workers, nearly all girls, work long hours for little or no pay. Many have no opportunity to go to school, or are forced to drop out because of the demands of their job. They are subject to verbal and physical abuse, and particularly vulnerable to sexual abuse. They may be fired for small infractions, losing not only their jobs, but their place of residence as well. The ILO estimates that more girls work as domestics than in any other form of child labour. Yet they have received little attention and even less protection. Government laws often exclude domestic workers from basic labour rights, labour ministries rarely monitor or investigate conditions of work in private households, and few programs addressing child labour include child domestics.

Child labour is a pervasive problem throughout the world, especially in developing countries. Africa and Asia together account for over 90 percent of total child employment. Child labour is especially prevalent in rural areas where the capacity to enforce minimum age requirements for schooling and work is lacking. Children work for a variety of reasons, the most important being poverty and the induced pressure upon them to escape from this plight. Though children are not well paid, they still serve as major contributors to family income in developing countries. Schooling problems also contribute to child labour, whether it is the inaccessibility of schools or the lack of quality education, which spurs parents to enter their children in more profitable pursuits. Traditional factors such as rigid cultural and social roles in certain countries further limit educational attainment and increase child labour. Working children are the objects of extreme exploitation in terms of toiling for long hours for minimal pay. Their work conditions are especially severe, often not providing the stimulation for proper physical and mental development. Many of these children endure lives of pure deprivation. However, there are problems with the intuitive solution of immediately abolishing child labour to prevent such abuse. First, there is no international agreement defining child labour, making it hard to isolate cases of abuse, let alone abolish them. Second, many children may have to work in order to attend school so abolishing child labour may only hinder their education. Any plan of abolishment depends on schooling. The state could help by making it worthwhile for a child to attend school, whether it is by providing students with nutritional supplements or increasing the quality and usefulness of obtaining an education. There must be an economic change in the condition of a struggling family to free a child from the responsibility of working. Family subsidies can help provide this support.

The 1959 Declaration on the Rights of the Child was the first United Nations statement devoted exclusively to the rights of children, but served more as a moral rather than legally binding framework. The special plight of girls was addressed in part by the Convention on the Elimination of All Forms of Discrimination Against Women, adopted in 1979. The Working Group on Contemporary Forms of Slavery annually addresses such issues as child labour and debt bondage. It took until the 1990s, however, for all of the pieces to come together in the form of the Convention on the Rights of the Child, which was adopted by the General Assembly in 1989. The Convention's 54 articles cover everything from a child's right to be free from sexual and economic exploitation, to the right to his or her own opinion, and to the right to education, health care, and economic opportunity. By September 1995, 178 countries had ratified the Convention. A dozen more, some of which had been created since the Convention was adopted six years earlier, were considering it. The International Covenant on Civil and Political Rights (ICCPR) states, "Every child shall have . . . the right to such measures of protection as are required by his status as a minor, on the part of his family, society and the State." The Convention on the Rights of the Child provides that children-all persons under eighteen "unless under the law applicable to the child, majority is attained earlier"-have a right "to be protected from performing any work that is likely to be hazardous or to interfere with the child's education, or to be harmful to the child's health or physical, mental, spiritual, moral or social development." All states parties to the Convention—every government in the world except for the United States and Somalia—are required to "undertake all appropriate legislative, administrative, and other measures for the implementation of the rights recognized in this Convention." Bonded labour is outlawed by the 1956 U.N. Supplementary Convention on the Abolition of Slavery, the Slave Trade, and Institutions and Practices Similar to Slavery.

In India, the problem of child labour continues to pose a challenge before the nation. Government has been taking various pro-active measures to tackle this problem. However, considering the magnitude and extent of the problem and that it is essentially a socio-economic problem inextricably linked to poverty and illiteracy, it requires concerted efforts from all sections of the society to make a dent in the problem. Way back in 1979, Government formed the first committee called Gurupadswamy Committee to study the issue of child labour and to suggest measures to tackle it. The Committee examined the problem in detail and made some far-reaching recommendations. It observed that as long as poverty continued, it would be difficult to totally eliminate child labour and hence, any attempt to abolish it through legal recourse would not be a practical proposition. The Committee felt that in the circumstances, the only alternative left was to ban child labour in hazardous areas and to regulate and ameliorate the conditions of work in other areas. It recommended that a multiple policy approach was required in dealing with the problems of working children. Based on the recommendations of Gurupadaswamy Committee, the Child Labour (Prohibition & Regulation) Act was enacted in 1986. The Act prohibits employment of children in certain specified hazardous occupations and processes and regulates the working conditions in others. The list of hazardous occupations and processes is progressively being expanded on the recommendation of Child Labour Technical Advisory Committee constituted under the Act. In consonance with the above approach, a National Policy on Child Labour was formulated in 1987. The Policy seeks to adopt a gradual and sequential approach with a focus on rehabilitation of children working in hazardous occupations and processes in the first instance. The Action Plan outlined in the Policy for tackling this problem is as follows:

- Legislative Action Plan for strict enforcement of Child Labour Act and other labour laws to ensure that children are not employed in hazardous employments, and that the working conditions of children working in non-hazardous areas are regulated in accordance with the provisions of the Child Labour Act. It also entails further identification of additional occupations and processes, which are detrimental to the health and safety of the children.
- Focusing of General Developmental Programmes for Benefiting Child Labour—As poverty is the root cause of child labour, the action plan emphasizes the need to cover these children and their families also under various poverty alleviation and employment generation schemes of the Government.
- Project Based Plan of Action envisages starting of projects in areas of high concentration of child labour. Pursuant to this, in 1988, the National Child Labour Project (NCLP) Scheme was launched in 9 districts of high child labour endemicity in the country. The Scheme envisages running of special schools for child labour withdrawn from work. In the special schools, these children are provided formal/non-formal education along with vocational training, a stipend of Rs.100 per month, supplementary nutrition and regular health check ups so as to prepare them to join regular mainstream schools. Under the Scheme, funds are given to the District Collectors for running special schools for child labour. Most of these schools are run by the NGOs in the district.

Government has accordingly been taking proactive steps to tackle this problem through strict enforcement of legislative provisions along with simultaneous rehabilitative measures. State Governments, which are the appropriate implementing authorities, have been conducting regular inspections and raids to detect cases of violations. Since poverty is the root cause of this problem, and enforcement alone cannot help solve it, Government has been laying a lot of emphasis on the rehabilitation of these children and on improving the economic conditions of their families. The coverage of the NCLP Scheme has increased from 12 districts in 1988 to 100 districts in the 9th Plan to 250 districts during the 10th Plan. An evaluation of the Scheme was carried out by independent agencies in coordination with V. V. Giri National Labour Institute in 2001. Based on the recommendations of the evaluation and experience of implementing the scheme since 1988, the strategy for implementing the scheme during the 10th Plan was devised. It aimed at greater convergence with the other developmental schemes and bringing qualitative changes in the Scheme. Some of the salient points of the 10th Plan Strategy are as follows:

- Focused and reinforced action to eliminate child labour in the hazardous occupations by the end of the Plan period.
- Expansion of National Child Labour Projects to additional 150 districts.
- Linking the child labour elimination efforts with the Scheme of Sarva Shiksha Abhiyan of Ministry of Human Resource Development to ensure that children in the age group of 5-8 years get directly admitted to regular schools and that the older working children are mainstreamed to the formal education system through special schools functioning under the NCLP Scheme.
- Convergence with other Schemes of the Departments of Education, Rural Development, Health and Women and Child Development for the ultimate attainment of the objective in a time bound manner.

The Government and the Ministry of Labour and Employment in particular, are rather serious in their efforts to fight and succeed in this direction. The number of districts covered under the NCLP Scheme has been increased from 100 to 250, as mentioned above in this note. In addition, 21 districts have been covered under INDUS, a similar Scheme for rehabilitation of child labour in cooperation with US Department of Labour. Implementation of this Project was recently reviewed during the visit of Mr. Steven Law, Deputy Secretary of State, from the USA. For the Districts not covered under these two Schemes, Government is also providing funds directly to the NGOs under the Ministry's Grants-in-aid Scheme for running Special Schools for rehabilitation of child labour, thereby providing for a greater role and cooperation of the civil society in combating this menace. Elimination of child labour is the single largest programme in this Ministry's activities. Apart from a major increase in the number of districts covered under the scheme, the priority of the Government in this direction is evident in the quantum jump in budgetary allocation during the 10th Plan. Government has allocated Rs. 602 crores for the Scheme during the 10th Plan, as against an expenditure of Rs. 178 crores in the 9th Plan. The resources set aside for combating this evil in the Ministry is around 50 per cent of its total annual budget. The implementation of NCLP and INDUS Schemes is being closely monitored through periodical reports, frequent visits and meetings with the District and State Government officials. The Government's commitment to achieve tangible results in this direction in a time bound manner is also evident from the fact that in the recent Regional Level Conferences of District Collectors held in Hyderabad, Pune, Mussoorie and Kolkata district-wise review of the Scheme was conducted at the level of Secretary. These Conferences provided an excellent opportunity to have one-to-one interaction with the Collectors, who play a pivotal role in the implementation of these Schemes in the District. Besides, these Conferences also helped in a big way in early operationalisation of Scheme in the newly selected 150 districts. The Government is committed to eliminate child labour in all its forms and is moving in this direction in a targeted manner. The multipronged strategy being followed by the Government to achieve this objective also found its echo during the recent discussions held in the Parliament on the Private Member's Bill tabled by Shri Iqbal Ahmed Saradgi. It was unanimously recognized therein that the problem of child labour, being inextricably linked with poverty and illiteracy, cannot be solved by legislation alone, and that a holistic, multipronged and concerted effort to tackle this problem will bring in the desired results. The Supreme Court of India, in its judgment dated 10th December, 1996 in Writ Petition (Civil) Number 465/1986, has given certain directions regarding the manner in which children working in the hazardous occupations are to be withdrawn from work and rehabilitated, and the manner in which the working conditions of children working in non-hazardous occupations are to be regulated and improved. The judgment of the Supreme Court envisages:

- Simultaneous action in all districts of the country;
- Survey for identification of working children (to be completed by June 10, 1997)
- Withdrawal of children working in hazardous industries and ensuring their education in appropriate institutions;
- Contribution of Rs.20, 000 per child to be paid by the offending employers of children to a welfare fund to be established for this purpose;
- Employment to one adult member of the family of the child so withdrawn from work, and if that is not possible a contribution of Rs.5000 to the welfare fund to be made by the State Government;

- Financial assistance to the families of the children so withdrawn to be paid out of the interest earnings on the corpus of Rs.20,000/25,000.00 deposited in the welfare fund as long as the child is actually sent to the schools;
- Regulating hours of work for children working in non-hazardous occupations so that their working hours do not exceed six hours per day and education for at least two hours is ensured. The entire expenditure on education is to be borne by the concerned employer;
- Planning and preparedness on the part of Central and State Governments in terms of strengthening of the existing administrative/regulatory/ enforcement frame-work (covering cost of additional manpower, training, mobility, computerization etc.) implying additional requirement of funds.

The Indian government has taken a step forward by enacting a law to ban domestic work and some other forms of labour by children under age 14, Human Rights Watch said today. The law goes into effect on October 10, 2006, but to be effective, the Indian authorities will need to improve upon their weak enforcement of existing child labour protections. The new law covers restaurant and hotel work as well as domestic labour. However, it provides no protection for children aged 14 to 18, who also face exploitation and abuse by their employers. Indian law prohibits the employment of children under age 14 in occupations deemed hazardous, a list that will now include domestic, hotel and restaurant work. Under the law, government officials must remove and rehabilitate children, and prosecute employers illegally using underage children. Employers of children under the age of 14 in India may face imprisonment under a new law effective in October. The child labour law extends an existing ban against employing children in hazardous industries. It will bar employing children as domestic servants, at roadside food stalls and in hospitals. Violators can be jailed for up to two years and fined, Britain's Daily Telegraph reports. The measure is designed to stop the exploitation of poor children, which includes violence, psychological trauma and sexual abuse. But children's rights groups wonder about the law's effectiveness because of the prevailing child labour culture. One group told the newspaper it would be respected only after the government finds alternative sources of income for poor families. Despite the existing ban applying to hazardous industries, many children still work in dangerous fireworks and match factories, or in wretched conditions, the report said. Indianews.com said there are no exact figures on the number of child workers in India, but the National Domestic Workers Movement estimates about 80 million children work as servants in Indian homes. The report said the International Labour Organization estimates India's domestic workforce accounts for up to 40 percent of child labour worldwide.

In addition, this Encyclopedia provides readers with a brief listing of acronyms on the subject, glossary of related terms, and a detailed bibliography for the purpose of further referencing and research. An appendix providing supporting documents is presented. A brief index is provided herein to make this encyclopedia user-friendly. It is believed that this publication would go a long way on elaborating upon the various multilateral and bilateral agreements on the subject under analysis. The editor would like to thank to our friends, colleagues and well wishers for extending help, assistance and also for enthusing our present efforts. Finally, we are thankful to our publishers for bringing out this encyclopedia superbly within stipulated time period. Constructive criticism and suggestions are welcome from all quarters for enhancing the quality and utility of this work.

V.K. Diwan

1

TOPICAL OVERVIEW

The following verse in the *yajurveda* throws a prism of light on friendly dealing and behaviour with all creatures of he world what to say of only human beings:—

दृते दृँह मा मित्रस्य मा चक्षुषा सर्वाणि भूतानि समीक्षन्ताम् ।

मित्रस्याहं चक्षुषा सर्वाणि भूतानि समीक्षे मित्रस्य चक्षुषा समीक्षामहे ।। (यजुर्वेद 36-18)

Oh God ! Let my eye view be firm in order that all creatures may look at me by friendly sight. In the same way I also may see all creatures with friendly sight and all of us creatures may see each or other in friendly view. (*Yajurveda* - 36, 18)

"Human Rights", says Claire Palley, "provide criteria for making value judgments—reflect normative judgments as to what is permissible to be done by free and responsible persons, acting either individually or collectively through the Government. Human Rights can be used to evaluate, the low of States by deciding whether the standards inherent in such rights are reflected in positive law."—[*Vide* The United Kingdom and Human Rights"—*Hamlyn Lectures*.]

Article 10.3 provides that special measures of protection and assistance should be taken on behalf of all children and young persons, without any discrimination for reasons of parentage or other conditions. Children and young persons should be protected from economic and social exploitation. Their employment in work harmful to their morals or health or dangerous to life or likely to hamper their normal development should be punishable by law. States should also set age limits below which the paid employment of child labour should be prohibited and punishable by law." [*Vide*, The International Covenant On Economic, Social and Cultural Rights, 1976.]

Constitution vision.—Law is an effective tool to translate the aspirations of common man into reality. Its significance and Sacredness should be preserved by all those who make and also by those for whom it is made. The Indian Constitution itself is a great social document. It underlines the ideals of Supremacy of Law ; Social, Economic and political justice, secularism and democracy. The fundamental rights guaranteed to Indian Citizens constitute the basis for a free and democratic society. The Directive principles contained in part IV, on the other hand, provide guidelines for the state to initiate measures to ensure welfare of the community. The physical integrity of life and liberty forms the most important aspect of individual freedom. It has been well safeguarded in the Constitution and liberally interpreted by law Courts. The doctrine of Rule of law enshrined in the Indian Constitution Seeks to balance individual rights with legal responsibility. It ensures equality before law and equal protection to all individuals and excludes the possibility of autocratic and totalitarian exercise of power by the State.

Status of Children.—"In States in which the rule of *jus soli* holds, exceptions of one kind or another are made in the cases of Children born to diplomatic officers and other public officials of foreign States. The general practice is confirmed by the convention on certain questions relating to the conflict of Nationality Laws, adopted at the Hague in 1930. Special difficulties due to the single operation of the Principal of jus sanguinis, have arisen in Connection with the nationality by birth of children of unknown parents, and numerous cases of Statelessness have resulted. The Hague Convention of 1930 provides that a child whose parents are both unknown shall have the nationality of the country of birth, that foundings shall be presumed to have been born on the territory of the State in which they were found, and in case of illegitimate child should lose its nationality of birth by reason of legitimation, the loss should by conditional upon acquiring the nationality of another country.

The lows of most states provide that minor children acquire the new nationality of their parents when the latter are naturalised abroad, and this rule is accepted with qualification by the Hague Convention of 1930, with the provisions that in the cases where the minor children do not acquire the nationality of their parents as a result of their parents' naturalisation. They shall retain their existing nationality. Under the low of the united States a child acquiring Citizenship by birth in the Country may lose it if taken during minority to the country of its parents origin where its parents resume their former allegiance and in like manner it may lose citizenship acquired jure sanguinis when it fails to meet certain residence requirements, and it may lose citizenship acquired through the naturalisation of its parents when they become naturalised in another country and the child does not acquire residence in the United States upon attaining the age of twenty three years. [*Vide* Charles G. Fenwick.]

Child—Meaning of.—Where the word child is used in correlation with father or parents, it means. As correlative to parent the off spring, male or female of human parents.[1]

As defined under the Dangerous Machines (Regulation) Act, 1983.—Section 3(a) of the Act defines 'Child' as under:—

(*a*) "*Child*" means a person who has not completed his fourteenth year of age."

Rights of the child.—It is hoped that the child of twenty first century would find the "heaven of freedom" depicted in the Gitanjali.[2]

Protection of Children.—Under the Universal Declaration of Human Rights, 1948, Article 25(2) provides that "Motherhood and Childhood are entitled to special care and assistance, whether born in or out of wedlock, shall enjoy the same social protection.

---

1. *Nanak Chand* v. *Sri Chandra Kishore Agarwala and Others*, AIR 1970 SC 446 : 1970 Cri LJ 522 ; 1970 (1) SCJ 176.
2. *M.C. Mehta* v. *State of Tamil Nadu*, AIR 1997 SC 669 : 1997 SCC (L & S) 49 : (1996) 6 SCC 756 : 1997 LLR 97 : (1997) II LLJ 724 (SC).

Protective Rights of Children

International Convention of the Rights of Child, 1990	Right envisaged and protected
Article 33	A child is entitled to be protected from use of narcotic drugs, and psychotropic substances and to be protected against used in illicit production and trafficking of such drugs.
Article 34	Children should be protected from against Sexual exploitation of all forms.
Article 35	They should be protected from abduction sale or trafficking, by all appropriate measures.
Article 36	They should be protected from all types of exploitation.
Article 38	Children who have not attained the age of fifteen years should not be recruited in armed forces even in times of emergency. In case of armed conflict they should be rehabilitated.

Rights to Development of Personality

International Convention of the Rights of Child, 1990	Right envisaged and protected
Article 18	Parents or legal guardians are primarily responsible for upbringing and development of children. The State is obliged to afford appropriate assistance to parents and legal guardians in the performance of such duties of parents and guardians.
Article 20	Children are entitled to get family environment. In case of bereavement in any circumstances of family, the State is obliged to give special protection and assistance.
Article 21	Adoption should be taken in the best interests of the child, being duly authorised by competent authority for the safeguard of the child.
Article 6	Survival and development of child must be ensured to the most possible extent.

Rights to Maintain and Develop Health

International Convention of the Rights of Child, 1990	Right envisaged and protected
Article 23	A mentally or physically retarded child has the right to

	enjoy a full and decent life, in conditions ensuring dignity promoting self-reliance and facilitating active participation in the community.
Article 24	A child is entitled to enjoy highest attainable standard of health, to treatment of illness, and malnutrition.
Article 27.1	A child has the right to a standard of of living adequate to his physical, mental and moral development.

Civil Rights and Liberties of Children

International Convention of the Rights of Child, 1990	Right envisaged and protected
Article 6	Every child has the inherent right to life and survival to the maximum extent.
Article 7	A child is entitled to be registered immediately after his birth and to get the nationality and home.
Articles 13 and 14	A child has the right to freedom of expression and thought, to seek, receive, import ideas, right to freedom of thought, conscience and religion.

Abolishing bonded Labour system.—The Bonded Labour System (Abolition) Act, 1976 has been brought by the Union of India for abolishing the system. In this Act, the Bonded labour system has been defined to mean the system of forced or partly forced labour under which a debtor enters or has, or is permitted to have entered, into an agreement with the creditor to the effect that—

(*i*) in consideration of an advance obtained by him or by any of his lineal ascendants or descendants (whether or not such advance is evidenced by way of document) and in consideration of the interest, if any, due on such advance ; or

(*ii*) in pursuance of any customary or social obligation ; or

(*iii*) in pursuance of an obligation devolving on him by succession ; or

(*iv*) for any economic consideration received by him or by way of his lineal ascendants, or descendants ; or

(*v*) by reason of his birth in any particular caste or community he would—

(*a*) render, by himself or through any member of his family, or any person dependent on him, labour or service to the creditor, or for the benefit of the creditor, for a specified period or for an unspecified period, either without wages on for nominal wages ;

(*b*) forfeit the freedom of employment or other means of livelihood for a specified period or for an unspecified period ;

(c) forfeit the right to more freely throught out the territory of India, or

(d) forfeit the right to appropriate or sell at market value any of the property or product of his labour or of a member of his family, or any person dependent on him and includes the system of forced, or partly forced labour under which a surety for debtor enters, or has or is presumed to have, entered into an agreement with the creditor to the effect that in the event of the failure of the debtor to repay the debt, he would render the banded labour on behalf of the debtor.

World Summit for Children.—On 30th September, 1990, a ten point programme for the rights of Children and improvement in their lives was laid down, in which the following programmes were included.

(i) Programme for solid national and international efforts for unchanging health and sanitation of children.

(ii) Programme promoting earlier ratification and implementation of the convention on the Rights of the child and world wide propagation about the rights of child.

(iii) Programmes for promoting the role and status by women and responsible family planning.

(iv) Programme attaining optional growth and development in childhood.

(v) Programme for enhancement of role of family in upbringing of child.

(vi) Programme reducing illiteracy and promoting education opportunities for all children.

(vii) Programme for providing protection to children during armed conflict and educating them in the values of peace under standing and dialogue.

(viii) Programme for amelioration of plight of children living in specially difficult circumstances.

(ix) Programme to protect environment, and

(x) Programme for world wide removal of poverty. This is a clear intention of the world organisation the U.N.O. to sow the seeds of world peace and prosperity without and discrimination of caste, creed, colour, religion, of nationality.

The plan action for implementing the world declaration on the survival protection and development of children of 1990, was adopted by the world summit for children along with the world. Declaration aforesaid. In this plan guidelines for the national Government, international organisations, bilateral aid agencies, non-Governmental organisations, and all other sectors of society of human beings have been laid down for formulating their action plan for the implementation of the world Declaration. The plan of Action aforesaid has insisted upon:—

(*a*) Concerned actions on national as well as international level for the achievement of the major goals for survival, protection and development of children by the year two ;

(*b*) The goal must be adopted to the specific conditions of each country for making them technically valid, logically feasible and financially realistic ;

(*c*) The efforts must be made to arouse broad public support and political commitment essential for achievement of the goal.

ILO—Constitution and Role.—"The Constitution of the International Labour Organisation, forming part of the Treaty of versailles, was based upon the principle that the Universal peace which was the object of the League of Nations could be established "only it is based upon social justice." Section I recited the urgent need of improving the conditions of Labour and stated. "The failure of any nations to adopt humane conditions of labour is an obstacle in the way of other nations which desire to improve the conditions their own countries. Acting in pursuance of this objective of social justice the successive General conferences of the organisation have adopted a long list of draft conventions and recommendations to be submitted to the member States. The subjects dealt with by these draft conventions and recommendations include the following problems of labour policy ; employment, general conditions of labour and work of women and children ; Industrial health safety and welfare ; social insurance ; Industrial relations ; administration of social legislation. Among the important conventions which have come into force are the conventions limiting the Hours of work in Industrial under takings to eight in the day and party eight in the week. The convention fixing the minimum age for Admission of Children to Industrial Employment, the convention concerning the Employment of women before and after child birth, and the convention concerning the employment of women during the night, all four adopted at Washington in 1919 ; the convention concerning workers compensation for occupational Diseases adopted at Genevea in 1925 ; and the convention ensuring benefit and allowances to the Involuntarily unemployed adopted at Geneva in 1934.

At the meeting of the General Conference of the ILO in 1944, a declaration of the aims and purposes of the organisation and of the principles which should inspire the policy of its members was adopted, known as "the Philadelphia character." In 1946, the organisations looking to the conclusion of an agreement with the United Nations by which it might be brought into relation with that body as a "Specialised agency", adopted and amended constitution. The agreement with the United Nations was signed on December 20, 1946." [*Vide* Charles G. Fenwick in his 'International Law'.]

ILO Efforts.—Regarding child labour ILO efforts are appreciable in this concern, whereas the convention on the rights of the child had recognised their following rights, that is:—

(*a*) right to life, to a name and to acquire nationality ;

(*b*) right to know and be cared for by his or her parents ;

(*c*) right to freedom of expression, thought, conscience, and religion ;

(*d*) right to association and peaceful assembly ;

(*e*) right to education ;

(*f*) right to the highest attainable standard of living adequate to his or her physical, mental spiritual, moral and social development ;

(*g*) right not to be separated from their parents against their will ;

(*h*) right of protection from economic exploitation and from employment in hazardous work, abstinence from drug use, and trafficking for sexual exploitation and abuses.

(*i*) right of minor and indigenous Children to have and maintain their own culture, religion and language ;

(*j*) right to enjoy full and decent life when mentally of physically disabled ;

(*k*) freedom from fortune and such other issues degenerating punishment and providing humanitarian juvenile justice to children below 18 years as are defined to be children under the convention.

1959 Declaration on Children's Right.—Following ten points have been put forth as follows:—

1. The Child shall enjoy all the rights set forth in this Declaration. All children without any exception whatsoever, shall be entitled to these rights without distinction or discrimination on account of race, colour, sex, language, religion, political or other opinion, national or social origin, property birth or other status whether of himself or of his family.

2. The child shall enjoy special protection and shall be given opportunities and facilities by low and other means, to enable him to develop physically, mentally, morally, spiritually and socially in a healthy and normal manner and in the conditions of freedom and dignity, in the enactment of laws for this purpose, the best interests of the Child shall be the paramount consideration.

3. The Child shall be entitled from his birth to a name and nationality.

4. The Child shall be enjoy the benefits of Social Security. He shall be entitled to grow and develop in health, to this end special care and protection shall be provided both to him and to his mother including adequate pre-natal and post-natal care. The Child shall have the right to adequate nutrition and medical services. Note that this provision undertaking the Declaration to be complied with by member States, is next to be impossible to be complied with in a capitalistic or monopolistic society having the tendency of exploiting the poor and remain rich and go on increasing their wealth by fair or foul means. This Declaration may remain a sermon to such capitalistic exploiters and remaining in power by hook or crook due to their enormous wealth.

5. The child who is physically, mentally or socially handicapped shall be given special treatment, education, and care required by the particular conditions.

6. The child for the full and harmonious development of his personality needs love and understanding he shall wherever possible grow up in the care and under the responsibility of his parents and in any case in an atmosphere of affection and a moral and material Security. A child of tender years shall not save in exceptional circumstances be separated from his mother. Society and public authorities shall have duty to extend particular care to children without a family and to those without means of support payment of State and other assistance towards the maintenance of children of large families is desirable.

7. The child is entitled to receive education, which shall be free and compulsory, at least in the elementary stages. He shall be given education which promotes his general culture and enable him on a basis of equal opportunity to develop his abilities, his individual judgment and his sense of moral and social responsibility lies in the first place with his parents.

The child shall have full opportunity for play and recreation, which should be directed to the same purposed as education. Society and the public authorities shall endeavour to promote the enjoyment of this right.

8. The child in all circumstances be among the first to receive protection and relief.

9. The child shall be protected against all forms of neglect cruelty, and exploitation. He shall not be the Subject of traffic, in any form. The child shall not be admitted to employment before the appropriate minimum age. He shall in no case be caused or permitted to engage in any occupation or employment which would prejudice his health or education, or interfere with his physical, mental or moral development.

10. The child shall be protected from practice which may foster racial, religious and any other form of discrimination. He shall be brought up in a spirit of understanding, tolerance, friendship among peoples, peace and Universal consciousness that his energy and talents should be directed to the service of his fellow men.

Human rights of children—International recognition.—The General Declaration of 1924 was made under the auspices of the League of Nations, in which the following five points were adopted :

1. The child should be given the means requisite for its normal developments both materially and spiritually.

2. The child that is hungry must be fed, the child that is sick must be helped, the child that is backward must be reclaimed, and the orphan and the wait must be sheltered and succoured.

3. The child must be first to receive relief in times of distress.

4. The child must be put in a position to each a likelihood and must be protected against every form of exploitation.

5. The Child must be brought up in the consciousness that its talents must be devoted to the service of its fellow men.

Laws Relating to Child Labour in India

(1) Constitutional Mandate.—

(a) Article 23.—Article 23 provides that—

1. Traffic in human beings and began and other similar forms of forced labour are prohibited and any contravention of this provision shall be an offence punishable in accordance with law.
2. Nothing in this Article shall prevent the State from imposing compulsory service for public purposes and in imposing such service the State shall not make any discrimination on the grounds only of religion, race, caste, or class or any of them.

This Article prohibits—

(*a*) traffic in human beings ;

(*b*) began, and

(*c*) other similar forms of forced labour,

(b) Article 24.—Article 24 bars employment of Children below the age of 14 years is factory, mine or any other hazardous works.

Article 24 prohibition the employment of children below the age of 14 years in any—

(*a*) factory

(*b*) mine, or

(*c*) other hazardous employment.

The Employment of Children Act, 1938, the Child Labour (Prohibition and Regulation) Act, 1986. The Factories Act, 1948, and the Mines Act, 1953, and similar other Acts prohibits the employment of Children below a certain age.

(i) Prohibited industries.—In *M.C. Mehta* v. *Union of India,*[1] the Court gave directions that no child be employed in match industries. Further, if laid down exhaustive guidelines for the education of children and for setting up a Child Labour Rehabilitation Welfare Fund. Other industries in respect of which the directions were given are diamond polishing, precious stone polishing, glass industry, brass-ware industry, carpet industry, lock-making industry and State industry.

(ii) Construction work—Hazardous work.—Construction work is a hazardous

1. (1996) 6 SCC 756

employment and no child below the age of 14 years can therefore be allowed to be employed in construction work by reason of the prohibition enacted in Article 24, and this Constitutional prohibition must be enforced by the Central Government.[1]

(iii) Curbing violation of fundamental rights.—Whenever any fundamental right which is enforceable against private individuals such as for example a fundamental right enacted in Article 17 or 23 or 24 is being violated, it is the Constitutional obligation of the State to take the necessary steps for the purpose of infederdicting such violation and ensuring observance of the fundamental right by the private individual who is transgressing the same. Of course, the person whose fundamental right is violated on always approach the Court for the purpose of enforcement of his fundamental right, but that cannot absolve the State from its constitutional obligation to see that there is no violation of the fundamental right of such person, particularly when he belongs to the weaker section of humanity and is unable to wage a legal battle against a strong and powerful opponent who is exploiting him.[2]

(iv) Salt mines employing minors as labourers.—Regarding child labour, the State Government issued notice to complain action taken against owner of salt mines and also directed to inform steps taken to ensure extension of facility of basic amenities to workers like grooves, gun boots, educational facilities and sufficient mobile Health Units.[3]

(c) Article 39.—Clauses (e) and (f) envisages that tender age of the Children are not abused and must not be forced by economic necessity to enter avocations unsuited to their age or strength and their childhood must be protected.

(d) Article 45.—Envisages free and compulsory education for all children until they complete the age of 14 years.

(2) Employment of Children Act, 1938.—[Repealed by Act 61 of 1986]. Even before the constitution, the aforesaid Act ensured protection to children from being employed and exploited.

(i) Prohibition against employment of Children under 1938 Act.—Prohibition against employment of children under Act 26 of 1938, did not apply to employment in construction industry. However, construction work being hazardous employment within of Article 24, children below 14 years cannot be employed in construction work notwithstanding absence of construction industry in the Schedule. [State Governments advised to take immediate steps for incursion of construction work in the Schedule of the Act.[4]

(ii) Employment in construction industry.—Construction industry is not a

---

1. *Labourers Working on Salal Hydro-Project* v. *State of J. & K.*, AIR 1984 SC 177 : 1983 Lab IC 502 : (1983) 2 SCC 181 : (1983) 2 SCWR 202.
2. *People's Union for Democratic Rights* v. *Union of India*, AIR 1982 SC 1473 : 1982 Lab IC 1646 : (1982) 2 SCC 494 : (1982) 2 SCWR 202.
3. *Narender Malar* v. *State of Gujarat*, 2003 (7) Scale 474.
4. *People's Union For Democratic Rights* v. *Union of India*, AIR 1982 SC 1473.

process specified in the Schedule attached to the Employment of Children Act, 1938. Prohibition against employment of children under the Act 26 of 1938, does not apply to employment in construction industry.[1]

(3) Child Labour (Protection and Regulation) Act, 1986.—The Act prohibition employment of children below age of 14 years in various specified occupations. However, the workshops where any process is carried on by occupier with the aid of his family and own schools which are established by or receiving assistance or recognition from the Government are exempted from the application of the Act.

(4) Children (Pledging of Labour) Act, 1933.—The Act prohibition the pledging the labour of children by agreement. The Royal Commission of Labour found evidence in such widely separated areas as Amritsar, Ahmedabad and Madras of the practice of pledging child labour, that is, the taking of advances by parents or guardians on agreements, written or oral, pledging the labour of their children. In some cases the Children. So pledged were subjected particularly to unsatisfactory working conditions. The Commission considered that the State would be justified in adopting strong measures to eradicate the evil, and this Act was brought to do so by imposing penalties on parents by agreements pledging the labour of children and of persons knowing employing children whose labour is so pledged.

(5) Factories Act, 1948.—'Young persons' under Section 29 the Act means a person who is either a child or an adolescent.

Section 22(2) prohibits employment of children to be allowed to do certain works.

FACTORIES ACT, 1948

Section	**Deals with**
(a) Section 22(2)	Prohibition a child to be allowed to do certain works.
(b) Section 23	Prohibition young person to be employed or dangerous machines.
(*c*) Section 27	Prohibition employment of women and children near cotton openers.
(*d*) Section 67	Prohibition employment of young children.
(*e*) Section 68	Provides for token to be supplied by employer and kept by non-adult workers.
(*f*) Section 69	Certificate of fitness to young person.
(*g*) Section 70	Provides for effect of certificate granted to an adolescent workman as an adult.

1. *Peoples Union for Democratic Rights* v. *Union of India*, AIR 1982 SC 1473 : (1982) 3 SCC 235 : 1982 Lab IC 1646.

(*h*) Section 71	Provides for working hours for children.
(*i*) Section 72	Provides for notice of periods of work for children.
(*j*) Section 73	Requires register of children to be maintained.
(*k*) Section 77	Declare that provisions of Chapter VII of the Factories Act shall be addition and not in derogation of Act of 1986.

(6) The Mines Act, 1952.—The Act prohibits presence of children in any part of a mine. Under Section 2(e), child means a person who has not completed his 14th year.

MINES ACT, 1952

Section	Deal with
(a) Section 68	Provides penalty for double employment of young person.
(b) Section 43	Empowers Inspector to requires medical examination of a person employed in a mine if a child or adolescent.
(c) Section 44	Provides for working hours for adolescents.
(d) Section 45	Prohibition employment of children.

(7) The Merchant Shipping Act, 1958.—The Section 109 of the Act prohibits child labours.

MERCHANT SHIPPING ACT, 1958

Section	Deal with
(a) Section 109	Prohibits employment of Children but with certain exception.
(b) Section 110	No young person to work as stoker or trimmer.
(c) Section 111	Provided for medical examination of young persons.
(d) Section 112	Requires maintenance of register of young persons of a ship.
(e) Section 113	Empowers Central Govèrnment to make rules respecting employment of young persons.

(8) The Motor Transport Workers Act, 1961.—Chapter VI of the Act provides against employment of young persons in the motor transport establishments.

MOTOR TRANSPORT WORKERS ACT, 1961

Section	Deals with
(a) Section 21	Prohibits employment of children in motor transport undertaking.

(b) Section 22	Provides for employment of adolescents as motor transport workers to carry tokens.
(c) Section 23	Provides for certificate of fitness.
(d) Section 24	Empowers inspectors to require medical examination of adolescents if employed.

(a) Implication of I.P.C.—Section 371 of the I.P.C. provides against habitual dealing with slaves that whoever habitually imports exports, removes, buys, sells, traffics or deals in slaves, shall be punished with imprisonment for life of with imprisonment of either description for a term not exceeding ten years and shall also be liable to fine.

2

A General Survey

Child labor or labour is the employment of children under an age determined by law or custom. This practice is considered exploitive by international organizations, such as the United Nations, and the International Labour Organization. The UN has stipulated, in article 32 of the Convention on the Rights of the Child that:

> States Parties recognize the right of the child to be protected from economic exploitation and from performing any work that is likely to be hazardous or to interfere with the child's education, or to be harmful to the child's health or physical, mental, spiritual, moral or social development.

In many countries, it is considered inappropriate or exploitative if a child below a certain age works, excluding household chores or school work. An employer is often not allowed to hire a child below a certain age. This minimum age depends on the country, such as in the United States, where the minimum age to work in an establishment without parents consent and restrictions is age 16.

Other forms of work include helping in the parents' business or having one's own small business, either selling small items or doing odd jobs. Some children work as a guide for tourists, sometimes combined with working for owners of shops and restaurants, bringing tourists to these businesses. More controversial forms of work include the military use of children, child prostitution, child actors and child singers. According to a UNICEF study, it is a myth that most child labor is in sweatshops that export goods to the rich countries. Most child labor is in the "informal sector" —"selling on the street, at work in agriculture or hidden away in houses — far from the reach of official labour inspectors and from media scrutiny."

The reasons a child would consent to do such work may vary greatly. An example of this consent to work would be if a child says he or she wants to work, such as because the earnings are attractive or if the child hates school, because such consent may not necessarily be informed consent. However, the workplace may still be an undesirable situation for a child or adult in the long run.

The use of children as laborers is now considered by wealthy countries as a human rights violation, and outlawed, while poorer countries may allow it. Poor families often rely on the labors of their children for survival and sometimes it is the only source of income. This type of work is often hidden because it is not in the industrial sector. Child labor is employment in substance agriculture, in the household, or in the urban informal sector. A related problem is that people are often more preoccupied with the long-term survival and well-being of their families than with their own direct, short term interests. Child labor prohibition has to address the dual challenge of providing children with both short-term income and long-term prospects.

Some youth rights groups, however, feel that prohibiting work below a certain age violates human rights, reducing their options and leaving them subject to the whims of those with money.

In the west, during the Industrial Revolution, use of child labour was commonplace, often in factories, but on the decline. In England and Scotland in 1788, about two-thirds of the workers in the new water-powered textile factories were children . Subsequently, largely due to the campaigning of Lord Shaftesbury, a series of Factory Acts were passed to restrict gradually the hours that children were allowed to work, and to improve safety. It is widely argued that the industrial revolution increased hardship for children. Historian E.P. Thompson notes in The Making of the English Working Class that child labor was not new, and had been "an intrinsic part of the agricultural and industrial economy before 1780", however he argues that "there was a drastic increase in the intensity of exploitation of child labour between 1780 and 1840, and every historian acquainted with the sources knows this is so. This was true in the mines, both in inefficient small-scale pits where the roadways were sometimes so narrow that children could not easily pass through them; where - as the coal face drew further away from the shaft - children were in demand as 'hurreyers' and to operate the ventilation ports. In the mills, the child and juvenile labour force grew yearly; and in several of the out-worker or 'dishonourable' trades the hours of labour became longer and work more intense."

Some historians have disagreed with this verdict. Economic historian Robert Hessen says:

> *"claims of increased misery...[are] based on ignorance of how squalid life actually had been earlier. Before children began earning money working in factories, they had been sent to live in parish poorhouses, apprenticed as unpaid household servants, rented out for backbreaking agricultural labor, or became beggars, vagrants, thieves, and prostitutes (Nutten) . The precapitalist "good old days" simply never existed"*

Laws were passed to prohibit child labor in the industrialized countries, however it is unclear whether this legislation is the principal cause of the decline in levels of juvenile employment. Research by Clark Nardinelli suggests that child labor was already decreasing in the United States and Western Europe prior to the passage of legislation, due to an increasing demand for educated and literate adults brought about by an increasing technological sophistication of industry. The demand for educated workers also provided an incentive for children to stay in school to meet the new demands of industry.

Concern has been raised about the buying public's moral complicity in buying products assembled or otherwise manufactured in developing countries with child labor. However, boycotting products manufactured through child labor may force these children to turn to more dangerous professions due to necessity, such as prostitution or agriculture. For example, a UNICEF study found that that 5,000 to 7,000 Nepalese children turned to prostitution after the United States banned that country's carpet exports in the 1990s. Also, after the Child Labor Deterrence Act was introduced in the US an estimated 50,000 children were dismissed from their garment industry jobs in Bangladesh, leaving many to resort to jobs such as "stone-crushing, street hustling, and prostitution," —"all of them more hazardous and exploitative than garment production" according to a UNICEF study. The study says that boycotts are "blunt instruments with long-term consequences that can actually harm rather than help the children involved."

Children's participation in economic activity was commonplace prior to the Industrial Revolution as children performed labor on their farms or for their families. Economists such as Milton Friedman argue that the Industrial Revolution saw a net decline in child labor, rather than an increase. According to this view, children began to work in factories, but greater numbers of children stopped working in agriculture. While accepting this overall child labor declined in this period, other commentators draw a qualitative distinction between domestic work and participation in the wider (waged) labor-market. The usefulness of the experience of the industrial revolution in making predictions about current trends has been disputed. Economic historian Hugh Cunningham notes that:

> *"Fifty years ago it might have been assumed that, just as child labour had declined in the developed world in the late nineteenth and early twentieth centuries, so it would also, in a trickle-down fashion, in the rest of the world. Its failure to do that, and its re-emergence in the developed world, raise questions about its role in any economy, whether national or global."*

Friedman and other market economists believe that the absence of child labor is a luxury that many poor states cannot yet afford. To prohibit it, is to prevent the economic growth necessary to relieve a society of the need for child labor. In poor societies these children will be put to work by their families by whatever means because they cannot afford to feed idle and unproductive children. Moreover, in addition to possibly increasing family costs on a depleted family income, parents may have to forego potential labor time and income, to care for idle children. Some argue that if industrial child labor is legally forbidden, then many children are relegated to working in more dangerous black market occupations such as prostitution.

The United States also has extensive child labor laws. In the 1990s every country in the world except for Somalia and the United States became a signatory to the Convention on the Rights of the Child, or CRC. The CRC provides the strongest, most consistent international legal language prohibiting illegal child labor.

Recent figures from the International Labour Organisation (ILO) show that:

- Globally, 1 in 6 children work
- 218 million children aged 5 - 17 are involved in child labour world wide
- 126 million children work in hazardous conditions
- The highest numbers of child labourers are in the Asia/Pacific region, where there are 122 million working children
- The highest proportion of child labourers is in Sub Saharan Africa, where 26% of children (49 million) are involved in work.

There has often been a tendency to focus on the visible forms of work, such as children who work in hazardous conditions, but this can obscure the many other ways in which children work. Rural working children, for example, are mainly engaged in agricultural activities and collecting water, fuel and fodder. In many countries, poor girls work as domestic servants for richer families. Almost everywhere, children, especially girls, perform unpaid work for their families. That work is done in the home or in family enterprises does not necessarily make it easier or more acceptable.

An estimated 246 million children are engaged in child labor around the world. Nearly 70 percent (171 million) of these children work in hazardous conditions — including working in mines, working with chemicals and pesticides in agriculture or with dangerous machinery. The vast majority of working children — about 70 percent — work in the agriculture sector. Millions of children work under horrific circumstances: they are trafficked, forced into debt bondage or other forms of slavery, forced into prostitution and/or pornography, or recruited as child soldiers in armed conflict.

Through the Convention on the Rights of the Child and the International Labor Organization Convention 182 on the Elimination of the Worst Forms of Child Labor, the world has condemned the economic exploitation of children and child labor. These international agreements define "child labor" as all children below 12 years of age working in any economic activities, those aged between 12 and 14 engaged in more than light work, and all children under 18 engaged in the worst forms of child labor. They condemn any form of labor that is likely to be hazardous or to interfere with the child's health, physical, mental, spiritual, moral or social development. The worst forms of child labor include trafficking of children, forced labor, using children in armed conflict, prostitution, pornography and drug trafficking.

Despite the international agreement the problem of child labor persists due to poverty, lack of political commitment to end it and weak legal and monitoring machnisms. Children caught in circumstances of child labor and economic explotitation face many threats to their health their lives and their futures.

It is important to distinguish between child labor and children working. The fact is that in many poor families, children must work to help support their families. UNICEF is not opposed to children (12 years and older) engaging in economic activities — as long as such work does not negatively affect their health and development, or interfere with their education.

UNICEF has long fought against child labor and exploitation. UNICEF's responses to child labor reflect the view that children are resilient, capable and active in their development. Building a protective environment for children requires a comprehensive strategy that combines access to free and good quality education, income-generation activities for families, community advocacy to change attitudes about child labor and strengthening government laws and policies.

U.S. Response to Child Labor

One U.S. response to child labor and abuse has been to address the issue of child trafficking. In 2000, the U.S. Congress enacted the *Trafficking Victims Protection Act* (TVPA). This legislation created a comprehensive framework for combating trafficking in persons abroad, as well as the trafficking of foreign nationals into the United States. In order to continue and strengthen U.S. efforts to fight trafficking that causes exploitation and abuse of children, a bipartisan group of Members of Congress led by Rep. Chris Smith introduced the *Trafficking Victims Protection Reauthorization Act of 2005*, H.R. 972. This bill reauthorizes funding for anti-trafficking programs here and abroad. It also addresses lessons from the aftermath of the devastating tsunami in South Asia by requiring the U.S. Government to develop trafficking prevention strategies for post-conflict and humanitarian crises.

LEGAL DEFINITIONS OF TERMS RELATED TO CHILD LABOUR

A child is defined as an individual under the age of 18 years, based on the 1989 United Nations Convention on the Rights of the Child and the ILO Convention on the Worst Forms of Child Labour, 1999 (No. 182). Since it is commonly accepted that a child under 5 years of age is too young to be engaged in work (although there are cases of exploitation or abuse by adults) or to start schooling, we considered only the child population aged 5-17 years for the purpose of our estimates. Age is measured in number of complete years at last birthday.

Child age groups were broken down in two different ways. For the estimates on children's work or economic activity we applied the commonly used categories 5-9 years of age, 10-14 years, and 15-17 years. For the presentation of data on child labour and hazardous child work, on the other hand, we divided the first two age brackets into 5-11 and 12-14 years, thereby following the logic of ILO Minimum Age Convention, 1973 (No. 138), which allows light work from the age of 12 years in a developing country context.

(a) Working Children

Work is defined in terms of economic activity in the sense of the System of National Accounts (SNA) 1993. This corresponds to the international definition of employment as adopted by the Thirteenth International Conference of Labour Statisticians.

Economic activity covers all market production (paid work) and certain types of non-market production (unpaid work), including production of goods for own use. Whether paid or unpaid, therefore, the activity or occupation could be pursued in either the formal or informal sector and in either urban or rural areas. For example, children engaged in unpaid activities in a market-oriented establishment operated by a relative living in the same household are considered as working in an economic activity. Children working as maids or other domestic workers in someone else's household are also considered economically active. Children engaged in domestic chores within their own households, however, are not classified as economically active.

In line with the international definition of employment, one hour of work during the reference week is sufficient to consider a person as being at work in economic activity during that week. Also included in the classification are individuals with a job but who are temporarily absent from work due to illness, vacation, or other reasons.

Note that the concept of "working children" based on economic activity excludes children seeking work or those who are currently unemployed.

Work was measured in relation to a reference week during the school year, as opposed to a longer reference period such as a year. The reference week is a more convenient reference period, since it permits a sharper measurement of economic activity and minimizes ambiguities due to the higher incidence of multiple status and changes in economic activity and work intensity that may arise during a longer reference period. Moreover, most sources of data on which the estimations rely have adopted the reference week as the basic reference period. A simple activity status classification was adopted for the purpose of our global estimation. The activity status was defined in terms of three categories with a maximum of two levels each:

1. At work in economic activity
   (a) At work only
   (b) At work and at school
2. At school, and not at work in economic activity
3. Neither at work nor at school
   (a) Household chores
   (b) Other (e.g. sick or disabled, at play, or in informal education)

At each level of classification, the activity statuses are meant to be exhaustive and mutually exclusive, so that each and every child should be classifiable according to one and only one status. According to this scheme, the classification into the category *"at work in economic activity"* takes precedence over the *"at school"* category. Thus, children combining work and school will be classified as *"at work"* at the basic level of the classification, but identified separately at the second level of the classification. To be considered *"at school"*, the child should be attending a regular educational institution during the reference week. School enrolment does not necessarily imply school attendance.

Work of a domestic nature (household chores) performed by children in their own household is considered to be non-economic activities, and thus lie outside the "production boundary" as defined by the United Nations System of National Accounts (1993 Rev. 3) for measuring GDP. Our estimates thus do not cover children working in non-economic activities. This is in line with international labour standards that provide for exceptions for household chores in the child's own household. The time children spend on these activities, however, can be substantial. In some cases, school enrolment or attendance is being thereby jeopardized. Unfortunately, data on the extent of non-economic child work are rather fragmented and not reliable enough to attempt a global estimation.

(b) Child Labour

Not all work performed by children is equivalent to "child labour" needing abolition. Work in the sense of "economic activity", as explained above, is a statistical definition. It does not necessarily match the provisions of international labour standards and national legislation. The Minimum Age Convention (No. 138) itself includes options meant, in some cases, to permit a flexible approach in light of given national conditions.

We need to draw (statistical) lines between

- acceptable forms of work by children (which may be regarded as positive), on the one hand, and child labour that needs to be eliminated, on the other; and between

- various forms of child labour and the WFCL, which require urgent action for elimination.

For the purposes of our global estimates for 2000 and 2004, a single set of cut-off criteria was used for all countries. Taking international standards into account, efforts were made wherever possible to use the average level or criteria prevailing in national legislation. The choice of one set of criteria for this estimation was intended purely for the purpose of assessing the extent of the problem quantitatively. Inevitably, some situations included in these estimates may in fact be allowed in terms of national or international standards, just as certain other situations *not* included may in fact represent child labour that requires elimination.

Our concept of child labour is based on Convention No. 138, which represents the most comprehensive and authoritative international definition of minimum age for admission to employment or work, implying "economic activity". Convention No. 138 stipulates that ratifying States fix a minimum age, and it defines a range of minimum ages below which no child should be allowed to work. Minimum age vary according to the level of development and according to the type of employment or work (Table 1).

TABLE 1

Minimum Ages According to ILO Convention No. 138

General minimum age	Light work	Hazardous work
In general:		
Not less than age of completion of compulsory schooling, and in any case not less than 15 years	13 years	18 years (16 years under certain strict conditions)
Where the economy and educational facilities are insufficiently developed:		
Not less than 14 years for an initial period conditions)	12 years	18 years (16 years under certain strict

As Table 1 indicates, the minimum age for employment or work should normally not be younger than 15 years, but developing countries may fix it at 14, and a number of countries have fixed it at 16 years. For our global estimates, we used the age of 15 as a cut-off point for all countries.

The same Convention exempts children from the ages of 12 or 13 years if engaged in "light work". For the purpose of our estimates, we used 12 years as the global cut-off for light work. Thus, all children aged 5-11 years working in economic activities are considered child labour that requires elimination. Working children aged 12-14 years are considered to be in child labour, unless they perform light work.

Light work is difficult to define. Convention No. 138, Article 7, stipulates that light work should neither

- be harmful to a child's health and development, nor
- prejudice attendance at school and participation in vocational training or "the capacity to benefit from the instruction received".

What does this mean in statistical terms? We decided on the following for the purpose of our estimates:

- Light work by children aged 12-14 years is work which is not hazardous in nature (see definition of hazardous work, below) and which does not exceed 14 hours per week. This cut-off point is supported by ILO Minimum Age (Non-Industrial Employment) Convention, 1932 (No. 33) and research findings regarding the impact of child labour on school attendance/performance and on health.

- Children aged 15-17 years are in principle allowed to work because they have reached and surpassed the general minimum age. If they are engaged in work that is hazardous due to its nature or conditions, however, their work becomes a WFCL in urgent need of elimination.

- "Child labour" as estimated in this document therefore comprises all children under 15 years of age who are economically active, excluding (i) those under 5 years of age and (ii) those aged 12-14 years who spend fewer than 14 hours a week on their jobs, unless their activities or occupations are hazardous by nature or circumstance. Added to this are children aged 15- 17 years, who are involved in hazardous work. Table 9 presents the forms of work classified according to the above principles.

TABLE 2

"Child labour" as Defined for the Purpose of the 2000 and 2004 Global Estimates

Age groups	*Forms of work*			
	Non-hazardous work (in non-hazardous industries & occupations and <43 hrs./week)		Worst forms of child labour	
	Light work	*Regular work*	*Hazardous work*	*Unconditional worst*
	(<14hrs/week)	(>14hrs/week and <43hrs/week)	(in specified hazardous industries & occupations plus >43hrs/week in	forms (trafficked children; children in forced & bonded labour,

	other industries and occupations)	armed conflict, prostitution & pornography, and illicit activities)
5-11		
12-14		
15-17		

Note: The blue areas are considered to be forms of child labour in need of elimination as per ILO Conventions Nos. 138 and 182.

(c) Hazardous Work and Other Worst Forms of Child Labour

Hazardous work by children is any activity or occupation which, by its nature or type, has or leads to adverse effects on the child's safety, physical or mental health, or moral development. Hazards could also derive from excessive workload, physical conditions of work, and/or work intensity in terms of the duration or hours of work even where the activity or occupation itself is known to be non-hazardous or "safe".

ILO Conventions Nos. 138 and 182 both define hazardous work only very generally as "likely to jeopardize/harm the health, safety or morals of children." The list of such work must be determined at the national level after tripartite consultation.

Taking account of national classifications of hazardous child work, where they exist, we established and applied for all countries the following criteria solely for the purpose of the estimates:

- Any child working in mining and construction was considered to be in hazardous work.
- Beyond mining and construction, a number of occupations were considered to be of a hazardous nature if they involved, for instance, work with heavy machinery or exposure to pesticides. The classification was based on (i) the stipulations contained in ILO Recommendation No. 190 accompanying the ILO Convention on the Worst Forms of Child Labour, 1999 (No. 182) and (ii) stipulations on hazardous work in national legislation.
- Any child younger than 18 years working 43 hours or more a week was considered to be in hazardous work (see also Recommendation No. 190, Para. 3.

Recommendation No. 190 on the Worst Forms of Child Labour (Excerpt):

II. Hazardous work

3. In determining the types of work referred to under Article 3 (d) of the Convention, and in identifying where they exist, consideration should be given, inter alia, to:

(a) work which exposes children to physical, psychological or sexual abuse;

(b) work underground, under water, at dangerous heights or in confined spaces;

(c) work with dangerous machinery, equipment and tools, or which involves the manual handling or transport of heavy loads;

(d) work in an unhealthy environment which may, for example, expose children to hazardous substances, agents or processes, or to temperatures, noise levels, or vibrations damaging to their health;

(e) work under particularly difficult conditions such as work for long hours or during the night or work where the child is unreasonably confined to the premises of the employer.

It is important to note that our *statistical determination of hazardous work* by children does *not* take into account the criterion set out in ILO Convention No. 138, Art. 3 that provides for exceptional authorization of work of a potentially hazardous nature under strict conditions from 16 years of age (ILO Recommendation No. 190, Para. 4 contains the same idea). For the purposes of this study, we decided to apply a single cut-off point of 18 years of age.

(d) Unconditional Worst Forms of Child Labour

Due to data imbalances, it was not possible to recalculate the extent of the unconditional WFCL in the 2004 global child labour estimates.

It is however important to note that the term "unconditional worst forms of child labour" refers to those forms covered by items (a) to (c) of Article 3 of ILO Convention No. 182 which read:

"(a) all forms of slavery or practices similar to slavery, such as the sale and trafficking of children, debt bondage and serfdom and forced or compulsory labour, including forced or compulsory recruitment, of children for use in armed conflict;

(b) the use, procuring or offering a child for prostitution, for the production of pornography or for pornographic performances;

(c) the use, procuring or offering of a child for illicit activities, in particular for the production and trafficking of drugs as defined in the relevant international treaties; ..."

CHILD LABOUR LEGISLATION AND SCENARIO

The International Labor Organization (ILO) estimates that 250 million children between the ages of five and fourteen work in developing countries – at least 120 million full time. Sixty-one percent of these are in Asia, 32 percent in Africa, and 7 percent in Latin America. Most working children in rural areas are found in agriculture; urban children work in trade and services, with fewer in manufacturing, construction and domestic service. Only an estimated 5 percent of child laborers work in export industries.

Article 32 of the Convention on the Rights of the Child protects children from economic exploitation and work that is likely to be hazardous to the child's development, or to interfere with the child's education. It calls on states to take legislative and other measures, including sanctions and penalties, to guarantee this protection to children.

Those addressing the issue of child labor are sometimes divided on how to proceed and consider a range of different approaches. Some urge that child labor be eliminated quickly and aggressively, including through the use of trade sanctions when countries or industries fail to act decisively. Some call for reforming the conditions in which children work with a view toward gradual elimination. Some believe that work plays an important and positive role in children's lives and in their relations with their families, and seek reform, but not an end to child labour.

A simple approach of requiring employers to discharge all child workers can lead to devastating results for children removed from the workplace. Children discharged from work can find themselves on the street in prostitution or crime, or working in even worse conditions and for less pay. In tackling the issue of child labor, consideration of the immediate and direct consequences for working children and their families cannot be underestimated. The removal of children from the workforce can have devastating results for children if not accompanied with nuanced adjustment programs for their rehabilitation, education, and direct assistance.

The trade sanction approach – seeking boycotts of employers or governments who permit the use of child labor, or banning the importation of goods made with child labor – is extremely difficult to monitor. Employers' assurances that they have not used child labor in manufacturing workplaces around the world are meaningless without effective and independent monitoring mechanisms in place. And trade sanctions or boycotts narrowly targeted to particular export industries, even if effective, have small impact, as only about 5 percent of child laborers work in export industries.

Child labor includes a range of situations from the clearly hazardous and exploitative, four year-old children tied to rug looms to keep them from running away, to the benign or positive, seventeen-year-olds helping out on the family farm or working after school to earn some pocket money. In many cases, as in the latter examples, children's work can be helpful to them and their families; money earned and the experience gained by children can be positive contributions to their development into responsible adults. This depends largely on the age of the child, the conditions in which the child works, and whether work prevents the child from going to school.

What is clear, and what the international community has agreed on, is that certain types of child labor are hazardous to the health, safety, and morals of children and should be banned. The ILO Convention concerning the Prohibition and Immediate Action for the Elimination of the Worst Forms of Child Labor (ILO Convention 182), adopted unanimously by the 174 member states of the ILO in June 1999, commits states who ratify it to take immediate steps to prohibit and eliminate "the worst forms of child labor," and to take effective measures to prevent children's engagement in it. The term child refers to anyone under the age of eighteen. Under the convention, the worst forms of child labor include the sale and trafficking of children, debt bondage, forced or compulsory labor (including the forced recruitment of children for use in armed conflict), using children for prostitution or production of pornography, using children for illegal activities, particularly drug trafficking, and other work which is likely to "harm the health, safety or morals of children."

Cognizant of the dangers of banning child labor without also providing children with alternatives to labor, the convention obligates states parties to ensure that children removed from the worst forms of child labor be given direct assistance to ensure their removal, rehabilitation, and social reintegration. Most importantly, the convention mandates that children removed from labor be ensured access to free basic education, and wherever possible and appropriate, vocational training.

Human Rights Watch has taken on the issue of child labor in areas where the rights abuses are clear and acute, and which fall within the new ILO Convention's definition of "worst forms of child labor." We have worked on bonded child laborers in India and Pakistan; the use of children as soldiers in armed conflicts around the world; and the employment of live-in domestic child servants in Sri Lanka. Throughout, Human Rights Watch has emphasized the importance of providing education and rehabilitation in assisting children removed from these worst forms of child labor to truly end the practice.

The importance of providing free and compulsory primary education cannot be underestimated in the fight to end the economic exploitation of children. The reasons are simple. Education opens up the whole future to a child, offering the chance for improved health, safety, and greater economic opportunity, and the full enjoyment of their rights

Agricultural work accounts for some 70 per cent of child labour worldwide, forcing children to work long hours, operate dangerous machinery, and carry loads that are too heavy for their growing bodies, the United Nations Food and Agriculture Organization (FAO) said today.

"Most working children in the world are found on farms and plantations, not in factories, sweatshops or urban areas," said Jennie Dey DePryck, Chief of

FAO's Rural Institutions and Participation Service, in a statement issued in Rome.

The FAO noted that agriculture is one of the world's three most hazardous work sectors, along with mining and construction.

"Some agricultural activities – mixing and applying pesticides, using certain types of machinery – are so dangerous that children should be clearly prohibited from engaging in them," said Parviz Koohafkan, Director of FAO's Rural Development Division.

He cautioned, however, that the issue is a complex one since not all of the agricultural work that children perform is harmful to their development and well-being.

"When it comes to subsistence and family agriculture, children's participation in family farm activities helps them learn valuable skills, build self-esteem and contribute to the generation of household income, which has a positive impact on their own livelihoods," Mr. Koohafkan said.

TRENDS IN GLOBAL CHILD LABOUR

Current Trends

The estimates regarding are based on an extrapolation of child labour data from 60 national household surveys. Key results are presented according to

- form of children's work,
- age group,
- sector of activity, and
- region.

Working children. The incidence of children's work in the sense of economic activity declined among all major age groups (see Table 3). About one-sixth of the total child population—i.e. 191 million children aged 5-14 years—was involved in some kind of economic activity in 2004. In total, there were some 20 million fewer working children in this age group than there had been four years earlier. Boys continue to be slightly more exposed to work than girls, especially in the older age groups.

Child labour. Child labour, a more restricted category than is "working children", excludes all children working legally in accordance with ILO Conventions Nos. 138 and 182. The global number of child labourers aged 5-17 years declined by 28 million from 246 million in 2000 to 218 million in 2004 (see Table 3). The incidence dropped to an average rate of 13.9 per cent. We note that gender differentials with regard to child labour become more pronounced with increasing age. Significantly more boys than girls are exposed to child labour in the older, 12- to 14-year and 15- to 17-year age groups.

Children in hazardous work. The number of children in this worst form of child labour (WFCL) dropped considerably, from an estimated 171 million in 2000 to 126 million in 2004 (see Table 3). The decrease was particularly strong among children in the 5- to 14-year-old age cohort. Boys continue to be more involved in dangerous jobs than girls.

Sectoral distribution of working children. Much of children's work is agricultural and rural in nature. We estimate that more than two-thirds (69 per cent) of all working children are involved in agriculture, compared to 22 per cent in services and 9 per cent in industry.

TABLE 3

Estimates of Various Forms of Children's Work, 2000 and 2004

Age Groups		*Child population*		*Working children*		*Child labourers*		*Children in hazardous work*	
		2000	2004	2000	2004	2000	2004	2000	2004
5-17	No. (million)	1531.4	1566.3	351.9	317.4	245.5	217.7	170.5	126.3
	Incidence (Percentage of age group)	100.0	100.0	23.0	20.3	16.0	13.9	11.1	8.1
	Percentage change from 2000 to 2004	—	2.3	—	-9.8	—	-11.3	—	-25.9
5-14	No. (million)	1199.4	1206.5	211.0	190.7	186.3	165.8	111.3	74.4
	Incidence (Percentage of age group)	100.0	100.0	17.6	15.8	15.5	13.7	9.3	6.2
	Percentage change from 2000 to 2004	—	0.6	—	-9.6	—	-11.0	—	-33.2
15-17	No. (million)	332.0	359.8	140.9	126.7	59.2	51.9	59.2	51.9
	Incidence (Percentage of age group)	100.0	100.0	42.4	35.2	17.8	14.4	17.8	14.4
	Percentage change from 2000 to 2004	8.4	—	-10.1	—	-12.3	—	-12.3	

Regional distribution of working children. The Asian-Pacific region continued to harbour the largest number of child workers, 122 million in total (see Table 4). It is followed by Sub-Saharan Africa (49.3 million) and Latin America and the Caribbean (5.7 million). Due to data gaps, there are no new estimates for the Middle East and North Africa and the group of industrialized countries. The number of child workers declined in Asia/Pacific and in Latin

America and the Caribbean, but not in Sub-Saharan Africa. The decline in the Latin American/Caribbean region was most significant. From 2000 to 2004, the region's number of child workers and it's child activity rate dropped to about one third of their previous levels. In the Asian-Pacific region, there was a slight decrease both in relative and absolute terms. The number of economically active children was reduced by 5 million in the four-year period under review. The regional activity rate also fell. The picture in Sub-Saharan Africa is more mixed. While the number of child workers increased slightly, the incidence of work dropped by more than two percentage points.

TABLE 4

Regional Trends in Children's Work, 2000 - 2004 (5 to 14 Year Olds)

Region	*Child population (million)*		*Economically active children (million)*		*Activity rate (%)*	
	2000	*2004*	*2000*	*2004*	*2000*	*2004*
Asia and the Pacific	655.1	650.0	127.3	122.3	19.4	18.8
Latin America and the Caribbean	108.1	111.0	17.4	5.7	16.1	5.1
Sub-Saharan Africa	166.8	186.8	48.0	49.3	28.8	26.4
Other regions	269.3	258.8	18.3	13.4	6.8	5.2
World	1'199.3	1'206.6	211.0	190.7	17.6	15.8

Child Labour in Africa

Some Key Data on Child Labour in the Region

- The ILO has recently estimated that some 217.7 million children ages 5 to 17 are engaged in child labour around the world. Of these, some 126.3 million are caught in the worst forms of child labour.
- Roughly 122.3 million children are economically active in Asia and the Pacific, 49.3 million in Sub-Saharan Africa, 5.7 million in Latin America and the Caribbean, and 13.4 million in other regions.
- Among working children ages 5 to 14 in the world, 69% are employed in the agricultural sector, 9% are employed in the industrial sector and the remaining 22% are employed in the services sector.
- Sub-Saharan Africa has the greatest incidence of economically active children: 26.4 percent of children ages 5 to 14 in the region are at work.
- In Africa, an estimated 50,000 children are in prostitution and pornography.
- Some 120,000 children under the age of 18 are thought to have been coerced into taking up arms as child soldiers, or military porters, messengers, cooks or sex slaves in Africa.

- Results from the Ghana National Child Labour Survey (IPEC-SIMPOC, 2001) indicate that 0.75 million or 27.6% of males, ages 5-14, work and 0.66 million or 26.3% of females, of the same age group, work resulting in 1.41 million or 27% of all children, ages 5 to 14, working.
- The Government of Kenya has recently reported that 1.9 million children, between the ages of 5-17, are working children. Only 3.2% of these children have attained a secondary school education and 12.7% have no formal schooling at all.
- Results from the Malawi National Child Labour (IPEC-SIMPOC, 2002) indicate that 0.39 million or 25.4% of males, ages 5-14, work and 0.34 million or 21.3% of females, of the same age group, work resulting in 0.73 million or 23.3% of all children, ages 5-14, working.
- Among the estimated 13, 4 million children aged between 5 and 17 years in South Africa in 1999, the extent of work-related activity was at least 36%.
- It is estimated that, in Tanzania mainland, there were 11,965,146 children ages 5-17, accounting for 36.7% of the projected national population of 32.6 million. Majority of these children (79.0%) live in the rural areas (2000/2001 integrated labour force and child labour survey)
- According to the Government of Zambia, there are some 595,000 child workers in Zambia. Of these, 58% are 14 or younger and, thus, ineligible for any form of employment under the Employment of Young Persons Act.
- In Zimbabwe, 26, 3% (1,225,868) of the children were involved in some economic activity of one nature or another.

Strategies

IPEC's strategies in Africa contribute to the ILO's priorities for the region, particularly poverty reduction, through mainstreaming of decent work in PRSPs and other poverty reduction programmes. The ILO priorities list children and youth as being most vulnerable. The IPEC programme targets some of the poorest among these groups. IPEC's work in Africa focuses on much needed capacity building, the strengthening of an Africa-wide movement against child labour and the provision of alternatives for children and their families. Large-scale national timebound programmes and multi-country programmes targeting specific WFCL have become important foci of IPEC's work in this region.

A new regional strategy has been developed for West and Central Africa concentrating on vocational training and apprenticeships as tools to combat child labour. Efforts also continue to encourage further ratifications of Conventions No. 182 and No. 138 and to assist member States to fulfil their obligations under these. On 12 June 2005, the governments and social partners of seven African countries (out of 14 countries globally) signed the Call to Action to commit their countries to eliminate child labour in the mines and quarries.

In the context of widespread and extreme poverty, families depend on children's income to help pay for basic needs, even survival. In addition, the widespread devastation caused by the HIV/AIDS pandemic, recurrent food crises and political unrest and conflict clearly exacerbate the problem.

There are still knowledge gaps on the magnitude and nature of the problem in Africa, although numerous WFCL are known to exist in many countries. Of particular concern are child trafficking, the use of children in armed conflict, mining, hazardous work in agriculture, commercial sexual exploitation and domestic labour. Children trapped in bondage and slavery have been reported in some areas.

IPEC Projects Active 2004-05

TBP Support Projects - 6:	Ghana, Kenya, Madagascar, Senegal, South Africa, and Tanzania
Country Programmes - 6:	Burkina Faso, Benin, Mali, Morocco, Niger, and Togo
SIMPOC National Surveys - 7:	Completed: Lesotho, Malawi, Uganda; Ongoing: Burkina Faso, Côte d'Ivoire, Mali, Senegal

Regional Projects Focusing on Children in Specific Worst Forms: 6

- Armed conflict - Phase 1: (Burundi, Congo, the Democratic Republic of Congo and Rwanda)
- Trafficking in children - Phases 1 & 2 (Benin, Burkina Faso, Cameroon, Cote d'Ivoire, Gabon, Ghana, Mali, Nigeria and Togo)
- Cocoa/commercial agriculture in West and Central Africa (Cameroon, Cote d'Ivoire, Ghana, Guinea and Nigeria)
- Commercial agriculture in eastern and southern Africa (Kenya, Malawi, Tanzania, Uganda and Zambia). (Completed 2005)
- Child domestic labour (Kenya, Tanzania, Uganda and Zambia)
- Prevention and Elimination of Child Labour in Mining in West Africa (Burkina Faso, Niger) (starting 2005)

Other Regional Projects: 4

- Regional capacity building (Ghana, Kenya, Nigeria, Uganda and Zambia, with some activities in Ethiopia, Malawi, South Africa and Tanzania)
- Regional project on skills training and vocational education (Ghana, Kenya, Tanzania)

- Regional project on vocational training and apprenticeship (Benin, Burkina Faso, Mali, Niger, Togo, Madagascar, Morocco, Senegal)
- Sub-regional project on combating HIV/AIDS and child labour in Sub-Saharan Africa (pilot projects in Uganda and Zambia)

Country Sectoral or Area-Based Projects Focusing on Children in Specific Worst Forms: 1

- Morocco: Worst forms of child labour in rural areas

DATASETS UNDERLYING THE 2004 GLOBAL CHILD LABOUR ESTIMATES

Estimates on Working Children in 2004

Number	*Country name*	*Source*	*Year*	*Region*
1.	Bangladesh	SIMPOC	2002-03	Asia and the Pacific
2.	Cambodia	SIMPOC	2002	Asia and the Pacific
3.	India	NSSO	1999-2000	Asia and the Pacific
4.	Mongolia	MICS	2000	Asia and the Pacific
5.	Philippines	SIMPOC	2002	Asia and the Pacific
6.	Portugal	SIMPOC	2001	Developed Economies
7.	Turkey	SIMPOC	1999	Developed Economies
8.	Yemen	Baseline Survey	2001	Middle East and North Africa
9.	Belize	SIMPOC	2001	Latin America and the Caribbean
10.	Bolivia	MICS	2000	Latin America and the Caribbean
11.	Brazil	PNAD	2003	Latin America and the Caribbean
12.	Colombia	SIMPOC	2001	Latin America and the Caribbean
13.	Costa Rica	SIMPOC	2002	Latin America and the Caribbean
14.	El Salvador	SIMPOC	2001	Latin America and the Caribbean
15.	Guatemala	SIMPOC	2000	Latin America and the Caribbean
16.	Venezuela	EHM, WB	2000	Latin America and the Caribbean
17.	Cameroon	LSMS	2001	Sub-Saharan Africa
18.	Congo, Democratic Republic	MICS	2000	Sub-Saharan Africa
19.	thiopia	WB	2000	Sub-Saharan Africa
20.	Ghana	SIMPOC	2000	Sub-Saharan Africa
21.	Kenya	MICS	2000	Sub-Saharan Africa
22.	Madagascar	WB	2001	Sub-Saharan Africa
23.	Malawi	SIMPOC	2002	Sub-Saharan Africa
24.	Lesotho	MICS	2000	Sub-Saharan Africa
25.	Senegal	MICS	2000	Sub-Saharan Africa
26.	Swaziland	MICS	2000	Sub-Saharan Africa
27.	Albania	MICS	2000	Transition Economies
28.	Azerbaijan	MICS	2000	Transition Economies

29.	Bosnia and Herzegovina	MICS	2000	Transition Economies
30.	Moldova	MICS	2000	Transition Economies
31.	Uzbekistan	MICS	2000	Transition Economies

Matched Sample countries

Number	*Country name*	*Period spread*	*Region*
1.	Bangladesh	1999-2003	Asia and the Pacific
2.	Cambodia	1996-2002	Asia and the Pacific
3.	India	1992-1999	Asia and the Pacific
4.	Philippines	1998-2002	Asia and the Pacific
5.	Portugal	1998-2001	Developed Economies
6.	Turkey	1994-1999	Developed Economies
7.	Yemen	1999-2001	Middle East and North Africa
8.	Bolivia	1999-2000	Latin America and the Caribbean
9.	Brazil	1998-2003	Latin America and the Caribbean
10.	Colombia	1998-2001	Latin America and the Caribbean
11.	Costa Rica	1998-2002	Latin America and the Caribbean
12.	El Salvador	1999-2001	Latin America and the Caribbean
13.	Cameroon	1996-2001	Sub-Saharan Africa
14.	Ghana	1997-2000	Sub-Saharan Africa
15.	Kenya	1999-2000	Sub-Saharan Africa
16.	Senegal	1995-2000	Sub-Saharan Africa
17.	Azerbaijan	1995-2000	Transition Economies

Estimates on Working Children in 2000

Number	*Country name*	*Source*	*Year*	*Region*
1.	Bangladesh	NSS	1999	Asia and the Pacific
2.	Cambodia	LSMS	1996	Asia and the Pacific
3.	India	NSS	1994	Asia and the Pacific
4.	Pakistan	Pre-SIMPOC	1996	Asia and the Pacific
5.	Philippines	LSMS	1998	Asia and the Pacific
6.	Sri Lanka	SIMPOC	1999	Asia and the Pacific
7.	Portugal	SIMPOC	1998	Developed Economies
8.	Turkey	Pre-SIMPOC	1994	Developed Economies
9.	Egypt	LSMS	1998	Middle East and North Africa
10.	Yemen	NSS	1997	Middle East and North Africa
11.	Bolivia	LSMS	1999	Latin America and the Caribbean
12.	Brazil	LSMS	1998	Latin America and the Caribbean

13.	Colombia	LSMS	1998	Latin America and the Caribbean
14.	Costa Rica	LSMS	1998	Latin America and the Caribbean
15.	El Salvador	LSMS	1999	Latin America and the Caribbean
16.	Mexico	LSMS	1996	Latin America and the Caribbean
17.	Paraguay	LSMS	1999	Latin America and the Caribbean
18.	Cameroon	LSMS	1996	Sub-Saharan Africa
19.	Ghana	LSMS	1997	Sub-Saharan Africa
20.	Kenya	SIMPOC	1999	Sub-Saharan Africa
21.	Mauritania	LSMS	1995	Sub-Saharan Africa
22.	Namibia	SIMPOC	1999	Sub-Saharan Africa
23.	Nigeria	SIMPOC	2000	Sub-Saharan Africa
24.	Senegal	LSMS	1995	Sub-Saharan Africa
25.	South Africa	SIMPOC	1999	Sub-Saharan Africa
26.	Zambia	SIMPOC	1999	Sub-Saharan Africa
27.	Azerbaijan	LSMS	1995	Transition Economies
28.	Kazakhstan	LSMS	1996	Transition Economies
29.	Ukraine	SIMPOC	1999	Transition Economies

First and Second Round Estimates on Child Labour and Children in Hazardous Work, 2004

Number	*Country name*	*Source*	*Year*	*Region*
1.	Bangladesh	SIMPOC	2002-03	Asia and the Pacific
2.	Cambodia	SIMPOC	2002	Asia and the Pacific
3.	India	NSSO	2000	Asia and the Pacific
4.	Philippines	SIMPOC	2001	Asia and the Pacific
5..	Portugal	SIMPOC	2001	Developed Economies
6.	Belize	SIMPOC	2001	Latin America and the Caribbean
7.	Brazil	SIMPOC	2001	Latin America and the Caribbean
8.	Colombia	SIMPOC	2001	Latin America and the Caribbean
9.	Costa Rica	SIMPOC	2002	Latin America and the Caribbean
10.	El Salvador	SIMPOC	2001	Latin America and the Caribbean
11.	Guatemala	SIMPOC	2000	Latin America and the Caribbean
12.	Honduras	SIMPOC	2002	Latin America and the Caribbean
13.	Jamaica	SIMPOC	2002	Latin America and the Caribbean
14.	Panama	SIMPOC	2000	Latin America and the Caribbean
15.	Venezuela	LSMS	2000	Latin America and the Caribbean
16.	Cameroon	LSMS	2001	Sub-Saharan Africa
17.	Ghana	SIMPOC	2000	Sub-Saharan Africa
18.	Malawi	SIMPOC	2002	Sub-Saharan Africa
19.	Tanzania	SIMPOC	2001	Sub-Saharan Africa

First Round Estimates

Number	*Country name*	*Source*	*Year*	*Region*
1.	Bangladesh	SIMPOC	2002-03	Asia and the Pacific
2.	Cambodia	SIMPOC	2002	Asia and the Pacific
3.	Philippines	SIMPOC	2001	Asia and the Pacific
4.	Portugal	SIMPOC	2001	Developed Economies
5.	Belize	SIMPOC	2001	Latin America and the Caribbean
6.	Colombia	SIMPOC	2001	Latin America and the Caribbean
7.	Costa Rica	SIMPOC	2002	Latin America and the Caribbean
8.	El Salvador	SIMPOC	2001	Latin America and the Caribbean
9.	Honduras	SIMPOC	2002	Latin America and the Caribbean
10.	Malawi	SIMPOC	2002	Sub-Saharan Africa

Second Round Estimates

Number	*Country name*	*Source*	*Year*	*Region*
1.	India	NSSO	2000	Asia and the Pacific
2.	Brazil	SIMPOC	2001	Latin America and the Caribbean
3.	Guatemala	SIMPOC	2000	Latin America and the Caribbean
4.	Jamaica	SIMPOC	2002	Latin America and the Caribbean
5.	Panama	SIMPOC	2000	Latin America and the Caribbean
6.	Venezuela	LSMS	2000	Latin America and the Caribbean
7.	Cameroon	LSMS	2001	Sub-Saharan Africa
8.	Ghana	SIMPOC	2000	Sub-Saharan Africa
9.	Tanzania	SIMPOC	2001	Sub-Saharan Africa

Matched Sample

Number	*Country name*	*Spread*	*Region*
1.	Cambodia	1996-2001	Asia and the Pacific
2.	India	1994-2000	Asia and the Pacific
3.	Philippines	1995-2001	Asia and the Pacific
4.	Brazil	1997-2001	Latin America and the Caribbean
5.	Colombia	1998-2001	Latin America and the Caribbean
6.	El Salvador	1998-2001	Latin America and the Caribbean
7.	Cameroon	1996-2001	Sub-Saharan Africa
8.	Ghana	1997-2000	Sub-Saharan Africa

CHILD LABOUR IN ASIA AND THE PACIFIC

Some Key Data on Child Labour in the Region

- The ILO has recently estimated that some 217.7 million children ages 5 to 17 are engagedb in child labour around the world. Of these, some 126.3 million are caught in the worst forms of child labour.
- Roughly 122.3 million children ages 5 to 14 are economically active in Asia and the Pacific, 49.3 million in Sub-Saharan Africa, 5.7 million in Latin America and the Caribbean, and 13.4 million in other regions.
- Among working children ages 5 to 14 in the world, 69% are employed in the agricultural sector, 9% are employed in the industrial sector and the remaining 22% are employed in the services sector.

With 122.3 million economically active children ages 5 to 14, the Asia and the Pacific region has the highest number of working children worldwide. Many worst forms of child labour are a problem in the region, including child trafficking, commercial sexual exploitation, bonded child labour, child domestic work, hazardous child labour, and the recruitment and use of children for armed conflict or drug trafficking. A high tolerance for child labour in many countries and political volatility and conflict in certain others (e.g. Afghanistan, Nepal, Indonesia and Sri Lanka) exacerbate the problem and can hinder the implementation of action against it. In addition, a large number of children in areas affected by the tsunami in Thailand, Indonesia, Sri Lanka and India are vulnerable to entering child labour.

- Results from the Bangladesh National Child Labour Survey (IPEC-SIMPOC, 2002-03) indicate that 3.4 million or 18.5% of males, ages 5-14, work and 1.3 million or 7.8% of females, of the same age group, work resulting in 4.7 million or 13.4% of all children, ages 5-14, working.
- The Cambodia Child Labour Survey (IPEC-SIMPOC, 2001) estimated that there were about 1,516,363 children aged 5-14 who can be considered "working children", about 44.8% of children in this age group. More boys than girls in the age groups 5-9 years old, 10-14 years old and 15-17 years old were working children.
- The total economically active child population between 5 and 17 years by current activity status was estimated at 68580 during 2002-03 in Mongolia. The overall child work rate is 10.1 percent. For the child population of aged 5-14 years, the child work ratio is 7.2 percent, but is considerably higher for the age group 15-17 years at 18.5 percent.
- Among the 40 million children aged 5-14 years in Pakistan, 3.3 million, i.e. 8.3 per cent, were economically active in 1996.
- Results from the Philippines Child Labour Survey (IPEC-SIMPOC,

2001) indicate that 1.4 million or 13.4% of males, ages 5-14, work and 0.8 million or 8.4% of females, of the same age group, work resulting in 2.2 million or 11.0% of all children, ages 5-14,working.

- In Sri Lanka, Child Activity Survey (1999) estimates that out of 4,344,770 children in the age group 5 - 17 years in Sri Lanka, 926,038 (21 percent) are engaged in some form of economic activity. The proportion of children who are engaged either in housekeeping activities or in education in addition to an economic activity is about 25 percent. The proportion of children engaged only in economic activities is 7.5%. The corresponding proportion for males is 9.4% and for females it is 4.2%. Out of all working children residing in the urban sector, 14.0% are engaged only in economic activities whereas the corresponding proportion in the rural sector is 7.1%.

Strategies

IPEC strategies in Asia, as elsewhere, are well in line with ILO priorities in the Region. As an integrated part of the ILO's programme in the countries, IPEC works towards mainstreaming child labour into government policies, strategies, plans and budgets. Child labour issues have been included in the national PRSPs in Cambodia, Indonesia, Nepal and Pakistan, and mainstreaming is being pursued in other countries, such as the Philippines and Viet Nam. Efforts are being made to integrate child labour and trafficking concerns into Education for All initiatives in Cambodia, China, India, Indonesia, Pakistan, the Philippines, Sri Lanka and Viet Nam. ILO priorities for the next biennium within the framework of fair globalization are: skills development, labour, migration, youth employment, collaboration with sub-regional and crossregional groupings (such as APEC and ASEAN), working out of poverty, advancing gender equality and addressing the needs of the most vulnerable - children, migrants and young women. These are all areas that offer potential for integrating child labour concerns within the broader Decent Work Agenda. Migrants, children and young women are among the most vulnerable.

Strategies such as capacity building of the social partners and IPEC implementing agencies, advocacy for adherence and implementation of ILO Conventions, awareness raising of the public and target groups and focused direct assistance are slowly but surely making inroads into the child labour problem.

Awareness and support for the eradication of the WFCL in a comprehensive manner is on the rise. Several national time-bound support projects are now being developed and implemented and an increasing number of regional sectoral programmes addressing child trafficking and child domestic work are in place. Progress is also being made with respect to children working in hazardous conditions. A regional tripartite workshop on the implementation of hazardous provisions of Conventions No. 138 and No. 182 was held in June 2005.

IPEC Projects - 2004-05

TBP Support Projects - 6 + 1:	Cambodia, Nepal, the Philippines, Indonesia (includes response to tsunami in Aceh province), Pakistan, Mongolia (starts 2005), Bangladesh (Prep-Phase)
Country Programmes - 3:	Lao PDR, Mongolia, and Viet Nam - (all completed 2004-05)
SIMPOC National Surveys-2:	Completed: Bangladesh, Mongolia

Country, Sectoral or Area-Based Projects Focusing on Children in Specific Worst Forms: 18

- Bangladesh (3): Garments (completed 2004), Hazardous sectors; Informal sector
- Cambodia (1): Hazardous sectors (completed 2004)
- Indonesia (2): Footwear, fishing (closed 2004)
- Philippines (1): Child soldiers;
- Pakistan (5): Carpet weaving, Soccer ball, Surgical instruments, Education and training, Media project
- India (3): Hazardous sectors covering four states, Andhra Pradesh State-based project, Sericulture industry in Karnataka State
- Nepal (1): Bonded labour
- Sri Lanka (2): Child soldiers; Prevention of child labour in the tsunami affected areas

Regional Sectoral Projects: 6

- APEC awareness raising campaign: eliminating the WFCL and providing educational opportunities (Indonesia, Philippines, Thailand and Viet Nam in Asia)
- Assessing the situation of children in the production, sales, and trafficking of drugs (Indonesia, the Philippines and Thailand). (Completed 2004)
- Child domestic workers (Cambodia, Indonesia, Pakistan and Sri Lanka)
- Child trafficking for labour and sexual exploitation, TICSA Phase II (Bangladesh, Nepal, Sri Lanka, Pakistan, Indonesia and Thailand)
- Trafficking in children and women in China
- Trafficking in children and women in the Mekong countries (Cambodia, Lao PDR, Thailand, Viet Nam, and Yunnan province in China), Phase II

CHILD LABOUR IN EUROPE AND CENTRAL ASIA

Although Europe and Central Asia do not have the sheer numbers of child labourers found in Asia and Africa, the problem is rapidly growing in the transition economies of Eastern and Central Europe and Central Asia. Contributing factors include the vulnerability of many families in the wake of the transition to market economies and the armed conflicts and political crises that have affected several countries in the region.

The most visible face of child labour can be seen in the numerous activities of street children and hazardous agricultural work. However, other WFCL also exist, as in the case of children from rural areas who are trafficked to urban centres or wealthier countries for labour exploitation, including commercial sexual exploitation.

IPEC Projects - 2004-05

TBP Support Projects - 1: Turkey

Country Programmes - 4: Albania, Russia, Turkey, Ukraine

SIMPOC National Surveys - 2: Completed: Georgia, Ongoing: Azerbaijan

Country Sectoral or Area-Based Projects Focusing on Children in Specific Worst Forms: 2

- Street children project, Phase 2 (St Petersburg, Russia)
- Street children project, Phase 1 (Leningrad region, Russia)

Regional Sectoral Projects: 4

- Trafficking in children in selected Balkan countries and the Ukraine, Phase 2 (Albania, Moldova, Romania, Ukraine)
- Worst Forms of Child Labour in Central Asian Republics (Kazakhstan, Kyrgyzstan, Tajikistan, Uzbekistan)
- Worst Forms of Child Labour projects in selected Stability Pact countries of Central and Eastern Europe (Core countries: Albania, Bulgaria, Kosovo, Moldova, Romania)
- Worst forms of child labour, initial phase (Leningrad region, Russia) Child Labour Facts

CHILD LABOUR IN ARAB STATES

Child labour is a significant problem in the region and there is growing evidence that its worst forms persist in many countries. The urban informal sector, seasonal agriculture, street work and domestic labour are of particular concern. Underlying this problem are rising poverty and widening income distribution differentials, an educational system that is unable to retain children, and uneven regional economic and social development that strongly favours urban areas. Although the gender gap in school enrolment has been slowly narrowing, inequity and illiteracy persist.

Working children in this region are vulnerable to participation in illicit activities such as drug trafficking and the commercial sex industry, recruitment by religious extremists, poor health, exposure to unsafe working environment, and lack of access to skills training.

With a focus on alleviating widespread poverty, accelerating development, improving the health and status of children and women, child labour and other issues concerning the large numbers of youth have begun to receive greater attention. In most Arab countries, the minimum age for employment in hazardous work has been raised from 16 to 18 years. All Middle East and North African countries have ratified ILO Convention No. 182. Ministries of labour and employers' and workers' organizations have established child labour units in Egypt, Jordan, Lebanon and Yemen. Other countries are still in the process of developing national plans of action to address the issue of exploitive child labour.

IPEC is supporting the Governments of Egypt, Jordan, Lebanon and Yemen to adopt and implement an explicit child labour policy, identify national priorities and realize objectives through a coherent national policy. Projects aiming at promoting access to quality basic education through the development of scholarship programmes, flexible schedules, and alternative curricula are being implemented.

Across the region, there is still a need to raise awareness of child labour among policy makers and civil societies and to collect more reliable and consistent data. Lack of coordination of efforts among governmental and non-governmental stakeholders, lack of good quality affordable schooling options, and lack of information sharing and community awareness of the dangers inherent in child labour are among the main barriers to successful elimination child labour.

IPEC Projects- 2004-05

TBP Support Projects - 1:	Lebanon and Yemen
Country Programmes - 3:	Egypt, Jordan, Lebanon

SECTORAL DISTRIBUTION OF CHILDREN'S WORK

The indicator for employment by sector—based on the International Standard Industrial Classification of All Economic Activities, Revisions 2 (1968) and 3 (1990)—breaks employment down into three broad groupings of economic activity: agriculture, industry, and services.

- *The agricultural sector* comprises activities in agriculture, hunting, forestry, and fishing. Children's work is primarily concentrated in agriculture, agriculture accounts for more than two-thirds (69 per cent) of all working children in the age group 5 to 14.

- *The industry sector* comprises mining and quarrying, manufacturing, construction, and public utilities (electricity, gas and water). Industry accounts for 9 per cent of working children.
- *The services sector* consists of wholesale and retail trade; restaurants and hotels; transport, storage, and communications; finance, insurance, real-estate, and business services; and community as well as social personal services. Services account for 22 per cent of working children.

WORKING CHILDREN AND THEIR REGIONAL DISTRIBUTION

Global Trend Estimation of the Number of Working Children

In 2002, we estimated the worldwide number of working children based on a sample of 29 countries with national household surveys conducted in the late 1990s. These surveys were designed either

- to measure child labour under the ILO's SIMPOC programme, or
- for broader purposes but containing special modules dealing with the employment of children or teenagers younger than 15 years of age.

Since the publication of the last estimates in 2002, 17 of the 29 countries have conducted a second survey to collect data on the work of children. These data present a matched sample to estimate the evolution of the number of working children in the world over the last four years. Furthermore, new data on the economic activity of children are available for a number of additional countries that have conducted special surveys under SIMPOC or other programmes since the 2002 publication. This larger set of data has been used to prepare regional trend estimates for working children for Asia and the Pacific, for Latin America and the Caribbean, and for Sub-Saharan Africa.

The next two sections present the methodologies underlying the estimation of global and regional trends. This is followed by an evaluation of the results using independent schoolenrolment data compiled by UNESCO.

The methodology first of all involves estimation of the changing incidence of working children, separately for boys and girls and for each age group (5-9, 10-14, and 15-17 years). These rates of change are then used to calculate the current incidence of children's work in each sex and age group. The results are finally applied to the total number of children published by the UN Population Division for 2004 to obtain the ILO current estimate of working children in the world.

The calculation of the global rate of change involves five steps:

1. **Incidence of working children.** Let xijk denote the number of working children in particular sex (i) and age category (j) in a sample country (k). The total number of children in that sex-age category is denoted by yijk. The incidence of working children is the percentage of children working in a particular sex-age category. It is defined by the following ratio:

$$r_{ijk} = 100 * x_{ijk} / y_{ijk}$$

In the process of calculating rijk for the 17 sample countries, the national data have been harmonized where the age limits differed from the standard age groups, and the missing data estimated where values for a particular age group were unavailable. The harmonization and the missing value methods are based on a modified version of the triangular model of Appendix 1 from *Every child counts*. The modified version is described separately in Annex 1 of the present report. This aims to harmonize the data for differences in survey methodologies in line with the logistic model described in Appendix 2 of *Every child counts*.

2. **Rate of change.** For two points in time to and t1, the rate of change of the incidence of working children is measured by the difference between the incidence rate at time to, and the incidence rate at time t1. It is expressed by

$$\Delta_{ijk} = r_{ijk}(t_1) - r_{ijk}(t_o).$$

Given that the time-lag between the national surveys differs from one country to another, the values of . have been harmonized to a standard time-lag of 4 years by simple proportional adjustment. Thus, for example, for a country with to = 1996 and t1 = 2002, the computed values of . are adjusted proportionally downward by the factor 4/(2002- 1996) = 4/6 = 2/3. The calculation of .ijk and the resulting values are shown in Annex 2.

3. **Test of statistical significance.** Observed changes of small magnitude may be due to the sampling and non-sampling errors inherent in sample surveys, and thus may not represent statistically significant evolutions in the incidence of working children. Similarly, abnormally large rates of change, in either direction, may not represent typical situations, and these should be treated as outliers in statistical calculations. Accordingly, the data used for global estimation, d, are plus or minus or zero values depending on the statistical significance of Δ measured in terms of the standard deviation. More precisely, the variable d is defined by

$$d = \begin{cases} 1 & \text{if } \Delta > \gamma\sigma \\ 0 & \text{if } |\Delta| \leq \gamma\sigma \\ -1 & \text{if } \Delta < -\gamma\sigma \end{cases}$$

where σ is the standard deviation of the Δ values, calculated over all sex and age groups and countries, and ã is a constant chosen such that the pattern of significant increases or decreases is smooth and not erratic across sex and age categories. A process of trial and error led to the choice of $\gamma = 7/24$, the harmonic average of the two values 1/2 and 1/12.

4. **Significant decline against significant increase.** The next step is to count, for each sex and age category, the number of countries that registered a significant increase in the incidence of working children (n+ ij), the number that registered a significant decline (nij), and the number that registered no significant change (no ij). The excess of increases over decreases is measured by For a description of logistic models, see Vittinghoff, E.: *Regression methods in biostatistics* (Springer, 2004).

$$n_{ij} = n^{+}_{ij} - n_{ij}$$

The results are presented in Table 3, below. The table indicates, for example, that for boys in the 5- to 9-year age group there is one more country showing a decline in the incidence of working children than there are countries showing increases. Similarly, for girls in the 15- to 17-year age group, the table indicates that there are six more countries registering a significant decline in the incidence of working children than there are countries registering significant increases.

TABLE 5

Excess of Significant Increases Over Significant Declines in the Incidence of Working Children in 17 Sample Countries (2000-2004)

Age group	*Boys*	*Girls*
5-9 yrs	-1	-1
10-14 yrs	-1	-2
15-17 yrs	-4	-6

5. The last step in the estimation of global change in the incidence of working children is to quantify the qualitative results shown in Table 3, above. This quantification is performed by evaluating the typical value of a significant decrease or significant increase over four years in a sample country, and assigning the resulting value to each unit reported in Table 10. The typical value is calculated by the median values of | . |

for cases where | . | > ã ó, over all sex and age categories. The calculation assumes that a typical significant increase has the same value as a typical significant decrease, except for the direction of the change, and this value is the same, on average, for boys and girls and for the three different age groups. The resulting common value is:

$$\text{median}(\,|\Delta| : |\Delta| > \gamma\,\sigma) = 0.25$$

For the estimation procedure to be as robust as possible, the median value calculated above is for a typical country, un-weighted for the population size of the country. Calculating a weighted median had been considered, but rejected due to the possible bias that the procedure could have introduced. Indeed, as the countries on which the calculations are made have not been selected on the basis of their size, each represents equally the other non-selected countries, independently of their size.

Multiplying this value for each entry of Table 3 and dividing by 17 for the total number of sample countries gives the estimated average global change in the incidence of working children by sex and age group, as shown in Table 6, below. Applying these estimates to the global incidence of working children for 2000 (*Every child counts*, we obtain the corresponding estimates for 2004.

TABLE 6

Estimated Global Change in the Incidence of Working Children (2000-2004)

Age group	*Boys*	*Girls*
5-9 yrs	-1.5%	-1.5%
10-14 yrs	-1.5%	-2.9%
15-17 yrs	-5.8%	-8.7%

TABLE 7

Estimated Global Incidence of Working Children (2004)

Age group	*Boys*	*Girls*
5-9 yrs	10.8%	10.5%
10-14 yrs	21.5%	20.0%
15-17 yrs	38.3%	32.0%

Finally, the resulting global estimates of the number of working children in 2004 are obtained by multiplying the incidence figures by the total number of children in each sex and age category published by the UN Population Division (2004 edition).23 Section 2, above, presents the results in detail.

Regional Breakdown of the Trend

The regional trends of the number of working children are estimated by combining the results of two methodologies:

(a) matched sample regional estimates, derived by applying the same methodology developed for the estimation of the global trend to the matched sample of countries in three regions (Asia and the Pacific, Latin America and the Caribbean, and Sub- Saharan Africa); and

(b) model-based regional estimates, derived by applying a logistic regression model to the full sample of countries, matched or unmatched, grouped into five categories (developed economies, Asia and the Pacific, Latin America and the Caribbean, Sub-Saharan Africa, and others). The regional trends are obtained by re-applying the logistic regression model to the sample countries used in the 2000 exercise reported in ILO, *Every child counts. New global estimates on child labour* (Geneva, IPEC, April 2002).

The two methods are further described in the following two sub-sections. A third sub-section describes the method used in combining the two sets of results.

Regional Estimates Based on a Matched Sample

Because of the data limitations, matched-sample estimates have been restricted to the age group of primary concern, i.e. children aged 5-14 years, and to the three major regions for which at least four matched sample countries exist:

Asia and the Pacific:

- Bangladesh – 1999 and 2002-3
- Cambodia – 1996 and 2002
- India – 1992 and 1999-2000
- Philippines – 1998 and 2002
- India – 1992 and 1999-2000

Latin America and the Caribbean:

- Bolivia – 1999 and 2000
- Brazil – 1998 and 2003
- Colombia – 1998 and 2001
- Costa Rica – 1998 and 2002
- El Salvador – 1999 and 2001

Sub-Saharan Africa:

- Cameroon – 1996 and 2001
- Ghana – 1997 and 2000
- Kenya – 1999 and 2000
- Senegal – 1995 and 2000

The estimates are calculated separately for boys and girls, and for the groups aged 5-9 and 10-14 years, before aggregating the results into a single category covering both girls and boys in the 5- to 14-year age group.

The first step in the regional estimation methodology involves examining—for each matched sample country in the region and for each sex and age category—the trend in the incidence of working children as harmonized for age group and methodological differences in the earlier estimation of the global trend. An account is made of (i) the number of matched sample countries with significant increase, (ii) the number with significant decrease, and (iii) the number with no significant movement. Statistical significance is determined in a fashion similar to that used in the global trend methodology, by measuring differences of trend that exceed a fixed fraction of the standard deviation of all incidence rates in the matched sample countries of the region irrespective of sex and age group. On the basis of these results, the difference between the number of countries with significant increases and the number of countries with significant decreases are calculated and reported for each region and each sex and age category, as shown in the table below.

TABLE 8

Regional Change in the Incidence of Working Children (More Matched Sample Countries are Showing Significant Decreases than Increases)

Sex and age group	*Asia and the Pacific*	*Latin America and the Caribbean*	*Sub-Saharan Africa*
Boys			
- 5 – 9 yrs	-2	-2	-1
- 10 –14 yrs	1	-1	-1
Girls			
- 5 – 9 yrs	-2	-1	-1
- 10 –14 yrs	-1	-1	-2
Median absolute value of a significant change	0.93%	10.40%	1.01%

Entry "-2", in the top row and first column of Table 8, indicates that there were two more countries showing a significant decline in the incidence of working children among 5- to 9-year-old boys in Asia and the Pacific than countries showing a significant increase among the same sex and age category in that region. Similarly, the last entry of the row, "-1", indicates that in Sub-Saharan Africa there was only one extra country showing a significant decline in the incidence of working children relative to the number showing a significant increase among the same sex and age category in that region. In general, the table indicates that, in every region and every sex and age category, the trend in the incidence of working children has been a decline, except for girls aged 10-14 years among the matched sample countries in Asia and the Pacific.

The last row of the table gives the median absolute value of a significant change in the incidence of working children, whether it is a significant increase or decrease. For example, a significant increase or decrease of the incidence of working children in a country in Asia and the Pacific is typically about 0.93 percentage points for any sex and age group. The largest median absolute value is in Latin America and the Caribbean, indicating that typically the matched sample countries in that region have exhibited by far the largest decline in the incidence of working children over all sex and age categories. Note that this rather significant decline may require further examination.

TABLE 9

Matched-Sample Calculation of the Number of Working Children in 2004 in Three Regions by Sex and Age Group ('000)

	Boys		*Girls*		*Total*
	5-9 yrs	*10-14 yrs*	*5-9 yrs*	*10-14 yrs*	
Asia and the Pacific					
— Population 2000	168 800	170 900	156 700	158 800	655 200
— Working children 2000	17 900	42 300	22 100	45 000	127 300
— Incidence rate 2000	10.60%	24.75%	14.10%	28.34%	
— Change 2000-2004	-1.86%	0.93%	-1.86%	-0.93%	
— Incidence rate 2004	8.74%	25.68%	12.24%	27.41%	
— Population 2004	166 178	170 145	155 142	158 491	649 956
— Working children 2004	14 531	43 695	18 995	43 438	120 660
Latin America and Caribbean					
— Population 2000	27 700	27 300	26 700	26 400	108 100
— Working children 2000	3 800	7 500	2 000	4 100	17 400
— Incidence rate 2000	13.72%	27.47%	7.49%	15.53%	
— Change 2000-2004	-20.80%	-10.40%	-10.40%	-10.40%	
— Incidence rate 2004	0.00%	17.07%	0.00%	5.13%	
— Population 2004	28 433	27 986	27 450	27 105	110 974
— Working children 2004	0	4 778	0	1 391	6 168
Sub-Saharan Africa					
— Population 2000	44 700	39 200	44 100	38 800	166 800
— Working children 2000	10 400	14 700	10 500	12 400	48 000

—	Incidence rate 2000	23.27%	37.50%	23.81%	31.96%	
—	Change 2000-2004	-1.01%	-1.01%	-1.01%	-2.02%	
—	Incidence rate 2004	22.26%	36.49%	22.80%	29.94%	
—	Population 2004	49 915	44 371	48 955	43 596	186 837
—	Working children 2004	11 109	16 191	11 162	13 052	51 514

Based on these estimated parameters, the next step consists of converting the values into equivalent estimated numbers of working children, as shown in Table 9, above. The starting point is the set of regional estimates of the number of working children for 2000 reported in *Every child counts: New global estimates on child labour* (Geneva, ILO/IPEC, 2002). For each region and sex and age category, the estimated change of incidence, derived in the present paper, is added to the incidence rate of working children in 2000, to obtain the resulting incidence rate in 2004. These incidence rates are then multiplied by the 2004 estimates of the number of children in each sex and age category for each region, according to the population estimates, 2004 edition, of the UN Population Division. The resulting estimates of the number of working children are added across the age groups and sex categories.

Thus we find that, in Asia and the Pacific, the matched sample estimate of the number of working children aged 5-14 years is about 121 million for 2004, a decrease from about 127 million in 2000. Similarly, in Latin America and the Caribbean, the matched sample estimate is 6.2 million working children in 2004, as opposed to 17.4 million in 2000. The corresponding estimates for Sub-Saharan Africa are 51.5 million and 48.0 million in 2004 and 2000, respectively.

Regional Estimates Based on the Full Sample

The method used to compute the model-based regional estimates of the trend in the numbers of working children is based on two separate logistic regressions:

- the national surveys used in the global estimation of the number of working children in 2000; and
- the subsequent national surveys, including the 17 matched surveys used for the global trend between 2000 and 2004.

To make the estimation more robust, a single group of children is used, namely those children aged 5-14 years. The constant coefficients of both regressions are then set in order to reflect the global estimate numbers in the years 2000 and 2004. The trend is measured by subtracting the proportion of working children in a given region in the second regression from the proportion in the first.

The Full-Sample Data

Region by region, the national surveys for the first regression are from the following countries:

- *Asia and the Pacific*—Bangladesh, Cambodia, India, Pakistan, the Philippines, and Sri Lanka.
- *Latin America*—Bolivia, Brazil, Columbia, Costa Rica, El Salvador, Mexico, and Paraguay.
- *The Middle East and Northern Africa*—Egypt and Yemen.
- *Sub-Saharan Africa*—Cameroon, Ghana, Kenya, Mauritania, Namibia, Nigeria, South Africa, Senegal, and Zambia.
- *Developed economies*—Portugal and Turkey.
- *Transition economies*—Azerbaijan, Kazakhstan, and Ukraine.

Region by region, the national surveys for the second regression are from these countries (* ndicates a matched survey):

- *Asia and the Pacific*—Bangladesh*, Cambodia*, India*, the Philippines,* and Mongolia.
- *Latin America*—Bolivia*, Belize, Brazil*, Colombia*, Costa Rica*, El Salvador*, Guatemala, Venezuela.
- *Middle East and Northern Africa*—Yemen*.
- *Sub-Saharan Africa*—Cameroon*, Congo, Ethiopia, Ghana*, Kenya*, Lesotho, Malawi, Madagascar, Senegal*, and Swaziland.
- *Developed economies*—Portugal* and Turkey*.
- *Transition economies*—Albania, Bosnia-Herzegovina, Georgia, Moldova, and Uzbekistan.

Annex 4 provides a listing of all data sources used.

For each survey, to compute the ratio of working children in that category, the total population and the total number of working children aged 5-14 years are summed from the following categories: boys 5-9, boys 10-14, girls 5-9, and girls 10-14 years.

The Logistic Model

The logistic regression model is given by

$$\log\left(\frac{p}{1-p}\right) = c + c_{AP}d_{AP} + c_{DE}d_{DE} + c_{LA}d_{LA} + c_{TE}d_{TE} + c_{ME}d_{ME}$$

where p is the ratio of working children in a country, c is the regression constant, c_{AP}, c_{DE}, c_{LA}, c_{TE} and c_{ME} are the coefficients for Asia and Pacific, developed economies, Latin America, transition economies, and Middle East and northern Africa, d_{AP}, d_{DE}, d_{LA}, d_{TE} and d_{ME} are the indicators for Asia and the Pacific, developed economies, Latin America, transition economies, and Middle East and northern Africa. Sub-Saharan Africa is used as reference, but this has no influence on the final results.

The proportion of working children in a region R is

$$p_R = \frac{\exp(c + c_R)}{1 + \exp(c + c_R)}.$$

From a lack of (matched) surveys, the regions "transition economies" and "Middle East", judged unreliable, are grouped together and independently of time. An estimated proportion pRW for this rest of the world (RW) and its corresponding regression coefficient cRW are estimated with

$$p_{RW} = \frac{p_{TE}^{(1)} pop_{TE}^{(2000)} + p_{ME}^{(1)} pop_{ME}^{(2000)} + p_{TE}^{(2)} pop_{TE}^{(2004)} + p_{ME}^{(2)} pop_{ME}^{(2004)}}{pop_{TE}^{(2000)} + p_{ME}^{(2000)} pop_{TE}^{(2004)++} + pop_{ME}^{(2004)}}$$

where) 200 (*X R pop* is the population of children 5-14 years old in region R in year 200X and) (*i* R p is the proportion of working children in region R estimated in the ith regression.

Final Combined Estimates

The following table presents the results of the full-sample logistic estimates described in the preceding section, and combines it with the matched sample regional results given earlier.

TABLE 10

Combining the Full-Sample Logistic Estimates and Matched Sample Estimates of Working Children (Aged 5-14 Years) by Region

Region	*Full-sample logistic estimate*	*Matched sample*		*Arithmetic average*
		Estimate	*Adjusted*[1]	
Asia and the Pacific	124 600	120 660	119 955	122 300
Latin America & Caribbean	5 300	6 168	6 132	5 700
Sub-Saharan Africa	47 400	51 514	51 213	49 300
Other regions	13 400	—	13 400	13 400
World Total	190 700	178 342	190 700	190 700

Note: Adjusted by pro-rata to the total of full-sample logistic estimates of the corresponding regions.

The two methods lead to similar results, although they are based on very different methodologies and essentially distinct sets of data. In order to combine the results into a single set, it is necessary to adjust one set to the total of the other. This is done here by adjusting the matched sample regional estimates to the total of the corresponding full-sample estimates, because the full-sample estimates have been derived by insuring correspondence to the world estimates. In that sense, the final regional estimates obtained in this paper are in fact the regional break-down of the global estimate obtained in section 2 of the report.

Distribution of Working Children by Sector of Economic Activity

The global estimation of the percentage of children working in the agricultural, industrial, and service sectors is based on data from the following countries: Bangladesh, Belize, Brazil, Cambodia, Cameroon, Columbia, Costa Rica, Ghana, Guatemala, India, the Philippines, Madagascar, Portugal, Turkey, and Venezuela.

The estimation is conducted similarly to that of the regional breakdown, using a logistic regression adjusted so that the percentages over all three sectors total 100. Ninety-five per cent confidence intervals were computed from 9,999 bootstrap replications.24 The result of the estimation is that 69 per cent of the working children aged 5-14 year work in the agricultural sector (with confidence intervals ranging from 59 to 80 per cent), 22 per cent in the service sector (CI: 14 to 30) and 9 per cent in the industrial sector (CI: 5 to 12).

Evaluation of the Results

In this final section, the global and regional estimates on working children are evaluated by comparing the estimated annual rates of change of the number of working children aged 5-14 years with the corresponding estimates of the number of children enrolled in primary and secondary education. We shall also review regional data on primary school-age children out of school for the time period relevant to our estimates.

TABLE 11

Comparison of Annual Change in Primary Education Enrolment (%) and Estimates of Annual Change in Working Children Aged 5-14 Years (%)

Enrolment rate in primary education, ISCED 1 % change 2000 to 2001	*Number of reporting countries*				
	Asia and the Pacific	*Latin American and Caribbean*	*Sub-Saharan Africa*	*Other regions*	*Total*
—	- 5	13	5	11	34
0-4	7	11	21	7	46
5-9	1	2	9	3	15
10+	2	1	5	2	10
Total	*15*	*27*	*40*	*23*	*105*

UNESCO % change in primary education enrolment, 2000-2001	2.3%	0.8%	3.9%	1.6%	2.3%
ILO % annual change in working children 5-14yrs old, 2000-2004	-1.0%	-24.3%	+0.7%	-7.5%	-2.5%

Source: UNESCO data from *Global education digest 2004. Comparing education statistics across the world* (UNESCO Institute of Statistics, Montreal, 2004), Table 2, pp. 50-59, and ILO data from the present report.

We note that the estimated negative global trend of working children derived in this report matches well with the UNESCO figures for the average global increase of enrolment in primary education. Comparison of the results by region, however, shows larger discrepancies, a result that could have been expected, given the limited number of matched sample observations within regions.

TABLE 12

Primary and Secondary Education, Change 1998/99 to 2002/03 (%)

Regions	*Net enrolment rate, primary education (change 1998/99 to 2002/03)*	*Net enrolment rate, total secondary (change 1998/99 to 2002/03)*	*Gross enrolment ratio, total secondary (change 1998/99 to 2002/03)*
Africa	7	3	3
Asia	not available	not available	5
South America	2	16	20

Source: UNESCO data from Global Education Digest 2005 Comparing Education Statistics Across the World, UNESCO Institute of Statistics, Montreal, 2005, Tables 3-5, pp. 54-83.

There is a clear link between child labour developments and trends in children's education, but the extent varies between individual countries and regions. Experience shows, for instance, that appropriate investment in primary and lower secondary education significantly decreases children's work participation rates. In Latin America and the Caribbean, 94 per cent of all primary school-age children are in school. The region has also made great strides towards increasing secondary schooling in the last few years. In contrast, Sub-Saharan Africa has the highest prevalence of primary school-age children out of school. Almost half of the children in West and Central Africa are out of school, and more than onethird in Eastern and Southern Africa. In South Asia, this proportion exceeds one-quarter.

TABLE 13

Primary School-Age Children Out of School by Region, 2001/02

Regions	*School-age population*	*Percentage of all children of primary school age*		*Absolute number of children out of school (thousands)*
		In school	*Out of school*	
Central and Eastern Europe/CIS	24,998	88.3	11.7	2,922
Middle East and North Africa	47,116	81.3	18.7	8,797
Eastern and Southern Africa	55,706	61.5	38.5	21,421
West and Central Africa	53,061	54.7	45.3	24,024
South Asia	162,720	74.0	26.0	42,294
East Asia and the Pacific	176,287	94.3	5.7	10,029
Latin America and the Caribbean	58,064	94.3	5.7	1,789
Industrialized countries	70,595	96.3	3.7	2,602
World	648,545	82.2	17.8	115,375

Source: UNESCO Institute for Statistics: Children out of school: Measuring exclusion from primary education (Montreal, UIS, 2005).

Global March Movement.—"The Global March Against Child Labour is a movement to mobilise worldwide efforts to protect and promote the rights of all children, especially the right to receive a free, meaningful education and to be free from economic exploitation and from performing any work that is likely to be harmful to the child's physical, mental spiritual, moral or social development."

Global March Against Child Labour is a movement born out of hope and the need felt by thousands of people across the globe—the desire to set children free from servitude.

The Global March movement began with a worldwide march when thousands of people marched together to jointly put forth the message against child labour. The march, which started on January 17, 1998, touched every corner of the globe built immense awareness and led to high level of participation from the masses. This march finally culminated at the ILO Conference in Geneva. The voice of the marchers was heard and reflected in the draft of the ILO Convention against the words forms of child labour. The following year, the Convention was unanimously adopted at the ILO Conference in Geneva. Today with 150 countries having ratified the convention so far, it has become the fastest ratified convention in the history of ILO. A large role in this was played by the Global March through our member partners.

With ILO conventions 138 and 182 as well as the UN Convention of Rights of the child forming the base of our movement the Global March also perceives education, and the Right to free and compulsory education of good quality for all children, as non negotiable. Therefore, the Global March also considers the EFA goals under the Dakar Framework an equally important international instrument and pushes for governments to achieve the goal of education for all.

Working on numbers is one thing and direct efforts to end child labour have always been a part of the Global March partner programmes. The Global March seeks to eliminate child labour by questioning, attaching and changing the very systems that compel children to work at the global, regional and national levels. What is key therefore, in the fight to end child labour is the need to advocate for policy changes. The Global March works on a three pronged strategy, or what we call a triangular paradigm. The three key processes affecting the future of the world, in particular our children, are the elimination of child labour. Education For All and poverty alleviation. Bringing together policy and action for a unified response to child labour, illiteracy and poverty is priority for the Global March.

The dedicated partners of the Global March movement form an effective network around the world. Acting as vigilant observers and lobbying with governments in their region, they form the backbone of the movement. The Global March International Secretariat is located in New Delhi, India.

Global March envisions a world free of child labour. It vows to fight for the rights of children in every corner of the world. These form the core beliefs which drive the movement ahead in every endeavour it undertakes.

Global March has shared a long association with the thousands of core marchers who participated in the historic worldwide march against child labour in 1998.

The core marchers continue to combine efforts with Global March in its fight for the rights of children.

Global March derives its strength from its efficient network of national and regional coordinators worldwide.

For an end to Child Labour.—Right from the drafting of ILO convention 182 on the Worst Forms of Child Labour, the Global March has been in the forefront of generating the mass support to make it the most effective tool in inspiring the worldwide actions to end child labour and its worst forms. During 1998-1999, the Convention Campaign focused on raising the profile of child labour issues and influencing decision-makers to adopt a strong and useful convention. Since the adoption in 1999, we have lobbied governments worldwide to accelerate the ratification process and kept child labour high in the world's agenda.

As of 1st April 2007, 14 of the 177 ILO member, countries have still NOT ratified this crucial convention. These countries are Afghanistan, Burma, Cuba,

Eritrea, Guinea-Buissau, Haiti, India, Kiribati (Rebpublic of), Sierra Leone, Soloman Islands, Somalia, Timor-Leste, Turkmenistan and Uzbekistan.

In 2002, Global March also published *Out of the Shadows,* an exhaustive country-wise report on the Worst Forms of Child Labour, as also the status of ratification of international conventions.

The Global March has now shifted it's focus to include the implementation of Convention 182 along with ratification. In order to achieve our goal of elimination of child labour, we need to see that Governments go beyond ratification and implement effective laws and programmes towards this end. We are currently working on an implementation report which will highlight as status of implementation of the conventions country wise.

(*a*) **Main Objective :**

* To accelerate actions by every nation in order to eliminate the words forms of child labour through monitoring faculitating. an lobbying for ratification and full implementation as ILO Convention 138 on the Minimum Age for Employment and ILR Convention 182 on the Worst Forms and Child Labour.

(*b*) **Achievements** :

* Ensuring the civil society participation in creating and implementing an effective international instrument in ending child labour.
* Motivating a number of governments to quickly ratify ILO Convention 182
* Broadening a network of civil society organisations working to end child labour and its worst forms.
* Improving relations and communication among IGOs, civil society organisations, trade unions and other stockholders to have better collaborated efforts in ending child labour.
* Providing expertise in lobbying and advocacy strategies.

Child labour in Agriculture sector.—Global March Against Child Labour, a world wide movement of child rights group, teacher organisations and trade unions active in 140 countries calls for urgent action to stop child labour in agriculture sector. An estimated 150 million children are engaged in a agriculture sector, which from 70% of the total child labour force in the world.

Agriculture is considered as a traditional medium of livelihood but the hazards in this sector remain unnoticed. The uncontrolled use of harmful chemicals like pesticides, insecticides and working with agricultural machinery damage the tender organs of working children and cause accidents. This also directly affects full time education, school retention and quality learning of these children. Children being the cheapest or free labour results in adult unemployment and low wages, which further fuels poverty. This situation is worsened by absence of legal enforcement or inadequate laws, inefficient schooling and health facilities.

Kailash Satyarthi, Chairperson Global March Against Child Labour said "it is unethical to eat delicious food and wear expensive clothes which are produced by half fed, half naked and even enslaved children trapped in agriculture world wide". For how long so called civilized human beings will continue consuming the earnings of their young children, which is not even practiced by animals and birds?" he asked.

Global March Against Child Labour with its partners demands a total eradication and rehabilitation of child labour in agriculture as it restricts education, health freedom and development of children. ILO convention on Worst Form of Child Labour (182) and Minimum Age of Employment (138) must be ratified and genuinely enforced by following the recommendations. The Civil society should be involved in planning, execution and monitoring of the National Action Plan substantiated with implementation mechanism and resources.

Governments must ensure free, compulsory and good quality of education with special focus on children working in agriculture. Minimum 6% of GDP must be earmarked for education including hiring and training teachers with decent wages. A comprehensive policy has to be worked out by the Government to integrate elimination of child labour in the education for all agenda as well as in poverty reduction strategy paper.

Many industries like chocolate, jute sugar, silk, coffee, tea, food involve children in the production and distribution. The corporate sector and national Government must ascertain the non employment of children in their production.

Global March will be observing this year World Day Against Child Labour (June 12th 2007 as Stop Child Labour in Agriculture Day. Through its members and partner organisation Global March Against Child Labour will be conducting rallies demonstrations public meetings, in many countries.

The Global March has decided to support the ILO campaign theme of "Child Labour in Agriculture". Child Labour in agriculture is a serious but largely ignored problem. It has been estimated that 70% of world's 218 million child labourers are involved in agricultural sector. In most cases agriculture is considered as a traditional medium of livelihood but the hazards in this sector, remain unnoticed. The uncontrolled use of harmful chemicals like pesticides, insecticides and working with agricultural machinery damage the tender organs of working children and cause accidents. This also directly affects full time education school retention and quality learning of these children. Children being the cheapest or free labour results in adult unemployment and low wages, which further fuels poverty. This situation is worsened by absence of legal enforcement or inadequate laws, inefficient schooling and health facilities.

In this context Global March should raise this issue at local, national and international level. We must demand a total eradication and rehabilitation of child labour in agriculture as it restricts education, health, freedom and development of children. ILO convention on Worst Form of Child Labour (182) and Minimum Age of Employment (138) must be ratified and genuinely enforced by following the ILO recommendations. The civil societies should be involved in planning execution and monitoring of the National Action Plan substantiated with implementation mechanism and resources.

Governments must ensure free, compulsory and good quality of education with special focus on children working in agriculture. Minimum 6% of GDP must be earmarked for education including hiring and training teachers with decent wages. A comprehensive policy has to be worked out by the Government to integrate elimination of child labour in the education for all agenda as well as in poverty reduction strategy paper.

Many corporations like chocolate, jute, sugar silk coffee, tea, food industry involve children in the production and distribution. The corporate sector and national Government must ascertain the non employment of children in their production. In this regard I would call upon you to observe the World Day Against Child Labour on 12th June, 2007 with full strength. You may plan your activities such as public hearing, media event, issuing press release, human chains, symposium or in-house discussion among the children, community and staff you work with.

(*a*) **Background Note**

These myths have to be broken

* That children working in the field are learning a skill
* That children using pesticides is just a task.
* That child labour in agriculture only exists in developing countries.......

These myths that have perpetuated for long, have to be broken for the sake of the children who are wasting there days and nights, proving that its not just a hobby or just helping their father or just a learning skill but its actually snatching their child hood.

Child labour in agriculture has become a global phenomenon. It is found in all regions of the world. Of an estimated 218 million child labourers 70% of them are working in agriculture. Nine out of ten children in rural areas are working in agriculture or are involved in the similar activities. Many of the world's child labourers in agriculture perform hazardous labour—work that can threaten their lives, limbs, health and general well-being. Agriculture is one of the three most dangerous sectors in which to work at any age, along with construction and mining in terms of work-related deaths and injuries, and this is especially true for children, whose lack of experience or training and still-developing bodies make them particularly vulnerable. It is found in both developed and developing countries and the trend to employ children in these fields has also become very common.

It is also a sector where many children are effectively denied education through factors which include lack of schools and teachers, lack of free education and so on.

Children become farm labourers around the worlds at an early age. Most statistical surveys only cover child workers aged 10 and above. Many children begin work it an earlier age, however, Rural children in particular girls, tend to begin work young at 5, 6 or 7 years of age.

In some countries, children under 10 are estimated to account for 20 per cent of child labour in rural areas. According to ILO report 73.3% boys and 78.8% girls are involved in agriculture and animal husbandry. The work that children perform in agriculture is often invisible and unacknowledged because they assist their parents or relatives on the family farm or they undertake piecework or work under a quota system on larger farms, or plantations, often as part of migrant worker families. Agriculture is historically and traditionally an under-regulated sector in many countries. This means that child labour laws—if they exist—are often less stringent in agricultural industries than in other industries. In some countries, adult and child workers in agriculture are not covered by or are exempt from safety and health laws covering other categories of adult workers.

Children are generally allowed to operate machinery and drive tractors at a younger age in agriculture than in other sectors. It degrades often harms and even kills children.

(*b*) **Some Glaring Facts**

(*i*) *Portugal*—According to the study, agriculture accounts for largest proportion of child labour in Portugal (49.2%) followed by : commerce (12.6%); and manufacturing (12.6% of which 3.8% in the textiles industry and 2.5% in the food industry).

In regional terms, Northern Portugal has most child labour, accounting for 51% of child labour, followed by the Centre of the country (25%) and Lisbon (10.5%).

In Portugal minors mainly work in the summer, with August being the peak month, followed by July and September.

(*ii*) *Child Labour and Cocoa Farming*—In November, 2001 the signatories, issued "the urgent need to identify and eliminate child labour in violation of International Labour Organisation "(ILO") Convention 182 with respect to the growing and processing of cocoa beans and their derivative products". They also recognized "the need to identify and eliminate practices in violation of ILO Convention 29 with equal urgency". The 2001 protocol included a commitment to establish a joint international foundation "to oversee and sustain efforts to eliminate the worst forms of child labour in the growing and processing of cocoa beans and their derivative products".

The International Cocoa Initiative (ICI) established under Swiss law in Geneva in 2002. In 2003, it began consulting a wide range of interested parties, from farmers to consumers, and, in 2004, a strategy was adopted and a program for action launched.

Despite cocoa companies repeated assurance that they would meet the target date, industry largely failed to meet its commitments and the deadline passed with the child labour situation virtually unchanged. Although lawmakers voiced their displeasure, cocoa companies faced no sanctions, instead, the industry negotiated an extended deadline giving it until July 2008 to implement a solution covering half of the cocoa-producing areas of Cote d'lvoire and Ghana.

While industry has specifically addressed the worst forms of child labour under ILO Convention No. 182 and forced labor under ILO Convention 29, it has not addressed other core labor rights in the agreement or in its activities, such as minimum age of employment under ILO Convention No. 138. Further, the industry-led initiative fails to call for concrete steps to ensure that farmers are getting a fair price for their product, which significantly impacts the use of child labour, as farmers are forced to reduce production costs and rely on the cheap labor of children.

(*iii*) *Egypt*—Cotton is the major cash crop, where over one million children work each year to manually remove pests from cotton plants. Children sometimes operate motorized pumps that saturate cotton plants with pesticides. Half a dozen children may help carry the pump's long hose, becoming heavily contaminated with pesticides in the process.

(*iv*) *Ecuador*—Nearly 600,000 children work in the rural sector. Children are working in banana fields and packing plants. 90% of child banana workers interviews by HRW stated that they continued working while fungicides were sprayed from airplanes flying overhead. They described trying to protect themselves by hiding under banana leaves, covering their faces with their shirts, or placing banana cartons on their heads. One boy said, "I went under the packing plaint roof until the (fumigation) plane left-less than an hour. I became intoxicated. My eyes were red. I was nauseous. I was dizzy. I had a headache. I vomited."

(*v*) *United States*—Estimated 300,000 children work as hired labourers in large-scale commercial agriculture, planting weeding, and picking apples, cotton cantaloupe, lettuce, asparagus, watermelons, chillies, and other crops.

(*vi*) *India*—There are 15 million child labourers working in agriculture. More than half, and possibly as many as 87 percent of these bonded child labourers work in agriculture, tending crops herding cattle, and performing other tasks for their "masters".

(*vii*) *Bangladesh*—According to Khairuzzaman Kamal Executive Director Bangladesh Manobadhikar Sangbadik Forum (BMSF)) estimates that nearly about 4 million children are involved with agriculture sector. It has been observed that the whole family work as bonded labour in which younger children are also involved.

(*viii*) *Sub-Saharan Africa*—Is the region with the highest incidence of child labour and is the only region that experienced an increase to 49.3 million.

The number of children and youth aged 5-17 in the number of child labourers between 2000 and 2004, from 48 million trapped in hazardous work decreased by 26 percent.

(*ix*) *West Africa*—Around 284,000 children work in hazardous conditions in West Africa's cocoa industry and some 2,500 may have been trafficked. The report, released on 26 July, is the first comprehensive report to examine child labour on cocoa farms in West Africa. It examined child labour on 1,500 cocoa farms in Cote d'lvoire, Ghana, Nigeria and Cameroon which collectively produce 70 per cent of the World's cocoa.

Industrial Revolution and child labour.—Since, 1788 when industrial revolution started, the burden to make profits was on children. To get more and more profit, children were used as cheap labour not only in factories but also in the production of the raw material, in agriculture. Starting from chocolate industry to textiles and food industry all are dependent on agriculture for raw materials. The major reason for hiring children has nothing to do with economic efficiency. Children are easier to manage than adults—although less skilled, they are less aware of their rights, less troublesome, less complaining and more flexible—and ultimately expendable.

For some employers they constitute a reserve of casual labour to be hired and fired at will. When their labour is illegal, they and their parents are less likely to complain to the authorities for fear of losing whatever meager income they bring to their families.

Moreover, some employers genuinely consider that they are doing a favour to the children whom they employ by offering them work and income. Thus, declaring child labour to be illegal may in some cases have the perverse effect of depriving child workers of much of the protection provided by labour legislation to adults. This only serves to highlight the point that prohibition alone will not suffice. Simple bans on child labour are not successful if they are not supplemented by a range of other measures.

It has to be understood that it is not the responsibility of children to develop a country but it's the responsibility of the country to develop a child. We need to put all the national and international legislation effectively.

Today there are many boycott calls by the NGO's civil societies and other organisations have raised concerned about the products assembled or otherwise manufactured in with child labour. Many ethical trading initiatives and consumer awareness programmes like Rugmark. International Cocoa Initiatives, have been successful in combating child labour but still a lot more has to be done.

The countries and cooperates should think of this issue seriously and abide by the agreements that they have made nationally and internationally. There should be proper monitoring system to check that there is no child labour used in the production of raw material as well as in any segment of supply chain.

Global March Call For Action:

(*a*) **Global March calls on all Governments to** :

* Ratify and implement ILO Convention 138 and 182 on the Worst Forms of Child Labour.
* Establish and vigorously enforce legislation to protect the rights of children.
* Budget allocation for the withdrawal rehabilitation and education of the children.
* Prompt and stringent action should be taken against the industries that are encouraging the use of child labour.
* Proper inspectoral system for monitoring the laws.
* There is no significant data available. A proper, research should be done to know the kind of work in which children are involved and the geographical area where child labour is rampant.

(*b*) **Global March Calls on all Regional, Sub-Regional, Multilateral and Bilateral Organisations to** :

* Set up significant funds for advocacy prevention, rehabilitation, and reintegration projects to combat child labour in agriculture.
* Work in collaboration and partnership with governmental organization and other NGO's.

(*c*) **Global March Calls all the Trade Unions to** :

* Ensure there is no illegal child labour and the adults are getting their "minimum wages".
* Report, withdraw and educate children engaged in mines and quarries.
* Lobby for the ratification and implementation of international conventions and government laws on child labour and minimum age of employment.

(*d*) **Global March Calls all the businesses to** :

* Ensure that there is no child labour involved in any segment of supply chain.
* Give minimum wages to the adult workers and ensure that labour laws are upheld in their businesses.

(*e*) **Global March Calls on All People to** :

* Educate themselves on the issue of child labour in agriculture and report any incidents of such crimes to appropriate authorities and to concerned NGO's.
* Boycott products and commodities that are likely to be tainted by the sweat of child labourers.

(*f*) **Proposed Activities Around the Globe**

* Public hearings on the state of child labour in the region.
* Press conference.
* Projecting profiles of child labourers in agriculture.
* Campaigning with Government to stop child labour in agriculture.
* National Scale Discussion program on the issue.
* Preparation of national (children's) declaration on the issue.
* Direct Programs in the real affected areas with the children.

(*g*) **Sources** :

* http://www.ilo.org/public/english/standards/relm/ilc/ilc95/pdf/rep-i-b.pdf
* http://www.eurofound.europa.eu/eiro/2002/07/feature/pt0207105.html
* An International Labour Organisation (ILO) study on child labour in Portugal (PTOO 12124N and PT9902128F) was presented in Lisbon in July 2002.

* http://www.antislavery.org/homepage/news/cocoareport290702.htm
* http://hrw.org/backgrounder/crp/back0610.htm
* http://www.antislavery.org/homepage/news/cocoareport290702.htm
* http://en.wikipedia.org/wiki/Cocoa_Protocol
* http://www.cocoainitiative.org/pages/default/asp?idm 1=63&idm2=81&pageid=81

Child Labour in Agriculture Targeted.—Every day more that 200 million children around the world spend time working at difficult and often dangerous task so that they and their family members can survive.

The most extreme forms of child labour involve children going enslaved, taken from their families, exposed to serious hazards and illnesses, sexually exploited or left to fend for themselves on the streets of the world's largesl cities.

On 12 June, the World Day Against Child Labour, Education International is calling attention to this massive violation of the rights of hundreds of millions children around the globe. EI is working with the Global Task Force on Child Labour which brings together UN agencies the World Bank and the Global March Against Child Labour, in a unique coalition rooted in shared commitment to prevent and eliminate child labour.

EI General Secretary Fred van Leeuwen noted that when children are forced to work and thus denied their right to an education, they are often doomed to unemployment and poverty in adulthood because they lack the skills needed for jobs that could support the next generation.

"Teachers unions around the world are determined to do our bit to stop the theft of childhood from so many youngsters", said van Leeuwen. "We are working with our member organisations to help develop programmes to keep children in school, because we know that free, quality education is the best preventive strategy."

Kailash Satyarthi, president of the Global March Against Child Labour, agreed: "Education is vital to all rights. It is vital to health, to reducing HIV and AIDS. It is vital to escaping poverty and contributing to the benefit of the society. We can't achieve any of the millennium Development Goals without education."

World Day Against Child Labour, 12 June, is a crucial day in the calendar for child labourers, teachers and their unions, and the international community. This year's theme is dedicated to eliminating child labour in fields and farms.

Harvest for the future : Agriculture without child labour is the title of a new publication brought out by EI and the ILO, through the International Programme on the Elimination of Child Labour (IPEC). It provides current facts and ideas teachers can use to support the growing movement to tackle child labour. The booklet contains exercises in English French, Spanish and Portuguese. Teachers and other concerned citizens will find this a useful tool to increase knowledge about child labour, provide practical exercises for classroom use or facilitate discussion within unions or civil society groups.

44 Lakh Children work in agriculture sector, 9 lakh exposed to risks— About 44 lakh children in Bangladesh are engaged in agricultural work and about 9 lakh of them are exposed to health hazards as they need to work for more than 57 hours a week, with earning not exceeding Tk 900 a month.

Of them, 61 per cent drop out before completing primary schooling and 40 per cent remain illiterate.

Most of the 7.4 million economically active children live in rural areas, according to the National Child Labour Survey.

Referring to the data, stakeholders in the Government, non-Government and international organisations at a seminar on Tuesday said children working in agriculture sector were exposed to the risks of fatal or non-fatal accidents and health problems.

Labour and employment and agriculture ministries, International Labour Organisation and Food and Agriculture Programme organised the seminar on child labour in agriculture at the Purbani Hotel in Dhaka marking World Day against Child Labour 2007.

This year's focus theme of the day was Harvest for the future agriculture without child labour.

The largest employment sector in Bangladesh agriculture remains the largest employer of child labourers, said Gopal Bhattacharya, ILO director in Bangladesh.

Lack of hard data on working children and inadequate knowledge and low awareness of the problem in general stand in the way of addressing the issue of child labour, he said.

To eliminate the worst forms of child labour in a time-bound manner, a national plan of action has been formulated involving the government and international organisations such as UNICEF and the Asian Development Bank, Bhattacharya said.

Bangladesh is yet to have a national child labour policy and the issue of working children has not been included in other related policies such as the Agricultural Policy 2007 and the Labour Law 2006.

The labour secretary, Ashfaque Hamid, however, said the national child labour policy was expected to be finalised soon.

The ILO studies show that 70 per cent of the child labourers worldwide were in the agriculture sector and more than 132 million girls and boys aged between 5 and 14 years work with farms and plantations, harvesting, spraying pesticides and tending livestock.

Bangladesh ratified the UN Convention on the Children's Right in 1990 and the ILO Convention 182 in 2001, which talk of prohibition and elimination of the worst forms of child labour by taking immediate action.

Bangladesh is, however, yet to ratify the Convention 138, which said the minimum age for entry into work should be not less than 15 years, and the Convention 184, which said children under 18 years of age should not be involved in hazardous agriculture works.

FAO representative in Bangladesh Ad Spijkers, Abdul Kader Howlader, representative, national coordinator committee on workers education, Sayed Naquib Muslim, additional agriculture secretary, and ABM Abdus Sattar, joint secretary of the labour ministry also spoke.

3

Child Domestic Labour : An Overview

Child Domestic Labour—An overview.—In India under the August, 2006 amendments to the Child Labour Act, Child Domestic Labour is includes in the list of hazardous occupations. While specific policies and programmes flowing from this ban on Child Domestic labour remain to be defined, this development marks the beginning of Government-supported action against child labour in this sector.

The Child Labour Prohibition Bill proposed by the Labour Ministry in 1998 remains under consideration by the National Human Rights Commission. If enacted into law, this Bill will raise the minimum age for employment to 15 uniformly for all sectors. At the same time it will make it mandatory for children under 15 to attend school.

1. Child Domestic Labour.—Child domestic labour refers to situations where children are engaged to perform domestic tasks in the home of a third party or employer that are exploitative. Whenever such exploitation is extreme and includes trafficking, slavery-like situations, or work that is hazardous and harmful to a child's physical or mental health it is considered one of the worst forms of child labour.

Domestic work undertaken by children under the legal minimum working age, as well as by children above the legal minimum age but under the age of 18 under slavery-like, hazardous or other exploitative conditions a form of child labour to be eliminated as defined in international treaties.

2. Child Domestic Labourers.—Child domestic servants are children under the age of 18 who work in households that are not their own undertaking household chores such as cooking, cleaning, taking care of other children, and running errands.

3. Child Domestic Labour is Hazardous.—Almost without exception, children who are in domestic labour are victims of exploitation, often of several different kinds. They are exploited economically ; forced to work long hours with no time off, low or no wages. They are exploited because they generally have no social or legal protection, and suffer harsh working conditions. They invariably are deprived of the rights due to them as children in International law, including the right to play, healthy, and freedom from sexual abuse and harassment, visits to or from their family, association with friends, decent accommodation, and protection from physical and mental abuse.

4. Child Domestic Labour is one of the Worst Forms of Child Labour.—Child domestic labour that is extremely hazardous to the child because of the tasks given, conditions of work or physical, emotional and sexual abuse ; practices similar to slavery such as debt bondage or forced labour, and child domestic labour into which a child has been trafficked.

Where a child under the age of 18 is engaged in domestic labour and works under conditions that are hazardous, then this constitutes a "worst form of child labour" and must be eliminated as a matter of urgency. This would also be true of situations where the child has been trafficked into domestic labour, or where debt bondage or other practices similar to slavery exist. The term worst form of child domestic labour is used for such exploitation, to reflect the extreme risk to the child and echoing the immediate elimination called for in the Worst Forms of Child Labour Convention, 1999 (No. 182).

Once a child is inside an employer's home, she is effectively hidden from view. As a result, employers of children in domestic service have total control over their lives. This is a high-risk situation for the child. Violence and abuse (of many different kinds) can take place behind closed doors, unnoticed by the outside world, and in such cases the child is considered to be in a worst form of child labour.

5. Understanding Child Domestic Labour

* Domestic work is among the lowest status, least regulated, and poorest remunerated of all occupations, whether performed by adults or children ;
* Most child domestics live in, and are under the exclusive, round the clock control of the employer, they have little freedom or free time ;
* About 90 percent of child domestics are girls, their powerlessness within the household.

6. Laws Specific to Child Domestic Labour.—In a recent development the Indian Central Government banned Child Domestic Labour in August, 2006 through an amendment to the Child Labour Prohibition and Regulation Act ("Child Labour Act"). Accordingly, Child Domestic Labour is now considered a hazardous occupation and is prohibited for children under the age of 14. The penalty for transgressors under the amended Act ranges from a fine to imprisonment for a several months. Previously, the only legal instrument that impacted this area was a government guidelines that urged all Government employees not to hire children.

It is worth nothing that in 2004, the Central Government has launched a welfare program on a pilot basis in 50 districts known as the Unorganized Sector Workers Social Security Scheme. The Scheme provides adult domestic workers with social security benefits such as old age pension, medical insurance and personal accidents insurance based on a monthly contribution by the workers, employer and the Government.[1] However, the scheme does not reach children in the domestic sector.[2]

1. Unorganizd Sector Workers Social Security Scheme Art. 7 (2004).
2. Pilot testing results indicate that the scheme's viability has been undermined because employees have not been contributing toward the fund. As a result, the scheme is in the process of being re-examined.

In India, legislative powers are distributed between the Central Government and State Government with some areas falling within the exclusive jurisdiction of each Governmental authority. All legislation concerning the subject of labour such as minimum wage, child labour and trade unions falls within the concurrent jurisdiction of both the central and state Governments.[1] As will be seen, in this survey's section on State Based Initiative,s a few states have independently enacted laws that specifically cover the domestic sector.

7. Other Relevant Laws—(a) *Protecting Child Rights*

(i) Safeguarding the Overall Well-Being of Children.—The Juvenile Justice (Care and Protection of Children) Act ("Juvenile Justice Act") consolidates the law relating to juveniles in conflict with legal authorities as well as children in need of care and protection. This is a central legislation enacted in 2000, and some states are still in the process of implementing this law. The Juvenile Justice Act defines a juvenile or child as any person under 18.[2] It provides for punishment in cases of child abuse or of exploitation of child employees and states in relevant part ; "Whoever having actual charge or control over a child, assaults, abandons, exposes or willfully neglects the child or causes or procures him to be assaulted, abandoned or neglected in a manner likely to cause such child unnecessary mental or physical suffering shall be punished.[3] As discussed earlier, in the case of a similar provision under Bangladesh law, the employer hiring a child domestic labourer can be seen to have actual charge or control over a child because of the live-in/work arrangement, which is a characteristic of this sector. Whether the protection of this Act can be extended to such situations remains clouded with uncertainty in the absence of enforcement information including definitive judgments.

In the context of work place exploitation the Act provides that: "Whoever ostensibly procures a child for the purpose of any employment and withholds the earning of the child or uses such earnings for his own purposes shall be punishable with a fine.[4] The section entitled Children in Need of Care and Protection requires the creation of child welfare committees to defend human rights, provide basic needs and rescue and rehabilitate children where necessary.[5] The elements of the definition of a Child in Need of Care and Protection relevant to domestic work are : "If someone who resides with a person (whether guardian of a child or not) and such a person has either threatened to kill or injure the child or has killed, abused or neglected some other child and there is a reasonable likelihood of the child in question being in danger of such treatment.[6] Additionally, a Child in Need of Care and Protection is also defined as "someone who is being or likely to be grossly

---

1. In case of inconsistency between laws, those enacted by the Central Government will prevail See Indian Constitution, Part XI Ch 1 Art. 254(1).
2. Juvenile Justice (Care and Protection of Children) Act Ch. 1 Art. 2(k)(2000).
3. Ibid. Ch. 1, Art. 2.
4. Ibid. Ch. II Art, 26.
5. Ibid. Ch. III, Arts. 29 and 31.
6. Ibid. Ch. 1, Art. 2(d)(ii).

abused, tortured or exploited for the purpose of sexual abuse or illegal acts.[1] As will be seen, the provisions of the Juvenile Justice Act represent the cornerstone of successful action undertaken to rescue and rehabilitate children working under oppressive conditions in the domestic sector in Karnataka State.

(ii) Right to Education, Rest and Leisure.—To be effective in protecting children, legal provisions should not only shield against these extreme forms of exploitation but should also extend to and penalize other forms of exploitation that are deemed socially unacceptable and that infringe upon fundamental child rights. These include fundamental rights forwarded by the CRC which even though has been ratified by India has not been fully adopted and as a consequence, some of the rights enshrined in this Convention enjoy limited jurisprudential force. Such rights include the right to be in contact with one's family, the right to rest and leisure and the right to be protected from hazardous work. Moreover, in contravention of the CRC and the ILO conventions there are no legal provisions requiring that child workers over minimum working age be provided with educational and vocational training.

In the context of the right to education, all children in India under the age of 14 have a constitutional right to free and compulsory education.[2] This harmonizes with CRC principles and practical efforts are underway to bring this right to fruition. This has been in the form of the Sarva Shiksha Abhiyan or Education for All initiative under which the Central Government in partnership with the State Governments all over the country plans on opening new schools and improving existing school facilities as well as the quality of education so as to provide elementary education for all children between the ages of 6-14 by the year 2010.[3] Additionally, on a legislative level, the Right to Education Bill, makes the provision of free and compulsory education for all children in the age group of 6-14 a legal right.[4] This Bill also prohibits the employment of children belonging to this age group.[5]

(b) *Protecting Workers Rights*

(i) Minimum Age.—In India, the Child Labour Act is the principal legislation prohibiting and regulating child labour. This law does not offer a blanket prohibition of child Labour in all industries, occupations and processes instead, it prohibits and regulates child labour in a limited group of sectors. A glimpse into the legislative history reveal the Government's reasons underlying this limitation. In 1979, the Government instituted its first special committee known as the Gurupadswamy committee to study the issue of child labour in India and provide recommendations to combat it. The study observed that child labour was a consequence of poverty and that legal prohibition, therefore, was not the solution. The committee's recommendations were therefore, to prohibit child labour in hazardous sectors and

---

1. Ibid. Ch. 1, Art. 2(d)(vi).
2. India Const. part IV, Art. 45.
3. More Information on the Government of India's Education for All initiative is available at http:/ www.ssa.nic.in (last visited Sept. 20, 2006).
4. Right to Education Bill, Ch. II, Art. 3 (2005).
5. Ibid, Ch. VIII, Art. 48.

to regulate working conditions in non-hazardous sectors.[1] Under the 2006 amendments to the Child Labour Act domestic work is recognized as a hazardous activity and is therefore, a prohibited occupation for children under 14.

(ii) Fair Remuneration and Social Protection.—The Minimum Wages Act fixes minimum wages in certain listed employments referred to as 'scheduled' employments and does not include domestic labour.[2] Karnataka is the first State to issue a notification that does prescribe minimum wages in this sector.[3] India also has an Equal Remuneration Act,the purpose of this Act is to eliminate wage discrimination between men and women but it does not limit such discrimination between adults and children over minimum working age for same or similar work.[4]

(iii) Freedom of Association.—The Indian Constitution provides that all citizens have the right to form associations and unions.[5] Under the Trade Unions Act in India, any person over 15 has the right to be a member of a trade union.[6] As a result, children over 14, who have the legal right to work in many sectors under national law, do not have the right to join unions. Consequently, many children in the domestic labour sector are deprived of this fundamental worker's right in contravention of ILO Convention No. 87, ICCPR and the ICESCR.

Although the 2006 amendments to the Child Labour Act prohibit Child Domestic Labour, the domestic labour sector has not yet been regulated to safeguard the fundamental rights of all persons above minimum age in this sector. To recapitulate, these are rights forwarded by ILO Convention No. 138 on minimum age and ILO Recommendation No. 146 together with the CRC, stipulating factors necessary to secure satisfactory standards for working children.

8. Combating the Worst Forms of Child Domestic Labour

(i) Forced Labour and Slavery.—Fundamental rights guaranteed under the Indian Constitution prohibit trafficking in human beings and forced labour.[7] Constitutional provisions are the Bonded Labour System (Abolition) Act outlaw bonded labour and void all agreements by virtue of which any person is required to do any work or render any service as a bonded labourer.[8] Effective implementation continues to be a challenge particularly in the arose of rural and informal economy where bonded labour is most prevalent. This is an area that invites rigorous law enforcement and well-formulated rehabilitation schemes focusing on fundamental human rights.

(ii) Trafficking.—Legislation specific to trafficking in India does not fully embody

1. Ibid.
2. Minimum Wages Act, Art. 3 (1948).
3. Ibid Art. 2(e).
4. Equal Remuneration Act, Ch. II, Art. 4 (1976).
5. India Const. Part III, Arts. 19(1)(c) and 19(4).
6. Trade Unions Act, Art. 21 (1926).
7. India Const. Part III, Art. 23(1).
8. Bonded Labour System Abolition Act Ch. II, Arts. 4 and 5 (1976).

the absolute prohibition on human trafficking enshrined in the Constitution. For example, existing laws, such as the Immoral Trafficking Prevention Act ("ITPA") legislate against trafficking in the context of prostitution.[1] As a result, the process of trafficking of children itself which can lead to other exploitative outcomes is not deemed an offence and can persist without corresponding sanctions. Additionally, the Act does not reflect the lower threshold established by the Palermo Protocoal for child trafficking nor does it adhere to the standards enshrined in ILO Convention No. 182 and the CRC which prohibit child trafficking for all purposes.

(iii) Hazardous Child Labour.—The Indian Constitution provides that : "No child below the age of 14 shall be employed in any factory or mine or engaged in any other hazardous employment.[2] As already stated, since the 2006 amendments to the Child Labour Act, Child Domestic Labour is now regarded as a hazardous form of child labour. However as pointed out, regulations defining hazardous working conditions need to be formulated to protect the rights of all workers in this sector.

(9) State Based Initiatives.—Recently, there have been a number of state-based initiatives in India to combat Child Domestic Labour. The following section summarizes the progress made and describes legislative efforts underway to address this sector :

(i) Andhra Pradesh.—In 2001, the Andhra Pradesh legislature adopted a unanimous resolution to eliminate child labour by the year 2004.[3] Even though child labour remains a challenge in this state, this resolution spanned important Government-sponsored educational, legislative and enforcement initiatives. As part of this campaign, the Government of Andhra Pradesh declared that any child out of school is a child labour.[4] While the State Government has launched several measures to combat child labour, few are directly focused on the domestic sector. One such measure is an amendment of the Civil Service Conduct Rules to abolish Child Labour in the domestic sector for State Government employees.

In 2003 the State Government proposed the Andhra Pradesh Child Labour Abolition and Compulsory Education Bill, which potentially impacts the domestic service sector.[5] Whole the draft legislation does not specifically mention Child Domestic Labour, it takes an expansive definition of child labour to mean "any child who is employed or working in any employment, occupation, process or activity which interferes with full-time schooling.[6] It also accords with ILO Convention No. 138 standards in establishing 15 as the minimum age for entry into employment. Moreover, in keeping with ILO Convention No. 182 it also prohibits the Worst Forms of Child Labour ; and therefore, the Worst Forms of Child Domestic

1. Immoral Trafficking Prevention Act, Art. 5(a) - (c) (1956).
2. Indian Cosnt. Part III, Art. 24.
3. Andhra Pradesh State Legislature Notice (2001).
4. Abolition of Child Labour in Andhra Pradesh at 1.
5. Andhra Pradesh Child Labour Abolition and Compuslory Education Bill (2003).
6. Ibid. Ch. 1 Cl. 2, Art. 3(a) (2003), Clause 2(1) defines a 'child' as any person who has not completed the age of fifteen years.

Labour. Furthermore, it protects the child's right to free and compulsory education as enshrined in ILO Convention No. 138 and the CRC.

However, the draft law does not seem to delineate the right for those children aged 15 to 18 *i.e.*, over minimum, working age which are at issue on account of the nuances associated with employment in the domestic sector. These are standards to ensure legitimate working condition including working hours to ensure adequate time for rest and leisure as well as the right to remain in contact with one's family as defined in the ILO conventions and the CRC.

The draft code vests law enforcement with fairly invasive monitoring powers and provides that inspectors can enter and search any premises including a house where there is reliable information that a child is working or upon a complaint made to the Child Labour Abolition Authority.[1] The question that follows is whether these powers are sufficient to monitor employment in domestic service. In this case, the law does not provide for continuous monitoring and instead takes a reactive approach in relying on external information to trigger enforcement action.

(ii) Goa.—The Goa Children's Act specifically prohibits employment for all Children under 14 in the domestic sector.[2] It also prescribes a fine of Rupees 50,000 for any person employing children in domestic labour.[3] Furthermore, it provides that the State needs to ensure that rehabilitation programs are in place before child labourers, defined as all working children under the age of 14, are released and placed in protective care facilities.[4]

(iii) Karnataka.—A recent pioneer in the fight against Child Domestic Labour, Karnataka is the only state in India to implement a Child Domestic Labour elimination project. Initiated in August 2004, in the city of Bangalore, and still in its pilot stages this project is a joint Initiative between the State Government, UNICEF and NGOs. Overall, this Intervention has also been reported to be quite successful in that over 750 children have been identified out of which 250 withdrawn from work and rehabilitated, many of whom have also been enrolled in formal schooling.[5]

The project adopts a multi-pronged approach spanning identification, release and rehabilitation of child domestic labourers together with law enforcement awareness raising. The two legal instruments that were critical to this endeavour include the Karnataka State Minimum Wage Notification for Domestic Workers ("Minimum Wage Notification") and the Juvenile Justice Act. The Minimum Wage Notification establishes a minimum wage for the domestic sector in prohibiting the employment of children below 14.[6] Legislative history reveals that a major concern

1. Ibid. Ch. 5 Cl. 15, Art. 2.
2. Goa Children's Act Art. 7(2)(c) (2003).
3. Ibid. Art. 7(5)(c).
4. Ibid. Arts. 7(3) and (4).
5. ILO Internal note on the progress of the Child Domestic Labour Elimination Project in Karnataka at 2.
6. Domestic Workers Notification arts 1, 2 and 6 (2004).

of the drafters was whether authorized labour inspectors enforcing minimum wage standards would compromise the privacy of the home.[1] To counter this concern, it was negotiated that the inspectors would not have the power to enter and inspect a home on their own and could only do so when directed by the Commissioner of Labour.[2] Although this enfeebled the protections provided, the legislation nonetheless had a positive impact in increasing the bargaining powers of domestic workers. Most notably, early this year domestic workers with the Karnataka Domestic Workers Movement, the local chapter of an India-wide NGO, submitted a memorandum to the Commissioner of Labour and rallied for the abolishment of child labour as well as for the payment of minimum wage and improved working conditions to ensure dignity of labour.[3] Central to the success of this project was the involvement of Childline, a hotline for children in need of aid and assistance run by an India-wide NGO supported by rescue operations of law enforcement agencies. This arrangement helped rescue children that were later presented in front of child welfare committee established under the Juvenile Justice Act. Reports indicate that over 80 children were rescued though Child Line and produced before child welfare committees and that to-date eight cases of abuse and violence have been filed against employers.

(iv) Kerala.—Although concrete legislative protection are yet to emerge, newspaper reports suggest that the Minimum Wages Act in Kerala will soon be amended to prescribe a minimum wage specifically for employment in the domestic sector.[4]

(v) Tamil Nadu.—According to the Tamil Nadu action plan, the State's objective is to eliminate child labour in all hazardous occupations by 2005 and all non-hazardous occupations by 2007.[5] Although this has resulted in many ad-hoc interventions to fight child labour at present policy measures aimed specifically at Child Domestic Labour appear to be limited.[6] However, the Tamil Nadu Manual Workers (Regulation of Employment and Conditions of Work) Act regulates the conditions of work and provides various welfare measures for manual workers including those in domestic work. It prohibits the employment of children under 16 in any scheduled employment including domestic labour.[7] The Tamil Nadu Manual Workers Social Security and Welfare Scheme also covers the domestic sector and provides workers with accident insurance, educational assistance, marriage expenses, maternity and limited health benefits as well as life insurance.[8]

1. Labour Administration and Child Labour Monitoring in the Informal Economy in India 20 (ILO 2005).
2. Ibid.
3. Domestic Workers Take out Rally in Support of Demands, The Hindu February, 2 2006.
4. Domestic Workers Day Observed, THE HINDU, January 10, 2006, available at http:// www.hindu.com 2006/01/10/stories/2006011001310200.htm.
5. Government of Tamil Nadu : *Child Labour Eradication Action Plan* (2003).
6. Based on an interview with Lally Ganesan, Assistant Commissioner of Labour, Tamil Nadu Government.
7. Tamil Nadu Manual Workers (Regulation of Employment and Conditions of Service) Act (1982).
8. Tamil Nadu Manual Workers Social Security and Welfare Scheme (2001).

Child Domestic Labour—Global Legal Regime.—Although international conventions do not directly legislate on the issue of Child Domestic Labour, the rights and protections available to child workers set forth below as children and as workers under International law can be construed using ILO and U.N. conventions. It is worth noting that ILO Recommendation No. 190 alludes to the practice of Child Domestic Labour in providing that States should design and implement action programs that give special attention to the problem of hidden work situations, in which girls are at special risk.[1]

10. Child Rights Enshrined in International Conventions :

(a) Safeguarding the Overall Well-Being of Children.—The U.N. Convention on the Rights of the Child ("CRC") is the principal International legal instrument detailing the rights of children. The rights at issue include non-discrimination on the grounds of race, colour, sex, language, religion, ethnic or social origin, disability, birth or other status.[2] Other fundamental rights are the right to know and be cared for by one's parents as well as the right to maintain personal relations and be in direct contact with parents on a regular basis.[3] Chidlren have a fundamental right to be protected from all forms of sexual exploitation and sexual abuse.[4] Protections that safeguard the overall well-being of children that are frequently compromised due to the nature of this practice are the right to enjoy the highest attainable standard of health and access to health care services.[5] This includes a right to a standard of living adequate for the child's physical, mental, spiritual, moral and social development.[6]

(b) Right to Education, Rest and Leisure.—Other rights that are infringed through Child Domestic Labour are the right of the child to education including free compulsory primary education as well as access to higher education and vocational training.[7] In addition, the right of the child to rest and leisure, to engage in play and recreational activities appropriate to the age of the child are also endangered.[8]

Additionally, ILO Recommendation No. 146 sets forth satisfactory standards that need to be considered in order to protect fundamental rights of working children over minimum age. It advises that a strict limitation of the hours spent at work in a day and in a week should be established including the prohibition of overtime so as to allow enough time for education, training and for rest during the day as well as leisure activities.[9] ILO Recommendation No. 146 further supports the granting of

1. ILO Recommendation No. 190, Worst Forms of Child Labour Recommendation Art. 2 (c)(iii), June 17, 1999 (hereinafter Recommendation No. 190).
2. Convention on the Rights of the Child, art. 2, Nov 20, 1989, 1577 U.N.T.S. 3 (hereinafter CRC).
3. Ibid. Arts. 7 and 9.
4. Ibid. Art. 34.
5. Ibid. Art. 24(1).
6. Ibid. Art. 27.
7. Ibid. Art. 28.
8. Ibid. Art. 31.
9. ILO Recommendation No. 146, supra note 4, Part IV, Art. 13(b).

12 hours of night rest and of customary weekly rest days as well as an annual holiday with pay of at least four weeks.[1]

11. Workers Rights Enshrined in International Conventions

(a) Minimum Age.—ILO Convention No. 138 determined the minimum age for employment which is a defining element of legitimate domestic work. In particular, it sets the minimum age for entry into any type of employment, including domestic labour at 15, which marks the completion of compulsory education. This requirement is entrenched in the principle that all persons should be equipped with a minimum level of education before they can start working on a full-time basis.[2] ILO Convention No. 138 also provides that children over 15, who have not completed compulsory schooling, can work in areas that are not likely to be harmful to their health and development and do not prejudice school attendance or participation in vocational training.[3] However, States with insufficiently developed economies and educational facilities are given some leeway and in such cases, the minimum age for employment can be lowered to 14. By establishing the legal minimum working age for entry into employment at 14/15 ILO Convention No. 138 implicitly requires that children below this age should be withdrawn from employment.

(b) Fair Remuneration and Social Protection.—Legitimate domestic work pertains to those situations where children over minimum age are employed under not apply to the domestic sector.[4] This is because working circumstances in this sector are hidden and inherently difficult to monitor and are likely to expose children under the age of 15, who are especially vulnerable by virtue of their age to exploitative conditions.

(b) Fair Remuneration and Social Protection.—Legitimate domestic work pertains to those situations where chidlren over minimum age are employed under working conditions that are maintained at a satisfactory standard. To ensure such conditions ILO Recommendation No. 146 requires that among other factors special attention should be given to the provision of fair remuneration bearing in mind the principle of equal pay for equal work.[5] CRC provisions lend support to this principle in requiring that the economic exploitation of children should be prohibited.[6] As noted earlier, Child Domestic Labour is often beyond the purview of regulations including minimum wage laws and workers in this sector are grossly underpaid. Other ILO Recommendation No. 146 factors include coverage by social security schemes, including employment injury, medical care, sickness and benefit schemes.[7]

1. Ibid. Part IV, Art. 13(c) and (d).
2. ILO Convention No. 138, supra note 4, Art. 3.
3. Ibid. Art. 7(2).
4. Ibid. Art. 7.
5. ILO Recommendation No. 146, supra note 4, Part IV, Art. 13(a).
6. CRC, supra note 14, Art. 32(1).
7. ILO Recommendation No. 146, supra note 4, Part IV, Art. 13(e).

The importance of maintaining satisfactory standards of safety and health as well as appropriate instruction and supervision, which are essential to the achievement of such working conditions, is also underscored within ILO Recommendation No. 146.[1]

(c) Freedom of Association.—Another fundamental workers right that is compromised not only in the context of child labour in domestic service but also more broadly in the informal economy is the right to freedom of association ILO conventions provide all workers with the right to freedom of association. More specifically, ILO Convention No. 87 provides that each member State shall take all necessary and appropriate measures to ensure that workers and employers may freely exercise the right to organize.[2] Other U.N. convention also support the right to freedom of association including the CRC, International Covenant on Civil and Political Rights ("ICCPR") and the International Covenant on Economic Social and Cultural Fights ("ICESCR").[3] As well be seen, laws in many South Asian countries do not expressly protect this fundamental right of child workers over minimum working age. Freedom of association is instrumental in helping older working children realize other rights and protections that are due to them under International law. On another level, organizing serves to counteract some of the negative features inherent in working in the domestic sector. By way of illustration, SUMAPI, a union of child domestic workers in the Philippines, has shown that organizing helps ease the sense of isolation and vulnerability that many children in this sector have to endure as it connects them to a greater network of people of the same age in similar circumstances.[4] Additionally, as demonstrated through the same example, unionizing has not only promoted advocacy and visibility of the issue but more importantly has empowered children to become their own spokes persons.[5] Lastly, SUMAPI shows that unionizing the domestic sector is probably the most efficient and effective self-monitoring tool.[6]

12. The Worst Forms of Child Domestic Labour Proscribed under International Law.—ILO Convention No. 182 establishes the Worst Forms of Child Labour some of which are relevant to Child Domestic Labour and qualify as the Worst Forms of Child Domestic Labour. In particular, this covers situation where children are trafficked into the domestic sector, and in a situation of debt bondage

1. Ibid. Part IV, Art. 13(1).
2. ILO, Convention No. 87, Freedom of Association and Protection of the Right to Organise, Art. 11, June 17, 1948, 68 U.N.T.S. 17 (hereinafter referred to as ILO Convention No. 87.
3. CRC, supra note 15, Art 15(1) : International Convention on Civil and Political Rights, Part III, Art. 22, March 23, 1976, 999 U.N.T.S. 171 (hereinafter referred to as ICCPR) International Covenant of Economic, Social and Cultural Rights, Art 8(1)(1), Dec. 16, 1966, 993 U.N.T.S. 3 (hereinafter referred to as ICESCR).
4. Child Domestic Labour and Emerging Good Practices to Combat in the South East and East Asia 74 (ILO Bangkok 2005), SUMAPI stands for Samahan at Ugnayan ng mga Manggagawang Pantahanan sa Pillipinas which roughly translates as Association and Linkage of House Helpers in the Philippines.
5. Ibid.
6. Child Domestic Labour in South East and East Asia, supra note 34, Art 75.

or of forced labour ; are trapped in slavery or slavery-like practices, or are working under hazardous conditions.[1] ILO Convention No. 182 requires member states to take steps to eliminate these Worst Forms or Child Labour and by inference the Worst Forms of Child Domestic Labour as a matter of urgency and urges that effective and time-bound measures should be taken to withdraw children as well as to provide assistance for their rehabilitation and social integration.[2]

(a) Forced Labour and Slavery.—In addition to ILO Convention No. 182, ILO Convention Nos. 29 and 105 urge States to take steps to suppress and refrain from the use of forced labour.[3] Furthermore, the U.N. Slavery Convention and the U.N. Supplementary Convention on the Abolition of Slavery require States to take all necessary steps to bring about the complete abolition of slavery in all its forms as well as debt bondage.[4]

(b) Trafficking.—The U.N. Protocol to Prevent, Suppress and Punish Trafficking in Persons ("Palermo Protocol") currently provides the most authoritative definition of trafficking in persons.[5] For child trafficking the Palermo Protocol sets a lower threshold and provides that child trafficking is the recruitment, transportation, transfer or receipt of a child for the purpose of exploitation.[6] This definition applies to all children, in other words all persons under 18, as defined in the CRC and dispenses with the requirement for deceptive or fraudulent means required to qualify as trafficking of persons.[7] Additionally the CRC also condemns trafficking of children and provides that State parties should take all appropriate measures to prevent the sale of or traffic in children for any purpose or in any form.[8]

(c) Hazardous Child Domestic Labour.—Although the international conventions do not define Hazardous Child Domestic Labour, ILO Recommendation

1. ILO Convention No. 182, supra note 5, Art 3.
2. Ibid. Arts 1 and 7(2)(b).
3. ILO Convention No. 29, Forced or Compuslory Labour, Art. 1(1), June 10, 1930, 39 U.N.T.S. 55 (hereinafter referred to as ILO Convention No. 29) ; ILO Convention No. 105, Art. 1, 320 U.N.T.S. 291 (hereinafter referred to as ILO Convention No. 105).
4. Slavery Convention, Art 2(b), March 9, 1927, 182 U.N.T.S. 51 ; Supplementary Convention on the Abolition of Slavery, the Slave Trade and Institutions and Practices Similar to Slavery, Art. 1(a), April 30, 1957, 226 U.N.T.S. 3.
5. Protocol to Prevent, Suppress and Punish Trafficking in Persons, especially Women and Children Supplementing the United Nations Convention against Transnational Organized Crime, Art. 3(a) 2000 U.N. Doc A/55/383 (hereinafter referred to as Palermo Protocol). "Trafficking in Persons shall mean the recruitment, transportation, transfer, harbouring or receipt of persons by means of the threat or use of force or other forms of coercion, or abduction, of fraud, of deception,or abuse of power or of a position of vulnerability or of the giving or receiving of payments or benefits to achieve the consent of a person having control over another person for the purpose of exploitation. Exploitation shall include, at a minimum, the exploitation of the prostitution of other or other forms of sexual exploitation, forced labour or services. Slavery or practices similar to slavery servitude or the removal of organs."
6. Ibid. Art 3(c).
7. Ibid.
8. CRC, supra note 15, Art. 35.

No. 190 provides guidelines that are useful in determining when Child Domestic Labour turns hazardous. Because it is one of the Worst Forms of Child Labour, ILO conventions make clear that no one clear 18 should be doing hazardous work. However, ILO Convention No. 138 does offer some latitude with older children (16 and over) who may be permitted to work under potentially hazardous conditions with sufficient training provided that adequate protections are taken to safeguard their health, safety and morals.[1]

ILO Convention No. 138 provides a general definition of Hazardous Child Labour as "work which by its nature or the circumstances in which it is carried out is likely to jeopardize the health, safety or morals of young persons.[2] ILO Recommendation No. 190, supplementing ILO Convention No. 182, provides indicia that are useful in specifically determining what constitutes Hazardous Child Labour and by inference Hazardous Child Domestic Labour. As indicated earlier, it provides in relevant part that consideration should be given to the following set of factors :

(*a*) Work which exposes children to physical, psychological or sexual abuse ;

(*b*) Work underground, under water, at dangerous heights or in confined spaces ;

(*c*) Work with dangerous machinery, equipment and tools or which involves the manual handling or transport of heavy loads ;

(*d*) Work in an unhealthy environment which may be example, expose children to hazardous substances, agents or processes or to temperature, noise levels, or vibrations damaging to health ;

(*e*) Work under particularly difficult conditions such as work for long hours or during the night or work where the child is unreasonably confined to the premises of the employer.[3]

The CRC also condemns Hazardous Child Labour and provides that children have a right to be protected from performing hazardous work that is likely to interfere with the child's education or is harmful to the child's health or development.[4] Furthermore the CRC also recognizes the right of children to be free from sexual exploitation and abuse which are encountered with a degree of frequency in this practice.[5] It also provides that States should take all appropriate measures to protect the child from physical or mental violence, neglect, abuse, maltreatment or exploitation.[6] As regards the last factor listed in ILO Convention No. 182, being 'unreasonably confined' is not merely a product of the live-in nature

1. ILO Convention No. 138, supra note 4, Arts 3(1) and 3(2) ; ILO Recommendation No. 190 supra note 14, Art. 11(4)
2. ILO Convention No. 138, supra note 4, Art. 3(1).
3. ILO Recommendation No. 190, supra note 14, Art. 11, $ 3(a)(e).
4. CRC, supra note 15, Art. 32(1).
5. CRC, supra note 15, Art. 34.
6. Ibid Art. 19.

of the domestic service employment relationship. It also relates to the deprivation of fundamental child right as a result of highly constrained terms of employment precluding a child's right to education, rest, leisure and contact with family.

(d) Monitoring the Domestic Sector.—Central to the realization of these rights is the issues of monitoring the domestic sector. ILO conventions and recommendation urge States to implement monitoring mechanisms to secure effective implementation. For instance, ILO Convention No. 182 requires States to establish appropriate mechanisms to monitor the implementation of its provisions.[1] ILO Recommendation No. 146 suggests measures to ensure the effective application of the minimum age standards including the strengthening of labour inspection and related service, by the special training of inspectors to defect abuses in employment or work of Children and young persons and to correct such abuses.[2] ILO Recommendation No. 146 lays emphasis on the role that inspectors can play in supplying information and advice on effective means of complying with relevant provisions as well as in securing enforcement.[3] Many argue that monitoring this sector is a challenge because of the difficulty in counterbalancing seemingly irreconcilable concerns. People's interest in protecting the privacy of their homes versus protecting the fundamental rights of children. However, international standards provide a precedent for transcending privacy interests where the protection of fundamental rights is at stake. In particular, ILO Convention No. 177 concerning Home Work regulates work carried out by a person in his or her home or in premises other than the work place of the employer and provides for a monitoring system whereby inspectors can enter a home to ensure the enforcement of labour standards.[4] This reinforces the argument for adopting a similar standard in the domestic sector where the protection of children's rights outweighs privacy interests as the home is also a work place.

13. Child Domestic Labour in South Asia—Reformatory Recommendations.—While some argue that regulating domestic work amounts to a legitimisation of Child Domestic Labour and that creating favourable working conditions will have the unintended effect of encouraging children to enter this sector, the ILO conventions and recommendations reflect broad consensus concerning the need to regulate this sector so as to control minimum age of employment as well as working hours and conditions. This would not only help to directly combat Child Domestic Labour but as stated, could also render this sector more attractive to adult workers, bolstering the movement to end child labour in this sector.

It is obviously desirable that a protective framework that is all-encompassing

1. ILO Convention No. 182, supra note 5, Art. 5.
2. ILO Recommendation No. 146, supra note 4, Part V, Art. 14(1)(a).
3. Ibid. Part V, Art. 14(3).
4. ILO Convention No. 177, Home Work, art 9(1) June, 20, 1996 (hereinafter referred to as ILO Convention No. 177), and ILO Recommendation No. 184. Home Work Recommendation, Art III(8), June 20, 1996, (hereinafter referred to as ILO Recommendation No. 184.

in respect of rights enshrined in ILO and U.N. conventions should be enacted but until such time as such a framework can be established legal recognition of even a subset of fundamental domestic workers rights such as minimum wage and minimum age for example could serve as preliminary steps towards fulfilling the need for comprehensive regulation in this sector. For instance, even in the limited instance of the minimum wage law in the Indian State of Karnataka the fact that the law did not provide a comprehensive inspection mechanism did not eclipse the benefits flowing from the legal protections that were provided which included establishing a minimum wage and prohibiting the domestic employment of children below 14.[1] Even if they were limited in scope, these measures served as an official recognition of the rights of domestic workers, whose increased bargaining power provided further stimulus to the movement for improved working conditions and the elimination of Child Domestic Labour. In contrast, keeping this sector unregulated would leave employers free to engage children of any age to pay them low wages and to treat them with scant respect for fundamental child rights and human rights more broadly. The point worth stressing again he is that defining legal parameters can help to counteract such practices and at the same time advance the creation of legitimate domestic work opportunities for all.

While the foregoing section identifies gaps and limitations under national law with regards to Child Domestic Labour in the countries surveyed, set of recommendations that summarize the international legal standard the may be applied in addressing these limitations. These recommendations recapitulate the legal framework already discussed in Section A of this paper.

Even if a legal framework is a necessary condition to defining and protecting child rights and workers rights, it is not alone sufficient in combating Child Domestic Labour. Durable solutions consist of a whole range of interventions directed at preventing children from entering domestic work or other exploitative sectors; identifying rescuing and rehabilitating those children in domestic work; and addressing the underlying dynamics of the problem through the creation of economic security and opportunity within vulnerable communities. Because such interventions are beyond the scope of this paper, they are not explored in the recommendations that follow which seek to define legitimate domestic work conditions within the framework of the ILO and U.N. conventions. Legitimate domestic work refers to those conditions where the persons employed are above the minimum age of employment and satisfactory working standards are maintained.

(a) Fixing a Legal Minimum Age for Entry into Domestic Work—

* ILO convention No. 138 states that a minimum age for entrance into any type of employment including domestic work, shall to be less that the age of completion of compulsory education and in any case, shall not be

1. The Karnataka Child Domestic Labour elimination project is described in detail on page 26.
2. ILO Convention No. 138, supra note 4, Art 2(3).

less than 15 years.[2] States with insufficiently developed economies and educational facilities are given some leeway and in such cases, the minimum age can be lowered to 14.[1] ILO Recommendation No. 146 provides that where the minimum age for employment is below 15 years, urgent steps should be taken to raise it to that level.[2]

* As a further exception ILO Convention No. 138 provides that national laws may permit the employment on light domestic work of persons who are 13-15 and have not completed their compulsory schooling. From a protection and policy point of view this is not a violable option for the domestic sector, because the working conditions in this sector are hidden difficult to monitor and can easily infringe fundamental child rights, running contrary to the object of the ILO conventions.[3]

* The minimum age requirement established by ILO Convention No. 138 implies that children below the minimum working age, *i.e.* children below the age of 15 on 14 (as the case may be) should be withdrawal from domestic work.

(b) Regulating Working Conditions to Ensure Satisfactory Working Standards—

* In order to ensure that the conditions under which children and young persons under the age of 18 are employed are maintained at a satisfactory standard, ILO Recommendation No. 146 provides that special attention should be given to :

  (*a*) The provisions of fair remuneration and its protection, bearing in mind the principle of equal pay for equal work;

  (*b*) The strict limitations of the hours spent at work in a day and in a week and the prohibition of overtime so as to allow enough time for education and training (including the time needed for homework related thereto), for rest during the day and for leisure activities;

  (*c*) The granting without possibility of exception save in genuine emergency, of a minimum consecutive period of 12 hours of night rest, and of customary weekly rest days;

  (*d*) Coverage by social security schemes, including employment injury, medical care and sickness benefit schemes, whatever the condition of employment or work may be;

  (*e*) The maintenance of satisfactory standards of safety and health and appropriate instruction and supervision.[4]

---

1. Ibid Art 2(4).
2. ILO Recommendation No. 146, supra note 4, Art. 11, Sec. 7(2).
3. ILO Conventions No. 138, supra note 4, Art. 7(1).
4. ILO Recommendation No. 146, supra note 4, Art. IV, Sec. 13.

* In addition, the CRC requires that States should respect the right of the child to education, health care services, rest and leisure and contract with parents on a regular basis.[1]

* Another fundamental workers right that should be granted to all children over minimum age in domestic work is the right to freedom of association. This right is supported by ILO Convention No. 87, CRC, ICCPR and the ICESCR.[2]

(c) *Enacting Laws and Policies to Eliminate the Worst Forms of Child Domestic Labour*—Ensuring legitimate conditions also requires the elimination of the Worst Forms of Child Domestic Labour :

* The Worst Forms of Child Domestic Labour can be inferred from the Worst Forms of child labour provided in ILO convention No. 182, which urges States to take effective measures to secure the prohibition and elimination as a matter of urgency.[3] States are also required to take time-bound measures to provide necessary and appropriate direct assistance for the removal of children from the Worst Forms of Child Labour and for their rehabilitation and social integration.[4] Based on the application of these provisions, the Worst Forms of Child Domestic Labour comprise of :

    (*a*) Slavery or practices similar to slavery such as the sale and trafficking of children, debt bondage and forced or compulsory labour; and

    (*b*) Hazardous work defined as work which by its nature or the circumstances in which it is carried out is likely to harm the health, safety or morals of children.[5]

Additionally, States should ensure that these worst Forms of Child Labour are considered to constitute criminal offences.[6]

* In determining Hazardous Child Domestic Labour consideration should be given to the following Hazardous Child Labour factors listed in ILO Recommendation No. 190 :

    (*a*) Work which exposes children to physical psychological or sexual abuse;

    (*b*) Work underground, under water at dangerous heights or in confined spaces;

    (*c*) Work with dangerous machinery equipment and tools or which involves that manual handling or transport of heavy loads;

1. CRC, supra note 15, Arts. 24(1), 31 and 9(3).
2. CRC, supra note 15, Art. 15(1) and (2); ILO Convention No. 87, supra note 31, Art. 11; ICCPR, supra note 33, Art. 22; ICESCR, supra note 31, Art. 8 (1)(1).
3. ILO Convention No. 182, supra note, Art. 1.
4. Ibid. Art. 7, Sec. 2(b).
5. Ibid Art. 3(a) and (d).
6. ILO Recommendation No. 190, supra note 4, Art. 12(a).

(*d*) Work in an unhealthy environment which may for example expose children to hazardous substances, agents of processes, or to temperatures noise, levels or vibrations damaging to their health;

(*e*) Work under particularly difficult conditions such as work for long hours or during the night of work where the child is unreasonably confined to the premises of the employer.[1]

In order to avoid unreasonably confining a child to the employer's premises as listed in ILO Recommendation No. 190 factor (e), employers should ensure implementation of satisfactory working standards detailed in ILO Recommendation No. 146 and the CRC.

* Both ILO Convention Nos. 138 and 182 specify that children below the age of 18 should not be employed in hazardous work.[2] An exception can be made to this rule for children from the age of 16 years after consultation with organizations of employers and workers to authorize employment or work of on condition that the health, safety and morals of the young persons concerned are fully protected and that the young persons have received adequate specific instruction and vocational training.[3] ILO Recommendation No. 146 as well emphasizes the importance of maintaining the minimum working age for hazardous occupations at 18 and provides in relevant part that where the minimum age for admission is below 18, immediate steps should be taken to raise it to that level.[4] In addition to the ILO Conventions, the CRC also recognizes the right of the child to be protected from performing hazardous work.[5]

(*d*) *Strenghening Enforcement Mechanisms*—

* The effective application of standards summarized in this section requires appropriate monitoring and enforcement mechanisms to ensure compliance. ILO Recommendation No. 146 requires the strenghening of labour inspection, for example by the special training of inspectors to detect abuses. Emphasis should be placed on the role of such inspectors in supplying information and advice on effective means of complying with relevant provisions.[6]

* ILO Convention No. 182 obliges states to monitor the implementation of steps to eliminate the Worst Forms of Child Labour.[7] Additionally interventions lead by the ILO across the world in the context of Child

1. Ibid part II, Art. 3(a) (e).
2. ILO convention No. 138, supra note 4, Art. 3(1); ILO Convention No. 182, supra note 5, Arts 1 and 2.
3. ILO Convention No. 138, Art. 3(3).
4. ILO Recommendation No. 146, supra note 4, Art. 111 (9).
5. CRC, supra note 15 Art. 32(1).
6. ILO Recommendation No. 146, supra note 4, Art. V(14).
7. ILO Convention No. 182, supra note 5, Art. 5.

Domestic Labour demonstrate that in addition to labour inspectors, effective monitoring mechanisms include working with community watch groups and trade unions among others.

* In addition to the foregoing points which recap the legal framework, birth registration is fundamental to law enforcement efforts directed at combating child labour as it plays a key role in enforcing minimum age legislation. It also impacts the child's right to education because unregistered children are unable to access educational opportunities in a timely manner. According to a UNICEF survey commissioned in 2000, South Asia has the largest number of unregistered children accounting for approximately 22.5 million or over 40% of the world's unregistered births.[1] This study also finds that 63% of the births went unregistered in South Asia.

1. Child Protection from violence, Exploitation and Abuse, available at http://www.unicef.org/protection/index_birthregistration.html(last visited Sept. 20, 2006).

4

STREET AND WORKING CHILDREN

Issues and Implication

Children in Difficult Circumstances—Concept and Definition.—Children in difficult circumstances include both the street children and the children working in inappropriate work processes and situations. The term `child labour' is generally used to refer to "any work by children (under 14 years of age, in case of India) that interfere with their full physical and mental development the opportunities for a desirable minimum of education and of their needed recreation". In reality, children do a variety of working widely divergent conditions. At one end of the continuum, it is palpably destructive or exploitative. At the other end the work may be beneficial providing or enhancing a child's physical mental spiritual moral or social development without interfering with schooling recreation and rest. Fyfe attempts to provide a distinction by differentiating between "Child Work" and "Child Labour". Child work is considered as permissible, while the child labour is prohibitive.

According to the U.N. Convention on the Rights of the Child (Article 32), "State parties recognize the right of the child to be protected from economic exploitation and from performing any work that is likely to be hazardous or to be harmful to the child's education or to be harmful to the child's health or physical mental spiritual moral and social development."

Child Labour, therefore, is the work, which involves, a degree of exploitation, *i.e.* physical, mental and economic. It denies the joy to children and access to social opportunities (like education, family love and attention), which eventually impairs the personality and creativity the evolution and growth of full being and the health and mental development of a child. The problem of child labour therefore, does not constitute the age or work of a child, but its exploitation and abuse. The perception of what constitutes exploitation or abuse can be subjective, as it is not easy to differentiate between the socialization aspects of a child's activity and its exploitative aspects.

Classification of Street Children.—UNICEF has defined street children :

> "Street children are those for whom the street (in the widest sense of the word, *i.e.* unoccupied dewellings, wastelands, etc.) more than their family has become their real home, a situation in which there is no protection, supervision or direction from responsible adults."

The operational categories of street children given by UNICEF are :

1. Children on the Street; Who have homes and mostly return to their families at the end of each day.
2. Children of the Street : These children have chosen the street as their home and it is there that they seek shelter, livelihood and companionship The have occasional contacts with their families.
3. Abandoned Children : Children who have severed all ties with their families.

Entire families living permanently on the streets confuse the UNICEF categorization. Therefore, the street children were broadly categorized taking into account their contacts with families. Three groups of street children have been classified for the purposes of this study.

(*i*) **Children on the Street**—Children who live with their families, whether it be on the street, in slums or wasteland or abandoned/derelict buildings, etc. but spend a lot of time working or hanging about on the street.

(*ii*) **Children of the Street**—The children of the street could be further classified into two groups.

(*a*) **Roofless**—Who live and work on the street (*i.e.* abandoned buildings, under bridges, railway stations, bus stands, in doorways, or in public parks), yet maintain occasional contacts with their families who may live in the same city, or other city or in rural areas. They see the street as their home and spend most of their lives on the streets, begging selling household goods, rag-picking, scavenging waste materials, shining shoes or washing cars to supplement their and their families incomes. They do often send money to their families.

(*b*) **Roofless Rootless**—Who live and work on the street (*i.e.* in the widest sense of the word) and have no family contacts whatsoever. These children have run away from their families to escape emotional and physical abuse (from an abusive stepmother/stepfather, or an alcoholic stepfather) and are presently roofless and rootless in the city. They have often been beaten or tortured due to neglect/estranged relationship with their families. They may be orphaned, abandoned or have broken families due to dislocation because of migration, wars, famine, natural disasters and poverty.

Classification of Working Children.—Working children can also be classified as :

(i) **Domestic work**—This includes the jobs undertaken by children for domestic purposes like caring for younger siblings cooking, cleaning, washing fetching water, etc. Girls in their families mostly perform these tasks. Although domestic service need not be hazardous, but children in domestic servitude may well be the most vulnerable and exploited children, as they are most difficult to protect, due to the hidden nature of the work. These children remain away from basic elementary education.

(*ii*) **Non-domestic and non-monetary work**—This is a major form of child activity in subsistence, economies, and encompasses farming, hunting gathering and household/cottage industrial activities. In an agrarian economy like India, children spend a great deal of time in such activities like looking after the cattle, grazing goats, collecting fodder and scaring away birds. They are gradually involved with full-time agricultural work. Naturally such children are deprived of schooling play and social activity, which impedes their mental development and creativity. Children under this category whether in agriculture, plantation or in cottage industry are engaged either independently or as part of family labour.

(*iii*) **Bonded child labour**—Tied or bonded labour is a manifestation of a "feudal or semi-feudal" structure of the society and the economy. Children are bonded both in the agriculture and in the unorganized sector. The principal feature is the pledging of children against a loan (small or large) or an agreement between the child's parents and the employer, whereby, the child would work throughout his or her life or part of life in exchange for money or food. There lifelong servitude never succeeds even in reducing the debt. Children are "lured away or pledged" by their parents for paltry sums of money. Most of them are kept in captivity, tortured and made to work 12 to 16 hours a day". The reasons for bondage could be immediate need for money (for purposes like medical treatment, repayment of earlier loan, marriage of daughters, etc.) or agreement to replace the bonded worker with a healthier sibling child worker.

(*iv*) **Wage labour**—Wage labour is one of the major types of work activity for children. Wage labour includes work in domestic service, cottage industries, manufacturing processes, industries, and other service activities. They work either as a part of the family labour force or as wage workers. They are often preferred to adults, because of low wages, docile nature and pliability. Wages are paid on a piece rate basis, applying tremendous pressure to work faster. Hours of work tend to be long.

(*v*) **Commercial and sexual exploitation of children.**—Commercial and sexual exploitation, especially for girls is common worldwide. Girls are lured or forced into this form of hazardous labour, which can verge on slavery. The physical and psychological damage inflicted by commercial sexual exploitation makes it one of the most hazardous forms of child labour. These children are not only subjected to risks of HIV/AIDS, sexually transmitted diseases, unwanted pregnancies and drug addiction but are also plunged into a distorted reality where violence and distrust, shame and rejection are the norms."

(*vi*) **The child combatant**—This is another form of labour exploitation, very much discussed currently at the national and international level. This could be the most difficult, challenge in the new millennium. There is a need to address the pull and push factors, which facilitate the recruitment of children as combatants. These factors range from education to gainful employment. There is a certain amount of self-prestige of being a hero. Even though we rehabilitate child combatants who have surrendered to Government forces, when they return to their community they rejoin as combatants, if they fail to secure the promised employment. We have to identify the most appropriate strategies to sustain their withdrawal and t prevent others from joining as combatants. We have to focus on the training of war trauma counsellors to address the psychological impact created in the minds of war combatants. Shelters and other supporting facilities should be in place to accommodate the victims.

The classification of children in difficult circumstances has been presented in (Diagram No. 1) identifying the children separately under Living Status, Work Situations and Work Activities.

Implications of Children Living on the Streets

Street children are susceptible to drug/alcoholic addiction and to inhalants, such as cobbler's glue correction fluid, gold/silver spray paint, nail polish, rubber, cement, permanent/dry erase markers and gasoline, which offers them an escape from reality and takes away hunger. In exchange, they invite a host of physical and psychological problems, including hallucinations, pulmonary edema, kidney failure and irreversible brain damage. Glue sniffing is a pragmatic response to an unlivable situation. Street children sniff glue because it takes away the children's hunger, cold and despair. It also gives them the courage to steal and engage in survival sex. But glue also causes irreparable damage and even death, and keeps kids stuck in the streets. Once addicted their personalities change. They become more aggressive. Glue destroys any future dreams these kids might have once envisaged for themselves. The become enslaved to the vapurs. In order to secure the regular dose of drugs/alcohol and inhalants they resort to pickpoketing, party thefts and even commit more serious crimes. Many of these kids eventually turn into hardened criminals controlled by organized crime rings for drug trafficking, prostitution and other unlawful activities, thus placing a heavy burden on the law and order machinery.

The street children are routinely detained illegally beaten and tortured by the employers, police and the society to extract maximum labour from them. Several factors contribute to this phenomenon like the inadequacy and non-implementation of legal safeguards, and the level of impunity that law enforcement officials enjoy. These street children are generally viewed as vagrants and criminals. While it is true that street children are sometimes involved in petty theft, drug trafficking prostitution and other criminal activities yet very few attempts are made to examine the root cause for such activities and provide the soothing and caring comfort to rehabilitate them. Street children are also easy targets for police atrocities. The responses from the authorities are to remove children forcibly from the streets, often to incarcerate them, and sometimes to resort to violent measures. Gross abuse is often quietly sanctioned against them. There are reports of street children being beaten tortured and even murdered by police. They are young, small, poor and ignorant of their rights and often have no family members who will come to their defence. It does not require much time or effort to detain and beat a child to extract a confession and the children are unlikely to register formal complaints.

Implication of Inappropriate Work for Children

Work has always been an important avenue of learning and socialization. Children have a powerful desire for competence, and this is expressed and satisfied through work as well as play. The work may be beneficial providing or enhancing a child's physical, mental spiritual, moral or social development. The productive use of children in the family work could provide the process of learning, the skills for a particular trade or craft. This could help the child to turn into a reasonably proficient craftsman or a skilled worker. Thus, the childhood work, paid or unpaid might become an investment for at least a modest future. Nearly all the child workers in this category live with their families. This category of child worker, without interfering with schooling (formal or non-formal), recreation and rest cannot be viewed as exploitative.

But at the same time the work by children, purely for profit motive cannot be justified at the cost of the child's health, education and mental physical and psychological development The work takes a heavy toll physically emotionally and intellectually. They are subjected to all kinds of occupational hazards and diseases, as they are frequently more vulnerable because of their growing bodies, their lower threshold for toxics and their lesser ability to respond effectively to hazards. Children are especially vulnerable to accidents because they have neither the awareness of the dangers nor knowledge of the precautions to be taken at work. It is often found that children and young workers tend to have more serious accidents than adults. The presence of children in these occupations will affect their life and limbs, their health, their psyche and their total development.

Children working long hours suffer from excessive fatigue and are susceptible to infectious diseases. Stunted growth is common among the working children. The work performed is frequently too demanding in relation to their size and strength, causing irreversible damage to their physical and physiological development, resulting in permanent disabilities, with serious consequences for their adult lives. In some occupations, children are exposed for long hours every day to toxic fumes or industrial waste. Children are particularly sensitive to exposure to solvents, lead, mercury and benzene. These toxic substances are handled by children in leather, construction activity, glass works, repair of automobiles, and mining activities.

The effects of repetitive action, postures of sitting, like in the case of carpet weaving can result in muscular-skeletal damage permanently. Carrying heavy loads or being forced to adopt unnatural positions at work can permanently distort or disable growing bodies. Some work situations expose children to unprotected machinery, the risk of explosions and industrial accidents like in case of fireworks, glasswork, etc. The work may damage their eyesight.

A less visible form of exploitation against children is commercial sexual exploitation. It is one of the most brutal forms of violence against children. The child victims suffer extreme physical psychological and emotional abuse, which have life-long threatening consequences. They risk early pregnancy, maternal mortality, sexually transmitted diseases and HIV/AIDS. Sexual exploitation of children has significant emotional ramifications as the victims are unable to return to a normal way of life and are psychologically scared by the experience. In Mumbai, India many young prostitutes were found to have sexually transmitted diseases with a significant proportion of cases having AIDS. The girls are often victims of beatings verbal abuse and sexual molestation and rape in the brothels.

The inappropriate work and living conditions in the streets of cities harms them indirectly by depriving them of positive experiences of future life. They remain bereft of education play and rest, the basic requirements for mental physical and psychological development. The opportunities lost for learning and growth, reduce their chances of prosperity in life and contributes to the perpetuation of increasing poverty and social under development from generation to generation.

Issues of the Street Children

The issues and needs of the children living and working on the streets of cities have attracted widespread international and national attention. There is no doubt that the most effective response to this is prevention through general support to families in poverty, creating broad-based awareness among the parents and society, addressing the factors underlying family disintegration that propel children into a life on the streets. In addition other preventive measures required are employment for adults support in times of crisis, strong childcare, programmes, relevant schooling and efforts to address the roots of domestic violence to keep families intact so that they fulfill responsibilities towards their children.

At the same time children already on the streets cannot be ignored and their rights must be vigorously defended. They need psychological support, relationships and a role in society along with other basic issues related to their survival, security and protection from a full range of civil rights, such as food, money shelter, clothes, healthcare, education, etc. They have the right like all other children to live in dignity, to health and education, to protection from abuse, exploitation silence and to voice their own feelings and sufferings (Articles 2 and 3 of the U.N. Convention on the Rights of the Child).

While evolving strategies for the rehabilitation of the street children one must understand their case histories and the assessment of their situation. Reasons for being on the street vary with each child. The sense of freedom may be intensely important to many of these children. Depriving them of this freedom may exacerbate matters especially when a child has strong ties to a group of peers. This involves establishing a relationship of trust with them providing them with a safe and supportive atmosphere. Institutionalization is definitely not the solution. Strategy has to be integrated with other services on the street.

Issues of Working Children

The presence of child labour is one of the major concerns facing the international community. There are determined efforts to respond to the issues and at the same time arrive at progressive solutions. The Convention on the Rights of the Child contains a number of provisions pertaining to children's work which together provide a framework for policy and action. The Convention requires that children be protected from all exploitative and hazardous work, and from work that interferes with their education and full development. To ensure this, the State is required to set minimum ages for employment and regulate working conditions (Article 32). The Convention also recognizes the right of children to the means for survival (Article 6). The uncomfortable reality in India is that children's work is often the only apparent avenue to their survival. In the context of widespread poverty and absence of a welfare system that guarantees a livelihood for children and their families, work remains the most viable option for many children. The responses from the state and the society must cover their protection as well as tackle the problems that make their work a necessity. The Convention calls to authorities to support parents in their effort to ensure their children's optimal development and adequate standard of living (Articles 18 and 27). The convention also guarantees access to free, relevant, high quality education, which is a critical element in resolving the issue of child labour. While governments and civil societies progress towards eradicating inappropriate child labour and presence of street children, they must address their concerns and ensure their access to education, a high quality of healthcare, rest and leisures, and acceptable working conditions (Articles 12, 24, 28, 31 and 32 of the Rights of the Child).

References

(a) Stein, E., Davis, J. (1940) (eds.), *Labour Problems in America*, F. Farrar and Richer, New York, pp. 112-113.

(b) Fyfe, Alec (1989) : *Child Labour*, Cambridge Polity Press.

(c) Nandna Reddy (1992) : *Street Children of Bangalore : A Situational Analysis*, NLI, NOIDA.

(d) Discussions with Don Bosco, Mumbai.

(e) Bequele, A. and W.E. Myers (1985) : *First Things First, in Child Labour : Eliminating Work Detrimental to Children*, UNICEF/ILO, Geneva, pp. 6-7.

(f) Bequele, A. and W.E. Myers (1985) : *First Things First, in Child Labour : Eliminating Work Detrimental to Children*, UNICEF/ILO, Geneva, pp. 6-7.

(g) ILO Report (1995), *Child Labour, Targeting the Intolerable.*

(h) Ibid.

(i) Casa Allanza Reports, *www. Casa allanza. org.*

(j) Human Rights Watch/Asia (1998), *Police Abuse and Killings of Street Children in India. Human Rights Watch/Children's Rights Project.*

(k) Ibid.

(l) Human Rights Watch/Asia (1998), *Police Abuse and Killings of Street Children in India. Human Rights Watch/Children's Rights Project.*

(m) Gilada, I.S. (1997) : "Child Prostitution : A Blot on Humanity", *Indian Health Organization.*

(n) Balance, C.S. and others (1994), *Urban Child in Distress : Global Predicaments and Innovative Strategies,* Florence, Italy, UNICEF International Child Development Centre, London.

Policy initiatives and Recommendations

(A) Policy Recommendations.—(*i*) The Government of India must adopt the 83rd Constitutional Amendment at the earliest recognizing elementary education as a fundamental right for all Indian citizens.

(*ii*) The Government of India should initiate the process for ratification of the ILO Convention No. 182, Elimination of the Worst Forms of Child Labour at the earliest.

(*iii*) Formation of a nodal agency to converge various activities related to the rehabilitation and education programmes for street and working children by Central and State Governments under various ministries. This will reduce duplication of activities and help in utilizing the activities and support judiciously and effectively.

(*iv*) The Government, local authority, civil society and NGOs should work together and coverage actions and programmes of various ministers such as Sarva Shiksha Abhiyan, National Literacy Mission, National Child Labour Projects and programmes of Street and destitute children, to effectively implement these programmes in a unified manner. An integral component of these programmes should be partnership with the community leaders to create mass mobilisation and community awareness.

(*v*) Non-formal education and other alternative education programmes should be viewed as a supplementary support for the formal education system in the initial stages. Ultimately mainstreaming of all children in formal education is the ultimate goal and NGOs should act as pressure groups to improve quality of education in the formal schools.

(*vi*) UNESCO as a lead agency must facilitate strengthening of national efforts to achieve the Dakar Framework of Action for accomplishing equitable access of education for all by 2015 A.D.

(*vii*) The Government of India in consultation with civil society and NGOs must formulate a National Plan of Action Incorporating details of programmes for achieving Education for All as stipulated under the Dakar Framework of Action by 2002 and seek UN support for the National Plan of Action.

(*viii*) The Government of India must increase budget allocations for elementary education at the level of 3 per cent to the total GDP to show its commitment for achieving Education For All at the earliest.

(*ix*) Accountability of NGOs and regular monitoring of activities must be made an integral component of funding for educational programmes under various Government schemes.

(B) Implementation for Action.—(*i*) Development of a uniform core content of curriculum along with area-specific curriculum and identification of area-specific teaching-learning materials. The curriculum should be introduced by all the NGOs Imparting the NFE programme. A committee of experts from central and state education departments NCERT, National Open School (NOS), education experts, area specific NGOs and experts could be given the task of developing the curriculum for various levels of NFE programme under the lead of NCERT or NOS.

(*ii*) A teacher-learning guide with details of methods of teaching, methodology for preparation of lessons for teachers and monthly targets or curriculum to be completed by the teachers should be prepared by the committee in consultation with the teachers from successful NGOs.

(*iii*) Regular training upgrades to the recruited teachers of all the NFE centres must be provided by Government education training institutions and other technical training Institutes. These centres should be equipped with facilities like library, teaching-learning equipment, development of teaching manuals and guides and other learning skills for the teachers. UNESCO and other UN agencies may take the lead in providing technical and financial assistance to build initial infrastructure and other capacities in these training centres.

(*iv*) All the recruited teachers should be given regular training upgrades at the beginning of the session. The training upgrades should be a regular in-built system of the NFE for at least once a year.

(*v*) Committed and motivated teachers, preferably from local areas and dominant existing social groups even with less formal education but with regular training upgrades should be given priority in recruitment.

(*vi*) The Sarva Shiksha Abhiyan Programme of the Government of India must incorporate provisions facilitating education for children without family support in the cities.

(*vii*) A mapping exercise must be undertaken to identify suitable locations and target groups (especially out-of-school children) for the NFE centres.

(*viii*) Partnership with local authorities and private school authorities should be explored to use the existing infrastructure, especially building structures for the NFE.

(*ix*) Partnership with local authority and private enterprises should be strengthened to provide vocational skills to the "of the street" category of children. Job placements of the trained children must be explored with the help of private enterprises.

(*x*) Priority should be made to enroll out-of-school children in the NFE centres, so that they could be streamlined into formal schooling after orientation courses in the NFE centres.

(*xi*) NFE education must be connected with the state education system to ensure smooth transition of the child from the NFE to the formal school system. The State Education Board should ease procedures for conducting examinations for these children. A set of model question papers should be circulated to the teachers and children well in advance.

(*xii*) NFE school teachers must undertake adult education programmes under the National Literacy Mission to create a proper rapport with the parents for discouraging drop-out rates.

(*xiii*) NFE courses must be for at least five days a week with 3 to 4 teaching hours per day.

(*xiv*) A minimum norm of two teachers for 50 enrolled must be ensured in each NFE centres.

(*xv*) To procure talented teachers, salaries of the teachers must be increased to the minimum of Rs. 1,500 to 2,000 per month depending upon the city and its cost of living.

(*xvi*) Networking of NGOs associated with the NFE in the region must be ensured for sharing knowledge and teaching experiences.

(*xvii*) Government funded NGOs must be assessed before funding. The assessment should consider NGOs' performance in the field of community awareness, rapport with the community.

(*xviii*) Accountability of the NGOs must be ensured through regular monitoring of the NFE centres with the help of evaluation studies conducted by researchers.

(*xix*) Funds should be released regularly without delays to the NGOs for smooth conduct of the NFE programme.

(*xx*) Specific funds should be allocated for Infrastructure development and procuring adequate teaching-learning materials to the NGOs.

(C) Research Studies and Improvement of Database.—(*i*) Regular studies should be conducted, especially in rural areas to enrich the database for arriving at meaningful generalizations. Support from UNESCO and other UN agencies may be sought for conducting such research studies.

(*ii*) Government should seek the support of the NGOs to create a strong database for conducting the research studies. NGOs should maintain and decipher the data to the researchers. It is therefore recommended that NGOs should maintain an adequate database regarding children enrolled—their age, sex, caste, previous work occupation, their attendance rate, drop-out rates, job placements, re-integration with families, avenues of services provided and enrolment into formal schools. The information should be supplied to the funding agencies as well as to the researchers by the NGOs as and when required. Help should also be given to the researchers to collect relevant information from the children, teachers and other stockholders.

Recommendations

Recommendation Addressed to	Broad Recommendation	Recommendation Number
Government of India	Adoption on 83rd Constitutional Amendment	I.1
	Adoption of ILO Convention No. 182	I.2
	Increase Budget Allocation for Elementary Education	I.8
Central and State Government Ministries	Development of Nodal Agency for the target group. The Nodal Agency should include several departments from various ministries working for the target group.	I.3
	Fixing accountability and regular monitoring of NFE centres.	I.9
Local Authority, Civil Society and Local Community	Convergence of various Government programmes for unified action and creation of partnership with local authority, civil society and local community	I.4
UNESCO and UN Agencies	Facilitating national efforts to prepare National Plan of Action for achieving Education for All	I.6, I.7
	Support for capacity building measures in training centres	II.3
Private Establishments Local Authority and Local Community and NGOs	Conducting Further Research	III. 1
	Help to NGOs for providing vocational skills and job placements to the children	II.9
	Provision of NFE building and other Infrastructure	II.8
State Government and Local Government	NFE examination connected to the formal system	II.11
Funding Agencies	Monitoring and Evaluation of NFE Sanction of NFE Centres	II, 7, II.18, II.19, II.20
	Guidelines for data maintenance	III.2

Central Government, State and Local Government, with support from UN agencies	Committee for preparation of uniform core curriculum content with area specific curriculum	II.1 II.2
	Training to teaching staff	II.3, II.4
	Provision of education for of the street' category of children in SSA	II.6
NGOs operating NFE Centres	Mapping of areas with target groups	II.7
	Priority to enroll out-of-school children	II.10
	Networking of NGOs	II.7
	Adult Education and NLM	II.12
	Operation Strategy for NFE	II.4, II.5, II.13, II.14, II.15, II.16

Government/Initiatives for the Working Children

The Government of India is greatly concerned about the magnitude and plight of the working children. India has stood for constitutional, statutory and development measures that are required to eliminate child labour. Six ILO Conventions related to child labour have been ratified. The framers of the Indian Constitution consciously incorporated relevant provision in the Constitution to secure labour protection for children (Articles 24 and 39(e) and (f)) and compulsory universal elementary education (Article 45). However, the basic goal of compulsory education up to the age of 14 years has yet to be achieved owing to lack of political commitment and will. Poor educational Infrastructure in the villages is the major hurdle in eradicating child labour. On the other hand, several legislations have been passed periodiclaly to prohibit or improve the working conditions of child labour. The legislations have started bearing fruits, but the situation demands strict enforcement along with creating conducive conditions for compulsory education.

The Government realized that mere legislation would be insufficient. It adopted the National Policy for Children (NPC) in August 1974. The policy stated, "It shall be the policy of the State to provide adequate service to children both before and after birth and through the period of their growth, to ensure their full physical, mental and social development" (NPC, 1979).

The Child Labour (Prohibition and Regulation) Act (CLA), 1986, was enacted with a view to rationalize earlier legislation on child labour, ensure elimination of child labour in hazardous employment, and regulate condition of child labour in non-hazardous industries. The major loopholes of the Act is that it only covers children in the organized sector and not the 90 per cent working in the unorganized sector. Moreover many occupations, which are hazardous, are not included in the Act.

The Government initiated several action-oriented programme to withdraw children form the hazardous work and prevent them entering the labour markets again. The most significant step in this direction was the adoption of the National Policy of Education (NPE-1986) and National Policy on Child Labour (1987). The policy was formualted is conjunction with the legal measures to address the social-economic issues, having a bearing on Child Labour and to provide a framework for a concrete programme of action. The policy encompasses action in the fields of education, health, nutrition, integrated child development and employment, Both these polcieis aimed at successfully rehabilitating child labour released from hazardous employment and to reduce the incidence of child labour progressively. The opening of special schools for imparting NFE and vocational training was the major recommendation of the two policies.

The National Child Labour Policy (NCLP) approved in 1987 envisaged a project based **Plan of Action** to reduce the incidence of child labour in the hazardous occuaptions. The basic objective was to rehabilitate the children withdrawn from hazardous employments. The Policy consisted of three main programmes :

Legal Action Plan : The purpose is to enforce effectively legal provision related to child labour under various laws of the country.

Focussing of general development programmes : The purpose is to effectively utilize the on going development progrmames of differnet departments/ministries for the benefit of the target families. Hence, converagence of actions from several departments was effectively desired.

Project-Based Plan of Action : The aim is to establish the special schools for the rehabilitation of the children withdrawn from the hazardous occupations in the areas of high concentration of child labour. Ten areas with high incidence of child labour in hazardous industries were initially identified. The industries identified were :

- The match Industry in Sivakasi, Tamil Nadu.
- The diamond polishing Industry in Surat, Gujarat.
- The precious stone polishing Industry in Jaipur (Rajasthan).
- The glass Industry in Firozabad (Uttar Pradesh).
- The brassware Industry in Moradabad (Uttar Pradesh).
- The handmade carpet Industry in Mirzapur-Bhadohi (Uttar Pradesh).
- The lock-making Industry in Aligarh (Uttar Pradesh).
- The handmade carpet Industry in Jammu and Kashmir.
- The slate Industry in Mandsaur (Madhya Pradesh).
- The Industry in Markapur (Madhya Pradesh).

A Project Society has been established in the National Child Labour Project areas for an Integration of various developmental programmes. The job of the Project Society is to :

- Effectively enforce child labour laws.
- Identification of areas for starting Non-Formal Education through the opening of the special schools.
- Creating public awareness, through adult education, income-generation and creating employment opportunties for the target families.

In the special schools, target children (children working in hazardous occupations, who have not completed 14 years of age) are to be enrolled. The scheme envisaged non-formal education, vocational training, supplementary nutrition, regular health care and stipends in case the children are withdrawn from prohibited employments and vocations. It also envisaged extension of benefits of the other State Government programmes for these school children and their familits by the district administration as far as possible. The desired teaching mode should preferably be non-formal with a condensed syllabus for a maximum period of 3 years. After the completion of the 3 years of special school education, children are expected to join the formal stream of education in the 6th standard. While appreciating the need for flexibility in the curriculum, the scheme felt the need to introduce some uniformity in the syllabus. The curriculum, course content and textual material needed was desired to be finalized at the State/district level by associating SCERT, DIET, DRU, UNICEF and other NGOs with experience in this field. The programme also stipualted imparting of age-appropriate craft and pre-vocational training, keeping in view the resources and market forces of the area, so that children unable to join formal schools after 14 years of age could start their own occupations.

The Government of India is implementing NCLP in 93 districts of the country as on June 2000. There are two types of special schools, one with an approved strength of 50 children and the other with 100 children. Each of the project societies has been sanctioned to run a specified number of schools. These schools are managed by the project society or alternatively the project runs these school through local NGOs. About 1,55,250 children were covered in 2,571 schools under the NCLP scheme. (Table No. IV.2)

In a landmark judgment, on 10 December, 1996 in writ petition (Civil) No. 465/1986, the Hon'ble Supreme Court of India has given the same directions, regarding the manner in which the children working in hazardous occuaptions as defined in (CLA, 86) are to be withdrawn from work and to be simultanesouly rehabilitated. The direction was also given to regulate and improve the working conditions in the non-hazardous occupations. Several measures were proposed by the Supreme Court to solve the problem of child labour. The measures include :

- Survey for identification of working children.
- Withdrawal of children working in hazardous industries and ensuring their education in appropriate Institutions.
- Contribution @ Rs. 20,000 per child to be paid by the offending employers of children to a welfare fund to be establsihed for this purpose.
- Employment of the one adult member of the family of a child so withdrawn from work and if that is not possible, a contribution of Rs. 5,000 per child to the welfare fund to be made by the State Government.
- Financial assistance to the families of the children so withdrawn to be paid out of the interest earnings on the surplus of Rs. 20,000/25,000 deposited in the welfare fund as long as the child is actually sent to school.
- Regulating hours of work for children working in non-hazardous occuaptions, so that their working hours do not exceed six hours per day and education for at least two hours is ensured. The entire education of the concerned is to be borne by the employer.

Coverage under the National Child Labour Project of India 1996-97

S. No.	State	District Covered	Sanctioned Schools	No. of Children Sanctioned	Actual Schools Functioning	Actual Coverage
1	Andhra Pradesh	20	807	43,550	610	36,249
2	Bihar	08	174	12,200	173	10,094
3	Gujarat	02	040	2,000	023	1,254
4	Karnataka	03	100	5,000	024	1,200
5	Madhya Pradesh	05	138	9,800	087	6,524
6	Maharashtra	02	074	3,700	024	1,200
7	Orissa	16	430	33,000	239	14,972
8	Rajasthan	02	060	3,000	054	2,700
9	Tamil Nadu	08	379	19,500	307	14,684
10	Uttar Pradesh	04	150	11,500	105	7,488
11	West Bengal	06	219	12,000	164	8,250
	Total	76	2571	1,55,250	1810	1,04,615

Source : Annual Report, 1996-97, Ministry of Labour, and Government of India.

International and Voluntary Sector Initiatives

Monetary and technical support has been provided to the Government and NGOs for various welfare programmes for the children in difficult circumstances by UN agencies and other International and national donor agencies. The support from UN agencies has come from ILO, UNESCO, UNICEF, UNIFEM, UNFPA, UNDP, and the World Bank. In addition to these, foreign Governmental agencies like USAID, DFID, the Norwegian and German Governments have also supported specific programmes in the specific areas.

International Labour Organization (ILO)

Two parallel programmes intended to build financial and human capacity of the Government and non-Government agencies were started in India with the support from ILO.

(i) International Programmes on the Elimination of Child Labour (IPEC).

(ii) Child Labour Action Support Programmes (CLASP).

IPEC a global Initiative of the ILO. It was launched in 1992 ; to support participating member countries in their national efforts to combat and eliminate child labour progressively based on ILO Conventions, in particular, Convention No. 138. The programmes have been implemented through Various Action Programmes, selected by the National Steering Committee of the Ministry of Labour. The Action Programme was characterized by :

- Setting up non-formal education centres for working children in these Identified areas.
- Supplementing nutritional and health care.
- Carry out awareness-raising project for the children, their parents and community and employers.
- Eliciting community support and involvement for substainability and continuation of welfare programmes.
- Training programmes for labour inspectors for effective enforcement of child labour legislation.

Under the ILO-IPEC programmes, a sum of US $6.9 million or 270 million rupees were made available to Central Employees' Organizations, Central Trade Union Organisations and NGOs between 1992-1999. This amount has been utilized under 160 projects benefiting about 100,000 children. The scheme is extended till 21 December, 2001 extendible by a further period of one year. The Government of Germany aided CLASP programmes. Assistance taken under this programmes has been used for the purpose of supporting on going activities under the National Policy on Child Labour.

United Nations International Children's Educational Fund (UNICEF)

UNICEF acknowledges the need to advocate the implementation of the Convention on the Rights of the Child in India and promote compulsory education.

A number of international seminars, symposia, workshops and conferences were organized or supported by UNICEF highlighting the problems of illiteracy among the children. UNICEF in India initiated curriculum programmes and supply of books for children. It funded studies identifying situational analysis of street children in major cities of India. Currently UNICEF is supporting the Bal Adhikar Paryojana Programmes providing need-based education to children out-of-schools in the carpet-weaving belt of Mirzapur and Bhadhoi. The aims and objectives of UNICEF programmes are to :

- Advocate revision and enforcement of legislation to prohibit child labour, particularly is hazardous industries ;
- Assist Central and State Governments for an action plan for the withdrawal and rehabilitation of child labour.
- Strengthen alliance between NGOs, media, Industry and legal set-up for social mobilisation in support of elimination of child labour.

United Nations Educational, Scientific and Cultural Organization (UNESCO)

UNESCO has been actively working for street and working children in India since the 1990 World Conference on Education for All, in Jomtien and the World Declaration on Education For All. The UNESCO's Education Programme for Children in need has enabled the organization to provide substantial funding and technical support for educational activities in favour of children in difficult circumstances. At the World Education Forum held in Dakar in April, 2000 UNESCO has been mandated as a lead agency supported by other official partners - the World Bank, UNFPA, UNDP and UNICEF, for promoting and ensuring the Education. For All movement. UNESCO is to play a key role in helping to co-ordinate policy planning at national, regional and international, regional and international levels to ensure that all children with special emphasis on girl and children in difficult circumstances from ethnic minorities have access to and complete free and compulsory primary education of good quality by 2015. The framework is also committed to achieve elimination of gender disparities in primary and secondary education by 2005 and achieve gender equality in education by 2015. At the national level, actions of concrete plans indicating technical assistance and aid for achieving Education. For all will be augmented for the countries that do not have co-ordination mechanisms. UNESCO aims to collaborate with Government and other agencies at the local level in encouraging the mobilization of the necessary resources, the establishment of sector analysis and project design and their implementation with the aid of experts. UNESCO is also devoted to holding regional and sub-regional technical meetings enabling all the bilateral and multilateral partners like the regional development banks, representatives of the Ministeries of Education and Finance, teachers' unions, the private sector, civil society foundations, and parents to discuss the regions' needs in terms of basic education and modalities of co-operation and financing within the framework of Education For All.

Within this framework, UNESCO has been supporting CINI ASHA and Don Bosco Ashalayam, NGOs based in Calcutta since 1997 on a framework of programmes to meet basic needs of street and working children's survival, growth and development. The active support from UNESCO has contributed significantly in providing rehabilitation and education for street and working children in Kolkata's urban agglomeration. UNESCO is also supporting PRAYAS, A Delhi-based NGO in preparing a project to develop innovative educational material to accomplish the needs of street and working children for education in urban surroundings. The educational material prepared will be tested for application by other NGOs in the country.

UNESCO has also supported the present study in the context of assessing the magnitude of out-of-school children in difficult circumstances, and to evaluate the present implementation of education and other rehabilitation programmes, undertaken by the Government and NGOs for these children. The aim is to prepare a coordinated strategy for achieving the Dakar Declaration of Education for All by 2015. UNESCO organized a workshop on 15 December, 2000 to discus the results of the study and have a concerted strategy after thorough discussions with the representatives from Government, NGOs, UN agencies, International Aid agencies, and other civil societies.

Other Agencies

The other UN agencies like UNDP and the World Bank are supporting educational projects in the Mirzapur-Bhadhoi carpet-weaving belt for out-of-school children. International Government agencies like USAID, DFID, the German and Norwegian Governments are also supporting several NGOs for education and rehabilitation schemes in several cities of the country. Other international donor agencies supporting child education and rehabilitation programmes are :

(*i*) Terra Des Hommes, Bread for the World, Rugmark Foundation, Care and Fair, Misesior (Germany).

(*ii*) Christian Aid, Anti Slavery-International, and Project Mala (United Kingdom).

(*iii*) Asian American Free Labour Institute, Child Labour Coalition and International Labour Rights Education and Research Fund, National Consumer League (United States).

(*iv*) Radda Barmer BLLF (Sweden).

(*v*) Save the Children (United Kingdom and Canada).

(*vi*) Alternative for India Development (United Kingdom).

(*vii*) Child Relief and You.

(*viii*) S.O.S. schools.

In addition to these, several national voluntary organizations are supporting the initiatives of NGOs through human resources, technical and monetary help. The South Asian Coalition on Child Servitude (SACCS), a conglomerate of NGOs working for children was actively associated with the 'Global March against Child Labour' for creating awareness against child labour. Several children were released from bondage and hazardous labour by the organization.

Education for street and working Children

(a) National Child Labour Project Schools.—The NCLP schools funded by the Ministry of Labour, under the IPEC and CLASP programme in the hazardous working processes have a 3-year non-formal education programme. These children are prepared to enter Class VI in the formal streams after completing 3 years of a condensed teaching programme. Most of these schools follow the State Education Board syllabus. But presently the books selected are of the pre-preparatory stage and may not give the required skills to get enrolled in Class VI. There is an urgent need to arrange appropriate textbooks for these children. Books having elementary reading of alphabets are being taught for one or two years in some NFE centres. A committee of experts should select the appropriate books for these children. Bal Adhikar Pariyojana, Nalanda with help from UNICEF, Lucknow has prepared a set of books for these classes. The books are in operation for NCLP schools in Bhadhoi. The committee should consider these books for operation after a proper review and tests are conducted on children. The books cover Hindi language reading and writing material, mathematics and elementary social science themes.

The teaching learning material used by other NFE centres are varied and need scrutiny from the experts. Since NGOs have to contribute significantly to the NFE programmes for some more time, till all children are enrolled in formal schools, preparation of universally accepted learning material is required. NGOs must pool in together and prepare acceptable teaching-learning materials with the help of Government, UN agencies and International funding agencies. The teaching-learning material prepared should be tested in all areas before being accepted universally. Help from experienced NGOs in this field should be sought.

(b) Success Stories of Some NGOs

(i) *MV Foundation.*—MV Foundation was established in 1987 to break the laboring cycle for the children aged 5-14 years, through community initiative by motivating parents and children to utilize formal schooling as a medium for his/her advancement. The aims is to send all out of school children to formal schools. The target groups are all out-of-school children in the age group 5-14 years. The strategy followed is different for the 5-8 year age group and for the 9-14 year age group. Parents of all children in the age group of 5-8 years are identified in the target region and are motivated for an Intensive enrollment drive in formal schools. About 90 per cent of the children in this age group are already in formal schools because of the MVF initiative. To ensure retention of the children in the schools, community involvement is sought. Several village committees like, the Parent Teacher Association, Village Education Committee and Mandal Education

Committee are promoted to act as pressure group to sensitize the administration towards education needs. These committees are also involved for monitoring and overseeing functioning of the schools. The district administration has already successfully replicated this model in 800 villages. Dedicated education activists handle the fieldwork programme components. They identify the child and are responsible for motivating the parents.

Children in the 9-14 year age group are initially motivated through the non-formal education centres, as they may not be able to catch up with the regular students. These NFE centres run bridge courses for a short duration in the residential camps. Children are persuaded to join these residential 'summer camps'. These camps are located in discued Government buildings. These camps are held separately for boys and girls, and vary in duration from 3 to 9 months, depending upon the child's receptive abilities. Study timings are from 9 a.m. to 5 p.m. In the evenings there are library sessions, review sessions and homework sessions. Responsibilities are given to children for organizing day-to-day chores. During 1991-98, 36 'Bridge Courses' were held covering 7,500 children. Ninety per cent of the children were rural child workers engaged as bonded labourers, cattleherds or shepherds, agricultural labourers harvesting cotton and orange flowers. At the end of the camp they are assured admission to the formal schools related to their age and learning capacity. The results demonstrate that all parents have an intense desire to educate children, provided quality teaching is given to them. They understand the value of dignity and confidence which education can give. It seeks to make creative use of local resources.

The success of the girl's camp to prepare girls to join formal school is spreading rapidly and parents are convinced of its success because they have witnessed it themselves.

(ii) *Cini Asha.*—CINI ASHA is a NGO based in Kolkata whose main objective is to mainstream street children, child labourers and children of sex workers into formal schools. The major goal of CINI ASHA is to improve the quality of life of the urban children living is socially disadvantaged and de-humanizing circumstances. The organization ensures that all children in the project area are enrolled and retained in formal schools. Some of the facilities provided by the organization are Drop-in-Centres, Night Shelters, short stay residential homes (Half-Way-House), Clinic, Sick Bay, HIV/AIDS prevention programmes for street children, preparatory centres and coaching centres for child labourers and evening centres for children of sex workers. Children who live on the platforms attend non-formal education classes in a small room given by the railway authorities. Working children from slum areas have been accommodated in non-formal education centres ; there is also a coaching centre where teachers conduct additional activities such as helping the children with their homework. The rehabilitation of the distressed children has been one of CINI ASHA's major thrust areas. Facilities like nutrition, education, recreation, counselling lockers, banking and vocational training are provided to the enrolled children.

CINI ASHA has managed mainstream, 1,500 street and working children from squatter settlements into formal schools. Their parents appreciated the educational experience for the children, which in turn have changed the lives of the families for the better. Their food habits have changed, consumption of alcohol has been reduced and gambling habits have changed. There is a heavy demand for such schools and pressure on the municipality has increased for increasing the number of schools and also for taking corrective measures to improve the quality of schooling.

(iii) *Project Mala.*—Project Mala was established in 1989, to educate and rehabilitate working children in carpet-weaving. It provides three-year non-formal education to children between the ages of 10 and 14, who are involved in carpet-weaving. This education is equivalent to 5 years in the formal primary system (levels I-V). The idea is that on completing the NFE, the child joins formal school for further education or will join the labour force, with more favourable terms as skilled workers. Adequate attention is paid to enrol girl students and children from marginal sections, especially backward classes and Scheduled Castes. Along with NFE, the Project Mala schools also provide technical skills by way of vocation training in the field of carpet-weaving and talloring. The parents have applauded the one-hour daily course on carpet-weaving and talloring. They consider the training as an asset, generating confidence among the children. Project Mala schools adopt Minimum Levels of Learning (MLL) curriculum designed by NCERT for non-formal education. It has inducted some aspects along with the Gandhian lines and is in accordance with guidelines laid down by the Government of India. It combines productive work with other forms of learning. The curriculum is child centred, providing basic primary skills for mathematics, language, social science and general sciences. Teachers attach significant importance to using teachings aids such as charts, posters, stories, songs, practical demonstration of skills, outdoor field tours and remedial teaching for children.

A discussion with parents and community members of the Mala school students indicated that they see a change in the children's behaviour, since they joined the Mala schools. Their health and physical appearance had changed for the better, their personal hygience habits had improved, they had becomes more alert, learnt things quicker and had confidence to face the challenges and spoke better. The influence was also found on their friends and siblings, as they also expressed motivation for learning. Mala schools have played a significant role in creating more demand for schools, as more and more children want to get enrolled in Mala schools or such other type of schools.

(iv) *Prayas.*—Prayas Juvenile Aid Centre was established in 1988. The target groups are both 'on the street' and 'of the street' categories of street children. The objective of the organization is to rehabilitate them and reduce the incidence of vagrancy and delinquency among them through a holistic approach comprising, shelter, food, clothing, care and protection, health support, community participation, reintegration with families, non-formal educations and imparting of vocational skills. The organization runs 3 shelter homes (one each for boys, girls a and custodial home for boys). The boys shelter home is a 24-hours open shelter home, where children spend their extra time. Girls' shelter home is restricted for only registered children. They are not allowed to move out unless reintegrated with families or provided a self-support mechanism. The girl's shelter home provides food, clothing, bedding, health care, non-formal education, library and vocational skill raining to the inmates. The organization also runs several non-formal education centres for 'on the street' children in identified slum squatters. They provide elementary education to out-of-school children as well as remedial support to the school-govers. The organization also imparts vocational skills like screen printing, cutting and tailoring, embroidery, beauty culture, book binding, art and crafts, candle-making and scooter repair. Emphasis is laid for mainstreaming the children from there slum areas after imparting basic elementary education. The other community participation activities are helping children of migrant workers by providing midday meals and non-formal education. The target children are also provided health services and imparted health awareness modules, through advocacy campaigns. Special awareness programmes for sex transmitted diseases. HIV/AIDs are given to the street children. The organization is associated with CHILDLINE in North Zone. The children in distress are immediately provided shelter in the homes. The efforts of Prayas have resulted in reintegration of several children with their families as well as creating self-support avenues for nearly 25 per cent of the children.

(v) *Salam Balak Trust.*—Salam Balak Trust, a Delhi-based NGO was established in 1989 to provide shelter and protection to street children loitering in and around New Delhi railway station. The target group are essentially 'of the street' children with minimum or no family contacts.

The objectives of the NGO are to provide counselling, basic necessities like shelter, food, health care, healthy living and sanitation. The organization has arranged reintegration of the children with families wherever possible.

Children Interested in education are put in separate shelter homes. These children are enrolled in Government/private schools and are also provided food, clothing and medical care. They are also given vocational skills. Children admitted in-between are given non-formal education and prepared for enrolments in formal schools. Children are encouraged to be in contact with families and even reunited after completing elementary schooling. Separate shelter homes for girls (aged 5-16 years) have been started to provide 'temporary safe space for girls in distressful circumstances. These girls are either reunited with their families or are getting education and vocational training to be rehabilitated back into the society. The girls are imparted non-formal education initially and are enrolled in formal Schools subsquently. The NFE covers alphabets, number and word formations. Vocational courses in embroidery and tailoring are also given to the girls. Efforts are made to provide recreation and counselling of basic awareness, especially health education on HIV/AIDS. Outdoor trips for cultural programmes and general awareness programmes are also arranged. Special discourses are given for health, hygiene and proper sanitation.

(vi) *The Vatsalya Foundation.*—The Vatsalya Foundation provides shelter, counselling, education, healthcare recreation and vocational training to the 'of the street' category of children. The organization has been able to reintegrate a number of street children with their families. They have also enrolled several children in the formal schools. The foundation provides technical skills to 'of the street' category of children. Several children have been enrolled in formal schools. The foundation provides computer-training courses to the enrolled children. Art lessons in he form of painting, drawings and preparation of handicrafts are given to the enrolled children. The major aim of the organization is to provide rehabilitation and protection from abuses to the 'of the street' category of children.

The children are independent and disciplined. A significant proportion of the children have been reintegrated with the society after job placements.

(vii) ***Don Bosco.***—The organization is working for the street and working children in several urban centres throughout the country such as Kolkata, Delhi, Mumbai, Chennai, Bangalore and Madurai. The organization has been striving to support street children to make them re-enter the maintenance of society. The project addresses entire socio-economic organization at two levels :

At the level of youngsters on the street by providing support to the child to grow and integrate into society.

By building a meaningful, social and political movement capable of challenging those situations that leave children abandoned on the streets.

The organization has successfully de-addicted several street children from drugs, inhalants and alcohol in their de-addiction centres. They have successfully provided technical skills to these children by imparting vocational skills and a seizable number of children have been able to earn their livelihood and stand on their own feet. These children have entered into adulthood with confidence and maturity. Many of them have their own families and provide formal education to their children.

(viii) ***Butterflies.***—Butterflies, a Delhi-based NGO, has been working for street and working children since 1988. Both 'on the street' and 'of the street' categories of street children are its target groups. The major objectives of the organization are to empower street children with elementary education and necessary skills to protect their rights as children. It also helps to provide necessary support for their reintegration with their families, keeping in view the principles of democracy and community participation.

The approach of the organization is to initiate contract with the target groups, through regular visits to their places of work and stay. Once the relationship is established, children are motivated to actively participate in the decision-making processes concerning their future life and create awareness towards child issues. The organizations role is initiator and supporting their decision through guidance and technical assistance. The activities are conducted on the streets or in parks, as they have to fixed centres. Help of school children and other youth groups is south for conducting the activity.

The other activities include saving schemes for children's earnings, formation of credit unions, quarterly, camps and get-together, health education, especially sex education and protection from sex transmitted diseases, HIV/AIDS, etc. The organization has developed 'Butterflies Restaurant's concept to support child entrepreneurship. This initiative helped them to gain confidence and generate employment of them.

(ix) ***The Indian Council for Child Welfare (Chennai, Tamil Nadu).***—The organization has multiple programmes for the development of street and working children. The programmes include creches for early childhood care, education for pre-school children to prepare them for schools,. transit schools for the working children to reorient them for enrolments in formal schools and rehabilitation of street children by providing shelter homes. These children are enrolled into non-formal education programmes initially and subsequently they are integrated with the formal education.

(x) ***The Hyderabad Council of Human Welfare (AP) : (HCHW-MARG).***—The organisation has worked effectively with street children since 1990. The major priority of the organization is rehabilitation of street children and protects them from abuse. The shelter homes serve as a platform to search for the child's talent and inner potential. The initial support in the shelter homes includes need-based education, food, clothing, healthcare, saving facility and job placement counselling. Measures for rehabilitation include vocational training, self-employment, and placements for street children and alternate ways of waste-picking.

(xi) ***Maya.***—Maya works to address the concerns of children and concentrates on slums and low-income areas of urban Bangalore. The approach is to enable and strengthen community members to address the needs of children through their own efforts rather then provide them with facilities and services. The activities include community run pre-schools, child development centres where facilities for non-formal education, exposure to creative and cultural activities, indoor and outdoor games and camp schools. The organization has created mass awareness for enrollments in schools.

(xii) ***Rag-Pickers' Education and Development Society.***—The main focus of the organization is to cover rag-pickers, domestic servants and street and working children living in slums. The organization provides shelter homes ; streamlines children into formal schools, value education and life skill education, concealing are recreation. The organization has helped many children who were mainly dependent upon rag picking. In this process many of them suffered from III health. The organization has made them aware about hygiene and health preventive measures. Many children who were addicted to inhalants have been saved by this organization.

— — — — — —

5

FLACTUAL MATRIX

Of all the world's children, one in seven is involved in child labour of some kind. For the past decade, this fact has moved the international community - in collaboration with the ILO - to mount one of the largest social reform movements ever seen. Now, the work of countless individuals and organizations is bearing results. According to the second Global Report on Child Labour prepared by the ILO, the end of child labour is now within our grasp.

Prepared under the ILO's Declaration on Fundamental Principles and Rights at Work and the International Programme on the Elimination of Child Labour (IPEC), the new report, entitled *"The end of child labour - Within reach"**, says we are beginning to see an encouraging reduction in child labour - especially its worst forms - in many parts of the world. What's more, the report says that if the current trends continue, child labour in its worst forms may be eliminated within the next decade.

The report indicates that the number of child labourers globally has fallen by 11 per cent over the last four years - or 28 million fewer than 2002. The sharpest decrease is in the area of hazardous work by children - where there has been a 26 per cent reduction overall, and 33 per cent fewer children between the ages of 5 and 14 endangering their lives in hazardous work.

This progress has not been automatic. It has taken political mobilization of workers, employers and governments combined with the practical action of parliaments, non-governmental organizations, local authorities, consumers and the public at large. This is truly a global movement against child labour.

Key Statistics

- The global number of child labourers in the age group 5-17 decreased from 246 million in 2000 to 218 million in 2004, a decrease of 11 per cent. The percentage of child labourers in this age group went down from 16 per cent (1 in 6) in 2000 to 14 per cent (1 in 7) in 2004.
- The number of children aged 5-17 engaged in hazardous work has declined by 26 per cent, from 171 million in 2000 to 126 million in 2004.

With 33 per cent, the decline in the age group 5-14 has even been sharper.

- Around 5 million children have benefited directly or indirectly from IPEC's work.
- Latin America and the Caribbean stand out in terms of a rapid decline of child labour. The number of children at work in the region has fallen by two-thirds over the last four years, with just 5 per cent of children ages 5-14 now engaged in work.
- With 26 per cent, or close to 50 million child workers, the proportion of children engaged in economic activities in sub-Saharan Africa is currently the highest of any region in the world.
- In the Asian-Pacific region, 122 million children ages 5-14 are engaged in work, 5 million fewer than four years ago. Less than 20 per cent of Asian children in that age group are now at work.
- In industrialized countries, about 2.5 million children under the age of 15 were at work in 2000.
- Almost 7 out of 10 working children are in the agricultural sector; whereas 22 per cent work in services and 9 per cent in industry, including mining, construction and manufacturing.
- The estimated cost of the elimination of child labour is US$760 billion over a 20-year period. The estimated benefit in terms of better education and health is over US$4 trillion. The economic benefits would therefore outweigh the costs by nearly 6 to 1, not to mention the unquantifiable social benefits to be gained.

Global Goals

The ILO urges member States to commit themselves to eradicating the worst forms of child labour by 2016. To do this, all countries are requested to design and put in place appropriate time-bound measures by 2008. The action plan is based on three pillars:

- supporting and mainstreaming national responses to child labour;
- deepening and strengthening the worldwide movement against child labour; and
- further integrating child labour concerns in overall ILO strategies to promote decent work for all.

If the trend observed over the last four years continues, the worst forms of child labour could be eliminated by 2016. Meeting the UN Millennium Development Goals by 2015 would further help to eradicate this scourge.

Global Action

The ILO's International Programme on the Elimination of Child Labour (IPEC) was created in 1992. By December 2005, it was operational in 86 countries, with an annual expenditure on technical cooperation projects that reached over US$70 million.

- IPEC is the largest programme of its kind globally and the biggest single operational programme of the ILO.
- IPEC has made a difference in countries like Brazil, Tanzania, Turkey and Thailand - just to name a few.

The number and range of IPEC's partners has also expanded over the years, and now includes other international and government agencies, employers and workers' organizations, private businesses, community-based organizations, NGOs, the media, parliamentarians, the judiciary, universities, religious groups and, of course, children and their families.

National and community action is crucial for the success of the IPEC programme. Through local authorities and municipalities, IPEC can reach children in the informal economy and small and medium-sized businesses that provide the bulk of employment, as well as promote integrated approaches to get children out of work and into school.

A Timeline on The Fight Against Child Labour

Eliminating child labour is an essential element in the ILO's goal of "Decent Work for All". The ILO tackles child labour not as an isolated issue but as an integral part of national efforts for economic and social development.

1919 The first International Labour Conference adopts the first international Convention against child labour, the Minimum Age (Industry) Convention (No. 5).

1930 Adoption of the first Forced Labour Convention (No. 29).

1973 Adoption of the Minimum Age Convention (No. 138).

1992 The ILO establishes the International Programme on the Elimination of Child Labour (IPEC).

1996 Stockholm Declaration and Agenda for Action: The elaboration of the principle that a crime against a child in one place is a crime anywhere. The ILO codifies this into an international standard by developing a convention three years later which spells out the role of enforcement and penalties.

1998 Adoption of the ILO Declaration on Fundamental Principles and Rights at Work: Freedom of association, abolition of forced labour, end of discrimination in the workplace and elimination of child labour. All

ILO member States pledge to uphold and promote these principles.

1999 Adoption of the ILO's Worst Forms of Child Labour Convention (No. 182). Focused world attention on the need to take immediate action to eradicate those forms of child labour that are hazardous and damaging to children's physical, mental or moral wellbeing. Convention 182 has been ratified by 9 out of 10 ILO member States while Convention 138 has been ratified by 4 out of 5 ILO Member States.

2001 The first Time Bound Programmes on the implementation of Convention 182 and 138 are launched by three countries. Over 20 countries are currently implementing time bound programmes with ILO support.

2002 The ILO publishes its first Global Report on Child Labour and establishes 12 June as World Day Against Child Labour. The Organization supports more than 80 countries in formulating their own programmes to combat child labour.

2004 First ILO global study on the costs and benefits of eliminating child labour says that economic benefits would outweigh costs by nearly 6 to 1.

2006 The ILO's second Global Report on Child Labour on child labour says that child labour is declining worldwide.

CONTEMPORARY COMPARATIVE GLOBAL TRENDS IN DIFFERENT CATEGORIES OF WORK BY CHILDREN

Previous sections have indicated that, from 2000 to 2004, all forms of children's involvement in work—economic activity, child labour, and hazardous work—were undergoing significant changes. Global incidence rates and the overall magnitude were decreasing, albeit at varying degrees. At the same time, the situation across the various regions was highly uneven. While some regions made significant progress—e.g. Latin America and the Caribbean—others, such as Sub-Saharan Africa, tended to stagnate. Unfortunately, the data at our disposal does not allow us to present regional estimates for the sub-categories of child labour and children in hazardous work.

How do declining rates in the various forms of work relate to one another, and how does the rate of decrease of, say, "children's work" compare to that of "child labour", taking into account age and sex differentials? Table 1 suggest the following:

The more harmful the work, the faster the decline.—The decline seems to accelerate with the degree of harm associated with the form of work. In other words, the more harmful the work, the faster the decline. Among the core group, aged 5-14 years, the number of working children declined by 9.6 per cent, from 211 million to 191 million.7 Among child labourers, however, the drop was greater than 10 per cent. The number of children in child labour slated for abolition decreased from 186 million in 7 For details on the 2000 figures quoted, see ILO/IPEC (2002), op.cit. 2000 to 166 million in 2004, which represents a decline of 11 per cent. The biggest decline is observed among children in hazardous work, a sub-category of the WFCL. The global number plummeted by about one-third in the 5-14 age group, from 111 million to 74 million children.

A trend towards less hazardous types of work.—As a result, and unsurprisingly, the number of children aged 5-14 years in non-hazardous child labour increased. This confirms the general trend towards less dangerous forms of work.

TABLE 1

Children in Economic Activity, Child Labour, and Hazardous Work (by Sex and Age Group), 2004

Sex & age group	*Econom children children (EAC) ('000s)*	*Child labour*	*Child labour as percent of EAC*	*Children in hazardous Work (CHW) ('000s)*	*CHW as per cent of EAC*	*CHW as per cent of child labour*
5-11	107'647	107'647	100	40'235	37.4	37.4
Boys	53'103	53'103	100	20'325	38.3	38.3
Girls	54'544	54'544	100	19'909	36.5	36.5
12-14	83'072	58'105	69.9	34'157	41.1	58.8
Boys	44'706	31'848	71.2	20'693	46.3	65.0
Girls	38'366	26'257	68.4	13'464	35.1	51.3
Total 5-14	190'719	165'752	86.9	74'392	39.0	44.9
Boys	97'809	84'951	86.9	41'018	41.9	48.3
Girls	92'910	80'801	87.0	33'374	35.9	41.3
Total 15-17	126'683	51'911	41.0	51'911	41.0	100
Boys	70'609	32'250	45.7	32'250	45.7	100
Girls	56'073	19'661	35.1	19'661	35.1	100
Total	317'402	217'663	68.6	126'302	39.8	58.0
Boys	168'418	117'201	69.6	73'268	43.5	62.5
Girls	148'983	100'462	67.4	53'035	35.6	52.8

CURRENT GLOBAL TRENDS IN CHILDREN'S WORK

(a) Children's Work by Age Group

In 2004, an estimated global population of 191 million children aged 5-14 years were at work. This accounts for less than one-sixth (15.8 per cent) of the world's population in that age group. The total economically active child population aged 5-17 years was estimated at 317 million.

As Table 2 shows, incidence of work among children declined in both absolute and relative terms. The trend is consistent across all major age groups. It means that

- fewer children were working in 2004 than there were four years earlier, and
- the percentage of working children among the total child population also declined.

TABLE 2

Global trend (2000-2004) in the number of working children 5-17 years old

	Population ('000)		*Number at work ('000)*		*Incidence rate*		*Change of incidence rate*
Year	*2000*	*2004*	*2000*	*2004*	*2000*	*2004*	
World	1'531'400	1'566'300	351'900	317'400	23.0%	20.3%	-2.7%
Boys	786'500	804'000	184'200	171'500	23.4%	21.3%	-2.1%
Girls	744'900	762'300	167'700	145'800	22.5%	19.1%	-3.4%
5-9	600'200	601'100	73'200	64'600	12.2%	10.7%	-1.5%
10-14	599'200	605'400	137'800	126'100	23.0%	20.8%	-2.2%
(5-14)	1'199'400	1'206'500	211'000	190'700	17.6%	15.8%	-1.8%
15-17	332'000	359'800	140'900	126'700	42.4%	35.2%	-7.2%

From 2000 to 2004, the number of working children in the most relevant, 5- to 14-year core age group declined by some 20 million. Among 15- to 17-year-olds, 14 million fewer children were at work. The incidence rate in the two age categories dropped from 17.6 to 15.8 per cent and from 42.4 to 35.2 per cent, respectively. It is interesting to note that the older the age group, the more pronounced was the downward change of incidence rate. Table 3 shows that incidence rates declined by 1.5 percentage points among the 5- to 9-year-olds versus 2.2 and 7.2 percentage points among those aged 10-14 and 15-17 years, respectively.

The terms "children's work", "working children", "children at work", and "economically active children" are used interchangeably in this publication. All denote a broader concept than child labour. It comprises all persons of either sex who furnish the supply of labour for the production of goods and services defined by the System of National Accounts during a specified reference period.

The notion of working children is based on the concept of economic activity, and encompasses most activities undertaken by children involving production of goods and services, whether

- for the market or not;
- paid or unpaid;
- part time or full time;
- performed on a casual or a regular basis;
- in the formal or informal sector;
- the activities are legal or illegal.

It excludes

- chores undertaken in the child's own household;
- activities that are part of schooling; and
- children seeking work for which they are available if it is offered.

(b) Children's Work by Sex

As was the case in 2000, the 2004 data do not reveal any major difference by sex in terms of overall magnitude of children's work and its relative incidence. Boys, especially in the older age groups, tend to be slightly more involved in work than are girls. The differentials, however, remain minor. Overall, in 2004, 172 million boys were working compared to 146 million girls. The incidence rate was about two percentage points higher among boys (21.3 per cent versus 19.1 per cent for girls).

The number of working children decreased among both sexes from 2000 to 2004. It is noteworthy that economic activity rates seem to have declined somewhat faster among girls than among boys. As Table 3 shows, the incidence rate among girls dropped by 3.4 percentage points compared to 2.1 percentage points among boys.

(c) Children's Work by Region

The regional activity rates and the extent of children's work by region, respectively. Both concentrate on the 5- to 14-year age group. We note that, while the Asia-Pacific region has the most child workers, the incidence is highest in Sub-Saharan Africa.

In 2004, an estimated 122.3 million children were at work in the Asia-Pacific region, compared to 49.3 million in Sub-Saharan Africa and 5.7 million in Latin America and the Caribbean. Reliable survey data were too limited to provide numbers for either the Middle East and North Africa (MENA) region or for the group of industrialized countries.

In terms of incidence, Sub-Saharan Africa ranks highest. About 1 in 4 children younger than 15 years works in the region (26.4 per cent). This compares to about 1 in 5 in the Asia-Pacific region (18.8 per cent) and 1 in 20 in Latin America and the Caribbean.

Table 4 reveal regional trends from 2000 to 2004. In Asia and the Pacific, the situation among working children has remained more or less stable, both in absolute and in relative terms. The incidence decreased slightly from 19.4 to 18.8 per cent. The absolute number of child workers dropped by 5 million to a total of 122 million. In Sub-Saharan Africa, we discern a more mixed development. While the incidence rate declined by 2.4 percentage points to 26.4 per cent, the absolute number of African child workers increased by 1.3 million to a total of 49.3 million. High population growth offset the relative progress in the region.

TABLE 3

Regional Trends in the Number of Working Children 5-14 Years Old (2000-2004)

	Population ('000)		*Number at Work ('000)*		*incidence rate*		*Change of Incidence rate*
	2000	*2004*	*2000*	*2004*	*2000*	*2004*	
World	1'199'400	1'206'600	211'000	190'700	17.6%	15.8%	-1.8%
Asia and the Pacific	655'100	650'000	127'300	122'300	19.4%	18.8%	-0.6%
Latin America and Caribbean	108'100	111'000	17'400	5'700	16.1%	5.1%	-11.0%
Sub-Saharan Africa	166'800	186'800	48'000	49'300	28.8%	26.4%	-2.4%
Other regions	269'300	258'800	18'300	13'400	6.8%	5.2%	-1.6%

Latin America, the region with the smallest population of working children, made the biggest progress in the four years following 2000. The incidence was reduced by 11 percentage points to 5.1 per cent, and the absolute number of working children aged 5-14 years dropped to 5.7 million.

CURRENT GLOBAL TRENDS IN CHILD LABOUR

(a) Child Labour by Age Group

We estimate that in 2004 there were about 218 million child labourers in the world. Three quarters of them (166 million) were younger than 15 years. As Table 5 shows, child labour is by no means only a problem among older children. In fact, 108 million—almost half of all child labourers in the world—were younger than 12 years.

Child labour declined during the period 2000 to 2004, reflecting trends in children's economic activity. The overall number decreased by 28 million from

246 to 218 million. The drop was most pronounced in the lower secondary-education, 12- to 14-year age cohort, leaving 18 million fewer child labourers.

TABLE 4

Global Number of Child Labourers by Major Age Group, 2000 and 2004

Major age group	*Child labour (in '000s), 2000*	*Child labour (in '000s), 2004*
5-11	109'700	107'647
12-14	76'600	58'105
Total 5-14	186'300	165'752
Total 15-17	59'200	51'911
Total 5-17	245'500	217'663

The worldwide incidence of child labour6 also dropped over the four-year period under observation from a rate of 16 per cent to 13.9 per cent.

(b) Child Labour by Sex

Data emerging over the last few years have shown that gender differentials with regard to the work children do increase both with age and with the dangers children face in the workplace. Generally, boys are more involved than are girls in child labour and hazardous work. Boys dominate in the older age groups.

Our estimates for 2004 corroborate these earlier findings. As Table 6 shows, child labour distribution by sex among those aged 5-11 years is almost on par. The gap widens, however, among those aged 12-14 years—about 55 per cent of child labourers in this category are boys.

The difference becomes most pronounced among youth aged 15-17 years. Here, boys clearly dominate and girls constitute only a little more than one third of child labourers (38 per cent).

Note that the distribution by sex remained largely unchanged in the period 2000 to 2004.

TABLE 5

Child Labour and Its Sex Distribution, 2004

Sex & age group	*Number of child labourers (in '000s)*	*Distribution by sex (%)*
5-11	107'647	100.0
Boys	53'103	49.3
Girls	54'544	50.7
12-14	58'105	100.0
Boys	31'848	54.8
Girls	26'257	45.2
Total 5-14	165'752	100.0

Boys	84'951	51.3
Girls	80'801	48.7
Total 15-17	51'911	100.0
Boys	32'250	62.1
Girls	19'661	37.9
Total 5-17	217'663	100.0
Boys	117'201	53.8
Girls	100'462	46.2

TABLE 6

Calculation of Change of the Incidence of Working Children by Sex and Age Group for 16 Sample Countries (2000-2004)

Country	*Sex*	*Age group*	*to*	*r(ijk)o*	*t1 r(ijk)*	*1 r(ijk)*	*1-r(ijk)*	*o .(ijk)*
Cameroun	1	5-9 yrs	1996	0.15	2001	0.00	-15%	-12%
Cameroun	1	10-14 yrs	1996	0.31	2001	0.11	-21%	-17%
Cameroun	1	15-17 yrs	1996	0.49	2001	0.24	-25%	-20%
Cameroun	2	5-9 yrs	1996	0.19	2001	0.00	-19%	-15%
Cameroun	2	10-14 yrs	1996	0.33	2001	0.11	-23%	-18%
Cameroun	2	15-17 yrs	1996	0.49	2001	0.22	-27%	-21%
Ghana	1	5-9 yrs	1997	0.13	2001	0.19	6%	6%
Ghana	1	10-14 yrs	1997	0.18	2001	0.38	20%	20%
Ghana	1	15-17 yrs	1997	0.32	2001	0.52	20%	20%
Ghana	2	5-9 yrs	1997	0.13	2001	0.16	3%	3%
Ghana	2	10-14 yrs	1997	0.21	2001	0.37	16%	16%
Ghana	2	15-17 yrs	1997	0.43	2001	0.48	5%	5%
Kenya	1	5-9 yrs	1999	0.14	2000	0.23	9%	37%
Kenya	1	10-14 yrs	1999	0.52	2000	0.46	-6%	-24%
Kenya	1	15-17 yrs	1999	0.65	2000	0.65	0%	-1%
Kenya	2	5-9 yrs	1999	0.13	2000	0.20	6%	24%
Kenya	2	10-14 yrs	1999	0.47	2000	0.42	-6%	-24%
Kenya	2	15-17 yrs	1999	0.60	2000	0.59	-1%	-5%
Sénégal	1	5-9 yrs	1995	0.53	2000	0.32	-21%	-17%
Sénégal	1	10-14 yrs	1995	0.56	2000	0.47	-8%	-6%
Sénégal	1	15-17 yrs	1995	0.58	2000	0.60	2%	2%
Sénégal	2	5-9 yrs	1995	0.36	2000	0.23	-13%	-10%
Sénégal	2	10-14 yrs	1995	0.41	2000	0.29	-11%	-9%
Sénégal	2	15-17 yrs	1995	0.46	2000	0.35	-11%	-9%
Bangladesh	1	5-9 yrs	1999	0.08	2002	0,02	-6%	-8%
Bangladesh	1	10-14 yrs	1999	0.33	2002	0.36	3%	4%

Country	Sex	Age group	to	r(ijk)o	t1 r(ijk)	1 r(ijk)	1-r(ijk)	o .(ijk)
Bangladesh	1	15-17 yrs	1999	0.52	2002	0.47	-5%	-6%
Bangladesh	2	5-9 yrs	1999	0.03	2002	0.01	-2%	-3%
Bangladesh	2	10-14 yrs	1999	0.27	2002	0.15	-12%	-16%
Bangladesh	2	15-17 yrs	1999	0.43	2002	0.22	-21%	-28%
Cambodia	1	5-9 yrs	1996	0.24	2002	0.26	2%	2%
Cambodia	1	10-14 yrs	1996	0.28	2002	0.65	37%	25%
Cambodia	1	15-17 yrs	1996	0.49	2002	0.83	34%	22%
Cambodia	2	5-9 yrs	1996	0.27	2002	0.25	-1%	-1%
Cambodia	2	10-14 yrs	1996	0.29	2002	0.64	35%	23%
Cambodia	2	15-17 yrs	1996	0.83	2002	0.84	1%	1%
India	1	5-9 yrs	1992	0.09	1999	5 0.01	-9%	-5%
India	1	10-14 yrs	1992	0.19	1999	.5 0.08	-11%	-6%
India	1	15-17 yrs	1992	0.43	1999	5 0.35	-8%	-4%
India	2	5-9 yrs	1992	0.15	1999	.5 0.01	-15%	-8%
India	2	10-14 yrs	1992	0.43	1999	.5 0.08	-35%	-19%
India	2	15-17 yrs	1992	0.76	1999.	5 0.22	-54%	-29%
Philippines	1	5-9 yrs	1998	0.12	2002	0.03	-9%	-9%
Philippines	1	10-14 yrs	1998	0.25	2002	0.23	-2%	-2%
Philippines	1	15-17 yrs	1998	0.37	2002	0.46	9%	9%
Philippines	2	5-9 yrs	1998	0.11	2002	0.02	-9%	-9%
Philippines	2	10-14 yrs	1998	0.17	2002	0.14	-3%	-3%
Philippines	2	15-17 yrs	1998	0.26	2002	0.28	2%	2%
Turkey	1	5-9 yrs	1994	0.03	1999	0.01	-2%	-2%
Turkey	1	10-14 yrs	1994	0.15	1999	0.08	-7%	-6%
Turkey	1	15-17 yrs	1994	0.53	1999	0.35	-18%	-15%
Turkey	2	5-9 yrs	1994	0.02	1999	0.01	-1%	-0%
Turkey	2	10-14 yrs	1994	0.11	1999	0.06	-6%	-4%
Turkey	2	15-17 yrs	1994	0.27	1999	0.21	-7%	-5%
Bolivia	1	5-9 yrs	1999	0.67	2000	0.17	-50%	-199%
Bolivia	1	10-14 yrs	1999	0.77	2000	0.35	-42%	-166%
Bolivia	1	15-17 yrs	1999	0.64	2000	0.49	-14%	-57%
Bolivia	2	5-9 yrs	1999	0.64	2000	0.16	-49%	-195%
Bolivia	2	10-14 yrs	1999	0.98	2000	0.29	-69%	-276%
Bolivia	2	15-17 yrs	1999	0.66	2000	0.40	-27%	-107%
Brazil	1	5-9 yrs	1998	0.11	2003	0.02	-9%	-7%
Brazil	1	10-14 yrs	1998	0.47	2003	0.14	-33%	-26%
Brazil	1	15-17 yrs	1998	0.81	2003	0.38	-42%	-34%
Brazil	2	5-9 yrs	1998	0.06	2003	0.01	-5%	-4%
Brazil	2	10-14 yrs	1998	0.27	2003	0.07	-20%	-16%

Country	Sex	Age group	to	r(ijk)o	t1 r(ijk)	1 r(ijk)	1-r(ijk)	o .(ijk)
Brazil	2	15-17 yrs	1998	0.48	2003	0.22	-26%	-21%
Colombia	1	5-9 yrs	1998	0.11	2001	0.07	-5%	-6%
Colombia	1	10-14 yrs	1998	0.16	2001	0.22	6%	8%
Colombia	1	15-17 yrs	1998	0.36	2001	0.40	5%	6%
Colombia	2	5-9 yrs	1998	0.02	2001	0.03	1%	2%
Colombia	2	10-14 yrs	1998	0.06	2001	0.10	4%	6%
Colombia	2	15-17 yrs	1998	0.24	2001	0.18	-5%	-7%
Costa Rica	1	5-9 yrs	1998	0.12	2002	0.01	-11%	-11%
Costa Rica	1	10-14 yrs	1998	0.19	2002	0.09	-10%	-10%
Costa Rica	1	15-17 yrs	1998	0.47	2002	0.40	-7%	-7%
Costa Rica	2	5-9 yrs	1998	0.03	2002	0.00	-2%	-2%
Costa Rica	2	10-14 yrs	1998	0.05	2002	0.03	-3%	-3%
Costa Rica	2	15-17 yrs	1998	0.25	2002	0.18	-7%	-7%
El Salvador	1	5-9 yrs	1999	0.30	2001	0.02	-27%	-54%
El Salvador	1	10-14 yrs	1999	0.34	2001	0.18	-16%	-32%
El Salvador	1	15-17 yrs	1999	0.56	2001	0.39	-17%	-35%
El Salvador	2	5-9 yrs	1999	0.08	2001	0.01	-7%	-14%
El Salvador	2	10-14 yrs	1999	0.17	2001	0.08	-9%	-18%
El Salvador	2	15-17 yrs	1999	0.25	2001	0.17	-8%	-17%
Yemen	1	5-9 yrs	1999	0.06	2001	0.16	10%	21%
Yemen	1	10-14 yrs	1999	0.24	2001	0.39	15%	30%
Yemen	1	15-17 yrs	1999	0.55	2001	0.58	3%	6%
Yemen	2	5-9 yrs	1999	0.09	2001	0.11	2%	4%
Yemen	2	10-14 yrs	1999	0.25	2001	0.31	6%	12%
Yemen	2	15-17 yrs	1999	0.29	2001	0.46	18%	35%
Azerbaijan	1	5-9 yrs	1995	0.00	2000	0.07	7%	5%
Azerbaijan	1	10-14 yrs	1995	0.00	2000	0.14	14%	12%
Azerbaijan	1	15-17 yrs	1995	0.22	2000	0.21	-1%	-1%
Azerbaijan	2	5-9 yrs	1995	0.00	2000	0.04	4%	3%
Azerbaijan	2	10-14 yrs	1995	0.00	2000	0.08	8%	7%
Azerbaijan	2	15-17 yrs	1995	0.25	2000	0.11	-13%	-11%

CURRENT GLOBAL TRENDS IN HAZARDOUS WORK BY CHILDREN

(a) Hazardous Work by Age Group

The majority of working children are in hazardous work. This means they are engaged in activities that endanger their safety, health, and moral development. We estimate that in 2004 126 million children were involved in this worst form of child labour. That from 2000 to 2004 the number of children in hazardous work declined by about 44 million, a significant decrease most apparent among children in the 5- to 14-year age group.

(b) Hazardous Work by Sex

As detailed in Section 2.2.2, above, boys tend to be involved in more dangerous jobs than are girls, especially at older ages. The older the age group, the more boys dominate in the child workforce. In the group aged 5-11 years, male and female participation is almost equivalent, but it declines significantly with increasing age. Among those aged 12-14 and 15-17 years, boys constitute more than 60 per cent of children in hazardous work.

CHILD LABOUR AND HAZARDOUS WORK: MAJOR ESTIMATION METHODOLOGIES

Many factors must be considered in statistically measuring child labour and children in hazardous work. Precise criteria must be specified and used consistently as definitions of indicators, ensuring that processes are defined in a cohesive and consistent manner.

Our statistical approach to child labour and children in hazardous work is guided by ILO Conventions Nos. 138 and 182. In 2002, within the same international legal framework, the ILO estimated the number of children in child labour and hazardous work based on national household surveys conducted in the late 1990s, either (i) specifically designed to measure child labour under the SIMPOC programme, or (ii) designed for broader purposes but containing special modules dealing with the employment of children.

The goal of the new child labour estimates is to (i) present a dynamic picture and (ii) depict child labour trends from 2000 to 2004. Estimates of change are based on matched and nonmatched sample parts. The extent of child labour and children in hazardous work is estimated strictly following the 2002 methodology (ILO/IPEC, 2002). The data sources and methodology underlying the estimation are presented in the next sub-section, and are followed by an evaluation of the results.

(a) Data Sources and Methodology

Estimates on child labour and children in hazardous work are based on 19 national household surveys conducted between 2000 and 2004. The data come from three sources:

- 16 surveys specifically designed to measure child labour and conducted under the SIMPOC programme in Bangladesh (2003), Belize (2001), Brazil (2001), Cambodia (2002), Colombia (2001), Costa Rica (2002), El Salvador (2001), Ghana (2000), Guatemala (2000), Honduras (2002),

Jamaica (2002), Malawi (2002), Panama (2000), the Philippines (2001), Portugal (2001), and Tanzania (2001);

- 2 surveys conducted as part of the World Bank programme of Living Standards Measurement Surveys (LSMS) in Cameroon (2001) and Venezuela (2000); and
- 1 survey conducted independently as part of the national statistical programme in India (NSSO, 2000).

Annex 4 provides a full listing of all surveys used.

The latter three surveys are a mixture of broad-based household and community surveys with modules on different social concerns including children's activities.

The key variables for which raw data were required for the purposes of the global estimates are the following:

- age groups (5-11, 12-14, and 15-17 years);
- sex;
- industry at most detailed classifications of ISIC Rev. 3 (UN, 1990);
- occupation at most detailed classifications of ISCO-88; and
- hours worked.

Global incidence of child labour. On the one hand, assuming a minimum age of 12 years for light work and a minimum age of 15 years for admission into employment or work, the global incidence of child labour includes

- children aged 5-11 years engaged in any economic activity;
- all working children aged 12-14 years except those in light work; and
- children aged 15-17 years in the worst forms of child labour (WFCL), including hazardous work.

Hazardous work, on the other hand, includes work performed for 43 hours or more per week as well as work in construction, mining and quarrying, and selected occupations considered hazardous in many countries25. Estimates for the number of children in hazardous work, therefore, include

- the number of economically active children in hazardous industries;
- those within non-hazardous industries but engaged in hazardous occupations; and
- those neither in hazardous industries nor in hazardous occupations, but who are working 43 hours or more per week.

These estimates thus require both detailed data at the industry and occupation levels, and judgements as to whether such work may, indeed, be classified as hazardous.

Most relevant data. The smallest or most detailed units or sub-units of the international standard classifications (ISIC) of economic activities and occupations are, respectively, the 4-digit level of ISIC Rev. 3 (United Nations 1990) and the 3- or 4-digit level of ISCO (International Standard Industrial Classification of Occupations) ISCO-88. Data sufficiently detailed for the 4-digit level of the ISIC and the 3- or 4- digit level of ISCO is rarely available, however. Thus, data of countries with the most detailed classifications (3-digit level, in our case) were considered a priority for constructing absolute numbers and rations in the first three rounds of estimation on child labour and hazardous work by children at the global level.

In this respect, out of all data sources, SIMPOC data collected explicitly for the purpose of making child labour estimates is the most relevant.

First-round estimates. Among countries for which required data at the 3-digit level classification of occupations is available within each digit level of ISIC, identification of hazardous and non-hazardous occupations is based on the stipulations of ILO Convention No. 182, Recommendation No. 190, and a compilation of occupations and working environments hazardous to child workers. The "non-hazardous" occupations at the 3-digit level were analyzed further by age group and hours worked. From this data, ratios of the number of child labourers and of the number of children in hazardous work were calculated by age group and sex. These constitute the first-round estimates, based on 10 SIMPOC surveys conducted in Bangladesh, Belize, Cambodia, Colombia, Costa Rica, El Salvador, Honduras, Malawi, the Philippines, and Portugal.

Second-round estimates. Among countries for which occupational data is available only at the 1-digit level, the ratios from the first-round estimates applied to the 1-digit occupation, by age group and sex, gives the number of children in hazardous work. These constitute the second-round estimates, based on 5 SIMPOC surveys, 2 LSMS, and 2 labour force surveys in Brazil, Cameroun, Ghana, Guatemala, India, Jamaica, Panama, Tanzania, and Venezuela.

Third-round estimates. During the third-round estimates, the totals produced for all occupations at the 1 digit level and for all countries are merged together into absolute numbers and single ratios of child labour and children in hazardous work are calculated. The final global estimates on child labour and hazardous child labour were extrapolated by applying these ratios to the global estimates of economically active children. Below is the estimation process for constructing global estimates of child labour and children in hazardous work.

(b) Evaluation

A significant limitation of the "child labour" and "children in hazardous work" estimates is the lack of adequate individual country-level raw data, which too often fails to include the required information. In this respect, the SIMPOC surveys—household-based national sample surveys whose target respondents are parents or guardians and children living in the same household—may be those most comprehensive in terms of serving the raw data needs and their relatively large sample sizes.

SIMPOC surveys.—The surveys are conducted as stand-alone surveys or as modules attached to other national household-based surveys such as labour force surveys. The statistics and information generated by these surveys address the following:

- both economic and non-economic activities of children;
- demographic and social characteristics of household numbers;
- working hours;
- nature of tasks;
- health and safety issues, including injuries at work;
- and perceptions of parents about children's work.

By making the sampling error of estimates less significant (ILO/IPEC, 2002), moreover, the typical SIMPOC survey "over-sampling" has positive effects for the global estimates.

For the purpose of the new global estimates, only 10 SIMPOC surveys were used to compute the relevant ratios in the first round: Bangladesh,26 Belize, Cambodia, Colombia, Costa Rica, El Salvador, Honduras, Malawi, the Philippines, and Portugal. The ratios obtained in the firstround estimates were applied to another relatively small number of surveys in the second round for calculating the final ratios in 9 countries: Brazil, Cameroon, Ghana, Guatemala, India, Jamaica, Panama, Tanzania, and Venezuela. Here, for analysis on industries, all the surveys (SIMPOC, LSMS, LFS) had data available. In particular, datasets for Brazil and India fortunately contained much of the needed information.

The final ratios were used in extrapolating the global estimates from the globally adjusted figures on the economically active children. Of the 19 surveys used, 15 are thus derived from SIMPOC surveys, and there are no major differences between the sources in the relevant datasets. Another positive factor affecting the quality of the final statistical results is the fact that the 3-digit ISCO analysis indicated a certain similarity of pattern in the activities and occupations of children in the SIMPOC surveys.

The survey reference years of the 10 countries included in the first round of the estimates ranged between 2000 and 2004. Out of the 19 surveys used, 8 form a matched sample with the median time spread of 4 years.27 However, the ratios for the different categories discussed above were computed without making adjustments for the variation in the reference periods.

With both the 2000 and 2004 global estimates on children in hazardous work, it was sometimes difficult to decide whether given activities or occupations should be judged hazardous or non-hazardous. In fact, because of important differences between countries in terms of economic structures and legislation, there is no "master list" that can always and unambiguously determine which activities are "hazardous" and which are not. Moreover, since specifying the hazardous nature or circumstances of activities or occupations was not an ISIC or ISCO objective when classifications were established as international standards, neither provides, even at the most detailed level, a clear distinction between hazardous or nonhazardous work. In this context, caution should be applied in those cases where categories may not be distinguished in the classification or depend on country characteristics. In all borderline situations, conservative decisions were made (see also ILO/IPEC, 2002).

Based on those factors mentioned above, to what extent may one compare the earlier estimates with the new ones? The following has to be noted:

- First, there is a slight difference between the data sources of the two estimates, both in scope and in depth. Eight of the nineteen surveys form a matched sample with the median time spread of four years.
- Second, the same extrapolation methods were used.
- Third, the new results are an independent estimate based on sample-matched and unmatched, which we regarded as the only viable option in view of the data material at hand.

Since the two estimates are derived from two independent samples, we used the Mann- Whitney test, a nonparametric means of detecting differences between them. In this sense, the statistical test is formed by counting all the bivariate pairs from the two samples in which one sample value is smaller than the other. More precisely, it asks whether the estimate of the probability demonstrates that the variables for the first group (2000 global estimates) are larger than the variables of the second group (2004 global estimates).

Hypothesis testing allows us to derive conclusions about the estimated probability and the ideas we are investigating, i.e. comparing the new global estimates on child labour and children in hazardous work with the old ones. It reveals a change in the incidence of this phenomenon, and shows whether the increase or decrease is statistically significant.

We focused the test on the list of the countries selected for the first-round estimates. Based on the estimates on children in hazardous work, the results of the test are as follows:

TABLE 7

Groups	*Obs*	*Rank sum*	*Expected*
2000 global estimates (GE)*	6	54	51
2004 global estimates (GE)**	10	82	85
Combined	16	136	136

* Children in hazardous work as per cent of economically active children (EAC) in 2000. Cambodia, Kenya, the Philippines, South Africa, Sri Lanka, and Turkey are the countries selected for the firstround estimates in 2000 global estimates.

** Children in hazardous work as per cent of EAC in 2004. Bangladesh, Belize, Cambodia, Colombia, Costa Rica, El Salvador, Honduras, Malawi, the Philippines, and Portugal are the countries selected for the first-round estimates in 2004 global estimates.

Unadjusted variance	85
Adjustment for ties	0
Adjusted variance	85

In the context of our exercise, the null hypothesis is that

H_o: hazardous work (group==2000 GE)

= hazardous work (group==2004 GE)

$z = 0.325$

Prob > $|z| = 0.7449$

Thus, the null and alternative hypotheses are

$H_o: P(X < Y) = 0.5$ and

$H_1: P(X < Y) < 0.5$

The estimated probability is that

P {hazardous work (group==2000 GE) > hazardous work (group==2004 GE)} = 0.550.

Based on the test of statistical significance (0.5), the Mann-Whitney test yields two main conclusions:

- one cannot reject the hypothesis that the two samples have similar distribution; and
- the estimate of the probability shows that the variables of the 2000 global estimates are larger than the variables of the 2004 global estimates—they indicate that the trend in the incidence of children in hazardous work has been a decline.

In other words, these results confirm statistically a downward trend between the previous estimates on children in hazardous work and the new ones.

HAZARDOUS OCCUPATIONS AND PROCESSES IN NATIONAL LEGISLATION

The following *occupations or processes* have been documented to expose children to hazards to an extent that countries have prohibited the admission of children below 18 years (or a lower age, where indicated) to these occupations or processes by law:

Work in abattoirs and meat rendering
Work in the aluminium industry (16 years)
Work on airport runways
Work with dangerous or wild animals
Archaeological excavations
Brick manufacture
Cable laying
Care for mentally disturbed persons
Carpet weaving (14 years)
Catering at railway stations (14 years)
Cinder-picking, clearing ash-pits (14 years)
Work with circular saws and other dangerous cutting machines
Work in commercial agriculture (as opposed to subsistence agriculture)
Work in construction and/or demolition
Work with cranes/hoists/lifting machinery
Work in crystal and/or glass manufacture
Domestic service (16 years)
Work in entertainment establishments (night clubs, bars, casinos, circuses, gambling halls)
Excavation work
Work with fire brigades and gas rescue services
Forestry work
Work with machinery in motion (operation, cleaning, repairs, etc.)
Manufacture of matches (16 years)
Maritime work
Mining, work in quarries, underground work
Oil prospecting/work with petroleum

Work with oxyacetylene blowpipes (16 years)
Work with pedal/crank operated equipment (16 years)
Work in salt and brine processes
Shipbuilding (16 years)
Soap manufacture (14 years)
Work with steam engines or equipment
Street trades
Work in sugar mills (16 years)
Work in tanneries
Work in textile industries (specific tasks)
Operating vehicles
Underwater work
Work in the water and gas industry
Work with heavy weights and loads
Welding and smelting of metals, metal working
Work at courts, prisons or as probation officers

Countries may also prohibit the exposure of children at work to certain *hazardous agents and products* below 18 years of age (or a lower age, where indicated). The following agents or products have been subject to such legal prohibition in a number of countries:

Alcohol production and/or sale
Asbestos
Benzene
Bleaching and chlorine
Cadmium
Cement
Chemicals, general provisions for exposure to
Chromium
Compressed air/gas
Electricity
Explosives
Fumes, dust, gas and other noxious substances
Infra-red and ultraviolet rays, laser, radio-frequency emissions
Lead/zinc metallurgy, white lead, lead in paint
Manganese

Marble, stone and gypsum

Mercury

Paints, solvents, shellac varnish, glue, enamel

Pathogenic agents, exposure to (hospital work, city cleaning, work related to sewers, handling

corpses, etc.)

Potassium and sodium

Radioactive substances or ionizing radiation

Rubber

Tar, asphalt, bitumen

Tobacco (inc. bidi and cigarette making) (16 years)

Finally, the admission to work below 18 years of age may also be prohibited on the basis of *hazards relating to the physical environment* in which the work takes place. Hazards that have given rise to a legal prohibition include:

Thermal stress (heat and/or cold)

Vibration and noise

Inadequate ventilation

Lack of light or abnormal levels of light

Increased or decreased air pressure

Ergonomic hazards

Accident hazards

INDIA COUNTRY REPORT

(a) Child Labour : Issues, Findings and Recommendations

- Even the official data has admitted that the magnitude of child labour has increased from 11.59 million in 1991 to 12.66 million in 2001 (Census 2001). However unofficial sources claim between 25 to 30 million child workers, as significant number of child workers in domestic and agriculture sector are not covered in the census.
- Sixty-five million children aged 6-14 years were not attending any educational institutions in India. (Census 2001, released in 2005) which were much higher than the education department estimates of 25 million children (MHRD-2002 data).
- The prosecution and conviction rates in contravention of Child Labour Act-1986 were few pointing out poor implementation of the act, due to administrative lapses and lacunae in the Act.
- The National Child Labour Project (NCLP) and the INDUS-USDOL project for supporting released child labourers from work has very little

synergy and co-ordination at the grassroots level with other welfare and poverty alleviation programmes. In the absence of such synergy, the enrolled children in the special schools do not complete full cycle of elementary education. Thus providing schooling without integrating other poverty alleviation programmes for the extreme poor families have not been successful. Moreover, the scale of coverage of both the NCLP and the INDUS-USDOL project and the magnitude of child Labour are mismatch and needs substantial scaling up.

- The quality of education and vocational training provided in majority of the NCLP special schools is below standard, due to limited monitoring either from labour department or from education department. The education component should be monitored by the education department for improving quality of education.
- On an average 20-25 percent aged 7-10 years were not attending schools and a large proportion of children aged 10-14 years drop-out of schools. The results strengthen the observation that due to awareness children get enrolled in the schools at ages 7-10 years, but eventually they drop out of schools either due to poor education quality or due to pressure from parents to work and sustain family livelihood. The empirical field survey results also depicit high drop out rates in the ages between 10-14 years.

(b) Poverty Labour force and unemployment Issues

- According to the Planning Commission 260 million people (26% of population) still live below the poverty line in India. Eighty three percent of these poor people are concentrated in Uttar Pradesh, Bihar, Madhya Pradesh, West Bengal, Orissa, Andhra Pradesh, Rajasthan and Assam. Significantly 84 percent of Out-of-school children (6-11 years) and 72 percent of child workers aged 5-14 years are also concentrated in these eight states. A close association (positive Correlation of 0.7325 and 0.4563) was found between Poverty incidence with percent out-of-school children and Percent child workers respectively among the states of India.
- The average monthly per capita consumer expenditure (MPCE) is not only very low US$13 in rural areas and US$ 24 in urban areas, but in-equity also exists in the MPCE, as the bottom 20% population have less than US$ 9 and US$12, MPCE in rural and urban areas respectively.
- Labour force participation declined for both males and females during 1983 to 1999-2000 and hence employment rates have declined for both gender groups across rural and urban areas but the decline was more for women in rural areas. Given the increase in the labour force, and a decline in the growth of employment in the nineties the incidence of unemployment has increased significantly.

(c) Child Labour-Human Deprivation Linkages

- The study suggests that combination of factors work together for prevalence of child labour. The factors identified through the multivariate analysis were education deprivation of the child and parents, food deficit at home, unemployment status of any family member for more than 6 months and families with no or less land. These variables explained 87% presence of child labour through the multivariate analysis. Therefore the elimination of child labour requires multi pronged strategy of making schools accessible, providing quality education in schools, attacking food deficit scenario at home through poverty alleviation programmes and providing employment to adults. The strict compliance and enforcement of child labour laws and other labour laws will automatically encourage adult employment along with provision of minimum stipulated wages.
- The empirical study reflected households with "Always food deficit at home" (proxy indicator for poverty) also recorded high proportion of child workers, out of school children and dropout rates from schools as compared to the households having "Break-Even or Surplus food at homes."
- The response of the parents for sending children to work and "problems faced by parent if child stops work" again reinforces the poverty as one of the major cause for sending children to work. About 70% and 50% parental responses indicate that children are pushed to work in order to maintain income levels for sustenance and survival of the families, in the absence of appropriate wages for adults and seasonality of work respectively. This supports the assertion that poverty is the key reason for perpetuation of child labour. However on the other hand child labour is the primary cause of poverty, as it pushes children early to premature work thereby denying children the opportunity to acquire the education and skills they need to obtain decent work and incomes as adults. The links are mostly straightforward and tend to run both ways. Poverty and lack of education provision constitute the principal common grounds. Even the latest ILO study reveals that children only earn 20 percent income of an adult earning, while cost-benefit analysis for educating a child works out seven times returns.

(d) Recommendations

(i) ***For International Community.***

- MDGs and child labour are intimately linked. The links are mostly straightforward and tend to run both ways. Poverty and lack of education provision constitute the principal common grounds. Indeed, it is poverty associated with social injustice and social exclusion that is not closely related to child labour. The absence of child labour from the MDG framework is a regrettable omission that needs to be corrected with a sense of urgency if the intent is to achieve the MDGs.

- Achieving the MDG and Dakar goals for poverty alleviation and universalization of primary and elementary education within the target time, would require scaling up of public investments, capacity building, domestic resource mobilization, and official development assistance. In view of the need for resource mobilization, high-income countries should increase official development assistance (ODA) to support the Millennium Development Goals, particularly in low-income countries, with improved ODA quality (including aid that is harmonized, predictable, and largely in the form of grants-based budget support). Each donor should reach 0.7 percent no later than 2015 to support the Goals and other development assistance priorities.
- International donors should identify more MGD "fast-track" countries for a rapid scale-up of official development assistance (ODA) in view of recognizing that many countries including India are already in a position for a massive scale-up on the basis of their good governance and absorptive capacity.
- Organizations that fund development projects in India, including the World Bank, should routinely include in all contracts a clause, enforceable by canceling the project, requiring compliance with international labour standards or domestic labour laws, whichever are higher. The World Bank should conduct a comprehensive review of all of its projects in India to determine whether child labour is in any way involved, directly or indirectly, and make the results public.
- Bodies such as the International Programme on the Elimination of Child Labour (IPEC), U.S. Department of Labour, the U.S. Agency for International Development (USAID), U.N. agencies, and others that fund projects aimed at reducing child labour should insist that local Governments in the areas where their projects operate enforce the child and bonded labour laws, and should contribute resources for capacity building, and technical assistance to local Governments to adequately enforce those laws.

(ii) ***For Government of India.***

- Incorporate multi-pronged approach by crafting effective synergy and coordination process between central and state Governments departments towards child labour elimination efforts. The central and State Governments should internalize the linking up processes of poverty alleviation, health support and elementary education in a unified manner to eliminate child labour supply and demand aspects effectively.
- Develop District Poverty Initiative Programmes (DPIP) for all backward districts having integrated component of livelihood strategies, focusing

most vulnerable rural communities, especially child labour and their families. The DPIP should be a community participatory project in line with the existing DPIP projects in Andhra Pradesh state.

- The SSA would require scaling up of public investments/budgets through domestic resource mobilization and official development assistance for improving school infrastructure, quality of teaching and school environments, to ensure full implementation of newly incorporated Article 21-A of the constitution, providing free and compulsory quality education to all children below 14 years.
- Review of the SSA and incorporate more budgetary allocations, in view of the 65 million out-of-school children aged 6-14 years as estimated by the Census-2001. The central Government should ensure the sustainability of SSA after the 10th Plan in view of the stipulated mandatory 50% contributions required from the state Government.
- The Government of India should take all possible steps to enforce the child labour and bonded labour laws. The child labour Act-1986 requires amendments to incorporate the requirements that all employers should have the onus to prove that any worker employed is above 14 years of age and the failure to have adequate proof should constitute a separate violation of the Act.
- Ratify ILO Convention No. 138 concerning the Minimum Age for Admission to Employment, ILO Convention No. 182 concerning the Prohibition and Immediate Action for the Elimination of the Worst Forms of Child Labour.

(e) The Magnitude and Estimate of Working Children in India

The statistics on the magnitude of working children is vastly inadequate in India. The Information on children working in informal sectors, or attending school,, who might also be working is difficult to procure. The collection of reliable data regarding child labour is limited also by the fact that, officially the work undertaken by children in domestic and informal sectors are excluded from the worker's category, as it is difficult to assess the productive value of such labour. Thus official child labour figures are always at such variance with statistics quoted by non-Governmental agencies.

The 1983 Operations Research Group of Baroda estimated the number of child workers at 44.5 million. The Planning Commission put the figure at around 20 million by the end of the year 2000. According to the National Sample Survey of 1987-88, the number of child workers was approximately 17.0 million (8.2 million males and 6.9 million females in rural areas : 1.2 million males and 0.8 million females in Urban areas)., Unofficial studies have put the number of child workers in India at around 100 million. Perhaps they have included all children out of schools as child workers.

The magnitude of child labour estimated by Government agencies like the Census of India and the National Sample Survey Organization (NSS) are presented for analysis purposes. The Census of India reported 5.37 per cent child labour numbering 11.28 million child workers (aged 5-14 years) in 1991. The estimates of NSS report (round 50th, 1993-94) also confirmed that 5.78 per cent of children (aged 5-14 years) were both principal and subsidiary status workers and 4.71 per cent were principal status workers.

The State of Andhra Pradesh (9.98 per cent) had the highest incidence of child labour followed by Mizoram (9.40 per cent), Karnataka (8.81 per cent), Madhya Pradesh (.08 per cent), Meghalaya (7.39 per cent) and Rajasthan 6.46 per cent). On the other hand, the states of Kerala (0.58 per cent), Delhi (1.27 per cent), Haryana (2.55 per cent), and Punjab (3.04 per cent) recorded the lowest proportion of child labour.

However the NSS survey reported high incidence of child labour (Principal Status) for Andhra Pradesh Rajasthan and Tamil Nadu. Insignificant changes in the proportion of child labour were observed by the survey for the other states compared to 1991 Census results, Proportion of child labour both (principal and subsidiary status) was recorded high for Himachal Pradesh, Tamil Nadu and Andhra Pradesh contrary to the general belief, as these states registered a lower proportion of out-of-school children by the NSS survey 1995-96. On scrutiny it was found that nearly 85-90 per cent of the child workers recorded by the NSS survey in Himachal Pradesh were subsidiary status workers. Similarly a significant proportion of reported child workers were also of subsidiary status in Andhra Pradesh and Tamil Nadu. This explains that children were doing part-time work in horticulture and agriculture activities for some time of the year, but at the same time they were attending schools. Himachal Pradesh has made remarkable progress towards universal elementary education. In fact the Education Department in the state has adjusted school timings and the vacation period taking into consideration the agricultural and other economic activity calendar. Thus the concept of part time child work and education has been strengthened provided children have easy access to schools. This model could be replicated in other rural areas of the country and would go a long way to achieve higher enrolment rates in the schools. Lok Jumbish in Rajasthan, Project Mala in Varanasi and CINI ASHA in Kolkata city are successfully working towards this goal.

To examine whether any relationship existed between the proportion of out-of-school children and proportion of child labour, Co-efficient of correlation was worked out for 32 States and Union Territories of the country for 1991 and 2000. There is a significant positive correlation between the two variables both for 1991 and 2000. In case of the year 2000, the relationship was worked out between the percentage out-of-school children and percentage of child labour (principal status only). Co-efficient of correlation in 1991 was + 0.60492 and it was + 0.420901 in 2000. The correlations were significant at 5 per cent level of significance. However, insignificant correlation was found between percentage of out-of-school children and percentage of child workers (when both principal and subsidiary status of child workers was added together) for 2000. This could be explained due to the presence of a large number of subsidiary workers, who were attending schools simultaneously. This shows that a higher proportion of out-of-school children also had a higher proportion of main child labour workers. Thus enrolment of children in schools will go a long way in curtailing the main child labour population. While help sought from children in the agricultural activity for some period of time may not affect school enrolments. But school time and hours should be adjusted keeping in view the agricultural calendar of the area, so that children may help parents in the agricultural activities or other activities that are not harmful to the child's mental and physical development.

TABLE 8

India : Estimated child Workers 1991 and (31 July) 2000

State	Child Workers 5-14		%Child Workers			Potential	%
	1991	2000	1991	1993 NSS (P+S)	1993 NSS (P)	Child Workers 2000*	
Andhra Pradesh	1661,940	2,364,000	9.98	13.06	11.66	7,433,960	41.05
Arunachal Pradesh	12.395	4,000	5.65	1.43	1.21	76,000	26.38
Assam	327,598	194,398	5.46	2.77	1,98	1,948,898	27.76
Bihar	942,245	836,215	3.99	3.09	2.76	15,465,275	57.14
Gujarat	523,585	340,256	5.26	3.10	2.17	2,754,976	25.10
Haryana	109,691	127,397	2.55	2.53	1.50	940,397	18.52
Himachal Pradesh	56,438	210,825	4.55	13.03	3.00	324,085	20.02
Jammu & Kashmir		132,554		5.53	2.55	2,529,554	25.32
Karnataka	976,247	1,171,297	8.81	9.73	7.67	4,421,557	36.72
Kerala	34,800	42,203	0.58	.70	.052	223,073	3.70
Madhya Pradesh	1.352,563	1,177,918	8.08	5.86	4.46	8,213,268	40.85
Maharashtra	1,068,418	911,643	5.73	4.30	3.50	3,879,783	18.30
Manipur	16,493	2,675	3.72	0.44	0.25	154,675	25.43
Meghalaya	34,633	14,170	7.39	2.41	1.59	143,530	25.73
Nagaland	16,476	5,820	5.29	1.43	1.12	103,500	25.42
Orissa	452,394	559,599	5.87	6.51	4.89	3,654,159	42.50
Punjab	142,868	118,070	3.04	2.24	1.80	908,720	17.23
Rajasthan	774,199	1,564,101	6.46	10.96	8.56	7,129,791	49.95

State	Child Workers 5-14		%Child Workers			Potential	%
	1991	2000	1991	1993 NSS (P+S)	1993 NSS (P)	Child Workers 2000*	
Sikkim	5,598	850	5.18	0.63	0.55	19,750	14.62
Tamil Nadu	578,889	949,591	4.83	7.76	6.92	2,662,771	21.75
Tripura	16,478	14,806	2.29	1.62	1.62	179,326	19.61
Uttar Pradesh	1,410,086	1,920,887	3.81	4.45	3.15	17,892,307	41.45
West Bengal	711,691	885,950	4.16	4.63	3.31	6,626,450	34.62
Andaman Islands	1,265	5,663	1.82	6.09	1.20	11.242	12.08
Chandigarh	1,870	000	1.40	0.00	0.00	21.400	10.00
Dadra & Nagar	4,416	699	13.2	1.52	1.52	16,799	36.51
Delhi	27,351	24,244	1.27	0.83	.083	316,344	10.82
Daman & Diu	941	147	3.89	0.42	0.42	5,047	29.68
Goa	4,656	6,737	1.95	1.75	0.00	22,137	5.74
Lakshadweep	34	000	0.27	00	0.00	340	20.00
Mizoram	16,411	3,266	9.40	1.42	0.71	58,466	25.42
Pondichery	2,680	3,577	1.54	1.33	1.33	17,027	6.32
INDIA	11,285,349	13,994,073	5.37	5.78	4.51	86,644,700	35.78

Note : F: Principal Worker, S : Subsidiary Worker

1. Child Workers 1991 based on C-Series Census data (Both Main and Marginal Workers)
2. Child Workers for 2000 was worked out taking the following inputs.
   a. State-wise projected child remain same for 2000 as on 31 July.
3. NSS data Round 50th (1992-93) depicting percentage of workers Principal Status (PS) and Subsidiary Status (S) among the children aged 5-9 and 10-14 groups. The percentage of workers was also assumed to continue for 2000. However, this may be an overestimation for 2000.
4. Potential child workers are estimated taking child workers (PS+S) and children out-of-school together into account.

The magnitude of estimated child workers and out-of-school children together in India was 86.64 million children for 2000. The magnitude of these children was high for Uttar Pradesh (17.89 million) followed by Bihar (15.4 million), Madhya Pradesh (8.21 million), Andhra Pradesh (7.4 million) and Rajasthan (7.12 million). The least potential child labour was for Kerala (0.22 million), Himachal Pradesh (0.32 million), Punjab (0.90 million) and Haryana (0.94 million). Thus education programmes are required for these potential working children. This task may not be achievable without the support from NGOs and other social organizations.

The selected cities and their aggiomerations together estimated 542,567 child workers in 2000. The estimated child workers were high for Kolkata (124,113) followed by Hyderabad (90,494), Mumbai (84,758), and Chennai (82,373). The magnitude of child workers in these cities and their aggiomerations depict the size of street children (of the street category), as mostly these categories of children are workers in these cities. However, this belies the claims of most of the NGOs that the magnitude of 'of the street category' children is over 2 million in the country. The potential child labour (which includes child labour and out-of-school children together) is 2.75 million in these selected cities. The magnitude of streed children covering both categories on the street and of the street are nearly 3 million in the major cities of the country, which requires immediate attention especially for education, health care, health education, shelter and regular counselling. The task is difficult and support from government and international agencies is required. NGOs, social organizations and civil society have to come forward and contribute significantly in this direction.

TABLE NO. 9

Urban Agglomerations-Estimated and Potential Child Workers for (31 July) 2000

Name of City	Estimated Child workers	% child workers to Child Population*	Potential Child Workers	% Potential Child Workers
Ahmedabad	20,826	1.96	179,406	16.96
Bangalore	56,944	4.35	227,122	17.34
Bhubaneswar	4,073	2.80	25,895	17.29
Hyderabad	90,494	6.81	289,820	21.80
Mumbai	84,758	2.13	403,100	10.12
Chennai	82,373	5.15	242,322	15.14
Sivakasi	1,549	5.15	8,169	27.14
Varanasi	11,469	3.20	97,488	27.19
Kanpur	23,587	3.20	185,752	25.19
Firozabad	2,998	3.20	17,991	19.19
Mirzapur	12,773	9.00	62,448	43.99
Kolkata	124,113	3.75	689,759	20.84
Delhi	26,610	0.88	328,998	10.87

Note :1.—The input data for estimated Child Workers for the Cities

a.—Estimated Child Population for 2000 in these cities.

b. * The percentage of child workers (aged 5-14 years) is based on NSS data for the urban areas in the states, where the city is located. It was assumed that the same percentage of child workers (PS+S) in the urban areas for the states would be in the cities selected.

c. Potential Child Workers is Estimated Child Workers and Children Out-of-Schools.

REPORT AND STATISTICS

(*a*) **Magnitude**—There are varying estimates of working children magnitude in India due to differing concepts and methods of estimation. The Census of India-1991 recorded 11.20 million working children, while the Census-2001 has recorded 12.66 million working children in the ages of 5-14 years. Ninety percent of the children workers were from rural areas. The proportion of working children to the child population aged 5-14 years, registered a marginal decline from 5.4 per cent to 5 per vent during 1991-2001.

The increase in the magnitude of child labour during 1991-2001 was in spite of tremendous efforts by government United Nations and other international agencies and NGOs for universalizing primary and elementary education and removing children from work through education and other rehabilitative interventions the results depicts that only education interventions without intergrating poverty alleviation programmes in the policy may not yield desired results of reducing child labour.

Andhra Pradesh state witnessed synergy of efforts between government, ILO trade unions and NGOs during 1991-2001 in scaling up education initiatives for out-of-school children but the strategy was not effective enough as the children dropped out without completing the full cycle of elementary education and joined back in the workforce. The 2001 reported marginal decline in the magnitude of child labour during 1991-2001, but it still recorded the second highest magnitude of child workers after Uttar Pradesh. The field work conducted in Andhra Pradesh, Bihar and Madhya Pradesh strengthens the view as a significant proportion of children have dropped out from schools without completing full cycle of elementary education. Majority of the dropped out children were from extreme poverty families and preferred children to work for family sustenance. Thus, the policy makers and planners need to incorporate and integrate poverty alleviation and strengthening livelihood opportunities along with education initiatives to release children from work.

(*b*) **Regional Pattern**—The regional variation of child workers suggests that high magnitude is found in Uttar Pradesh, Andhra Pradesh, Rajasthan, Bihar and Madhya Pradesh in 2001. Among the larger states the proportion of working children in the age group of 5-14 years was high in Andhra Pradesh, Madhya Pradesh, Rajasthan and Karnataka.

(*c*) **Magnitude of Out-of-School Children**—All children not attending schools are potential child workers and they need to be addressed in a holistic framework.

According to the latest census figures of 2001 released in August 2005, out of 226 million children aged 6-14 years, 65.3 million children (29%) were not attending any educational institutes at the time of the survey. The proportion of out-of-school boys was 25% while it was 33% for girls. In spite of the official age of 6 years for enrolling children in class I, a significant proportion of children aged 6 years (60 percent) were not attending schools. On an average 20-25 percent aged 7-10 years were not attending schools and a large proportion of children aged 10-14 years drop out of schools. The results strengthen the observation that due to awareness children get enrolled in the schools at ages 7-10 years, but eventually they drop out of schools either due to poor education quality or due to pressure from parents to work and sustain family livelihoods. The field survey results also depicit high drop out rates in the ages between 10-14 years.

Magnitude of child workers (Census 2001) figures with the out-of-school children (Education Department Household Survey Data for SSA, 2002) figures depicts serious anomalies. In the case of Andhra Pradesh the Census data recorded 0.943 million main child workers aged 5-14 years, while the Education data recorded only 0.642 million out-of-school children for Andhra Pradesh. Similarly in the case of Andhra Pradesh, Rajasthan and Madhya Pradesh the Census data recorded 1.36 million, 1.26 million and 1.06 million child workers (main+marginal workers) aged 5-14 years respectively, while the Education data recorded only 0.642 million, 1.06 million and 0.742 million out of school children respectively for Andhra Pradesh Rajasthan and Madhya Pradesh. Therefore, out-of-school children estimated by the Education Department survey for SSA, seem to be grossly under estimated and it requires review and subsequently SSA budget estimates need revision.

(*d*) **Work Activities.**—Out of the 12.66 million working children in 2001, about 5.77 million children were classified as main workers and the rest 6.88 million children were as marginal workers. Most of the working children are engaged in agricultural activities as wage labourers or cultivators. Manufacturing processing, servicing and repairs in the household industries engaged 3% child workers, while 3% child workers were engaged in factory work and the other 15% working children were engaged in service sector, mostly as domestic workers, and in small trade activities. Working children are usually classified in terms of work situations in domestic work, non-domestic and non-monetary work, bonded labour work, wage work in hazardous and non-hazardous occupations and commercial sexual exploitation work. Each work situation has deep-rooted consequences on their human rights, healthcare and future economic production processes. Some of the hazardous processes and occupations, where child labourers are found in large numbers are :

(*e*) **Hazardous Occupations**—

* Agriculture hybrid cotton seed production
* Agricultural allied processes Bidi making, making thread from silk cocoon.

* Mining Mica and slate
* Manufacturing processes carpet weaving silk and other cotton weaving leather, electric bulb making, glass and bangle making, sports especially ball stitching gem and diamond cutting and polishing, lock making
* Construction-manual labour, brick making and chipping, stone breaking
* Service industries domestic services, transport and garages, hotels and restaurants, sexual abuse and exploitation

(*f*) **Case Study of Hybrid Cotton Seed Production in Andhra Pradesh**—Hybrid cottonseed production is characterized as highly labour-intensive mating method, and girl children are engaged in most of its operations. Children are employed on a long-term contract basis through advances and loans extended to their parents by local seed producers, who have agreements with the large national and multinational seed companies. Children are made to work long hours and are paid less than market and official minimum wates. They are also exposed to poisonous pesticides used in high quantities in cottonseed cultivation. The India Committee of the Netherlands study indicated that, the situation of child labour in the farms producing hybrid seed for multi national companies (MNCs) is not significantly different from other farms producing seed for local companies. Out of 174 farms surveyed, 44 farms produce seed for MNCs. A total of 272 children were employed in these farms during 2003-04 crop seasons. Children constitute 53.5% of total workforce. On an average 5.5 children were employed in one acre seed farm. Girls account for nearly 72% of the total child labour population."

CHILD LABOUR ELIMINATION : GOVERNMENT POLICY AND INITIATIVES

The Ministry of Labour at the centre and the corresponding ministry at the states are responsible for adopting constitutional statutory and development measures, that are required to eliminate child labour. Six ILO conventions related to child labour have been ratified. However, ratification of the ILO Convention No. 182 is still pending.

(*g*) **Child Labour Act, 1986**—It seeks to ban employment of children working in certain hazardous occupations; the hazardous occupations are identified and reviewed by the expert committee from time to time. The Act also regulates the work of children in certain other industries. However, there is no specific or all encompassing prohibition on the work for children,. There are sectors such as domestic service, agriculture, urban and rural informal sectors where children work in large numbers.

(*h*) **Bonded Labour System (Abolition Act 1976)**—The Bonded Labour System (Abolition) Act purports to abolish all debt agreements and obligations arising out of India's longstanding bonded labour system. It frees all bonded laboures, cancels any outstanding debts against them, prohibits the creation of new bondage agreements and orders the economic rehabilitation of freed bonded labourers by the State.

(*i*) **The Supreme Court directions in 1996**—It gave directions for immediate identification of children in hazardous occupations and their subsequent rehabilitation, including providing appropriate education to the released children.

(*j*)**The National Child Labour Policy**—The National Child Labour Policy-1987 addresses the complex issue of child through the legislative action plan by implementing Child labour Act, 1986 and project based action plan in areas of high concentration of child labour. Under the project-based action plan the released children from the hazardous occupations are provided educational services in specially designed Non-formal education centres under the centrally sponsored National Child Labour Project (NCLP). The NCLP. The NCLP is currently in operation in 100 districts in 13 states, in the areas of high concentration of child labour throughout the country. Till September, 2004-05, 4077 special NFE schools are in operation throughout the country, with a total enrolment of 203,850 children.

* Analysis of the implementation of Child Labour Act-1986 reveals that Act has several loopholes, because of which conviction rates are low. Only 1543 prosecutions have been registered, out of which only 278 were convicted and 181 cases were acquitted, while the other cases are still pending. The onus of proving the age of child for the administration is difficult. The law should put the onus of proving age of employee on the employer. Moreover the provision of child can work in family units also makes it difficult to prosecute the offender.
* The policy envisages general development programme for families, but very little co-ordination and synergy was evinced at the grassroots level to identify the parents of target groups and provide benefits of poverty alleviation scheme on priority basis.
* The vocational training provided to the enrolled children under the NCLP has not been very useful as no synergy and coordination was observed with the poverty alleviation programmes of the rural development ministry to provide employment avenues or marketing support to the parents of the children as envisaged in the NCLP.
* The scale of support provided through the NCLP and the magnitude of child labour are mismatch and needs substantial scaling up.

International Response—The UN agencies and other international bi-lateral and multi-lateral agencies support Government of India and a large number of NGOs in developing micro projects for releasing child labour from hazardous occupations and providing educational support to released children and develop capacity building and provide livelihood support to families through vocational training. ILO has taken significant initiatives under the IPEC programme by supporting as many as 175 major projects against child labour. Currently ILO is targeting 80,000 children at risk of hazardous employment in brick manufacturing stone quarring bidi manufacturing footwear manufacturing fireworks manufacturing, manufacturing of matches, silk manufacturing lock making brassware and glassware production through the INDUS project. The project also addresses the employment generation and skills development needs of 10,000 parents. It seeks to work with two major programmes of the Government of India; the NCLPs and the Sarva Shiksha Abhiyan (SSA).

(*k*) **The World Bank**—The World Bank has developed successful partnership with government of India to create the environment for broad based social and economic growth which is an essential element of the process of eliminating child labour. A Review of World Bank Lending for Children and its Bearing on Child Labour indicated that the World Bank and Asian Development Bank supported six major projects related to primary and elementary education in India, having a credit of US$ 1239 million. Major objective of the projects was improving physical access to schools, developing infrastructure, supporting quality and learning outcomes and supporting policy change and capacity building.

The World Bank also supported District Poverty Innovation Projects (DPIPs) in Rajasthan, Madhya Pradesh, Andhra Pradesh, Jharkhand and Tamil Nadu during the period 2000-2005. These projects have a special component on release and rehabilitation of hard to reach children and for creating employment opportunities for the parents of these hard to reach children.

(*l*) **Non-Government Organizations and Civil Society Response**—NGO movement in India has been very strong in creating pressure on government to address the social development issues and create awareness for child rights. The Bachpan Bachao Andolan (BBA) and its partner's organizations under the banner of South Asian Coalition on Child Servitude (SACCS) have been in the forefront for creating awareness towards child rights. The major activities of BBA and SACCS partners has been to release and withdraw children from the worst forms of labour particularly from bondage and forced labor, through direct action, secret raids, legal intervention, persuasion and pressure building while ensuring their social psychological economic and statutory rehabilitation through quality transitory rehabilitation measures and state efforts. Keeping in view the holistic vision for child rights and child development Bal Mitra Gram-BMG (Child Friendly Village strategy is extended in 75 villages as a demonstration for other replicable projects) intervention has been one of the successful project of BBA. Other NGOs like M.F. Foundation, Pratham, CREDA, Project Mala, CINI-ASHA and other regional NGOs have demonstrated project based approach. The main focus has been to provide educational support out-of-school children, through bridge course/camp schools/non formal schools and mainstream the children in formal schools.

TABLE 10

Child Labour Population, 1991-2001

State	Child Workers 1991	Child Workers 2001	% Workers 1991	% Workers 2001	Change 1991-2001
Andhra Pradesh	1,661,940	13,633,339	9.98	7.7	-2.28
Arunachal Pradesh	12.395	18,482	5.65	6.06	0.41
Assam	327,598	351416	5.46	5.07	-0.39
Bihar	942,245	111,7500	3.99	4.68	0.69
Chattisgarh		364572		6.96	6.96
Delhi	27351	41899	1.27	1.35	0.08
Goa	4656	4138	1.95	1.82	-0.13
Gujarat	523,585	4,85,530	5.26	4.28	-0.98
Haryana	109,691	253491	2.55	4.78	2.23
Himachal Pradesh	56,438	10,7774	4.55	8.14	3.59
Jammu & Kashmir		17,5630		6.62	6.62
Jharkhand		407200		5.47	5.47
Karnataka	976,247	822665	8.81	6.91	-1.90
Kerala	34,800	26156	0.58	0.47	-0.11
Madhya Pradesh	1.352,563	1065259	8.08	6.71	-1.37
Maharashstra	1,068,418	764075	5.73	3.54	-2.19
Orissa	452,394	377594	5.87	4.37	-1.50
Punjab	142,868	177268	3.04	3.23	0.19
Rajasthan	774,199	1262570	6.46	8.25	1.79
Sikkim	5598	16547	5.18	12.04	6.86
Tamil Nadu	578,889	418801	4.83	3.61	-1.22
Tripura	16,478	21756	2.29	2.79	0.50
Uttar Pradesh	1,410,086	1927997	3.81	4.04	0.23
Uttranchal		70183		324	3.24
West Bengal	711,691	857087	4.16	4.5	0.34
INDIA	**11285349**	**12666377**	**5.37**	**5**	**-0.37**

Source : Census of India Tables on Workers 2001

TABLE 11

Education Child Labour Elimination Projects Supported by the World Bank 1990-2005

Project	Loan/ Credit/ Grant	Amount US$ Million	Sector	Percent Amount stipulated 1	2	3
Second District Primary Education Project-1996	Credit	260	Education	35	43	22
Uttar Pradesh Second Education Basic Project-1997	Credit	59	Education	32	68	
Third District Primary Education Project-1997	Credit	152	Education	52	38	10
Rajasthan District Primary Education Project-1999	Credit	86	Education	20	45	35
Uttar Pradesh Third District Education Project-1999	Credit	182	Education	37	30	33
Elementary Education-2004	Credit	500	Elem.Education			
All Education Projects	1239					

Source : The World Bank Project Paper.

1 : Improving Physical Access 2 : Supporting learning outcomes 3 : Supporting Policy Change.

TABLE 12

Regression Coefficients and odd ratios

Variable	Regression Coefficient	Standard Error	Odd Ratios
Age			
5-9 years	0.00		1.00
10-12 years	0.67***	0.06	1.76
12-14 years	0.77***	0.04	2.16
Child Education			
No Schooling	0.00		1.00
1-5 years	-.25***	0.08	0.78
5+ years	0.62***	0.14	0.52
Mothers Education			
No Schooling	0.00		1.0
1-5 years	-0.28***	0.11	0.79
5 + years	-0.48***	0.17	0.64
Father Schooling			
No Schooling	0.00		1.0
1-5 years	-0.18*	0.09	0.86
5 + years	-0.58***	0.12	0.54
Food deficit			
Always deficit	0.00		1.0

Variable	Regression Coefficient	Standard Error	Odd Ratios
Somewhat Deficit	-0.18*	0.07	0.86
Sufficient	-0.43***	0.18	0.23
Adult Employed			
Last 3 months	0.00		1.0
3-6 months	0.36***	0.09	1.56
6+ months	0.77***	0.05	1.98
Land Ownership			
Landless	0.00		1.0
Up to 100	0.09	0.07	0.65
Above 100	0.44***	0.11	0.43

TABLE 13

State-wise Distribution of Working Children according to 1971, 1981, 1991 and 2001 Census in the age group 5-14 years

S.No.	Name of the State/UT	1971	1981	1991	2001****
1.	Andhra Pradesh	1627492	1951312	1661,940	13,633,339
2.	Assam	239349	**	327,598	351416
3.	Bihar	1059359	1101764	942,245	1117500
4.	Gujarat	518061	616913	523585	485530
5.	Haryana	137826	194189	109691	253491
6.	Himachal Pradesh	71384	99624	56,438	107774
7.	Jammu & Kashmir	70489	258437	**	175630
8.	Karnataka	808719	1131530	976247	822615
9.	Kerala	111801	92854	34800	26156
10.	Madhya Pradesh	1112319	1698597	1352563	1065259
11.	Maharashstra	988357	1557756	1068427	764075
12.	Chattisgarh				364572
13.	Manipur	16380	20217	16493	28836
14.	Meghalaya	30440	44916	34633	53940
15.	Jharkhand				407200
16.	Uttranchal				70183
17.	Nagaland	13726	16235	16467	45874
18.	Orissa	492477	702293	452394	377594

S.No.	Name of the State/UT	1971	1981	1991	2001****
19.	Punjab	232774	216939	142868	177268
20.	Rajasthan	587389	819605	774199	1262570
21.	Sikkim	15661	8561	5,598	16457
22.	Tamil Nadu	713305	975055	578,889	418801
23.	Tripura	17490	24204	16,478	21756
24.	Uttar Pradesh	1326726	1434675	1410086	1927997
25.	West Bengal	511443	605263	711691	857087
26.	Andaman & Nicobar Islands	572	1309	1,265	1960
27.	Arunachal Pradesh	17925	17950	12395	18482
28.	Chandigarh	1086	1986	1,870	3779
29.	Dadra & Nagar Haveli	3102	3615	4416	4274
30.	Delhi	17120	25717	27,351	41899
31.	Daman & Diu	7391	9378	941	729
32.	Goa			4,656	4138
33.	Lakshadweep	97	56	34	27
34.	Mizoram	***	6314	16,411	26265
35.	Pondichery	3725	3606	2,680	1904
	Total	**10753985**	**13640870**	**11285349**	**12666377**

Note : * 1971 Census figures of Assam includes figures of Mizoram.

** Census could not be conducted.

*** Census figures 1971 in respect of Mizoram included under Assam.

*** includes marginal workers also.

Initiatives towards Elimination of Child Labour—Action Plan and Present Strategy—The problem of child labour continues to pose a challenge before the nation. Government has been taking various poractive measures to tackle this problem. However, considering the magnitude and extent of the problem and that it is essentially a socio-economic problem inextricably linked to poverty and illiteracy, it requires concerted efforts from all sections of the society to make a dent in the problem.

Way back in 1979, Government formed the first committee called Gurpadswamy Committee to study the issue of child labour and to suggest measures to tackle it. The Committee examined the problem in detail and made some far-reaching recommendations. It observed that as long as poverty continued, it would be difficult to totally eliminate child labour and hence, any attempt to abolish it through legal recourse would not be a practical proposition. The committee felt that in the circumstances, the only alternative left was to ban child labour in hazardous areas and to regulate and ameliorate the conditions of work in other areas. It recommended that a multiple policy policy approach was required in dealing with the problems of working children.

Based on the recommendations of Gurupadaswamy Committee, the Child Labour (Prohibition & Regulation) Act was enacted in 1986. The Act prohibits employment of children in certain specified hazardous occupations and processes and regulates the working conditions in others. The list of hazardous occupations and processes is progressively being expanded on the recommendation of Child Labour Technical Advisory Committee constituted under the Act.

In consonance with the above approach, a National Policy on Child Labour was formulated in 1987. The Policy seeks to adopt a gradual and sequential approach with a focus on rehabilitation of children working in hazardous occupations and processes in the first instance. The Action Plan outlined in the Policy for tackling this problem is as follows :

(*a*) **Legislative Action Plan**—for strict enforcement of Child Labour Act and other labour laws to ensure that children are not employed in hazardous employments, and that the working conditions of children working in non-hazardous areas are regulated in accordance with the provisions of the Child Labour Act. It also entails further identification of additional occupations and processes, which are detrimental to the health and safety of the children.

(*b*) **Focusing of General Development Programmes for Benefiting Child Labour**—As poverty is the root cause of child labour, the action plan emphasizes the need to cover these children and their families also under various poverty alleviation and employment generation schemes of the Government.

(*c*) **Project Based Plan of Action**—envisages starting of projects in areas of high concentration of child labour. Pursuant to this, in 1988, the National Child Labour Project (NCLP)) Scheme was launched in 9 districts of high child labour endmicity in the country. The Scheme envisages running of special schools for child labour withdrawn from work. In the special schools, these children are provided formal/non-formal education along with vocational training, a stipend of Rs. 100 per month, supplementary nutrition and regular health check ups so as to prepare them to join regular mainstream schools. Under the Scheme, funds are given to the District Collectors for running special schools for child labour. Most of these schools are run by the NGOs in the district.

Government has accordingly been taking poractive steps to tackle this problem through strict enforcement of legislative provisions along with simultaneous rehabilitative measures. State Governments, which are the appropriate implementing authorities, have been conducting regular inspections and raids to detect cases of violations. Since poverty is the root cause of this problem, and enforcement alone cannot help solve it, Government has been laying a lot of emphasis on the rehabilitation of these children and on improving the economics of their families.

The coverage of the NCLP Scheme has increased from 12 districts in 1988 to 100 districts in the 9th Plan to 250 districts during the 10th Plan.

Strategy for the elimination of child labour under the 10th Plan.—An evaluation of the Scheme was carried out by independent agencies in coordination with V.V. Giri National Labour Institute in 2001. Based on the recommendations of the evaluation and experience of implementing the scheme since 1988, the strategy for implementing the scheme during the 10th Plan was devised. It aimed at greater convergence with the other developmental schemes and bringing qualitative changes in the Scheme. Some of the salient points of the 10th Plan Strategy are as follows :

* Focused and reinforced action to eliminate child labour in the hazardous occupations by the end of the Plan period.
* Expansion of National Child Labour Projects to additional 150 districts.
* Linking the child labour elimination efforts with the Scheme of Sarva Shiksha Abhiyan of Ministry of Human Resource Development to ensure that children in the age group of 5-8 years get directly admitted to regular schools and that the older working children are mainstreamed to the formal education system through special schools functioning under the NCLP Scheme.
* Convergence with other Schemes of the Departments of Education, Rural Development, Health and Women and Child Development for the ultimate attainment of the objective in a time bound manner.

The Government and the Ministry of Labour and Employment in particular, are rather serious in their efforts to fight and succeed in this direction. The number of districts covered under the NCLP Scheme has been increased from 100 to 250, as mentioned above in this note. In addition, 21 districts have been covered under INDUS, a similar Scheme for rehabilitation of child labour in cooperation with US Department of Labour. Implementation of this Project was recently reviewed during the visit of Mr. Steven Law, Deputy Secretary of State from the USA. For the Districts not covered under these two Schemes, Government is also providing funds, directly to the NGOs under the Ministry's Grants-in-Scheme for running Special Schools for rehabilitation of child labour, thereby providing for a greater role and cooperation of the civil society in combating this menace.

Elimination of child labour is the single largest programme in this Ministry's activities. Apart from a major increase in the number of districts covered under the scheme the priority of the Government in this direction is evidence the quantum jump in budgetary allocation during the 10th Plan. Government has allocated Rs. 602 crores for the Scheme during the 10th Plan, as against an expenditure of Rs. 178 crores in the 9th Plan. The resources set aside for combating this evil in the Ministry is around 50 per cent of its total annual budget.

The implementation of NCLP and INDUS Schemes is being closely monitored through periodical reports, frequent visits and meetings with the District and State Government officials. The Government's commitment to achieve tangible results in this direction in a time bound manner is also evident from the fact that in the recent Regional Level Conferences of District Collectors held in Hyderabad, Pune, Mussoorie and Kolkata district-wise review of the Scheme was conducted at the level of Secretary. These Conference provided an excellent opportunity to have one-to-one interaction with the collectors, who play a pivotal role in the implementation of these Schemes in the District. Beside, these conferences also helped in a big way in early operationalisation of Scheme in the newly selected 150 districts.

The Government is committed to eliminate child labour in all its forms and is moving in this direction in a targeted manner. The multipronged strategy being followed by the Government to achieve this objective also found its echo during the recent discussions held in the Parliament on the Private Member's Bill tabled by Shri Iqbal Ahmed Saradgi. It was unanimously recognized therein that the problem of child labour, being inextricably linked with poverty and illiteracy, cannot be solved by legislation, alone, and that a holistic, multipronged and concerted effort to tackle this problem will bring in the desired results.

TABLE 14

Statement showing the Budget Allocation and Actual Expenditure Incurred Under all Schemes of Child Labour During the Period from 2000-01 to 2005-06

Year	Budget Allocation	Expenditure (in lakhs)
2000-2001	3600.00	3803.69
2001-2002	6700.00	6191.67
2002-2003	8010.00	6513.77
2003-2004	7243.00	6739.66
2004-2005	9905.00	9315.80
2005-2006	12479.00	5664.00*

**Expenditure incurred up to 30.6.2005*

TABLE 15

Statement Showing the Plan-wise Allocation Under NCLP Scheme

Plan Period	Allocation (in lakhs)
1992-1997 (Eighth Plan)	1500.00
1997-2002 (Ninth Plan)	24960.00
2002-2007 (Tenth Plan)	60200.00

TABLE 16

Statement Showing BE/RE and Actual Expenditure under Various Schemes Implemented by Child Labour Division During 2000-01, 2001-02, 2002-03, 2003-04 and 2004-05

(*a*) **National Child Labour Project Scheme Including Grant-in-Aid to Voluntary Agencies**

Year	BE (Rs. in crores)	RE (Rs. in crores)	Actual Expenditure (Rs. in crores)
2000-01	35.90	35.90	37.98
2001-02	61.90	61.86	61.86
2002-03	70.00	65.10	65.10
2003-04	67.38	66.90	66.77
2004-05	89.00	89.00	81.69
2005-06	99.74		

(*b*) **Strengthening of Child Labour Cell**

Year	BE (Rs. in crores)	RE (Rs. in crores)	Actual Expenditure (Rs. in crores)
2000-01	0.10	0.10	0.05
2001-02	0.10	0.05	0.05
2002-03	0.10	0.10	0.03
2003-04	0.05	0.05	0.05
2004-05	0.05	0.05	0.05
2005-06	0.05		

(*c*) **Indo-US Matching Grant (Now Renamed as Indus Project)**

(Project was launched on 16.2.2004)

Year	BE (Rs. in crores)	RE (Rs. in crores)	Actual Expenditure (Rs. in crores)
2000-01	...	...	...
2001-02	5.00	0.00	Nil
2002-03	10.00	5.00	Nil
2003-04	5.00	1.00	0.57
2004-05	10.00	9.07	10.00
2005-06	25.00		

Table 17

Allocation iN the Tenth Plan Period Under Various Schemes Implemented by Child Labour Division

S.No.	Name of the Scheme	Allocation in the Tenth Plan Period (Rs. in crores)
1.	National Child Labour Project Scheme including Grant-in-aid to Voluntary agencies	*602.00
2.	Indo US Matching Grant (renamed as Indus Project)	65.00
3.	Strenghening of Child Labour Cell	0.50
	Total	667.50

*(NCLP-Rs. 592.50 crores; GIA-Rs. 7.50 crores).

6

INTERNATIONAL LEGAL INITIATIVES

FORCED LABOUR (INDIRECT COMPULSION) RECOMMENDATION, 1930

Date of adoption 28:06:1930

The General Conference of the International Labour Organisation,

Having been convened at Geneva by the Governing Body of the International Labour Office, and having met in its Fourteenth Session on 10 June 1930, and

Having decided upon the adoption of certain proposals with regard to indirect compulsion to labour, which is included in the first item on the agenda of the Session, and

Having determined that these proposals should take the form of a Recommendation,

adopts this twenty-eighth day of June of the year one thousand nine hundred thirty, the following Recommendation, which may be cited as the Forced Labour (Indirect Compulsion) Recommendation, 1930, to be submitted to the Members of the International Labour Organisation for consideration with a view to effect being given to it by national legislation or otherwise, in accordance with the provisions of the Constitution of the International Labour Organisation:

Having adopted a Convention concerning forced or compulsory labour, and

Desiring to supplement this Convention by a statement of the principles which appear best fitted to guide the policy of the Members in endeavouring to avoid any indirect compulsion to labour which would lay too heavy a burden upon the populations of territories to which the Convention may apply,

The Conference recommends that each Member should take the following principles into consideration:

I

The amount of labour available, the capacities for labour of the population, and the evil effects which too sudden changes in the habits of life and labour may have on the social conditions of the population, are factors which should be taken into consideration in deciding questions connected with the economic development of territories in a primitive stage of development, and, in particular, when deciding upon:

(a) increases in the number and extent of industrial, mining and agricultural undertakings in such territories;

(b) the non-indigenous settlement, if any, which is to be permitted;

(c) the granting of forest or other concessions, with or without the character of monopolies.

II

The desirability of avoiding indirect means of artificially increasing the economic pressure upon populations to seek wage-earning employment, and particularly such means as:

(a) imposing such taxation upon populations as would have the effect of compelling them to seek wage-earning employment with private undertakings;

(b) imposing such restrictions on the possession, occupation, or use of land as would have the effect of rendering difficult the gaining of a living by independent cultivation;

(c) extending abusively the generally accepted meaning of vagrancy;

(d) adopting such pass laws as would have the effect of placing workers in the service of others in a position of advantage as compared with that of other workers.

III

The desirability of avoiding any restrictions on the voluntary flow of labour from one form of employment to another or from one district to another which might have the indirect effect of compelling workers to take employment in particular industries or districts, except where such restrictions are considered necessary in the interest of the population or of the workers concerned.

(WITHDRAWN) FORCED LABOUR (REGULATION) RECOMMENDATION, 1930

Date of adoption 28:06:1930

The General Conference of the International Labour Organization, Having been convened in Geneva by the Governing Body of the International Labour Office, and having met in its 92nd Session on 1 June 2004, and Following consideration of the proposal for the withdrawal of several international labour Recommendations, which is the seventh item on the agenda of this session, decides this sixteenth day of June of the year two thousand and four to withdraw the Forced Labour (Regulation) Recommendation, 1930 (No. 36). The Director-General of the International Labour Office shall notify all Members of the International Labour Organization as well as the Secretary-General of the United Nations of this decision to withdraw the instrument. The English and French versions of the text of this decision are equally authoritative.

The General Conference of the International Labour Organisation,

Having been convened at Geneva by the Governing Body of the International Labour Office, and having met in its Fourteenth Session on 10 June 1930, and

Having decided upon the adoption of certain proposals with regard to the regulation of forced or compulsory labour, which is included in the first item on the agenda of the Session, and

Having determined that these proposals should take the form of a Recommendation,

adopts this twenty-eighth day of June of the year one thousand nine hundred thirty, the following Recommendation, which may be cited as the Forced Labour (Regulation) Recommendation, 1930, to be submitted to the Members of the International Labour Organisation for consideration with a view to effect being given to it by national legislation or otherwise, in accordance with the provisions of the Constitution of the International Labour Organisation:

Having adopted a Convention concerning forced or compulsory labour, and

Desiring to give expression to certain principles and rules relating to forced or compulsory labour which appear to be of a nature to render the application of the said Convention more effective,

The Conference recommends that each Member should take the following principles and rules into consideration:

I

Any regulations issued in application of the Convention concerning forced or compulsory labour, as well as any other legal provisions or administrative orders, existing at the time of the ratification of the said Convention or thereafter enacted, governing the employment of forced or compulsory labour, including any laws or administrative orders concerning compensation or indemnification for sickness, injury to, or death of workers taken for forced or compulsory labour, should be printed by the competent authority in such one or more native languages as will convey their import to the workers concerned and to the population from which the workers are to be drawn. Such printed texts should be widely exhibited and, if necessary, arrangements made for their oral communication to the workers and to the population concerned; copies should also be made available to the workers concerned and to others at cost price.

II

Recourse to forced or compulsory labour should be so regulated as not to imperil the food supply of the community concerned.

III

When recourse is had to forced or compulsory labour all possible measures should be taken to ensure that the imposition of such labour in no case leads indirectly to the illegal employment of women and children on forced or compulsory labour.

IV

All possible measures should be taken to reduce the necessity for recourse to forced or compulsory labour for the transport of persons or goods. Such recourse should be prohibited when and where animal or mechanical transport is available.

V

All possible steps should be taken to see that no alcoholic temptations are placed in the way of workers engaged in forced or compulsory labour.

MINIMUM AGE RECOMMENDATION, 1973

Date of adoption 26:06:1973

The General Conference of the International Labour Organisation,

Having been convened at Geneva by the Governing Body of the International Labour Office, and having met in its Fifty-eighth Session on 6 June 1973, and

Recognising that the effective abolition of child labour and the progressive raising of the minimum age for admission to employment constitute only one aspect of the protection and advancement of children and young persons, and

Noting the concern of the whole United Nations system with such protection and advancement, and

Having adopted the Minimum Age Convention, 1973, and

Desirous to define further certain elements of policy which are the concern of the International Labour Organisation, and

Having decided upon the adoption of certain proposals regarding minimum age for admission to employment, which is the fourth item on the agenda of the session, and

Having determined that these proposals shall take the form of a Recommendation supplementing the Minimum Age Convention, 1973,

adopts this twenty-sixth day of June of the year one thousand nine hundred and seventy-three, the following Recommendation, which may be cited as the Minimum Age Recommendation, 1973:

I. National Policy

1. To ensure the success of the national policy provided for in Article 1 of the Minimum Age Convention, 1973, high priority should be given to planning for and meeting the needs of children and youth in national development policies and programmes and to the progressive extension of the inter-related measures necessary to provide the best possible conditions of physical and mental growth for children and young persons.

2. In this connection special attention should be given to such areas of planning and policy as the following:

(a) firm national commitment to full employment, in accordance with the Employment Policy Convention and Recommendation, 1964, and the taking of measures designed to promote employment-oriented development in rural and urban areas;

(b) the progressive extension of other economic and social measures to alleviate poverty wherever it exists and to ensure family living standards and income which are such as to make it unnecessary to have recourse to the economic activity of children;

(c) the development and progressive extension, without any discrimination, of social security and family welfare measures aimed at ensuring child maintenance, including children's allowances;

(d) the development and progressive extension of adequate facilities for education and vocational orientation and training appropriate in form and content to the needs of the children and young persons concerned;

(e) the development and progressive extension of appropriate facilities for the protection and welfare of children and young persons, including employed young persons, and for the promotion of their development.

3. Particular account should as necessary be taken of the needs of children and young persons who do not have families or do not live with their own families and of migrant children and young persons who live and travel with their families. Measures taken to that end should include the provision of fellowships and vocational training.

4. Full-time attendance at school or participation in approved vocational orientation or training programmes should be required and effectively ensured up to an age at least equal to that specified for admission to employment in accordance with Article 2 of the Minimum Age Convention, 1973.

5. (1) Consideration should be given to measures such as preparatory training, not involving hazards, for types of employment or work in respect of which the minimum age prescribed in accordance with Article 3 of the Minimum Age Convention, 1973, is higher than the age of completion of compulsory full-time schooling.

(2) Analogous measures should be envisaged where the professional exigencies of a particular occupation include a minimum age for admission which is higher than the age of completion of compulsory full-time schooling.

II. Minimum Age

6. The minimum age should be fixed at the same level for all sectors of economic activity.

7. (1) Members should take as their objective the progressive raising to 16 years of the minimum age for admission to employment or work specified in pursuance of Article 2 of the Minimum Age Convention, 1973.

(2) Where the minimum age for employment or work covered by Article 2 of the Minimum Age Convention, 1973, is still below 15 years, urgent steps should be taken to raise it to that level.

8. Where it is not immediately feasible to fix a minimum age for all employment in agriculture and in related activities in rural areas, a minimum age should be fixed at least for employment on plantations and in the other agricultural undertakings referred to in Article 5, paragraph 3, of the Minimum Age Convention, 1973.

III. Hazardous Employment or Work

9. Where the minimum age for admission to types of employment or work which are likely to jeopardise the health, safety or morals of young persons is still below 18 years, immediate steps should be taken to raise it to that level.

10. (1) In determining the types of employment or work to which Article 3 of the Minimum Age Convention, 1973, applies, full account should be taken of relevant international labour standards, such as those concerning dangerous substances, agents or processes (including ionising radiations), the lifting of heavy weights and underground work.

(2) The list of the types of employment or work in question should be re-

examined periodically and revised as necessary, particularly in the light of advancing scientific and technological knowledge.

11. Where, by reference to Article 5 of the Minimum Age Convention, 1973, a minimum age is not immediately fixed for certain branches of economic activity or types of undertakings, appropriate minimum age provisions should be made applicable therein to types of employment or work presenting hazards for young persons.

IV. Conditions of Employment

12. (1) Measures should be taken to ensure that the conditions in which children and young persons under the age of 18 years are employed or work reach and are maintained at a satisfactory standard. These conditions should be supervised closely.

(2) Measures should likewise be taken to safeguard and supervise the conditions in which children and young persons undergo vocational orientation and training within undertakings, training institutions and schools for vocational or technical education and to formulate standards for their protection and development.

13. (1) In connection with the application of the preceding Paragraph, as well as in giving effect to Article 7, paragraph 3, of the Minimum Age Convention, 1973, special attention should be given to—

(a) the provision of fair remuneration and its protection, bearing in mind the principle of equal pay for equal work;

(b) the strict limitation of the hours spent at work in a day and in a week, and the prohibition of overtime, so as to allow enough time for education and training (including the time needed for homework related thereto), for rest during the day and for leisure activities;

(c) the granting, without possibility of exception save in genuine emergency, of a minimum consecutive period of 12 hours' night rest, and of customary weekly rest days;

(d) the granting of an annual holiday with pay of at least four weeks and, in any case, not shorter than that granted to adults;

(e) coverage by social security schemes, including employment injury, medical care and sickness benefit schemes, whatever the conditions of employment or work may be;

(f) the maintenance of satisfactory standards of safety and health and appropriate instruction and supervision.

(2) Subparagraph (1) of this Paragraph applies to young seafarers in so far as they are not covered in respect of the matters dealt with therein by

international labour Conventions or Recommendations specifically concerned with maritime employment.

V. Enforcement

14. (1) Measures to ensure the effective application of the Minimum Age Convention, 1973, and of this Recommendation should include—

(a) the strengthening as necessary of labour inspection and related services, for instance by the special training of inspectors to detect abuses in the employment or work of children and young persons and to correct such abuses; and

(b) the strengthening of services for the improvement and inspection of training in undertakings.

(2) Emphasis should be placed on the role which can be played by inspectors in supplying information and advice on effective means of complying with relevant provisions as well as in securing their enforcement.

(3) Labour inspection and inspection of training in undertakings should be closely co-ordinated to provide the greatest economic efficiency and, generally, the labour administration services should work in close co-operation with the services responsible for the education, training, welfare and guidance of children and young persons.

15. Special attention should be paid—

(a) to the enforcement of provisions concerning employment in hazardous types of employment or work; and

(b) in so far as education or training is compulsory, to the prevention of the employment or work of children and young persons during the hours when instruction is available.

16. The following measures should be taken to facilitate the verification of ages:

(a) the public authorities should maintain an effective system of birth registration, which should include the issue of birth certificates;

(b) employers should be required to keep and to make available to the competent authority registers or other documents indicating the names and ages or dates of birth, duly certified wherever possible, not only of children and young persons employed by them but also of those receiving vocational orientation or training in their undertakings;

(c) children and young persons working in the streets, in outside stalls, in public places, in itinerant occupations or in other circumstances which make the checking of employers' records impracticable should be issued licences or other documents indicating their eligibility for such work.

MINIMUM AGE CONVENTION, 1973

Date of Adoption :26:06:1973

The General Conference of the International Labour Organisation,

Having been convened at Geneva by the Governing Body of the International Labour Office, and having met in its Fifty-eighth Session on 6 June 1973, and

Having decided upon the adoption of certain proposals with regard to minimum age for admission to employment, which is the fourth item on the agenda of the session, and

Noting the terms of the Minimum Age (Industry) Convention, 1919, the Minimum Age (Sea) Convention, 1920, the Minimum Age (Agriculture) Convention, 1921, the Minimum Age (Trimmers and Stokers) Convention, 1921, the Minimum Age (Non-Industrial Employment) Convention, 1932, the Minimum Age (Sea) Convention (Revised), 1936, the Minimum Age (Industry) Convention (Revised), 1937, the Minimum Age (Non-Industrial Employment) Convention (Revised), 1937, the Minimum Age (Fishermen) Convention, 1959, and the Minimum Age (Underground Work) Convention, 1965, and

Considering that the time has come to establish a general instrument on the subject, which would gradually replace the existing ones applicable to limited economic sectors, with a view to achieving the total abolition of child labour, and

Having determined that these proposals shall take the form of an international Convention,

adopts this twenty-sixth day of June of the year one thousand nine hundred and seventy-three the following Convention, which may be cited as the Minimum Age Convention, 1973:

Article 1

Each Member for which this Convention is in force undertakes to pursue a national policy designed to ensure the effective abolition of child labour and to raise progressively the minimum age for admission to employment or work to a level consistent with the fullest physical and mental development of young persons.

Article 2

1. Each Member which ratifies this Convention shall specify, in a declaration appended to its ratification, a minimum age for admission to employment or work within its territory and on means of transport registered in its territory; subject to Articles 4 to 8 of this Convention, no one under that age shall be admitted to employment or work in any occupation.

2. Each Member which has ratified this Convention may subsequently notify the Director-General of the International Labour Office, by further declarations, that it specifies a minimum age higher than that previously specified.

3. The minimum age specified in pursuance of paragraph 1 of this Article shall not be less than the age of completion of compulsory schooling and, in any case, shall not be less than 15 years.

4. Notwithstanding the provisions of paragraph 3 of this Article, a Member whose economy and educational facilities are insufficiently developed may, after consultation with the organisations of employers and workers concerned, where such exist, initially specify a minimum age of 14 years.

5. Each Member which has specified a minimum age of 14 years in pursuance of the provisions of the preceding paragraph shall include in its reports on the application of this Convention submitted under article 22 of the Constitution of the International Labour Organisation a statement—

(a) that its reason for doing so subsists; or

(b) that it renounces its right to avail itself of the provisions in question as from a stated date.

Article 3

1. The minimum age for admission to any type of employment or work which by its nature or the circumstances in which it is carried out is likely to jeopardise the health, safety or morals of young persons shall not be less than 18 years.

2. The types of employment or work to which paragraph 1 of this Article applies shall be determined by national laws or regulations or by the competent authority, after consultation with the organisations of employers and workers concerned, where such exist.

3. Notwithstanding the provisions of paragraph 1 of this Article, national laws or regulations or the competent authority may, after consultation with the organisations of employers and workers concerned, where such exist, authorise employment or work as from the age of 16 years on condition that the health, safety and morals of the young persons concerned are fully protected and that the young persons have received adequate specific instruction or vocational training in the relevant branch of activity.

Article 4

1. In so far as necessary, the competent authority, after consultation with the organisations of employers and workers concerned, where such exist, may exclude from the application of this Convention limited categories of employment or work in respect of which special and substantial problems of application arise.

2. Each Member which ratifies this Convention shall list in its first report on the application of the Convention submitted under article 22 of the Constitution of the International Labour Organisation any categories which may have been excluded in pursuance of paragraph 1 of this Article, giving the reasons for such exclusion, and shall state in subsequent reports the position of its law and practice in respect of the categories excluded and the extent to which effect has been given or is proposed to be given to the Convention in respect of such categories.

3. Employment or work covered by Article 3 of this Convention shall not be excluded from the application of the Convention in pursuance of this Article.

Article 5

1. A Member whose economy and administrative facilities are insufficiently developed may, after consultation with the organisations of employers and workers concerned, where such exist, initially limit the scope of application of this Convention.

2. Each Member which avails itself of the provisions of paragraph 1 of this Article shall specify, in a declaration appended to its ratification, the branches of economic activity or types of undertakings to which it will apply the provisions of the Convention.

3. The provisions of the Convention shall be applicable as a minimum to the following: mining and quarrying; manufacturing; construction; electricity, gas and water; sanitary services; transport, storage and communication; and plantations and other agricultural undertakings mainly producing for commercial purposes, but excluding family and small-scale holdings producing for local consumption and not regularly employing hired workers.

4. Any Member which has limited the scope of application of this Convention in pursuance of this Article—

(a) shall indicate in its reports under Article 22 of the Constitution of the International Labour Organisation the general position as regards the employment or work of young persons and children in the branches of activity which are excluded from the scope of application of this Convention and any progress which may have been made towards wider application of the provisions of the Convention;

(b) may at any time formally extend the scope of application by a declaration addressed to the Director-General of the International Labour Office.

Article 6

This Convention does not apply to work done by children and young persons in schools for general, vocational or technical education or in other training institutions, or to work done by persons at least 14 years of age in undertakings, where such work is carried out in accordance with conditions prescribed by the competent authority, after consultation with the organisations of employers and workers concerned, where such exist, and is an integral part of—

(a) a course of education or training for which a school or training institution is primarily responsible;

(b) a programme of training mainly or entirely in an undertaking, which programme has been approved by the competent authority; or

(c) a programme of guidance or orientation designed to facilitate the choice of an occupation or of a line of training.

Article 7

1. National laws or regulations may permit the employment or work of persons 13 to 15 years of age on light work which is—

(a) not likely to be harmful to their health or development; and

(b) not such as to prejudice their attendance at school, their participation in vocational orientation or training programmes approved by the competent authority or their capacity to benefit from the instruction received.

2. National laws or regulations may also permit the employment or work of persons who are at least 15 years of age but have not yet completed their compulsory schooling on work which meets the requirements set forth in sub-paragraphs (a) and (b) of paragraph 1 of this Article.

3. The competent authority shall determine the activities in which employment or work may be permitted under paragraphs 1 and 2 of this Article and shall prescribe the number of hours during which and the conditions in which such employment or work may be undertaken.

4. Notwithstanding the provisions of paragraphs 1 and 2 of this Article, a Member which has availed itself of the provisions of paragraph 4 of Article 2 may, for as long as it continues to do so, substitute the ages 12 and 14 for the ages 13 and 15 in paragraph 1 and the age 14 for the age 15 in paragraph 2 of this Article.

Article 8

1. After consultation with the organisations of employers and workers concerned, where such exist, the competent authority may, by permits granted in individual cases, allow exceptions to the prohibition of employment or work provided for in Article 2 of this Convention, for such purposes as participation in artistic performances.

2. Permits so granted shall limit the number of hours during which and prescribe the conditions in which employment or work is allowed.

Article 9

1. All necessary measures, including the provision of appropriate penalties, shall be taken by the competent authority to ensure the effective enforcement of the provisions of this Convention.

2. National laws or regulations or the competent authority shall define the persons responsible for compliance with the provisions giving effect to the Convention.

3. National laws or regulations or the competent authority shall prescribe the registers or other documents which shall be kept and made available by the employer; such registers or documents shall contain the names and ages or dates of birth, duly certified wherever possible, of persons whom he employs or who work for him and who are less than 18 years of age.

Article 10

1. This Convention revises, on the terms set forth in this Article, the Minimum Age (Industry) Convention, 1919, the Minimum Age (Sea) Convention, 1920, the Minimum Age (Agriculture) Convention, 1921, the Minimum Age (Trimmers and Stokers) Convention, 1921, the Minimum Age (Non-Industrial Employment) Convention, 1932, the Minimum Age (Sea) Convention (Revised), 1936, the Minimum Age (Industry) Convention (Revised), 1937, the Minimum Age (Non-Industrial Employment) Convention (Revised), 1937, the Minimum Age (Fishermen) Convention, 1959, and the Minimum Age (Underground Work) Convention, 1965.

2. The coming into force of this Convention shall not close the Minimum Age (Sea) Convention (Revised), 1936, the Minimum Age (Industry) Convention (Revised), 1937, the Minimum Age (Non-Industrial Employment) Convention (Revised), 1937, the Minimum Age (Fishermen) Convention, 1959, or the Minimum Age (Underground Work) Convention, 1965, to further ratification.

3. The Minimum Age (Industry) Convention, 1919, the Minimum Age (Sea) Convention, 1920, the Minimum Age (Agriculture) Convention, 1921, and the Minimum Age (Trimmers and Stokers) Convention, 1921, shall be closed to further ratification when all the parties thereto have consented to such closing by ratification of this Convention or by a declaration communicated to the Director-General of the International Labour Office.

4. When the obligations of this Convention are accepted—

(a) by a Member which is a party to the Minimum Age (Industry) Convention (Revised), 1937, and a minimum age of not less than 15 years is specified in pursuance of Article 2 of this Convention, this shall ipso jure involve the immediate denunciation of that Convention,

(b) in respect of non-industrial employment as defined in the Minimum

Age (Non-Industrial Employment) Convention, 1932, by a Member which is a party to that Convention, this shall ipso jure involve the immediate denunciation of that Convention,

(c) in respect of non-industrial employment as defined in the Minimum Age (Non-Industrial Employment) Convention (Revised), 1937, by a Member which is a party to that Convention, and a minimum age of not less than 15 years is specified in pursuance of Article 2 of this Convention, this shall ipso jure involve the immediate denunciation of that Convention,

(d) in respect of maritime employment, by a Member which is a party to the Minimum Age (Sea) Convention (Revised), 1936, and a minimum age of not less than 15 years is specified in pursuance of Article 2 of this Convention or the Member specifies that Article 3 of this Convention applies to maritime employment, this shall ipso jure involve the immediate denunciation of that Convention,

(e) in respect of employment in maritime fishing, by a Member which is a party to the Minimum Age (Fishermen) Convention, 1959, and a minimum age of not less than 15 years is specified in pursuance of Article 2 of this Convention or the Member specifies that Article 3 of this Convention applies to employment in maritime fishing, this shall ipso jure involve the immediate denunciation of that Convention,

(f) by a Member which is a party to the Minimum Age (Underground Work) Convention, 1965, and a minimum age of not less than the age specified in pursuance of that Convention is specified in pursuance of Article 2 of this Convention or the Member specifies that such an age applies to employment underground in mines in virtue of Article 3 of this Convention, this shall ipso jure involve the immediate denunciation of that Convention,

if and when this Convention shall have come into force.

5. Acceptance of the obligations of this Convention—

(a) shall involve the denunciation of the Minimum Age (Industry) Convention, 1919, in accordance with Article 12 thereof,

(b) in respect of agriculture shall involve the denunciation of the Minimum Age (Agriculture) Convention, 1921, in accordance with Article 9 thereof,

(c) in respect of maritime employment shall involve the denunciation of the Minimum Age (Sea) Convention, 1920, in accordance with Article 10 thereof, and of the Minimum Age (Trimmers and Stokers) Convention, 1921, in accordance with Article 12 thereof,

if and when this Convention shall have come into force.

Article 11

The formal ratifications of this Convention shall be communicated to the Director-General of the International Labour Office for registration.

Article 12

1. This Convention shall be binding only upon those Members of the International Labour Organisation whose ratifications have been registered with the Director-General.

2. It shall come into force twelve months after the date on which the ratifications of two Members have been registered with the Director-General.

3. Thereafter, this Convention shall come into force for any Member twelve months after the date on which its ratifications has been registered.

Article 13

1. A Member which has ratified this Convention may denounce it after the expiration of ten years from the date on which the Convention first comes into force, by an act communicated to the Director-General of the International Labour Office for registration. Such denunciation shall not take effect until one year after the date on which it is registered.

2. Each Member which has ratified this Convention and which does not, within the year following the expiration of the period of ten years mentioned in the preceding paragraph, exercise the right of denunciation provided for in this Article, will be bound for another period of ten years and, thereafter, may denounce this Convention at the expiration of each period of ten years under the terms provided for in this Article.

Article 14

1. The Director-General of the International Labour Office shall notify all Members of the International Labour Organisation of the registration of all ratifications and denunciations communicated to him by the Members of the Organisation.

2. When notifying the Members of the Organisation of the registration of the second ratification communicated to him, the Director-General shall draw the attention of the Members of the Organisation to the date upon which the Convention will come into force.

Article 15

The Director-General of the International Labour Office shall communicate to the Secretary-General of the United Nations for registration in accordance with Article 102 of the Charter of the United Nations full particulars of all ratifications and acts of denunciation registered by him in accordance with the provisions of the preceding Articles.

Article 16

At such times as it may consider necessary the Governing Body of the International Labour Office shall present to the General Conference a report on the working of this Convention and shall examine the desirability of placing on the agenda of the Conference the question of its revision in whole or in part.

Article 17

1. Should the Conference adopt a new Convention revising this Convention in whole or in part, then, unless the new Convention otherwise provides:

(a) the ratification by a Member of the new revising Convention shall ipso jure involve the immediate denunciation of this Convention, notwithstanding the provisions of Article 13 above, if and when the new revising Convention shall have come into force;

(b) as from the date when the new revising Convention comes into force this Convention shall cease to be open to ratification by the Members.

2. This Convention shall in any case remain in force in its actual form and content for those Members which have ratified it but have not ratified the revising Convention.

Article 18

The English and French versions of the text of this Convention are equally authoritative.

RATIFICATION OF MINIMUM AGE CONVENTION LIST

Country	*Ratification date*	*Status*
Albania	16:02:1998	ratified
Algeria	30:04:1984	ratified
Angola	13:06:2001	ratified
Antigua and Barbuda	17:03:1983	ratified
Argentina	11:11:1996	ratified
Armenia	27:01:2006	ratified
Austria	18:09:2000	ratified
Azerbaijan	19:05:1992	ratified
Bahamas	31:10:2001	ratified
Barbados	04:01:2000	ratified
Belarus	03:05:1979	ratified
Belgium	19:04:1988	ratified
Belize	06:03:2000	ratified
Benin	11:06:2001	ratified
Bolivia	11:06:1997	ratified

Country	*Ratification date*	*Status*
Bosnia and Herzegovina	02:06:1993	ratified
Botswana	05:06:1997	ratified
Brazil	28:06:2001	ratified
Bulgaria	23:04:1980	ratified
Burkina Faso	11:02:1999	ratified
Burundi	19:07:2000	ratified
Cambodia	23:08:1999	ratified
Cameroon	13:08:2001	ratified
Central African Republic	28:06:2000	ratified
Chad	21:03:2005	ratified
Chile	01:02:1999	ratified
China	28:04:1999	ratified
Colombia	02:02:2001	ratified
Comoros	17:03:2004	ratified
Congo	26:11:1999	ratified
Democratic Republic of the Congo	20:06:2001	ratified
Costa Rica	11:06:1976	ratified
Côte d'Ivoire	07:02:2003	ratified
Croatia	08:10:1991	ratified
Cuba	07:03:1975	ratified
Cyprus	02:10:1997	ratified
Denmark	13:11:1997	ratified
Djibouti	14:06:2005	ratified
Dominica	27:09:1983	ratified
Dominican Republic	15:06:1999	ratified
Ecuador	19:09:2000	ratified
Egypt	09:06:1999	ratified
El Salvador	23:01:1996	ratified
Equatorial Guinea	12:06:1985	ratified
Eritrea	22:02:2000	ratified
Ethiopia	27:05:1999	ratified
Fiji	03:01:2003	ratified
Finland	13:01:1976	ratified
France	13:07:1990	ratified
Gambia	04:09:2000	ratified
Georgia	23:09:1996	ratified
Germany	08:04:1976	ratified
Greece	14:03:1986	ratified

Country	*Ratification date*	*Status*
Grenada	14:05:2003	ratified
Guatemala	27:04:1990	ratified
Guinea	06:06:2003	ratified
Guyana	15:04:1998	ratified
Honduras	09:06:1980	ratified
Hungary	28:05:1998	ratified
Iceland	06:12:1999	ratified
Indonesia	07:06:1999	ratified
Iraq	13:02:1985	ratified
Ireland	22:06:1978	ratified
Israel	21:06:1979	ratified
Italy	28:07:1981	ratified
Jamaica	13:10:2003	ratified
Japan	05:06:2000	ratified
Jordan	23:03:1998	ratified
Kazakhstan	18:05:2001	ratified
Kenya	09:04:1979	ratified
Republic of Korea	28:01:1999	ratified
Kuwait	15:11:1999	ratified
Kyrgyzstan	31:03:1992	ratified
Lao People's Democratic Republic	13:06:2005	ratified
Latvia	02:06:2006	ratified
Lebanon	10:06:2003	ratified
Lesotho	14:06:2001	ratified
Libyan Arab Jamahiriya	19:06:1975	ratified
Lithuania	22:06:1998	ratified
Luxembourg	24:03:1977	ratified
The former Yugoslav Republic of Macedonia	17:11:1991	ratified
Madagascar	31:05:2000	ratified
Malawi	19:11:1999	ratified
Malaysia	09:09:1997	ratified
Mali	11:03:2002	ratified
Malta	09:06:1988	ratified
Mauritania	03:12:2001	ratified
Mauritius	30:07:1990	ratified
Republic of Moldova	21:09:1999	ratified
Mongolia	16:12:2002	ratified
Morocco	06:01:2000	ratified

Country	*Ratification date*	*Status*
Mozambique	16:06:2003	ratified
Namibia	15:11:2000	ratified
Nepal	30:05:1997	ratified
Netherlands	14:09:1976	ratified
Nicaragua	02:11:1981	ratified
Niger	04:12:1978	ratified
Nigeria	02:10:2002	ratified
Norway	08:07:1980	ratified
Oman	21:07:2005	ratified
Pakistan	06:07:2006	ratified
Panama	31:10:2000	ratified
Papua New Guinea	02:06:2000	ratified
Paraguay	03:03:2004	ratified
Peru	13:11:2002	ratified
Philippines	04:06:1998	ratified
Poland	22:03:1978	ratified
Portugal	20:05:1998	ratified
Qatar	03:01:2006	ratified
Romania	19:11:1975	ratified
Russian Federation	03:05:1979	ratified
Rwanda	15:04:1981	ratified
Saint Kitts and Nevis	03:06:2005	ratified
Saint Vincent and the Grenadines	25:07:2006	ratified
San Marino	01:02:1995	ratified
Sao Tome and Principe	04:05:2005	ratified
Senegal	15:12:1999	ratified
Serbia	24:11:2000	ratified
Seychelles	07:03:2000	ratified
Singapore	07:11:2005	ratified
Slovakia	29:09:1997	ratified
Slovenia	29:05:1992	ratified
South Africa	30:03:2000	ratified
Spain	16:05:1977	ratified
Sri Lanka	11:02:2000	ratified
Sudan	07:03:2002	ratified
Swaziland	23:10:2002	ratified
Sweden	23:04:1990	ratified
Switzerland	17:08:1999	ratified

Country	*Ratification date*	*Status*
Syrian Arab Republic	18:09:2001	ratified
Tajikistan	26:11:1993	ratified
Tanzania United Republic of	16:12:1998	ratified
Thailand	11:05:2004	ratified
Togo	16:03:1984	ratified
Trinidad and Tobago	03:09:2004	ratified
Tunisia	19:10:1995	ratified
Turkey	30:10:1998	ratified
Uganda	25:03:2003	ratified
Ukraine	03:05:1979	ratified
United Arab Emirates	02:10:1998	ratified
United Kingdom	07:06:2000	ratified
Uruguay	02:06:1977	ratified
Bolivarian Republic of Venezuela	15:07:1987	ratified
Viet Nam	24:06:2003	ratified
Yemen	15:06:2000	ratified
Zambia	09:02:1976	ratified
Zimbabwe	06:06:2000	ratified

ILO DECLARATION ON FUNDAMENTAL PRINCIPLES AND RIGHTS AT WORK

The ILO Declaration on Fundamental Principles and Rights at Work aims to ensure that social progress goes hand in hand with economic progress and development.

The Declaration is a promotional instrument - and a reaffirmation by the ILO's government, employer and worker constituents of central beliefs set out in the organization's Constitution.

Adopted in 1998, the Declaration commits Member States to respect and promote principles and rights in four categories, whether or not they have ratified the relevant Conventions. These categories are: freedom of association and the effective recognition of the right to collective bargaining, the elimination of forced or compulsory labour, the abolition of child labour and the elimination of discrimination in respect of employment and occupation.

The Declaration makes it clear that these rights are universal, and that they apply to all people in all States - regardless of the level of economic development. It particularly mentions groups with special needs, including the unemployed and migrant workers. It recognizes that economic growth alone is not enough to ensure equity, social progress and to eradicate poverty.

This commitment is supported by a Follow-up procedure. Member States that have not ratified one or more of the core Conventions are asked each year to report on the status of the relevant rights and principles within their borders, noting impediments to ratification, and areas where assistance may be required. These reports are reviewed by the Committee of Independent Expert Advisers. In turn, their observations are considered by the ILO's Governing Body.

The Declaration and its Follow-up provides three ways to help countries, employers and workers achieve the full realisation of the Declaration¿s objective. Firstly, there is an Annual Review composed of reports from countries that have not yet ratified one or more of the ILO Conventions that directly relate to the specific principles and rights stated in the Declaration. This reporting process provides Governments with an opportunity to state what measures they have taken towards achieving respect for the Declaration. It also gives organizations of employers and workers a chance to voice their views on progress made and actions taken.

Next, the Global Report each year provides a dynamic global picture of the current situation of the principles and rights expressed in the Declaration. The Global Report is an objective view of the global and regional trends on the issues relevant to the Declaration and serves to highlight those areas that require greater attention. It serves as a basis for determining priorities for technical cooperation. Technical cooperation projects, the third way to give effect to the Declaration, are designed to address identifiable needs in relation to the Declaration and to strengthen local capacities thereby translating principles into practice.

The Declaration¿s principles and rights are gaining wider recognition among organizations, communities, and enterprises. These fundamental principles and rights provide benchmarks for responsible business conduct, and are incorporated into the ILO¿s own Tripartite Declaration of Principles concerning Multinational Enterprises and Social Policy. The OECD¿s Guidelines for Multinational Enterprises emphasize the principles and rights found in the ILO Declaration and the UN Global Compact promotes them as universal values to be achieved in business dealings around the world. A growing number of private sector codes of conduct and similar initiatives also refer to the fundamental principles and rights at work.

ILO DECLARATION ON FUNDAMENTAL PRINCIPLES AND RIGHTS AT WORK

86th Session, Geneva, June 1998

Whereas the ILO was founded in the conviction that social justice is essential to universal and lasting peace;

Whereas economic growth is essential but not sufficient to ensure equity, social progress and the eradication of poverty, confirming the need for the ILO to promote strong social policies, justice and democratic institutions;

Whereas the ILO should, now more than ever, draw upon all its standard-setting, technical cooperation and research resources in all its areas of competence, in particular employment, vocational training and working conditions, to ensure that, in the context of a global strategy for economic and social development, economic and social policies are mutually reinforcing components in order to create broad-based sustainable development;

Whereas the ILO should give special attention to the problems of persons with special social needs, particularly the unemployed and migrant workers, and mobilize and encourage international, regional and national efforts aimed at resolving their problems, and promote effective policies aimed at job creation;

Whereas, in seeking to maintain the link between social progress and economic growth, the guarantee of fundamental principles and rights at work is of particular significance in that it enables the persons concerned, to claim freely and on the basis of equality of opportunity, their fair share of the wealth which they have helped to generate, and to achieve fully their human potential;

Whereas the ILO is the constitutionally mandated international organization and the competent body to set and deal with international labour standards, and enjoys universal support and acknowledgement in promoting Fundamental Rights at Work as the expression of its constitutional principles;

Whereas it is urgent, in a situation of growing economic interdependence, to reaffirm the immutable nature of the fundamental principles and rights embodied in the Constitution of the Organization and to promote their universal application;

The International Labour Conference

1. Recalls:

(a) that in freely joining the ILO, all Members have endorsed the principles and rights set out in its Constitution and in the Declaration of Philadelphia, and have undertaken to work towards attaining the overall objectives of the Organization to the best of their resources and fully in line with their specific circumstances;

(b) that these principles and rights have been expressed and developed in the form of specific rights and obligations in Conventions recognized as fundamental both inside and outside the Organization.

2. Declares that all Members, even if they have not ratified the Conventions in question, have an obligation arising from the very fact of membership in the Organization to respect, to promote and to realize, in good faith and in accordance

with the Constitution, the principles concerning the fundamental rights which are the subject of those Conventions, namely:

(a) freedom of association and the effective recognition of the right to collective bargaining;

(b) the elimination of all forms of forced or compulsory labour;

(c) the effective abolition of child labour; and

(d) the elimination of discrimination in respect of employment and occupation.

3. Recognizes the obligation on the Organization to assist its Members, in response to their established and expressed needs, in order to attain these objectives by making full use of its constitutional, operational and budgetary resources, including, by the mobilization of external resources and support, as well as by encouraging other international organizations with which the ILO has established relations, pursuant to article 12 of its Constitution, to support these efforts:

(a) by offering technical cooperation and advisory services to promote the ratification and implementation of the fundamental Conventions;

(b) by assisting those Members not yet in a position to ratify some or all of these Conventions in their efforts to respect, to promote and to realize the principles concerning fundamental rights which are the subject of these Conventions; and

(c) by helping the Members in their efforts to create a climate for economic and social development.

4. Decides that, to give full effect to this Declaration, a promotional follow-up, which is meaningful and effective, shall be implemented in accordance with the measures specified in the annex hereto, which shall be considered as an integral part of this Declaration.

5. Stresses that labour standards should not be used for protectionist trade purposes, and that nothing in this Declaration and its follow-up shall be invoked or otherwise used for such purposes; in addition, the comparative advantage of any country should in no way be called into question by this Declaration and its follow-up.

FOLLOW-UP TO THE DECLARATION

I. Overall Purpose

1. The aim of the follow-up described below is to encourage the efforts made by the Members of the Organization to promote the fundamental principles and rights enshrined in the Constitution of the ILO and the Declaration of Philadelphia and reaffirmed in this Declaration.

2. In line with this objective, which is of a strictly promotional nature, this follow-up will allow the identification of areas in which the assistance of the Organization through its technical cooperation activities may prove useful to its Members to help them implement these fundamental principles and rights. It is not a substitute for the established supervisory mechanisms, nor shall it impede their functioning; consequently, specific situations within the purview of those mechanisms shall not be examined or re-examined within the framework of this follow-up.

3. The two aspects of this follow-up, described below, are based on existing procedures: the annual follow-up concerning non-ratified fundamental Conventions will entail merely some adaptation of the present modalities of application of article 19, paragraph 5(e), of the Constitution; and the Global Report will serve to obtain the best results from the procedures carried out pursuant to the Constitution.

II. Annual Follow-Up Concerning Non-Ratified Fundamental Conventions

A. Purpose and Scope

1. The purpose is to provide an opportunity to review each year, by means of simplified procedures to replace the four-year review introduced by the Governing Body in 1995, the efforts made in accordance with the Declaration by Members which have not yet ratified all the fundamental Conventions.

2. The follow-up will cover each year the four areas of fundamental principles and rights specified in the Declaration.

B. Modalities

1. The follow-up will be based on reports requested from Members under article 19, paragraph 5(e), of the Constitution. The report forms will be drawn up so as to obtain information from governments which have not ratified one or more of the fundamental Conventions, on any changes which may have taken place in their law and practice, taking due account of article 23 of the Constitution and established practice.

2. These reports, as compiled by the Office, will be reviewed by the Governing Body.

3. With a view to presenting an introduction to the reports thus compiled, drawing attention to any aspects which might call for a more in-depth discussion, the Office may call upon a group of experts appointed for this purpose by the Governing Body.

4. Adjustments to the Governing Body's existing procedures should be examined to allow Members which are not represented on the Governing Body to provide, in the most appropriate way, clarifications which might prove necessary

or useful during Governing Body discussions to supplement the information contained in their reports.

III. Global Report

A. Purpose and Scope

1. The purpose of this report is to provide a dynamic global picture relating to each category of fundamental principles and rights noted during the preceding four-year period, and to serve as a basis for assessing the effectiveness of the assistance provided by the Organization, and for determining priorities for the following period, in the form of action plans for technical cooperation designed in particular to mobilize the internal and external resources necessary to carry them out.

2. The report will cover, each year, one of the four categories of fundamental principles and rights in turn.

B. Modalitie

1. The report will be drawn up under the responsibility of the Director-General on the basis of official information, or information gathered and assessed in accordance with established procedures. In the case of States which have not ratified the fundamental Conventions, it will be based in particular on the findings of the aforementioned annual follow-up. In the case of Members which have ratified the Conventions concerned, the report will be based in particular on reports as dealt with pursuant to article 22 of the Constitution.

2. This report will be submitted to the Conference for tripartite discussion as a report of the Director-General. The Conference may deal with this report separately from reports under article 12 of its Standing Orders, and may discuss it during a sitting devoted entirely to this report, or in any other appropriate way. It will then be for the Governing Body, at an early session, to draw conclusions from this discussion concerning the priorities and plans of action for technical cooperation to be implemented for the following four-year period.

IV. It is Understood That

1. Proposals shall be made for amendments to the Standing Orders of the Governing Body and the Conference which are required to implement the preceding provisions.

2. The Conference shall, in due course, review the operation of this follow-up in the light of the experience acquired to assess whether it has adequately fulfilled the overall purpose articulated in Part I.

- The foregoing is the ILO Declaration on Fundamental Principles and Rights at Work and its Follow-up duly adopted by the General Conference of the International Labour Organization during its Eighty-sixth Session which was held at Geneva and declared closed the 18 June 1998. In faith whereof we have appended our signatures this nineteenth day of June 1998.

WORST FORMS OF CHILD LABOUR CONVENTION, 1999

Date of Adoption:17:06:1999

The General Conference of the International Labour Organization

- Having been convened at Geneva by the Governing Body of the International Labour Office, and having met in its 87th Session on 1 June 1999.
- Considering the need to adopt new instruments for the prohibition and elimination of the worst forms of child labour, as the main priority for national and international action, including international cooperation and assistance, to complement the Convention and the Recommendation concerning Minimum Age for Admission to Employment, 1973, which remain fundamental instruments on child labour.
- Considering that the effective elimination of the worst forms of child labour requires immediate and comprehensive action, taking into account the importance of free basic education and the need to remove the children concerned from all such work and to provide for their rehabilitation and social integration while addressing the needs of their families.
- Recalling the resolution concerning the elimination of child labour adopted by the International Labour Conference at its 83rd Session in 1996.
- Recognizing that child labour is to a great extent caused by poverty and that the long-term solution lies in sustained economic growth leading to social progress, in particular poverty alleviation and universal education.
- Recalling the Convention on the Rights of the Child adopted by the United Nations General Assembly on 20 November 1989.
- Recalling the ILO Declaration on Fundamental Principles and Rights at Work and its Follow-up, adopted by the International Labour Conference at its 86th Session in 1998.
- Recalling that some of the worst forms of child labour are covered by other international instruments, in particular the Forced Labour Convention, 1930, and the United Nations Supplementary Convention on the Abolition of Slavery, the Slave Trade, and Institutions and Practices Similar to Slavery, 1956.
- Having decided upon the adoption of certain proposals with regard to child labour, which is the fourth item on the agenda of the session.

- Having determined that these proposals shall take the form of an international Convention.

adopts this seventeenth day of June of the year one thousand nine hundred and ninety-nine the following Convention, which may be cited as the Worst Forms of Child Labour Convention.

Article 1

Each Member which ratifies this Convention shall take immediate and effective measures to secure the prohibition and elimination of the worst forms of child labour as a matter of urgency.

Article 2

For the purposes of this Convention, the term *child* shall apply to all persons under the age of 18.

Article 3

For the purposes of this Convention, the term *the worst forms of child labour* comprises:

(a) all forms of slavery or practices similar to slavery, such as the sale and trafficking of children, debt bondage and serfdom and forced or compulsory labour, including forced or compulsory recruitment of children for use in armed conflict;

(b) the use, procuring or offering of a child for prostitution, for the production of pornography or for pornographic performances;

(c) the use, procuring or offering of a child for illicit activities, in particular for the production and trafficking of drugs as defined in the relevant international treaties;

(d) work which, by its nature or the circumstances in which it is carried out, is likely to harm the health, safety or morals of children.

Article 4

1. The types of work referred to under Article 3(d) shall be determined by national laws or regulations or by the competent authority, after consultation with the organizations of employers and workers concerned, taking into consideration relevant international standards, in particular Paragraphs 3 and 4 of the Worst Forms of Child Labour Recommendation, 1999.

2. The competent authority, after consultation with the organizations of employers and workers concerned, shall identify where the types of work so determined exist.

3. The list of the types of work determined under paragraph 1 of this Article shall be periodically examined and revised as necessary, in consultation with the organizations of employers and workers concerned.

Article 5

Each Member shall, after consultation with employers' and workers' organizations, establish or designate appropriate mechanisms to monitor the implementation of the provisions giving effect to this Convention.

Article 6

1. Each Member shall design and implement programmes of action to eliminate as a priority the worst forms of child labour.

2. Such programmes of action shall be designed and implemented in consultation with relevant government institutions and employers' and workers' organizations, taking into consideration the views of other concerned groups as appropriate.

Article 7

1. Each Member shall take all necessary measures to ensure the effective implementation and enforcement of the provisions giving effect to this Convention including the provision and application of penal sanctions or, as appropriate, other sanctions.

2. Each Member shall, taking into account the importance of education in eliminating child labour, take effective and time-bound measures to:

(a) prevent the engagement of children in the worst forms of child labour;

(b) provide the necessary and appropriate direct assistance for the removal of children from the worst forms of child labour and for their rehabilitation and social integration;

(c) ensure access to free basic education, and, wherever possible and appropriate, vocational training, for all children removed from the worst forms of child labour;

(d) identify and reach out to children at special risk; and

(e) take account of the special situation of girls.

3. Each Member shall designate the competent authority responsible for the implementation of the provisions giving effect to this Convention.

Article 8

Members shall take appropriate steps to assist one another in giving effect to the provisions of this Convention through enhanced international cooperation and/or assistance including support for social and economic development, poverty eradication programmes and universal education.

Article 9

The formal ratifications of this Convention shall be communicated to the Director-General of the International Labour Office for registration.

Article 10

1. This Convention shall be binding only upon those Members of the International Labour Organization whose ratifications have been registered with the Director-General of the International Labour Office.

2. It shall come into force 12 months after the date on which the ratifications of two Members have been registered with the Director-General.

3. Thereafter, this Convention shall come into force for any Member 12 months after the date on which its ratification has been registered.

Article 11

1. A Member which has ratified this Convention may denounce it after the expiration of ten years from the date on which the Convention first comes into force, by an act communicated to the Director-General of the International Labour Office for registration. Such denunciation shall not take effect until one year after the date on which it is registered.

2. Each Member which has ratified this Convention and which does not, within the year following the expiration of the period of ten years mentioned in the preceding paragraph, exercise the right of denunciation provided for in this Article, will be bound for another period of ten years and, thereafter, may denounce this Convention at the expiration of each period of ten years under the terms provided for in this Article.

Article 12

1. The Director-General of the International Labour Office shall notify all Members of the International Labour Organization of the registration of all ratifications and acts of denunciation communicated by the Members of the Organization.

2. When notifying the Members of the Organization of the registration of the second ratification, the Director-General shall draw the attention of the Members of the Organization to the date upon which the Convention shall come into force.

Article 13

The Director-General of the International Labour Office shall communicate to the Secretary-General of the United Nations, for registration in accordance with article 102 of the Charter of the United Nations, full particulars of all ratifications and acts of denunciation registered by the Director-General in accordance with the provisions of the preceding Articles.

Article 14

At such times as it may consider necessary, the Governing Body of the International Labour Office shall present to the General Conference a report on the working of this Convention and shall examine the desirability of placing on the agenda of the Conference the question of its revision in whole or in part.

Article 15

1. Should the Conference adopt a new Convention revising this Convention in whole or in part, then, unless the new Convention otherwise provides —

(a) the ratification by a Member of the new revising Convention shall ipso jure involve the immediate denunciation of this Convention, notwithstanding the provisions of Article 11 above, if and when the new revising Convention shall have come into force;

(b) as from the date when the new revising Convention comes into force, this Convention shall cease to be open to ratification by the Members.

2. This Convention shall in any case remain in force in its actual form and content for those Members which have ratified it but have not ratified the revising Convention.

Article 16

The English and French versions of the text of this Convention are equally authoritative.

THE CONVENTION ON THE WORST FORMS OF CHILD LABOUR

ILO Convention No. 182, against the Worst Forms of Child Labour, comes into force on 19 November 2000. The Convention comes into force on this day because, under the Convention's rules, this is exactly 12 months after the date on which the ILO officially registered the second ratification of the C. 182. The first ratification of the Convention was by the Seychelles on 28 September 1999. The second ratification was by Malawi on 19 November 1999.

For each of the other countries whose ratification of the Convention has been registered, it comes into force 12 months after the date of registration of the ratification. For example, the USA's ratification of C.182 occurred on 2 December 1999. Therefore the Convention comes into force for the USA on 2 December 2000.

The ILO registers a ratification of C.182 only after receiving a formal "instrument of ratification", which is a document signed by a head-of-state. The registration of ratification can sometimes be much later than the day when a country officially decides to ratify.

For Countries Which have Ratified...

- When the new child labour Convention is ratified and in force for a country, the country should do as its provisions say, in both law and practice. For example, C.182 declares that, "Each Member which ratifies this Convention shall take immediate and effective measures to secure the prohibition and elimination of the worst forms of child labour as a matter of urgency." The necessary actions range from a reform of laws and their enforcement, to practical and direct help to children and their families.

- In addition, the government is obliged to report regularly to the ILO how the new Convention is applied. For C.182, a ratified country must report every two years. This provides a basis for regular supervision. This report has to be copied to employers' and workers' organizations and they can make comments on it.
- The government, which has ratified also, has to be accountable for any allegation of non-observance raised by procedures, called "representation", or "complaints" under the ILO Constitution. These can be initiated by employers, workers or another country that has ratified the Convention.

For Countries Which have Not Yet Tatified...

- For the fundamental ILO Conventions, countries that have not yet ratified them are asked to send Annual Reports on their law and practice to the ILO, within the framework of follow-up to the ILO Declaration on Fundamental Principles and Rights at Work. The new child labour Convention is a fundamental ILO Convention, and starting with the 2001 reporting cycle, there will be an ILO Global Report on child labour to be discussed at the International Labour Conference in 2002.
- It is also possible for the Governing Body to ask for reports on unratified Conventions to have a general survey made.

WORST FORMS OF CHILD LABOUR RECOMMENDATION, 1999

Date of Adoption:17:06:1999

The General Conference of the International Labour Organization,

Having been convened at Geneva by the Governing Body of the International Labour Office, and having met in its Eighty-seventh Session on 1 June 1999, and

Having adopted the Worst Forms of Child Labour Convention, 1999, and

Having decided upon the adoption of certain proposals with regard to child labour, which is the fourth item on the agenda of the session, and

Having determined that these proposals shall take the form of a Recommendation supplementing the Worst Forms of Child Labour Convention, 1999;

adopts this seventeenth day of June of the year one thousand nine hundred and ninety-nine the following Recommendation, which may be cited as the Worst Forms of Child Labour Recommendation, 1999.

1. The provisions of this Recommendation supplement those of the Worst Forms of Child Labour Convention, 1999 (hereafter referred to as "the Convention"), and should be applied in conjunction with them.

I. Programmes of action

2. The programmes of action referred to in Article 6 of the Convention should be designed and implemented as a matter of urgency, in consultation with relevant government institutions and employers' and workers' organizations, taking into consideration the views of the children directly affected by the worst forms of child labour, their families and, as appropriate, other concerned groups committed to the aims of the Convention and this Recommendation. Such programmes should aim at, inter alia:

(a) identifying and denouncing the worst forms of child labour;

(b) preventing the engagement of children in or removing them from the worst forms of child labour, protecting them from reprisals and providing for their rehabilitation and social integration through measures which address their educational, physical and psychological needs;

(c) giving special attention to:

  (i) younger children;

  (ii) the girl child;

  (iii) the problem of hidden work situations, in which girls are at special risk;

  (iv) other groups of children with special vulnerabilities or needs;

(d) identifying, reaching out to and working with communities where children are at special risk;

(e) informing, sensitizing and mobilizing public opinion and concerned groups, including children and their families.

II. Hazardous Work

3. In determining the types of work referred to under Article 3(d) of the Convention, and in identifying where they exist, consideration should be given, inter alia, to:

(a) work which exposes children to physical, psychological or sexual abuse;

(b) work underground, under water, at dangerous heights or in confined spaces;

(c) work with dangerous machinery, equipment and tools, or which involves the manual handling or transport of heavy loads;

(d) work in an unhealthy environment which may, for example, expose children to hazardous substances, agents or processes, or to temperatures, noise levels, or vibrations damaging to their health;

(e) work under particularly difficult conditions such as work for long hours or during the night or work where the child is unreasonably confined to the premises of the employer.

4. For the types of work referred to under Article 3(d) of the Convention and Paragraph 3 above, national laws or regulations or the competent authority could, after consultation with the workers' and employers' organizations concerned, authorize employment or work as from the age of 16 on condition that the health, safety and morals of the children concerned are fully protected, and that the children have received adequate specific instruction or vocational training in the relevant branch of activity.

III. Implementation

5. (1) Detailed information and statistical data on the nature and extent of child labour should be compiled and kept up to date to serve as a basis for determining priorities for national action for the abolition of child labour, in particular for the prohibition and elimination of its worst forms as a matter of urgency.

(2) As far as possible, such information and statistical data should include data disaggregated by sex, age group, occupation, branch of economic activity, status in employment, school attendance and geographical location. The importance of an effective system of birth registration, including the issuing of birth certificates, should be taken into account.

(3) Relevant data concerning violations of national provisions for the prohibition and elimination of the worst forms of child labour should be compiled and kept up to date.

6. The compilation and processing of the information and data referred to in Paragraph 5 above should be carried out with due regard for the right to privacy.

7. The information compiled under Paragraph 5 above should be communicated to the International Labour Office on a regular basis.

8. Members should establish or designate appropriate national mechanisms to monitor the implementation of national provisions for the prohibition and elimination of the worst forms of child labour, after consultation with employers' and workers' organizations.

9. Members should ensure that the competent authorities which have responsibilities for implementing national provisions for the prohibition and elimination of the worst forms of child labour cooperate with each other and coordinate their activities.

10. National laws or regulations or the competent authority should determine the persons to be held responsible in the event of non-compliance with national provisions for the prohibition and elimination of the worst forms of child labour.

11. Members should, in so far as it is compatible with national law, cooperate with international efforts aimed at the prohibition and elimination of the worst forms of child labour as a matter of urgency by:

(a) gathering and exchanging information concerning criminal offences, including those involving international networks;

(b) detecting and prosecuting those involved in the sale and trafficking of children, or in the use, procuring or offering of children for illicit activities, for prostitution, for the production of pornography or for pornographic performances;

(c) registering perpetrators of such offences.

12. Members should provide that the following worst forms of child labour are criminal offences:

(a) all forms of slavery or practices similar to slavery, such as the sale and trafficking of children, debt bondage and serfdom and forced or compulsory labour, including forced or compulsory recruitment of children for use in armed conflict;

(b) the use, procuring or offering of a child for prostitution, for the production of pornography or for pornographic performances; and

(c) the use, procuring or offering of a child for illicit activities, in particular for the production and trafficking of drugs as defined in the relevant international treaties, or for activities which involve the unlawful carrying or use of firearms or other weapons.

13. Members should ensure that penalties including, where appropriate, criminal penalties are applied for violations of the national provisions for the prohibition and elimination of any type of work referred to in Article 3(d) of the Convention.

14. Members should also provide as a matter of urgency for other criminal, civil or administrative remedies, where appropriate, to ensure the effective enforcement of national provisions for the prohibition and elimination of the worst forms of child labour, such as special supervision of enterprises which have used the worst forms of child labour, and, in cases of persistent violation, consideration of temporary or permanent revoking of permits to operate.

15. Other measures aimed at the prohibition and elimination of the worst forms of child labour might include the following:

(a) informing, sensitizing and mobilizing the general public, including national and local political leaders, parliamentarians and the judiciary;

(b) involving and training employers' and workers' organizations and civic organizations;

(c) providing appropriate training for the government officials concerned, especially inspectors and law enforcement officials, and for other relevant professionals;

(d) providing for the prosecution in their own country of the Member's nationals who commit offences under its national provisions for the prohibition and immediate elimination of the worst forms of child labour even when these offences are committed in another country;

(e) simplifying legal and administrative procedures and ensuring that they are appropriate and prompt;

(f) encouraging the development of policies by undertakings to promote the aims of the Convention;

(g) monitoring and giving publicity to best practices on the elimination of child labour;

(h) giving publicity to legal or other provisions on child labour in the different languages or dialects;

(i) establishing special complaints procedures and making provisions to protect from discrimination and reprisals those who legitimately expose violations of the provisions of the Convention, as well as establishing helplines or points of contact and ombudspersons;

(j) adopting appropriate measures to improve the educational infrastructure and the training of teachers to meet the needs of boys and girls;

(k) as far as possible, taking into account in national programmes of action:

   (i) the need for job creation and vocational training for the parents and adults in the families of children working in the conditions covered by the Convention; and

   (ii) the need for sensitizing parents to the problem of children working in such conditions.

16. Enhanced international cooperation and/or assistance among Members for the prohibition and effective elimination of the worst forms of child labour should complement national efforts and may, as appropriate, be developed and implemented in consultation with employers' and workers' organizations. Such international cooperation and/or assistance should include:

(a) mobilizing resources for national or international programmes;

(b) mutual legal assistance;

(c) technical assistance including the exchange of information;

(d) support for social and economic development, poverty eradication programmes and universal education.

Supplemented: C182 Complementary to the Worst Forms of Child Labour Convention, 1999.

WORKERS CONSULTATION ON CHILD DOMESTIC LABOUR

ILO Geneva, 1-3 February 2006

Final Statement

- Work in the domestic sector, and child domestic labour in particular, is an area where all the fundamental rights in the ILO Declaration are under threat. It is a large challenge confronting trade unions in all parts of the world.
- Child domestic labour, to be eliminated under ILO Conventions Nos. 138 and 182, is domestic work undertaken by children under the legal minimum working age, as well as by children above the legal minimum age but under the age of 18 under slavery-like, hazardous or other exploitative conditions, including child domestic labour that is a result of trafficking.
- Trade unions have a vital role to play in the elimination of child domestic labour; in particular by organizing domestic workers, who are key actors in this struggle.
- All domestic workers must have the right to organize and should have the right to be affiliated to trade unions, as long as they are above the minimum legal age for admission to work. Adolescent domestic workers should be encouraged to join trade unions in the framework of a trade union policy that is inclusive of young workers.
- Child domestic labour is also, in many cases, the consequence of the migration from the rural areas to the cities. Trade unions that work in these areas, including agricultural workers' unions, have a special role to play. This includes promoting public policies that promote equal opportunities in education and health for rural children.
- Education is crucial in elimination of CDL and teachers and their organizations are vital strategic partners.
- At the national, regional and international level, trade unions should lobby for legislation that prohibits children's work in the domestic sector below the national minimum age, and extends protection to working children above that minimum age.
- The ILO can support the trade union movement in their struggle against CDL with programs and projects aimed at strengthening the

institutional capacity of the trade union movement. including their capacity to participate meaningfully in discussion regarding poverty reduction policies.

I

ILO DIRECTOR-GENERAL'S MESSAGE

Juan Somavia - 4 May 2006

Launch of the Global Report on Child Labour

Thank you for coming together as the ILO launches a major new global report on child labour.

We have some encouraging news to share. Despite the difficulty of the struggle, we are beginning to see signs of a reduction in child labour - especially its hazardous forms - in many parts of the world.

Our report indicates that the number of child labourers globally has fallen by I I per cent over the last four years. That's 28 million fewer children at work. And the sharpest decline is in the area of hazardous work by children where we have seen a 26 percent reduction.

Far more than a compilation of statistics, this report is a story of dignity and hope. It tells us that more girls and boys around the world are on the path from workrooms to classrooms: out of exploitation toward real opportunity.

That is the rightful path for every child. But paving it hasn't been easy. There has been denial, doubting and indifference along the way. Many claimed progress was not possible. Child labour, they said, is just a fact of life. Well, it is not. And, a growing community of conscience has pressed on.

Courageous women and men spurring grassroots movements for action. Committed communities joining hands to say child labour has no place where we live. Visionary leaders who have committed the resources to make things happen. Consumers rejecting products made by the hands of children. Employer and worker organizations contributing their voices and full support.

Children and youth in schools mobilizing in solidarity and becoming one of the biggest social forces of all to expose and end child labour. Together, they represent the emergence of a genuine worldwide movement against child labour.

And they are the real heroes. Their efforts have been coupled with increased political will.

The ILO Convention on the worst forms of child labour has seen the most ratifications in the shortest time for any Convention in ILO history — 159 ratifications in seven short years. And at last year's UN World Summit, global leaders endorsed the elimination of child labour as a major element in achieving the Millennium Development Goals. It is a sound investment. Research indicates that the benefits of eliminating child labour exceed the costs by six to one.Now is not the time to relent. It is the time to redouble our efforts. It is the time to take our work to the next level. That is why our report sets out the goal of eliminating the worst forms of child labour in the next ten years. It can be done. In fact, more than 30 countries have already set similar or even earlier target dates.

Decent work for parents. Quality education for children. Real opportunity for young people. Dignity for all. Getting there is difficult and complex. But this report signals hope. In this 21 century, no child should be brutalized by exploitation or be placed in hazardous work. No child should be denied access to education. No child should have to work for his or her survival.

We all have a responsibility to build that future. And we are on the right track. Let's keep up the momentum. Let's resolve to keep investing in the struggle for the right of every child to their childhood.

I invite you to take an active part in this struggle. We must overcome obstacles with persistence and conviction.

II

STANDARDIZATION OF AGE GROUPS

Age groupings in the raw data from national surveys may differ from the standard age groups adopted for the present study in any one of three situations:

- where the available data is grouped in a broader category than prescribed, e.g. where the national data is for those aged 15-19 years, while the required age group is 15-17 years;
- where the available data is grouped in a narrower category than prescribed, e.g. where the national data is for those aged 6-9 years, with no information regarding 5-year-olds; and
- where no national data exists for the required age groups, e.g. where no data is available for the 15- to 17-year age category.

The age groups may be standardized with the help of a model for the percentage of children at work as a function of age.

Method

Our model assumes that the percentage of children at work is a linear function of the age of the children, and that the distribution of children with respect to their ages is uniform within a group. For each problematic situation, one model is fitted on the basis of the two nearest available age groups.

Let us define s and c as the slope and constant of the linear function f of the percentage y as a function of age x. We have y = x*s+c. Regardless of the slope, the percentage of working children in a group age with interval a-b will be equal to the percentage of working children for its mean age m = (a+b+1)/2. Given the percentages y1 and y2 and midpoints m1 and m2 of the nearest available age groups, the slope and constant can be estimated with s = (y2-y1)/(m2-m1) and c = y1–m1*s.

Finally, the percentage of working children for the age group of interest with midpoint m is simply computed with m*s+c.

The method is not limited to the percentage of working children. It can be applied also to the percentages of children studying, combining both work and study or doing neither.

Application

In the present study, the age group 5-9 years is too narrow for Yemen. The available age group is limited to the 6- to 9-year-olds. In this case, the available age groups 6-9 and 10-14 years were used to estimate the ratio for the 5- to 9-year age group.

TABLE 1

Estimated Ratio for the Age Group 5-9 Years for Yemen

		Available age groups		*Estimated a.g.*
Country	*Sex*	*6-9*	*10-14*	*5-9*
Yemen	boys	0.190	0.394	0.164
Yemen	girls	0.130	0.308	0.114

Note: The estimated ratio for the age group 5-9 is computed from the available ratios for age groups 6-9 and 10-14 years.

Another problem is the missing age group 15-17 years for Azerbaijan, Kenya, Senegal, and Yemen. For these countries, the age groups 5-9 and 10-14 are used to estimate the ratio for the age group 15-17 years.

TABLE 2

Estimated ratio for the age group 15-17 years

		Available age groups		*Estimated a.g.*
Country	*Sex*	*5-9*	*10-14*	*15-17*
Azerbaijan	boys	0.065	0.144	0.207
Azerbaijan	girls	0.043	0.082	0.114
Kenya	boys	0.234	0.464	0.648

		Available age groups		*Estimated a.g.*
Country	*Sex*	*5-9*	*10-14*	*15-17*
Kenya	girls	0.195	0.416	0.592
Senegal	boys	0.321	0.474	0.596
Senegal	girls	0.228	0.294	0.346
Yemen	boys	0.164	0.394	0.578
Yemen	girls	0.114	0.308	0.462

Note: The estimated ratio for the age group 15-17 years is computed from the available ratios for age groups 5-9 and 10-14 years.

Our study requires input from 17 countries for 3 age categories and both sexes. That amounts to a total of 102 ratios. This method was used to complete or adapt 10 of these values, just shy of 10 per cent.

Validation

The method is validated with the use of extra information. An approximation of the ratio of children at work is available on the age group 12-14 years. The same ratio is estimated with the help of the method. The average absolute difference between the two is 8.2 per cent, with a standard deviation of 7.2 and a median of 5.0.

We find the result satisfactory. It is at least much better than carrying the closest observed value (the ratio of age group 10-14 years).

TABLE 3

Comparison of Ratio of Children at Work Aged 12-14 Years Estimated by the Model with an Approximation Measured from Extra Information

		Available ratios		*12-14 age group*		
Country	X	*X-9 yrs.*	*10-14 yrs.*	*Estimated*	*Measured*	*Difference*
Albania	7	0.277	0.491	0.545	0.547	-0.4%
Azerbaijan	5	0.065	0.144	0.160	0.162	-1.2%
Bolivia	5	0.171	0.350	0.386	0.371	4.0%
Bosnia and H.	5	0.112	0.269	0.301	0.306	-1.6%
Madagascar	6	0.201	0.305	0.328	0.326	0.6%
Moldova	5	0.195	0.393	0.433	0.446	-2.9%
Mongolia	5	0.200	0.249	0.258	0.249	3.6%
Senegal	5	0.321	0.474	0.505	0.481	5.0%
Uzbekistan	6	0.115	0.267	0.301	0.291	3.4%
Yemen	6	0.187	0.394	0.440	0.458	-3.9%

		Available ratios		12-14 age group		
Country	X	X-9 yrs.	10-14 yrs.	Estimated	Measured	Difference
Congo	5	0.001	0.405	0.485	0.447	8.5%
Turkey	5	0.007	0.081	0.096	0.122	-21.3%
Cameroon	5	0.000	0.106	0.127	0.164	-22.6%
Brazil	5	0.017	0.138	0.162	0.172	-5.8%
India	5	0.005	0.079	0.094	0.111	-15.3%
Belize	5	0.026	0.123	0.142	0.164	-13.4%
Costa Rica	5	0.014	0.089	0.104	0.127	-18.1%
El Salvador	5	0.025	0.179	0.210	0.234	-10.3%
Guatemala	5	0.068	0.365	0.424	0.446	-4.9%
Malawi	5	0.153	0.366	0.409	0.495	-17.4%
Philippines	5	0.029	0.234	0.275	0.277	-0.7%
Bangladesh	5	0.019	0.358	0.425	0.516	-17.6%
Cambodia	5	0.259	0.654	0.733	0.695	5.5%

Note: The method estimates the ratio for the 12- to 14-year age group using the ratios for the age group of 9- year-olds and younger and the ratio for the 10- to 14-year age group. The difference is computed with (estimatedmeasured)/ measured. E.g., for Bolivia, the ratios of children at work for age groups 5-9 and 10-14 years are 0.171 and 0.350, respectively. From these values, the method estimates the ratio for the age group 12-14 years to be 0.386. From the extra information, we have measured a ratio of 0.371. The difference between these values is computed with (0.386 – 0.371)/0.371 = 4%.

III

REPORT IV (2A) CHILD LABOUR

Fourth Item on the Agenda: International Labour Office Geneva

Introduction

The first discussion of the question of child labour took place at the 86th Session (1998) of the International Labour Conference. Following that discussion, and in accordance with article 39 of the Standing Orders of the Conference, the International Labour Office prepared and communicated to the governments of member States a report containing a proposed Convention and a proposed Recommendation concerning the prohibition and immediate elimination of the worst forms of child labour, based on the conclusions adopted by the Conference at its 86th Session.

Governments were invited to send any amendments or comments they might wish to make so as to reach the Office by 30 November 1998 at the latest, or to inform it, by the same date, whether they considered that the proposed texts constituted a satisfactory basis for discussion by the Conference at its 87th Session (1999).

At the time of drawing up this report, the Office had received replies from the governments of the following 83 member States: Argentina, Australia, Austria, Bahrain, Bangladesh, Belarus, Belgium, Benin, Bolivia, Botswana, Brazil, Bulgaria, Canada, Cape Verde, Chile, China, Colombia, Croatia, Cyprus, Czech Republic, Denmark, Ecuador, Egypt, El Salvador, Estonia, Ethiopia, Finland, France, Germany, Greece, Haiti, Hungary, India, Indonesia, Ireland, Italy, Japan, Jordan, Kenya, Republic of Korea, Kuwait, Latvia, Lebanon, Madagascar, Malaysia, Mali, Mauritius, Mexico, Morocco, Myanmar, Netherlands, New Zealand, Norway, Pakistan, Peru, Poland, Portugal, Qatar, Romania, Saudi Arabia, Senegal, Slovakia, South Africa, Spain, Sri Lanka, Sudan, Sweden, Switzerland, Syrian Arab Republic, United Republic of Tanzania, Thailand, Togo, Tunisia, Turkey, Uganda, Ukraine, United Arab Emirates, United Kingdom, United States, Venezuela, Yemen, Zambia, Zimbabwe, as well as from the Holy See.

In accordance with article 39, paragraph 6, of the Standing Orders of the Conference, governments were requested to consult the most representative organizations of employers and workers before finalizing their replies and to indicate which organizations were consulted.

The governments of the following 49 member States stated that the most representative organizations of employers and workers had been consulted: Bangladesh, Belarus, Belgium, Benin, Brazil, Bulgaria, Canada, Chile, China, Croatia, Cyprus, Czech Republic, Denmark, Egypt, El Salvador, Estonia, Finland, France, Germany, Greece, Hungary, Indonesia, Ireland, Italy, Japan, Jordan, Kenya, Republic of Korea, Latvia, Mauritius, Myanmar, Netherlands, New Zealand, Norway, Portugal, Slovakia, South Africa, Spain, Sweden, Switzerland, Syrian Arab Republic, United Republic of Tanzania, Togo, Turkey, United Arab Emirates, United Kingdom, United States, Venezuela, Zimbabwe.

In the case of the following 37 member States the replies of employers' and workers' organizations were incorporated into those of the government, were appended or were communicated directly to the Office: Bangladesh, Belarus, Belgium, Brazil, Bulgaria, Canada, Chile, Croatia, Czech Republic, Denmark, Egypt, Estonia, Finland, France, Germany, Greece, Hungary, Indonesia, Ireland, Italy, Japan, Jordan, Kenya, Republic of Korea, Netherlands, New Zealand, Norway, Portugal, South Africa, Spain, Sweden, Switzerland, Syrian Arab Republic, Turkey, United States, Venezuela, Zimbabwe.

The United Nations Committee on the Rights of the Child formulated comments during its 20th Session. These are summarized below.

To ensure that the English and French texts of the proposed Convention and proposed Recommendation concerning the prohibition and immediate elimination of the worst forms of child labour are in the hands of the governments within the time-limit laid down in article 39, paragraph 7, of the Standing Orders of the Conference, these texts have already been published in a separate volume, Report IV (2B), that has been sent to them. The present volume, Report IV (2A), which has been drawn up on the basis of the replies from governments and from employers' and workers' organizations, contains the essential points of their observations. It is divided into three sections: the first comprises their general observations on the proposed texts, while the second and third sections contain their observations on the proposed Convention and proposed Recommendation, with the Office commentaries on these observations.

Replies Received and Commentaries

The substance of the replies received on the proposed Convention and the proposed Recommendation concerning child labour is given below. The replies are followed, where appropriate, by brief Office commentaries.

The governments of the following 35 member States stated that they had no observations to put forward at the moment or that they considered that the proposed texts constituted a satisfactory basis for discussion at the 87th Session of the International Labour Conference: Belarus, Belgium, Bulgaria, Cape Verde, China, Colombia, Cyprus, Finland, France, Hungary, Ireland, Kenya, Kuwait, Latvia, Lebanon, Mali, Myanmar, Netherlands, New Zealand, Peru, Poland, Qatar, Romania, Saudi Arabia, Slovakia, Switzerland, United Republic of Tanzania, Thailand, Togo, Ukraine, United Arab Emirates, United Kingdom, United States, Yemen, Zambia. Some of the countries which considered the texts a satisfactory basis for discussion also commented on the texts and replied to the questions raised in the Office commentary in Report IV (1).

GENERAL OBSERVATIONS

Australia

The Government supports the adoption of a Convention, supplemented by a Recommendation, concerning the prohibition and elimination of the worst forms of child labour. It is important that distinct attention be given to the most extreme and serious part of this problem and the proposed Convention and Recommendation should provide a focal point for achieving this. The new Convention should be flexible and not overly prescriptive to ensure that there are no obstacles to ratification among ILO member States. The Convention should also be concisely stated, principles-based, and clearly focused on extreme forms of child labour. The Government also supports a Recommendation that would provide guidance for member States on the implementation of the Convention. However, the provisions of the proposed Recommendation should not be regarded as compulsory. Member States should have some flexibility as to the way in which the Convention is implemented.

Bahrain

The title of the instrument should be "Prohibition of child labour", "Elimination of child labour" or "Prohibition and elimination of child labour". The expression "immediate abolition of the worst forms of child labour" is ambiguous and raises many questions, as it is aimed at banning the worst forms of child labour yet allows everything else. Furthermore, what constitutes unacceptable and acceptable work is open to disagreement. If the proposed Convention seeks to protect children by prohibiting work for those below a given age, the prohibition should be comprehensive to achieve protection. For countries which have difficulties in applying the prohibition overnight, it should be gradually implemented within a given time frame. In light of progress reports, this period could be extended or adapted to take into account the conditions of a given region or country. On the eve of the third millennium, the ban should not be restricted to "the worst forms of child labour", but to all forms of employment, because child labour is a serious threat to the future of humanity. A child must be able to learn and develop, and therefore work should be prohibited. Children have only one childhood to live and they cannot wait. If humanity is to give them the best it has to offer, it must be now. The ILO should make combating child labour its top priority, supported by the adoption of a clear and transparent Convention that calls for the elimination of child labour.

Belgium

National Labour Council (CNT). New instruments focusing on the worst forms of child labour are needed. These instruments should rely on the Minimum Age Convention, 1973 (No. 138), which remains one of the core ILO Conventions and a key instrument in the fight against child labour. The proposed new Convention should deal with the fundamental principles of the fight against the most extreme forms of child labour.

Bolivia

Both a Convention and a Recommendation should be adopted. While there is legislation in Bolivia on work that is prohibited for children, it is barely enforced, if at all. More than laying down standards, child labour policies should be aimed at enforcing them. Policies to prohibit and eliminate the worst forms of child labour should also be aimed at offering options through programmes to protect the child's psychological and social development. Without such real and effective protection, efforts could be counterproductive and increase the clandestine nature of child labour and hence the exploitation of children.

Brazil

National Confederation of Commerce (CNC). The employers on the Committee on Child Labour were satisfied with the high quality of the debates and the progress made during the first discussion. However, this was with the reservation that the instruments should be concise, simple, focused, realistic and easy to understand, so that they can receive wide support and be ratified by the highest possible number of member States, both developed and developing. In short, the texts deserve the employers' support. Some questions remain, however, which should be resolved with a view to a flexible Convention which gives the greatest opportunity for ample ratification by member States.

Bulgaria

The Government considers positively the texts of the proposed Convention and proposed Recommendation.

Canada

Canada gives overall support for the intent and principles of the proposed instruments. However, in view of the Government's commitment to a clear and concise Convention that can be ratified and implemented by Canada and a large number of member States, it raises a number of questions on the proposed text below.

Canadian Labour Congress (CLC). The CLC agrees that however well discussions at the 1998 Session of the International Labour Conference proceeded, many challenges remain. There are a number of weaknesses in the current text of both the proposed Convention and the proposed Recommendation concerning access to basic education, the definition of hazardous work and enforcement. The potential for "watering down" tripartism is also a serious concern.

Chile

Chile takes a positive view of the proposed text, which represents the spirit of the United Nations Convention on the Rights of the Child and reflects a considerable effort and contribution to child protection.

Croatia

The Government fully supports the adoption of new instruments concerning the prohibition of child labour.

Croatian Association of Employers. The Association agrees with the proposed texts and stresses the importance of education in the complete elimination of child labour, which is a long-term objective. It is necessary to concentrate on developing instruments that could directly influence the elimination of extreme forms of child labour. Such instruments should be practical and capable of being effectively applied in countries in transition and in industrialized countries, taking into account supervision and implementation.

Union of Autonomous Trade Unions of Croatia (SSSH), Confederation of Independent Trade Unions of Croatia (KNSH), Croatian Association of Trade Unions (HUS), Federation of Croatian Trade Unions of Public Services (MATICA). The amendments that were made to the texts subsequent to the 86th Session of the International Labour Conference are accepted.

Czech Republic

Provisions concerning the prohibition and immediate elimination of extreme forms of child labour contained in both instruments will markedly contribute to the protection of the rights of the child.

Denmark

It is unclear how the proposed Convention should be delimited in relation to the proposed Recommendation.

Egypt

The proposed Recommendation should be annexed to the proposed Convention and not supplement it, since the application of the proposed Convention together with the proposed Recommendation would contradict article 19 of the ILO Constitution, which stipulates that a Recommendation is not binding for States which have ratified the Convention to which it is attached, but is only for guidance. Moreover, the proposed Recommendation includes small details which may obstruct ratification of the proposed Convention by a number of States, and hence the purpose of the proposed Convention would not be fulfilled. The Government supports the text of the proposed Recommendation; however, the "worst forms of child labour" referred to in the proposed Convention under Article 3(a), (b) and (c) do not exist in Egypt in the work environment.

Federation of Egyptian Industries. The Federation supports the proposed Convention and Recommendation because the goals in the Preamble are widely echoed in the policy of the Federation and its continuous efforts to protect children.

El Salvador

The proposed text reflects the debate that took place during the first discussion. The Government agrees with it, with a few minor proposed modifications.

Estonia

Estonian Association of Trade Unions. The phrase "abolition of the worst forms of child labour" is preferred over "the prohibition and immediate elimination of the worst forms of child labour" as it is more precise, shorter and clearer, and has also been used in relation to earlier ILO labour standards, such as the abolition of forced labour.

Finland

The changes made by the Office are essentially technical in nature and intended to clarify the meaning and assist in the interpretation of the texts. Finland completely agrees with the need to deal with the prohibition and immediate elimination of the worst forms of child labour. However, providing appropriate opportunities for young people to gain work experience should not be condemned.

The proposed Convention and Recommendation do not address the use of the Internet in the exploitation of children, for example paedophilia and the sale and trafficking of children. The international community should investigate ways to intervene more effectively in such activities. The complexity of the problem must not prevent research or the development of international cooperation to find a solution.

Confederation of Finnish Industry and Employers (TT) and Employers' Confederation of Service Industries in Finland (PT). Children's participation in working life has a long history and deep cultural roots in many countries. Such participation also has implications for the economic development of these countries. It would therefore be a mistake to seek to ban all forms of work by children. Attention should rather be focused on extreme cases and the forms of work which are most harmful to the well-being of children. The ILO's existing instruments already cover these worst forms of labour. The demands imposed by these instruments are, however, unrealistically high for many countries, which has resulted in a low level of ratification. It is therefore particularly important to keep the demands realistic.

Central Organization of Finnish Trade Unions (SAK), Finnish Confederation of Salaried Employees (STTK) and Confederation of Unions for Academic Professions (AKAVA). The proposed Convention and Recommendation and some of the changes proposed by the Office form a good basis for the decisive second discussion. The SAK, STTK and AKAVA support the use of the expression "worst forms of child labour" rather than "extreme" or "intolerable" and the proposed title "Convention concerning the prohibition and immediate elimination of the worst forms of child labour", as it clearly and immediately indicates the content of the proposed Convention.

France

The Government wholly supports the proposed new instruments on the elimination of the worst forms of child labour. France has always agreed with initiatives aimed at the eradication of child labour within the framework of relevant ILO standards, and has very protective national legislation regarding the work of persons under the age of 18. The proposed instruments should not replace but should be consistent with Convention No. 138, which should remain the fundamental ILO Convention for the abolition of child labour.

Movement of French Enterprises (MEDEF). The MEDEF considers favourably the implementation of an international legal instrument on the worst forms of child labour. The content of the texts for the proposed Convention and Recommendation remains very much in line with the texts submitted for discussion to the 86th Session (1998) of the International Labour Conference. However, the draft text of the proposed Recommendation continues to pose a problem of compatibility with the French legislation governing apprenticeships.

Germany

The proposed text is an appropriate basis for the adoption of instruments that will enable as many member States as possible to make an international commitment to eliminate, as soon as possible, the worst forms of child labour.

Confederation of German Employers' Associations (BDA). The BDA favours adopting standards for the immediate abolition of the worst forms of child labour. Such a standard-setting measure will establish a meaningful and important priority in the worldwide fight against child labour. The proposed texts are a usable basis for discussions at the 87th Session of the Conference. The purpose of the proposed Convention should be to define the worst forms of child labour and the measures required for their immediate elimination clearly and realistically enough to make their implementation and ratification a feasible and desirable goal for a large number of ILO member States. The proposed Recommendation should suggest practical and relevant measures for implementation.

Haiti

The texts of the proposed Convention and Recommendation have been positively received by the Government, employers' and workers' organizations. The document constitutes a very satisfactory basis for discussion and reflects appropriately the relevant resolutions adopted by the member States of the ILO, which are fully supported by the Government.

India

Child labour is one of the most serious violations of children's rights. Child labour is not only a social problem but also an economic one. In addition to compulsory schooling, empowerment and economic betterment of the poor parents are also considered essential to eliminate this social evil. The problem needs to be addressed in a very comprehensive manner and effective measures to eliminate child labour have to be taken in a phased manner. It was in this context and spirit that the Government supported the ILO's initiative to adopt fresh instruments to eliminate the worst forms of child labour immediately. Although reservations relating to Article 3 exist, the Government generally supports the proposed text of the Convention and Recommendation.

Indonesia

The instrument should be in the form of a Recommendation, therefore comments are made only on the proposed Recommendation. Paragraphs 1 to 15 of the proposed Recommendation constitute a satisfactory basis for discussion. However, further amendments or comments from the respective parties may be submitted during the second discussion.

Ireland

Irish Congress of Trade Unions (ICTU). The Preamble of the proposed Convention states that Convention No. 138 remains the fundamental ILO instrument on child labour and that the new Convention should complement Convention No. 138, which sets 18 as the minimum age for hazardous work. The wording of the new Convention should not in any way set a lower standard than that established in Convention No. 138, and there should be consistency between the provisions of the two Conventions. There was insufficient time for a thorough discussion on the proposed Recommendation at the 1998 Session of the Conference owing to the length of time taken for the debate on the proposed Convention. References are welcomed to the need for clear requirements for action in the national programmes to remove and rehabilitate child labourers and ensure their access to basic education, the use of penal and other sanctions for violations, the need for special attention to the situation of girls and the need for international cooperation to implement the Convention. See also comments under Articles 2 and 7(2)(b).

Services Industrial Professional Technical Union (SIPTU). The Union is pleased that the emphasis advocated on eliminating the forms of exploitation that particularly affect girl workers has been adequately reflected in the proposed text. It is also pleasing that the particular problems created for young domestic workers whose work is often invisible and does not allow for the possibility of returning home each day has been fully recognized as a form of hazardous work to be made subject to the provisions of this Convention. It is further noted that the request for measures to ensure, at the national level, that children who are victims of the worst forms of child labour have easy access to ombudspersons and SOS telephone lines has been reflected in Paragraph 14(g) of the proposed Recommendation. As an Irish supporter of the Global March Against Child Labour, the SIPTU urges governments to give absolute priority to the immediate elimination of the worst forms of child labour; to set up, without delay, national commissions that are entrusted with the task of creating the infrastructure necessary for the implementation of the proposed Convention; and to ratify the Convention at the earliest opportunity.

Italy

The texts, following the deliberations of the 86th Session of the Conference, have been substantially improved. Fundamental passages, such as the recognition of free basic education as an instrument to achieve the rehabilitation and social reintegration of child workers and as an alternative to involvement in work, are now included in the text at the end of the Preamble. Equally fundamental is the recognition that the ultimate objective of the instruments being adopted, together with the Minimum Age Convention and Recommendation, 1973, is the total elimination of child labour. Another important and fundamental aspect is the recognition of the particularly serious situation of girls, the exploitation of whom is often hidden in homes, and which escapes the public monitoring and censure it deserves because it is justified by usage, customs and practices, which make it no less reprehensible. Since the issue of child soldiers was not resolved during the first discussion, the Government notes with satisfaction that countries are being asked specific questions on the matter.

Italian General Confederation of Employers in Commerce, Tourism and Services (CONFCOMMERCIO). The Confederation highlights its considerable interest in the proposed Convention and Recommendation and concurs with the content in general and the amendments approved by the Committee on Child Labour.

Italian General Confederation of Labour (CGIL), Italian Confederation of Workers' Unions (CISL) and Italian Labour Union (UIL). These organizations welcome the general outcome of the first discussion.

Japan

Solving the problem of child labour is one of the most important tasks imposed on the entire world society. Efforts are being made by international organizations, including the United Nations, to develop international instruments and promote technical cooperation. The Government also recognizes the need to make an active contribution to the solution of this problem. Under such circumstances, it seems appropriate for the ILO to adopt international instruments for the immediate elimination of the worst forms of child labour. This will encourage efforts to eliminate child labour in many countries and will enable technical cooperation activities of international organizations, including the ILO, to be more effective. The ILO should facilitate effective measures consistent with the activities of other international organizations, including those of the United Nations working group on the draft optional protocol to the Convention on the Rights of the Child, to avoid excessive administrative burdens, duplication and confusion in each country. The new instruments should focus on areas where the ILO can use its expertise and should cover fundamental matters that can be easily applied by member States.

Japan Federation of Employers' Associations (NIKKEIREN). The Federation supports the Government's comments. The Convention should provide only basic minimum principles to ensure universal ratification and application.

Japanese Trade Union Confederation (JTUC-RENGO). The Confederation supports the proposed texts and recognizes the importance of adopting a Convention and Recommendation aimed at combating child labour, which is a universal problem requiring an immediate solution.

Jordan

Amman Chamber of Industry. Countries will need time after the adoption of the proposed Convention and Recommendation to determine what work a child may undertake, to adapt to the requirements of the instruments and amend legislation if necessary. This could take two to four years.

Federation of Jordanian Chambers of Commerce. The proposed Convention completes the provisions of Convention No. 138 and requires immediate measures to suppress the most oppressive forms of child labour, while the proposed Recommendation contains guidance for steps to be taken. The main purpose of Convention No. 138 is to abolish child labour completely, which takes time, while the proposed Convention deals with certain forms of child labour that cannot be condoned, such as forced labour, dangerous work, prostitution and pornography. It should be noted that any income earned by a child or any member of a family, especially in most developing countries, is a source of livelihood for the whole family.

Kenya

Central Organization of Trade Unions (COTU). The general impact of the proposed Convention is that it covers the "worst forms" of child labour as contained in Convention No. 138, which is less focused. The wording in the new Convention should not provide room for flexibility by setting a lower standard than that laid down in Convention No. 138.

Republic of Korea

The Government strongly supports the ILO's endeavour to eliminate the worst forms of child labour and protect the basic human rights of children. The proposed Convention and Recommendation, which are the products of the heated debates and sincere explorations by representatives from governments and workers' and employers' organizations throughout the world, embody the representatives' commitment to abolishing the worst forms of child labour. However, to make this universal desire a reality, a large number of countries must be able to ratify and implement the proposed Convention and Recommendation. This factor should, without fail, be considered in the second discussion.

Federation of Korean Trade Unions (FKTU). The FKTU has no special observation on the proposed Convention and Recommendation. However, recalling that the embargo in the early 1990s on the import of Pakistani carpets, imposed by industrialized countries as a way of eliminating the use of Pakistani children for weaving carpets, forced hundreds of thousands of child carpet weavers into the street, the FKTU emphasizes that industrialized countries and international organizations need to give support to building facilities and programmes for education.

Kuwait

The proposed texts appear to complement the Minimum Age Convention and Recommendation, 1973, and the United Nations Convention on the Rights of the Child, adopted in 1989, as well as all other international conventions on the subject. The proposed texts were established to eliminate all forms of child labour which could, owing to the conditions in which such work is performed, place children at risk or endanger their health, safety or psychological well-being. Consequently, as the texts of the proposed Convention and Recommendation are among national and international priorities, they are an adequate basis for discussion.

Malaysia

The general nature of the provisions in the proposed Convention would provide flexibility to enable ratifying States to formulate their own policies and legislation, thereby encouraging wide ratification. In the absence of a comprehensive definition for Article 3(d), for example, the wide variations among member States concerning health and safety standards based on facilities, technical expertise, enforcement capacity, level of economic development and other social and cultural factors will have an impact. Due consideration should be given to these factors and a flexible approach should be adopted when evaluating the compliance of member States with the Convention. The ILO has a key role in helping member States to comply through its technical cooperation programmes and other relevant means.

Mali

The Government fully supports the ideals embodied in the texts of the proposed Convention and Recommendation and considers them a solid basis for discussion.

Mexico

Many of the activities referred to as the "worst forms of child labour" in the proposed instruments do not constitute child labour, but are crimes against children, and therefore come under criminal law. A distinction should be drawn between exploitation of children and economic exploitation of children's labour, as is done in the United Nations Convention on the Rights of the Child (articles 32 to 35). The former concept comes under the criminal law of each State and the latter falls within the labour sphere. Action against the exploitation of children is being carried out by the United Nations Commission on Human Rights, UNICEF and Interpol. To adopt provisions on the matter could result in a duplication of efforts and contradictions between the ILO and Interpol and other agencies. The inclusion of a large number of criminal aspects in the proposed Convention could lead to problems in application and contradictions, and thus constitute an obstacle to ratification. The ILO should therefore focus its efforts on work which jeopardizes the safety and health of children. Situations which constitute criminal offences rather than labour should be eliminated from the definition. The need for flexibility and realism has been highlighted. To this end the instruments should define the "worst forms of child labour" as forced or compulsory labour, debt bondage and serfdom; and any other type of work or activity which, by its nature or the circumstances in which it is carried out, is likely to jeopardize the health, safety or morals of children. The instruments should then fix the minimum age, hours and conditions of work and the application of penalties, and in doing so take account of the provisions on child labour in the legislation of each State.

Moreover, the instrument adopted should be a Recommendation. Explicit reference to "immediate elimination" of the worst forms of child labour could constitute an obstacle to ratification, since States vary in their level of development and cannot commit themselves to this objective. A more realistic solution would include requiring States to take the necessary measures to prohibit immediately and eliminate progressively the worst forms of child labour. The experience of the International Programme on the Elimination of Child Labour (IPEC) shows that elimination is a process which includes different phases in the short, medium and long term. "Immediate" should therefore be inserted before "prohibition" and "progressive" before "elimination" wherever they occur, so that reference is made to "immediate prohibition and progressive elimination".

Morocco

The proposed Convention should be modified on certain points.

Netherlands

While the proposed texts are a solid basis for discussion at the 87th Session of the Conference in June 1999, the proposed Convention could be improved. For instance, not only social partners, but also other non-governmental organizations (NGOs) have an important role to play in the elimination of the worst forms of child labour. The worst forms of child labour are often invisible and located in the informal sector where the possibilities for intervention by "official" social partners are limited. Especially in these situations the full efforts of other concerned groups, provided they have sufficient support, credibility and knowledge, are needed to eliminate child labour. The role of these "other concerned groups, as appropriate" should explicitly be recognized in the proposed Convention, for instance in Article 4 (both paragraphs) and especially in Article 6, paragraph 2.

Netherlands Trade Union Confederation (FNV). The Confederation disagrees with the opinion of the Government above on references to "other concerned groups" in the proposed Convention.

New Zealand

The Government reconfirms its strong support for the development of instruments to address the worst forms of child labour and generally supports the texts in Report IV(1) as a basis for discussion by the Conference at its 87th Session in June 1999. However, comments are made below on the formulations proposed by the Office, and on some aspects of the texts that are not clear, or require expansion or amendment.

New Zealand Employers' Federation (NZEF). In its 1997 response to the ILO's questionnaire on child labour, the NZEF expressed doubt as to whether the introduction of a Convention on child labour would achieve the effect intended by its promoters. Instead, the Federation proposed that the abolition of all exploitative forms of child labour be accepted as a first principle which every country, on becoming a Member of the ILO, would promise to uphold. Should a country not be in a position to guarantee abolition, it would be required to promise to aspire to the complete elimination of all exploitative forms of child labour. In the NZEF's view, requiring promises of this kind would likely be a more effective deterrent than introducing a Convention which member States might well be reluctant to ratify. The NZEF recognizes, however, that the general view of the Conference was in favour of a new Convention and Recommendation and so offers its comments on the Government's report on that basis.

Peru

The Government finds the proposed Convention appropriate for discussion at the 87th Session of the Conference and agrees with the proposed Recommendation, except for the comments below.

Portugal

The proposed text is a satisfactory basis for the second discussion. Observations on specific points are given below under the relevant provisions.

Confederation of Portuguese Industry (CIP). During the first discussion, the Confederation said that instead of adopting new international standards to achieve the elimination of illicit child labour, effective means of action should be taken at the national level. Nevertheless, child labour in itself should not be confused with the "extreme" forms, the "worst" forms or the "most intolerable" forms of such work, which must be eliminated. Therefore, the elimination of child labour in all its forms, in view of the importance of the education and training of young people, should be considered, but in a long-term perspective. The discussion of this problem focuses, then, on extreme forms of child labour. If a new international instrument is adopted on this subject, it is essential that it be realistic, simple and precise and that it reflect adequately all the economic and practical implications, enabling it to be ratified by the highest possible number of member States. There are reservations about the texts of the proposed Convention and Recommendation, which do not constitute a sufficiently appropriate basis for the discussion of this subject at the next session of the Conference.

General Confederation of Portuguese Workers (CGTP-IN). The proposed new ILO Convention and Recommendation on child labour have as their specific aim the prohibition and immediate elimination of the "worst forms of child labour" and are intended to complement the Minimum Age Convention and Recommendation, 1973, which will continue to be the fundamental ILO instruments in this area. The proposed texts, therefore, have a very specific and restricted objective. They do not contain any references to the fact that all forms of child labour are intrinsically reprehensible, that the final objective continues to be the ultimate abolition of all child labour and that these instruments represent just one small step in this direction. It would be impossible, in fact useless, to approve instruments which call for the immediate abolition of all forms of child labour, as they would meet with little or no acceptance by ILO Members. It is fundamental that the Preamble to the proposed Convention include a clear and express reference in this respect, that would in fact simply reflect the positions that the ILO has always taken, since its inception in 1919, in relation to child labour. Furthermore, the proposed Recommendation, not having the same binding nature as the proposed Convention, could include more advanced provisions in respect of the progressive elimination of all forms of child labour. The expression chosen to delimit the scope of the instruments – "the worst forms of child labour" – is not the most ideal one, in that it involves an implicit value judgement: if there are worse forms, there are also better forms of child labour which are therefore more acceptable – a particularly disturbing idea in the context of the fight against child labour. In reality, however, whatever the expression chosen – "extreme forms", "intolerable forms", "most abusive forms" – there is still a value element because the problem does not lie in the expression used, but in the actual fact of qualifying certain types of child labour as more acceptable than others. The main shortcoming in the proposed instruments is their scope, which is too restricted and, moreover, liable to give the idea that the other forms of child labour not mentioned could, in some way, be acceptable. However, even taking as inevitable the need to restrict the scope of the proposed Convention to the "worst forms of child labour", it is imperative that the definition of what constitutes these forms of work be absolutely clear and objective, on the one hand corresponding strictly to situations considered to be work in the true sense and, on the other, to as broad a range as possible of situations involving child labour. Therefore, it is necessary first of all not to lose sight of the fact that the Conference is defining "forms of labour", which means that other forms of child exploitation, however disgusting and intolerable they may be (such as prostitution or the use of children in illicit activities such as drug trafficking), do not fall within this sphere, because they do not correspond to the concept of work. In spite of the proposed Convention, and other international instruments condemning these forms of child exploitation, it does not seem appropriate to define them as "forms of labour". Secondly, given that the proposed Convention defines a child as any person under the age of 18, it is essential that the "worst forms of child labour" to be abolished immediately include work (of any kind) performed by very young children – let us say under the age of 12 years, with the reservation that any age limit established will always be a random one, but no more so than the boundary between the worst and the best forms of child labour. A distinction is made in this particular case between a child in the strict sense of the word and an adolescent. Certainly no one will question that the use of children of 6 or 7 years of age for work is, objectively and irrespective of the type of work in question, more intolerable than work performed by an adolescent of 15 or 16 years of age or more. The younger the child is, the more his or her physical and mental development will be affected, as well as access to school, and the more flagrant the violation of his or her most basic rights will be. Lastly, work which, by its nature or the circumstances in which it is carried out, is likely to jeopardize the health, safety or morals of children, as provided in Article 3(d), should be specifically defined in the proposed Convention instead of the proposed Recommendation, given that the proposed Convention is a binding instrument. Likewise, the proposed Convention should list these types of work (see the list included in the proposed Recommendation – Paragraph 3) and should stipulate their immediate prohibition and elimination, in keeping with the objectives of the proposed Convention. As for the rest, the Confederation does not disagree in principle, although the Members' obligations should be more clearly formulated, making it clear that the main obligation to which they will become bound through ratification will be the immediate elimination of these forms of child labour and not merely their legal prohibition; in other words, it will not be enough to publish laws prohibiting them (remember that in most countries child labour is already prohibited), but it will be necessary effectively to monitor their practical application through the use of coercive measures (the application of sanctions, preferably penal ones); furthermore, the removal of children from work will imply the existence of alternatives for these children, namely in terms of education. Although the CGTP-IN agrees with the reasoning that brought the ILO to approve the proposed Convention and Recommendation, it could and should go further.

South Africa

New standards in the form of a Convention supplemented by a Recommendation should be adopted.

Business South Africa (BSA). BSA supports the adoption of a Convention and a Recommendation on the immediate abolition of the worst forms of child labour. It supports the formulation of a Convention that would lead to universal ratification. In addition to supplementing the proposed Convention, the proposed Recommendation should be drafted so that it could be used as a stand-alone document in countries that have not ratified the Convention. All comments on particular provisions should be seen against this background.

Sri Lanka

The Government recommends adoption of the new Convention. The principal objective of the proposed Convention is to a large extent in conformity with the objective of recently enacted legislation, the National Child Protection Authority Act, which "provides for the establishment of an authority for the formulation of a national policy on the prevention of child abuse and the protection and treatment of children who are victims of such abuse", and for the coordination and monitoring of action against all forms of child abuse.

Sweden

The Swedish tripartite ILO committee supports a Convention supplemented by a Recommendation. The texts proposed are in close agreement with the conclusions adopted by the Conference in 1998. There is an urgent need for the new Convention concerning the prohibition and immediate elimination of the worst forms of child labour to be included among the fundamental ILO Conventions referred to by the World Summit for Social Development in Copenhagen in 1995 and also the ILO Declaration on Fundamental Principles and Rights at Work. The United Nations Convention on the Rights of the Child should be the starting-point for continuing work by the ILO, and a stronger link could be made to it in the proposed Convention. It would be logical if the proposed Convention came to be regarded as a refinement of Article 32(1) of the Convention on the Rights of the Child, in the same way that Convention No. 138 is in relation to Article 32(2). Such an interaction could have a great impact, given, among other things, that 191 States have acceded to the Convention on the Rights of the Child. It would also be of great benefit to the work of the United Nations Committee on the Rights of the Child and UNICEF if it could be said that Article 32(1) is made clearer by the new Convention. See also comments below under the Preamble.

Swedish Employers' Confederation (SAF). There must be a short, simple and generally worded instrument which can be ratified by as many States as possible immediately after its adoption by the Conference in June 1999.

Switzerland

The Government of Switzerland fully supports the elaboration of a new Convention and new Recommendation on the worst forms of child labour.

Confederation of Swiss Employers (UPS). The UPS fully supports the adoption of international instruments concerning the elimination of the worst forms of child labour. These instruments should be concise and well targeted in order to be understood, accepted and ratified by as many member States as possible. The proposed texts constitute a satisfactory basis for a second discussion in 1999.

Federation of Swiss Salaried Employees' Association (FSE/VSA). The FSE/VSA welcomes the Conference's initiative to develop an international instrument which will concentrate on the elimination of the worst forms of child labour.

Swiss Confederation of Christian Trade Unions (CSC/CNG). The outcome of the first discussion was positive even if there is still a need to discuss in depth the role of education and the use of children for military purposes.

Turkey

Confederation of Progressive Trade Unions of Turkey (DÝSK). The proposed Convention and Recommendation concerning the prohibition and immediate elimination of the worst forms of child labour are appropriate and the Confederation endorses the texts. However, the proposed Convention would come closer to its objective if the following points are added. First, any type of work which keeps children from school must be recognized as one of the worst forms of child labour. The essential and inalienable right to education can be a fundamental criterion in response to the argument made by countries that children are obliged to work since they would otherwise be driven to prostitution or starvation. Second, the views of the children affected by child labour and of their families must be sought and included in future action programmes designed to prevent child labour. Finally, the practice of arming children and sending them to war must also be defined as "hazardous work". The fact that children are being used in wars is a totally unacceptable situation. In fact, sending children to war is a practice which is prohibited in various international human rights instruments. Inclusion of the practice of sending children to fight in wars in the scope of the ILO Convention and its definition as a practice which must be prohibited and immediately eliminated would strengthen other international laws and initiatives in the field.

United Kingdom

The text of the report is broadly in line with the United Kingdom's views reflected in the conclusions of the Committee on Child Labour at the 86th Session of the Conference. The Government is therefore of the opinion that the proposed texts of the instruments provide a suitable basis for discussion at the 87th Session of the Conference in June 1999. The comments below under the relevant provisions therefore focus on the amendments introduced by the Office.

United States

While the texts of the proposed Convention and Recommendation are, on the whole, a satisfactory basis for discussion by the Conference at its 87th Session in June 1999, comments and suggested amendments are proposed in furtherance of the widely subscribed view that the new instruments be crafted to permit broad ratification. These comments and amendments have been agreed on a tripartite basis. The ILO must create a Convention that is strong and meaningful but that can be ratified and implemented by the widest possible number of member States. All comments below flow from this fundamental idea. It is imperative to adopt an instrument which creates immediate and concrete obligations for member States to stop the worst forms of child labour. The objective, then, must be to keep the proposed Convention narrowly focused and action-oriented, in plain language and without duplication. It should emphasize outcomes and provide a framework sufficiently flexible to accommodate appropriate diversity in national policies and practices. The aim of the proposed Convention clearly is the elimination of the worst forms of child labour, i.e. work that is the most harmful and performed by the most vulnerable children. For this reason, the proposed Convention must not be a restatement or a revision of Convention No. 138, which will remain the basic ILO standard on child labour. Rather, the new instrument should be viewed as applicable to a subset of the types of labour covered by Convention No. 138. Such a view does not compromise Convention No. 138. In fact, it permits consistency with Convention No. 138 where appropriate, and going beyond it where necessary. Attempts to incorporate the language of Convention No. 138 would be counterproductive as they could render the proposed

Convention unratifiable for countries that have encountered difficulties in ratifying Convention No. 138. In this regard, any work proposed to be banned in addition to bonded labour and work in the sex and drug industries must be of the same severity as these imminently harmful and readily identifiable work categories. The third and fourth paragraphs of the Preamble to the proposed Convention refer to the "prohibition and effective elimination of the worst forms of child labour" and explain that "effective elimination of the worst forms of child labour requires immediate and comprehensive action". This is the correct approach, since it is unrealistic to expect that the worst forms of child labour can in all cases be eliminated immediately. During the first discussion, some delegates considered that "immediate" means "as soon as possible", but this is by no means the accepted definition of the term. The language of the proposed Convention and Recommendation should be fully understandable to all who will read them, and the proposed Convention's provisions should lend themselves to "immediate" and as wide as possible ratification by all member States. Therefore, the title of the draft instruments should be changed to "the proposed Convention and the proposed Recommendation concerning the prohibition and effective elimination of the worst forms of child labour" and all other references to "immediate" elimination should be replaced with "effective" elimination. The focus of the instruments is thereby placed on urgent and comprehensive measures, provisions which would be immediately applicable, the aim of which is the total elimination of the worst forms of child labour. Finally, no provisions should be moved from the proposed Recommendation into the proposed Convention, because it would diminish the likelihood of ratification by member States.

Venezuela

Confederation of Autonomous Trade Unions (CODESA). Any legitimate activity engaged in by children anywhere in the world and which warrants the supervision of the government must be conducive to their full physical, mental, spiritual, moral and intellectual development. The instrument adopted by the Conference should not focus only on negative aspects, such as stressing that its objective is the elimination of the worst forms of child labour or the immediate elimination of any particular type of work, but should also emphasize positive aspects. For example, the governments and civil societies of countries where poverty is seen as making child labour necessary should devise forms of child labour that are culturally based, such as theatrical activities and other activities that develop the child's artistic talents and skills, such as music, poetry and painting. Such activities should be strictly supervised by the State.

Holy See

Taking into consideration its status of observer and without intervening directly in the debate on the new legal instruments, the Holy See confirms its full support to the objectives of the proposed new international standards concerning the prohibition and elimination of the worst forms of child labour.

United Nations Committee on the Rights of the Child

The Committee welcomes the close cooperation it has established with the ILO regarding the implementation of existing norms as well as the drafting of new norms to eliminate the worst forms of child labour. The Committee wishes to emphasize that the Convention on the Rights of the Child has now reached near-universal ratification (191 States parties) and that its principles and provisions, especially its Article 32, call upon States parties to duly take into account other existing international instruments, including with regard to the minimum age for admission to employment, regulation of hours and conditions of employment and the provision of appropriate sanctions. The Committee has taken note of the text of the proposed new Convention concerning the prohibition and immediate elimination of the worst forms of child labour. It strongly welcomes the fact that the text of the proposed Convention integrates many recommendations and comments made by the Committee during its thematic discussion on the economic exploitation of children held at its fourth session in 1993 and in its letter dated 12 February 1997 to the Director-General of the ILO (request to reply to the ILO questionnaire regarding the drafting of a proposed Convention concerning the prohibition and immediate elimination of the worst forms of child labour). Specific comments on Articles 3 and 5 appear below.

Office Commentary

The general observations reinforce the overwhelming support for new ILO standards specifically focused on the worst forms of child labour. The replies also indicate that the texts of the proposed Convention and Recommendation are a good basis for discussion during the 1999 session of the International Labour Conference. Nevertheless, amendments have been suggested on several points and there is a divergence of opinion on some key issues.

It should be noted at the outset that the Proposed Conclusions discussed by the Conference Committee in 1998 had referred to "extreme" forms of child labour. The Committee, however, amended the reference to read the "worst" forms of child labour. This continues to be accepted, although some reservations have been reiterated about the possible implication that certain types of child labour are more acceptable than others.

The desire is expressed again in the general observations to have a short, focused Convention, dealing with basic principles and capable of being ratified in all member States. It is also suggested that it should define the worst forms of child labour and the measures required for their immediate elimination clearly and realistically enough to make their implementation and ratification feasible, that it should be among the fundamental ILO Conventions, and that it should create immediate and concrete obligations that are narrowly focused and action-oriented.

The determination of what constitutes "the worst forms of child labour" remains at the heart of the debate. A major issue is whether the extreme or worst forms of child labour have adequately been identified and separated out from other forms or kinds of child labour. This debate is centred around the definition in Article 3(d) of the proposed Convention and whether further clarity should be provided by referring more directly in the Convention to the kinds of work considered likely to jeopardize the health, safety or morals of children, or whether the flexibility in Article 4 for national determination is sufficient and appropriate. Other issues to come before the Conference relate to the inclusion of access to basic education and a direct reference to child soldiers or other involvement of children in armed conflict or military activity in the definition of the worst forms of child labour.

There are also differences of opinion on the time frame within which the worst forms of child labour are to be eliminated, and the meaning to be given to the relevant phrases in the Preamble (immediate and comprehensive action for effective elimination), in Article 1 (measures for immediate elimination) and in Article 7 (effective and time-bound measures).

The relationship between the new standards and the Minimum Age Convention, 1973 (No. 138), is another central issue. Concerns are raised in particular with respect to the references to Convention No. 138 in the Preamble and to the similarities between Articles 3(d) and 4 concerning the definition of the worst forms of child labour, and the provisions in Article 3 of Convention No. 138 on the higher minimum age for hazardous work. Generally, commentators elaborate on different principles that they believe should govern the relationship between the instruments. Some replies reiterate the importance of making it clear that the new Convention does not replace or undermine Convention No. 138, but that it is consistent with it, and that Convention No. 138 remains the fundamental ILO Convention for the total abolition of child labour. Others are concerned that a repetition of, or too close a link with, provisions in Convention No. 138 is inappropriate and might result in the adoption of provisions which could pose similar obstacles to ratification, or that references to child labour in general are inappropriate because some forms of work by children are acceptable. These issues are discussed below in the commentary on the Preamble and Articles 3 and 4.

In general, an underlying concern is whether the value added of a new Convention has been clearly established. As drafted, the proposed Convention differs from existing standards in that it focuses on the worst forms of child labour, requiring priority action in the form of immediate elimination; explicitly lists some of these worst forms while allowing flexibility at the national level to determine which hazards bring other work into the category of the worst forms; provides for monitoring mechanisms and programmes of action; requires measures of prevention, rehabilitation and reintegration; stipulates that special attention shall be given to children at special risk and the situation of girls; and calls for international cooperation and assistance.

The Office has taken note of the proposals for drafting changes made by governments and employers' and workers' organizations. However, a minimal number of changes have been made to the texts, given that on most issues the present text is accepted by the majority or there is not sufficient agreement to support one particular change over another. In some instances, the Office offers, merely for consideration, some possible alternatives under the relevant provisions below to address some of the concerns raised in the comments.

IV

OBSERVATIONS ON THE PROPOSED CONVENTION CONCERNING THE PROHIBITION AND IMMEDIATE ELIMINATION OF THE WORST FORMS OF CHILD LABOUR

The General Conference of the International Labour Organization,

Having been convened at Geneva by the Governing Body of the International Labour Office, and having met in its 87th Session on 1 June 1999, and

Considering the need to adopt new instruments for the prohibition and effective elimination of the worst forms of child labour, as the main priority for national and international action, to complement the Convention and Recommendation concerning Minimum Age for Admission to Employment, 1973, which remain the fundamental instruments with a view to achieving the total abolition of child labour, and

Considering that the effective elimination of the worst forms of child labour requires immediate and comprehensive action, taking into account the importance of basic education and the need to remove the concerned children from work and to provide for their rehabilitation and social reintegration, and

Recalling the Convention on the Rights of the Child adopted by the United Nations General Assembly on 20 November 1989, the Copenhagen Declaration on Social Development and the Programme of Action of the World Summit for Social Development, 1995, and the Beijing Declaration and Platform for Action of the Fourth World Conference on Women, 1995, and

Recalling that some of the worst forms of child labour are covered by other international instruments, in particular the Forced Labour Convention, 1930, and the United Nations Supplementary Convention on the Abolition of Slavery, the Slave Trade, and Institutions and Practices Similar to Slavery, 1956, and

Recalling the relevant provisions of the Labour Inspection Convention,

1947, and the Human Resources Development Convention and Recommendation, 1975, as well as the Declaration on Equality of Opportunity and Treatment for Women Workers, adopted by the International Labour Conference in 1975, and

Having decided upon the adoption of certain proposals with regard to child labour, which is the fourth item on the agenda of the session, and

Having determined that these proposals shall take the form of an international Convention;

adopts this day of June of the year one thousand nine hundred and ninety-nine the following Convention, which may be cited as the Immediate Abolition of the Worst Forms of Child Labour Convention, 1999:

Observations on the Preamble

Argentina. Third and fourth paragraphs: Agrees with the original proposal "immediate elimination".

Australia. Concerning the drafting changes made in the third and fourth paragraphs, the Government does not object to the reference to "effective elimination" of the worst forms of child labour as the main priority for national and international action or to the format in the fourth paragraph providing an explanation of what is involved in the effective elimination of such labour. The Government does not support including at the end of the third paragraph the text "... with a view to achieving the total abolition of child labour". While the purpose is to align the text with the Preamble to Convention No. 138, the focus should be kept on the aims and purposes of the new instrument and not on the aim of another standard. The adoption of the new instrument should not be seen just as a step in achieving the objective of effective abolition of all forms of child labour, which, with limited exceptions, is the subject of Convention No. 138. The reference in the fourth paragraph to the "need to remove the concerned children from work" should be amended to read "from such work" to make it clear that it is not proposed that children be removed from all work.

Bahrain. Include a reference to the Universal Declaration of Human Rights, 1948, as it is one of the most widely known and influential documents in the field of human rights. Reference should also be made to the United Nations International Convention on the Elimination of All Forms of Racial Discrimination, 1965.

Belgium. Agrees to the changes made by the Office to align the texts of the third and fourth paragraphs with the title of the proposed Convention.

CNT. Regrets that the Preamble does not stress the need for collaboration and coordination between the ILO and other organizations of the United Nations system.

Brazil. CNC. The Preamble should be as concise as possible, avoiding references to instruments relating to other issues, such as human resources development and equality of opportunity and treatment for women workers.

Bulgaria. Wholly supports the text of the Preamble.

Canada. Amend the third paragraph, which begins "Considering the need to adopt", to clarify the double objective of Convention No. 138, which is to abolish child labour and raise progressively the minimum age for admission to employment. This would indicate that the proposed Convention does not require the abolition of all forms of work by children. Insert the word "such" before "work" in the fourth paragraph, to clarify the intention to remove children from the worst forms of child labour, not from all work.

Canadian Employers Council (CEC). Agrees with the Office's proposed rewording. Third paragraph: The addition of the words "with a view to achieving the total abolition of child labour" when referring to Convention No. 138 is misleading, as that Convention allows some forms of child labour such as "light work". Furthermore, notwithstanding allowed exceptions under Convention No. 138, it has not received broad acceptance. Many member States (including Canada) have not ratified it and probably will never do so and some ratifying Members have made few efforts to implement it. Finally, many employers and citizens do not support the total abolition of child labour in Canada. Part-time activities such as paper routes, babysitting and the like are generally regarded as beneficial to children of appropriate age. Canadian employers do, however, support wholeheartedly the total abolition of the worst forms of child labour (subject to an acceptable definition of the classes of activities it would encompass). Fourth paragraph: Move the adjective "concerned" to after "children".

Chile. Agrees with the Office's new formulation of the two paragraphs, which originally contained an element of duplication. The proposed change in the second of these contributes to the comprehension of the proposed instrument by explaining and putting into context the meaning of the term "effective elimination".

United Trades Confederation of Small and Medium-sized Enterprise, Service and Craft Industries of Chile (CONUPIA). The term "as a priority" should be expanded and improved by establishing times and deadlines.

Croatia. The Night Work of Young Persons (Non-Industrial Occupations) Convention, 1946, and the Night Work of Young Persons (Industry) Convention (Revised), 1948, should be added to the seventh paragraph of the Preamble. The definition of the worst forms of child labour includes any type of work which could jeopardize the health of children, and Paragraph 3(e) of the proposed Recommendation specifically refers to night work as hazardous.

Denmark. Maintain the reference to "immediate and comprehensive action" in the third paragraph, because the text proposed by the Office does not emphasize that action must be taken immediately, only that effective elimination must be achieved.

Ecuador. Agrees.

Egypt. Approves of the Preamble. Suggests including in the fourth paragraph the phrase "to reduce poverty" after "the importance of basic education".

Egyptian Trade Union Federation. Agrees with the text of the Preamble. However, the numbers, not only the title and date, of Conventions and Recommendations referred to should be included, so they can be retrieved more easily. In addition, add: "in order to alleviate poverty and fight unemployment" to the fourth paragraph after "comprehensive action".

El Salvador. Reference should be made to all the relevant international declarations, programmes and platforms of action, Conventions and Recommendations, and to the importance of basic education in the removal of children from work and their rehabilitation and social reintegration.

Finland. At the June 1998 Session of the Conference, Finland supported including references to other international conventions, such as the United Nations Convention on the Rights of the Child, which has an important role in implementing the new Convention. Finland supports the references in the Preamble to internationally important agreements of which Finland is a signatory and the important role of basic education in the prevention and elimination of child labour. Basic education is one of the most important tools available to development cooperation programmes which aim to reduce and eliminate the use of child labour. Removing the double reference to "comprehensive action" in the third and fourth paragraphs has improved the language of the text. The Government strongly supports the recommended wording "with a view to achieving the total abolition of child labour". A reference to the conclusions of the International Conference on Child Labour held in Oslo from 27 to 30 October 1997 should be included in the fifth paragraph, and a reference to the Discrimination (Employment and Occupation) Convention, 1958 (No. 111), which deals with discrimination in access to employment, training and working conditions, should be included in the seventh paragraph.

Federation of Finnish Enterprises (SY). See comment under Article 7.

France. French Democratic Confederation of Labour (CFDT). Taking children out of work and reintegrating them into society is important. Governments should take immediate global measures. A reference to poverty in the Preamble would be inappropriate since poverty is one of a number of factors that contribute to child labour and should not be presented as being the principal one.

Germany. Supports changes made by the Office, which appear to be appropriate.

BDA. The references to the Copenhagen Declaration on Social Development, the Programme of Action of the World Summit for Social Development, 1995, the Beijing Declaration and Platform for Action of the Fourth World Conference on Women, 1995, and the Declaration on Equality of Opportunity and Treatment for Women Workers should be deleted. The Preamble should be short and restricted to subject matter of recognizable relevance; the relevance of these declarations to the subject of the proposed Convention is not clear since they have nothing directly to do with its subject matter.

German Confederation of Trade Unions (DGB). Third paragraph: The reference to Convention No. 138 is particularly relevant with regard to the general minimum age (18 years) laid down in the proposed Convention. Convention No. 138 sets the minimum age for hazardous work at 18 years, the general age for admission to employment at 15 (14 years initially in countries whose economy is insufficiently developed). Light work may be performed by persons 13 years of age (or 12 years initially in view of the level of economic development). The following three main objections arise with regard to a minimum age of 18 years: general objections based on the impact of the proposed Convention on the employment of persons aged between 15 (14) and 18; possible impact on participation of persons aged under 18 in vocational training measures, especially in cases in which trainees are involved in activities at the workplace; and a possible conflict between the provisions of the proposed Convention and the legislation on the age of consent (legal age for sexual activity) in several countries. This concerns participation in commercial sexual activities/prostitution of persons aged under 18 but over the legal age of consent. The proposed Convention should supplement Convention No. 138, and its provisions concerning the employment/training of persons aged between 15 (14) and 18 in non-hazardous work should be taken into account in the application and interpretation of the new Convention. Apart from this, the provisions of the proposed instrument bear a considerable resemblance to Convention No. 138, since the minimum age of 18 only applies to the worst forms of child labour. Fourth paragraph: This was the subject of heated debate in the first discussion, with objections raised mainly against the requirement to take immediate action. The DGB stressed that this should not be taken to mean that all cases of the worst forms of child labour would immediately disappear, but rather that immediate and comprehensive action should be taken by governments, i.e. that appropriate measures must be taken immediately. Although the Workers' group agrees that clearer wording in some places might be helpful, the wording proposed by the Office does contain some substantive changes that call for further discussion. Some governments were clearly in favour of an explicit reference to poverty as a cause of child labour. The Workers' group agreed that poverty was a consequence and a cause of child labour and suggested a compromise text to the effect that ratifying States would be assisted in applying the provisions of the Convention by the ILO in cooperation with other institutions. The compromise text was rejected by the Committee. The Workers' group decided not to pursue the reference to poverty further, since poverty could serve as a pretext for not applying the Convention fully, and poverty is only one of many factors causing child labour and therefore should not be put forward as the only main factor.

Greece. Agrees to the changes made by the Office in the third and fourth paragraphs.

National Confederation of Greek Trade. Agrees to the changes made by the Office in the third and fourth paragraphs.

Ireland. ICTU. The proposed Convention stresses that immediate elimination of the worst forms of child labour requires comprehensive action and that the children affected should be removed from work, rehabilitated and reintegrated into society. There was considerable debate on this issue in the first discussion, in particular objections from certain governments to the requirement for immediate action. The Workers' group stressed that they did not believe that this should be interpreted to mean that all cases of the worst forms of child labour would disappear immediately, but that immediate and comprehensive action should be taken by governments – that is, action should be taken without delay. The Office has endeavoured to redraft the relevant sections in the Preamble and operative part of the proposed Convention (Preamble and Article 6). While the ICTU accepts that some clarification of language in certain paragraphs might be useful, the wording proposed by the Office could be seen to involve rather more substantial changes on this issue than is necessary. Some governments argued strongly during the first discussion for clear references in the Convention to poverty as a cause of child labour. The Workers' group accepted that child labour is both a consequence and a cause of poverty and proposed compromise language which would require ratifying countries to support cooperation between the ILO and other institutions to implement the provisions of the Convention. The compromise proposal was not accepted by the Committee. The ICTU does not believe that a proposal for the inclusion of a reference to poverty in the Convention should be agreed, as some governments could use poverty as an excuse to avoid fully implementing the requirements of the Convention. Because poverty is one of many factors which causes child labour, it should not be presented as being the only major factor. The ICTU supports the proposal to include a reference to the Discrimination (Employment and Occupation) Convention, 1958 (No. 111), in the Preamble along with a reference to the conclusions of the International Conference on Child Labour held in Oslo from 27 to 30 October 1997.

Italy. Agrees with the change made by the Office and is very pleased with the formulation of the third preambular paragraph which states that the effective elimination of the worst forms of child labour is "the main priority for national and international action" but "with a view to achieving the total abolition of child labour". The term "to remove from work" used in the proposed text should be interpreted in the broadest possible sense: to remove from extreme forms of work on a priority basis, as part of comprehensive action to remove children from work.

CGIL, CISL and UIL. It is appropriate that the proposed Convention refers to the worst forms of child labour rather than the most intolerable or extreme forms. Agree that the new instruments supplement Convention No. 138 and Recommendation No. 146, which remain fundamental instruments. Suggest that the third preambular paragraph should keep the following words: "for the prohibition and immediate and comprehensive action for the ...". The following paragraph should also remain as the Committee approved it. As regards the question of removal from work, which also appears in Article 7, paragraph 2, the formulation should stay as it is. It is proposed to. insert in the Preamble a reference to the conclusions of the International Conference on Child Labour held in Oslo in 1997 and Convention No. 111.

Kenya. COTU. Fourth paragraph: The words "immediate and comprehensive" suggest bold action without delay or urgent action in an holistic way. The social partners need to make serious comments on this issue. Poverty should be cited for its special relevance in three ways: as a consequence and cause of child labour, as a factor that must be eliminated, and because of its relationship to social justice, which must be promoted. This will give full meaning to the words "comprehensive action".

Madagascar. Approves the proposed text. The fight against child labour requires comprehensive action that should be undertaken within the global framework of the ongoing programme on poverty eradication. This includes education and rehabilitation.

Mexico. The title of the new instrument, which should be a Recommendation only, should be "Recommendation concerning the immediate prohibition and progressive elimination of the worst forms of child labour". First, second, fifth, sixth, seventh and eighth paragraphs: Retain. Third paragraph: Delete "to adopt new instruments" and replace "complement" with "strengthen". Insert a new fourth paragraph: "Considering that there is a radical difference between the terms 'exploitation of children' and 'economic exploitation of child labour', the first referring to situations involving crimes and offences against children and the second to activities which are among the forms of labour to which this Recommendation refers as the worst forms of child labour". Existing proposed fourth paragraph: Replace the term "effective" by "progressive". Tenth paragraph: Replace the words "Immediate Abolition" with "Immediate Prohibition and Progressive Elimination".

Morocco. Replace "national and international action" by "national action, and international cooperation and assistance".

New Zealand. The Preamble contains unnecessary references to other international instruments. Although it is useful to recall existing instruments dealing with similar matters, it is also desirable to use the drafting of new instruments to move forward and make progress on issues within the contemporary context. The United Nations Convention on the Rights of the Child, 1989, is the key instrument relating to children, and therefore the Preamble needs to explicitly link the purpose of the proposed Convention with the fundamental rights set out in the Convention on the Rights of the Child. It is suggested therefore that the Preamble refer to the core principles contained in that Convention which have specific relevance to the proposed Convention, such as article 3 concerning the best interests of the child and article 12 dealing with the right of the child to be heard in matters affecting the child. Including such a reference in the Preamble would highlight the fundamental purpose of the proposed Convention, which is to protect child workers from harm, and link it to the cornerstone instrument which sets out children's rights. The Government supports the revised texts in the third and fourth paragraphs, regarding the use of "effective elimination" and "prohibition and immediate and comprehensive action". Concerning the third paragraph, which draws a relationship between Convention No. 138 and the proposed Convention, the Government does not support the formulation recommended by the Office. Firstly, all forms of child labour are not harmful, and therefore "to achieve the total abolition of child labour" should not be included (in New Zealand there is a long-established practice of the employment of children in part-time/holiday work, i.e. outside school hours, such as newspaper rounds and fruit picking). Secondly, despite recent ratifications, Convention No. 138 has yet to gain broad acceptance. It may therefore be counterproductive to the goal of universal ratification of the proposed Convention if the text of the latter is aligned too closely with that of Convention No. 138.

NZEF. Agrees with the Government that the Preamble contains unnecessary references to earlier international instruments. While these instruments may cover some of the worst forms of child labour, the fact that they have not enjoyed universal ratification, and that inappropriate forms of child labour continue to exist, indicates a lack of success in achieving the end they were intended to achieve. Reference to such instruments is unlikely, therefore, to be particularly effective in encouraging ratification of a new Convention, which should be accepted or rejected on its own merits. The NZEF disagrees with the Government that the Preamble should refer to the core principles contained in the Convention on the Rights of the Child. That Convention's potential difficulties of interpretation make it desirable that any instrument developed by the ILO be judged on its own merits and ratified (or not) accordingly. The NZEF supports the proposed textual revision in the third and fourth paragraphs, which it agrees are tautological, and agrees with the Government's opposition to the reference in the third paragraph to Convention No. 138, as there are forms of "child labour" in New Zealand that have never traditionally been considered harmful. Rather, they are looked upon as an effective way of helping young people to become aware of the world of work and its accruing rights and responsibilities. Jobs of this kind may only be performed on a part-time or casual basis, may not involve hazardous work, and may in no circumstances interfere with a young person's schooling.

New Zealand Council of Trade Unions (NZCTU). Supports the changes in the proposed text of the Convention from the words "immediate elimination" to "immediate and comprehensive action" in the third and fourth paragraphs, as it is sufficiently clear that action to be taken by governments is to be done without delay. Concerning the third paragraph, the NZCTU agrees that Convention No. 138 is the fundamental ILO instrument on child labour and that the new Convention should complement it. The NZCTU notes that the Government does not support the words "to achieve the total abolition of child labour" for the reason that not all forms of work undertaken by children are hazardous or harmful. New Zealand has a long-established practice of children working part time after school and during the holidays. However, neither Convention No. 138 nor the proposed new Convention on the worst forms of child labour are intended to eliminate all work undertaken by children. The proposed new Convention is designed with a specific focus on eliminating the worst forms of child labour, not all forms of work undertaken by children. Although Convention No. 138 is broader, it is implicit in its provisions that not all forms of work undertaken by children are considered to be harmful. This is evidenced by its benchmarks for admission into employment. For example, all children over the age of 15 years are permitted to perform non-hazardous work, and children between 13 and 15 years of age may undertake light work. Hazardous work is restricted to persons over 18 years of age. The NZCTU does not believe that the words "total abolition of child labour" are intended to capture all forms of work undertaken by children. It therefore supports the current wording recommended by the Office.

Norway. The Preamble should mention that harmful child labour, including the worst forms of child labour, is prohibited by the Convention on the Rights of the Child. The reference to that Convention in the fifth paragraph is general and it is not mentioned in the sixth paragraph, which refers to other instruments that deal with some of the worst forms of child labour. It is important to point out that States already have an obligation to prevent these forms of child labour under article 32 of the Convention on the Rights of the Child. There should also be a reference to the conclusions adopted by the International Conference on Child Labour in 1997, especially the Agenda for Action.

Portugal. The Government agrees with the changes made by the Office in the third and fourth paragraphs, which simplify the text without affecting its content.

CIP. The Preamble is too extensive, including references to the Convention on the Rights of the Child and to other international instruments, which, contrary to the desired aim, does not confer greater clarity or simplicity on the text.

CGTP-IN. The Preamble should state expressly and clearly that all forms of child labour are intrinsically reprehensible and that the ILO's final objective is the short-term abolition of all forms of child labour.

Senegal. Fourth paragraph: Suggests replacing the words "immediate and comprehensive action" with "a vast alliance".

South Africa. Supports the Office's change to the third paragraph to include "with a view to achieving the total abolition of child labour".

BSA. Including the words "total abolition of child labour" in the third paragraph, allegedly to bring the new proposed Convention in line with Convention No. 138, could become a stumbling block to the universal ratification of the proposed Convention. Either this reference should be deleted or a definition should be given to explain the meaning in relation to the proposed Convention. It is surely not the intention to prohibit all child labour under the age of 18, something that would, for instance, even prohibit a youngster from earning pocket money during school holidays. The explicit reference to various other international instruments in the Preamble could also act as a deterrent to ratification, in particular where mention is made of international instruments that have not been accepted, adopted or ratified by the countries concerned.

Spain. The Government objects to the way in which the Preamble reflects a tendency to prohibit all child labour for those under 18 years of age, given that the aim of the proposed Convention is to focus on the "worst forms" of child labour. If the instrument concentrates on the worst forms of child labour, the result will be different from one that focuses on child labour in general, in which case the age limit could be lower. More specifically, the reference in the third paragraph to the Minimum Age Convention and Recommendation, 1973, to the effect that they "remain the fundamental instruments with a view to achieving the total abolition of child labour", is confusing. Taking into account that Article 2 defines "child" as "all persons under the age of 18", the inevitable conclusion is that the third preambular paragraph provides that ratifying States undertake the goal of achieving the "total elimination" of child labour for persons under 18. Likewise, this paragraph appears to indicate that ratifying States undertake to achieve the "total abolition" of child labour of persons under 18, an objective which is not only philosophically questionable, but out of place in a Convention which should focus on the worst or extreme forms of child labour and, by doing so, attract unanimous support among member States. The declarations and programmes of action referred to in the fifth paragraph, such as the Copenhagen Declaration on Social Development and the Programme of Action of the World Summit for Social Development, 1995, and the Beijing Declaration and Platform for Action of the Fourth World Conference on Women, 1995, are not legal instruments, and governments are not bound by them. If these references are included in the proposed Convention, ratifying States would have to adjust their strategies and programmes to them. Furthermore, whenever the proposed Convention refers to the "total abolition of child labour" or "the need to remove ... children from work", it should be stated and not forgotten that reference is always made to "the worst forms" of child labour. A Convention on the worst or extreme forms of child labour should be clear, concise and comprehensible.

Spanish Employers' Confederation (CEOE). The changes by the Office in the third and fourth paragraphs are an improvement as they eliminate the duplication mentioned while retaining the sense of the amendments accepted in the Committee. Using "prohibition and immediate and comprehensive action" instead of "immediate elimination of the worst forms of child labour" is supported, given the difficulties the latter would pose for certain countries where child labour is endemic. The changes made by the Office in the third paragraph also preserve the spirit of the agreement reached in the Committee on the complementarity between this proposed Convention and the Minimum Age Convention and Recommendation, 1973.

Sudan. During the 1998 Session of the Conference there were lengthy discussions about the expression "immediate elimination". Although this phrase has been replaced in the Articles of the proposed Convention by "take measures to secure the prohibition and immediate elimination", it has been included in the title. Considering that the immediate elimination of the worst forms of child labour requires measures and action to be taken, the present title is not in conformity with the reality of the situation or the text of Article 1. Thus, the proposed Convention should be called "Measures for the Immediate Elimination of the Worst Forms of Child Labour Convention, 1999".

Sweden. The United Nations Convention on the Rights of the Child should be given a paragraph to itself. Binding instruments should be mentioned consecutively and references to conferences and meetings should be separate.

Tunisia. Agrees with the deletion of the reference to "immediate and comprehensive action" in the Preamble.

Uganda. Third and fourth paragraphs: Comprehensive action may require time and resources to set up necessary infrastructure and mechanisms and sensitize all parties. The prohibition preceding the elimination of the worst forms of child labour may be difficult, especially in the African context, where creating the necessary infrastructure and mechanisms and sensitizing the people is in a preliminary stage. It would be more appropriate to have the comprehensive action before the prohibition and the paragraph could read: "for the effective elimination and prohibition of the worst forms of child labour".

United Kingdom. Agrees with the Office's revision. It is clearer and preserves the sense that immediate "action" is required, not immediate elimination of the worst forms of child labour. This is the correct approach as, apart from not being a practical possibility in any case, a commitment to eliminate the worst forms immediately would make ratification unlikely for many member States. However, the title of the Convention still refers to "immediate elimination" and this should be changed. Immediate elimination is impractical and unenforceable at the present time.

United States. Does not support adding language regarding the total abolition of child labour. Even though this phrase is taken from the Preamble to Convention

No. 138, it is unnecessary because the total elimination of child labour is not the aim of the proposed Convention, and the adjective is potentially confusing. As noted above under *General observations*, the proposed Convention should be neither a restatement nor a revision of Convention No. 138. Furthermore, its provisions should be easily understood. Similarly, while the Preamble should acknowledge that the proposed Convention will complement Convention No. 138, the negotiating history should nevertheless make it clear that this proposed Convention is completely separate from the requirements of Convention No. 138, since the proposed Convention should focus on the elimination of only the worst forms of work. The last part of the third paragraph should read: "which remain[s] the comprehensive instrument[s] on child labour". Agrees with the comments made during the first discussion to the effect that a shorter, plainer Preamble would be preferable and could therefore support proposals for limiting the references to international instruments solely to ILO Conventions Nos. 138 and 29 and the United Nations Convention on the Rights of the Child. For the same reasons, recalling the relevant provisions of Conventions Nos. 81 and 142 and the Declaration on Equality of Opportunity and Treatment for Women Workers is unnecessary. In the last paragraph of the Preamble, in keeping with comments made above on the term "immediate elimination", the proposed Convention should be cited simply as the "Abolition of the Worst Forms of Child Labour Convention, 1999".

Venezuela. Venezuelan Federation of Chambers of Commerce and Manufacturers' Associations (FEDECAMARAS). Agrees with the use of the phrase "immediate and comprehensive action".

Office Commentary

In general, the comments show a difference of opinion on the appropriate references to be made in the Preamble and the reasons for doing so and raise some questions about the status of the Preamble.

The Meaning and Effect of the Preamble

The Preamble is not an operative part of the instrument, meaning that it does not have legal force. It can be helpful, however, in interpreting ambiguities within the text. Under international treaty law, the basic principle of interpretation is that a "treaty shall be interpreted in good faith in accordance with the ordinary meaning to be given to the terms of the treaty in their context and in the light of its object and purpose". The Preamble forms part of the context of the Convention and is relevant in determining its overall object and purpose.

Use of the Preamble to Establish the Relationship of New Instruments to Existing Instruments

International labour Conventions are designed to form a coherent body of minimum standards in the field of competence of the International Labour Organization. The standard-setting body, the International Labour Conference, takes care to ensure that there is neither duplication of nor conflict between the provisions of different Conventions; one means regularly used by it is to refer in the Preamble to relevant existing texts and to define, again in the Preamble, the legislative gap which the new instrument is designed to fill.

The Office had therefore suggested a short Preamble which would provide the reader with an introduction to the reason for adopting a new instrument and the context in which it is being adopted. This was intended to avoid confusion, to keep the Preamble focused, and to refer only to the other particularly relevant instruments that cover the same subject and might give rise to some question as to its relationship with the other instruments.

The comments reveal a preference for a shorter Preamble but also some continued disagreement over the appropriate references. Some replies suggest deletions from the list, while others suggest additions.

Reference to Convention No. 138 in the Third Preambular Paragraph

Following the first discussion, the end of the third preambular paragraph was revised by the Office. The reference to "the Convention and Recommendation concerning Minimum Age for Admission to Employment, 1973, which remain the fundamental instruments for the abolition of child labour" is amended to read: "which remain the fundamental instruments with a view to achieving the total abolition of child labour". The purpose was to correctly reflect the language of the Preamble to the Minimum Age Convention, 1973 (No. 138).

The Office has retained the reference as an accurate restatement of the purpose of Convention No. 138 from its own Preamble, which is supported by most of those who commented. Those who object do so because they consider that the language may imply that immediate action is to be taken to abolish all forms of child labour or they do not view all "child labour" as inappropriate and thus do not want the reference made. However, the new instrument does not apply to all forms of child labour and the aims of the two Conventions are different.

The divergence of views on this point may be reduced if the term "child labour" is seen as referring not to all work by children, but rather to work which is prohibited by ILO standards. This is how the Office understands the term. Under Convention No. 138, for example, allowable work is subject to minimum ages. Whether it is to be prohibited depends on the age of the child, the kind of work, the circumstances in which it is carried out, whether it jeopardizes safety, health or morals, whether it prejudices attendance at school, and the like. Work which does not conflict with the standard is allowed. Some countries give examples of work which they believe is suitable for children but imply that it is the kind of work prohibited by Convention No. 138 as child labour. It appears that some of the examples given would not be prohibited by Convention No. 138 and thus would not be understood as "child labour".

Third and Fourth Preambular Paragraphs

As commented upon in Report IV(1), the texts in the two preambular paragraphs of the proposed Convention beginning "Considering ..." (third and fourth paragraphs) were revised by amendments in the Committee during the first discussion. The compromise reached on the language of the Preamble was to refer to new instruments "for the prohibition and for immediate and comprehensive action for the elimination of the worst forms of child labour", rather than to the "immediate elimination" of such forms. In the next preambular paragraph it was stated that "effective elimination of the worst forms of child labour requires comprehensive action, taking into account the importance of basic education and the need for the removal from work and the rehabilitation and social reintegration of the children concerned". There was thus an element of duplication in that both paragraphs referred to the need for "comprehensive action", a need which (according to the second of the two paragraphs) stems from the need for "effective elimination".

The Office had been invited to review the drafting of these paragraphs. In doing so, it redrafted them to keep the references to "effective elimination" and "prohibition and immediate and comprehensive action" that had been decided upon by the Committee, but to avoid the duplication. The first of the two paragraphs now refers to the need for new instruments "for the prohibition and effective elimination of the worst forms of child labour" as the main priority for national and international action, and the second explains what is entailed by "effective elimination", namely "immediate and comprehensive action, taking into account the importance of basic education and the need to remove the concerned children from work and to provide for their rehabilitation and social reintegration".

There is considerable support for this in the comments, and the changes have accordingly been maintained. It is emphasized, however, that it reflects the Committee's decisions taken on the Preamble. In the operative part of the Convention, in Article 1, the Committee decided that the Convention should require "measures to secure the prohibition and immediate elimination of the worst forms of child labour". It is this obligation laid down in the operative part of the Convention from which the title has been derived. The title will, of course, eventually reflect the final decisions to be taken by the Conference.

Concerning the fourth preambular paragraph, a question was raised in the Committee's Drafting Committee about the meaning of "removal from work" in the second of the two paragraphs and in Article 7, paragraph 2(b), and whether the intent was to remove children in the worst forms of child labour from such forms or from all work.

A substantial number of replies want the insertion of "such" before "work", arguing that the purpose of the new Convention is to focus on the worst forms of child labour and that it should not interfere with work allowed under Convention No. 138. While some note that in many cases it would be desirable for children who are removed from the worst forms of child labour to be rehabilitated, attend school and no longer work, this might not be practical in all circumstances, and therefore there should be the possibility of older children switching to acceptable work.

Those who want to retain the reference to work in general, however, strike the balance the other way. Children in the worst forms should not be moved around the labour market. Moving them into other work could carry with it the threat of a return to the worst forms or prevent them from being properly rehabilitated or given a chance of obtaining an education. Given the difference of opinion, the text has not been changed, but it is a matter which the Conference may wish to consider.

Fifth and Seventh Preambular Paragraphs

The Office has made changes to the fifth and seventh paragraphs beginning "Recalling ...". The reference to the Convention on the Rights of the Child has been given more emphasis in a separate paragraph. The other references have been regrouped to give more prominence to the legal documents. The Declarations and Programme of Action have been separated into one paragraph, now the eighth preambular paragraph.

Several commentators argue for deletion of the references to the Copenhagen Declaration on Social Development and the Programme of Action of the World Summit for Social Development, 1995, the Beijing Declaration and Platform for Action of the Fourth World Conference on Women, 1995, the Human Resources Development Convention and Recommendation, 1975, as well as the Declaration on Equality of Opportunity and Treatment for Women Workers, adopted by the International Labour Conference in 1975, in favour of retaining only the most significant and particular legal instruments. Some additions were also suggested. Except for the reordering of these provisions, the Office has not made changes, leaving the decision to the Conference. However, it invites the Conference to consider a shorter, more focused Preamble.

Title

There are a few suggestions to change the title, for example by deleting the reference to "immediate" elimination. Since the title is drawn from the obligation laid down in the Convention, it has been maintained and it is left for the Conference to decide, depending upon the final text. It is suggested, however, that "immediacy" of action is a distinguishing feature of the new standards and is thus a clear indication of their purpose.

Article 1

Each Member which ratifies this Convention shall take measures to secure the prohibition and immediate elimination of the worst forms of child labour.

Observations on Article 1

Austria. Insert after the word "measures" the words "under Articles 5 to 8". This would make it clear that Articles 5 to 8 apply only to member States which have ratified the proposed Convention.

Bolivia. National legal provisions specify the types of work prohibited for minors, which will be elaborated on by a forthcoming Children's and Adolescents' Code.

Bulgaria. Agrees.

Ecuador. Agrees.

Egypt. Supports the text of the Article, but it should come after Articles 2 and 3, since it is more convenient to have the definitions at the beginning of the proposed Convention before the main provisions.

Egyptian Trade Union Federation. Agrees.

El Salvador. Agrees.

Jordan. Federation of Jordanian Chambers of Commerce. National legislation prohibits the employment of children under 17 in activities that are dangerous, exhausting or harmful to their health. However, these laws do not conform to the requirement to take immediate measures to secure the elimination of the worst forms of child labour.

Mexico. Mexico favours a Recommendation only and this should read as follows in it: "Each Member shall take the necessary measures for the immediate prohibition and progressive elimination of the worst forms of child labour."

Morocco. There is a discrepancy between the reference to the "effective elimination" of the worst forms of child labour in the second paragraph of the Preamble and the reference to their "immediate elimination" in Article 1. This could lead to conflicting interpretations, and the text should therefore only refer to one of these two terms.

Norway. The phrase "take measures" seems unnecessarily indecisive. In Article 7 the phrase "take all necessary measures" is used. It is difficult to see why the implementation obligation is weaker in Article 1 than in Article 7, when the substance of the obligation is the same.

Peru. Given the country's present social and economic situation, it has to allow minors to work from the age of 12, with the express authorization of the competent authority and provided it does not interfere with their school work or development. However, Peru intends to work towards the progressive elimination of child labour.

South Africa. Supports the proposed text.

Spain. It is not realistic to secure the immediate elimination of the worst forms of child labour. It is one thing to adopt immediate measures and another to eliminate immediately the reality of child labour in its worst manifestations, which requires time, and above all, the elimination of poverty. To state this is tantamount to saying that all ratifying governments shall take measures to secure the immediate elimination of crime or drug trafficking. The following qualified formulation is suggested: "Each Member which ratifies this Convention shall take measures to secure the prohibition and promote the immediate and effective elimination of the worst forms of child labour."

Syrian Arab Republic. Move the word "immediate" to in front of "measures", to give the text greater flexibility.

United States. The correct approach to the proposed Convention is to focus on immediate and comprehensive action for the effective elimination of the worst forms of child labour, thus the following formulation is proposed: "Each Member which ratifies this Convention shall take immediate and comprehensive measures to secure the prohibition and effective elimination of the worst forms of child labour."

Office Commentary

The comments on this Article are not numerous, implying its general acceptance. However, there is not a common thread among those that did comment. Some support it as it is, one prefers a stronger formulation such as "all necessary measures", others refer to the necessity for more progressive action and yet another suggests that it be aligned with the wording of the Preamble to refer to immediate and comprehensive measures to secure the prohibition and "effective" elimination, instead of "immediate" elimination, of the worst forms of child labour.

Concerning the meaning of "immediate", the Office notes the dictionary definition, which assigns the meaning of done at once or without delay.

In the light of the comments also made on the provision concerning "time-bound" measures in Article 7, there seems to be considerable support for the emphasis being placed on immediate action or measures. (There is also distinct support, however, especially among workers' organizations, to maintain the reference to "immediate" elimination, on the understanding that some time-bound measures are also required.) The spirit of the Article suggests that immediate measures are required to achieve the goal of effective elimination; however, the text could be understood as allowing a certain time for measures to be taken but requiring their result to be immediate. The meaning might be clarified by placing the word "immediate" before the word "measures", and referring to "effective" rather than to "immediate" elimination (see below).

The rationale for the new instruments has been that there are forms of child labour that cannot be tolerated and therefore cannot be subject to progressive elimination. This is consistent with the resolution concerning the elimination of child labour adopted by the International Labour Conference in 1996 which stressed, within the context of the progressive elimination of child labour, the need to immediately proceed with the abolition of its most intolerable aspects. To immediately proceed implies taking immediate measures without waiting for progress on achieving longer-term goals such as universal compulsory education and poverty alleviation.

At the same time, effective elimination would seem to require both immediate and time-bound measures, and the replies reflect a coalition around this view. Immediate measures would include, for example, removal from intolerable situations. As soon as children are found, for instance, in bondage, in a brothel or deep in a mine, they are to be removed and emergency measures, if nothing else, are to be taken until further assistance and rehabilitation can be provided. Other measures could then be taken, for example for prevention, that could require a certain time frame for implementation and should be time-bound, as stated in many of the comments. Prevention, rehabilitation and social reintegration as called for in Article 7 could have immediate and time-bound aspects. Some examples are given in the box.

The Office has not introduced changes, but invites the Conference to consider which of the adjectives in brackets best expresses the intent in the following proposition:

> Each Member which ratifies this Convention shall take [immediate] measures to secure the prohibition and [effective] [immediate] elimination of the worst forms of child labour.

Article 2

For the purposes of this Convention, the term "child" shall apply to all persons under the age of 18.

Observations on Article 2

Australia. The definition of "child" is not exactly the same as that in the Convention on the Rights of the Child. This is an issue that may need to be revisited in the second discussion.

Bahrain. Several ILO minimum age Conventions provide various types of protection for children, especially for hazardous work, and prohibit overtime employment, paying children wages based on piece-work or output and other forms of protection. These Conventions must be legally harmonized with the text of this Article to avoid conflict between the ages stipulated in other Conventions and that set by the proposed Convention. Despite the degree of flexibility available in the provisions of Convention No. 138, many countries have had trouble ratifying it. It may be necessary to reconcile the differences between Convention

No. 138 and this Article to promote ratification and go beyond the compulsory education age limit, so that a child may receive a minimum of education. Countries should be able to derogate from this Article, according to their specific economic situations, degree of development and circumstances.

Bangladesh. The term "child" should apply to all persons under the age of 14 instead of 18.

Bolivia. It is correct to apply the term "child" to persons under the age of 18, since the protection of the State should last until that age. From the viewpoint of human biological, psychological and social development, however, it is not correct, since a distinction should be drawn before the age of 18 between children and adolescents. The preliminary draft of proposed national legislation, the Children's and Adolescents' Code, considers any human being from conception to the age of 12 to be a child and from the age of 12 to 18 to be an adolescent.

Bulgaria. Agrees with the proposed texts.

Canada. CEC. The selection of 18 as the age for defining children to whom the proposed Convention will apply will be the subject of further debate at the 1999 Session of the Conference. This is particularly so concerning the definition of the types of work "likely to jeopardize the health, safety and morals of children". Many governments appear to favour exclusions, for example for cases where children under 18, but over a stated age such as 16, receive adequate training and are provided with the appropriate safety equipment.

Croatia. Replace "shall apply to" with "shall mean" to be in accordance with article 1 of the United Nations Convention on the Rights of the Child and to clarify the definition of the term – child".

Czech Republic. Federation of Entrepreneurs in the Construction Industry. When defining the minimum age for work, including light work, there should be a distinction between "children" and "teenagers".

Ecuador. Agrees.

Egypt. Agrees, as it is in accordance with the definition of "child" under Egyptian law.

Egyptian Trade Union Federation. Agrees.

El Salvador. Agrees.

Finland. TT and PT. The age of 18 is so high that it could potentially hamper ratification of the proposed Convention in a number of countries.

Germany. BDA. In view of the differing practical and legal situations in some countries, the definition of "child" as any person under the age of 18 is unnecessarily strict and could be an obstacle to implementation and ratification. A definition allowing a gradual approach should be adopted instead. Based on the wording of Article 2, paragraphs 4 and 5, of Convention No. 138, countries whose economies and educational facilities are insufficiently developed (or, in the wording of article 19(3) of the ILO Constitution, "those countries in which climatic conditions, the imperfect development of industrial organization, or other special circumstances make the industrial conditions substantially different") might be allowed for the purpose of this Convention initially to define as "children" all persons under the age of 16. Reports submitted under article 22 of the ILO Constitution will then be required to indicate whether the reasons for limiting the scope of application in this way still subsist or whether no further use is to be made of this exemption clause as from a stated date.

Hungary. Union of Agrarian Employers. Include an additional category for juveniles.

Ireland. ICTU. The following three main concerns have been raised about setting the age at 18: (i) general concern over the impact of the new Convention on employment of persons above the basic minimum age for employment, 15 (or 14) years, and below 18 years; (ii) the possible impact on the involvement of persons under 18 years in vocational training, especially where trainees are involved in activities in workplaces; and (iii) the potential for conflict between the provisions of the new Convention and "age of consent" laws (i.e. the lawful age for sexual activity) in several countries, concerning involvement in commercial sexual activity/prostitution of persons under 18 years but above the legal age of consent. Concerning the general impact on employment and vocational training, the new Convention would complement Convention No. 138. The provisions in Convention No. 138 concerning employment/training of those between 15 (14) years and 18 years of age in non-hazardous activities would be taken into account in the application and interpretation of the new Convention. In any case, the provisions contained in the current draft are very similar to the existing provisions in Convention No. 138, as the 18-year benchmark only applies to the worst forms of child labour. Concerning age of consent, while national law may set an age lower than 18 years for lawful sexual activity (and thus potentially for commercial sexual activity/prostitution), commercial sexual activity would in any case fall within the definition of hazardous work (owing to the potential for infectious disease, violence, etc.). To this extent, the new Convention would, in effect, reiterate the meaning of the existing provisions in Convention No. 138.

Jordan. The term "child" should apply to all persons under the age of 16.

Amman Chamber of Industry. The age should be 16 because traditionally in Jordan, as in other developing countries, a child who reaches the age of 16 is deemed fit to undertake some forms of labour. To set the age at 18 does an injustice to children in the 16-18 age group, especially those who cannot join educational institutions. Failure to employ them represents a social burden, especially as unemployment leads to vagrancy and behavioural and moral deviance. The new Convention should allow for the employment of adolescents in developing countries in appropriate work that would not exhaust them. Vocational training institutions should be made to accept all those over the age of 15, which requires extending the scope of activities in these institutions and providing the young people with technical and financial support. Children in the 16-18 age group could be employed in different handicrafts for a limited number of hours a day while protecting their social rights by enrolling them in vocational training institutions.

Malaysia. See comment under Article 3.

Mexico. Insert a heading "Frame of reference" before this provision. One of the main obstacles to ratification of Convention No. 138 is that in some countries the minimum age is lower than that set in the Convention. Therefore the minimum age in the proposed instruments should be flexible according to those fixed by national legislation or, in any case, reflect those in Convention No. 138. Considering that the 86th Session of the Conference adopted a resolution concerning youth employment, which includes young persons between 15 and 24 years of age, fixing the age in the new instruments at 18 years could lead to confusion given the different ages in national legislation. The age limits for hazardous work in Convention No. 138 should serve as an example for child labour and are applicable to many countries. There are activities considered as criminal offences which are punishable irrespective of the age of the person committing them. To set a general minimum age of 18 years could be interpreted as condoning these activities for those aged over 18 years. This Article should be inserted after Article 3 and separated into two parts. The first part should provide that for activities considered as the worst forms of child labour in Article 3(d), account should be taken of the provisions on the minimum age for hazardous work in Article 3 of the Minimum Age Convention, 1973. The second part should provide that for the illicit work and the criminal activities described in Article 3(a) to (c), the term "child" shall apply to all persons under the age of 18. Mexico favours a Recommendation only, thus references to Articles should be replaced by references to Paragraphs throughout.

New Zealand. NZEF. For clarity, the proposed Convention should state what upper age limit is to apply with respect to the word "child".

Pakistan. Fixing the age limit at 18 may not be suited to the economic, social and legal systems of most member States, including Pakistan. For those member States which have economic and social conditions that are not ripe enough, it will be difficult to comply with the proposed instruments. An inflexible limit of age 18, accompanied by a very broad definition of what constitutes the worst forms of child labour, may inhibit the ability of a number of member States to ratify or accept the proposed Convention or Recommendation. Thus, fixing an age limit could be left to member States to establish in accordance with national law and practice.

South Africa. Supports the proposed text. The South African Constitution defines "child" as all persons under 18.

Spain. Applying the term "child" to all persons under the age of 18, irrespective of whether they have attained majority or the age of emancipation, is too rigid, especially since the provisions of the proposed Convention do not give any other indications as to age and may contradict those of paragraph 3 of Article 3 of Convention No. 138, which allows persons aged 16 to perform hazardous work under certain conditions. Moreover, since the proposed Convention deals with matters that are purely criminal in scope (illegal activities, prostitution, pornography, drug trafficking, etc.), the rigid definition of a child as any person under the age of 18 may give rise to serious legal difficulties in ratification. In defining the term "child" a distinction should be drawn between the worst forms of child labour set out in Article 3, subparagraphs (a), (b) and (c), and the hazardous work referred to in subparagraph (d). Both groups need protection, but not in the same way. Regarding the work described in subparagraph (d), there should be a connection between the age limit laid down for compulsory education and the minimum age for hazardous work. It should be borne in mind that the proposed Convention lays down minimum standards and that a strict limitation to age 18 may give rise to problems for States in ratification or application, unless reference is made to the "worst forms of child labour" in Article 3(a), (b) and (c) only.

United States. Supports the proposed text, to the extent that the definitional aspect of the proposed Convention is not expanded.

Office Commentary

The majority of observations support the provision as it is, and so no change has been introduced. However, several object either to the age itself, or to referring to persons under the age of 18 as children, preferring that a distinction be made between children and young persons or adolescents. The definition is for "the purposes of this Convention" and thus is not offering a general definition of "child". It refers to all persons under the age of 18, which includes categorizations of persons under that age such as children, young persons and adolescents.

Some objections to age 18 appear to be based on a misunderstanding about the designation of age 18 for the purposes of the proposed Convention. The proposed Convention does not apply to all work by children, but only to the worst forms of child labour. Because the subject of the proposed Convention is work that is so intolerable, so bad that no child or young person should be engaged in it, the age of 18 was chosen to be consistent with the higher minimum age laid down in Convention No. 138 for hazardous work and the general definition of "child" in the Convention on the Rights of the Child. It does not in any way affect the minimum ages in Convention No. 138, which allows lower ages, down to 12 or 13 for light work.

This issue is also addressed in the commentary on Article 3.

Article 3

For the purposes of this Convention, the expression "the worst forms of child labour" comprises:

(a) all forms of slavery or practices similar to slavery, such as the sale and trafficking of children, forced or compulsory labour, debt bondage and serfdom;

(b) the use, procuring or offering of a child for prostitution, for the production of pornography or for pornographic performances;

(c) the use, procuring or offering of a child for illegal activities, in particular for the production and trafficking of narcotic drugs and psychotropic substances as defined in the relevant international treaties;

(d) any other type of work or activity which, by its nature or the circumstances in which it is carried out, is likely to jeopardize the health, safety or morals of children.

Observations on Article 3

Argentina. The proposed Convention should include a ban on the participation of children in armed conflicts. Subparagraph (c): Supports a definition of drugs as worded in article 33 of the United Nations Convention on the Rights of the Child. Subparagraph (d): Add "or (compulsory) basic education" after "morals".

Australia. It is noted that the discussion of the issue of children in armed conflict, as combatants, has been deferred until the second (1999) discussion. Participation of children in armed conflict is an important issue and is certainly appropriate for discussion. Subparagraph (c): Prefers the term "illicit" to "illegal" because "illicit" could cover activities that may be lawful in some States but not permissible with respect to the objectives of the proposed Convention. "Illegal" would not cover cases in which there is a minor illegality in what is essentially a lawful activity and therefore not in the worst forms of child labour. Supports the simplification of the text to refer to "production and trafficking of drugs as defined in the relevant international treaties".

Austria. Subparagraph (b): Since the whole purpose of child pornography is to make money by satisfying persons with abnormal sexual tendencies, the list should include the consumption of child pornography. The same applies to prostitution, in so far as consumption is not already included in the concept of "use ... for prostitution". This wording would place States under the obligation to take measures against prostitution in connection with sex tourism or child pornography over the Internet, for example as is done by some European countries, which would also help the main countries concerned in Asia and Latin America to combat these extreme forms of exploitation of children. Subparagraph (d): Welcomes the reference to work or activity which is likely to jeopardize the health, safety or morals of children. This makes it clear that it is meant to include work in which such hazards are probable, but do not yet have to be expressly proven. Therefore, proposed amendments referring to clearly proven hazards (for example, which "jeopardize" instead of "are likely to jeopardize") should be rejected in the discussion. The activities listed in Paragraph 3 of the proposed Recommendation should be included in Article 3 of the proposed Convention, at least by way of examples. Alternatively, a reference to particularly hazardous branches of industry should be made in brackets, such as textiles, mining, ceramic and glass industries, match and fireworks industries and deep-sea fishing. At least in regard to hazardous work a distinction should be drawn between children and young persons following Convention No. 138, and the proposed instrument should provide that hazardous work shall be prohibited for children under a certain age, but may be performed under certain conditions by young persons. Wider ratification could be achieved, since this would make it clear in express terms (and not only by interpretation as is now the case) that certain work does not have to be prohibited for persons aged over 16 just because the proposed Convention applies to all persons under 18 years of age.

Bahrain. The introductory paragraph should read: "For the purposes of this Convention, the following could be considered as 'the worst forms of child labour':". The worst forms of child labour should not be limited to the forms explicitly listed but should be a list of examples to which others could be added. This proposed amendment would be in line with the text of paragraph 2 of Article 4, which allows countries to revise the list.

Belgium. The Government prefers to abstain at this time on the issue of children in armed conflicts, as combatants, as child soldiers or in military activities, as constituting one of the worst forms of child labour. It is more appropriate to wait for the results of the current discussions of the working group on a draft optional protocol to the Convention on the Rights of the Child on involvement of children in armed conflicts. Paragraph (c): Agrees with the simplified formulation of the "in particular" phrase proposed by the Office.

CNT. The reference to "work and activities which expose children to physical, emotional or sexual abuse" in Paragraph 3(a) of the proposed Recommendation should be in Article 3 of the proposed Convention instead. Subparagraph (d): Add a reference to the "elimination of the use of children in any type of work which, by its nature or the circumstances in which it is carried out, is likely to jeopardize their education, at least up to the statutory age of compulsory education set by relevant national legislation".

Benin. The use of children as child soldiers is a practice that exists in various countries involved in armed conflicts. It is a specific and well-known situation which is likely to jeopardize their health, safety and morals. There should be an explicit reference to the use of children in armed conflicts or in military activities as constituting one of the worst forms of child labour. Subparagraph (d): This includes all unspecified or unknown types of activity.

Bolivia. A clear distinction should be drawn between criminal offences and child labour. There are activities in which the child is a victim or object of the work done by other persons, while in other cases the child is the worker. Thus, the sale and trafficking of children and prostitution are criminal offences, the victims of which are children, and should not be considered as "worst forms of child labour".

Botswana. Prefers an explicit reference to the involvement of children in military activities. Due to the hazardous nature of such activities, the involvement of children in them requires serious action aimed at halting the practice.

Brazil. It does not seem appropriate to include the participation of children in armed conflicts in an instrument that aims to regulate child labour. The subject is already amply covered in the United Nations Convention on the Rights of the Child (article 39), and in paragraph 25 of the Plan of Action for Implementing the World Declaration on the Survival, Protection and Development of Children in the 1990s. More specifically, the Vienna Declaration and Programme of Action of 1993 provides, in paragraph 50, that: "The World Conference on Human Rights strongly supports the proposal that the Secretary-General initiate a study into means of improving the protection of children in armed conflicts ... Measures should include protection for children against indiscriminate use of all weapons of war, especially anti-personnel mines ... The Conference calls on the Committee on the Rights of the Child to study the question of raising the minimum age of recruitment into armed forces." Lastly, resolution 1994/91 of the Commission on Human Rights established the working group on a draft optional protocol to the Convention on the Rights of the Child on involvement of children in armed conflicts, a decision supported by Brazil.

Bulgaria. Article 3 should explicitly provide that the participation of children in armed conflicts as combatants or as child soldiers, or their use in military activities, constitutes one of the worst forms of child labour. It represents a threat to their lives. Subparagraph (c): Supports replacing the word "illegal" with "illicit". This should provide a much broader legal coverage for various cases that are not considered as criminal acts by the national legislation of different countries. This change of terminology is preferable for the establishment of penal and other sanctions.

Canada. The Government questions the need for a reference to child soldiers in the proposed Convention, given the ongoing discussions on children in armed conflicts within the Convention on the Rights of the Child and its proposed optional protocol. However, if a reference to child soldiers is included, it is preferred that language is used which characterizes the use of children in active combat or the participation of children in hostilities as one of the worst forms of child labour, but not language which calls for its criminalization in domestic law. Subparagraph (a): Would like confirmation that "sale and trafficking" should not be interpreted to cover issues outside the worst forms of child labour, such as adoptions. Subparagraph (c): This is very broad and vague because of the use and placement of the undefined term "illegal activities". Suggests instead the following: "the use, procuring or offering of a child in the production and trafficking of narcotic drugs and psychotropic substances, as defined in the relevant international treaties". If necessary, "and for other illegal activities" could be added at the end of the Article; however, there should be confirmation that this would refer to activities designated illegal in national law. Disagrees with replacing "illegal" with "illicit", as this is an undefined term. Subparagraph (d): Given the broad nature of this subparagraph, and the provisions of Paragraph 11 of the proposed Recommendation, the Government would like confirmation that there is no requirement for the activities in this subparagraph to be criminalized as long as there are other appropriate penalties, such as administrative, civil and labour penalties.

CEC. Subparagraph (c): The distinction between "illegal" and "illicit" activities and the resulting implications are difficult to comprehend, thus retain "illegal" and add "illicit" to cover those activities which are prohibited by national laws as well as those which, though not the subject of specific prohibition, are nevertheless considered illicit (with its moral connotation). Limiting the applicability to "illicit" could generate endless academic debate without the effective elimination of activities sought to be addressed by the subparagraph. The Office's proposal to simplify the "in particular" phrase requires a careful review of the definition of "drugs" in the relevant treaties. Regarding the issue of children in armed conflict, relying on the phrase "likely to jeopardize the health, safety or morals", in subparagraph (d) is not sufficient to protect children from some of the excesses of war witnessed in recent years involving young children. Without specific reference to this modern-day blight governments could inadvertently or intentionally fail to address this serious problem. It is suggested to prohibit separately the participation of children in armed conflict as combatants (whether formally as members of armies or militias or on a more ad hoc basis) and in non-combat military activities which are likely to jeopardize their health, safety or morals. In this way, children could be air and sea cadets though under the age of 18. More thought is required on this issue to ensure that the excesses are clearly prohibited while retaining a Convention that can be ratified. The CEC would thus support a clear reference to the issue of children placed in intolerable situations owing to armed conflicts in the definition of the worst forms of child labour; however, as employers do not have particular expertise or knowledge of the scope of the broader issue of "military activities", it would seek the advice of the Canadian Government's experts on current military activities involving children under 18 in Canada.

CLC. Presses for the inclusion of a reference to "work which jeopardizes access to basic education" in the definition of the worst forms of child labour, and for the inclusion in the proposed Convention of the detailed definition of hazardous work contained in the proposed Recommendation, to specify more clearly what should, as a minimum, be considered as hazardous work.

Chile. Regarding the participation of children in armed conflicts, agrees that this specific situation would come under Article 4 as a type of activity or work that is likely to jeopardize the safety, health or morals of boys or girls. Nevertheless, it is important that an agreement be reached to mention these types of situation, particularly given their gravity and the irreparable damage they cause boys and girls who are involved in them. It would be useful to mention them to give an even stronger negative moral connotation and to raise awareness about their effects on children. Subparagraph (d): Add the adjectives used in article 32(1) of the Convention on the Rights of the Child, which states: "States parties recognize the right of the child to be protected from economic exploitation and from performing any work that is likely to be hazardous or to interfere with the child's education; or to be harmful to the child's health or physical, mental, spiritual, moral or social development." This would clarify more precisely what is meant by "the worst forms of child labour", at the same time as bringing the proposed Convention more into line with the Convention on the Rights of the Child. In addition, the term "physical integrity" should be added after "health", to provide for specific situations of physical exploitation to which boys and girls may be exposed. The term "image" should also be added to the definition so that the worst forms of child labour include those that harm the image of boys and girls, as image is an asset belonging to children which can be harmed or undermined by being shown, for example, on television, in advertisements or in connection with controversial issues. This damage to image becomes a stigma for the child throughout development, with a series of negative repercussions which the child is unable to evaluate when involved in situations such as those being considered here. Agrees with the inclusion of a direct reference to "the use, procuring or offering of a child for the production and trafficking of drugs", linking these activities to the term "illicit". The term "illicit" makes it easier to assess this type of activity, as it covers a greater number of situations (as a result of its moral connotation) and at the same time allows this subparagraph to be applied in countries where the production and trafficking of narcotic drugs has not been declared illegal.

CONUPIA. Subparagraph (c): This should be applied in a broader form taking into account anything relating to criminal activities, as there is a tendency for criminal networks to use children to carry out criminal activities, since children do not, under national law, bear criminal liability for such acts. It would be very useful if the proposed Convention could help to ensure that progress is made towards providing penalties for using children in criminal activities, for which there is inadequate provision in international law. Subparagraph (d): Replace "health" with "overall development of the child", as a broader concept of "health" should be applied, rather than one which is apparently based on strictly biological criteria and fails to take into account aspects relating to psychological and social development. The use of children in armed conflicts should be included under the worst forms of child labour. A reference could be made to the Convention on the Rights of the Child as the basis for the prohibition of the use of children in armed conflicts, given that it protects children in situations which are detrimental to their welfare and development. It would also be possible to cite research in psychology which has shown the damage that children may suffer in this type of social conflict.

Croatia. The Article refers to different forms of work and conditions. It should refer to the work of children instead of criminal offences, particularly because Paragraph 11 of the proposed Recommendation states that the forms of child labour listed in clauses (a) to (c) should be regarded as criminal offences. It is unclear who the perpetrators are and who should be punished. It could be implied that children should be punished. Therefore the changes below should be made. Subparagraph (a): Replace "practices" with "work under the conditions" and replace "forced or compulsory labour, debt bondage and serfdom" with "and debt bondage, forced or compulsory labour and serfage". Subparagraphs (b) and (c): Replace "the use, procuring or offering of a child" with "the engaging of a child used, procured or offered". Subparagraph (c): Replace "for the production" with "in the production".

Working Group of Trade Union Confederations. Insert clauses (a) to (e) of Paragraph 3 of the proposed Recommendation before subparagraph (d) of this Article to provide greater legal force and a clearer explanation of the expression "the worst forms of child labour".

Czech Republic. Subparagraphs (a) to (c): These types of work probably constitute criminal offences in most countries, as is the case in the Czech Republic.

Denmark. The term "child soldier" should be part of the definition. In 1998, Denmark decided to raise the age limit for military service in the armed forces to age 18. It had been possible for 17-year-olds to perform duty as private first class/private first class trainees, conscripts and volunteers in the Home Guard. As of 1 January 1999, conscripts will not be able to be called to the first collective service until they reach age 18. The minimum age for the Home Guards will be changed to 18 with the next amendment of the Home Guard Act. Thus, there is no objection to including "all forms of military activity", provided, however, that the age limit of 18 in Article 2 is not raised. The wording "all forms of activity which involve the use of violence" and "all forms of military activity" are suggested. The final decision should be seen in the light of the discussion in the working group on a draft optional protocol to the Convention on the Rights of the Child on involvement of children in armed conflicts. Subparagraph (d): Add clauses by moving Paragraph 3 from the proposed Recommendation to the proposed Convention.

Danish Employers' Confederation (DA). Lacking access to education is not comparable to the crude abuses of children covered by this Article, therefore, lacking access to education should not be part of the definition. Light work is acceptable for persons under the age of 15, when it takes place under acceptable working conditions.

Federation of Danish Trade Unions (LO). Add lacking access to basic education as part of the definition of the worst forms of child labour in a new subparagraph.

Ecuador. Eighteen-year-olds are generally already undergoing military service or instruction, whether compulsory or optional. This type of military instruction should therefore not be considered as one of the worst forms of child labour. Military or pre-military instruction is voluntary or optional, so there is no manifest intention to disregard children's rights when they participate in this type of activity. Voluntary or optional pre-military instruction involves children between the ages of 14 and 18. It is therefore suggested that such instruction be permitted from a specified age, from the age of puberty recognized by law, or from the end of compulsory education. In so far as military or pre-military activity is voluntary and authorized, the kind of strictly civic work involved warrants special treatment, and it would be difficult to stipulate exactly to what extent it might be said to constitute forced labour.

Egypt. This should be moved to become Article 1. Subparagraphs (a) to (c): These forms of child labour do not exist in Egypt. If they do exist, they would be considered contrary to morality and would fall under the provisions of penal law.

Federation of Egyptian Industries. Subparagraphs (a) to (c): Prohibiting these activities is in harmony with the views of the social partners, and more specifically the teachings of the holy faiths that ban exploitation of children and their exposure to such activities. In Egyptian society, thanks to its values and traditions, such practices are unknown. The Egyptian Penal Code penalizes such child exploitation.

Egyptian Trade Union Federation. Agrees.

El Salvador. Agrees with the proposed text.

Estonia. The use of children in the military or for military activities could be added to subparagraph (a) or added as a separate new subparagraph (e).

Estonian Association of Trade Unions. Agrees with the Government.

Ethiopia. Involving children in armed conflicts should be included as one of the worst forms of child labour, as the practice fulfils all the terms indicated in the proposed instruments. It can severely affect and jeopardize the health, safety, morals, and all other aspects of children's development, including their education. Above all, such practices are becoming common in the African continent, where children have been forcibly drilled in such phenomenon and suffer from the atrocities evolving from it.

Finland. At the June 1998 Session of the Conference, Finland and other Nordic countries expressed reservations over leaving the definition of dangerous work to individual national authorities. The parties to the new Convention should agree on a common definition of what is meant by the worst forms of child labour. The activities referred to in subparagraphs (a) to (c) are crimes under Finnish law. The forms of dangerous work detailed in Paragraph 3 of the proposed Recommendation should be included in the proposed Convention, where appropriate, for instance at the end of Article 3. The forms and conditions of dangerous work should be listed differently, separating those which are totally prohibited from those which can be done if special measures are taken to ensure safety. A blanket prohibition could have unfortunate consequences for children by preventing them from studying and preparing for a trade. Subparagraph (b): Particularly when considering the content of Article 3 from the perspective of sexual equality, there are many situations which could be covered by this subparagraph, such as the sale and trafficking of children, the use of children and young people in the sex industry in general (various different forms) and the enticement with false promises of children and young persons into situations which could possibly lead to their involvement in prostitution and/or pornography. Thus the effectiveness of this subparagraph will largely depend on how it is interpreted. Subparagraph (c): The Government supports the proposals made by the Office to use "illicit" and the changes after "in particular". Subparagraph (d): Add "work which jeopardizes access to basic education". This is not intended to mean that every ratifying State would have to provide education, but work which prevents a child from taking advantage of available education should be included in the definition of the worst forms of child labour.

TT and PT. Subparagraph (d): Jeopardizing the health, safety and morals of children can be manifested in different degrees. The most immediate evils should be tackled first.

France. MEDEF. Underlines the necessity to ensure that the specific situation of apprentices is taken into consideration so that it does not fit the definition of the "worst forms" of child labour.

CFDT. A specific reference to children in armed conflicts should be included. The detailed definition of hazardous work should be transferred from the text of the proposed Recommendation to the proposed Convention. The expression "the worst forms of child labour" should also comprise "any type of work which jeopardizes access to primary education". Subparagraph (b): The CFDT continues to express its concern regarding the use of the word "prostitution" in an ILO Convention. It would be more appropriate to refer to "sexual exploitation, whether commercial or not".

Germany. Subparagraph (c): Supports the proposals made by the Office, in particular to replace the term "illegal" with "illicit".

BDA. Subparagraph (c): Delete "psychotropic substances", to avoid complicating this provision. Agrees with the simplified formulation of the "in particular" phrase proposed by the Office. Subparagraph (d): To make it clear that the reference is not to any child labour but to the "worst" forms of it, the hazardous nature of work should be more restricted by inserting "to a particular degree" before "jeopardize" or "to such an extent as not to be tolerable under any circumstances" after "morals of children". Furthermore, the subparagraph should refer to "the life, health or morals" of children, rather than to "the health, safety or morals". Unlike "health" and "morals", "safety" is not in itself a right susceptible of legal protection (safety for what?). It is vague and as such could lead to differences of opinion regarding interpretation. Prohibiting the use of children in armed conflicts, as combatants, as child soldiers or in military activities appears to be unnecessary, since such cases are already covered by subparagraph (d).

DGB. During the first discussion the DGB favoured a detailed definition of hazardous work in the text of the proposed Convention, as defined in the proposed Recommendation, to state more specifically what should be considered, as a minimum, hazardous work. The Conference may not accept this view in 1999, thus the detailed definition should remain in the proposed Recommendation. In this case, the detailed definition could in practice continue to apply to the proposed Convention, since the Committee of Experts on the Application of Conventions and Recommendations normally takes the provisions of relevant Recommendations into account when interpreting the meaning of a Convention. Subparagraph (b): Prefers the term "commercial sexual exploitation" in this context. However, during the last session of the Conference there were objections to this on the grounds that forms of sexual exploitation that do not involve any commercial transactions could be excluded. If no agreement can be reached on another appropriate wording, the present draft will be accepted. Agrees with the Office's proposal of the term "illicit" and the resulting amendments. During the first discussion the DGB proposed that a special reference be made to children in armed conflict in the proposed Convention, but this was not retained. The Committee agreed to discuss this subject again in 1999. The DGB agrees with the Office's view that this form of exploitation would in any case be covered by the definitions of forced labour and hazardous work or activities likely to jeopardize their health, safety or morals. The importance of education, in particular of access to basic education, is mentioned in several parts of the proposed Convention and Recommendation. However, the proposal to include work which jeopardizes access to basic education in the definition of the worst forms of child labour was rejected. This will be an important point for discussion in 1999 and the Workers' group will press once again for the inclusion of this aspect in the definition. It must be made clear, however, that the intention is not for the proposed Convention to require governments to ensure universal basic education, but rather for work which by its nature systematically bars children's access to basic education to come under the definition and hence to be verified in the context of the procedure for the application of the Convention under Articles 4 and 6.

Greece. Opposes the participation of children in military service, armed forces or armed conflicts. Subparagraph (c): Agrees to the amendment suggested by the Office to use the word "illicit" and to the simplification of the subparagraph.

General Confederation of Small and Medium-sized Entrepreneurs, Craftsmen and Tradesmen of Greece. Accepts the use of the word "illicit". Proposes to add a specific subparagraph (e) to prohibit the use of children in armed conflicts, as combatants, as child soldiers or in military activities. This issue should be mentioned in a separate subparagraph as in the case of child prostitution, slavery, sale and trafficking of children, serfdom and the use of children for illicit activities.

Haiti. As regards the participation of children in military activities, it is important to adopt appropriate legal provisions.

Hungary. Union of Agrarian Employers. In defining the worst forms of child labour categories used for vocational education should be used. Specifying age groups for the different activities would allow for fine-tuning of regulations.

India. Subparagraph (a): Exacting of all forms of forced or compulsory labour is prohibited as a penal offence under the Forced Labour Convention, 1930 (No. 29). The above Convention also envisages suppression of the use of forced or compulsory labour in all its forms, irrespective of age, in the shortest possible time. This Convention has achieved one of the highest levels of ratification and acceptability. In view of the above, prohibition and suppression of forced and compulsory labour need not be included. Subparagraph (d): The worst forms of child labour have been elaborated in subparagraphs (a) to (c) very clearly and specifically without giving any room for ambiguity of interpretation or representation. After having defined a "child" under Article 2 and the worst forms of child labour under subparagraphs (a) to (c), there is no need to include undefined areas in the definition of worst forms of child labour through subparagraph (d). This will only lead to ambiguity as well as dilution of the already defined areas. Therefore, it is felt that the deletion of this subparagraph, and consequently Article 4, will not undermine the spirit and objective of the proposed instruments. As guidelines to member States in further identifying hazardous work, Paragraph 3 of the Recommendation can remain.

Ireland. ICTU. During the first discussion, the Workers' group proposal to refer specifically to children in armed conflict in the definition was not accepted, but the Committee agreed that this issue would be discussed again in 1999. In any case, the definitions of forced labour and hazardous work or activity which were included in the text would cover this form of exploitation. Subparagraph (b): Prefers to use the term "commercial sexual exploitation". There is some concern, however, that this term could exclude forms of sexual exploitation which do not involve commercial transactions and if it is not possible to find a suitable alternative wording, the ICTU would support the existing draft text. Subparagraph (d): Welcomes the deletion of a restrictive clause which would have limited the definition of hazardous work by referring to work or activity which is so hazardous that children "should not be used or engaged in it under any circumstances". The deletion of this phrase extends the scope of the Convention considerably. The ICTU strongly supports including the current detailed definition of hazardous work (in Paragraph 3 of the Recommendation) in the text of the Convention to specify more clearly what should, as a minimum, be considered as hazardous work. While the importance of education, in particular access to basic education, is referred to in several parts of the proposed Convention and Recommendation, "work which jeopardizes access to basic education" should be included in the definition of the worst forms of child labour. This does not mean that this Convention would impose a requirement on governments to provide universal basic education. The purpose is that work which, by its nature, systematically denies children access to basic education would come within the definition and would thus need to be considered under the tripartite procedures set out in Articles 4 and 6. The ICTU would urge the Government to consider the argument made by the Government member of Sweden during the first discussion "that there was a difference between saying that education was a 'tool' to prevent and address the problem of child labour and its worst forms, and whether the prevention of access to education was so serious a danger as to warrant including it in the definition of the worst forms".(6) The proposed consultative process to determine what falls within the definition of the worst forms of child labour currently considers problems concerning health, safety and morals. It would be inappropriate not to mention education as a criterion when work or conditions of work would result in systematically preventing a child of school age from going to school. This Convention must address this type of treatment.

SIPTU. Subparagraph (d): Whereas Paragraph 2(b) of the Recommendation notes the importance of social reintegration measures which address the educational needs of children freed from the worst forms of child labour, it is regrettable that work which systematically deprives children of access to education at all is not included in the definition of the worst forms of child labour. A reference to work which systematically denies the child access to basic education should be added to the definition of "worst forms of child labour". This provision would not require governments to provide universal education. Work which by its nature, owing to the number of hours worked, the time of work or its location, deprives a child of access to educational facilities that would otherwise be available to him or her is without doubt one of the worst possible disservices to the future of that child, as it condemns the child to suffer a permanent handicap as a member of society. It remains a matter of concern that "hazardous work" has not been defined to include the most hazardous form of all, armed combat. In view of the wide-scale use of children in warfare in many parts of the world, the ILO is called upon to add the weight of the proposed Convention to the global effort to eliminate this practice. There is no justification for treating the military differently from all other employers. The definition of "work in an unhealthy environment" in Paragraph 3(d) of the Recommendation should include work that exposes children to risking their lives in military conflict.

Italy. Proposes to divide the Article into more subparagraphs, with a specific reference to pornographic activities as distinct from other forms of illicit activities. Subparagraph (c): Agrees with the use of the term "illicit". Considers it important that the reference to activities related to the production and trafficking of drugs remains in the text of the Convention. Proposes to insert before subparagraph (d) the following text: "the use, procuring and offering of children as combatants or soldiers with a view to their involvement in military activities with the intention of employing these children in war or armed conflicts".

CONFCOMMERCIO. Agrees with the replacement of the term "illegal" with "illicit". It is preferable to mention explicitly in a subparagraph the issue of children in armed conflicts, as combatants or soldiers, as well as their use in military activities. It is insufficient to have a general reference to activities that jeopardize the safety, health and morals of children or to forced and compulsory labour.

CGIL, CISL and UIL. A reference to children in armed conflicts should be included among the worst forms of child labour. The definition of hazardous work in the Recommendation should be moved to the Convention to specify more clearly an initial list of types of hazardous work. Subparagraph (d): Hazardous work should include all kinds of work which could "jeopardize or deny access to basic education".

Japan. Subparagraph (c): Use of "illicit" in place of "illegal" is likely to unnecessarily extend the scope of the applicable activities, and seems to be inappropriate. While issues concerning children in armed conflict, as combatants, as child soldiers or in military activities are important, it should be noted that the debate still continues in the United Nations working group on a draft optional protocol to the Convention on the Rights of the Child on involvement of children in armed conflicts. The working group initially discussed the proposal to raise the minimum age uniformly for participation in hostile actions and military recruitment. After four sessions, however, it failed to reach an agreement because military recruitment ages and the systems of enlistment in the army, for example, compulsory draft systems, volunteer systems, or a combination, differ from country to country. Considering that debate, it is difficult to establish a clearly defined provision that can be agreed upon at the ILO, in particular if such provision applies to all persons under the age of 18. Even if such provision is established, it does not contribute to the solution of the overall problem of the worst forms of child labour and it may deter many countries from ratifying the Convention. Furthermore, the present draft appropriately addresses the problem because the subject is covered by Article 3(d), if each country so determines in accordance with Article 4. For these reasons, the subject should not be explicitly mentioned in the Convention.

JTUC-RENGO. Subparagraph (c): Replace "illegal" with "illicit". Add a new subparagraph as follows: "work which jeopardizes access to basic education;".

Jordan. Amman Chamber of Industry. The Ministry of Labour in cooperation with employers and workers should establish a list of the worst forms of child labour which should be suppressed immediately. As agreed through consultation with the social partners, other forms of child labour should be left open.

Federation of Jordanian Chambers of Commerce. National legislation prohibits the employment of children under 17 in activities that are dangerous, exhausting or harmful to their health. However, these laws do not conform to the description of the worst forms of child labour in the proposed Convention.

Kenya. COTU. Subparagraph (d): Insert "and systematically" before "jeopardize" and "access to basic education as well as" after "jeopardize". This is to highlight the fact that any work which interferes with or impedes or is an obstacle to the right to education constitutes one of the worst forms of child labour. Furthermore, the right to education implies the development of full human potential, which is a major concern of Kenyan trade unions, who are focused on the quality of the workers of tomorrow. If this amendment is not accepted on the grounds that it imposes on governments the duty to provide universal basic education, the alternative would be to require the national consultations under paragraph 1 of Article 4 to give attention to work which, by its nature, systematically denies children access to basic education by inserting the words "taking into account the right to basic education and" before "relevant international standards".

Republic of Korea. There is some disagreement as to whether the "participation of children in military activities" should be referred to in Article 3. In some parts of the world where the use of child soldiers is a serious problem, eliminating it is a pressing task. The issue of child soldiers goes beyond the reach of this Convention because it would excessively expand the range of labour. Moreover, even if the relevant provision is not directly expressed, protection of children from being used as soldiers would be ensured under subparagraph (a), which prohibits forced labour, and subpara-graph (d), as the Office has pointed out. Subparagraph (c): Needs to be changed, considering its excessively broad scope and the content of the other three subparagraphs (a), (b) and (d). Rather than including "in particular for the production and trafficking of narcotic drugs and psychotropic substances" as an example of illegal activities, the provision should be more concrete and limited to the production and trafficking of drugs. The other activities should be included in subparagraph (d). The United Nations Convention on the Rights of the Child, in article 33, only stipulates the prevention of the use of children in the illicit production and trafficking of such substances. In addition, considering that the Convention on the Rights of the Child, which deals comprehensively with the rights of children, does not contain wide-ranging provisions for the protection of children from being used for "illegal activities", and that Article 3(d) of the proposed Convention has a broad scope, it would be inappropriate to include "the use, procuring or offering of a child for illegal activities" as a worst form of child labour to be eliminated. Therefore, subparagraph (c) should be revised as follows: "the use, procuring or offering of a child for illicit production and trafficking of narcotic drugs and psychotropic substances as defined in the relevant international treaties".

Lebanon. Introductory paragraph: Add either the expression "for instance" or "in a non-exhaustive manner" after "the worst forms of child labour comprises", as this Article contains issues that cannot be limited. Subparagraph (c): Add "[and] precursors" after "narcotic drugs and psychotropic substances". Add "[and] the transportation, offering, and distribution thereof in any way whatsoever" at the end of the subparagraph. Subparagraph (d): Add "or is likely to hinder their physical or social development" at the end of the subparagraph, in keeping with the Convention on the Rights of the Child.

Madagascar. The participation of children in military service, armed forces or in armed conflicts would be contrary to the Convention. Subparagraph (c): Prefers to use the words "illegal activities". The "in particular" phrase should be maintained as in the proposed text.

Malaysia. Convention No. 138 defines a "child" as a person below 15 years of age and a "young person" as one between 15 and 18 years of age. Ratifying States of both Convention No. 138 and the proposed Convention will face a problem when determining permissible jobs or employment for a child, since there is no specific definition or a complete guideline that could be applied for "the worst forms of child labour". The implication in the proposed Convention, taking into account Convention No. 138, is that those below 18 years of age are allowed to work but are barred only from engaging in "the worst forms of child labour". Member States with differing cultural and social status should be allowed to determine conditions which could be construed as "the worst forms of child labour". Subparagraphs (a) to (b): In Malaysia, matters raised in the proposed Convention, such as the sale and trafficking of children, pornography, prostitution, etc., are already provided for in legislation that is being administered by government agencies other than the Ministry of Human Resources, including the Police, Social Welfare Department, Religious Department, Women Affairs Department (Hawa) and others.

Mali. Considers the word "illicit" more appropriate than "illegal" because it should provide a much broader coverage for various cases. The use of children in armed conflicts, as combatants, as child soldiers or in military activities constitutes one of the worst forms of child labour and therefore should be mentioned in the text.

Mauritius. Subparagraph (d): Insert the words "growth and development" after the word "safety".

Mexico. After "the worst forms of child labour" insert "referring to economic exploitation of child labour". Replace "comprises" with "should comprise". Separate this Article into two Paragraphs of the Recommendation, as Mexico favours a Recommendation only. The first Paragraph should provide that the expression "'the worst forms of child labour', referring to economic exploitation of child labour, should comprise: (a) forced or compulsory labour, debt bondage and serfdom; (b) any other type of work or activity which, by its nature or the circumstances in which it is carried out, is likely to jeopardize the health, safety or morals of children". The second Paragraph should include the following: "(1) The situations referring to exploitation of children and considered as criminal offences should comprise: (a) all forms of slavery or practices similar to slavery, such as the sale and trafficking of children; (b) the use, procuring or offering of a child for prostitution, for the production of pornography or for pornographic performances; (c) the use, procuring or offering of a child for illegal activities, in particular for the production and trafficking of narcotic drugs and psychotropic substances as defined in the relevant international treaties. (2) Penalties should be applied for the criminal forms referred to above in accordance with the national law and practice of each Member." Regarding the issue of children in armed conflict, article 38 of the United Nations Convention on the Rights of the Child makes a separate provision on the concept. To include it in the proposed Convention or Recommendation would contradict the scope and age limits of that Convention on the subject.

Morocco. Add another subparagraph before subparagraph (d) to read as follows: "Any type of activity involving children directly or indirectly in armed conflicts."

Netherlands. An explicit reference to children in armed conflicts is not required since they are already covered by this Article. An alternative option might be to add in Paragraph 3 of the proposed Recommendation on hazardous work, a clause on "participation of children in armed conflicts". The relationship between child labour and education is complicated. The FNV and several NGOs believe that "work which jeopardizes access to available basic education" should be included in this Article. Such a proposal is not acceptable to the Government and was not accepted by the Conference in 1998. As an alternative option, the FNV would suggest that under Article 4, paragraph 1, the national consultations give attention to work which, by its nature, systematically denies access to basic education. Some NGOs suggest adding the following clause to Paragraph 3 of the proposed Recommendation: "work that jeopardizes access to available basic education". Such suggestions deserve further consideration. Subparagraph (c): Supports replacing "illegal" by "illicit".

FNV. See Government's reply above.

New Zealand. Subparagraph (b): The wording should be consistent with the draft optional protocol to the Convention on the Rights of the Child on the sale of children, child prostitution and child pornography. While a final draft of this definition is not yet available, the draft optional protocol is linked to article 34 of the Convention on the Rights of the Child, and a definition could therefore be based on the language of that article, to read as follows: "(b) the use, inducement, coercion, procuring or offering of a child for unlawful sexual activities including prostitution, the production of pornography or pornographic performances". The above formulation widens the range of sexual activities which might be covered to include situations where the child is not engaged in sexual activity, but where his or her employment is exploited for sexual purposes. Subparagraph (c): While there is no objection to replacing the word "illicit" with "illegal", it is difficult to ascertain whether the change in wording will, in fact, change the meaning. The word "illicit" in English is commonly defined as being an activity that is illegal. There does not, as Report IV(1) would suggest, appear to be any further "moral connotation" attached to the word which would include undesirable activity which is not illegal, and which would exclude an illegal activity which is not necessarily morally reprehensible, for example the breach of copyright. Subparagraph (d): The word "morals" is too subjective, and could be replaced by more comprehensive wording. Accordingly, the following is proposed: "any other type of work or activity which, by its nature or the circumstances in which it is carried out, is likely to jeopardize the development, health, safety and psychological well-being of children". Involvement of children in armed conflicts, as combatants, as child soldiers or in a military activity, would fall under subparagraph (d), and therefore a specific reference is unnecessary.

NZEF. Subparagraph (b): Agrees with the Government that for purposes of consistency, this could be worded as article 34 of the Convention on the Rights of the Child. While the NZEF, unlike the Government, accepts the report's argument that the word "illicit" has a more moral connotation than the word "illegal", it does not agree that the use of "illicit" would necessarily cover situations such as drug trafficking not prohibited by national law, while leaving an "illegal" performance in a play where a breach of copyright was involved outside the ambit of the proposed Convention. Something which is illegal must, necessarily, be illicit and though the contrary need not be true, it is still difficult to see how, whatever word is used, a country could take action in respect of an activity which occurred within its borders but which national law did not forbid. Consequently, the NZEF has no particular preference for the use of either word. Subparagraph (d): Disagrees with the Government that the word "morals" is too subjective and would be better replaced by the words "development" and "psychological well-being", since these are words of very uncertain interpretation. It is, for example, an assumption that participation in military service would necessarily jeopardize either a young person's development or her or his psychological well-being or even, provided it were not participation in armed combat, safety and health. It might be supposed, however, that such participation would have a bad effect on the young person's morals, as that term has been, and still is, generally interpreted.

NZCTU. Subparagraph (b): Agrees with the Government that article 34 of the Convention on the Rights of the Child is a more useful formulation that would broaden the scope of the proposed Article. Subparagraph (d): Agrees that the word "morals" is too subjective and supports the wording proposed by the Government. Suggests that "work which by its nature systematically denies children access to basic education" should be added to the definition of the "worst forms of child labour". This proposed addition to the definition would also need to be considered in the context of Articles 4 and 6.

Norway. It is a great improvement that the importance of education is now addressed in the text. However, "work that deprives children of access to basic education" should be one of the worst forms of child labour. Also, it would be a great achievement if the text contained a direct reference to the participation of children in armed conflict as one of the worst forms of child labour.

Pakistan. Some of the worst forms of child labour are manifestations deeply rooted in poverty, parental unemployment and parental illiteracy. No society can eliminate them overnight or merely legislate them away, even with the best political will. Sometimes action to eradicate child labour can drive children into greater destitution. There is no doubt that providing children with education is an important factor in eliminating the worst forms of child labour. However, while providing universal education is an obligation of every State in accordance with the Universal Declaration of Human Rights, as well as all signatories to the Convention on the Rights of the Child, it would be difficult to agree that any work which hinders the education of a child should be included in the definition of the worst forms of child labour.

Peru. Participation in armed conflict is one of the worst risks to which a minor can be exposed; in Peru only persons approaching the age of 18 are called up for military service. Subparagraph (c): Agrees that it is more appropriate to use the term "illicit" than "illegal"; this would be in accordance with the United Nations treaties on drugs and the Convention on the Rights of the Child.

Portugal. Subparagraph (d): The enlistment of children in armed conflicts, as combatants, as child soldiers or in military activities, is fully covered by subparagraph (d). This solution is advantageous because it would also cover the use of children in activities of a non-military nature but which pose the same danger of physical confrontation and use of arms, for example in private security activities.

CIP. Subparagraph (d): The definition of the type of work which, by its nature or the circumstances in which it is carried out, is likely to jeopardize the health, safety or morals of children, is a subject that Convention No. 138 refers to the national legislation of member States. It is therefore not necessary to make provision for it in the proposed Convention.

CGTP-IN. It is forms of "labour" that are being defined. Other forms of child exploitation, however disgusting and intolerable they might be (such as prostitution or the use of children in illicit activities such as drug trafficking), do not fall within this sphere, as they do not correspond to the concept of work. In spite of the condemnation of these forms of child exploitation in the proposed Convention and other international instruments, it does not seem appropriate to define them as "forms of labour". Subparagraph (d): On the basis of the principle that the exclusive aim of the proposed Convention is the immediate elimination of the worst forms of child labour, the definition of what constitutes these forms of labour should be as broad and precise as possible, leaving nothing to the discretion of the Members which ratify the Convention. Because it is a binding instrument, the proposed Convention should list these types of work, as defined in Paragraph 3 of the proposed Recommendation, and should stipulate their immediate prohibition and elimination in keeping with its objectives.

Senegal. As regards illicit activities, the wording of article 33 of the United Nations Convention on the Rights of the Child appropriately defines the expression. The definition of illicit activities will have to be in conformity with the wording of relevant United Nations drug treaties. Although the involvement of children in armed conflicts, as combatants or child soldiers, constitutes an example of forced or compulsory labour, it must be expressly classified as one of the worst forms of child labour. Subparagraph (d): Should read "safety and morals", instead of "or", to show it is cumulative.

South Africa. Subparagraph (a): Include a reference to children involved in military activity as one of the worst forms of child labour in the new Convention, even if other international documents deal with the issue. Supports the formulation that was suggested by the Government member of Italy during the first discussion: "all forms of activity which involve the use of violence, including all forms of military activity". This formulation could also include the use of children by gangs. Subparagraph (c): Forms of illegal activity, for example, selling stolen goods, should also be included in a definition of the worst forms of child labour. Would such types of illegal activity also be covered by the term "illicit"? Both "illegal" and "illicit" could be included.

BSA. Subparagraph (c): During the debate at the 1998 Session of the Conference it was indicated that the word "illegal" is problematic in countries where the production and trafficking of narcotic drugs and psychotropic substances are legal. If this means that universal ratification would be jeopardized, then the word "illicit" should be used. However, as far as the situation in South Africa is concerned, the interpretation of the clause would not be affected by using "illicit" instead of "illegal". Subparagraph (d): It could be argued that this covers children in armed and military combat/service. Any explicit reference to armed and military combat/service could jeopardize universal ratification of the proposed Convention and more could be achieved by relying on subparagraph (d), together with domestic legislation in the various countries.

Spain. This Article includes purely illegal or criminal activities among the worst forms of child "labour". To call selling drugs "labour" is contrary to logic and to the law. Moreover, including purely criminal matters in an ILO Convention seems inappropriate, as this is not the best forum for this kind of discussion. A clear distinction should be drawn in two major paragraphs between what is really considered hazardous child labour, adapting it to Convention No. 138 to ensure strict consistency, and criminal and illicit activities for commercial purposes, which would come under, and are already incorporated in, national criminal legislation. Subparagraph (a): The sale and trafficking of children should not be considered as child labour but as activities using children for commercial purposes. Subparagraph (b): Similarly, these types of activities should be distinguished from labour. Remove the reference to illegal activities and draft a new separate subparagraph (c). New subparagraph (c): "the use, procuring or offering of a child for illicit activities in general, and in particular for the production and trafficking of narcotic drugs and psychotropic substances as defined in the relevant international treaties". It is better to refer to "illicit" than "illegal" as the term "illicit activities" could refer to kinds of activities that are contrary to the law or morals, other than the production and trafficking of drugs. Special attention should be given to the possibility of explicitly referring to involvement of children in armed conflicts as combatants, as soldiers or in military activities. Subparagraph (d) is somewhat unclear, since it does not include the exceptions laid down in Convention No. 138 (paragraph 3 of Article 3), which allow persons under 18 years of age to work in hazardous activities, in particular with apprenticeships in mind.

CEOE. The issue of child soldiers was deferred to the second discussion in 1999, since it was not clear whether this could be considered as "labour" and hence be the subject of an ILO Convention. The Committee wondered whether it should be the subject of another kind of treaty or convention. It also runs counter to the practice in some industrialized countries that allows volunteer service from the age of 16. Subparagraph (c): Supports the Office's proposal as it is clearer.

Sri Lanka. The involvement of child combatants in armed conflicts, as soldiers or as military activists, constitutes one of the major forms of child abuse. This is a phenomenon prevalent in most of the countries where armed conflicts exist. There are instances where children even as young as 12 are conscripted. They are conscripted by force and, when caught while escaping, are severely punished. Children are engaged in activities that endanger their lives and the trauma and deleterious effects they undergo are enormous. Given the magnitude of the problem, and the potential threats it poses in jeopardizing the life, health, safety and morals of the child, it is proposed to mention this issue explicitly. The National Child Protection Authority Act of 1998 explicitly identifies this as a form of "child abuse".

Sweden. Subparagraph (c): Supports the use of "illicit" instead of "illegal". Insert a new subparagraph before subparagraph (d) that reads: "the use of children, forced or otherwise, recruited into armed forces for whatever purpose". Subparagraph (d): Add: "or to interfere with the child's education, as determined in Article 4(1)" at the end.

Switzerland. The situation of children in armed conflicts should be considered as one of the worst forms of child labour and be explicitly mentioned in this Article and not in Article 4, which deals with national legislation. Swiss NGOs also support such a reference. The right to education must absolutely be mentioned in the proposed new Convention. Whether such a reference should be made in Article 3 or 7, or in a specific provision of the proposed Convention, will be debated during the second discussion and a decision will be taken, hopefully by consensus. Subparagraph (c): Agrees with the Office's proposal to use the word "illicit" instead of "illegal", and to simplify the "in particular" phrase.

CSC/CNG. Favours mentioning the use of children in military activities. Because such a reference should be as broad as possible, it is proposed to refer to "the use of children in military activities". Subparagraph (c): Agrees with the Office's proposals to use the word "illicit" instead of "illegal", and to simplify the subparagraph. Subparagraph (d): Access to education should be mentioned. This reference should not be an obstacle to ratification as it does not imply that member States have an obligation to "guarantee" such access.

FSE/VSA. Subparagraph (c): Supports the Office's suggestion to refer to "illicit" instead of "illegal" activities. The suggested formulation of the phrase beginning "in particular" is also clear. Subparagraph (d): The situation of children in armed conflicts clearly comes under (d). However, it is both right and important to cite clearly the deployment of children in armed conflicts in a separate subparagraph and not to leave it to individual member States to define this circumstance themselves.

Syrian Arab Republic. Subparagraph (d): Shorten, while retaining its objectives and not leaving any scope for questioning the existence of the danger, as follows: "any type of work or activity that may jeopardize the health, safety or morals of children".

Ministry of Industry. During the first discussion in 1998, the Conference Committee decided to postpone discussion of children in armed conflict to the second discussion in 1999. A variety of opinions were expressed, the majority of which viewed the Committee as competent to deal with the issue. While war and conflict cannot be considered as employment, the social partners should determine their position on the matter and reaffirm the need to protect children during armed conflicts, and the need for those children to at least be able to defend themselves, should their mental, psychological, physical or moral well-being be endangered. Subparagraph (c): There is no reason to include these activities because as long as they are illegal, they are prohibited *ab initio*. The subparagraph should stress national legislation in member States to strengthen deterrent measures.

Tunisia. Favours mentioning the participation of children in armed conflicts, as combatants, as child soldiers or in military activities. Such a reference should be located between subparagraphs (c) and (d). Subparagraph (c): Agrees with the Office's proposed amendment.

Turkey. Employing children in armed conflicts, or in any kind of military activities as combatants, as well as recruiting and training them for these purposes, should be inserted as one of "the worst forms of child labour".

DÝSK. See comment under *General observations*.

Uganda. Children in armed conflict are a very vulnerable category of children and one of the most complex to handle. Interventions for their specific needs do not only include basic education, withdrawal and their reintegration into society, but should also involve conflict resolution and making peace by all nations. The reference in the Preamble to the kind of comprehensive action envisaged to address the worst forms of child labour does not make any reference to conflict resolution or making peace. This special problem remains complex and requires deeper debate. Subparagraph (c): Supports the Office's proposal to use "illicit" instead of "illegal", since it harmonizes the English and French texts and is more consistent with the wording of United Nations treaties.

United Kingdom. The first two paragraphs of the Office's commentary in Report IV(1) end by suggesting "illicit" rather than "illegal". This, together with the simplified text proposed, would be acceptable. It is consistent with the United Nations Convention on the Rights of the Child and it is understood that it includes things which are unlawful as well as those which are morally wrong. It is considered that the original version of the report was illogical as, by introducing in subparagraph (c) the idea of procuring a child for illegal activities, it could appear to suggest that slavery, forced labour and child prostitution in subparagraphs (a) and (b) might be legal. The proposed amendment avoids this. The application of the Convention should not cover military service by persons under the age of 18, particularly as negotiations are currently in progress for an optional protocol to the Convention on the Rights of the Child on involvement of children in armed conflicts. The Office commented that military combat is captured by subparagraph (d), which refers to work jeopardizing health and safety. If the ILO

Convention does address the issue of military service it should do so explicitly, in keeping with the terms and focus of the Convention on the worst situations. The Government believes that the worst situations would involve young children who are forcibly recruited and involved in combat.

United States. Opposes the application of the proposed Convention to military service by persons under the age of 18, given current negotiations for an optional protocol to the United Nations Convention on the Rights of the Child on involvement of children in armed conflicts. Such efforts need not, and should not, be duplicated. If, however, the proposed Convention were to address the issue of military service, it should do so explicitly, in a provision that, in keeping with the proposed Convention's subject, focuses on the worst situations. Those situations involve young children who are forcibly recruited and involved in combat. Subparagraphs (a) and (b): Accepts these subparagraphs as presently drafted. Subparagraph (c): To afford as broad an interpretation as possible of this provision, the following text is suggested: "the use, procuring or offering of a child for illegal activities, as defined in the relevant treaties, including the production and trafficking of narcotic drugs and psychotropic substances;". Paragraph 11(c) of the proposed Recommendation should be revised accordingly. Regarding the use of the term "illegal" or "illicit", either term is acceptable. The simplified reference to drugs is also acceptable, provided that the relevant treaties now footnoted remain footnoted in Report IV(2A). Subparagraph (d): As currently formulated, this is open to the criticism that it is insufficiently focused on the truly worst forms of child labour. By tracking broadly-sweeping language in Convention No. 138, this subparagraph could (but need not) be read to present the same sort of obstacles to ratification that have prevented many member States from ratifying Convention No. 138. This problem is evident from Members' comments and from the discussions in the Committee on Child Labour in 1998. In this respect, subparagraph (d) is distinguishable from subparagraphs (a) to (c), which contain suggested prohibitions that are clearly defined and that address readily identifiable types of exploitation. This subparagraph can, and should, be interpreted as addressing in a focused way forms of child labour that are of the same severity as those covered by subparagraphs (a) to (c). Within the context of the proposed Convention, it is understood that the proper focus of subparagraph (d) is work that poses an imminent danger to the health, safety, or morals of children. Like the work referred to elsewhere in Article 3, such work necessarily exploits children and exposes them to harm. Regarding access to basic education, it would be appropriate for the proposed Convention, in a focused way, to address the relationship between child labour and access to education. Subparagraph (d) should be modified to address the harm to younger children caused by forms of work that necessarily deny them access to basic education (appropriately defined) that would otherwise be available to them, taking into account the compulsory education requirements of the competent authorities of the member States. The undefined word "activity" should be deleted as it unnecessarily broadens the scope of the proposed Convention beyond the regulation of children's work. There is no clear justification in either the preparatory documents or the record of the discussions in the Committee on Child Labour for including this alternative phrasing in this provision. In contrast, the term "work" can be understood to include employment situations covered by national labour laws and other child-protection statutes, and can be readily catalogued for enforcement.

Venezuela. Subparagraph (b): Opposes the reference to prostitution, the production of pornography and pornographic performances as forms of work because this degrades the very concept of labour and the use of children for such activities is a crime against childhood and a violation of the human rights of children that merits universal condemnation and repudiation. Considering prostitution as a form of labour legitimizes an activity that is supposed to be eliminated, and fundamentally contradicts the very spirit of the proposed Convention. As subparagraph (d) refers to any activity "which, by its nature or the circumstances in which it is carried out, is likely to jeopardize the ... morals of children", it is possible to work towards the eradication of these activities without these crimes needing to be defined as a form of labour, even if they are described as one of the "worst". The same applies to the participation of children in armed conflicts or as combatants.

FEDECAMARAS. Wholeheartedly supports the elimination of the intolerable forms of child labour listed in Article 3(a), (b) and (c) of the proposed Convention.

Zimbabwe. If the proposed Convention is to focus on the worst forms of child labour, the issue of child soldiers in armed conflicts or engaging in military activities should be explicitly mentioned under this Article, rather than leaving it to be dealt with under Article 4.

RELATED HUMAN RIGHTS LAWS TO CHILD LABOUR

Slavery Convention—*Entry into Force 9 March 1927, in Accordance with Article 12*

Status of Ratifications, Reservations and Declarations

Whereas the signatories of the General Act of the Brussels Conference of 1889-90 declared that they were equally animated by the firm intention of putting an end to the traffic in African slaves,

Whereas the signatories of the Convention of Saint-Germain-en-Laye of 1919, to revise the General Act of Berlin of 1885 and the General Act and Declaration of Brussels of 1890, affirmed their intention of securing the complete suppression of slavery in all its forrns and of the slave trade by land and sea,

Taking into consideration the report of the Temporary Slavery Commission appointed by the Council of the League of Nations on June 12th, 1924,

Desiring to complete and extend the work accomplished under the Brussels Act and to find a means of giving practical effect throughout the world to such intentions as were expressed in regard to slave trade and slavery by the signatories of the Con ven tion of Saint-Germain-en-Laye, and recognising that it is necessary to conclude to that end more detailed arrangements than are contained in that Convention,

Considering, moreover, that it is necessary to prevent forced labour from developing into conditions analogous to slavery, have decided to conclude a Convention and have accordingly appointed as their Plenipotentiaries [names omitted]

... have agreed as follows:

Article 1

For the purpose of the present Convention, the following definitions are agreed upon:

1. Slavery is the status or condition of a person over whom any or all of the powers attaching to the right of ownership are exercised.
2. The slave trade includes all acts involved in the capture, acquisition or disposal of a person with intent to reduce him to slavery; all acts involved in the acquisition of a slave with a view to selling or exchanging him; all acts of disposal by sale or exchange of a slave acquired with a view to being sold or exchanged, and, in general, every act of trade or transport in slaves.

Article 2

The High Contracting Parties undertake, each in respect of the territories placed under its sovereignty, jurisdiction, protection, suzerainty or tutelage, so far as they have not already taken the necessary steps:

(a) To prevent and suppress the slave trade;

(b) To bring about, progressively and as soon as possible, the complete abolition of slavery in all its forrns.

Article 3

The High Contracting Parties undertake to adopt all appropriate measures with a view to preventing and suppressing the embarkation, disembarkation and transport of slaves in their territorial waters and upon all vessels flying their respective flags.

The High Contracting Parties undertake to negotiate as soon as possible a general Convention with regard to the slave trade which will give them rights and impose upon them duties of the same nature as those provided for in the Convention of June 17th, 1925, relative to the International Trade in Arms (Articles

12, 20, 21, 22, 23, 24 and paragraphs 3, 4 and 5 of Section II of Annex II), with the necessary adaptations, it being understood that this general Convention will not place the ships (even of small tonnage) of any High Contracting Parties in a position different from that of the other High Contracting Parties.

It is also understood that, before or after the coming into force of this general Convention, the High Contracting Parties are entirely free to conclude between themselves, without, however, derogating from the principles laid down in the preceding paragraph, such special agreements as, by reason of their peculiar situation, might appear to be suitable in order to bring about as soon as possible the complete disappearance of the slave trade.

Article 4

The High Contracting Parties shall give to one another every assistance with the object of securing the abolition of slavery and the slave trade.

Article 5

The High Contracting Parties recognise that recourse to compulsory or forced labour may have grave consequences and undertake, each in respect of the territories placed under its sovereignty, jurisdiction, protection, suzerainty or tutelage, to take all necessary measures to prevent compulsory or forced labour from developing into conditions analogous to slavery.

It is agreed that:

1. Subject to the transitional provisions laid down in paragraph(2) below, compulsory or forced labour may only be exacted for public purposes.
2. In territories in which compulsory or forced labour for other than public purposes still survives, the High Contracting Parties shall endeavour progressively and as soon as possible to put an end to the practice. So long as such forced or compulsory labour exists, this labour shall invariably be of an exceptional character, shall always receive adequate remuneration, and shall not involve the removal of the labourers from their usual place of residence.
3. In all cases, the responsibility for any recourse to compulsory or forced labour shall rest with the competent central authorities of the territory concerned.

Article 6

Those of the High Contracting Parties whose laws do not at present make adquate provision for the punishment of infractions of laws and regulations enacted with a view to giving effect to the purposes of the present Convention undertake to adopt the necessary measures in order that severe penalties may be imposed in respect of such infractions.

Article 7

The High Contracting Parties undertake to communicate to each other and to the Secretary-General of the League of Nations any laws and regulations which they may enact with a view to the application of the provisions of the present Convention.

Article 8

The High Contracting Parties agree that disputes arising between them relating to the interpretation or application of this Convention shall, if they cannot be settled by direct negotiation, be referred for decision to the Permanent Court of International Justice. In case either or both of the States Parties to such a dispute should not be Parties to the Protocol of December 16th, 1920, relating to the Permanent Court of International Justice, the dispute shall be referred, at the choice of the Parties and in accordance with the constitutional procedure of each State, either to the Permanent Court of International Justice or to a court of arbitration constituted in accordance with the Convention of October 18th, 1907, for the Pacific Settlement of International Disputes, or to some other court of arbitration.

Article 9

At the time of signature or of ratification or of accession, any High Contracting Party may declare that its acceptance of the present Convention does not bind some or all of the territories placed under its sovereignty, jurisdiction, protection, suzerainty or tutelage in respect of all or any provisions of the Convention; it may subsequently accede separately on behalf of any one of them or in respect of any provision to which any one of them is not a Party.

Article 10

In the event of a High Contracting Party wishing to denounce the present Convention, the denunciation shall be notified in writing to the SecretaryGeneral of the League of Nations, who will at once communicate a certified true copy of the notification to all the other High Contracting Parties, informing them of the date on which it was received.

The denunciation shall only have effect in regard to the notifying State, and one year after the notification has reached the Secretary-General of the League of Nations.

Denunciation may also be made separately in respect of any territory placed under its sovereignty, jurisdiction, protection, suzerainty or tutelage.

Article 11

The present Convention, which will bear this day's date and of which the French and English texts are both authentic, will remain open for signature by the States Members of the League of Nations until April 1st, 1927.

The Secretary-General of the League of Nations will subsequently bring the present Convention to the notice of States which have not signed it, including States which are not Members of the League of Nations, and invite them to accede thereto.

A State desiring to accede to the Convention shall notify its intention in writing to the Secretary-General of the League of Nations and transmit to him the instrument of accession, which shall be deposited in the archives of the League.

The Secretary-General shall immediately transmit to all the other High Contracting Parties a certified true copy of the notification and of the instrument of accession, informing them of the date on which he received them.

Article 12

The present Convention will be ratified and the instruments of ratification shall be deposited in the office of the Secretary-General of the League of Nations. The Secretary-General will inform all the High Contracting Parties of such deposit.

The Convention will come into operation for each State on the date of the deposit of its ratification or of its accession.

IN FAITH WHEREOF the Plenipotentiaries signed the present Convention.

DONE at Geneva the twenty-fifth day of September, one thousand nine hundred and twenty-six , in one copy, which will be deposited in the archives of the League of Nations. A certified copy shall be forwarded to each signatory State.

ABOLITION OF FORCED LABOUR CONVENTION

Adopted on 25 June 1957 by the General Conference of the International Labour Organisation at Its Fortieth Session

Entry into Force, 17 January 1959, in Accordance with Article 4

Status of Ratifications (ILO Database on International Labour Standards) *

The General Conference of the International Labour Organisation,

Having been convened at Geneva by the Governing Body of the International Labour Office, and having met in its fortieth session on 5 June 1957, and

Having considered the question of forced labour, which is the fourth item on the agenda of the session, and

Having noted the provisions of the Forced Labour Convention, 1930, and

Having noted that the Slavery Convention, 1926, provides that all necessary measures shall be taken to prevent compulsory or forced labour from developing into conditions analogous to slavery and that the Supplementary Convention on the Abolition of Slavery, the Slave Trade, and Institutions and Practices Similar to Slavery, 1956, provides for the complete abolition of debt bondage and serfdom, and

Having noted that the Protection of Wages Convention, 1949, provides that wages shall be paid regularly and prohibits methods of payment which deprive the worker of a genuine possibility of terminating his employment, and

Having decided upon the adoption of further proposals with regard to the abolition of certain forms of forced or compulsory labour constituting a violation of the rights of man referred to in the Charter of the United Nations and enunciated by the Universal Declaration of Human Rights, and

Having determined that these proposals shall take the form of an international Convention,

Adopts this twenty-fifth day of June of the year one thousand nine hundred and fifty-seven the following Convention, which may be cited as the Abolition of Forced Labour Convention, 1957:

Article 1

Each Member of the International Labour Organisation which ratifies this Convention undertakes to suppress and not to make use of any form of forced or compulsory labour:

(a) As a means of political coercion or education or as a punishment for holding or expressing political views or views ideologically opposed to the established political, social or economic system;

(b) As a method of mobilising and using labour for purposes of economic development;

(c) As a means of labour discipline;

(d) As a punishment for having participated in strikes;

(e) As a means of racial, social, national or religious discrimination.

Article 2

Each Member of the International Labour Organisation which ratifies this Convention undertakes to take effective measures to secure the immediate and complete abolition of forced or compulsory labour as specified in article 1 of this Convention.

Article 3

The formal ratifications of this Convention shall be communicated to the Director-General of the International Labour Office for registration.

Article 4

1. This Convention shall be binding only upon those Members of the International Labour Organisation whose ratifications have been registered with the Director-General.

2. It shall come into force twelve months after the date on which the ratifications of two Members have been registered with the Director-General.

3. Thereafter, this Convention shall come into force for any Member twelve months after the date on which its ratification has been registered.

Article 5

1 . A Member which has ratified this Convention may denounce it after the expiration of ten years from the date on which the Convention first comes into force, by an act communicated to the Director-General of the International Labour Office for registration. Such denunciation shall not take effect until one year after the date on which it is registered.

2. Each Member which has ratified this Convention and which does not, within the year following the expiration of the period of ten years mentioned in the preceding paragraph, exercise the right of denunciation provided for in this article, will be bound for another period of five years and, thereafter, may denounce this Convention at the expiration of each period of five years under the terms provided for in this article.

Article 6

1. The Director-General of the International Labour Office shall notify all Members of the International Labour Organisation of the registration of all ratifications and denunciations communicated to him by the Members of the Organisation.

2. When notifying the Members of the Organisation of the registration of the second ratification communicated to him the Director-General shall draw the attention of the Members of the Organisation to the date upon which the Convention will come into force.

Article 7

The Director-General of the International Labour Office shall communicate to the Secretary-General of the United Nations for registration in accordance with Article 102 of the Charter of the United Nations full particulars of all ratifications and acts of denunciation registered by him in accordance with the provisions of the preceding articles.

Article 8

At such times as it may consider necessary the Governing Body of the International Labour Office shall present to the General Conference a report on the working of the Convention and shall examine the desirability of placing on the agenda of the Conference the question of its revision in whole or in part.

1. Should the Conference adopt a new Convention revising this Convention in whole or in part, then, unless the new Convention otherwise provides:

(a) The ratification by a Member of the new revising Convention shall *ipso jure* involve the immediate denunciation of this Convention, notwithstanding the provisions of article 5 above, if and when the new revising Convention shall have come into force;

(b) As from the date when the new revising Convention comes into force this Convention shall cease to be open to ratification by the Members.

2. This Convention shall in any case remain in force in its actual form and content for those Members which have ratified it but have not ratified the revising Convention.

Article 10

The English and French versions of the text of this Convention are equally authoritative.

The foregoing is the authentic text of the Convention duly adopted by the General Conference of the International Labour Organisation during its fortieth session which was held at Geneva and declared closed the twenty-seventh day of June 1957.

IN FAITH WHEREOF we have appended our signatures this fourth day of July 1957.

DECLARATION OF THE RIGHTS OF THE CHILD

Proclaimed by General Assembly Resolution 1386(XIV) of 20 November 1959

Whereas the peoples of the United Nations have, in the Charter, reaffirmed their faith in fundamental human rights and in the dignity and worth of the human person, and have determined to promote social progress and better standards of life in larger freedom,

Whereas the United Nations has, in the Universal Declaration of Human Rights, proclaimed that everyone is entitled to all the rights and freedoms set forth therein, without distinction of any kind, such as race, colour, sex, language, religion, political or other opinion, national or social origin, property, birth or other status,

Whereas the child, by reason of his physical and mental immaturity, needs special safeguards and care, including appropriate legal protection, before as well as after birth,

Whereas the need for such special safeguards has been stated in the Geneva Declaration of the Rights of the Child of 1924, and recognized in the Universal Declaration of Human Rights and in the statutes of specialized agencies and international organizations concerned with the welfare of children,

Whereas mankind owes to the child the best it has to give,

Now therefore,

The General Assembly

Proclaims this Declaration of the Rights of the Child to the end that he may have a happy childhood and enjoy for his own good and for the good of society the rights and freedoms herein set forth, and calls upon parents, upon men and women as individuals, and upon voluntary organizations, local authorities and national Governments to recognize these rights and strive for their observance by legislative and other measures progressively taken in accordance with the following principles:

Principle 1

The child shall enjoy all the rights set forth in this Declaration. Every child, without any exception whatsoever, shall be entitled to these rights, without distinction or discrimination on account of race, colour, sex, language, religion, political or other opinion, national or social origin, property, birth or other status, whether of himself or of his family.

Principle 2

The child shall enjoy special protection, and shall be given opportunities and facilities, by law and by other means, to enable him to develop physically, mentally, morally, spiritually and socially in a healthy and normal manner and in conditions of freedom and dignity. In the enactment of laws for this purpose, the best interests of the child shall be the paramount consideration.

Principle 3

The child shall be entitled from his birth to a name and a nationality.

Principle 4

The child shall enjoy the benefits of social security. He shall be entitled to grow and develop in health; to this end, special care and protection shall be provided both to him and to his mother, including adequate pre-natal and post-natal care. The child shall have the right to adequate nutrition, housing, recreation and medical services.

Principle 5

The child who is physically, mentally or socially handicapped shall be given the special treatment, education and care required by his particular condition.

Principle 6

The child, for the full and harmonious development of his personality, needs love and understanding. He shall, wherever possible, grow up in the care and under the responsibility of his parents, and, in any case, in an atmosphere of affection and of moral and material security; a child of tender years shall not, save in exceptional circumstances, be separated from his mother. Society and the public authorities shall have the duty to extend particular care to children without a family and to those without adequate means of support. Payment of State and other assistance towards the maintenance of children of large families is desirable.

Principle 7

The child is entitled to receive education, which shall be free and compulsory, at least in the elementary stages. He shall be given an education which will promote his general culture and enable him, on a basis of equal opportunity, to develop his abilities, his individual judgement, and his sense of moral and social responsibility, and to become a useful member of society.

The best interests of the child shall be the guiding principle of those responsible for his education and guidance; that responsibility lies in the first place with his parents.

The child shall have full opportunity for play and recreation, which should be directed to the same purposes as education; society and the public authorities shall endeavour to promote the enjoyment of this right.

Principle 8

The child shall in all circumstances be among the first to receive protection and relief.

Principle 9

The child shall be protected against all forms of neglect, cruelty and exploitation. He shall not be the subject of traffic, in any form.

The child shall not be admitted to employment before an appropriate minimum age; he shall in no case be caused or permitted to engage in any occupation or employment which would prejudice his health or education, or interfere with his physical, mental or moral development.

Principle 10

The child shall be protected from practices which may foster racial, religious and any other form of discrimination. He shall be brought up in a spirit of understanding, tolerance, friendship among peoples, peace and universal brotherhood, and in full consciousness that his energy and talents should be devoted to the service of his fellow men.

UNITED NATIONS STANDARD MINIMUM RULES FOR THE ADMINISTRATION OF JUVENILE JUSTICE

("The Beijing Rules")

Adopted by General Assembly Resolution 40/33of 29 November 1985

PART ONE

General Principles

1. Fundamental Perspectives

1.1 Member States shall seek, in conformity with their respective general interests, to further the well-being of the juvenile and her or his family.

1.2 Member States shall endeavour to develop conditions that will ensure for the juvenile a meaningful life in the community, which, during that period in life when she or he is most susceptible to deviant behaviour, will foster a process of personal development and education that is as free from crime and delinquency as possible.

1.3 Sufficient attention shall be given to positive measures that involve the full mobilization of all possible resources, including the family, volunteers and other community groups, as well as schools and other community institutions, for the purpose of promoting the well-being of the juvenile, with a view to reducing the need for intervention under the law, and of effectively, fairly and humanely dealing with the juvenile in conflict with the law.

1.4 Juvenile justice shall be conceived as an integral part of the national development process of each country, within a comprehensive framework of social justice for all juveniles, thus, at the same time, contributing to the protection of the young and the maintenance of a peaceful order in society.

1.5 These Rules shall be implemented in the context of economic, social and cultural conditions prevailing in each Member State.

1.6 Juvenile justice services shall be systematically developed and coordinated with a view to improving and sustaining the competence of personnel involved in the services, including their methods, approaches and attitudes.

Commentary

These broad fundamental perspectives refer to comprehensive social policy in general and aim at promoting juvenile welfare to the greatest possible extent, which will minimize the necessity of intervention by the juvenile justice system, and in turn, will reduce the harm that may be caused by any intervention. Such care measures for the young, before the onset of delinquency, are basic policy requisites designed to obviate the need for the application of the Rules.

Rules 1.1 to 1.3 point to the important role that a constructive social policy for juveniles will play, inter alia, in the prevention of juvenile crime and delinquency. Rule 1.4 defines juvenile justice as an integral part of social justice for juveniles, while rule 1.6 refers to the necessity of constantly improving juvenile justice, without falling behind the development of progressive social policy for juveniles in general and bearing in mind the need for consistent improvement of staff services.

Rule 1.5 seeks to take account of existing conditions in Member States which would cause the manner of implementation of particular rules necessarily to be different from the manner adopted in other States.

2. Scope of the Rules and Definitions Used

2.1 The following Standard Minimum Rules shall be applied to juvenile offenders impartially, without distinction of any kind, for example as to race, colour, sex, language, religion, political or other opinions, national or social origin, property, birth or other status.

2.2 For purposes of these Rules, the following definitions shall be applied by Member States in a manner which is compatible with their respective legal systems and concepts:

(a) A juvenile is a child or young person who, under the respective legal systems, may be dealt with for an offence in a manner which is different from an adult;

(b) An offence is any behaviour (act or omission) that is punishable by law under the respective legal systems;

(c) A juvenile offender is a child or young person who is alleged to have committed or who has been found to have committed an offence.

2.3 Efforts shall be made to establish, in each national jurisdiction, a set of laws, rules and provisions specifically applicable to juvenile offenders and institutions and bodies entrusted with the functions of the administration of juvenile justice and designed:

(a) To meet the varying needs of juvenile offenders, while protecting their basic rights;

(b) To meet the needs of society;

(c) To implement the following rules thoroughly and fairly.

Commentary

The Standard Minimum Rules are deliberately formulated so as to be applicable within different legal systems and, at the same time, to set some minimum standards for the handling of juvenile offenders under any definition of a juvenile and under any system of dealing with juvenile offenders. The Rules are always to be applied impartially and without distinction of any kind.

Rule 2.1 therefore stresses the importance of the Rules always being applied impartially and without distinction of any kind. The rule follows the formulation of principle 2 of the Declaration of the Rights of the Child.

Rule 2.2 defines "juvenile" and "offence" as the components of the notion of the "juvenile offender", who is the main subject of these Standard Minimum Rules (see, however, also rules 3 and 4). It should be noted that age limits will depend on, and are explicitly made dependent on, each respective legal system, thus fully respecting the economic, social, political, cultural and legal systems of Member States. This makes for a wide variety of ages coming under the definition of "juvenile", ranging from 7 years to 18 years or above. Such a variety seems inevitable in view of the different national legal systems and does not diminish the impact of these Standard Minimum Rules.

Rule 2.3 is addressed to the necessity of specific national legislation for the optimal implementation of these Standard Minimum Rules, both legally and practically.

3. Extension of the Rules

3.1 The relevant provisions of the Rules shall be applied not only to juvenile offenders but also to juveniles who may be proceeded against for any specific behaviour that would not be punishable if committed by an adult.

3.2 Efforts shall be made to extend the principles embodied in the Rules to all juveniles who are dealt with in welfare and care proceedings.

3.3 Efforts shall also be made to extend the principles embodied in the Rules to young adult offenders.

Commentary

Rule 3 extends the protection afforded by the Standard Minimum Rules for the Administration of Juvenile Justice to cover:

(a) The so-called "status offences" prescribed in various national legal systems where the range of behaviour considered to be an offence is wider for juveniles than it is for adults (for example, truancy, school and family disobedience, public drunkenness, etc.) (rule 3.1);

(b) Juvenile welfare and care proceedings (rule 3.2);

(c) Proceedings dealing with young adult offenders, depending of course on each given age limit (rule 3.3).

The extension of the Rules to cover these three areas seems to be justified. Rule 3.1 provides minimum guarantees in those fields, and rule 3.2 is considered a desirable step in the direction of more fair, equitable and humane justice for all juveniles in conflict with the law.

4. Age of Criminal Responsibility

4.1 In those legal systems recognizing the concept of the age of criminal responsibility for juveniles, the beginning of that age shall not be fixed at too low an age level, bearing in mind the facts of emotional, mental and intellectual maturity.

Commentary

The minimum age of criminal responsibility differs widely owing to history and culture. The modern approach would be to consider whether a child can live up to the moral and psychological components of criminal responsibility; that is, whether a child, by virtue of her or his individual discernment and understanding, can be held responsible for essentially antisocial be ha vi our. If the age of criminal responsibility is fixed too low or if there is no lower age limit at all, the notion of responsibility would become meaningless. In general, there is a close relationship between the notion of responsibility for delinquent or criminal behaviour and other social rights and responsibilities (such as marital status, civil majority, etc.).

Efforts should therefore be made to agree on a reasonable lowest age limit that is applicable internationally.

5. Aims of Juvenile Justice

5. 1 The juvenile justice system shall emphasize the well-being of the juvenile and shall ensure that any reaction to juvenile offenders shall always be in proportion to the circumstances of both the offenders and the offence.

Commentary

Rule 5 refers to two of the most important objectives of juvenile justice. The first objective is the promotion of the well-being of the juvenile. This is the main focus of those legal systems in which juvenile offenders are dealt with by family courts or administrative authorities, but the well-being of the juvenile should also be emphasized in legal systems that follow the criminal court model, thus contributing to the avoidance of merely punitive sanctions. (See also rule 14.)

The second objective is "the principle of proportionality". This principle is well-known as an instrument for curbing punitive sanctions, mostly expressed in terms of just deserts in relation to the gravity of the offence. The response to young offenders should be based on the consideration not only of the gravity of the offence but also of personal circumstances. The individual circumstances of the offender (for example social status, family situation, the harm caused by the offence or other factors affecting personal circumstances) should influence the proportionality of the reactions (for example by having regard to the offender's endeavour to indemnify the victim or to her or his willingness to turn to wholesome and useful life).

By the same token, reactions aiming to ensure the welfare of the young offender may go beyond necessity and therefore infringe upon the fundamental rights of the young individual, as has been observed in some juvenile justice systems. Here, too, the proportionality of the reaction to the circumstances of both the offender and the offence, including the victim, should be safeguarded.

In essence, rule 5 calls for no less and no more than a fair reaction in any given cases of juvenile delinquency and crime. The issues combined in the rule may help to stimulate development in both regards: new and innovative types of reactions are as desirable as precautions against any undue widening of the net of formal social control over juveniles.

6. *Scope of Discretion*

6.1 In view of the varying special needs of juveniles as well as the variety of measures available, appropriate scope for discretion shall be allowed at all stages of proceedings and at the different levels of juvenile justice administration, including investigation, prosecution, adjudication and the follow-up of dispositions.

6.2 Efforts shall be made, however, to ensure sufficient accountability at all stages and levels in the exercise of any such discretion.

6.3 Those who exercise discretion shall be specially qualified or trained to exercise it judiciously and in accordance with their functions and mandates.

Commentary

Rules 6.1, 6.2 and 6.3 combine several important features of effective, fair and humane juvenile justice administration: the need to permit the exercise of discretionary power at all significant levels of processing so that those who make determinations can take the actions deemed to be most appropriate in each individual case; and the need to provide checks and balances in order to curb any abuses of discretionary power and to safeguard the rights of the young offender. Accountability and professionalism are instruments best apt to curb broad discretion. Thus, professional qualifications and expert training are emphasized here as a valuable means of ensuring the judicious exercise of discretion in matters of juvenile offenders. (See also rules 1.6 and 2.2.) The formulation of specific guidelines on the exercise of discretion and the provision of systems of review, appeal and the like in order to permit scrutiny of decisions and accountability are emphasized in this context. Such mechanisms are not specified here, as they do not easily lend themselves to incorporation into international standard minimum rules, which cannot possibly cover all differences in justice systems.

7. *Rights of Juveniles*

7.1 Basic procedural safeguards such as the presumption of innocence, the right to be notified of the charges, the right to remain silent, the right to counsel, the right to the presence of a parent or guardian, the right to confront and cross-examine witnesses and the right to appeal to a higher authority shall be guaranteed at all stages of proceedings.

Commentary

Rule 7.1 emphasizes some important points that represent essential elements for a fair and just trial and that are internationally recognized in existing human rights instruments (See also rule 14.). The presumption of innocence, for instance, is also to be found in article 11 of the Universal Declaration of Human rights and in article 14, paragraph 2, of the International Covenant on Civil and Political Rights. Rules 14 seq. of these Standard Minimum Rules specify issues that are important for proceedings in juvenile cases, in particular, while rule 7.1 affirms the most basic procedural safeguards in a general way.

8. Protection of Privacy

8.1 The juvenile's right to privacy shall be respected at all stages in order to avoid harm being caused to her or him by undue publicity or by the process of labelling.

8.2 In principle, no information that may lead to the identification of a juvenile offender shall be published.

Commentary

Rule 8 stresses the importance of the protection of the juvenile's right to privacy. Young persons are particularly susceptible to stigmatization. Criminological research into labelling processes has provided evidence of the detrimental effects (of different kinds) resulting from the permanent identification of young persons as "delinquent" or "criminal".

Rule 8 stresses the importance of protecting the juvenile from the adverse effects that may result from the publication in the mass media of information about the case (for example the names of young offenders, alleged or convicted). The interest of the individual should be protected and upheld, at least in principle (The general contents of rule 8 are further specified in rule 2 1.).

9. Saving Clause

9.1 Nothing in these Rules shall be interpreted as precluding the application of the Standard Minimum Rules for the Treatment of Prisoners adopted by the United Nations and other human rights instruments and standards recognized by the international community that relate to the care and protection of the young.

Commentary

Rule 9 is meant to avoid any misunderstanding in interpreting and implementing the present Rules in conformity with principles contained in relevant existing or emerging international human rights instruments and standards- such as the Universal Declaration of Human Rights, the International Covenant on Economic, Social and Cultural Rights and the International Covenant on Civil and Political Rights, and the Declaration of the Rights of the Child and the draft convention on the rights of the child. It should be understood that the application of the present Rules is without prejudice to any such international instruments which may contain provisions of wider application (See also rule 27.).

PART TWO

Investigation and Prosecution

10. Initial Contact

10.1 Upon the apprehension of a juvenile, her or his parents or guardian shall be immediately notified of such apprehension, and, where such immediate notification is not possible, the parents or guardian shall be notified within the shortest possible time thereafter.

10.2 A judge or other competent official or body shall, without delay, consider the issue of release.

10.3 Contacts between the law enforcement agencies and a juvenile offender shall be managed in such a way as to respect the legal status of the juvenile, promote the well-being of the juvenile and avoid harm to her or hi m, with due regard to the circumstances of the case.

Commentary

Rule 10.1 is in principle contained in rule 92 of the Standard Minimum Rules for the Treatment of Prisoners.

The question of release (rule 10.2) shall be considered without delay by a judge or other competent official. The latter refers to any person or institution in the broadest sense of the term, including community boards or police authorities having power to release an arrested person. (See also the International Covenant on Civil and Political Rights, article 9, paragraph 3.)

Rule 10.3 deals with some fundamental aspects of the procedures and behaviour on the part of the police and other law enforcement officials in cases of juvenile crime. To "avoid harm" admittedly is flexible wording and covers many features of possible interaction (for example the use of harsh language, physical violence or exposure to the environment). Involvement in juvenile justice processes in itself can be "harmful" to juveniles; the term "avoid harm" should be broadly interpreted, therefore, as doing the least harm possible to the juvenile in the first instance, as well as any additional or undue harm. This is especially important in the initial contact with law enforcement agencies, which might profoundly influence the juvenile's attitude towards the State and society. Moreover, the success of any further intervention is largely dependent on such initial contacts. Compassion and kind firmness are important in these situations.

11. Diversion

11.1 Consideration shall be given, wherever appropriate, to dealing with juvenile offenders without resorting to formal trial by the competent authority, referred to in rule 14.1 below.

11.2 The police, the prosecution or other agencies dealing with juvenile cases shall be empowered to dispose of such cases, at their discretion, without recourse to formal hearings, in accordance with the criteria laid down for that purpose in the respective legal system and also in accordance with the principles contained in these Rules.

11.3 Any diversion involving referral to appropriate community or other services shall require the consent of the juvenile, or her or his parents or guardian, provided that such decision to refer a case shall be subject to review by a competent authority, upon application.

11.4 In order to facilitate the discretionary disposition of juvenile cases, efforts shall be made to provide for community programmes, such as temporary supervision and guidance, restitution, and compensation of victims.

Commentary

Diversion, involving removal from criminal justice processing and, frequently, redirection to community support services, is commonly practised on a formal and informal basis in many legal systems. This practice serves to hinder the negative effects of subsequent proceedings in juvenile justice administration (for example the stigma of conviction and sentence). In many cases, non-intervention would be the best response. Thus, diversion at the outset and without referral to alternative (social) services may be the optimal response. This is especially the case where the offence is of a non-serious nature and where the family, the school or other informal social control institutions have already reacted, or are likely to react, in an appropriate and constructive manner.

As stated in rule 11.2, diversion may be used at any point of decision-making-by the police, the prosecution or other agencies such as the courts, tribunals, boards or councils. It may be exercised by one authority or several or all authorities, according to the rules and policies of the respective systems and in line with the present Rules. It need not necessarily be limited to petty cases, thus rendering diversion an important instrument.

Rule 11.3 stresses the important requirement of securing the consent of the young offender (or the parent or guardian) to the recommended diversionary measure(s). (Diversion to community service without such consent would contradict the Abolition of Forced Labour Convention.) However, this consent should not be left unchallengeable, since it might sometimes be given out of sheer desperation on the part of the juvenile. The rule underlines that care should be taken to minimize the potential for coercion and intimidation at all levels in the diversion process. Juveniles should not feel pressured (for example in order to avoid court appearance) or be pressured into consenting to diversion programmes. Thus, it is advocated that provision should be made for an objective appraisal of the appropriateness of dispositions involving young offenders by a "competent authority upon application". (The "competent authority,' may be different from that referred to in rule 14.)

Rule 11.4 recommends the provision of viable alternatives to juvenile justice processing in the form of community-based diversion. Programmes that involve settlement by victim restitution and those that seek to avoid future conflict with the law through temporary supervision and guidance are especially commended. The merits of individual cases would make diversion appropriate, even when more serious offences have been committed (for example first offence, the act having been committed under peer pressure, etc.).

12. Specialization Within the Police

12.1 In order to best fulfil their functions, police officers who frequently or exclusively deal with juveniles or who are primarily engaged in the prevention of juvenile crime shall be specially instructed and trained. In large cities, special police units should be established for that purpose.

Commentary

Rule 12 draws attention to the need for specialized training for all law enforcement officials who are involved in the administration of juvenile justice. As police are the first point of contact with the juvenile justice system, it is most important that they act in an informed and appropriate manner.

While the relationship between urbanization and crime is clearly complex, an increase in juvenile crime has been associated with the growth of large cities, particularly with rapid and unplanned growth. Specialized police units would therefore be indispensable, not only in the interest of implementing specific principles contained in the present instrument (such as rule 1.6) but more generally for improving the prevention and control of juvenile crime and the handling of juvenile offenders.

13. Detention Pending Trial

13.1 Detention pending trial shall be used only as a measure of last resort and for the shortest possible period of time.

13.2 Whenever possible, detention pending trial shall be replaced by alternative measures, such as close supervision, intensive care or placement with a family or in an educational setting or home.

13.3 Juveniles under detention pending trial shall be entitled to all rights and guarantees of the Standard Minimum Rules for the Treatment of Prisoners adopted by the United Nations.

13.4 Juveniles under detention pending trial shall be kept separate from adults and shall be detained in a separate institution or in a separate part of an institution also holding adults.

13.5 While in custody, juveniles shall receive care, protection and all necessary individual assistance-social, educational, vocational, psychological, medical and physical-that they may require in view of their age, sex and personality.

Commentary

The danger to juveniles of"criminal contamination" while in detention pending trial must not be underestimated. It is therefore important to stress the need for alternative measures. By doing so, rule 13.1 encourages the devising of new and innovative measures to avoid such detention in the interest of the well-being of the juvenile. Juveniles under detention pending trial are entitled to all the rights and guarantees of the Standard Minimum Rules for the Treatment of Prisoners as well as the International Covenant on Civil and Political Rights, especially article 9 and article 10, paragraphs 2 (b) and 3.

Rule 13.4 does not prevent States from taking other measures against the negative influences of adult offenders which are at least as effective as the measures mentioned in the rule.

Different forms of assistance that may become necessary have been enumerated to draw attention to the broad range of particular needs of young detainees to be addressed (for example females or males, drug addicts, alcoholics, mentally ill juveniles, young persons suffering from the trauma, for example, of arrest, etc.).

Varying physical and psychological characteristics of young detainees may warrant classification measures by which some are kept separate while in detention pending trial, thus contributing to the avoidance of victimization and rendering more appropriate assistance.

The Sixth United Nations Congress on the Prevention of Crime and the Treatment of Offenders, in its resolution 4 on juvenile justice standards, specified that the Rules, inter alia, should reflect the basic principle that pre-trial detention should be used only as a last resort, that no minors should be held in a facility where they are vulnerable to the negative influences of adult detainees and that account should always be taken of the needs particular to their stage of development.

PART THREE

Adjudication and Disposition

14. Competent Authority to Adjudicate

14.1 Where the case of a juvenile offender has not been diverted (under rule 11), she or he shall be dealt with by the competent authority (court, tribunal, board, council, etc.) according to the principles of a fair and just trial.

14.2 The proceedings shall be conducive to the best interests of the juvenile and shall be conducted in an atmosphere of understanding, which shall allow the juvenile to participate therein and to express herself or himself freely.

Commentary

It is difficult to formulate a definition of the competent body or person that would universally describe an adjudicating authority. "Competent authority" is meant to include those who preside over courts or tribunals (composed of a single judge or of several members), including professional and lay magistrates as well as administrative boards (for example the Scottish and Scandinavian systems) or other more informal community and conflict resolution agencies of an adjudicatory nature.

The procedure for dealing with juvenile offenders shall in any case follow the minimum standards that are applied almost universally for any criminal defendant under the procedure known as "due process of law". In accordance with due process, a "fair and just trial" includes such basic safeguards as the presumption of innocence, the presentation and examination of witnesses, the common legal defences, the right to remain silent, the right to have the last word in a hearing, the right to appeal, etc. (See also rule 7.1.)

15. Legal Counsel, Parents and Guardians

15.1 Throughout the proceedings the juvenile shall have the right to be represented by a legal adviser or to apply for free legal aid where there is provision for such aid in the country.

15.2 The parents or the guardian shall be entitled to participate in the proceedings and may be required by the competent authority to attend them in the interest of the juvenile. They may, however, be denied participation by the competent authority if there are reasons to assume that such exclusion is necessary in the interest of the juvenile.

Commentary

Rule 15.1 uses terminology similar to that found in rule 93 of the Standard Minimum Rules for the Treatment of Prisoners. Whereas legal counsel and free legal aid are needed to assure the juvenile legal assistance, the right of the parents or guardian to participate as stated in rule 15.2 should be viewed as general psychological and emotional assistance to the juvenile-a function extending throughout the procedure.

The competent authority's search for an adequate disposition of the case may pro fit, in particular, fro m the co-operation of the legal representatives of the juvenile (or, for that matter, some other personal assistant who the juvenile can and does really trust). Such concern can be thwarted if the presence of parents or guardians at the hearings plays a negative role, for instance, if they display a hostile attitude towards the juvenile, hence, the possibility of their exclusion must be provided for.

16. Social Inquiry Reports

16.1 In all cases except those involving minor offences, before the competent authority renders a final disposition prior to sentencing, the background and circumstances in which the juvenile is living or the conditions under which the offence has been committed shall be properly investigated so as to facilitate judicious adjudication of the case by the competent authority.

Commentary

Social inquiry reports (social reports or pre-sentence reports) are an indispensable aid in most legal proceedings involving juveniles. The competent authority should be informed of relevant facts about the juvenile, such as social an d family background, school career, educational experiences, etc. For this purpose, some jurisdictions use special social services or personnel attached to the court or board. Other personnel, including probation officers, may serve the same function. The rule therefore requires that adequate social services should be available to deliver social inquiry reports of a qualified nature.

17. Guiding Principles in Adjudication and Disposition

17.1 The disposition of the competent authority shall be guided by the following principles:

(a) The reaction taken shall always be in proportion not only to the circumstances and the gravity of the offence but also to the circumstances and the needs of the juvenile as well as to the needs of the society;

(b) Restrictions on the personal liberty of the juvenile shall be imposed only after careful consideration and shall be limited to the possible minimum;

(c) Deprivation of personal liberty shall not be imposed unless the juvenile is adjudicated of a serious act involving violence against another person or of persistence in committing other serious offences and unless there is no other appropriate response;

(d) The well-being of the juvenile shall be the guiding factor in the consideration of her or his case. 17.2 Capital punishment shall not be imposed for any crime committed by juveniles.

17.3 Juveniles shall not be subject to corporal punishment.

17.4 The competent authority shall have the power to discontinue the proceedings at any time.

Commentary

The main difficulty in formulating guidelines for the adjudication of young persons stems from the fact that there are unresolved conflicts of a philosophical nature, such as the following:

(a) Rehabilitation versus just desert;

(b) Assistance versus repression and punishment;

(c) Reaction according to the singular merits of an individual case versus reaction according to the protection of society in general;

(d) General deterrence versus individual incapacitation.

The conflict between these approaches is more pronounced in juvenile cases than in adult cases. With the variety of causes and reactions characterizing juvenile cases, these alternatives become intricately interwoven.

It is not the function of the Standard Minimum Rules for the Administration of Juvenile Justice to prescribe which approach is to be followed but rather to identify one that is most closely in consonance with internationally accepted principles. Therefore the essential elements as laid down in rule 17.1 , in particular in subparagraphs (a) and (c), are mainly to be understood as practical guidelines that should ensure a common starting point; if heeded by the concerned authorities (see also rule 5), they could contribute considerably to ensuring that the fundamental rights of juvenile offenders are protected, especially the fundamental rights of personal development and education.

Rule 17.1 (b) implies that strictly punitive approaches are not appropriate. Whereas in adult cases, and possibly also in cases of severe offences by juveniles, just desert and retributive sanctions might be considered to have some merit, in juvenile cases such considerations should always be outweighed by the interest of safeguarding the well-being and the future of the young person.

In line with resolution 8 of the Sixth United Nations Congress, rule 17.1 (b) encourages the use of alternatives to institutionalization to the maximum extent possible, bearing in mind the need to respond to the specific requirements of the young. Thus, full use should be made of the range of existing alternative sanctions and new alternative sanctions should be developed, bearing the public safety in mind. Probation should be granted to the greatest possible extent via suspended sentences, conditional sentences, board orders and other dispositions.

Rule 17.1 (c) corresponds to one of the guiding principles in resolution 4 of the Sixth Congress which aims at avoiding incarceration in the case of juveniles unless there is no other appropriate response that will protect the public safety

The provision prohibiting capital punishment in rule 17.2 is in accordance with article 6, paragraph 5, of the International Covenant on Civil and Political Rights.

The provision against corporal punishment is in line with article 7 of the International Covenant on Civil and Political Rights and the Declaration on the Protection of All Persons from Being Subjected to Torture and Other Cruel, Inhuman or Degrading Treatment or Punishment, as well as the Convention against Torture and Other Cruel, Inhuman or Degrading Treatment or Punishment and the draft convention on the rights of the child.

The power to discontinue the proceedings at any time (rule 17.4) is a characteristic inherent in the handling of juvenile offenders as opposed to adults. At any time, circumstances may become known to the competent authority which would make a complete cessation of the intervention appear to be the best disposition of the case.

18. Various Disposition Measures

18.1 A large variety of disposition measures shall be made available to the competent authority, allowing for flexibility so as to avoid institutionalization to the greatest extent possible. Such measures, some of which may be combined, include:

(a) Care, guidance and supervision orders;

(b) Probation;

(c) Community service orders;

(d) Financial penalties, compensation and restitution;

(e) Intermediate treatment and other treatment orders;

(f) Orders to participate in group counselling and similar activities;

(g) Orders concerning foster care, living communities or other educational settings;

(h) Other relevant orders.

18.2 No juvenile shall be removed from parental supervision, whether partly or entirely, unless the circumstances of her or his case make this necessary.

Commentary

Rule 18.1 attempts to enumerate some of the important reactions and sanctions that have been practised and proved successful thus far, in different legal systems. On the whole they represent promising opinions that deserve replication and further development. The rule does not enumerate staffing requirements because of possible shortages of adequate staff in some regions; in those regions measures requiring less staff may be tried or developed.

The examples given in rule 18.1 have in common, above all, a reliance on and an appeal to the community for the effective implementation of alternative dispositions. Community-based correction is a traditional measure that has taken on many aspects. On that basis, relevant authorities should be encouraged to offer community-based services.

Rule 18.2 points to the importance of the family which, according to article 10, paragraph l, of the International Covenant on Economic, Social and Cultural

Rights, is "the natural and fundamental group unit of society". Within the family, the parents have not only the right but also the responsibility to care for and supervise their children. Rule 18.2, therefore, requires that the separation of children from their parents is a measure of last resort. It may be resorted to only when the facts of the case clearly warrant this grave step (for example child abuse).

19. Least Possible Use of Institutionalization

19.1 The placement of a juvenile in an institution shall always be a disposition of last resort and for the minimum necessary period.

Commentary

Progressive criminology advocates the use of non-institutional over institutional treatment. Little or no difference has been found in terms of the success of institutionalization as compared to non-institutionalization. The many adverse influences on an individual that seem unavoidable within any institutional setting evidently cannot be outbalanced by treatment efforts. This is especially the case for juveniles, who are vulnerable to negative influences. Moreover, the negative effects, not only of loss of liberty but also of separation from the usual social environment, are certainly more acute for juveniles than for adults because of their early stage of development.

Rule 19 aims at restricting institutionalization in two regards: in quantity ("last resort,,) and in time ("minimum necessary period"). Rule 19 reflects one of the basic guiding principles of resolution 4 of the Sixth United Nations Congress: a juvenile offender should not be incarcerated unless there is no other appropriate response. The rule, therefore, makes the appeal that if a juvenile must be institutionalized, the loss of liberty should be restricted to the least possible degree, with special institutional arrangements for confinement and bearing in mind the differences in kinds of offenders, offences and institutions. In fact, priority should be given to "open" over "closed" institutions. Furthermore, any facility should be of a correctional or educational rather than of a prison type.

20. Avoidance of Unnecessary Delay

20.1 Each case shall from the outset be handled expeditiously, without any unnecessary delay.

Commentary

The speedy conduct of formal procedures in juvenile cases is a paramount concern. Otherwise whatever good may be achieved by the procedure and the disposition is at risk. As time passes, the juvenile will find it increasingly difficult, if not impossible, to relate the procedure and disposition to the offence, both intellectually and psychologically.

21. Records

21.1 Records of juvenile offenders shall be kept strictly confidential and closed to third parties. Access to such records shall be limited to persons directly concerned with the disposition of the case at hand or other duly authorized persons.

21.2 Records of juvenile offenders shall not be used in adult proceedings in subsequent cases involving the same offender.

Commentary

The rule attempts to achieve a balance between conflicting interests connected with records or files: those of the police, prosecution and other authorities in improving control versus the interests of the juvenile offender. (See also rule 8.) "Other duly authorized persons" would generally include among others, researchers.

22. Need for professionalism and training

22.1 Professional education, in-service training, refresher courses and other appropriate modes of instruction shall be utilized to establish and maintain the necessary professional competence of all personnel dealing with juvenile cases.

22.2 Juvenile justice personnel shall reflect the diversity of juveniles who come into contact with the juvenile justice system. Efforts shall be made to ensure the fair representation of women and minorities in juvenile justice agencies.

Commentary

The authorities competent for disposition may be persons with very different backgrounds (magistrates in the United Kingdom of Great Britain and Northern Ireland and in regions influenced by the common law system; legally trained judges in countries using Roman law and in regions influenced by them; and elsewhere elected or appointed laymen or jurists, members of community-based boards, etc.). For all these authorities, a minimum training in law, sociology, psychology, criminology and behavioural sciences would be required. This is considered as important as the organizational specialization and independence of the competent authority.

For social workers and probation officers, it might not be feasible to require professional specialization as a prerequisite for taking over any function dealing with juvenile offenders. Thus, professional on-the job instruction would be minimum qualifications.

Professional qualifications are an essential element in ensuring the impartial and effective administration of juvenile justice. Accordingly, it is necessary to improve the recruitment, advancement and professional training of personnel and to provide them with the necessary means to enable them to properly fulfil their functions.

All political, social, sexual, racial, religious, cultural or any other kind of discrimination in the selection, appointment and advancement of juvenile justice personnel should be avoided in order to achieve impartiality in the administration of juvenile justice. This was recommended by the Sixth Congress. Furthermore, the Sixth Congress called on Member States to ensure the fair and equal treatment of women as criminal justice personnel and recommended that special measures should be taken to recruit, train and facilitate the advancement of female personnel in juvenile justice administration.

PART FOUR

Non-Institutional Treatment

23. Effective Implementation of Disposition

23.1 Appropriate provisions shall be made for the implementation of orders of the competent authority, as referred to in rule 14.1 above, by that authority itself or by some other authority as circumstances may require

23.2 Such provisions shall include the power to modify the orders as the competent authority may deem necessary from time to time, provided that such modification shall be determined in accordance with the principles contained in these Rules.

Commentary

Disposition in juvenile cases, more so than in adult cases, tends to influence the offender's life for a long period of time. Thus, it is important that the competent authority or an independent body (parole board, probation office, youth welfare institutions or others) with qualifications equal to those of the competent authority that originally disposed of the case should monitor the implementation of the disposition. In some countries, a juge de l'execution des peines has been installed for this purpose.

The composition, powers and functions of the authority must be flexible; they are described in general terms in rule 23 in order to ensure wide acceptability.

24. Provision of Needed Assistance

24.1 Efforts shall be made to provide juveniles, at all stages of the proceedings, with necessary assistance such as lodging, education or vocational training, employment or any other assistance, helpful and practical, in order to facilitate the rehabilitative process.

Commentary

The promotion of the well-being of the juvenile is of paramount consideration. Thus, rule 24 emphasizes the importance of providing requisite facilities, services and other necessary assistance as may further the best interests of the juvenile throughout the rehabilitative process.

25. Mobilization of Volunteers and Other Community Services

25.1 Volunteers, voluntary organizations, local institutions and other community resources shall be called upon to contribute effectively to the rehabilitation of the juvenile in a community setting and, as far as possible, within the family unit.

Commentary

This rule reflects the need for a rehabilitative orientation of all work with juvenile offenders. Co-operation with the community is indispensable if the directives of the competent authority are to be carried out effectively. Volunteers and voluntary services, in particular, have proved to be valuable resources but are at present underutilized. In some instances, the co-operation of ex-offenders (including ex-addicts) can be of considerable assistance.

Rule 25 emanates from the principles laid down in rules 1.1 to 1.6 and follows the relevant provisions of the International Covenant on Civil and Political Rights.

PART FIVE

Institutional Treatment

26. Objectives of Institutional Treatment

26.1 The objective of training and treatment of juveniles placed in institutions is to provide care, protection, education and vocational skills, with a view to assisting them to assume socially constructive and productive roles in society.

26.2 Juveniles in institutions shall receive care, protection and all necessary assistance-social, educational, vocational, psychological, medical and physical-that they may require because of their age, sex, and personality and in the interest of their wholesome development .

26.3 Juveniles in institutions shall be kept separate from adults and shall be detained in a separate institution or in a separate part of an institution also holding adults.

26.4 Young female offenders placed in an institution deserve special attention as to their personal needs and problems. They shall by no means receive less care, protection, assistance, treatment and training than young male offenders. Their fair treatment shall be ensured.

26.5 In the interest and well-being of the institutionalized juvenile, the parents or guardians shall have a right of access.

26.6 Inter-ministerial and inter-departmental co-operation shall be fostered for the purpose of providing adequate academic or, as appropriate, vocational training to institutionalized juveniles, with a view to ensuring that they do no leave the institution at an educational disadvantage.

Commentary

The objectives of institutional treatment as stipulated in rules 26.1 and 26.2 would be acceptable to any system and culture. However, they have not yet been attained everywhere, and much more has to be done in this respect.

Medical and psychological assistance, in particular, are extremely important for institutionalized drug addicts, violent and mentally ill young persons.

The avoidance of negative influences through adult offenders and the safeguarding of the well-being of juveniles in an institutional setting, as stipulated in rule 26.3, are in line with one of the basic guiding principles of the Rules, as set out by the Sixth Congress in its resolution 4. The rule does not prevent States from taking other measures against the negative influences of adult offenders, which are at least as effective as the measures mentioned in the rule. (See also rule 13.4)

Rule 26.4 addresses the fact that female offenders normally receive less attention than their male counterparts. as pointed out by the Sixth Congress. In particular, resolution 9 of the Sixth Congress calls for the fair treatment of female offenders at every stage of criminal justice processes and for special attention to their particular problems and needs while in custody. Moreover, this rule should also be considered in the light of the Caracas Declaration of the Sixth Congress, which, inter alia, calls for equal treatment in criminal justice administration, and against the background of the Declaration on the Elimination of Discrimination against Women and the Convention on the Elimination of All Forms of Discrimination against Women.

The right of access (rule 26.5) follows from the provisions of rules 7.1, 10.1, 15.2 and 18.2. Inter-ministerial and inter-departmental co-operation (rule 26.6) are of particular importance in the interest of generally enhancing the quality of institutional treatment and training.

27. Application of the Standard Minimum Rules for the Treatment of Prisoners adopted by the United Nations

27.1 The Standard Minimum Rules for the Treatment of Prisoners and related recommendations shall be applicable as far as relevant to the treatment of juvenile offenders in institutions, including those in detention pending adjudication.

27.2 Efforts shall be made to implement the relevant principles laid down in the Standard Minimum Rules for the Treatment of Prisoners to the largest possible extent so as to meet the varying needs of juveniles specific to their age, sex and personality.

Commentary

The Standard Minimum Rules for the Treatment of Prisoners were among the first instruments of this kind to be promulgated by the United Nations. It is generally agreed that they have had a world-wide impact. Although there are still countries where implementation is more an aspiration than a fact, those Standard Minimum Rules continue to be an important influence in the humane and equitable administration of correctional institutions.

Some essential protections covering juvenile offenders in institutions are contained in the Standard Minimum Rules for the Treatment of Prisoners (accommodation, architecture, bedding, clothing, complaints and requests, contact with the outside world, food, medical care, religious service, separation of ages, staffing, work, etc.) as are provisions concerning punishment and discipline, and restraint for dangerous offenders. It would not be appropriate to modify those Standard Minimum Rules according to the particular characteristics of institutions for juvenile offenders within the scope of the Standard Minimum Rules for the Administration of Juvenile Justice.

Rule 27 focuses on the necessary requirements for juveniles in institutions (rule 27.1) as well as on the varying needs specific to their age, sex and personality (rule 27.2). Thus, the objectives and content of the rule interrelate to the relevant provisions of the Standard Minimum Rules for the Treatment of Prisoners.

28. Frequent and early recourse to conditional release

28.1 Conditional release from an institution shall be used by the appropriate authority to the greatest possible extent, and shall be granted at the earliest possible time.

28.2 Juveniles released conditionally from an institution shall be assisted and supervised by an appropriate authority and shall receive full support by the community.

Commentary

The power to order conditional release may rest with the competent authority, as mentioned in rule 14.1 or with some other authority. In view of this, it is adequate to refer here to the "appropriate,' rather than to the "competent" authority.

Circumstances permitting, conditional release shall be preferred to serving a full sentence. Upon evidence of satisfactory progress towards rehabilitation, even offenders who had been deemed dangerous at the time of their institutionalization can be conditionally released whenever feasible. Like probation , such release may be conditional on the satisfactory fulfilment of the requirements specified by the relevant authorities for a period of time established in the decision, for example relating to "good behaviour" of the offender, attendance in community programmes, residence in half-way houses, etc.

In the case of offenders conditionally released from an institution, assistance and supervision by a probation or other officer (particularly where probation has not yet been adopted) should be provided and community support should be encouraged.

29. Semi-Institutional Arrangements

29.1 Efforts shall be made to provide semi-institutional arrangements, such as half-way houses, educational homes, day-time training centres and other such appropriate arrangements that may assist juveniles in their proper reintegration into society.

Commentary

The importance of care following a period of institutionalization should not be underestimated. This rule emphasizes the necessity of forming a net of semi-institutional arrangements.

This rule also emphasizes the need for a diverse range of facilities and services designed to meet the different needs of young offenders re-entering the community and to provide guidance and structural support as an important step towards successful reintegration into society.

PART SIX

Research, Planning, Policy Formulation and Evaluation

30. Research as a Basis for Planning, Policy Formulation and Evaluation

30.1 Efforts shall be made to organize and promote necessary research as a basis for effective planning and policy formulation.

30.2 Efforts shall be made to review and appraise periodically the trends, problems and causes of juvenile delinquency and crime as well as the varying particular needs of juveniles in custody.

30.3 Efforts shall be made to establish a regular evaluative research mechanism built into the system of juvenile justice administration and to collect and analyse relevant data and information for appropriate assessment and future improvement and reform of the administration.

30.4 The delivery of services in juvenile justice administration shall be systematically planned and implemented as an integral part of national development efforts.

Commentary

The utilization of research as a basis for an informed juvenile justice policy is widely acknowledged as an important mechanism for keeping practices abreast of advances in knowledge and the continuing development and improvement of the juvenile justice system. The mutual feedback between research and policy is especially important in juvenile justice. With rapid and often drastic changes in the life-styles of the young and in the forms and dimensions of juvenile crime, the societal and justice responses to juvenile crime and delinquency quickly become outmoded and inadequate.

Rule 30 thus establishes standards for integrating research into the process of policy formulation and application in juvenile justice administration. The rule draws particular attention to the need for regular review and evaluation of existing programmes and measures and for planning within the broader context of overall development objectives.

A constant appraisal of the needs of juveniles, as well as the trends and problems of delinquency, is a prerequisite for improving the methods of formulating appropriate policies and establishing adequate interventions, at both formal and informal levels. In this context, research by independent persons and bodies should be facilitated by responsible agencies, and it may be valuable to obtain and to take into account the views of juveniles themselves, not only those who come into contact with the system.

The process of planning must particularly emphasize a more effective and equitable system for the delivery of necessary services. Towards that end, there should be a comprehensive and regular assessment of the wide-ranging, particular needs and problems of juveniles and an identification of clear-cut priori ties. In that connection, there should also be a co-ordination in the use of existing resources, including alternatives and community support that would be suitable in setting up specific procedures designed to implement and monitor established programmes.

DECLARATION OF BASIC PRINCIPLES OF JUSTICE FOR VICTIMS OF CRIME AND ABUSE OF POWER

Adopted by General Assembly Resolution 40/34 of 29 November 1985

A. Victims of Crime

1. "Victims" means persons who, individually or collectively, have suffered harm, including physical or mental injury, emotional suffering, economic loss or substantial impairment of their fundamental rights, through acts or omissions that are in violation of criminal laws operative within Member States, including those laws proscribing criminal abuse of power.

2. A person may be considered a victim, under this Declaration, regardless of whether the perpetrator is identified, apprehended, prosecuted or convicted and regardless of the familial relationship between the perpetrator and the victim. The term "victim" also includes, where appropriate, the immediate family or dependants of the direct victim and persons who have suffered harm in intervening to assist victims in distress or to prevent victimization.

3. The provisions contained herein shall be applicable to all, without distinction of any kind, such as race, colour, sex, age, language, religion, nationality, political

or other opinion, cultural beliefs or practices, property, birth or family status, ethnic or social origin, and disability.

Access to Justice and Fair Treatment

4. Victims should be treated with compassion and respect for their dignity. They are entitled to access to the mechanisms of justice and to prompt redress, as provided for by national legislation, for the harm that they have suffered.

5. Judicial and administrative mechanisms should be established and strengthened where necessary to enable victims to obtain redress through formal or informal procedures that are expeditious, fair, inexpensive and accessible. Victims should be informed of their rights in seeking redress through such mechanisms.

6. The responsiveness of judicial and administrative processes to the needs of victims should be facilitated by:

(a) Informing victims of their role and the scope, timing and progress of the proceedings and of the disposition of their cases, especially where serious crimes are involved and where they have requested such information;

(b) Allowing the views and concerns of victims to be presented and considered at appropriate stages of the proceedings where their personal interests are affected, without prejudice to the accused and consistent with the relevant national criminal justice system;

(c) Providing proper assistance to victims throughout the legal process;

(d) Taking measures to minimize inconvenience to victims, protect their privacy, when necessary, and ensure their safety, as well as that of their families and witnesses on their behalf, from intimidation and retaliation;

(e) Avoiding unnecessary delay in the disposition of cases and the execution of orders or decrees granting awards to victims.

7. Informal mechanisms for the resolution of disputes, including mediation, arbitration and customary justice or indigenous practices, should be utilized where appropriate to facilitate conciliation and redress for victims.

Restitution

8. Offenders or third parties responsible for their behaviour should, where appropriate, make fair restitution to victims, their families or dependants. Such restitution should include the return of property or payment for the harm or loss suffered, reimbursement of expenses incurred as a result of the victimization, the provision of services and the restoration of rights.

9. Governments should review their practices, regulations and laws to consider

restitution as an available sentencing option in criminal cases, in addition to other criminal sanctions.

10. In cases of substantial harm to the environment, restitution, if ordered, should include, as far as possible, restoration of the environment, reconstruction of the infrastructure, replacement of community facilities and reimbursement of the expenses of relocation, whenever such harm results in the dislocation of a community.

11. Where public officials or other agents acting in an official or quasi-official capacity have violated national criminal laws, the victims should receive restitution from the State whose officials or agents were responsible for the harm inflicted. In cases where the Government under whose authority the victimizing act or omission occurred is no longer in existence, the State or Government successor in title should provide restitution to the victims.

Compensation

12. When compensation is not fully available from the offender or other sources, States should endeavour to provide financial compensation to:

(a) Victims who have sustained significant bodily injury or impairment of physical or mental health as a result of serious crimes;

(b) The family, in particular dependants of persons who have died or become physically or mentally incapacitated as a result of such victimization.

13. The establishment, strengthening and expansion of national funds for compensation to victims should be encouraged. Where appropriate, other funds may also be established for this purpose, including in those cases where the State of which the victim is a national is not in a position to compensate the victim for the harm.

Assistance

14. Victims should receive the necessary material, medical, psychological and social assistance through governmental, voluntary, community-based and indigenous means.

15. Victims should be informed of the availability of health and social services and other relevant assistance and be readily afforded access to them.

16. Police, justice, health, social service and other personnel concerned should receive training to sensitize them to the needs of victims, and guidelines to ensure proper and prompt aid.

17. In providing services and assistance to victims, attention should be given to those who have special needs because of the nature of the harm inflicted or because of factors such as those mentioned in paragraph 3 above.

B. Victims of Abuse of Power

18. "Victims" means persons who, individually or collectively, have suffered harm, including physical or mental injury, emotional suffering, economic loss or substantial impairment of their fundamental rights, through acts or omissions that do not yet constitute violations of national criminal laws but of internationally recognized norms relating to human rights.

19. States should consider incorporating into the national law norms proscribing abuses of power and providing remedies to victims of such abuses. In particular, such remedies should include restitution and/or compensation, and necessary material, medical, psychological and social assistance and support.

20. States should consider negotiating multilateral international treaties relating to victims, as defined in paragraph 18.

21. States should periodically review existing legislation and practices to ensure their responsiveness to changing circumstances, should enact and enforce, if necessary, legislation proscribing acts that constitute serious abuses of political or economic power, as well as promoting policies and mechanisms for the prevention of such acts, and should develop and make readily available appropriate rights and remedies for victims of such acts.

UNITED NATIONS GUIDELINES FOR THE PREVENTION OF JUVENILE DELINQUENCY (THE RIYADH GUIDELINES)

Adopted and Proclaimed by General Assembly Resolution 45/112 of 14 December 1990

I. Fundamental Principles

1. The prevention of juvenile delinquency is an essential part of crime prevention in society. By engaging in lawful, socially useful activities and adopting a humanistic orientation towards society and outlook on life, young persons can develop non-criminogenic attitudes.

2. The successful prevention of juvenile delinquency requires efforts on the part of the entire society to ensure the harmonious development of adolescents, with respect for and promotion of their personality from early childhood.

3. For the purposes of the interpretation of the present Guidelines, a child-centred orientation should be pursued. Young persons should have an active role and partnership within society and should not be considered as mere objects of socialization or control.

4. In the implementation of the present Guidelines, in accordance with national legal systems, the well-being of young persons from their early childhood should be the focus of any preventive programme.

5. The need for and importance of progressive delinquency prevention

policies and the systematic study and the elaboration of measures should be recognized. These should avoid criminalizing and penalizing a child for behaviour that does not cause serious damage to the development of the child or harm to others. Such policies and measures should involve:

(a) The provision of opportunities, in particular educational opportunities, to meet the varying needs of young persons and to serve as a supportive framework for safeguarding the personal development of all young persons, particularly those who are demonstrably endangered or at social risk and are in need of special care and protection;

(b) Specialized philosophies and approaches for delinquency prevention, on the basis of laws, processes, institutions, facilities and a service delivery network aimed at reducing the motivation, need and opportunity for, or conditions giving rise to, the commission of infractions;

(c) Official intervention to be pursued primarily in the overall interest of the young person and guided by fairness and equity;

(d) Safeguarding the well-being, development, rights and interests of all young persons;

(e) Consideration that youthful behaviour or conduct that does not conform to overall social norms and values is often part of the maturation and growth process and tends to disappear spontaneously in most individuals with the transition to adulthood;

(f) Awareness that, in the predominant opinion of experts, labelling a young person as "deviant", "delinquent" or "pre-delinquent" often contributes to the development of a consistent pattern of undesirable behaviour by young persons.

6. Community-based services and programmes should be developed for the prevention of juvenile delinquency, particularly where no agencies have yet been established. Formal agencies of social control should only be utilized as a means of last resort.

II. Scope of the Guidelines

7. The present Guidelines should be interpreted and implemented within the broad framework of the Universal Declaration of Human Rights, the International Covenant on Economic, Social and Cultural Rights, the International Covenant on Civil and Political Rights, the Declaration of the Rights of the Child and the Convention on the Rights of the Child, and in the context of the United Nations Standard Minimum Rules for the Administration of Juvenile Justice (The Beijing Rules), as well as other instruments and norms relating to the rights, interests and well-being of all children and young persons.

8. The present Guidelines should also be implemented in the context of the economic, social and cultural conditions prevailing in each Member State.

III. General Prevention

9. Comprehensive prevention plans should be instituted at every level of Government and include the following:

(a) In-depth analyses of the problem and inventories of programmes, services, facilities and resources available;

(b) Well-defined responsibilities for the qualified agencies, institutions and personnel involved in preventive efforts;

(c) Mechanisms for the appropriate co-ordination of prevention efforts between governmental and non-governmental agencies;

(d) Policies, programmes and strategies based on prognostic studies to be continuously monitored and carefully evaluated in the course of implementation;

(e) Methods for effectively reducing the opportunity to commit delinquent acts;

(f) Community involvement through a wide range of services and programmes;

(g) Close interdisciplinary co-operation between national, State, provincial and local governments, with the involvement of the private sector representative citizens of the community to be served, and labour, child-care, health education, social, law enforcement and judicial agencies in taking concerted action to prevent juvenile delinquency and youth crime;

(h) Youth participation in delinquency prevention policies and processes, including recourse to community resources, youth self-help, and victim compensation and assistance programmes;

(i) Specialized personnel at all levels.

IV. Socialization Processes

10. Emphasis should be placed on preventive policies facilitating the successful socialization and integration of all children and young persons, in particular through the family, the community, peer groups, schools, vocational training and the world of work, as well as through voluntary organizations. Due respect should be given to the proper personal development of children and young persons, and they should be accepted as full and equal partners in socialization and integration processes.

A. Family

11. Every society should place a high priority on the needs and well-being of the family and of all its members.

12. Since the family is the central unit responsible for the primary socialization of children, governmental and social efforts to preserve the integrity of the family, including the extended family, should be pursued. The society has a

responsibility to assist the family in providing care and protection and in ensuring the physical and mental well-being of children. Adequate arrangements including day-care should be provided.

13. Governments should establish policies that are conducive to the bringing up of children in stable and settled family environments. Families in need of assistance in the resolution of conditions of instability or conflict should be provided with requisite services.

14. Where a stable and settled family environment is lacking and when community efforts to assist parents in this regard have failed and the extended family cannot fulfil this role, alternative placements, including foster care and adoption, should be considered. Such placements should replicate, to the extent possible, a stable and settled family environment, while, at the same time, establishing a sense of permanency for children, thus avoiding problems associated with "foster drift".

15. Special attention should be given to children of families affected by problems brought about by rapid and uneven economic, social and cultural change, in particular the children of indigenous, migrant and refugee families. As such changes may disrupt the social capacity of the family to secure the traditional rearing and nurturing of children, often as a result of role and culture conflict, innovative and socially constructive modalities for the socialization of children have to be designed.

16. Measures should be taken and programmes developed to provide families with the opportunity to learn about parental roles and obligations as regards child development and child care, promoting positive parent-child relationships, sensitizing parents to the problems of children and young persons and encouraging their involvement in family and community-based activities.

17. Governments should take measures to promote family cohesion and harmony and to discourage the separation of children from their parents, unless circumstances affecting the welfare and future of the child leave no viable alternative.

18. It is important to emphasize the socialization function of the family and extended family; it is also equally important to recognize the future role, responsibilities, participation and partnership of young persons in society.

19. In ensuring the right of the child to proper socialization, Governments and other agencies should rely on existing social and legal agencies, but, whenever traditional institutions and customs are no longer effective, they should also provide and allow for innovative measures.

B. Education

20. Governments are under an obligation to make public education accessible to all young persons.

21. Education systems should, in addition to their academic and vocational

training activities, devote particular attention to the following:

(a) Teaching of basic values and developing respect for the child's own cultural identity and patterns, for the social values of the country in which the child is living, for civilizations different from the child's own and for human rights and fundamental freedoms;

(b) Promotion and development of the personality, talents and mental and physical abilities of young people to their fullest potential;

(c) Involvement of young persons as active and effective participants in, rather than mere objects of, the educational process;

(d) Undertaking activities that foster a sense of identity with and of belonging to the school and the community;

(e) Encouragement of young persons to understand and respect diverse views and opinions, as well as cultural and other differences;

(f) Provision of information and guidance regarding vocational training, employment opportunities and career development;

(g) Provision of positive emotional support to young persons and the avoidance of psychological maltreatment;

(h) Avoidance of harsh disciplinary measures, particularly corporal punishment.

22. Educational systems should seek to work together with parents, community organizations and agencies concerned with the activities of young persons.

23. Young persons and their families should be informed about the law and their rights and responsibilities under the law, as well as the universal value system, including United Nations instruments.

24. Educational systems should extend particular care and attention to young persons who are at social risk. Specialized prevention programmes and educational materials, curricula, approaches and tools should be developed and fully utilized.

25. Special attention should be given to comprehensive policies and strategies for the prevention of alcohol, drug and other substance abuse by young persons. Teachers and other professionals should be equipped and trained to prevent and deal with these problems. Information on the use and abuse of drugs, including alcohol, should be made available to the student body.

26. Schools should serve as resource and referral centres for the provision of medical, counselling and other services to young persons, particularly those with special needs and suffering from abuse, neglect, victimization and exploitation.

27. Through a variety of educational programmes, teachers and other adults and the student body should be sensitized to the problems, needs and perceptions of young persons, particularly those belonging to underprivileged, disadvantaged, ethnic or other minority and low-income groups.

28. School systems should attempt to meet and promote the highest professional

and educational standards with respect to curricula, teaching and learning methods and approaches, and the recruitment and training of qualified teachers. Regular monitoring and assessment of performance by the appropriate professional organizations and authorities should be ensured.

29. School systems should plan, develop and implement extracurricular activities of interest to young persons, in co-operation with community groups.

30. Special assistance should be given to children and young persons who find it difficult to comply with attendance codes, and to "drop-outs".

31. Schools should promote policies and rules that are fair and just; students should be represented in bodies formulating school policy, including policy on discipline, and decision-making.

C. Community

32. Community-based services and programmes which respond to the special needs, problems, interests and concerns of young persons and which offer appropriate counselling and guidance to young persons and their families should be developed, or strengthened where they exist.

33. Communities should provide, or strengthen where they exist, a wide range of community-based support measures for young persons, including community development centres, recreational facilities and services to respond to the special problems of children who are at social risk. In providing these helping measures, respect for individual rights should be ensured.

34. Special facilities should be set up to provide adequate shelter for young persons who are no longer able to live at home or who do not have homes to live in.

35. A range of services and helping measures should be provided to deal with the difficulties experienced by young persons in the transition to adulthood. Such services should include special programmes for young drug abusers which emphasize care, counselling, assistance and therapy-oriented interventions.

36. Voluntary organizations providing services for young persons should be given financial and other support by Governments and other institutions.

37. Youth organizations should be created or strengthened at the local level and given full participatory status in the management of community affairs. These organizations should encourage youth to organize collective and voluntary projects, particularly projects aimed at helping young persons in need of assistance.

38. Government agencies should take special responsibility and provide necessary services for homeless or street children; information about local facilities, accommodation, employment and other forms and sources of help should be made readily available to young persons.

39. A wide range of recreational facilities and services of particular interest to young persons should be established and made easily accessible to them.

D. Mass Media

40. The mass media should be encouraged to ensure that young persons have access to information and material from a diversity of national and international sources.

41. The mass media should be encouraged to portray the positive contribution of young persons to society.

42. The mass media should be encouraged to disseminate information on the existence of services, facilities and opportunities for young persons in society.

43. The mass media generally, and the television and film media in particular, should be encouraged to minimize the level of pornography, drugs and violence portrayed and to display violence and exploitation disfavourably, as well as to avoid demeaning and degrading presentations, especially of children, women and interpersonal relations, and to promote egalitarian principles and roles.

44. The mass media should be aware of its extensive social role and responsibility, as well as its influence, in communications relating to youthful drug and alcohol abuse. It should use its power for drug abuse prevention by relaying consistent messages through a balanced approach. Effective drug awareness campaigns at all levels should be promoted.

V. Social Policy

45. Government agencies should give high priority to plans and programmes for young persons and should provide sufficient funds and other resources for the effective delivery of services, facilities and staff for adequate medical and mental health care, nutrition, housing and other relevant services, including drug and alcohol abuse prevention and treatment, ensuring that such resources reach and actually benefit young persons.

46. The institutionalization of young persons should be a measure of last resort and for the minimum necessary period, and the best interests of the young person should be of paramount importance. Criteria authorizing formal intervention of this type should be strictly defined and limited to the following situations: (a) where the child or young person has suffered harm that has been inflicted by the parents or guardians; (b) where the child or young person has been sexually, physically or emotionally abused by the parents or guardians; (c) where the child or young person has been neglected, abandoned or exploited by the parents or guardians; (d) where the child or young person is threatened by physical or moral danger due to the behaviour of the parents or guardians; and (e) where a serious physical or psychological danger to the child or young person has manifested itself in his or her own behaviour and neither the parents, the guardians, the juvenile himself or herself nor non-residential community services can meet the danger by means other than institutionalization.

47. Government agencies should provide young persons with the opportunity of continuing in full-time education, funded by the State where parents or

guardians are unable to support the young persons, and of receiving work experience.

48. Programmes to prevent delinquency should be planned and developed on the basis of reliable, scientific research findings, and periodically monitored, evaluated and adjusted accordingly.

49. Scientific information should be disseminated to the professional community and to the public at large about the sort of behaviour or situation which indicates or may result in physical and psychological victimization, harm and abuse, as well as exploitation, of young persons.

50. Generally, participation in plans and programmes should be voluntary. Young persons themselves should be involved in their formulation, development and implementation.

51. Government should begin or continue to explore, develop and implement policies, measures and strategies within and outside the criminal justice system to prevent domestic violence against and affecting young persons and to ensure fair treatment to these victims of domestic violence.

VI. Legislation and Juvenile Justice Administration

52. Governments should enact and enforce specific laws and procedures to promote and protect the rights and well-being of all young persons.

53. Legislation preventing the victimization, abuse, exploitation and the use for criminal activities of children and young persons should be enacted and enforced.

54. No child or young person should be subjected to harsh or degrading correction or punishment measures at home, in schools or in any other institutions.

55. Legislation and enforcement aimed at restricting and controlling accessibility of weapons of any sort to children and young persons should be pursued.

56. In order to prevent further stigmatization, victimization and criminalization of young persons, legislation should be enacted to ensure that any conduct not considered an offence or not penalized if committed by an adult is not considered an offence and not penalized if committed by a young person.

57. Consideration should be given to the establishment of an office of ombudsman or similar independent organ, which would ensure that the status, rights and interests of young persons are upheld and that proper referral to available services is made. The ombudsman or other organ designated would also supervise the implementation of the Riyadh Guidelines, the Beijing Rules and the Rules for the Protection of Juveniles Deprived of their Liberty. The ombudsman or other organ would, at regular intervals, publish a report on the progress made and on the difficulties encountered in the implementation of the instrument. Child advocacy services should also be established.

58. Law enforcement and other relevant personnel, of both sexes, should be trained to respond to the special needs of young persons and should be familiar with and use, to the maximum extent possible, programmes and referral possibilities for the diversion of young persons from the justice system.

59. Legislation should be enacted and strictly enforced to protect children and young persons from drug abuse and drug traffickers.

VII. Research, Policy Development and Co-Ordination

60. Efforts should be made and appropriate mechanisms established to promote, on both a multidisciplinary and an intradisciplinary basis, interaction and co-ordination between economic, social, education and health agencies and services, the justice system, youth, community and development agencies and other relevant institutions.

61. The exchange of information, experience and expertise gained through projects, programmes, practices and initiatives relating to youth crime, delinquency prevention and juvenile justice should be intensified at the national, regional and international levels.

62. Regional and international co-operation on matters of youth crime, delinquency prevention and juvenile justice involving practitioners, experts and decision makers should be further developed and strengthened.

63. Technical and scientific co-operation on practical and policy-related matters, particularly in training, pilot and demonstration projects, and on specific issues concerning the prevention of youth crime and juvenile delinquency should be strongly supported by all Governments, the United Nations system and other concerned organizations.

64. Collaboration should be encouraged in undertaking scientific research with respect to effective modalities for youth crime and juvenile delinquency prevention and the findings of such research should be widely disseminated and evaluated.

65. Appropriate United Nations bodies, institutes, agencies and offices should pursue close collaboration and co-ordination on various questions related to children juvenile justice and youth crime and juvenile delinquency prevention.

66. On the basis of the present Guidelines, the United Nations Secretariat, in co-operation with interested institutions, should play an active role in the conduct of research, scientific collaboration, the formulation of policy options and the review and monitoring of their implementation, and should serve as a source of reliable information on effective modalities for delinquency prevention.

7

A Report of Convention on Child Labour

REPORT OF THE COMMITTEE ON CHILD LABOUR (CORR.)

87th Session Geneva, June 1999

Introduction

1. The Committee was originally composed of 217 members (94 Government members, 50 Employer members and 73 Worker members). To achieve equality of voting strength, each Government member entitled to vote was allotted 3,650 votes, each Employer member 6,643 votes and each Worker member 4,550 votes. The composition of the Committee was modified nine times during the session and the number of votes attributed to each member was adjusted accordingly.[1]

2. The Committee elected its Officers as follows:

Chairperson:	Mr. A. Atsain (Government member, Côte d'Ivoire);
Vice-Chairpersons:	Mr. B. Botha (Employer member, South Africa) and Mr. L. Trotman (Worker member, Barbados);
Reporter:	Mrs. M. Niven (Government member, United Kingdom).

3. At its tenth sitting, the Committee appointed a Drafting Committee composed of the following members: Mr. A. Anderson (Government member, Australia), Mrs. A. Benhamou (Employer member, France), Mr. S. Steyne (Worker member, United Kingdom), and the Reporter of the Committee, Mrs. M. Niven (Government member, United Kingdom).

4. The Committee held 20 sittings and had before it Reports VI(1) and VI(2A) and (2B), prepared by the Office on the fourth item on the agenda of the Conference: "Child labour".

5. The representative of the Secretary-General presented Report IV(2A), which contained summaries of the comments received from governments, after

consultations with the most representative organizations of workers and employers, on the texts prepared by the Office following the 86th Session of the International Labour Conference, in 1998, and Report IV(2B) which contained the text of the Proposed Convention and Recommendation.

6. The representative of the Secretary-General recalled the decisions taken by the Conference the previous year. These were that there should be a legally binding Convention, supplemented by a Recommendation, obliging States ratifying the Convention to take measures to secure the prohibition and immediate elimination of the worst forms of child labour. The Convention should be short, precise and contain basic principles capable of being ratified and effectively implemented. The determination of the types of work deemed to be hazardous or likely to jeopardize the health, safety or morals of children should be made at national level. Access to education should not be a criterion for the definition of the worst forms of child labour, but its importance should be taken into account when taking measures of prevention, removal, rehabilitation and reintegration. Finally, the subject of child soldiers should be deferred to the second discussion.

7. The representative of the Secretary-General noted the exceptionally large response to the text of the proposed Convention and Recommendation and pointed out that the comments showed overwhelming support for a new Convention and Recommendation on the prohibition and elimination of the worst forms of child labour. The replies also indicated that the texts of the proposed Convention and Recommendation were a good basis for the second discussion, with consensus on many issues, notably on the principle that there are forms of child labour that cannot be tolerated anywhere and that these should be the priority for national and international action.

8. There was divergence of opinion on some key issues, but the text had been only minimally changed by the Office, as the replies indicated that on most issues the proposed text was accepted by the majority of member States and that, where there were differences, there was insufficient agreement to support one particular position over another. He emphasized that the proposed Convention was concerned first and foremost with situations that could not be tolerated under any circumstances. It applied to all young persons under the age of 18, and would oblige member States which ratified the Convention to take measures to prohibit and immediately eliminate the worst forms of child labour. These worst forms comprised: (i) all forms of slavery and practices similar to slavery, such as the sale and trafficking of children, forced or compulsory labour, debt bondage and serfdom; (ii) the use, procurement or offering of a child for prostitution, production of pornography or pornographic performances; (iii) the use, procurement or offering of a child for illicit activities, in particular for the production and trafficking of drugs; and (iv) work which, by its nature or the circumstances in which it was carried out, was likely to jeopardize the health, safety or morals of children.

9. The proposed Convention required that countries design and implement programmes of action to eliminate the worst forms of child labour and that all necessary measures be taken to ensure the effective implementation and enforcement of the provisions of the Convention, including monitoring mechanisms, appropriate sanctions, and measures of prevention, removal, rehabilitation and social reintegration. Particular attention was to be given to the special situation of girls and of other children at special risk. Finally, it required member States to take steps to assist one another in giving effect to the provisions of the Convention. The proposed Recommendation provided further guidance concerning the definition of hazardous work, the elements of a programme of action, and provisions designed to aid effective enforcement and implementation.

10. The representative of the Secretary-General highlighted some of the major issues likely to come up during the second discussion. The first concerned whether all hazardous work covered by the Minimum Age Convention, 1973 (No. 138), should be covered by the new Convention. Some had felt that the new Convention had a more limited scope and was concerned with hazardous work which posed imminent danger or with work which should not be tolerated under any circumstances. Others, especially workers' organizations, had expressed a wish to give specific examples in the Convention of work likely to jeopardize the health, safety or morals of children, such as the criteria set out in Paragraph 3 of the proposed Recommendation.

11. The explicit inclusion or not of child soldiers and the use of children in armed conflicts was the second major issue. The third contentious issue was whether the denial of access to education should be a criterion for determining the worst forms of child labour. Some governments and workers' organizations wished to reconsider the issue and suggested various formulations, such as specifying, as a worst form of child labour, work that systematically denied children access to education, whilst some governments and employers' organizations opposed this on the basis that it would broaden the scope of the new Convention to include all child labour.

12. The fourth issue was the relationship between immediate and time-bound measures. The final issue related to the possible role of non-governmental organizations (NGOs) and other concerned groups. Several governments had stated that broader consultations should be required in the Convention and there was support from some workers' organizations for consultations with the concerned children and their families.

13. The representative of the Secretary-General concluded by stressing the historical significance of the second discussion on the worst forms of child labour, as new instruments would add to the body of international law begun by the International Labour Organization in 1919, which had culminated in 1973 with the adoption of the comprehensive Minimum Age Convention (No. 138), the ILO's fundamental Convention for the elimination of child labour. He drew

attention to the growing international consensus for clearer priorities nationally and internationally to tackle the problem of the worst forms of child labour, as reflected especially in the resolution concerning the elimination of child labour, adopted in 1996 by the International Labour Conference. The resolution had reaffirmed the long-standing policy of the ILO to put an end to child labour, and called for policies to "immediately proceed to put an end to the most intolerable aspects of child labour, namely the employment of children in slave-like and bonded conditions and in dangerous and hazardous work, the exploitation of very young children, and the commercial sexual exploitation of children".

General Discussion

14. The Employer Vice-Chairperson expressed the Employer members' desire for a universally ratifiable and meaningful Convention. It should not be a repetition of Convention No. 138, but should be concise, simple, understandable, unambiguous, focused and realistic. The reasons for this were that children themselves had to feel and be protected, that anything less than full ratification would result in the continuation of practices which injure, maim and kill children, and that unrealistic, ambiguous and complicated instruments would result in confusion, uncertainty, avoidance and excuses. He stressed that the Employer members remained committed to these intentions.

15. He referred to the issues already agreed upon which the representative of the Secretary-General had outlined earlier noting, in particular, that age 18 was appropriate as the Convention did not refer to all work, only its worst forms, was consistent with the higher minimum age in Convention No. 138 and did not affect its other minimum ages, and was also consistent with the definition of "child" in the United Nations Convention on the Rights of the Child. There was, however, some unease amongst the Employer members regarding the age of 18, contrasting this, for example, with the lower minimum age for marrying. He called on all those present not to unravel what had been agreed, as this would almost certainly result in repeating the previous year's work.

16. He also stated that some issues required further debate, including the possibility of a shorter, more concise and meaningful Preamble, the need for a common understanding of the words "immediate", "effective" and "time-bound", the issues of the inclusion of child soldiers and the wording on education and whether they would promote or hinder ratification, and the role of NGOs.

17. The Employer Vice-Chairperson stressed that the Employer members were committed to finding consensus on these issues and that they also remained committed to the development of a universally ratifiable and immediately implementable Convention. The questions under consideration were life and death issues relating to the protection of children. He considered that the new Convention was fundamental to the ILO's reputation.

18. The Worker Vice-Chairperson expressed the willingness of the Worker

members to work for a ratifiable instrument. The Worker members did not want an instrument resulting in an advantageous position for one or the other group; they wanted to develop an instrument that could be presented before the conscience of the world and effect change. The instruments should be dealt with expeditiously for the sake of the children and in order to take care of their future. He stated that child labour could not be addressed in isolation from the ILO's Declaration on Fundamental Principles and Rights at Work and its Follow-up, adopted by the International Labour Conference at its 86th Session, Geneva, 1998. He noted the presence of the NGOs and the participants in the Global March against Child Labour. The children had brought demands that could not be overlooked.

19. The Worker Vice-Chairperson referred to the reply to the Government of Canada in the Office Commentary in Report IV(2A), *Child Labour*, under Article 4, paragraph 1, concerning possible complaints based on the omission of types of work from the list to be determined and the role of the Committee of Experts on the Application of Conventions and Recommendations in interpreting it. The Worker members indicated their intention to request a clarification.

20. The Worker Vice-Chairperson emphasized that the Worker members were open to dialogue and discussion and had conducted discussions over the past year with many parties all around the world. He stated that much could be achieved from informal dialogue and recalled that the Committee on Child Labour had not had a single vote during the first discussion and that he hoped to repeat that record this year. He considered that the instrument under discussion would be a flagship for the ILO, which would heighten the ILO's reputation throughout the world. The ILO was the one institution that reflected the views of employers' and workers' organizations; and it played a central role in the promotion of social dialogue to maintain democracy.

21. The Worker Vice-Chairperson emphasized that child labour was a human rights issue which needed the framework of the Convention to be operationalized. The proposed instrument was not intended to reword Convention No. 138, but to complement it. Nor was the instrument intended to be used to vilify governments that permitted child labour. However, whatever the reasons for the existence of child labour, immediate action had to be taken to deal with its worst forms. He reiterated that the focus of discussion was the worst forms of child labour, not the abolition of all forms of child labour.

22. The Worker Vice-Chairperson highlighted the issues that would be raised by the Worker members, namely, those related to education, child soldiers, the nature of hazardous work, social reintegration and the special situation of girls. He spoke of the advisory and interpretive role of the Committee of Experts on the Application of Conventions and Recommendations, pointing out the importance of the record of Committee members' contributions in the Committee's Report, which would subsequently be used to guide interpretation. Everyone

wanted the Convention, but the important question was what would happen after adoption of the instrument and what the governments, employers' and workers' organizations would do. Monitoring mechanisms could be envisaged at national level made up of governments, employers' and workers' organizations with NGOs selected after consultation with the social partners; NGOs should not be left out once the Convention was adopted. Reporting mechanisms to bring attention to violations of provisions giving effect to the Convention were also important. There was a need to protect those who reported abuses concerning the worst forms of child labour to make reporting effective.

23. The Government member of the Netherlands, speaking on behalf of the Government members of Australia, Austria, Belgium, Canada, Denmark, Finland, France, Germany, Greece, Hungary, Ireland, Japan, Luxembourg, Netherlands, New Zealand, Norway, Portugal, San Marino, Spain, Sweden, Switzerland, Turkey, United Kingdom and United States, stressed the importance of the instruments under consideration and the great need for clear international commitments to combat exploitative forms of child labour. The first discussion had indicated that the vast majority of Committee members considered the proposed text to be a satisfactory basis for discussion. The new instruments were to focus exclusively on forms of child labour so exploitative and hazardous that no child should be engaged in them. The text of the new Convention needed to be short, clear and concise and it should aim at universal ratification by ILO member States. The new Convention was to complement and be consistent with Convention No. 138; it should also avoid inconsistencies with other international instruments dealing with child labour. The importance of international cooperation and assistance was reaffirmed. She anticipated debates concerning the definition of the worst forms of child labour; the level of detail desirable in the new Convention; and the degree of flexibility to be accorded to the national authorities in determining the worst forms of child labour.

24. The Government member of Switzerland stated her Government firmly believed the adoption of the new instruments was fundamental to the fight against child labour. She recalled that the President of Switzerland had recently announced that Switzerland was likely to ratify Convention No. 138 in 1999, and that it had supported the ILO's International Programme on the Elimination of Child Labour (IPEC), since 1998. She stated that the Government of Switzerland supported the role played by NGOs and other voluntary organizations in this area. Referring to the proposed instruments, she stated that her Government considered that appropriate sanctions, including penal sanctions, were required and called for international cooperation and assistance in addressing the problem.

25. The Government member of India confirmed his Government's commitment to the full eradication of all forms of child labour, beginning with the most exploitative and hazardous ones. He expressed support for a new instrument which could be ratified and implemented and had a clear, well-defined scope.

All governments had to take immediate action to eliminate the worst forms of child labour, bearing in mind their socio-economic context and specific situation regarding child labour. Precipitate actions could drive children into even deeper forms of exploitation and should be avoided. He stressed that child labour could only be eliminated gradually and that efforts must take into consideration the level of development of each country and be directly linked to the level of international cooperation necessary to promote socio-economic development and the eradication of poverty. He stressed the importance of the multi-dimensional approach contained in the resolution concerning the elimination of child labour adopted by the International Labour Conference in 1996 and the need to include these elements in the text under discussion. Adequate resources needed to be mobilized and the ILO should support job-creation and poverty-eradication programmes. The new instruments should not address the problem of the worst forms of child labour purely in a political and civil rights context. The Convention should combine in a balanced manner elements relating to the eradication of poverty, unemployment and illiteracy which were directly linked to the ILO's efforts to gradually secure the realization of economic and social rights, alongside political and civil freedoms. He indicated that the main areas where changes would be essential to the draft text would be as follows:

- the title as well as Article 1 had to make it clear that the Convention addressed immediate and effective action for the prohibition and elimination of the worst forms of child labour;
- the complex nature of the phenomenon had to be reflected in the Preamble primarily with consensus language of the 1996 ILO resolution;
- the scope of the convention should remain focused on the worst and most hazardous forms of child labour and there should be no prescriptive age limit that would undermine ratification prospects;
- provisions related to the national implementation of the Convention had to reflect the complex nature of the phenomenon and not create untenable legal obligations for enforcement. The Convention clearly had to indicate that alongside appropriate national legislation, only multidimensional strategies to provide access to educational opportunities (particularly in the 5-14 age group), avenues for gainful employment of parents, eradication of parental illiteracy and protection of all rights of the child contained in the United Nations Convention on the Rights of the Child could effectively eliminate certain manifestations of the worst forms of child labour;
- any references to access to education had to reflect that governmental responsibility lay in facilitating the availability of this economic and social right in a progressive and developmental context. They also had to indicate that the implementation of desired goals such as compulsory

primary education had to be seen in conjunction with the availability of resources, including through enhanced international cooperation;

- draft Article 8 of the Convention had to be reinforced through language that explicitly endorsed international cooperation, solidarity and assistance for eradicating poverty and promoting socio-economic development.

26. The Government member of Egypt commented on the very important role played by the ILO in the fight against child labour both at the normative level and through the practical assistance provided by IPEC. She emphasized that poverty remained one of the basic reasons why children had to work and called for a greater focus on national policies and compulsory primary education. She announced her Government's ratification of Convention No. 138 and confirmed Egypt's commitment to respect relevant international standards, which was reflected in recent ministerial decisions. There should be further expansion of ILO's technical assistance programmes in favour of developing countries in their efforts to eliminate child labour.

27. The Government member of China underscored the importance of addressing the worst forms of child labour and confirmed the importance his Government attached to the protection of children. He recalled the ratification in December 1998 of Convention No. 138, which demonstrated China's determination to eliminate the problem. China supported the adoption of the new instruments. A new Convention should be clear, concise, and flexible to make universal ratification more likely. He reaffirmed that poverty was the underlying cause of child labour in many developing countries and called upon the ILO to provide more assistance to countries facing the problem, to allow them to strengthen their economies.

28. The Government member of Japan said that solving the problem of child labour was one of the most important issues facing the world today. He stated that in May 1999 the Japanese Parliament had passed new legislation on punishment for child prostitution and pornography, and that this had enhanced protection of chidren. He stressed that a new Convention should contain only those principles which were essential to eliminate the worst forms of child labour, so that it would be ratifiable by as many countries as possible.

29. The Government member of the Islamic Republic of Iran considered child labour to be a dominant issue of our time. At least 120 million children were working throughout the world, the overwhelming majority of them in developing countries. He cited poverty as the driving force behind child labour. However, there were reasons to be optimistic in view of the emerging consensus on the obligation to combat child labour, especially its intolerable forms. The Islamic Republic of Iran had been able to take successful action against child labour, and its incidence was very low. International organizations, and the ILO

in particular, should provide assistance to countries struggling with child labour problems and help them develop comprehensive programmes. These should include statistical work and research, awareness-raising activities and the improvement of education, health and other social services.

30. The Government member of France reaffirmed her Government's dedication to the adoption of a new Convention and emphasized the need to make it one of the ILO's core standards as laid down in the ILO Declaration on Fundamental Principles and Rights at Work and its Follow-up. Child labour was not only an economic and social problem, but also a moral one. Recent initiatives against child labour undertaken by her country included a report on child labour in France, a new draft law to respect children's rights and an increased contribution to IPEC.

31. The Government member of Pakistan stressed her Government's commitment to eliminating the worst forms of child labour. A flexible instrument with clear definitions of the worst forms was needed in order to ensure a maximum number of ratifications. The United Nations Convention on the Rights of the Child served as an example in this regard. Any work it was proposed to ban in addition to bonded labour and work in the sex and drugs trade had to be of the same severity as those readily identifiable activities. She also emphasized that the title of the Convention should be modified to bring out the need for prohibition and immediate measures, as opposed to the immediate elimination of the worst forms of child labour.

32. The Government member of Canada reiterated strong Canadian support for the intent and principles of the proposed instruments which had to be simple and focused on the elimination of the worst forms of child labour and allow for immediate and universal ratification. The Global March against Child Labour had provided an even greater incentive to arrive at agreement. She stated that Canada would seek consistency in the references to child labour and the worst forms.

33. The Government member of Sudan emphasized the importance of the child labour issue and cautioned against reopening last year's general discussion. Sudan had recently taken a number of important steps against child labour. These included the establishment of a Council on the Protection of Children, action programmes and improved child support services.

34. The Government member of Norway called for a clearer specification of hazardous types of work and for sufficient flexibility and a stronger reflection of the importance of education in the proposed Convention. The issue of child soldiers should be included and reference to "other concerned groups" reinforced. The Agenda of Action emerging from the 1997 Oslo Conference on Child Labour was cited as a useful tool for international and national action against child labour. Norway contributed to the IPEC programme and would continue to do

so in the future. The ILO remained a cornerstone in worldwide efforts to eliminate child labour, but inter-agency cooperation needed to be strengthened.

35. The Government member of Senegal stated that poverty, instability and war in the African region had created a high demand for cheap labour. Child labour undermined children's education and integration into society, therefore there was a need for strong instruments. Children worked in agriculture, cattle raising, as domestic servants, with their families in the informal sector, and as apprentices from the age of six or seven in handicrafts, workshops, and construction sites in unhealthy environments under hazardous working conditions. The Government member of Senegal expressed support for the substance of the proposed Convention. She emphasized the need for a follow-up mechanism, and for providing legal and financial assistance by the ILO where necessary. The Preamble should stress the advantages of concrete action regarding training and education. She hoped the ILO would commit itself to promotional action.

36. The Government member of Lebanon repeated that her Government had enacted a law prohibiting admission to employment for children who had not completed age 15 and hazardous work for children under the age of 17 or 18, depending on the nature of the activities performed. The Government, along with employers' and workers' organizations, had established a national strategy on child labour. The Government believed that the proposed Convention and Recommendation should be clear and flexible and the proposed Recommendation should complement the Convention. She questioned the use of the phrase "applied in conjunction with" in Paragraph 1 of the proposed Recommendation and questioned whether "should" was the proper word in a Recommendation as Recommendations provided guidelines and were not binding instruments.

37. The Government member of Ethiopia, speaking on behalf of the members of the African Group on the Committee, strongly supported the unanimous adoption of the proposed Convention. He recalled a number of African meetings on child labour which had enabled the development of an African common position that demanded urgent action be taken against the worst forms of child labour. Poverty and social deprivation had contributed to the rapid increase in the number of children seriously affected by child labour on the continent. He stated that the members of the African Group on the Committee would be guided by the decisions passed by the Labour and Social Affairs Commission of the Organization of African Unity (OAU) and the African Charter on the Rights and Welfare of the Child, which stated in Article 15 that "every child shall be protected from all forms of economic exploitation and from performing any work that is likely to be hazardous or to interfere with the child's physical, mental, spiritual, moral or social development". The Group would propose several changes to the texts, including an explicit reference to the recruitment and use of children in armed conflict in the definition of the worst forms of child labour; a reference to civil society in the Convention; more explicit language

regarding the need for increased technical and financial assistance to complement national efforts aimed at the effective elimination of the worst forms of child labour; and reference to the eradication of poverty, since this was the principal root cause of the worst forms of child labour. Lastly, there was a need to emphasize the need for education with regard to prevention, rehabilitation and reintegration. The need for a concise, ratifiable Convention should not preclude the inclusion of important issues such as poverty eradication measures.

38. The Government member of Morocco emphasized the need to combat poverty in order to eliminate child labour. He stated that the instruments should be clear and that an explanation should be given of how the implementation of this instrument could affect member States. He also noted the need for technical cooperation and financial assistance. He further stated that the involvement of children in armed conflict had to be addressed for the sake of the credibility of the instruments. He also recalled the measures the Government of Morocco had been taking for the protection of children such as the ratification of Convention No. 138, the establishment of a parliament for children and the implementation of a cooperation programme in the framework of IPEC's activities.

39. The Government member of South Africa endorsed the statement made on behalf of the members of the African Group on the Committee. He stated that the South African Constitution ensured that "every child has the right to be protected from exploitative labour practices". South Africa supported an effective and targeted Convention that supplemented Convention No. 138. He summarized his Government's position on several issues. First, an explicit reference to the prohibition of involvement of children in armed conflict should be made because it affected more than 300,000 children in approximately 30 conflicts in the world. Those children had difficulty demobilizing once peace was restored as they had become accustomed to violence and experienced severe problems when they returned home. The use of child soldiers should be considered an illegal activity. The involvement of children in armed conflict was clearly work which by its nature or circumstances in which it was carried out was likely to jeopardize the health, safety or morals of children. This had been documented by the United Nations Study on the Impact of Armed Conflict on Children (51st Session, 1996). Convention No. 138 established a minimum age of 18 for such dangerous work. Second, a reference should be made to access to education as it was central to the prohibition and elimination of the worst forms of child labour. A lack of commitment to provide basic education could unintentionally result in children who were withdrawn from the worst forms of child labour ending up on the street. Third, the proposed Convention should provide clearer guidelines for hazardous work, such as those contained in Article 5, paragraph 3, of Convention No. 138 which indicated the industries or sectors of the economy to which the Convention must as a minimum apply, notably, mining and quarrying; manufacturing; construction; electricity, gas and water; sanitary services; transport, storage, and communication;

and plantations and other agricultural undertakings mainly producing for commercial purposes. Such determination at the international level should not preclude additions at the national level. Fourth, there was no contradiction between the concepts of immediate measures and time-bound measures; the Convention should require States to take immediate measures, such as bringing their law and practice into line with international standards, and setting up the necessary institutional capacity and programmes aimed at prohibiting and eliminating the worst forms of child labour. However, the effective elimination of child labour needed well-conceived, strictly time-bound programmes. Fifth, formulating and implementing strategies for the prohibition and elimination of the worst forms of child labour should be done with the full participation of employers' and workers' organizations, civil society, community leaders and NGOs. Finally, the proposed Convention was expected to fall within the scope of the ILO Declaration on Fundamental Principles and Rights at Work and its Follow-up.

40. The Government member of the Syrian Arab Republic stated that children represented the future and hope of mankind and that they had to be protected to respect their integrity. He favoured the adoption of the Convention and Recommendation to provide a regulatory framework to abolish child labour. All States had a right to a decent standard of economic development but this had to be achieved without child labour. His Government had ratified a number of international instruments and had enacted laws against slavery and practices akin to slavery, sale and trafficking of children, child prostitution, child pornography and violence against children which were severely punished. The Government of the Syrian Arab Republic had also enacted legislation providing compulsory free education and sanctioning parents or guardians who did not send their children to school. The instruments should be flexible, clear, straightforward and easily understood and should avoid obstacles to ratification. The worst forms of child labour should be abolished as soon as possible. He also stated that Article 3(d) and Article 4 needed to be brought into line to avoid the risk of activities being defined as hazardous work in one country but not in another. It should be understood that child labour was remunerated work and this implied that unremunerated work by children was not covered. He also considered that poverty was the root cause of child labour, but other causes also needed to be studied. Parents and guardians needed to be made aware of the issue in order to protect their children.

41. The Government member of the United States commented that the proposed Convention on the worst forms of child labour was an important addition to international labour standards, which historically had addressed the issue of child labour. He noted that the Report of the Director-General to this Session of the ILC foresaw strong action against the worst forms of child labour as an important element for the ILO in future. He stated that the United States Government

had accelerated its contributions to IPEC and its action against child labour reflected the personal commitment of the President. He welcomed the presence of two young Americans among participants in the Global March. They had served as a reminder that developed countries, too, had to be vigilant, and the United States had renewed its attention to the issue within the country. He considered that the proposed Convention should be a well-targeted instrument on the worst forms of child labour and be complementary to and consistent with Convention No. 138, while not duplicating its provisions. It should not present technical obstacles to ratification and should strengthen commitment to joint action to eliminate child labour. The definition of hazardous work in Article 3(d) should be different from that in Convention No. 138, should be clear and achievable, and not present technical barriers to ratification. He said this would permit a clearer approach to Article 4, paragraph 1, and would avoid any paradoxical outcomes. Recalling the debate on the age of eligibility for military service, he thought it inadvisable to add unnecessary obstacles to ratification. The intention of the Convention was not to limit traditional national military training and voluntary service consistent with current international law. International legal obligations set an age limit of 15 years, which admittedly was low; but in trying to address these issues it would be prudent not to establish a norm that would prove unworkable or counter-productive. The emphasis should be on the coerced or criminal imposition of military activity. He further stated that education was fundamental to ending child labour, and that it was appropriately addressed in Article 7, though the United States was willing to consider ways to emphasize it further. He concluded by stating that concerning means of action the United States was willing to consider ways of strengthening the obligation for cooperation within the ILO, with other international organizations, and with NGOs and the public at large, who had much to contribute to this effort.

42. The Government member of Bangladesh commented that while there was no doubt that child labour was detrimental to children and that all children should attend school, the reality was different. Poverty was the primary cause of child labour, exacerbated by other factors such as the lack of schools and the inability of families to afford schooling. Socio-economic considerations had to be taken into account when formulating interventions targeting the worst forms of child labour. Legislation was important but insufficient by itself. Policy interventions should be aimed at development, education and social mobilization. The Convention should be flexible and should allow decisions regarding what constituted hazardous work to be made at the national level. He stated that the Government of Bangladesh had demonstrated the political will to address child labour and had instituted national machinery to protect children against abandonment, neglect, economic exploitation and other abuse. With the assistance of IPEC and UNICEF, action by the Bangladeshi Garment Manufacturers Association had now rendered the ready-made garment sector of Bangladesh almost free of child labour.

43. The Government member of Sri Lanka hoped for a Convention that could be ratified and implemented by all member States, whether developed or developing. He recalled the debate on the title of the proposed Convention during the first discussion, and reiterated his support for the position taken by the Governments of India and Pakistan that this should be renamed "Immediate action for the abolition of the worst forms of child labour Convention, 1999". He also suggested that the age to which the Convention would apply should be to those under 15, in line with the age of compulsory education in Sri Lanka and many other countries. Child labour was to be found in the informal sector, not the formal sector, in Sri Lanka as in other developing countries. He considered that poverty was a major cause of child labour and that this needed to be addressed through the generation of employment, foreign capital investment and poverty alleviation programmes; he called for an international fund to this end, financed by a percentage of member States' GNP. The elimination of child labour required the active participation and cooperation not only of governments but also of NGOs, employers' and workers' groups. He also supported the inclusion of child soldiers in the Convention. He reiterated the full support of the Government of Sri Lanka for the proposed Convention, and recalled the recent establishment of a child protection task force in Sri Lanka.

44. The Government member of the Russian Federation confirmed that his Government was in favour of drawing up a Convention complemented by a Recommendation on the worst forms of child labour. He stressed the need for a short, clear, unambiguous and generally acceptable instrument which would permit universal ratification. The Convention should prohibit only the worst forms of child labour and there should be a clearer definition of these forms. However, he doubted the advisability of including a reference to child soldiers, given that this issue was being addressed through the consideration of a United Nations draft optional protocol to the Convention on the Rights of the Child on the involvement of children in armed conflicts. He commented that if the proposed Convention before the Committee were to be adopted without substantive change it would be a significant step, as it would go further than Convention No. 138. The Preamble should reflect the relation between the new Convention and Convention No. 138 and a comparison of the provisions of each Convention should be made on the basis of general norms in line with international treaties. He stated that the current Convention should be in line with the ILO Declaration on Fundamental Principles and Rights at Work and its Follow-up.

45. The Government member of Namibia reported on the decisions taken during the April 1999 Session of the OAU Labour and Social Affairs Commission, chaired by his Government. There was consensus on a large number of issues, although there was some divergence on the definition of hazardous work and the criterion for its determination contained in the proposed instruments. The April Session had recognized four major outstanding issues, namely: the question

of child soldiers; the role of education; hazardous work; and the role of NGOs and other concerned groups. It had also been decided to adopt a common African position during the discussion at the 87th Session of the International Labour Conference. The meeting had also urged support for the proposed new Convention and the promotion of African participation in ratification and implementation of the new instruments. Important issues to the African members were the prohibition of the recruitment and use of children in armed conflict, the inclusion of NGOs in the application of the provisions of the Convention, and the need for increased technical and financial assistance.

46. The Government member of Yemen pointed to poverty as a major cause of child labour. The demographic explosion in developing countries, the question of globalization and structural adjustment policies had generated unemployment and had negative repercussions on the child labour situation. Normative work had to be complemented by the support of industrialized countries, which should face up to their moral and humanitarian responsibilities emerging from the globalization process. He highlighted the central role of his Government in identifying and fighting the worst forms of child labour. The Government of Yemen had ratified all relevant Conventions and expressed its support for the new Convention. There were some questions concerning the interpretation of Article 3 of the proposed Convention.

47. The Government member of Chile expressed his Government's support for the adoption of the proposed instruments, which were considered integral to efforts to eliminate child labour. He stated they were complementary to Convention No. 138, and pointed out that the United Nations Convention on the Rights of the Child was the most complete legal instrument for the protection of children's rights. The standards contained in that Convention needed to be adequately reflected in the text for adoption, namely, mentioning explicitly prohibition of the worst forms of child labour and the obligation on States to protect children against economic exploitation and from performing any work that was likely to be hazardous or to interfere with their education, or be harmful to their health and development; to effectively guarantee their right to education and to ensure they were not enrolled in armed conflicts. He also hoped that the new instruments would be ratified by as many countries as possible.

48. The Government member of Eritrea outlined measures taken by his Government to eliminate child labour. After formal independence in 1993, the Government officially announced compulsory primary education and established programmes of financial support to children to enable their school attendance, with priority for orphans, children with disabilities and street children; and a rehabilitation project and training for homeless adolescents with problems. The Government of Eritrea had signed the United Nations Convention on the Rights of the Child, and its draft Labour Code posed restrictions on the employment of

young people. It supported measures by the ILO and the international community to eliminate the worst forms of child labour.

49. The Government member of Saudi Arabia considered that poverty was the main if not the sole cause of child labour, and that it resulted in parents letting their children work in order to boost their low family incomes. This meant that children stopped going to school and risked getting involved in dangerous or morally reprehensible work. In his view, the Convention should make provision for assistance to families with low incomes, as this would help reduce child labour.

50. The Government member of Tunisia outlined action taken by his Government to consolidate measures to protect children and promote their rights, including the establishment of the school-leaving age at 16; the ratification of the United Nations Convention on the Rights of the Child; the creation of a National Council on Children's Affairs, with representatives from ministries concerned, from organizations concerned with children and from the trade union movement, with the aim of contributing to strategies to protect and promote children's physical and psychological health, education and leisure, protecting them from exploitation and abuse and enhancing the role of the family. The Government had promulgated a child protection code and had ratified Convention No. 138 in 1995. The Government of Tunisia supported the adoption of flexible instruments likely to attract a large number of ratifications and to be readily and effectively applied.

51. The Government member of Uruguay supported the aims of the proposed texts as a complement to Convention No. 138. She expressed her Government's support for the inclusion of child soldiers as among the victims of the worst forms of child labour listed in Article 3 of the proposed Convention, as this was one of the most dangerous forms of work; and for raising the age of eligibility for involvement in the armed forces. She welcomed the fact that the members of the African Group on the Committee would be presenting a draft amendment covering the recruitment and involvement of children in warfare. Her Government was also ready to accept, in the context of the present Convention, the reference only to participation and was open to the recruitment of persons to the armed forces under the age of 18 for the purposes of vocational training only, as a way of enabling national legislation to adapt gradually to this new international standard.

52. The Government member of Zimbabwe stated that she joined other countries in their commitment to the care and protection of children. Along with a traditionally protective culture, a supportive NGO constituency and positive national legislation, her country was working towards making children's rights a reality. However, unless poverty was addressed, legislation would eliminate child labour on paper only. The Convention should be a practical instrument and programming tool aimed at gradually eliminating poverty and providing children

with the means, not only of survival, but of development. The Government member of Zimbabwe recognized the importance of basic primary education and free education was being targeted to destitute families. She concluded that there was a need to protect children from damaging experiences, and this included their participation in all forms of military conflict.

53. The Government member of Ethiopia stated that the future of all countries depended on their children. It was unthinkable to expect sustained development without giving due attention to the welfare of children. The worst forms of child labour characterized by exploitation, serious abuse, excessive long hours, low or no pay, inadequate working conditions and exposure to occupational hazards should be prohibited and eliminated. For these reasons the Ethiopian Government strongly supported unanimous approval and ratification of the proposed Convention and Recommendation. The instruments should not seek to revise or replace existing standards on child labour but rather expressly refer and reaffirm their complementary nature. The Convention should take into account the reality of widespread poverty and underdevelopment and the need for continued and increased international cooperation. The Government member of Ethiopia also emphasized the disturbing trend of recruiting and using children in armed hostilities. Children were not only victims of violence in situations of armed conflicts, but also served as instruments of violence, trained or indoctrinated to kill and abuse other children and adults. Recruiting and using children for warfare not only destroyed their moral values but also inclucated a culture of violence and intolerance. This in turn made rehabilitation, reconstruction and reconciliation even more daunting tasks. The proposed Convention should incorporate the recruitment for and the use of children in armed conflict as a worst form of child labour; showing the resolve of the world community to prohibit and eliminate this heinous practice. He concluded by informing the Committee that Ethiopia had recently ratified Convention No. 138, together with the Equal Remuneration Convention, 1957 (No. 100) and the Abolition of Forced Labour Convention, 1951 (No. 105), bringing to six the number of fundamental ILO Conventions ratified by Ethiopia.

54. The general discussion was concluded by brief comments from the Employer and Worker Vice-Chairpersons. The Employer Vice-Chairperson noted the commitment of the Committee to reach a consensus but regretted the lack of focus and precision in much of the general discussion. The Employer members were particularly concerned about the issues of child soldiers, the role of NGOs and Article 3(d) on hazardous work. They also regarded Article 7, paragraph 2, as problematic since it could put an obligation on States to set up programmes to ensure free, basic education while there were still 25 countries in the world without compulsory education in place. He encouraged the countries concerned to consider this Article carefully. Another area of concern was the frequently mentioned link between poverty and child labour. While he recognized that

there was no doubt about this interrelationship, he appealed to the Committee to concentrate on the worst forms of child labour for which poverty could not provide an excuse for inaction.

55. The Worker Vice-Chairperson expressed disappointment at the lack of consistency between the intentions expressed in the general discussion and the content of the first amendments submitted. These amendments cast some doubt on whether the Committee would be able to arrive at a Convention at all. He recalled the level of international attention focused on the work of the Committee and appealed to its members to consider the consequences of failure to reach agreement.

56. The representative speaking on behalf of NGOs from the Americas pointed out that there were some 30 million children working in the Americas, many of them in hazardous conditions such as in brick-manufacturing, quarrying, mining, agriculture, in factories, building sites and as domestic servants. Poverty was the primary cause of child labour, and far-reaching and radical changes were necessary to address the issue. The proposed Convention on the worst forms of child labour was one such measure. She stated that Article 3 of the Convention was welcome, however, it should reckon with the fact that 75 per cent of working children in the region did not attend school. Article 32 of the United Nations Convention on the Rights of the Child recognized the importance of including as harmful, work which denied access to schooling and she appealed for consistency in international instruments relating to children's rights. She also appealed for an inclusion in Article 3 of the proposed Convention a reference to children in armed conflict as this, by its nature, was harmful to a child. She concluded that eliminating child labour required broad consensus, coordination and action of all governments, employers' and workers' organizations, NGOs and child workers themselves.

57. The representative speaking on behalf of African-based NGOs commended the new Convention for setting the age to which the Convention would apply at 18, in conformity with the United Nations Convention on the Rights of the Child and with Convention No. 138. She considered that education was crucial to successfully tackling the problem of child labour, and that without it the vicious cycle of poverty would not be broken. She noted the role of civil society in the fight against child labour, commenting that for the Convention to systematically exclude their participation would be an oversight. She stressed the need to include in the proposed Convention practices which were particular to the situation in Africa, including all forms of traditional, cultural, religious practices and rituals that predispose children to child labour, such as arranged and forced child marriages, offering of children to shrines, and mock child marriages; the use of children in slave-like and invisible domestic work; and the use, procuring or offering of a child for armed conflict.

58. The representative speaking on behalf of Asian-based NGOs reiterated the Global March's call for all governments, employers' and workers' organizations to unite with the child workers, their families and communities to combat exploitative child labour. She stated that, in keeping with the spirit of the United Nations Convention on the Rights of the Child, these working children had the right to be protected from exploitative and hazardous work and abuse. Most child labourers in the Asian region worked in the informal sector, largely hidden from view, so it was important that the new Convention and national plans of action should address child labour in these areas. She stated that Governments needed to develop basic education which was child-centred, relevant and accessible to the poor, and to strengthen informal and vocational education for children once they were removed from hazardous working conditions and bonded labour. She commented that it was imperative for working children, their families, communities, concerned NGOs and civic organizations to be seen as active partners and collaborators in national plans of action on the new Convention. She concluded with a call for governments, and employers' and workers' organizations to ensure that it was translated into practical action in their own countries.

59. The representative speaking on behalf of European-based NGOs welcomed the new Convention, which she believed would provide a legal framework to help reinforce the activities of civic organizations working on the issue. She stressed that the worst forms of child labour were not found only in developing countries and pointed to the thousands of asylum-seekers, refugee and migrant children working in hazardous forms of labour in Europe. The new Convention would be missing an essential component if it did not specifically prohibit child participation in armed conflict irrespective of how they were recruited. She considered that all children had a right to basic education, which was essential to their development and future prospects. She noted with pleasure that the Report of the Director-General to the Conference referred to the possibility of expanding social dialogue to include civic organizations, and stated her concern that the proposed new Convention did not reflect that important role in combating child labour. She pointed out that IPEC included NGOs amongst its main partners at the country level, and called for the views of children and families directly affected by the worst forms of child labour and of relevant civil society organizations to be taken into account, when determining types of hazardous work and when designing, implementing and monitoring action programmes.

60. The representative speaking on behalf of the Global March against Child Labour reiterated its support to governments, employers' and workers' organizations to achieve rapid ratification and implementation of the new Convention. He pointed out the need to differentiate between the issue of poverty and child labour, and urged all parties concerned to take immediate measures to put an end to the worst forms of child labour. Education was considered a

fundamental right for children and experience had shown that educational programmes could also be offered in countries where a large portion of the population lived below the poverty line. He concluded by urging member States to consider the elimination of the worst forms of child labour as a moral and social commitment. The Worker Vice-Chairperson indicated that the organizers of the Global March had been in constant discussion with the Worker members about reaching an agreement on language acceptable to them.

CONSIDERATION OF THE PROPOSED TEXTS CONTAINED IN REPORT IV(2B)

A. Proposed Convention Concerning the Prohibition and Immediate Elimination of the Worst Forms of Child Labour

Title

61. A series of amendments were submitted and discussed concerning whether the title should refer to "immediate prohibition", but not "immediate elimination"; "immediate measures for elimination", rather than "immediate elimination"; "effective" elimination, instead of "immediate" elimination; and "prohibition and elimination" without any reference to "immediate". As the discussion below reveals, consensus was reached on the phrase "prohibition and immediate action for the elimination" of the worst forms of child labour.

62. The Employer members submitted an amendment to replace the word "concerning" by "on" and delete the word "immediate". The Employer members argued that while it was necessary to refer to urgency and immediacy of action in the body of the text of the Convention, its title should remain simple and concise.

63. The Worker members pointed to the need to keep the word "concerning" as this was the term commonly used in other ILO Conventions. They strongly opposed the second part of the amendment on the grounds that the requirement of immediacy for the elimination of the worst forms of child labour was an essential element of the proposed Convention. The deletion of "immediate" was also opposed by the Government member of Ethiopia. The Government member of India suggested a subamendment to insert "measures for the" so that the reference would be to immediate "measures for the" elimination of the worst forms of child labour. The Government members of Ethiopia and Zimbabwe supported the subamendment but the Employer and Worker members opposed it. The Government member of Switzerland opposed both the amendment and the subamendment. The Employer members withdrew the amendment.

64. The Government members of Bolivia, Colombia, Ecuador and Venezuela submitted a similar amendment to delete "immediate". The Government member of Colombia speaking on behalf of the abovementioned countries expressed concern about the future implementation of the Convention with the title as

proposed. He anticipated difficulties for the international community if the title did not correspond to the results produced by the instrument itself. Given their commitment to eliminating the worst forms of child labour, they withdrew the amendment but emphasized that the terminology would create obstacles for the implementation of the Convention.

65. The Government member of Morocco submitted an amendment to insert the word "immediate" before the word "prohibition" and replace the word "immediate" with the word "effective" before the word "elimination", so that the title would read as follows: "Proposed Convention concerning the immediate prohibition and effective elimination of the worst forms of child labour". The amendment would better reflect that prohibition of the worst forms of child labour through legislative means could be immediate, whereas their elimination required time. The Government member of India supported the amendment indicating the need to adopt an instrument which contained achievable goals. The Worker and the Employer members opposed the amendment, as did the Government members of Canada, Finland, Netherlands, Switzerland and Zimbabwe, while the Government member of Angola supported it. The Government member of Nigeria supported the first part of the amendment and proposed a subamendment to change the second part to read: "effective measures for the elimination". The Government member of Morocco supported the subamendment, but in view of the insufficient support indicated for the amendment, withdrew it.

66. The Government member of Ethiopia on behalf of the Government members of the African Group on the Committee submitted an amendment to insert after the word "immediate" the words "measures for the". He referred to the previous discussions and confirmed that the title should refer to immediate measures for elimination, not immediate elimination. The Worker members opposed the amendment, reaffirming that the commitment was to immediate elimination, but that it was understood that immediate elimination did not mean today, but rather without delay or as soon as possible. The Government member of Egypt pointed out there was a general consensus to take immediate steps against the worst forms of child labour and that the new Convention should be a flexible instrument capable of being rapidly ratified by many member States. The Government members of China, Colombia, Cuba, India, Lebanon, Namibia, Spain and the Syrian Arab Republic supported the amendment confirming the need to urgently adopt measures to eliminate the worst forms of child labour. The Employer members also supported the amendment. The Worker members, while recognizing the support for the amendment suggested that "immediate action" was preferable to "immediate measures" and established a closer link between the Title and the wording in the Preamble and better reflected the concept of an ongoing process to eliminate the worst forms of child labour. The Government member of Ethiopia on behalf of the members of the African Group on the Committee opposed the subamendment, while the Government member of the Sudan supported it.

67. The Government member of the Netherlands proposed a subamendment whereby the title would read: "Proposed Convention concerning immediate measures for the prohibition and effective elimination of the worst forms of child labour", in an effort to facilitate the discussions. However, the Worker members believed such proposals weakened the intention of the instruments. They recalled the great expectations of the outside world concerning the proposed instruments and that the title should convey a strong and clear message about what the new ILO instruments intended to do about the worst forms of child labour.

68. The Government member of France agreed and reiterated the need to focus on central issues and not go back on the consensus that had been reached the previous year. She thus supported retaining the title in the Office text. The Government members of Argentina, Belgium, Canada, Italy, Norway, Poland and Uruguay also expressed their support for the existing title. In view of this show of support, the Employer members also decided to support the existing title.

69. The Government members of Spain and Rwanda continued to support the amendment proposed by the Government member of Ethiopia, as the title should make a clear statement to the public with achievable and realistic aims. The Government member of Bolivia, speaking on behalf of Colombia, Ecuador and Venezuela agreed with the Government member of Spain, believing that the instruments should be viable and achievable.

70. The Worker members reiterated their conviction that the title should convey a strong message to the world, and that the word "immediate" clearly conveyed the sense of "without delay". In the light of the strong support for retaining the original title, the Government member of the Netherlands withdrew her subamendment. A show of hands by Government members indicated majority support for maintaining the original title, but the Government member of Ethiopia stated that the members of the African Group on the Committee preferred to retain the intention of their amendment and to this end they could accept the proposal that had been made by the Worker members to replace the word "measures" by "action".

71. The Worker members stressed their wish for consensus on the aims of the instruments as did the Employer members in supporting this subamendment. The Government member of the Netherlands on behalf of several other Government members also supported it. The subamendment was adopted, as was the amendment as subamended.

72. The Title as amended was adopted.

Preamble

Preambular Paragraphs 1 and 2

73. Preambular paragraphs 1 and 2 were adopted without change.

Preambular Paragraph 3

74. An amendment submitted by the Employer members proposed to delete the word "effective" before "elimination" and to replace the words "with a view to achieving the total abolition of child labour" with "on child labour". Their intention was to ensure a simple, readily understood instrument. The second part of their amendment sought, in the interests of clarity, to move away from the words taken directly from the Preamble to Convention No. 138, which referred to the total abolition of child labour as defined in that Convention, but which could be misunderstood by the general public to refer to all work done by children.

75. The Government member of Canada spoke to a similar amendment, which was to be submitted by the Government members of Australia, Canada, Germany, Hungary, Ireland, Japan, Netherlands, New Zealand, Portugal, San Marino, Spain, Turkey, United Kingdom and United States, to delete the words "which remain the fundamental instruments with a view to achieving the total abolition of child labour". They considered the phrase a commentary on Convention No. 138 which was unnecessary, and pointed out that no other instruments mentioned in the Preamble had such a commentary.

76. The Worker members opposed the amendment and stated that Convention No. 138 was the governing standard on child labour, which remained fundamental to child labour, and that the resolution of 1996 went to its heart. The principle it represented, the total abolition of child labour, needed to be stated for it to be adhered to.

77. The Employer members opposed the amendment proposed by the Government member of Canada and the abovementioned group of Governments, maintaining their amendment. The Government member of Egypt considered the fundamental nature of Convention No. 138 needed to be emphasized. The Government member of India argued that the Employer members' amendment oversimplified the text, as it no longer linked the aim of Convention No. 138 with any specific intention concerning child labour.

78. The Government members of Cuba, Ethiopia, Finland, France, Italy, Lebanon, South Africa and Uruguay opposed the amendments in favour of keeping the Office text. The Government member of France stated that the wording was taken directly from Convention No. 138 and that it would be strange to question such wording. Furthermore, the wording reflected the previous year's decision regarding the link between Convention No. 138 and the new Convention, which was important to recall in the Preamble. The Government member of Switzerland, supported by the Government member of Turkey, agreed with the Government member of France and noted that the Preamble was not a legally binding part of the instrument. She stated that her Government had erroneously been included on the proposed amendment submitted by Canada and the other Governments mentioned.

79. The Government members of Colombia and Hungary supported the amendment submitted by the Government member of Canada and others, stating that the key word in this paragraph was "complement". When reference was made to other international instruments in the text of a Convention, added qualifications or interpretations were not given.

80. The Government member of Canada, speaking on behalf of the Government members of Australia, Canada, Germany, Hungary, Ireland, Japan, Netherlands, New Zealand, Portugal, San Marino, Spain, Turkey, United Kingdom and the United States, suggested a subamendment to delete the word "the" before "fundamental instruments" in the preceding phrase in the title. The phrase in the title would thus read : "... which remain fundamental instruments on child labour, and". The Worker members agreed to support the subamendment in the interests of reaching consensus. Support was also voiced by the Government members of Argentina, Denmark, Finland, Rwanda, and Switzerland, but the Government members of Cuba, Egypt, Ethiopia, France, India and South Africa felt that the proposed subamendment would weaken the intent of the text and the reference to Convention No. 138 and Recommendation No. 146 as "the" fundamental instruments should remain. Following an appeal by the Worker members to concentrate on more substantive matters in the proposed Convention, the amendment as subamended was adopted by consensus, thus the reference read as follows: "to complement the Convention and Recommendation concerning Minimum Age for Admission to Employment, 1973, which remain fundamental instruments on child labour,".

81. The Government members of Egypt and Ethiopia withdrew an amendment to replace "national and international action" by "national action and international cooperation", in favour of the amendment being submitted next by the Government member of Morocco. The Government member of Morocco submitted an amendment to delete "and international" after "national" and to insert "international cooperation and assistance" after the word "action".

82. The insertion of "international cooperation and assistance" to replace "international action" sought to clarify which kind of international action was to be taken and the methods needed to support the efforts of the States involved to achieve the elimination of the worst forms of child labour.

83. The Employer members expressed some disagreement with the proposal, indicating that the question was covered in greater detail in Article 8 of the proposed Convention. The Worker members recognized the strong call made by several developing countries for technical and monetary support in addressing the problem of poverty eradication and elimination of the worst forms of child labour. While confirming the intent of the Workers to give considerable attention to the question of international cooperation and assistance under Article 8, the

Worker members considered it unnecessary to include a similar reference in the Preamble and thus opposed the amendment.

84. The Government member of Sweden proposed a subamendment to retain the words "international action" and to insert the words "including international cooperation and assistance". The Government member of the Netherlands, speaking on behalf of the members of the Group of Industrialized Market Economies (IMEC) (Australia, Austria, Belgium, Canada, Denmark, Finland, France, Germany, Greece, Ireland, Italy, Japan, Luxembourg, Netherlands, New Zealand, Norway, Portugal, Spain, Sweden, Switzerland, Turkey, United Kingdom and United States), supported the subamendment, as did the Government members of South Africa and the United States. The subamendment was also supported by the Worker members and the Employer members. The amendment as subamended read as follows: "as the main priority for national and international action, including international cooperation and assistance". The amendment as subamended was adopted.

85. Preambular paragraph 3 was adopted as amended.

Preambular Paragraph 4

86. The Employer members submitted an amendment to delete the word "effective" before the word "elimination" to ensure consistency with the text adopted in Preambular paragraph 3. The Worker members supported the amendment. The Government member of the Netherlands, speaking on behalf of the members of the IMEC Group on the Committee, opposed the amendment stating that the provision should be consistent with the language in Article 1 of Convention No. 138. The Government members of Argentina and India also opposed the amendment. The Employer members withdrew the amendment.

87. The Worker members submitted an amendment to insert "free" before "basic education", to mention explicitly the importance of free basic education. The Government member of the Netherlands, speaking on behalf of the members of the IMEC Group on the Committee, supported the amendment. The Government members of Bolivia, Cuba, Ethiopia, India, Lebanon, Syrian Arab Republic and Venezuela supported the amendment. The Government member of Chile, also speaking on behalf of the Government members of Brazil and Uruguay, supported the amendment and added that it was consistent with Article 22 of the United Nations Convention on the Rights of the Child. The Employer members also supported the amendment but recalled that there were countries without compulsory education systems. The amendment was adopted.

88. The Government member of Canada, speaking on behalf of Australia, Belgium, Canada, Denmark, Finland, Germany, Hungary, Ireland, Italy, Japan, Netherlands, New Zealand, Norway, San Marino, Spain, Sweden, Switzerland, Turkey, United Kingdom and United States, submitted an amendment to refer to

the removal of children from "such" work, meaning from the worst forms of child labour rather than all work, and to replace the word "reintegration" with the word "integration", since many of the children engaged in the worst forms of child labour had not yet been integrated into society.

89. The Employer members supported the amendment, while the Worker members supported the change to "integration", but opposed the insertion of "such" work. The Worker Vice-Chairperson referred to cases in which child workers had been removed from one "worst form" only to find themselves in another and emphasized the objective of creating the necessary environment for rehabilitation and educational opportunities and other integrative measures. To address these concerns the Government member of Sweden proposed a subamendment to insert the word "all" before the words "such work", which was supported by the Government member of the United States and by the Employer members. The Worker Vice-Chairperson stated that the Worker members would accept the subamendment in the spirit of compromise and emphasized that there was a measure of protection ensured because the new Convention was in the context of Convention No. 138, which protected children and provided for minimum ages. The Government members of Argentina, Cuba and Venezuela suggested that a better definition was needed in Spanish which would be addressed by the Drafting Committee. The amendment as subamended was adopted.

90. The Worker members submitted an amendment to add "while supporting the needs of their families" at the end of the paragraph. The needs of the families of children engaged in the worst forms of child labour needed to be taken into account to ensure that well-intended actions did not have unintended and harmful consequences.

91. The Employer members stated that they were not against the suggestion but questioned the usefulness of the amendment since social integration encompassed a wide range of actions, including support to families.

92. The Government members of Ethiopia and India supported the amendment. The Government member of Sweden supported the idea, but suggested "taking into account" rather than "supporting" as one could speak of support to families or of taking their needs into account, but not of supporting their needs.

93. The Worker members opposed the subamendment as it changed the meaning of the proposed amendment.

94. The Government member of the Netherlands, speaking on behalf of the Government members of Australia, Austria, Belgium, Canada, Denmark, Finland, France, Germany, Greece, Hungary, Ireland, Japan, Luxemburg, Netherlands, New Zealand, Norway, Portugal, San Marino, Spain, Switzerland, Turkey, United Kingdom and United States, supported the subamendment as did the Government members of Egypt, Pakistan and Venezuela, as it made the point more clear. To

meet the concerns of the Worker members, however the Government member of the United States suggested an alternative might be to replace "supporting" with "addressing" or with "while responding to the needs of".

95. The Government member of Argentina was concerned that it might imply that Governments were under an obligation to provide subsidies to the families of children in the worst forms of child labour and also pointed out that there were children without families. The Government member of Venezuela also referred to the problem of street children who had no families.

96. The Worker members agreed to the proposal to replace "supporting" with "addressing". The Employer members also supported it. The subamendment was adopted as was the amendment as subamended.

97. The Government member of Pakistan expressed concern regarding the implications for implementation, particularly economic. The Government member of Bolivia shared the same concern. The Government member of Hungary pointed out that the Preamble was not a legally binding part of the text, and so there were no implications for implementation.

98. Preambular paragraph 4 was adopted as amended and read as follows:

Considering that the effective elimination of the worst forms of child labour requires immediate and comprehensive action, taking into account the importance of free basic education and the need to remove the concerned children from all such work and to provide for their rehabilitation and social integration, while addressing the needs of their families.

Proposed New Preambular Paragraph after Preambular Paragraph 4

99. The members of the African Group on the Committee, and the Government members of Australia, China, India, Indonesia, Japan, Republic of Korea, Malaysia, New Zealand, Pakistan and Singapore submitted identical amendments to insert a new Preambular paragraph 5, to read: "Recognizing that child labour is to a great extent caused by poverty and that the long-term solution lies in sustained economic growth leading to social progress, in particular poverty alleviation and universal education, and".

100. The Government member of Ethiopia, speaking on behalf of the members of the African Group on the Committee, explained that a reference to poverty was not an excuse for inaction, but a recognition of the reasons for child labour. Poverty and social deprivation had contributed immensely to the increase in child labour, particularly in Africa, and the amendment was submitted to reflect the fact that poverty was a principal causal factor of child labour. This was indicated in the resolution concerning the elimination of child labour adopted at the 83th Session of the International Labour Conference in 1996, from which the text of the amendment had been taken.

101. The Government member of India, speaking on behalf of the majority of members of the Asia-Pacific Group on the Committee, echoed the sentiments of the Government member of Ethiopia, and added that whilst some of the worst forms of child labour were a consequence of the denial of political and civil rights, others such as those defined as hazardous work, were frequently rooted in poverty and socio-economic circumstances, including inadequacy of resources to provide for economic and social rights. It was not a question of making excuses. Poverty could not justify the denial of any human rights, but was frequently a reason for their absence from the lives of countless millions as economic and social rights could only be promoted and secured progressively.

102. The Employer members stated that there were concerns about the complex relationship between poverty and child labour and its worst forms, but after a long debate the previous year it had been decided that it was inappropriate for poverty to be linked in this manner to the elimination of the worst forms of child labour. Moreover, there had been support for a short and concise Preamble. However, the issue had grown in importance since the first discussion and the Employer members were not opposed to its inclusion in some form.

103. The Worker members stated that poverty was both a cause and a consequence of the worst forms of child labour. It was inappropriate to lift one paragraph from the 1996 resolution concerning the elimination of child labour. It would be more appropriate to mention the resolution itself.

104. The Government member of the United States commented that the interrelationship between poverty and child labour was complex and still not well understood and that the proposed amendment did not capture that complexity. If one were to address, permit or explain the existence of child labour as a response to poverty, there would be both poverty and child labour for ever. He suggested it would be better to say that child labour was "both a cause and a consequence of poverty" rather than "to a great extent caused by poverty" and that the long-term solution "includes" rather than "lies in" economic growth. He opposed including a reference to the resolution in the Preamble; it was counter to keeping the Preamble short and the debate on the elimination of child labour had advanced considerably since adoption of that resolution.

105. The Worker Vice-Chairperson reiterated that certain aspects of child labour had to be eliminated without delay and for which poverty was not an excuse. The Government member of the Netherlands recalled the Worker members' earlier suggestion that the Preamble refer to the full 1996 resolution on the elimination of child labour, while the Government member of Ethiopia disagreed as the members of the African Group on the Committee had wished to refer in particular to poverty eradication and not in its place to the resolution in general. The Government member of India agreed with the Government member of Ethiopia.

Proposed New Paragraphs after Preambular Paragraph 4, Preambular Paragraph 5, a Proposed New Paragraph after Preambular Paragraph 5, Preambular Paragraphs 6 and 7 and Preambular Paragraph 8

106. Considerable discussion followed on how to reconcile the various view points. The Government member of India presented a proposal which incorporated a number of changes that had been agreed upon by many Government members, and by the Employer and Worker members as a result of consultations. The proposal consisted of:

(a) a specific reference to the 1996 resolution concerning the elimination of child labour;

(b) the adoption of the amendment submitted by the Government member of Ethiopia, on behalf of the members of the African Group on the Committee, to include the following new Preambular paragraph:

"Recognizing that child labour is to a great extent caused by poverty and that the long-term solution lies in sustained economic growth leading to social progress, in particular poverty alleviation and universal education, and".

(c) the adoption of the amendment presented by the Government members of Australia, Austria, Belgium, Canada, Denmark, Finland, France, Germany, Hungary, Ireland, Japan, Luxembourg, Netherlands, New Zealand, Norway, Portugal, San Marino, Spain, Sweden, Switzerland, Turkey, United Kingdom and United States, to add a new Preambular paragraph after paragraph 5 recalling the ILO Declaration on Fundamental Principles and Rights at Work and its Follow-up;

(d) the adoption of amendments submitted by the Employer members to delete Preambular paragraphs 7 and 8;

(e) withdrawal of an amendment by the Government members of China, India, Indonesia, Japan, Republic of Korea, Malaysia, Pakistan and Papua New Guinea to include a paragraph from the 1996 resolution on the international community addressing the root cause of child labour, and;

(f) withdrawal of the amendment by the Government members of Australia, China, India, Indonesia, Japan, Republic of Korea, Malaysia, New Zealand, Pakistan, Papua New Guinea and Singapore to add a paragraph from the 1996 resolution on the shared responsibility for the progressive elimination of child labour.

107. The Worker Vice-Chairperson expressed support for the composite proposal. He stated the Worker members' intention to submit an amendment at an appropriate point in the body of the text which would give effect to the provisions of the Convention to enhance international cooperation and assistance,

including support for social and economic development, for poverty eradication and for universal education.

108. The Government member of Lebanon stated she was favourable to the maintaining of the reference in Preambular paragraph 8 to the Copenhagen Summit on Social Development. The Government member of Uruguay, speaking also on behalf of the Government member of Chile, expressed concern about the Spanish text and stated that she preferred maintaining a reference to the Copenhagen Declaration on Social Development and the Programme of Action of the World Summit for Social Development, 1995, and the Beijing Declaration and Platform for Action of the Fourth World Conference on Women, 1995 in Preambular paragraph 8. Not having the text of the 1996 resolution in front of her she did not know whether that resolution made reference to those instruments, but if it did, then she would accept the proposal.

109. The Government member of the Netherlands, on behalf of the members of the IMEC Group on the Committee, indicated their support. The Government member of Ethiopia, on behalf of the members of the African Group on the Committee, stated their agreement but noted that they agreed to delete Preambular paragraph 8 only because it was part of the entire proposal. The Government member of Mexico declared her surprise that references to gender issues, in particular to the Beijing Declaration and Platform for Action of the Fourth World Conference on Women, 1995 were being deleted from the text. In response, the Worker members maintained that gender issues were taken into account by referring to the 1996 resolution and the ILO Declaration on Fundamental Principles and Rights at Work and its Follow-up and there should be no implication that they were not aware and supportive of gender issues. The Government member of Pakistan reluctantly agreed with the proposal. She made it clear that accepting the reference to the Declaration on Fundamental Principles and Rights at Work and its Follow-up did not change her Government's position on the Declaration that had been stated at the time of its adoption.

110. The changes noted in (a) to (f) above were adopted by consensus with the following effect.

111. A new Preambular paragraph after paragraph 4 was adopted: "Recalling the resolution concerning the elimination of child labour adopted at the 83rd Session of the International Labour Conference in 1996".

112. A second new Preambular paragraph after paragraph 4 was adopted: "Recognizing that child labour is to a great extent caused by poverty and that the long-term solution lies in sustained economic growth leading to social progress, in particular poverty alleviation and universal education, and".

113. Preambular paragraph 5 was adopted without change.

114. A new Preambular paragraph after paragraph 5 was adopted: "Recalling

the ILO Declaration on Fundamental Principles and Rights at Work and its Follow-up, adopted by the International Labour Conference in 1998,".

115. Preambular paragraph 6 was adopted without change.

116. Preambular paragraph 7 was deleted.

117. Preambular paragraph 8 was deleted.

Preambular Paragraph 9

118. The Employer members withdrew their amendment to add "the worst forms of" before the word "child", in view of the fact that the Conference agenda item was on child labour.

119. Preambular paragraph 9 was adopted without change.

Preambular Paragraph 10

120. Preambular paragraph 10 was adopted without change.

Preambular Paragraph 11

121. Three amendments concerning the short title of the proposed Convention were discussed together. The Government member of Ethiopia and other Government members of the African Group on the Committee proposed replacing the word "Abolition" by the words "Measures for the Elimination", to be consistent with the long title. The Government members of Australia, China, India, Indonesia, Japan, the Republic of Korea, Malaysia, New Zealand, Pakistan and Singapore proposed to insert the words "and effective action for" after the word "immediate". The Employer members proposed to replace the words "Immediate Abolition" by the words "Prohibition and Elimination".

122. The Government member of the Netherlands, on behalf of a number of the members of the IMEC Group on the Committee, and the Government members of Cuba and Uruguay supported retaining the full title which had been agreed upon in this part of the text as well, rather than having a different short title. The Government member of Sweden stated that it was customary for the Conference to adopt a short title and proposed a subamendment so that the proposed Convention would be referred to as the the "Worst Forms of Child Labour Convention, 1999"; this was seconded by the Government member of Pakistan. The Legal Adviser stated that for the sake of convenience it had been customary since the 1920s for international labour standards to be known by shorter titles. The official title reflected the content of a Convention and the short title was used in the list of titles of Conventions and in documents.123. The Employer members, the Worker members and the Government members of Argentina, Bolivia, Finland and Lebanon supported the subamendment. After an indicative show of hands, the subamendment was adopted which replaced the three pending amendments.

124. Preambular paragraph 11 was adopted as amended.

125. The Government members of Egypt and Pakistan expressed their reservations about the reference to international action, as this reference could lend itself to misinterpretation or abuse. They stated that this reference could only be understood in conjunction with Article 8.

126. The Preamble was adopted as amended.

Article 1

127. The Worker members submitted an amendment to provide that "all necessary and effective" measures would be required. The addition would signal in stronger language the need for concrete action. The amendment was supported by the Government members of Argentina and Finland but opposed by the Employer members and the Government member of the Netherlands. A discussion ensued, taking into account several other amendments submitted to this Article concerning the deletion or placement of "immediate" and whether measures should be "effective".

128. After consultations, the Government member of the Netherlands proposed a subamendment which inserted the words "immediate and effective" before "measures", deleted the word "immediate" before "elimination" and added at the end of the Article the words "as a matter of urgency.". The Article as subamended thus would read: "Each member which ratifies this Convention shall take immediate and effective measures to secure the prohibition and elimination of the worst forms of child labour as a matter of urgency." The subamendment was supported by the Employer members and the Worker members. Following an indicative show of support, the subamendment was adopted. The amendment as subamended was adopted.

129. Article 1 was adopted as amended.

Proposal Concerning Articles 2, 3, 4, 6 and 7 of the Proposed Convention and Paragraph 3 and a New Paragraph 4 of the Proposed Recommendation

130. Given the number of important issues represented by the amendments submitted to Articles 2, 3, 4, 6 and 7 of the proposed Convention, the Committee decided to allow time for extensive group meetings and an informal tripartite working group to work toward consensus on a number of key issues in these Articles, in particular, the age of children to which the Convention would apply, the definition of hazardous work, the determination of hazardous work (Article 4 of the Convention and Paragraph 3 of the Recommendation), the explicit inclusion of children in armed conflict, the role of education in Article 3 and Article 7, and the role of NGOs or other members of civil society. As a result of the consultations, the Government member of Australia presented a comprehensive proposal which included amendments agreed upon by many Government members and by the Employer and Worker members. These proposed amendments related to Articles 2, 3, 4, 6 and 7 of the proposed Convention and Paragraph 3 and a

proposed new Paragraph 4 in the proposed Recommendation. The proposal was as follows:

(a) No amendment to Article 2;

(b) Article 3, subparagraph (a): after the words "of children" replace the existing text with the words "debt bondage and serfdom and forced or compulsory labour, including forced or compulsory recruitment of children for use in armed conflict;";

(c) Article 3, subparagraph (d): replace the word "jeopardize" with the word "harm";

(d) Article 4, paragraph 1: replace the words "taking into account" with the words "fully taking into consideration" and add after the words "international standards" the words "in particular Paragraphs 3 and 4 of the Recommendation [on the worst forms of child labour];

(e) Article 4, paragraph 3: replace the word "after" with the word "in";

(f) Article 6, paragraph 2: add at the end of the paragraph the following words: "taking into consideration the views of other concerned groups as appropriate.";

(g) Article 7, paragraph 2, subparagraph (b): after "removal", replace the words "from work" with the words "from the worst forms of child labour"; and delete the following words at the end of the subparagraph: "through, inter alia, access to free basic education";

(h) Article 7, paragraph 2: insert a new subparagraph (c) as follows: "ensure access to free basic education and, wherever possible and appropriate, vocational training, for all children removed from the worst forms of child labour;";

(i) Paragraph 3 of the proposed Recommendation: replace the words "as a minimum" with the words "inter alia";

(j) Paragraph 3, subparagraph (a): replace the word "emotional" with the word "psychological";

(k) Paragraph 3, subparagraph (e): replace the words "which does not allow for the possibility of returning home each day" with the words "where the child is unreasonably confined to the premises of the employer.";

(l) After Paragraph 3, insert a new Paragraph under the title "Hazardous Work", as follows:

Notwithstanding Article 2 of the Convention, for the types of work referred to under Article 3(d) of the Convention, national laws or regulations, or the competent authority, may, after consultation with the workers' and employers' organizations concerned, authorize employment or work as from the age of 16 years, on condition that the health, safety and morals of the children concerned are fully protected, and that the young persons have received adequate specific instruction or vocational training in the relevant branch of activity.

131. The Committee agreed that it accepted the principle of the proposal coming from the informal working group and that it would be considered as a whole. Before the specific provisions of the proposal from the informal working group were considered, several members commented on the proposal. The Employer members and the Worker members supported the proposal. Nevertheless, the Worker members were concerned about a number of points. Regarding the issue of children in armed conflict, some Worker members — notably the members from the Americas — were very disappointed with the manner in which it was proposed to deal with this most hazardous form of child labour. They felt that an injustice was being done to children by not having a broader provision for all children in armed conflict and that it would be necessary to return to this issue because wars would continue. The Worker members were also concerned about a reference in Article 6 to "other concerned groups as appropriate". They were reluctant to agree with its inclusion because they considered some governments were responsible for the repression of trade unions and deaths of some trade unionists and were more open to consulting with NGOs than trade unions. They felt that "other concerned groups" should mean groups sincerely committed to the abolition of the worst forms of child labour. The Worker Vice-Chairperson proposed a subamendment to the proposal for Article 4, paragraph 1, namely, to delete the word "fully".

132. The Government member of the Netherlands, speaking on behalf of the members of the IMEC Group on the Committee, and the Government member of India, speaking on behalf of the members of the Asia-Pacific Group on the Committee, and the Government member of Guatemala, speaking on behalf of the members of the Latin American Group on the Committee, supported in principle the proposal but requested legal advice on various issues. The Government member of Ethiopia, speaking on behalf of the members of the African Group on the Committee, supported the proposal and welcomed the deletion of the word "fully" suggested by the Worker members. Regarding the issue of children in armed conflict, the Government member of Ethiopia stated that the proposal did not reflect the views of the members of the African Group on the Committee concerning children in armed conflict, which they considered the most hazardous and injurious form of child labour.

133. The Government member of Australia, on behalf of the members of the informal working group, posed several questions to the Legal Adviser that had been raised by members of the Committee during consultations. First, regarding Article 4, paragraph 1, he questioned the effect of the reference to Paragraphs 3

and 4 of the Recommendation in this provision of the Convention. Second, also referring to Article 4, paragraph 1, he asked what was meant by "relevant international standards". Third, referring to Article 4, paragraph 3, and the use of the phrase "in consultation with", he sought advice on what was required of ratifying member States. Finally, he wanted clarification on the links between Article 3(a) of the proposed Convention concerning the worst forms of child labour and the Forced Labour Convention, 1930 (No. 29) and what the legal requirements and obligations were for member States that ratified the proposed Convention.

134. The Government member of Egypt presented a further question to the Legal Adviser regarding the new Paragraph proposed for the Recommendation starting with "Notwithstanding Article 2 of the Convention,". He questioned whether it was legally correct to include in a Recommendation an exception to an Article in a Convention.

135. Concerning the question on the nature of the obligation arising from a reference to a Recommendation in a Convention, the Deputy Legal Adviser stated that though it was infrequent, a number of international labour Conventions made such references to ILO Recommendations as well as to United Nations Recommendations. He explained that such references did not make it mandatory for Governments to comply with the provisions of the Recommendations, and that in this case, it was a procedural obligation to take into consideration the contents of the Recommendation in question. The content of a Recommendation did not become binding by such reference. With regard to which international instruments were relevant, the representative of the Legal Adviser said that these were too numerous to list, but for example there were standards concerning toxic substances, dangerous processes, heavy weight, night work and so on. Such reference did not oblige member States that had not ratified these instruments to comply with them, merely to take them into account. Regarding the question on the meaning of "in consultation with", he stated that the obligation to consult was commonly included in international labour standards and was an element of the decision-making process. Under such a provision, Governments were obliged to consult with the social partners before a decision was taken but were not obliged by the result of the consultation. However, Governments had to consult and to consider the elements discussed in good faith because consultation without consideration would not respect the spirit of the obligation. He noted that the difference between "in" consultation with and "after" consultation with was minimal, and reflected the discontinuous (after) or the continuous (in) character of the consultative process.

136. Referring to the link between Article 3(a) and Convention No. 29, he stated that each Convention was autonomous and unless there was a specific reference they remained autonomous. He noted that the definition of forced labour contained in Article 2 of Convention No. 29 remained valid for the

purposes of the proposed Convention unless it defined the term differently. Convention No. 29 did not define debt bondage and serfdom, which were defined in United Nations instruments. Regarding the proposed new Paragraph after Paragraph 3 in the Recommendation, he stated that the text before the Committee could not be included in the Recommendation as drafted, because a Recommendation could not create derogation to an obligation contained in a Convention. He stated that the Employer and Worker members had agreed to modify the text accordingly. The proposed new wording was as follows: "For the types of work referred to under Article 3(d) of the Convention and Paragraph 3 of the Recommendation, national laws or regulations, or the competent authority, could, after consultation with the workers' and employers' organizations concerned, authorize employment or work as from the age of 16 years, on condition that the health, safety and morals of the children concerned are fully protected, and that the young persons have received adequate specific instruction or vocational training in the relevant branch of activity."

137. The Government member of Argentina requested legal advice concerning the proposed text of Article 3(a) in relation to the Forced Labour Convention, 1930 (No. 29) as Convention No. 29 made an exception for military service.

138. A representative of the Legal Adviser stated that Convention No. 29 did not exclude all compulsory military service, and that work carried out by conscripts for non-military purposes was considered as forced labour prohibited under Convention No. 29. The definition of forced or compulsory labour under Convention No. 29 did not specifically refer to "forced or compulsory recruitment of children for use in armed conflict". Therefore, it would be clearer if the word "and" were used in Article 3(a) instead of the word "including". Nevertheless, it was for the Committee to decide.

139. The Government member of Hungary stated his objections to the working methods of the Committee. He considered them inefficient, undemocratic and irregular. Some member States were effectively excluded from group representation as they did not readily belong to a particular informal government group, as these were determined primarily by geographical considerations. Furthermore, he felt such attachment to groups should be voluntary. He hoped a precedent was not being set for the Committee's future work as much remained to be discussed in plenary sittings of the Committee. He considered that decisions regarding what should be included or excluded from the text should be made in plenary, not in small informal groups, which had the additional disadvantage of denying the social partners the opportunity of hearing the arguments and counter-arguments of their counterparts. Finally, he stressed the importance of discussion in plenary, so as to ensure a record of the decisions taken, which was necessary for future interpretation of the instruments after their adoption and ratification. The Government member of Lebanon expressed her concern that the working methods were depriving the delegates of the opportunity to express their views

and to seek clarification especially if the package deal were not to be further discussed in the Committee plenary.

140. The Worker Vice-Chairperson strongly objected to the assessment of the Government member of Hungary. He stated that all the groups had arrived at proposals to amend the texts only after full consultation with the members of their individual groups and that Government members did have the opportunity to state their positions in plenary. He stated that the Worker members were participating in working methods which promoted open and frank discussion in an informal forum and which were aimed at reaching consensus on very important issues in the proposed Convention and Recommendation. This consensus was critical to achieving wide support for the instruments, rapid ratification and effective implementation.

141. The Government member of Australia indicated that there were still a number of questions on which clarification was sought from the Legal Adviser. Five issues appeared to be most important: first, to clarify the meaning of the term "other concerned groups" in light of the tripartite nature of the ILO; second, to explain whether in Article 3 the use of language addressing criminal acts of adults would present a legal difficulty in view of the intention to define the worst forms of child labour; third, to explore the implications of the draft provision in the proposal to Article 3(a) on forced or compulsory recruitment of children in armed conflict for member States which allowed compulsory military service as of the age of 17, particularly in the event of armed conflict or military intervention; fourth, to clarify the implications of Article 2 for member States with legislation defining differently the age bracket of childhood; and lastly, to explain whether, in view of Articles 2 and 3(d) of the proposed Convention, ratifying member States would be able to invoke the flexiblility provision set out in a proposed new Paragraph 4 of the Recommendation when determining the types of work as provided for in Article 4, paragraph 1.

142. Other Government members had further questions. The Government member of Colombia asked whether the stipulation of Article 4 to consult with workers' and employers' organizations would be binding. The Government member of the Russian Federation sought clarification as to whether there were rules in the ILO or an established practice which would attach particular importance to the views of the Legal Adviser on the draft instruments, as compared to other legal interpretations, especially in cases of draft international treaties.

143. In responding, the Deputy Legal Adviser explained that the draft instruments, as amended, did not spell out the meaning of "other concerned groups". These could, for example, be parents' organizations, children's associations or organizations for the defence of children. A number of other Conventions, such as the Vocational Rehabilitation and Employment (Disabled Persons) Convention, 1983 (No. 159) and the Minimum Wage Fixing Convention, 1970 (No. 131) included similar references to other concerned groups or qualified

persons. The above notwithstanding, Article 6, paragraph 2, fully respected the role of the tripartite constituents and accorded them a clear priority in the consultation process. In responding to the related question of the Government member of Colombia, he explained that while Article 4, paragraph 1, would make it binding for ratifying member States to include the social partners in the process leading up to a decision, the decision itself would be taken by the Government only. On the question regarding legal difficulties arising from the language used in Article 3 to address criminal acts by adults, he explained by example. Children making bricks in conditions of debt bondage were engaged in a worst form of child labour and were victims of it; whereas the adult who put them to such work was a criminal profiting from such work. In regard to the question of children recruited for lawful compulsory military service at the age of 17 and their potential participation in armed conflict, he noted that this was a very hypothetical question. ILO Conventions were universal texts expressed in general terms and as such could not envisage all possible situations that might occur. The purpose of the proposal on Article 3(a) was to cover forced or compulsory recruitment of children for use in armed conflict. This was all that could be said from a legal point of view. Concerning the issue of potential conflict of the draft Convention's definition of "child" with existing national legislation, the Legal Adviser recalled that Article 2 of the draft Convention stipulated only that the term "child" should apply to all persons under the age of 18 for the purposes of this Convention. It did not matter which designation national law gave to persons under the age of 18, on the understanding that all such persons were covered by the proposed Convention. Moreover, Article 2 corresponded to the definition of "child" in Article 1 of the United Nations Convention on the Rights of the Child which was almost universally ratified. Regarding the last question expressed by the Government member of Australia, Article 4, paragraph 1, provided flexibility in that the determination of types of work was left to the discretion of member States subject to two procedural requirements, namely consultation with employers' and workers' organizations concerned and the need to take into consideration relevant international standards. The latter would not imply any obligation to ratify or respect the relevant standards. Additionally, there was the requirement to make the determination in good faith consistent with the obligation on ratifying States under the international law of treaties to implement in good faith the Conventions that they ratify.

144. In responding to the question raised by the Government member of the Russian Federation concerning whether there were any rules or established procedure of the Organization which attached any particular significance to the opinion of the Legal Adviser in view of other rules of interpretation of international treaties, the Legal Adviser referred to Article 63, paragraph 2(f), of the Standing Orders which provided for the possibility of a motion to ask for the opinion of the Legal Adviser. He also pointed out that the Legal Adviser served exclusively the Conference during its duration, and not the Office.

145. The Government member of Cuba stressed the importance of reconciling the language used in Article 3(a) with regard to criminal acts and the definition of the worst forms of child labour. She noted that the activities of the children subject to sale and trafficking of children, for example, were not child labour but crimes against children. She also voiced concern that the draft provision of Article 3 on children in armed conflict which, she thought, had a very limited scope, could contradict Article 38 of the United Nations Convention on the Rights of the Child, and jeopardize the ongoing discussions on the draft optional protocol to that Convention on the involvement of children in armed conflicts. The Government member of Colombia expressed similar concerns.

146. The Government member of Lebanon questioned whether the legal obligations under Article 3(a) differed in the case of voluntary recruitment. The Government member of Hungary suggested that it was for the Committee to interpret what it meant in view of the Legal Adviser's statement, not for the Legal Adviser to tell the Committee what the Committee meant.

147. Many Government members expressed satisfaction with the Legal Adviser's explanations.

148. The Committee examined as a whole the particular provisions and Articles affected by the proposal in the proposed Convention, which were Articles 2, 3, 4, 6 and 7. The discussions on Article 5 and Article 8, though occurring in non-sequential order, are reported below in the order of the Articles in the Convention.

Article 2

149. An amendment by the Employer members to insert "Exclusively" at the beginning of the Article was withdrawn. The Government member of India announced the withdrawal of an amendment submitted by the Government members of India, Indonesia, Lebanon, Malaysia and Pakistan to take account of Article 3 of Convention No. 138. The decision was made on the basis that Article 3, subparagraph (d) and Article 4, paragraph 1, provided for a national determination of hazardous work which would constitute the worst forms of child labour.

150. Article 2 was adopted without change.

Article 3(a)

151. The Government member of the United States sought the understanding of the Committee on some important points. He indicated that the text that referred to the "forced or compulsory recruitment of children for use in armed conflict" as a worst form of child labour proposed under Article 3(a) was a most important and positive addition to the Convention. It addressed effectively an essential concern: the abduction, coercion, and forced or involuntary recruitment of children for use as participants in armed conflict. The adoption of the above

text would make the Convention stronger and would significantly strengthen current international standards concerning forced or compulsory enlistment. It would in no way undermine other international standards on the subject. He stated that the United States and some other countries permitted the lawful recruitment of 17-year-olds to volunteer — with parental consent — to serve in the armed forces, including when armed conflict was regrettably necessary. He did not believe that such voluntary enlistment in lawful national military service was the basis of the concern which had resulted in this text.

152. He noted that there was no other obligation related to genuine service in armed forces, and/or lawful national military service contained or contemplated under Article 3(d) on hazardous work. In summarizing his intervention, the Government member of the United States requested the Committee's confirmation of the abovementioned understanding on two points that: Article 3(a) did not apply to 16- and 17-year-olds who lawfully volunteered for service in a nation's armed forces, and that Article 3(d) covering "hazardous work" did not impose any additional obligation in regard to the engagement of children in lawful military activities.

153. The Deputy Legal Adviser confirmed that the statements made by the Government member of the United States were not in contradiction with what he had said earlier concerning the scope of Article 3(a) (forced or compulsory recruitment of children for use in armed conflict) and the relation between Articles 3(d) and 4, paragraph 1, of the proposed Convention.

154. The Government member of Norway, speaking on behalf of the Government members of Canada, Denmark, France, Italy, Mexico, Spain and Uruguay, stressed the importance of providing the utmost protection for children. Speaking to an amendment that would regard all involvement of children in armed conflict as a worst form of child labour, she argued that a restrictive formulation introduced the question of how to determine whether participation is truly voluntary or involuntary and how to protect the children involved. She expressed disappointment and deep regret for the impossibility of providing a basic level of protection to this group of children. However, she believed that an explicit reference to children in armed conflict in the new ILO instrument was a positive step both towards the protection of children and in strengthening the ILO's mandate on this subject. In the interest of consensus and with the expectation that this issue would be addressed in a comprehensive manner in the context of the draft optional protocol on the involvement of children in armed conflict, the amendment was withdrawn.

155. The Government member of Cuba, speaking on behalf of the Government members of Egypt, Guatemala, India and Venezuela, withdrew an amendment to Article 3(a), to insert the words "for any purpose or in any form" after the words "the sale and trafficking of children".

156. The Government members of Australia, Austria, Belgium, Finland, Germany, Hungary, Ireland, Luxemburg, Netherlands, New Zealand, Portugal, San Marino, Sweden, Turkey, United Kingdom and United States had submitted an amendment to replace the existing text after the words "of children" with the words "debt bondage and serfdom and forced or compulsory labour, including the forced or compulsory use of children in military activities;". The Government member of the Netherlands, speaking on behalf of the Government members sponsoring the amendment, withdrew it in favour of the text in the proposal and said that this question should continue to be discussed in other relevant United Nations fora, particularly by the Working group on the draft optional protocol on the involvement of children in armed conflicts.

157. The Government member of Switzerland supported the consensus solution regarding an explicit mention of children involved in armed conflict. She believed that an explicit reference to child soldiers in the new Convention was appropriate and the recruitment and involvement of children in armed conflict could be defined as a worst form of child labour. Switzerland confirmed its commitment to work for a ban on involvement of persons under the age of 18 in armed conflicts, inter alia in the Working group of the United Nations on the draft optional protocol on the involvement of children in armed conflicts. The Government member of Hungary shared the same view.

158. The Worker members stated their position on this question, namely, that there should be no war at all. Money spent on warheads and instruments of destruction should instead be used to help develop humankind. Children in particular should not be exposed to this unnecessary evil. However, the Worker members had made a concession in the interest of consensus in order to address the needs of the children who required the most immediate help and concerted attention.

159. The Government member of the Russian Federation, while indicating support for the consensus solution, expressed his disappointment with the proposed wording. The text excluded only the forced or compulsory recruitment of all children and, most importantly, did not prevent the actual participation by and use of all children in armed conflicts. He signalled that the appearance of this wording in an international Convention could jeopardize the work on the draft optional protocol on the involvement of children in armed conflicts.

160. The Government member of the United States noted that there had been no objections to the understandings as expressed in his previous statement, understood that the Committee concurred, and on that basis he was prepared to move forward.

161. The Government member of Cuba supported the statement that had been made by the Worker members concerning the wasted resources on war and arms races and confirmed her Government's commitment to put the interests of

children first. She reiterated that the issue of children in armed conflict was being discussed in the Human Rights Commission in a wide, precise and detailed manner, as the matter was more pertinent. She further emphasized that, in honour of the highest interest of childhood in Cuba, she hoped that no more military aggression would put Cuban children in danger.

162. The Government member of France expressed deep regret that the text of the proposal did not bar involvement in armed conflicts of volunteers below the age of 18. She felt that the appropriate instrument for extending protection to this very vulnerable category of children was the draft optional protocol on the involvement of children in armed conflicts and hoped that the discussions on this ILO Convention would not hamper work in other United Nations fora.

163. Article 3(a) as amended by the proposal from the informal working group was adopted to read as follows: "all forms of slavery or practices similar to slavery, such as the sale and trafficking of children, debt bondage and serfdom and forced or compulsory labour, including forced or compulsory recruitment of children for use in armed conflict;".

Article 3(b)

164. The Government members of Denmark, Finland, Germany, New Zealand, Norway, Spain, Sweden and United Kingdom had submitted an amendment to replace the word "use" with the word "exploitation". The Government member of the United Kingdom withdrew the amendment but noted that her Government would have preferred the word "exploitation" which would have made it clearer that the use of a child prostitute by a client was covered where it amounted to exploitation. She considered that the existing wording, "use for prostitution", did not cover the use by a client of a child prostitute, only the use made of the child by the procurer for prostitution. The Government member of Germany supported the withdrawal of the amendment but noted that she assumed the word "use" would also cover the use by a client if the child was below the national age of sexual consent.

165. Article 3(b) was adopted without change.

Article 3(c)

166. The Government member of Canada, on behalf of the Government members of Canada, Ireland, Japan, Netherlands and Spain, withdrew an amendment to delete the words "for illicit activities, in particular" and after the words "international treaties" to insert the words "and for other illegal activities". They had proposed the amendment because they preferred retaining the word "illegal" which they considered provided a clearer definition.

167. Article 3(c) was adopted without change.

Article 3, Proposed New Subparagraph after Article 3(c)

168. Several amendments were submitted to add a new subparagraph on the

issue of children in armed conflict. As this had been discussed and included as part of the agreed proposal including Article 3(a), several members of the Committee withdrew amendments. The Worker members withdrew an amendment to add "the use, procuring or offering of a child for armed conflict;". Likewise the Government member of Ethiopia, speaking on behalf of the members of the African Group on the Committee withdrew an amendment to include "the recruitment for and the use of children in armed conflicts;". The Government member of Ethiopia, speaking on behalf of the members of the African Group on the Committee, stated that the participation of children in armed conflicts and their exposure to such violence denied children their basic rights including the right to life, education, family care and a peaceful environment. This form of child labour or employment resulted in children being killed, injured and seriously traumatized. This grave situation seriously affected the activities in which the child victims lived and rendered post-conflict rehabilitation and peace-building even more daunting. For these reasons, the members of the African Group on the Committee had proposed a clear and direct prohibition on the participation of children in armed conflict. He noted that the formulation in the proposal before the Committee did not include all aspects of the problem they had sought to address and they were disappointed by that. However, in a spirit of understanding and consensus building, the amendment was withdrawn. He also noted that the compromise adopted on this issue did not adversely affect the ongoing work in the United Nations towards the adoption of the draft optional protocol to the Convention on the Rights of the Child on involvement of children in armed conflicts.

169. The Government member of Canada, speaking on behalf of the Government members of Canada, Denmark, France, Italy, Mexico, Norway, Spain and Uruguay, also withdrew an amendment to include "the use of children to participate in hostilities in an armed conflict;". She supported the statement made by the Government member of Norway in the discussion on Article 3(a).

170. The Worker members had proposed the inclusion of a new subparagraph to read: "work which, by its nature or circumstances in which it is carried out, systematically denies a child access to basic education." They noted that most Government and Employer members had in principle supported the principle that a child denied access to basic education was denied the ability to develop. However, in view of the practical difficulties experienced by children in some countries, for instance, merely surviving, they withdrew the amendment, though they retained their conviction on this issue.

Article 3(d)

171. The Employer members withdrew an amendment to replace the words "is likely to jeopardize" with the words "will harm".The Government member of Spain requested clarification on the meaning of the phrase "likely to harm". He

referred to the Spanish translation and wanted to know the degree of probability expressed by the word "likely". The Employer Vice-Chairperson stated that "likely to" referred to probability and "may" referred to possibility. Thus, Spain stated that the translation should be "probable" and should be reviewed by the Drafting Committee. The Government member of Uruguay referred to the use of the word "other" in the Spanish text that was not included in the English. This was also referred to the Drafting Committee.

172. The Employer members stated that they wanted to make it clear that the proposed Convention should not require governments to intervene in situations in which children worked for their parents on bona fide family farms or holdings. The Employer members recognized that there could be instances in which children were employed on farms that were not bona fide family farms. In such situations parents had little or no control over working conditions and therefore could not protect their children from abuse and exploitation. There could also be situations in which title to, or effective control of, land was held by a family, but the family employed children who were also subject to abusive working conditions. These latter situations — unlike bona fide family farms and holdings — were intended to be addressed by this Convention.

173. The Worker Vice-Chairperson noted that this reference to sectoral coverage, though meant as an understanding of the Employers for the record, posed some concern. The Worker members recognized that there were differences between bona fide family farms and those farms that misused that title and in effect were not family and thus engaging workers, including children, in contradiction of standards for good working conditions. The proposed Convention should not be interpreted in any way to allow the abuse of children by not extending coverage to such situations. The Worker members distinguished family farms that did not interfere with children's schooling and which were truly within a protected family environment. In some countries there were farms of hundreds of acres which were exploiting non-related persons and were still referred to as family farms.

174. The Government member of India, speaking on behalf of the Government members of Australia, China, India, Japan, Republic of Korea, Malaysia, New Zealand, Pakistan, Philippines, Singapore and Thailand, referred to their amendment to delete the remaining text after the words "carried out", and to replace it with the words: "is hazardous to the health, safety or morals of children, as determined by national laws or regulations, or by the competent authority, after consultation with the organizations of employers and workers concerned, taking into account relevant international standards." They had intended to unify the content of Article 3(d) and Article 4, paragraph 1, and preferred the word "jeopardize" to the word "harm". However, as their concerns were met by the text of the agreed proposal they withdrew the amendment.

175. The Government member of Sweden, speaking on behalf of the Government members of Austria, Belgium, Denmark, Italy, Luxembourg, Netherlands, Norway, Portugal, Sweden, Turkey and United States, referred to a similar amendment to delete the remaining text after the word "circumstances", and to replace it with the words: "is determined by national laws or regulations, or by the competent authority, taking into account relevant international standards, after consultation with the organizations of employers and workers concerned, as likely to harm the health, safety or morals of children." The amendment was withdrawn in favour of the agreed proposal for this Article.

176. The Worker members withdrew an amendment which would have moved Paragraph 3 of the proposed Recommendation into this Article, with the addition of "(f) work where the child is delivered to and wholly dependent on the employer". However, as the agreed proposal contained a reference to this Paragraph, they could withdraw it.

177. Article 3(d) was adopted as amended to read as follows: "work which, by its nature or the circumstances in which it is carried out, is likely to harm the health, safety or morals of children."

Article 3, Proposed new Subparagrap after Subparagraph (d)

178. An amendment submitted by the Government members of Austria, Belgium, Canada, Denmark, Finland, France, Germany, Ireland, Italy, Luxembourg, Netherlands, New Zealand, Norway, San Marino, Spain, Sweden, Switzerland, Turkey, United Kingdom and United States to insert after subparagraph (d) a new subparagraph to read: "work which systematically deprives children of access to education in accordance with applicable compulsory education requirements as established by national laws or regulations or by the competent authority." was withdrawn by the Government member of the Netherlands speaking on behalf of the co-sponsors. She noted that the amendment was being withdrawn with some regret as the co-sponsors would have preferred the definition of hazardous work to include a reference to the denial of access to basic education. The Government member of Switzerland supported the comments of the Government member of the Netherlands.

179. The Government member of India stated that his Government attached a great deal of importance to free, basic education. However, the amendment would have made the Convention unimplementable and unratifiable as it would have expanded the scope of the Convention to virtually all forms of child labour which were rooted in poverty, as all working children in these circumstances were unable to attend school. To do so would be tantamount to imposing sanctions on poverty, while ignoring the fact that economic and social rights such as free basic education were achievable only progressively and in a developmental context.

180. Article 3 was adopted as amended.

Article 4, Paragraph 1

181. An amendment submitted by the Government members of Austria, Belgium, Denmark, Italy, Luxembourg, Netherlands, Norway, Portugal, Sweden, Turkey and United States to replace the text of Article 4, paragraph 1, with the proposed text of Paragraph 3 of the Recommendation was withdrawn. Identical proposed amendments by the Worker members and by the Government members of Australia, China, India, Japan, Republic of Korea, Lebanon, Malaysia, New Zealand, Pakistan, Philippines, Singapore and Thailand to delete the paragraph entirely were withdrawn. Also withdrawn was an amendment submitted by the Government member of Ethiopia acting on behalf of the members of the African Group on the Committee to insert the words "which are most representative" after the word "concerned,".

182. An amendment submitted by the Government members of Austria, Belgium, Germany, Ireland, Italy, Netherlands, New Zealand, Norway, Portugal, Switzerland and United Kingdom proposed to insert after the words "workers concerned," the words "as well as other groups of civil society, as appropriate." The Government member of Switzerland, speaking on behalf of the co-sponsors, stated that whilst they would have preferred to have these other groups mentioned in Article 4 in the interests of consensus and bearing in mind that Article 6 of the proposal had in principle been agreed, they withdrew their proposed amendment.

183. An amendment submitted by the Government member of Ethiopia, on behalf of the members of the African Group on the Committee, to delete the words "taking into account relevant international standards" was withdrawn. These Government members had been concerned about the possible legal obligations of the clause but had been reassured by the advice of a Representative of the Legal Adviser, as stated above.

184. The Government member of Egypt wished to state for the record that he fully supported the comments of the Government member of Ethiopia, and would be making a fuller statement regarding this issue later in the proceedings.

185. The Government member of Hungary suggested that the Drafting Committee might wish to change the reference to international standards to international instruments, to conform with other ILO Conventions. The Government member of India cautioned against such a recommendation as this was not an editorial issue but one of substance. The language had been chosen for very specific reasons and it should be retained to reflect those reasons.

186. Paragraph 1 of Article 4 was adopted as amended.

Article 4, Proposed New Paragraph after Paragraph 1

187. An amendment submitted by the Employer members to insert a new paragraph to read "Notwithstanding the provisions of Article 2, for the types of work referred to under Article 3(d), national law or regulation, or the competent

authority, may, after consultation with the workers' and employers' organizations concerned, authorize employment or work as from the age of 16 years, on condition that the health, safety and morals of the children concerned are fully protected, and that the young persons have received adequate specific instruction or vocational training in the relevant branch of activity." was withdrawn.

Article 4, Paragraph 2

188. The Worker members withdrew three amendments: to replace the word "after" with the word "in", to replace the words "so determined" with the words "referred to in Article 3(d)", and to add the words "taking into account relevant international standards" at the end of the paragraph.

189. The Government members of Australia, China, India, Japan, Republic of Korea, Lebanon, Malaysia, New Zealand, Pakistan, Philippines, Singapore and Thailand also withdrew an amendment to delete the remaining text after the words "types of work" and replace this with the words: "determined in Article 3(d) exist."

190. Paragraph 2 of Article 4 was adopted unchanged.

Article 4, Paragraph 3

191. Amendments submitted by the Government members of Canada, Denmark, Finland, Ireland, Netherlands, Norway, Spain, Sweden, Switzerland, Turkey and United Kingdom to insert the words "or activity" after the words "of work" and to insert the words "by the competent authority," after the word "necessary," were withdrawn in favour of the text in the proposal. An amendment to replace the words "paragraph 1 of this Article" with the words "Article 3(d)", submitted by the Government members of Australia, China, India, Japan, Republic of Korea, Lebanon, Malaysia, New Zealand, Pakistan, Philippines, Singapore and Thailand, was also withdrawn.

192. Paragraph 3 of Article 4 was adopted as amended.

193. Article 4 was adopted as amended.

Article 5

194. The Worker members submitted an amendment to include after "each Member" the words "in consultation with employers' and workers' organizations" in order to underscore the need for tripartite consultation. The amendment was supported by the Employer members and the Government members of Cuba and Mexico. The Government member of India, speaking on behalf of the members of the Asia-Pacific Group on the Committee, supported it in principle but proposed to replace the words "in consultation with" by "after consultation with" to make it consistent with language used in other Articles. The subamendment was supported by the Worker members and the Government member of Spain. The Government member of the Netherlands reserved her Government's position

because of possible legislative implications of the proposal. She was supported by the Government members of Canada, Colombia, and Sweden. The Government member of Colombia sought clarification from the Legal Adviser on the meaning of the term "appropriate mechanisms", in particular whether these would be national or international in scope. The Deputy Legal Adviser responded by stating that the draft instruments did not define the nature of the mechanisms but required the establishment or designation of a national mechanism.

195. The Government member of the Netherlands suggested a further subamendment to include the words "as appropriate" after the reference to workers' and employers' organizations. The subamendment was strongly opposed by the Worker members who in turn proposed to replace the words "as appropriate" by "concerned".

196. The Committee called on the Legal Adviser to elaborate on the possible legal implications both of the amendment proposed by the Worker members and the subamendment suggested by the Government member of the Netherlands. The Deputy Legal Adviser explained that consultations with the social partners, as proposed by the Worker members, would be an element in the decision-making process. The State, however, would not be bound by the views presented in the consultation process. If the words "as appropriate" were added, as suggested in the subamendment presented by the Government member of the Netherlands, it would make the consultation optional and thus leave it to the State to decide whether or not such consultations be undertaken.

197. In the light of the Legal Adviser's clarifications the Government member of the Netherlands withdrew her subamendment. She stated that though she had initially considered suggesting a further subamendment to include, after the reference to workers' and employers' organizations, the words "and other concerned groups", she had decided not to do so, in a spirit of compromise.

198. The Government members of Colombia and Sweden then also lent their support to the amendment as proposed by the Worker members. The Government member of Colombia added that this was done on the understanding that when criminal law was being redrafted, there would be no obligation on governments to consult with the social partners. The Employer members reiterated their support. The amendment as subamended was adopted.

199. Article 5 was adopted as amended and read: "Each Member, after consultations with employers' and workers' organizations, shall establish or designate appropriate mechanisms to monitor the implementation of the provisions giving effect to this Convention.".

200. Article 5 was adopted as amended.

Article 6, Paragraph 1

201. No amendments were submitted for Article 6, paragraph 1, and the paragraph was adopted unchanged.

Article 6, Paragraph 2

202. An amendment submitted by the Worker members to insert, after the word "organizations", the words: "taking into account the views of children directly affected by the worst forms of child labour and their families, and, where appropriate, those of other concerned groups committed to the aims of the Convention" was withdrawn. However, the Worker Vice-Chairperson stated that he would be making some comments on the nature of tripartism and on the role of other concerned groups such as the Global March later in the proceedings.

203. The Government member of the Netherlands, speaking on behalf of the Government members of Australia, Austria, Belgium, Finland, France, Germany, Greece, Hungary, Ireland, Italy, Netherlands, New Zealand, Norway, Portugal, San Marino, Spain, Sweden, Switzerland, Turkey, United Kingdom and United States, withdrew an amendment to insert after the word "organizations", the words "and other concerned groups, as appropriate" They stressed that under no circumstances did that group of Government members question the tripartite nature of the International Labour Organization.

204. Paragraph 2 of Article 6 was adopted as amended and read: "Such programmes of action shall be designed and implemented in consultation with relevant government institutions and employers' and workers' organizations, taking into consideration the views of other concerned groups as appropriate.".

205. Article 6 was adopted as amended.

Article 7, Paragraph 1

206. Two amendments submitted by the Government members of Denmark and Japan to remove the requirement for penal sanctions were considered at the same time. The Government member of Denmark stated that the amendment would allow countries which did not provide penal sanctions to conform to the Convention. Denmark would need to change its criminal laws to provide sanctions, for example, for pornographic films that may have used children whose age was difficult to prove. The Government member of Japan added that the text without the amendment might impede ratification by many countries. The Worker members opposed the amendment. It seemed that the word "including" implied that other measures could be taken prior to the imposition of sanctions. The Employer members also expressed doubt regarding the meaning of the amendment, and therefore also opposed it. The Government member of India stated that when addressing human rights issues, such as this Convention was, the stronger language was preferable and believed the Office text provided better safeguards. The Government member of Denmark withdrew the amendment.

207. The Government member of Ethiopia, speaking on behalf of the members of the African Group on the Committee, submitted an amendment concerning the translations in French and Spanish of "provision and application" and withdrew it in favour of it being considered by the Drafting Committee.

208. The Government member of Germany, speaking also on behalf of the Government member of Austria, proposed an amendment aimed at ensuring that the child victims of child labour would not be subject to criminal prosecution. In order not to put into question the overall consensus, the amendment was withdrawn because it might cause problems in the case of activities which might be considered as a criminal offence for a child as well as for an adult.209. Article 7, paragraph 1, was adopted without change.

Article 7, Paragraph 2

210. An amendment submitted by the Government members of Austria, Canada, Hungary, Netherlands, Sweden, Turkey, United Kingdom and United States, to delete the words ", taking into account the importance of education in eliminating child labour," and another amendment submitted by the Government members of Bangladesh, China, India, Indonesia, Lebanon, Malaysia, Pakistan and Philippines to replace the same words by "adopt comprehensive and multidimensional approaches, and" were withdrawn.

211. An amendment submitted by the Government members of Bangladesh, China, India, Indonesia, Lebanon, Malaysia, Pakistan and Philippines, to delete the words "and time-bound" was also withdrawn. The Government member of India, speaking on behalf of the co-sponsors of the amendment stated that the Government members now preferred the original text as the proposed Convention recognized in other provisions that action to eliminate the worst forms of child labour needed to be immediate and effective. He added that any programme of action would have to be multidimensional, with mutually reinforcing cohesive programmes which would necessarily have to be implemented in a time-bound manner. He raised this, since an amendment submitted by the Government members of Austria, Canada, Hungary, Netherlands, Sweden, Turkey, United Kingdom and United States, to replace the word "time-bound" with the word "immediate" would compromise this fact.

212. The representative of the Netherlands, speaking on behalf of the co-sponsors of that amendment, commented that the amendment had been submitted to keep the language of this Article consistent with Article 1 of the proposed Convention, which spoke of "immediate" action. However they withdrew the amendment as "time-bound" was the language agreed to in the proposal. The Worker members also agreed.

213. The introductory part of paragraph 2 was adopted without change.

Article 7, Paragraph 2(a)

214. An amendment submitted by the Government member of Ethiopia, on behalf of the members of the African Group on the Committee, to replace the words "children from engaging" with the words "the engagement of children", was withdrawn, as the sponsors had been assured that the intention conveyed by

their formulation was no different from that in the original text. However, after support from the Worker members, and the Government members of the Netherlands and India, and no objections from the Employer members, the amendment was reintroduced and adopted as a clearer formulation of what was meant by placing the emphasis on action against those who would engage children in the worst forms of child labour.

215. Article 7, paragraph 2(a) was adopted as amended to read: "prevent the engagement of children in the worst forms of child labour;".

Article 7, Paragraph 2(b)

216. An amendment submitted by the Government of Ethiopia acting on behalf of the members of the African Group on the Committee to replace the word "work" with the words "the worst forms of child labour, and for their" and two amendments submitted by the Government members of Austria, Canada, Hungary, Netherlands, Sweden, Turkey, United Kingdom and United States to replace the word "work" with the words "the worst forms of child labour" and to insert the word "simultaneous" after the words "from work," were withdrawn in favour of the text in the proposal.

217. An amendment submitted by the Government members of Austria, Canada, Hungary, Netherlands, Sweden, Turkey, United Kingdom and United States to replace the word "reintegration" with the word "integration" was adopted, to conform to the wording adopted in Preambular paragraph 4.

218. Several amendments were withdrawn concerning the reference to free basic education as the agreed proposal had dealt with the issue in a new subparagraph (c). The withdrawn amendments included an amendment by the Employer members to delete the words "through, inter alia, access to free basic education"; an amendment submitted by the Government members of Austria, Canada, Hungary, Netherlands, Sweden, Turkey, United Kingdom and United States to delete the words "free basic"; and an amendment submitted by the Worker members to insert "and vocational training consistent with other relevant international standards". It was clear to the Employers that "Basic education" means primary education, plus one year: in other words, eight or nine years of schooling, such education being curriculum-based and not age-based.

219. Article 7, paragraph 2(b), was adopted as amended to read: "provide the necessary and appropriate direct assistance for their removal from the worst forms of child labour, rehabilitation and social integration;".

Article 7, Proposed New Paragraph after Paragraph (b)

220. The Committee adopted a new subparagraph (c) as part of the agreed proposal for Article 7 to: "ensure access to free basic education and, wherever possible and appropriate, vocational training, for all children removed from the worst forms of child labour".

Article 7, Paragraph 2(c)

221. The Worker members withdrew an amendment to insert the words "including those in hidden work situations" after the words "special risk". The Employer members also withdrew an amendment to delete the words "and reach out to", as did the Government member of Ethiopia on behalf of the members of the African Group on the Committee, to replace the words "reach out to" with the words "have a direct contact with".

222. The Government member of the Netherlands was disappointed that the Worker members had withdrawn the amendment to include a reference to children in "hidden work situations" as she was about to support it. There was a particular concern for children in these situations, such as child domestic workers. The Government member of Norway agreed. The Government members of Austria, Germany and Sweden also expressed their support.

223. The Employer members and the Government member of India were glad that the amendment had been withdrawn; the Government member of India added that, whilst they appreciated that there was a great deal of concern regarding domestic work, there was insufficient clarity or information regarding what was meant by "hidden work" to be able to address it. Moreover, this type of work was to be addressed in Paragraph 3(e) of the Recommendation, so it was unnecessary to mention it here given that it was unclear where hidden work situations started and ended.

224. The Government member of the Netherlands refuted the claim that little was known about the nature of hidden work, and cited some examples of publications on domestic work.

225. The Government member of Hungary reintroduced the Worker members' amendment to add the words "including those in hidden work situations" after the words "special risk" with support from the Government member of the Netherlands. The Employer members argued that the situation with the amendment was problematic because "hidden work" was not clearly defined and they believed that it was covered by Article 7, paragraphs 2(c) and (d). Furthermore, it could lead to a longer list to include other difficult situations. The Government member of Guatemala, supported by the Government member of Cuba, stressed the importance of addressing hidden work situations but felt that the issue was adequately addressed in Paragraph 3 of the proposed Recommendation. The Government member of Lebanon opposed the amendment because she believed it was difficult to identify hidden work situations and a long list might be needed to identify groups of children "at special risk". She also questioned who the authority would be to reach out to these hidden work situations. The Government member of Ethiopia, speaking on behalf of the members of the African Group on the Committee, stated that despite his strong feeling about the problem of hidden work, which referred mainly to domestic work, this amendment

added ambiguity to the text and therefore the members of the African Group on the Committee opposed it.

226. The Government member of Pakistan, while recognizing the concern expressed by some in the Committee, felt however that "hidden work" could not be included in a legal document without a clear definition. The Government member of Egypt also opposed the amendment as there was no clear definition of hidden work.

227. The Government member of the Netherlands asked for confirmation that the Committee agreed that hidden work situations were covered by Article 7, paragraphs 2(c) and (d). The Government member of India did not agree with this statement. The Government member of Hungary stated that hidden work situations, including domestic work, were covered by Article 7, paragraphs 2(c) and (d) and he therefore withdrew the amendment. The Government member of Egypt disagreed with his statement.

228. The Government member of the Netherlands, speaking on behalf of the Government members of Austria, Canada, Hungary, Sweden, Turkey, United Kingdom and United States withdrew an amendment to add the words "and children from vulnerable groups" after the words "special risk", because it was adequately covered by Article 7, paragraph 2(c). The Government member of Cuba stated that "children at special risk" included street children, minority children, children with disabilities and children deprived of their liberty. In addition, the Government member of Ethiopia, speaking on behalf of the members of the African Group on the Committee, withdrew an amendment to add the words "and their families" after the words "special risk".

229. Article 7, paragraph 2(c), was adopted without change.

Article 7, Paragraph 2(d)

230. Article 7, paragraph 2(d), was adopted without change.

Article 7, Paragraph 3

231. The Worker members withdrew an amendment to insert the words "and publicize the time-bound measures" after the word "Convention". They wished to draw attention to the need to make all parties, including the ILO, workers and employers, aware of the time-bound measures that governments were taking, and to the fact that they considered this a prerequisite for full implementation of the proposed Convention.

232. Article 7, paragraph 3, was adopted without change.

233. Article 7 was adopted as amended.

Article 8

234. In introducing the discussion on Article 8, the Chairperson referred to

formal and informal discussions which had taken place during the adoption of the Preamble. An attempt had been made to bring an agreed text to the Committee. The Worker members submitted the following composite text based on several amendments that had been submitted to Article 8: "Members shall take appropriate steps to give effect to the provisions of this Convention through enhanced international cooperation and assistance including support for social and economic development, poverty eradication programmes and universal education".

235. The Government member of India cited informal discussions on the possible redrafting of Article 8 and referred to a specific amendment submitted by a number of countries belonging to the Asia-Pacific Group on the Committee on a Preambular paragraph which would have referred to the subject of international cooperation. That amendment had been withdrawn on the basis of a statement by the Worker members that this question would be reflected in Article 8. He confirmed the strong support of most of the members of the Asia-Pacific Group for the text proposed by the Worker members.

236. The Government member of Ethiopia supported the proposed formulation, as did the Employer members. The Government member of Norway, speaking on behalf of the Government member of Sweden, while indicating general support for the text, expressed some reservations about the word "enhanced". She referred to the substantial contributions made by the two countries to support developing countries and her apprehension about accepting a legal obligation to increase financial contributions. The Government member of the United Kingdom supported the second part of the proposed text but was concerned that the language of the first part did not give sufficient emphasis to steps at the national level to give effect to the provisions of the Convention. She submitted a subamendment to insert the word "including" after the word "Convention". Referring to the concerns expressed by the previous speaker concerning the word "enhanced", she argued that the word did not necessarily imply the provision of more financial resources but could refer, for example, to better targeted interventions and programmes.

237. The Government member of the Netherlands supported the subamendment proposed by the Government member of the United Kingdom and also suggested the deletion of the word "enhanced". The Government member of Hungary opposed the inclusion of the word "including", arguing that the Article was concerned essentially with international cooperation and assistance. He also submitted a subamendment to delete the word "enhanced". The Government member of Ethiopia, speaking on behalf of the members of the African Group on the Committee, emphasized the need for cooperation on legal and judicial matters and wanted the word "enhanced" to be retained. He also stated that, as the purpose of the Article was international cooperation and assistance, the addition of the word "including" would render Article 8 unnecessary as there were preceding Articles on national obligations. The Worker members referred to previous discussions on the same subject and confirmed their request

for an Article with strong language underscoring the need for global and international action against the worst forms of child labour. The Worker members reaffirmed that poverty anywhere constituted a danger to prosperity everywhere. He recalled the language adopted in Article 7, paragraph 1, and stressed the need to combine national and international action. The Government members of Cuba and India welcomed the statement of the Worker members and expressed concern regarding some governments' need to reconsider the text discussed in conjunction with the adoption of the relevant Preambular paragraphs. Referring to the subamendment submitted by the Government member of the United Kingdom, the Government member of India opposed the proposal and recalled the references to national obligations included in Article 7, paragraph 1. He also supported the proposal to retain the word "enhanced" on the basis of the explanations previously offered by the Government member of the United Kingdom to the effect that this did not refer only to financial assistance. The Government member of the Netherlands, on behalf of the members of the IMEC Group on the Committee, and the Government members of Germany and Sweden indicated their wish for further group consultation on the proposed text. She reiterated the full commitment of the IMEC Group of the Committee to the principle of member States assisting one another in giving effect to the provisions of the Convention through international cooperation or assistance.

238. The Government member of India recalled the broad support for the proposal submitted by the Worker members and the members of the Asia-Pacific Group on the Committee. It was a balanced proposal, providing for flexibility and leaving it to individual member States to decide on the nature of such cooperation and assistance. He noted that international cooperation in this context should not be viewed in terms of a donor-recipient equation, but rather as a partnership on an equal footing from which all parties would stand to benefit.

239. The Government member of Ethiopia, speaking on behalf of the members of the African Group on the Committee, supported the position expressed by the Government member of India and the text proposed by the Worker members.

240. The Government member of Australia proposed a new subamendment: "Members shall take appropriate steps to assist one another in giving effect to the provisions of this Convention through enhanced international cooperation or assistance including support for social and economic development, poverty eradication programmes and universal education."

241. A discussion ensued, based on this new subamendment and the earlier proposals. The Government member of Germany supported the subamendment though he would have preferred the original Office text. He considered that strictly speaking, the more appropriate place for Article 8 was in a Recommendation, not in a Convention. He also recalled that the Government of Germany had always been willing to assist countries where child labour was a problem. Further

support for the new subamendment was also expressed from the Government members of Italy, New Zealand, United Kingdom and the members of the Latin American Group on the Committee.

242. The Government member of Hungary requested the Legal Adviser's view on how far the provisions in the subamendment would create a binding obligation for ratifying member States to assist one another. The Deputy Legal Adviser stressed the idea of partnership contained in the spirit of the Article. He explained that no obligation would arise from either proposal for ratifying member States in relation to a particular level or form of cooperation or assistance. There was only an obligation to take appropriate steps towards enhanced international partnership, and it was up to individual States to decide on those appropriate steps.

243. The Government member of the United States considered the subamendment proposed by the Government member of Australia a good basis for further discussion. He understood that "partnerships" as referred to by the representative of the Legal Adviser meant "working together," and that Article 8 encouraged members to work together to meet the goals of the Convention. He further understood that in no way did Article 8 require any member to provide any specific form or amount of cooperation or assistance. No legal obligation was created as to the nature of such cooperation or assistance and therefore the matter was left entirely to the discretion of individual member States.

244. The Government member of India maintained that he strongly opposed the wording "international cooperation or assistance", as contained in the subamendment. Cooperation encompassed assistance and he therefore suggested a further subamendment which replaced the word "or" linking cooperation with assistance by the word "and". He was supported by the Government member of Finland. The Government member of Australia responded that there was a need for greater flexibility and that the word "or" reflected this need.

245. The Worker members noted that cooperation and assistance should not be seen purely in economic and financial terms. While these represented an important dimension, there were also other forms of assistance such as international legal assistance which had to be taken into account when considering the Article. In order to arrive at a compromise solution, he suggested a further subamendment which included both "and" and "or" and read as "international cooperation and/or assistance". The Government member of Hungary noted that "and/or" would effectively mean "or".

246. The Government member of Hungary had wished to hear whether the Committee had agreed with the Legal Adviser's opinion on the legal consequences of the text proposed by the Government member of Australia, but there had been no disagreement.

247. The Government member of Australia, speaking on behalf of the members

of the IMEC Group on the Committee and other members, stated their support for the subamendment submitted by the Worker members. The Employer members also supported the subamendment.

248. The Government member of Ethiopia, speaking on behalf of members of the African Group on the Committee, expressed their disappointment with the position adopted by some members on this issue. He reluctantly agreed to the amendment submitted by the Government member of Australia and subamended by the Worker members to include "and/or". He outlined his Group's understanding that, under Article 8, the obligations of ratifying member States were cumulative requirements necessary for the implementation of the provisions of the Convention; the Article was an essential component of the Convention and he asked all ratifying member States to respect it in good faith.

249. The Government member of India fully endorsed the statement made on behalf of the members of the African Group on the Committee, and confirmed the particular importance attached to this Article by the vast majority of the members of the Asia-Pacific Group on the Committee. Referring to the nature of obligations entailed by the Convention, he stressed that obligations are the same for each Article. While expressing some reservations on the proposed formulation, in a spirit of compromise he supported the text of the Article as subamended by the Worker members. He wished to state his disagreement with the Government member of Hungary's statement that no delegation had objected or responded to his enquiry and reaffirmed his understanding that there was an obligation under the Convention for members to assist each other. The Government member of Chile, speaking on behalf of the Government members of Argentina, Brazil, Chile, Mexico, Uruguay and Venezuela, supported the consensus that had emerged in support of the subamendment submitted by the Worker members, as did the Government member of Colombia. The Chairperson noted that there was unanimity on the text proposed for Article 8 and that, therefore, the Committee had agreed to withdraw all other amendments submitted on Article 8.

250. Article 8 was adopted as amended to read: "Members shall take appropriate steps to assist one another in giving effect to the provisions of this Convention through enhanced international cooperation and/or assistance including support for social and economic development, poverty eradication programmes and universal education."

Proposed New Article after Article 8

251. The Worker members submitted an amendment to add a new Article after Article 8 to read as follows: "Members shall take appropriate steps to promote enhanced cooperation and assistance between the ILO and other international institutions in order to promote the realization of the aims of this Convention.". The Worker members referred to the important role played by international financial institutions and expressed the dissatisfaction of workers'

organizations as regards the assistance received by developing countries. He referred to the position of the Secretary-General of the United Nations, who had affirmed that it was impossible to build economic development without the development of the people of the beneficiary countries. The ILO with its unique tripartite structure and being the institution concerned with such subjects as the elimination of child labour had a special role in promoting social objectives. He strongly encouraged the ILO to intensify its efforts and take a leading role in reducing poverty and ensuring that all work was decent work.

252. The Government member of India said he understood and supported the feelings which had led to the Worker members' position. He recognized that there had been occasions when certain programmes of international agencies had failed to achieve positive results. He also underlined the difficulties encountered by the ILO in promoting international labour standards where jobs were difficult to create or maintain. He appreciated the direction of the strategic objectives presented by the Director-General of the ILO, particularly the emphasis on employment generation to eradicate poverty and ensure social progress. Referring to the obligations deriving from the ratification of this Convention, he believed that they would be the responsibility of ratifying member States and therefore did not see how the amendment if adopted could lead to its realization. With this in mind, he asked the Worker members to withdraw the amendment. The Employer members agreed with the statement made by the Government member of India. The Worker members expressed their appreciation of the various views expressed and withdrew their amendment, while reaffirming the need for complementary international action towards the immediate elimination of the worst forms of child labour.

253. The Chairperson expressed his great satisfaction for the work completed and submitted the Convention to the Committee for adoption.

254. The Convention was adopted as amended.

255. After the proposed Convention was adopted, the Government member of Egypt stated that Egypt had accepted the text of the proposed Convention but would like to put on record a number of points. Concerning Preambular paragraph 3, the phrase "international action" could only be interpreted in light of Article 8. This had clearly been stated during the deliberations of the Committee on this paragraph, moreover the Committee's intent was clear in considering this phrase to refer exclusively to action undertaken with the consent of all concerned governments. Nevertheless, his Government had reservations on this wording because it could be misinterpreted or abused. Referring to Article 3(a), he supported the statement made by the Government member of Ethiopia on behalf of the members of the African Group on the Committee. With regard to Article 3(d), he favoured using the same language as Article 3, paragraph 1, of Convention No. 138, and was concerned that using different wording in describing the same

activities could create confusion in the application of both Conventions. He added that his Government did not interpret the substitution of "jeopardize" with "harm" as adding any new obligations or widening the scope of the proposed Convention as compared to Convention No. 138. This remark also applied equally to Article 4, paragraph 1, where the phrase "taking into consideration relevant international standards" was added. As for the reference to Paragraph 3 in the Recommendation in Article 4, paragraph 1, of the proposed Convention, he stressed that his Government considered the interpretation given by the Legal Adviser to be the only correct interpretation. Referring to the proposed new Paragraph 4 in the Recommendation which was paraphrased from Article 3, paragraph 3, of Convention No. 138, he considered that this Paragraph should have been included in the proposed Convention. Nevertheless, he stated that since reference had been made to this Paragraph in the proposed Convention it was his Government's interpretation that it carried the same legal weight as if it had been included in the proposed Convention, and that hence, the proposed Convention did not add any new requirements regarding the determination of the minimum age for hazardous work. Concerning Article 8, he supported the statements made by the Government members of Ethiopia and India during the Committee's discussion on the Article.

B. Proposed Recommendation Concerning the Prohibition and Immediate Elimination of the Worst Forms of Child Labour

Title

256. Two amendments were proposed by the Government member of Ethiopia, on behalf of the members of the African Group on the Committee, and by the Government member of India, on behalf of the Government members of Australia, China, India, Indonesia, Japan, Lebanon, Malaysia, New Zealand and Pakistan, to add "action for" after the word "immediate" in order to align the title of the Recommendation with that of the Convention. The Employer members and Worker members supported the amendment, which was adopted. The Worker members proposed a subamendment to add the word "the" after "action for". The subamendment was adopted.

257. The title was adopted as amended.

Preambular Paragraph 1

258. Preambular Paragraph 1 was adopted without change.

Preambular Paragraph 2

Preambular Paragraph 2 was adopted without change.

Preambular Paragraph 3

260. Preambular Paragraph 3 was adopted as amended to conform to the title adopted for the Convention: "the Worst Forms of Child Labour Convention, 1999, and".

Preambular Paragraph 4

Preambular Paragraph 4 was adopted without change.

Preambular Paragraph 5

262. Preambular Paragraph 5 was adopted as amended, to conform to the reference to the title of the Convention: "these proposals shall take the form of a Recommendation supplementing the Worst Forms of Child Labour Convention, 1999;".

Preambular Paragraph 6

The Employer members and the Government member of Ethiopia, on behalf of the members of the African Group on the Committee, submitted identical amendments to delete "the Immediate Abolition of" to align the text with that of the Convention. The amendments were adopted.

264. Preambular Paragraph 6 was adopted as amended.

265. The Preamble was adopted as amended.

Paragraph 1

266. The Employer members proposed an amendment to delete the words ", and should be applied in conjunction with them" which they considered to be superfluous as the word "supplement" covered this phrase. The Government member of Lebanon questioned the meaning of the expression "should be applied in conjunction with them." She recalled that the provisions of the Recommendation were only guidelines which were not binding but complemented those of the Convention. The Worker members disagreed and opposed the amendment. The Employer members withdrew the amendment.

267. The Committee modified the title to conform to the short title adopted for the Convention. Paragraph 1 was adopted as amended to read: "The provisions of this Recommendation supplement those of the Worst Forms of Child Labour Convention, 1999; (hereafter referred to as 'the Convention'), and should be applied in conjunction with them."

Paragraph 2

268. The Worker members submitted an amendment to add the words ", as a matter of urgency," after the word "implemented", in order to align the text of the Recommendation with that of Article 1 of the Convention which included the same phrase. The Employer members, the Government members of the Netherlands and Austria, and the Government member of Mexico, speaking on behalf of the Government members of Argentina, Bolivia, Brazil, Chile, Colombia, Cuba, Dominican Republic, Guatemala, Mexico and Uruguay, supported the amendment. The Government of India recalled the lengthy debate on this wording in the Convention and stated that the members of the Asia-Pacific Group on the Committee fully supported the amendment. He called on the Worker members to display

understanding when the deletion of the word "immediate" would be proposed later in other provisions of the Recommendation. The amendment was adopted.

269. The Worker members proposed an amendment to replace the existing text after the words "organizations" with ", taking into consideration the views of the children directly affected by the worst forms of child labour and their families, and, as appropriate, other concerned groups committed to the aims of this Convention.". Regarding the phrase "as appropriate, other concerned groups committed to the aims of this Convention", they wanted to make it clear that the reference was to groups that were committed to abolishing the worst forms of child labour. The Government member of Ethiopia, speaking on behalf of the members of the African Group on the Committee, supported the amendment. The Government member of the Netherlands endorsed the amendment and stated that they had wanted such a reference in the Convention and supported this reference in the Recommendation. The Government member of Sweden supported the amendment and proposed a subamendment to change "this Convention" to "the Convention and Recommendation"; this was supported by the Worker members. The Government member of Switzerland supported the amendment as her Government supported the participation of other groups.

270. The Government member of India, on behalf of the members of the Asia-Pacific Group on the Committee, stated that they fully supported the spirit of the amendment, but that considering that there were approximately two and a half million children in the worst forms of child labour in India, taking account of their views and their parents' views would pose a logistical problem. Thus, the Government member of India proposed to subamend the amendment by deleting "the children directly affected by the worst forms of child labour and their families, and, as appropriate,". The Government member of the United Kingdom supported the Worker members' amendment and expressed surprise that India did not support it, because India was at the forefront in involving children and their families in the implementation of programmes dealing with the worst forms of child labour. The Government member of India acknowledged that his Government did involve children and their families as much as possible but stated that the large number involved created a logistical problem.

271. The Employer members were also concerned with the mechanisms that would be used to consider the views of children and their families and the broad nature of this recommendation.

272. The Government member of Mexico supported the Worker members' amendment and recalled Article 12 of the United Nations Convention on the Rights of the Child which provides that children have the right to participate in decisions that affect them. The Government members of Argentina, Canada and France also supported the Worker members' amendment.

273. The Employer members proposed the wording "in so far as possible"

instead of "as appropriate". The Government member of the United Kingdom supported the Indian amendment and proposed deleting the second reference to "as appropriate". This was opposed by the Government member of Finland who supported the Worker members' amendment. The Government member of India supported the proposal made by the United Kingdom. The Government member of the Dominican Republic supported the Worker members' amendment. The Government member of Zimbabwe also supported the Worker members' amendment and pointed out that although the Recommendation included guidelines that Governments should strive to achieve, they were not legally bound by them.

274. The Government member of India restated that they were not opposing the amendment or the idea behind it. They had proposed amending the text to take account of the practical problem that may result and to ensure that the Recommendation did not include something that was not feasible.

275. A show of hands by Government members indicated that there was broad support for the amendment. The Government member of India withdrew his subamendment. However, the Employer members reiterated that they were concerned about the practicalities of how such a recommendation would be carried out. The Government member of Finland, while maintaining his support for the Worker members' amendment, stated that, if this would pave the way for a compromise, one could add words "as far as possible" to qualify the provisions. The Government member of Spain agreed with the Employer members' concerns, and stated that designing programmes of action was one thing and implementing them was another. If a country were to design a programme of action against the worst forms of child labour, it would be impractical to solicit the views of all children concerned. The Government member of Colombia also supported these views and commented that it would be almost impossible, for example, to take into consideration the views of children who were the victims of trafficking. He therefore had supported the subamendment proposed by the Government member of India.

276. The Government member of Switzerland remarked that a Recommendation spoke to the ideal practice and governments were not obliged to undertake the measures laid out in Recommendations, merely take them into consideration. Most member States had expressed support for this ideal, and she therefore appealed to the Employer members to support the amendment.

277. The Worker members, quoting from Article 12 of the United Nations Convention on the Rights of the Child, pointed out that most member States had already entered into a commitment to allow children the opportunity to express their views, and that this need not be directly with each individual child but through other appropriate mechanisms. There had been considerable support for their amendment and they were not willing to withdraw it.

278. The Employer members stated that they had never been against the proposal, merely that they had wished for further discussion regarding the practicalities of consultation and could now support it. The amendment as subamended was adopted.

279. An amendment submitted by the Government member of Ethiopia, acting on behalf of the members of the African Group on the Committee, to delete the words "as appropriate" was withdrawn, and the introductory part to Paragraph 2 as amended was adopted.

Paragraph 2(a)

280. An amendment was submitted by the Government member of Ethiopia, acting on behalf of the members of the African Group on the Committee, to insert after the word "identifying", the word "prohibiting" to reflect that identification was not sufficient, as one of the main aims of the Convention was to prohibit the worst forms of child labour.

281. The Worker members stated that whilst they agreed with the spirit of the proposed amendment, prohibition was a legislative issue, and it was addressed elsewhere, in the instruments. The Government member of Ethiopia withdrew the amendment.

282. Paragraph 2(a) was adopted without change.

Paragraph 2(b)

283. The Government member of India noted that an amendment had been adopted to Article 7, paragraph 2(a), to change the phrase "from engaging in" to "the engagement of", and for the sake of consistency this should also be amended in clause (b) of Paragraph 2. Similarly, the word "emotional" had been replaced with "psychological". The Government member of the United Kingdom made the same point regarding the word "reintegration" which had been changed elsewhere to "integration". The Committee agreed to delete "emotional" and substitute "psychological". The Chairman stated that the other points would be included and brought to the attention of the Drafting Committee.

284. Paragraph 2(b) was adopted as amended.

Paragraph 2(c) and 2(c)(i)

285. Paragraph 2(c) and 2 (c)(i) were adopted without change.

Paragraph 2(c)(ii)

286. The Government member of India, speaking on behalf of the Government members of China, India, Indonesia, Japan, Lebanon, Malaysia and Pakistan withdrew an amendment to replace the words "the problem of hidden work situations" with the word "work". Despite their preference for the deletion of this language, they had agreed to do so to reach consensus.

Proposed new Sub-Clause after Paragraph 2(c)(ii)

287. The Government member of Ethiopia, acting on behalf of the members of the African Group on the Committee, submitted an amendment to insert a new subclause after paragraph 2(c)(ii), to read "(iii) the girl child;". They stated that it was clear that girls were particularly vulnerable to and subject to the worst forms of child labour, and attention should be drawn to this by including an explicit subclause on the girl child.

288. The proposal received overwhelming support from the Government members of Bolivia, Canada, Cuba, Finland, Guatemala, Mexico, the Netherlands, Switzerland, the United Kingdom, and from India, speaking on behalf of the members of the Asia-Pacific Group on the Committee. The Employer members also supported the amendment, as did the Worker members. However, they suggested that the subclause would more appropriately come before 2(c)(ii) and become new subclause (ii). The Government member of Ethiopia stated that this proposal was an improvement on their original amendment and the amendment was adopted as subamended.

Paragraph 2(c)(iii) and (iv)

289. Subclauses (iii) and (iv) were adopted without change.

290. Paragraph 2(c) was adopted as amended.

Paragraph 2(d)

291. An amendment was submitted by the Government member of Ethiopia, acting on behalf of the Government members of the African Group on the Committee, to replace the words "reaching out to" with the words "working with". The Government member of Ethiopia explained that the phrase "reaching out" did not suggest clearly enough the need for the involvement of children and their communities in programmes of action.

292. The Government member of the United Kingdom supported the amendment but the Worker members stated that the amendment changed the intention, as "reaching out" was more proactive and was intended to suggest that programmes of action should aim at actively seeking out and working with children and their communities. The Government member of the Netherlands agreed with the Worker members' interpretation and suggested that both phrases could be used, so that the clause would read: "(d) identifying, reaching out to and working with communities where children are at special risk;".

293. The Government member of Ethiopia had no objections to this subamendment, and neither did the Employer members. The Government member of Bolivia also supported the proposal and asked that the Drafting Committee change the word "descubrir" in the Spanish text since it had a clandestine connotation. The amendment as subamended was adopted.

294. Paragraph 2(d) was adopted as amended.

Paragraph 2(e)

295. Paragraph 2(e) was adopted without change.

296. Paragraph 2 was adopted as amended.

Paragraph 3

297. Paragraph 3 was part of the proposal that had been received by the Committee from the informal tripartite working group, as was new Paragraph 4 below.

298. The Employer members submitted an amendment to replace the words "as a minimum" with the words "inter alia". The members of the Committee unanimously supported the amendment which was adopted as was the first part of the Paragraph as amended.

Paragraph 3(a)

299. The Employer members proposed to replace the word "emotional" with the word "psychological". The amendment was adopted and Paragraph 3(a) was adopted as amended.

Paragraph 3(b)

300. Paragraph 3(b) was adopted without change.

Paragraph 3(c)

301. Paragraph 3(c) was adopted without change.

Paragraph 3(d)

302. Paragraph 3(d) was adopted without change.

Paragraph 3(e)

303. The Employer members proposed replacing the words "which does not allow for the possibility of returning home each day" with the words "where the child is unreasonably confined to the premises of the employer". This was adopted and Paragraph 3(e) was adopted as amended to read: "work under particularly difficult conditions such as work for long hours or during the night or work where the child is unreasonably confined to the premises of the employer."

304. Paragraph 3 was adopted as amended.

Proposed New Paragraph after Paragraph 3

305. The Employer members submitted an amendment (included in the agreed proposal) to add a new Paragraph after Paragraph 3 to read:

For the types of work referred to under Article 3(d) of the Convention and Paragraph 3 of the Recommendation, national laws or regulations or the competent authority could, after consultation with the workers' and employers' organizations concerned, authorize employment or work as from the age of 16 years on condition that the health, safety and morals of the children concerned are fully protected, and that the young persons have received adequate specific instruction or vocational training in the relevant branch of activity.

The Government member of India stated that although this wording had been discussed and agreed upon by the members of the Committee, he wished to point out that the introductory words "For the types of work" differed slightly from those used in Paragraph 3 which started "In determining the types of work", and suggested aligning the texts. The Employer Vice-Chairperson stated that he believed the wording was different because the meaning was different. Following a discussion on the drafting, the amendment was adopted.

306. New Paragraph 4 was adopted.

Paragraph 4(1)

307. The Government member of Ethiopia, acting on behalf of the members of the African Group on the Committee, submitted an amendment to delete the word "immediate" before the word "elimination". He referred to previous discussions on the concept of immediate elimination. The Government member of Norway proposed a subamendment to move the word "immediate" before the word "prohibition".The proposal was supported by the Government member of the Netherlands. The Government member of India, speaking on behalf of the members of the Asia-Pacific Group on the Committee, said that his group had submitted an identical amendment. The Worker members expressed initial support for the amendment proposed by the members of the African Group on the Committee provided that this deletion did not harm the intent of the instruments. They then referred to an amendment they had submitted to add the words "as a matter of urgency." at the end of the sentence, and asked for the two amendments to be considered together. The Government member of the Netherlands supported the amendment with some regret, as did the Government member of Norway who withdrew their subamendment. The Employer members also supported the formulation containing the two amendments, which were adopted.

308. The Government members of Canada, Denmark, Norway and Switzerland submitted an amendment to replace the existing Paragraph with the following text: "As far as possible, detailed information and statistical data on the nature and extent of the worst forms of child labour should be compiled and kept up to date to serve as a basis for determining priorities for national action for its prohibition and immediate elimination.". The Government member of Canada referred to the possible difficulties of some countries in collecting statistical information and stressed the importance of the collection of data itself, not how they were disaggregated. Priority should be given to the collection of statistics on the worst forms of child labour. The Worker members were puzzled by the use of the words "As far as possible", and argued that the proposed language suggested the relevant institutions could minimize their efforts. He asked the

Government members concerned to recognize the urgency of this aspect and withdraw the amendment. The Government member of Spain supported the amendment, but added that it implied that there was no distinction between all forms of child labour and its worst forms. The Worker members expressed some doubts about the capacities of certain countries to separate information about forms of child labour that required immediate elimination and other forms.

309. The Government member of the Netherlands opposed the amendment and argued that it was also essential to start compiling information on all forms of child labour as a preventive measure. The Government member of Mexico also opposed the amendment and recalled that the United Nations Commission for Human Rights and other human rights mechanisms systematically referred to the fact that national and international programmes of action to combat, inter alia, prostitution, sale and trafficking of children and the use of children in pornography had not been carried out effectively because of the lack of statistical information. The members of the African Group on the Committee, as well as the Government members of India and the United Kingdom, expressed their preference for the existing text as previously amended by the Worker members. In a spirit of cooperation and consensus and having noted the position expressed by various members, the Government member of Canada withdrew the amendment.

310. The Government member of Ethiopia, speaking on behalf of the members of the African Group on the Committee, withdrew an amendment to insert the words "and international cooperation" after the word "action".

311. Paragraph 4(1) was adopted as amended to read: "Detailed information and statistical data on the nature and extent of child labour should be compiled and kept up to date to serve as a basis for determining priorities for national action for the abolition of child labour, in particular for the prohibition and elimination of its worst forms as a matter of urgency.".

Paragraph 4(2)

312. The Worker members submitted an amendment to add the words ", school attendance, and geographical location, and should take into account the importance of an effective system of birth registration, which should include issuing of a birth certificate.". The Worker members explained that this formulation would help to identify the areas where information should be collected and used effectively. The Employer members supported the amendment. The Government members of Canada, Italy, Netherlands, Switzerland and the United Kingdom supported the amendment as did the Government member of Chile on behalf of the members of the Latin American Group on the Committee. The Government member of India, speaking on behalf of the majority of the members of the Asia-Pacific Group on the Committee, stated their surprise at the level of detail included in the amendment and considered that national authorities should be left to decide how best to handle these matters. The Government member of

Bolivia supported the position expressed by the Government member of India. While supporting the proposal submitted by the Worker members, the Government member of Ethiopia, speaking on behalf of the members of the African Group on the Committee, reported that various members of this Group had signalled they would encounter practical difficulties in implementing the provisions of this amendment, especially the issuing of birth certificates. The Government member of Australia proposed a subamendment to improve the readability of the provision: "As far as possible, such information and statistical data should include data disaggregated by sex, age group, occupation, branch of economic activity, status in employment, school attendance and geographical location. The importance of an effective system of birth registration, which should include issuing of a birth certificate, should be taken into account.". The Employer and Worker members supported the subamendment and the amendment was adopted as subamended. The Worker members withdrew an amendment to insert the words "as a minimum" after the word "include".

313. Paragraph 4(2) was adopted as amended.

Paragraph 4(3)

314. The Government member of Ethiopia, acting on behalf of the members of the African Group on the Committee, submitted an amendment to delete the word "immediate" before the word "elimination". He referred to the arguments presented during the adoption of Paragraph 4(1).

315. The Worker members noted that the Paragraph addressed the question of violations, and the removal of the word "immediate" would expose governments to a wider interpretation of their obligations. The Government member of Ethiopia confirmed that the objective was to take immediate action. The Employer members supported the amendment as did the Government member of India. The Worker members also supported the amendment. The amendment was adopted.

316. Paragraph 4(3) was adopted as amended.

317. Paragraph 4 was adopted as amended.

Paragraph 5

318. Paragraph 5 was adopted without change.

Paragraph 6

319. Paragraph 6 was adopted without change.

Paragraph 7

320. The members of the Asia-Pacific Group and the African Group on the Committee submitted an amendment to delete the word "immediate" before the word "elimination" in order to make it consistent with earlier Articles and Paragraphs in the instruments. It was supported by the Employer and Worker members and a majority of Government members and was adopted.

321. The Government members of Bolivia, Colombia and Venezuela submitted an amendment to delete the words "and, as appropriate, other concerned groups", in order to ensure consistency with the proposed text of the Convention and to reflect the tripartite structure of the ILO, since it was related to the monitoring of the Convention. The amendment was supported by the Employer and Worker members and the Government members of Cuba, India, and Mexico. It was opposed by the Government member of the Netherlands, on behalf of the members of the IMEC Group on the Committee. A subamendment proposed by the Government member of the Netherlands to delete the entire Paragraph, in view of its similarity to Article 5 of the Convention, was supported by the Government members of Denmark, Finland, Guatemala and Switzerland, but opposed by both the Worker and Employer members and the Government members of Bolivia and Mexico on the grounds that it had to be in the Recommendation because not all member States would ratify the Convention. The subamendment was withdrawn and the amendment adopted. A subamendment submitted by the Worker members to insert after "concerned groups" the words "committed to the aims of the Convention" was withdrawn as no longer necessary.

322. Paragraph 7 was adopted as amended and read: "Members should establish or designate appropriate national mechanisms to monitor the implementation of national provisions for the prohibition and elimination of the worst forms of child labour after consultation with employers' and workers' organizations."

Paragraph 8

323. Identical amendments were submitted by the Government member of Ethiopia, on behalf of the members of the African Group on the Committee, and by the Government members of China, India and Indonesia, as well as the other members of the Asia-Pacific Group on the Committee, to delete the word "immediate" before the word "elimination". The Government member of Ethiopia explained that this was consistent with the deletion of "immediate" in the title and in previous Articles and Paragraphs, and the Government member of India echoed his sentiments. The amendments were adopted.

324. Paragraph 8 was adopted as amended.

Paragraph 9

325. Identical amendments were submitted by the Government member of Ethiopia, on behalf of the Government members of the African Group on the Committee, and by the Government members of China, India and Indonesia, as well as the other members of the Asia-Pacific Group on the Committee, to delete the word "immediate" before the word "elimination", for the same reasons as in the previous paragraph. The amendments were adopted.

326. An amendment was submitted by the Government member of Colombia,

and supported by Bolivia and Cuba, to replace the words "in the event of non-compliance" with the words "for compliance". The Government member of Colombia explained that he did not know how the competent authority could take steps to determine the persons held to be responsible in the event of non-compliance of national provisions, as persons were usually held responsible for compliance. Following an explanation by the Representative of the Secretary-General that the Paragraph had been formulated in the negative to prevent child victims from being subject to penalties, while ensuring those responsible for their victimization were held responsible, the Government member of Colombia withdrew the amendment.

327. Paragraph 9 was adopted as amended.

Paragraph 10

328. Identical amendments were submitted by the Government members of China, India, Indonesia, as well as other members of the Asia-Pacific Group on the Committee, and by the Government member of Ethiopia, on behalf of the members of the African Group on the Committee, to delete the word "immediate" before the word "elimination". The Government member of Ethiopia stated that, as previously, the reason was to ensure consistency in the text.

329. The Worker members urged the Government member of Ethiopia to rethink his position with regard to this Paragraph, as the immediacy of the need for action to eliminate child labour was in danger of being lost as a result of the deletion of all references to "immediate". He wished to emphasize that the context of each provision needed to be considered. Following a discussion regarding the most suitable language, the Committee adopted a proposal put by the Government member of Pakistan to insert the words "as a matter of urgency," after "the worst forms of child labour", as this was consistent with amendments to the text of the Convention. The amendment as subamended was adopted.

Paragraph 10(a), (b) and (c)

330. Clauses (a), (b) and (c) were adopted without change.

331. Paragraph 10 was adopted as amended.

Paragraph 11

332. The introductory part of Paragraph 11 was adopted without change.

Paragraph 11(a)

333. The Government member of Ethiopia, speaking on behalf of the members of the African Group on the Committee proposed aligning the text with Article 3(a) of the Convention by replacing the words "forced or compulsory labour, debt bondage and serfdom" with the following words: "debt bondage and serfdom and forced or compulsory labour, including forced or compulsory recruitment of children for use in armed conflict". The Employer and Worker members and the

Government member of India, on behalf of the members of the Asia-Pacific Group on the Committee, supported the amendment. The amendment was adopted.

334. Paragraph 11(a) was adopted as amended.

Paragraph 11(b)

335. Paragraph 11(b) was adopted without change.

Paragraph 11(c)

336. The Worker members proposed adding: ", or in illicit activities which involve the carrying or use of firearms or other weapons" at the end of the sentence. The Worker Vice-Chairperson stated that the Committee members had agreed that drug trafficking and similar forms of illicit behaviour needed to be addressed. The use of guns was another illicit activity that should be deplored. A discussion ensued on whether "illicit", "illegal" or "unlawful" was the appropriate wording and whether the amendment was restricted to the context of the production and trafficking of drugs. The Government member of the United States proposed including the word "unlawful" before the word "carrying". The Worker Vice-Chairperson stated that as the clause was referring to illicit activities, the word "unlawful" was not necessary. No child should be involved in illicit activities or be used to carry guns or be a "gun runner". The Employer Vice-Chairperson stated that it was not clear that the amendment was related to drug trafficking. The Government member of Hungary proposed a subamendment to replace the amendment with ", or for activities which involve the unlawful carrying or use of firearms or other weapons".

337. The Employer and Worker members and the Government members of Cuba, Portugal and United States supported the subamendment. The amendment was adopted as subamended and Paragraph 11(c) was adopted as amended.

338. Paragraph 11 was adopted as amended.

Paragraph 12

339. The Government member of Ethiopia, speaking on behalf of the members of the African Group on the Committee, and the Government member of India, speaking on behalf of the Government members of China, India, Indonesia, Japan, Lebanon, Malaysia, Pakistan, Papua New Guinea and Singapore, proposed deleting the word "immediate". The Employer members supported the amendment. The Worker members pointed out that although it could be appropriate to align the text in this instance, the deletion of the word "immediate" was not appropriate on every occasion, as it could change the meaning of the text. The Worker members supported the amendment, and the amendment was adopted.

340. Paragraph 12 was adopted as amended.

Paragraph 13

341. In light of the previous comments made by the Worker members, the

Government member of India, speaking on behalf of the members of China, India, Indonesia, Japan, Lebanon, Malaysia, Pakistan, Papua New Guinea and Singapore, proposed modifying their original amendment to delete the word "immediate" and by adding "as a matter of urgency" at the end of the Paragraph. This was supported by the Government member of Ethiopia, speaking on behalf of the members of the African Group on the Committee, who had submitted a similar amendment. The Employer members supported the amendment as subamended. The Worker members proposed formulating the sentence in line with the wording agreed upon in the Convention, that was to include "immediate measures for" before "elimination" and "as a matter of urgency" at the end. Following a brief discussion that included several proposals on appropriate wording, the Government member of the United Kingdom proposed inserting "as a matter of urgency" after the word "provide". The Worker members supported the proposal as did the Employer members and the amendment as subamended was adopted.

342. The Worker members submitted an amendment to add the following words at the end of the sentence:", such as special supervision of enterprises which have used the worst forms of child labour, and, in cases of persistent violation, consideration of temporary or permanent revoking of permits to operate". The Worker members stated that this provision was aimed at enterprises that would be glad to pay fines and continue engaging in practices of abusing children, such as their use in pornography or prostitution, which were lucrative for the operators. Therefore, the Worker members wanted to provide the possibility for revoking the permits of persistent violators. The Employer members expressed concern about the difficulty of applying the provision given the complexity of criminal codes. The Government members of Canada and the United Kingdom appreciated the spirit of the amendment and supported it. The Government member of Cuba stated that consideration should be given to the current preparation of the United Nations draft optional protocol to the Convention on the Rights of the Child on the sale of children, child prostitution and child pornography, which was along the same lines as this amendment. The Government member of the Dominican Republic welcomed the amendment because it included coverage of juridical persons. He stated that action should be taken by ministries of labour to ensure that inspectors were effective. The Government member of India, speaking on behalf of the members of the Asia-Pacific Group on the Committee, supported the amendment but questioned what was envisaged by the phrase "special supervision", in view of the fact that monitoring mechanisms were included in Paragraph 7. The Government members of Portugal, Switzerland and Norway supported the amendment.

343. The Government member of Hungary expressed concern over the word "enterprise" which referred to a legal entity and would not cover self-employed entrepreneurs. He proposed replacing it with "employers or establishments".

The Worker members and the Government members of Colombia and Austria supported the subamendment. The Government member of Ethiopia expressed support but was concerned with the word "persistent" because this might result in delay when dealing with the worst forms of child labour. The Employer Vice-Chairperson opposed the subamendment as it could cast a derogatory meaning on the term "employer". He proposed "individuals or establishments". The Government member of Hungary pointed out that labour inspectors did not inspect individuals: they inspected people who employed others. Following a discussion about the appropriate terms and the meaning of various proposals such as "legal and natural persons", "enterprises" and "establishments", the Government member of Hungary withdrew the subamendment, and the amendment was adopted.

344. Paragraph 13 was adopted as amended.

Paragraph 14

345. Identical amendments were submitted by the Government member of Ethiopia, acting on behalf of the members of the African Group on the Committee, and by the Government members of China, India, Indonesia, Japan, Lebanon, Malaysia, Pakistan, Papua New Guinea and Singapore, to delete the word "immediate", to ensure consistency with the remainder of the text.

346. The amendment was supported by the Employer and Worker members. The amendment was adopted, and the introductory part of the Paragraph was adopted as amended.

Paragraph 14(a)

347. An amendment was submitted by the Government members of Ireland, Netherlands, New Zealand and United Kingdom, to insert "and mobilizing" after "sensitizing". The Government member of the United Kingdom explained that this would be consistent with the wording of Paragraph 2(e) of the Recommendation, and would reflect the common understanding that information and sensitization rarely lead to change without mobilization.

348. The Employer members supported the amendment. The Worker members commented that the amendment would have been more properly addressed in clause (b) of the same Paragraph, since they believed that Government members should be interested in helping to strengthen the capacity of employers' and workers' organizations to give effect to the provisions of the Convention. However, they were happy to support the amendment.

349. The amendment was adopted and Paragraph 14(a) was adopted as amended.

Paragraph 14(b) and 14(c)

350. Clauses (b) and (c) were adopted without change.

351. The Government member of Bolivia stated that whilst they had not submitted an amendment to this effect, Paragraph 14(b) would have been more consistent and complete with the addition of the word "national" before the words "civic organizations".

Paragraph 14(d)

352. An amendment submitted by the Government members of Canada and Denmark to delete the Paragraph was withdrawn.

353. An amendment was submitted by the Government members of Ireland, Netherlands and the United Kingdom, to refer to Member's nationals in the singular rather than to "Members' nationals". The Government member of the United Kingdom said that the amendment better reflected the intention that a Member's own nationals would be liable to prosecution in their own country for offences committed elsewhere. However, the plural "Members' " could require member States to prosecute all other member States' nationals, not merely their own.

354. The Worker and Employer members supported the amendment, as did the Government member of Ethiopia. The Government member of Mexico agreed and requested that the Drafting Committee reconsider the Spanish text.

355. The Government member of Pakistan stated that this provision should not prejudice the work on the United Nations draft optional protocol to the Convention on the Rights of the Child on the sale of children, child prostitution and child pornography.

356. The amendment was adopted and Paragraph 14(d) was adopted as amended.

Paragraph 14(e)

357. Paragraph 14(e) was adopted without change.

Paragraph 14, proposed new clause after clause (e)

358. An amendment was submitted by the Worker members to insert a new clause after clause (e), to read as follows: "encouraging the development of policies by undertakings to promote the aims of the Convention;".

359. The Worker members stated that establishments which were seeking to promote policies aimed at the elimination of the worst forms of child labour should be encouraged to do so, within the framework of national legislation. The Worker Vice-Chairperson said that he recognized the limitations of the word "undertakings", and was open to alternatives.

360. The Government member of India stated that, in principle, they were in favour of the amendment, but would prefer an alternative word to "undertakings". The Employer members pointed out that the word "undertakings" was consistent

with other ILO instruments, and were happy to support the amendment as it stood. The Government member of India withdrew his reservations since it appeared that there was appropriate precedent for use of the term.

361. The Government members of Mexico, Switzerland and Uruguay drew attention to the terms used in the French and Spanish texts, and requested that the Drafting Committee reconsider those to maintain consistency between the three texts.

362. The amendment was adopted and a new clause following clause (e) was adopted.

Paragraph 14(f)

363. The Worker members submitted an amendment to insert the words "monitoring and" before the words "giving publicity". The amendment was supported by the Committee and adopted.

364. The Government members of China, India, Indonesia, Japan, Lebanon, Malaysia, Pakistan, Papua New Guinea and Singapore submitted an amendment to insert the words "elimination of" before child labour in order to clarify that the best practices were those on the "elimination" of child labour. The amendment was supported by the Committee and adopted.

365. Paragraph 14(f) was adopted as amended.

Paragraph 14(g) and 14(h)

366. Paragraph 14(g) and 14(h) were adopted without change.

Paragraph 14, Proposed New Clause after Clause (h)

367. The Government members of Argentina, Bolivia, Brazil, Chile, Cuba, Dominican Republic, Guatemala, Mexico and Uruguay submitted an amendment to insert a new clause after clause (h) to read: "adopting appropriate measures to improve the educational infrastructure and training of teachers to meet the needs of boys and girls." It was stated that the proposed amendment covered all levels of education, including vocational training, and applied to education offered to children rescued from the worst forms of child labour. Boys and girls were mentioned so that their different needs would be addressed. The amendment was supported by the Employer and Worker members and the Government members of India and the United Kingdom and adopted.

368. The new clause after clause (h) was adopted.

Paragraph 14, Proposed New Clause after Clause (h)

369. An amendment was submitted by the Government members of Cuba, Guatemala, Mexico and Uruguay, to insert another new clause after clause (h) to read: "taking account, in national action programmes, of job promotion and vocational training for the parents of the boys and girls working in these conditions

and of awareness-raising of the parents on the problem." The intention was to highlight the important role of the family in combating the worst forms of child labour by providing them with opportunities for enhanced income and to become more aware of the detrimental effects of work on children. The Government member of Pakistan argued that the objectives set forth in the proposed clause could be difficult to achieve for some developing countries and suggested subamending it by inserting the words "as far as possible" after the words "vocational training". Following discussion, the Government member of Sweden submitted a subamendment to replace the words "boys and girls" by the word "children". This was considered along with other proposed subamendments seeking to widen the scope of the term "parents" by referring variously to "adults in families of the boys and girls", or to "fathers, mothers and other adults in the family". There was general agreement in the Committee on the principle of the proposed changes. The amendment was adopted as subamended to take account "as far as possible" of job promotion and vocational training for parents "and adults" in the families of the children. Because of the complexity of the agreed text, it was referred to the Drafting Committee to improve and reconcile the English, French and Spanish formulations.

370. The new clause after clause (h) was adopted as amended.

371. Paragraph 14 was adopted as amended.

Paragraph 15

372. The Government member of Ethiopia, on behalf of the members of the African Group on the Committee, submitted an amendment to replace the word "or" with the word "and". The Employer members and the Government member of India supported the amendment. The Worker members underscored the need for consistency with Article 8 of the Convention, and therefore proposed replacing the word "and" with "and/or". The Government members of Australia and United States supported this subamendment. Following an indicative show of support, the amendment was adopted as subamended.

373. The Government member of Ethiopia, on behalf of the members of the African Group on the Committee, submitted an amendment to replace the word "immediate" with the word "effective". He said that this was intended to ensure consistency with Articles previously adopted. The Employer and Worker members supported the amendment which was adopted.

374. In light of the adoption of the previous amendment the Government members of China, India, Indonesia, Japan, Lebanon, Malaysia, Pakistan, Papua New Guinea and Singapore withdrew an amendment to delete the word "immediate".

375. The Government member of Ethiopia, on behalf of the members of the African Group on the Committee, submitted an amendment to add the words

"complement national efforts and" after the world "should". He explained that the amendment was aimed at ensuring consistency with the text of the Convention. The Worker members accepted this formulation but submitted a subamendment to add the following text: "be developed and implemented in consultation with employers' and workers' organizations. Such cooperation and/or assistance should".

376. The Government member of India opposed the subamendment and argued that the problem of child labour mostly occurred in unorganized sectors where employers' and workers' organizations were not always active. He suggested that governments had a broad responsibility throughout society to promote social and economic development and poverty eradication. He explained that it would not always be feasible for governments to consult with the social partners on these aspects and asked the Worker members to reconsider the subamendment.

377. The Worker members presented some examples of poverty alleviation programmes aimed at the elimination of the worst forms of child labour where national trade union centres or employers' organizations had played a major role. The Government member of Ethiopia stated that the members of the African Group on the Committee disagreed with the subamendment. The Government members of Australia, Bolivia, Dominican Republic, Egypt, New Zealand and Pakistan supported the position expressed by the Government member of India and considered the proposal impractical. The Employer members underscored the constructive role played by their national organizations in implementing programmes of action against child labour and supported the Worker members' subamendment. In a spirit of compromise, the Government member of the United States proposed that the sponsors withdraw the proposed amendment, and return to the original text which also was supported by the Government member of Switzerland.

378. The Government member of India restated his support for the amendment and reaffirmed that international cooperation programmes in the area of eradicating the worst forms of child labour must be in conformity with, and must complement, national programmes. The Employer members expressed surprise at the opposition to tripartite arrangements expressed by many governments, and submitted a subsubamendment to provide that there be consultation with employers' and workers' organizations "as apropriate". The Government member of India suggested "and, as appropriate" be inserted before "national efforts". The Government members of the Dominican Republic and Switzerland and supported the proposal made by the Government member of India.

379. The Government member of Ethiopia, on behalf of the members of the African Group on the Committee, proposed to insert "may" before "as appropriate". The Employer and Worker members agreed to the proposal. The amendment as subamended by the Workers, as subamended by the Government member of India and as further subamended by the members of the African Group on the Committee, was adopted.

380. The introduction of Paragraph 15 was adopted as subamended to read: "International cooperation and/or assistance among Members for the prohibition and effective elimination of the worst forms of child labour should complement national efforts and may, as appropriate, be developed and implemented in consultation with employers' and workers' organizations. Such international cooperation and/or assistance should include:".

Paragraph 15, Clauses (a), (b) and (c)

381. Clauses (a), (b) and (c) were adopted without change.

Paragraph 15, Proposed New Clause after Clause (c)

382. The Government member of Ethiopia, on behalf of the members of the African Group on the Committee, submitted an amendment to add after clause (c) a new clause to read: "enhanced assistance, including support for social and economic development, poverty eradication programmes and universal education.". He said that the amendment was submitted to keep the text of the Recommendation consistent with the language adopted in Article 8 of the proposed Convention. The Employer and Worker members and the Government members of India and Bolivia supported the amendment. The Government member of the United Kingdom proposed a subamendment to delete the words "enhanced assistance, including" to facilitate the readability of the entire Paragraph. This was supported by the Government members of Netherlands, Switzerland and the United States. The Government member of India submitted a subamendment to insert "Enhanced" at the beginning of Paragraph 15. This subamendment was adopted and the amendment as subamended was adopted. The new clause (d) was adopted as amended to read: "support for social and economic development, poverty eradication programmes and universal education."

383. Paragraph 15 was adopted as amended.

384. The Recommendation as amended was adopted.

385. At the end of the discussion, the Secretary-General of the Conference briefly addressed the members of the Committee. He underscored the historical contribution being made by the work of the Committee. Through this Convention, the ILO would propose a global instrument to combat child labour, with the strong and broad support of the tripartite delegations. The world had been waiting for this Convention which promoted universally accepted values. He believed that the Convention would transcend negotiation and would have a profound direct impact upon the life of many people, particularly children.

Adoption of the Report and the Proposed Convention and Recommendation

386. At its twentieth sitting, the Committee adopted its report, subject to changes requested by various members, as well as the proposed Convention and

Recommendation as they had been amended by the Drafting Committee. Before presentation of the report, members of the Committee made closing statements.

387. The Employer Vice-Chairperson noted that the discussions in the Committee had been unusual in many ways. There had been little conflict, no votes had been cast, and there was an effort to proceed by consensus. He noted however that the Employer members had been opposed to the reference to child soldiers, the linking of education to the definition of the worst forms of child labour, and the inclusion of NGOs in the consultation process required by the Convention. The Employer members strongly supported the objective of ending the use of children in military or armed forces of any kind. But they believed that the United Nations and its Working group on an optional protocol to the Convention on the Rights of the Child on the involvement of children in armed conflicts was the appropriate forum to discuss these matters. The Employer members called on the United Nations to speedily end the use of children in wars. The Employer members valued education highly and recognized the important role of education in keeping children out of work. They were concerned, however, that linking education to the definition of the worst forms of child labour would delay ratification of the Convention. The Employers called on States parties which had already committed themselves to the provision of free compulsory education to meet this commitment as soon as possible. They also called on the international community to support this effort. Finally, while the Employer members recognized the important role of NGOs in the fight against child labour, it was important that the tripartite nature of the ILO was not undermined.

388. The Worker Vice-Chairperson expressed his appreciation for the large degree of commitment of the Government and Employer members to the development of a ratifiable and implementable Convention and Recommendation. The new Convention was a human rights Convention, and poverty could not be put forward as an excuse for not ratifying or implementing it. Key to its successful implementation would be the universal provision of at least eight years of basic education. He emphasized the urgency of taking action and called on the international community to strongly cooperate and step up its efforts to provide resources to help eliminate the worst forms of child labour.

389. The Government member of India: My delegation would like to take this opportunity to place on record a few observations regarding the deliberations of this Committee and elements of the draft Convention and Recommendation on the worst forms of child labour.

Allow me to first of all express our deep appreciation to the spokespersons of the Workers' and Employers' groups, Mr. Trottman and Mr. Botha, as well as all Government members of this Committee, for participating in these negotiations in a constructive spirit. This has facilitated our search for solutions to the many difficult issues that were before us and has enabled us to forge a consensus. We believe that this will in turn promote greater understanding of the complexity of the issues covered by this draft Convention as well as the practical considerations related to efforts to eliminate the worst forms of child labour.

We would also like to congratulate you, Mr. Chairman, for your most able stewardship of the work of this Committee which has in no small measure contributed to the success of our endeavours.

Further, we would like to express our appreciation to the secretariat for its excellent support which in our view merits special commendation.

At the outset of this meeting, my delegation had stressed the need for an instrument which is implementable and ratifiable, sensitive to the poverty dimension of the phenomenon of child labour in its worst forms, and recognizes that in addition to national action, there must be an element of international cooperation and solidarity to address socio-economic development and to eradicate poverty which is most frequently the root cause of child labour. We had cautioned against inflexible prescriptions, an unduly broad scope and unrealistic or unattainable objectives.

Mr. Chairman, the outcome we have reached does not meet all the concerns that had been raised by my delegation. However, we do believe that it broadly reflects a balance of concerns raised by the tripartite members of this Committee, and, therefore, are prepared to support the draft Convention and Recommendation.

Allow me to offer some observations on the draft text of these instruments.

The title of the document and of the draft Convention as well as Article 1 clearly define the objective of this instrument, which is to address measures for the prohibition and elimination of the worst forms of child labour. We believe that this recognition is of critical importance as the phenomenon of the worst forms of child labour, when it is rooted in poverty, cannot be eliminated overnight or merely legislated away. The most effective way of addressing the problem is to progressively eradicate the root cause, which is poverty, through national action and international cooperation. We welcome the fact that these aspects are fully recognized in the draft Convention. At the same time, we recognize in equal measure the need to undertake immediate steps for the elimination of the worst forms of child labour, and to deal with this issue as a matter of urgency.

390. We had supported the need for a clear and well-defined scope of the draft Convention. The definitions of the worst forms of child labour which are to be covered by this draft Convention, as contained in Article 3, continue to be rather broad. However, we welcome the fact that this Article reaffirms a number of fundamental political and civil rights of the child which must be enforced in all circumstances. In the area of hazardous work where child labour is most likely to be rooted in poverty, determination of the worst forms is to be made by competent national authorities after consultation with tripartite partners at the

national level. This will provide the instrument with a measure of flexibility as well as the capacity to address the specificities of the situation prevailing in each national context.

391. Articles 5, 6 and 7 address national responsibility for giving effect to the provisions of the draft Convention. We have noted the emphasis placed on education as an essential component of the removal of children from the worst forms of child labour and their durable rehabilitation.

Regarding access to education, we would like to stress that governmental responsibility lies in facilitating the availability of this economic and social right in a progressive and developmental context, an aspect fully recognized by Article 28 of the Convention on the Rights of the Child. The implementation of goals such as free and compulsory basic education must also be seen in conjunction with national economic circumstances and the availability of resources as provided under Article 2 of the International Covenant on Economic, Social and Cultural Rights, including through enhanced international cooperation and assistance.

My delegation would like to reiterate that this draft Convention does not create any new binding obligations in respect of economic and social rights which by their nature cannot be legally guaranteed and enforced. That these rights can be fully realized only in a progressive manner is well recognized under international human rights law, and it is our belief that the implementation of this draft Convention must also conform to relevant international standards established by the International Covenant on ESC Rights and the Convention on the Rights of the Child.

In this context, we would once again like to make it clear that the symptoms of poverty do not constitute deliberate violations of human rights by states. Virtually all forms of child labour which involve the absence of the child from school are rooted in poverty, parental unemployment or underemployment, or parental illiteracy. It is not possible to penalize such absence from school because this would involve penalizing or imposing sanctions on poverty. It would also be tantamount to labelling poverty as the worst form of child labour. This phenomenon cannot be eliminated by condemning poverty. We are firmly convinced that the ILO, as an organization committed to social progress and social justice and recognizing that poverty anywhere is a threat to prosperity everywhere, will never embrance arguments that undermine its fundamental objectives and evade the shared responsibility of all its Members to secure them.

The ultimate answer to the problem of child labour lies in the eradication of poverty, unemployment and illiteracy by progressively securing the realization of economic and social rights. This is a long-standing goal to which the ILO must recommit itself with renewed vigour. Only multi-dimensional strategies that provide access to educational opportunities, open avenues for gainful employment for parents, eradicate parental illiteracy, and ensure the protection of all rights of the child contained in the Convention on the Rights of the Child, can eventually eliminate the worst forms of child labour, wherever it occurs as a symptom of poverty.

My delegation attaches particular importance to Article 8 of the draft Convention. We welcome the fact that the language of this Article has been considerably strengthened to explicitly endorse international cooperation and assistance for eradicating poverty, promoting socio-economic development and realizing universal education. We would like to reiterate that the obligation contained in this Article is no different from those arising from other articles that define national responsibilities, and that in the overall context of eradicating poverty as a root cause of child labour, obligations for national action and international cooperation contained in this draft Convention are indivisible and inter-related.

392. Mr. Chairman, my delegation attaches importance to the problem of the involvement of children in armed conflict. Such involvement can cause irreparable harm to the psyche of the child and invariably threatens the child's right to life. We would have preferred to see stronger language in the text of the draft Convention. While noting that this issue is dealt with in the context of forced or compulsory recruitment, we believe that the relevant provision in the draft Convention is without prejudice to a more comprehensive treatment of the matter through an optional Protocol of the CRC on the involvement of children in armed conflict, the early conclusion of which we strongly support.

393. The draft Convention and Recommendation contain references to consultation required to be undertaken by national authorities. We respect the tripartite nature of the ILO and would like to affirm that the obligation to undertake such consultations relates only to employers' and workers' organizations. Thereafter, the responsibility for decision-making rests with the competent national authorities alone. While we attach importance to the views of civil society at large, we would not like to see the erosion of the tripartite structure of the ILO. We have also pointed out the practical difficulties regarding some of the elements in the draft Recommendation which call for wider consultation. Our clear preference would have been to avoid elements which raise difficulties of a practical nature and are unimplementable. We believe that insertion of such language can only erode the value of the Recommendation.

394. We have heard with attention issues which have been raised by some delegations related to "hidden work" or "domestic work". These are relatively new concepts which are yet to be clearly understood and defined within the tripartite structures of the ILO. They should not be confused with the worst forms of child labour. We also believe that the situations of "special risk" referred to in the draft Convention and Recommendation should not be seen as incorporating the undefined concepts of "hidden" or "domestic work".

In conclusion, Mr. Chairman, allow me to reaffirm that my Government is committed to the full eradication of all forms of child labour, beginning with its most exploitative and hazardous forms. We see the new instrument on the worst forms of child labour which this Committee has drafted as a culmination of initiatives which my Government has supported in the International Labour Conference since 1996. As the Director-General of the ILO has stated, this Committee has been entrusted with a historic opportunity. We believe that we have not failed the children of the world whose tender years are crushed and lives blighted by the worst forms of child labour. We would like to express the hope that this draft Convention will provide a major impetus to national action and international cooperation and assistance to eradicate the worst forms of child labour. There is nothing more precious for any nation or society than the protection and well-being of its children and their capacity to achieve their full potential as adults. This recognition must underpin our efforts, individual and collective, to give effect to the provisions of this draft Convention.

395. The Government member of the Netherlands, on behalf of the Government members of Australia, Austria, Belgium, Canada, Denmark, Finland, France, Germany, Greece Hungary, Ireland, Italy, Japan Luxembourg, Netherlands, New Zealand, Norway, Portugal, San Marino, Spain, Sweden, Switzerland, Turkey, United Kingdom and United States, expressed satisfaction with the work carried out by the Committee in reaching a satisfactory compromise text for a Convention and a Recommendation and considered the major relevant issues were adequately reflected.

396. The instruments represented a first step towards the setting of international standards on the issue of child soldiers. A basis had been laid for the Working group on the optional protocol to the United Nations Convention on the Rights of the Child on involvement of children in armed conflicts to make further progress.

397. The Government member of the Netherlands, speaking on behalf of the abovementioned member States, reiterated their full commitment to tripartism and welcomed the agreement to involve other groups that work towards the aims of the Convention in the design and implementation of programmes of action. She assured the Committee that IMEC members would continue to be fully committed to the principle of all members assisting one another in giving effect to the provisions of the Convention on the worst forms of child labour through international cooperation and/or assistance. It was their understanding, based upon the opinion of the Legal Adviser, that Article 8 of the Convention addressed the need for all members to work together to meet the goals of the Convention.

398. The Government member of the Netherlands recognized that child labour was to a great extent caused by poverty and that in its turn child labour

perpetuated poverty. The members of the Committee should acknowledge, however, that poverty could under no circumstances be used as an excuse for condoning the worst forms of child labour. She strongly endorsed the enhanced emphasis in the Convention on the crucial role of education and vocational training in the elimination of child labour. She considered this Convention to be one of the ILO's fundamental labour standards and that it should be included in the campaign to promote ratification of fundamental labour standards.

399. The Government member of Ethiopia, speaking on behalf of the members of the African Group on the Committee, reiterated their wholehearted support the Committee for the adoption of the new Convention and Recommendation. He expressed their satisfaction that the Committee had adopted the instruments without a vote after making the necessary compromises. He noted that the report reflected the understandings and positions of the members of the African Group on the Committee on some issues.

400. The Government member of Pakistan: I would like to congratulate this Committee for its success in ensuring that the 87th Session of the International Labour Conference adopts the Convention and the Recommendation on the worst forms of child labour. All concerned have worked very hard to achieve consensus through compromises from all sides. The final draft before us today may not be the best document from the point of view of all concerned, but it does attempt to deal with all the questions that need answers for the elimination of the worst forms of child labour.

Our delegation has repeatedly said in all discussions, and during the negotiating process on the draft Convention and Recommendation that it was essential to focus on the objective of the entire exercise. The objective was to have a Convention which deals with the worst forms of child labour. We were, therefore, concerned during the negotiating process, when at times, we appeared to lose focus of our objective and tried to extend into areas that dealt with child labour per se and not with its worst forms only. We would sincerely hope that in the implementation of the Convention all concerned would continue to concentrate on the worst forms of child labour and not attempt to extend its import to areas that are beyond its framework.

A unanimous concern expressed by all participants during the negotiating process, that the new Convention should be flexible and not overly prescriptive, must also be borne in mind in the implementation of the Convention. Such display of flexibility by all concerned would ensure the greatest number of ratifications of the Convention by ILO constituent states. In this context, we would like to refer, once again, to the comment by the United States delegation in its submission to the Office, that any work proposed to be banned in addition to bonded labour and work in the sex and drug industries, must be of the same severity as these imminently harmful and readily identifiable categories. This comment would greatly assist us in the identification of what falls under the definition of "hazardous work". We also agree with them that the aim of the Convention clearly is the elimination of the worst forms of child labour i.e. work that is the most harmful and performed by the most vulnerable children. It is clear to us that the definition of hazardous work as included in the Recommendation being adopted with the Convention must not be interpreted loosely. It is important that each country in consultation with workers and employers determine such work, bearing in mind the economic, social and developmental levels. It is our objective to achieve the elimination of the worst forms of child labour and not to use the definition to disallow children to work with their families in the agricultural sector.

The flexibility provided in Paragraph 4 of the Recommendation with regard to the definition of the child under Article 2 of the Convention, and the importance of allowing the competent authority within a country, after consultations with workers and employers concerned, to authorize employment or work, as from the age of 16 years under specific conditions, would greatly assist developing countries. Such flexibility would ensure greater ratification.

We must also underscore the fact that a Recommendation to a Convention only provides guidance to member States on the implementation of the Convention and is not binding on them. This has been clarified in article 19 of the ILO Constitution. The Recommendation cannot be considered to become legally binding by virtue of the language in Paragraph 1 of the Recommendation which says that the provisions of this Recommendation supplement those of the Convention and should be "applied in conjunction with them". The Office has categorically confirmed this in Report IV(2A).

We fully appreciate the underlying concern to provide support and assistance to families of children involved in the worst forms of child labour. A number of programmes being undertaken in Pakistan, in the context of the elimination of child labour, do take this concern into account. It must, nevertheless, be stated for the record that some of the obligations on member States with regard to providing assistance and support to families of children may be somewhat difficult to implement, especially by developing countries.

The provisions of Article 8 of the Convention recognize the importance of shared international responsibility towards the elimination of the worst forms of child labour through programmes of cooperation and assistance. These programmes must take a holistic view of the problem of child labour. Child labour cannot be considered as an isolated tragedy that takes place without any relevance to the overall economic situation of some countries. The Preamble of the Convention recognizes the linkages between poverty and child labour and paragraph 8 of the Convention underscores the obligations at the international level to assist countries in eliminating the worst forms of child labour.

Pakistan, Mr. Chairman, is committed to the elimination of child labour. We have undertaken extensive programmes in the context of ILO-IPEC, through bilateral efforts as well as efforts by the Government and employers to deal with this problem. Out commitment to work towards the agreed target within the SARC region to eliminate child labour by the year 2010 is visible also at the highest political level. Pakistan is perhaps amongst the few countries where financial assistance is provided by the Government through its own funds to contribute towards the elimination of child labour.

We, therefore, welcome the adoption of an instrument which will assist countries in taking measures for the elimination of the worst forms of child labour. In this context, we appreciate the recognition by those involved in the work on this Convention, that child labour or even its worst forms, cannot be wished away with one stroke of the pen. We must express our appreciation to the Workers' and Employers' groups for their understanding that all cases of worst forms of child labour would not disappear immediately, but that immediate and effective measures need to be taken to secure the prohibition and subsequent elimination of the worst forms of child labour.

401. The Government member of the United Kingdom stated her support of the adoption of this new ILO Convention, and believed that it would be both effective and widely ratifiable. She noted the compromises made but did not believe they would detract from the role that the Convention would have in enhancing the protection of children affected by the worst forms of child labour, and in promoting the best interests of the child. She believed that the commitments to appropriate consultation with all groups affected by the worst forms of child labour, and to enhanced cooperation between member countries would greatly increase the possibilities for maximizing the effectiveness, efficiency and impact of national and international interventions aimed at combating the worst forms of child labour. Nevertheless, there were issues which had caused some concern. In particular, she stated that the United Kingdom cared deeply about the problem of child soldiers. She stated that the current minimum international age standard on recruitment and participation in armed conflicts was too low. The forced or compulsory recruitment of children for use in armed conflict was undoubtedly one of the worst forms of child labour and the Government member of the United Kingdom considered that this aspect of the child soldiers issue came within the ambit of the new Convention and that including it would not prejudice the work currently on the abovementioned optional protocol. The Government member of the United Kingdom believed that the enlistment of volunteers in the armed forces was fundamentally different from the abusive, exploitative, forced or coercive involvement of children in armed conflict.

402. The Government member of the United Kingdom also expressed concern about the issue of child domestic workers but she recognized that there were enormous difficulties in defining what was meant by "hidden work". She believed

that there were now provisions within the text of the Convention which would offer protection to children exploited in domestic work, and believed that implementation of the Convention would improve the possibilities for all countries to bring "hidden work" into the light and to fight against it in its worst forms. She also welcomed the strengthened references in the text to the crucial importance of education in the elimination of harmful child labour.

403. The Government member of the United States: First, let me associate myself with the remarks of the Netherlands concerning the scope and application of the Convention.

As we all know, the Committee dealt responsibly and effectively with a number of very difficult issues. We have a Convention that we can be proud of — and one that can be widely ratified.

I want to specially commend the Workers' and the Employers' groups for their ability to work together and to help keep the Government members on the right course. On issues like hazardous work, child soldiers, family and small farms, and basic education — just to name a few — it was cooperation between the workers and employers that let us agree and compromise positions and avoid potential and unnecessary obstacles. I thank Mr. Trottman and Mr. Botha for all of their efforts. We share their views and understandings. Let me also thank the Government group coordinators, especially our coordinator, Alette van Leur of the Netherlands, for their skill and dedication.

Finally, Mr. Chairman, let me thank you and the Office staff for your leadership, expertise and — not least — your patience.

404. The Government member of the Dominican Republic expressed the commitment of his Government to ratifying the Worst Forms of Child Labour Convention, 1999. He noted that all members of the Committee had the task of convincing the members of their respective law-making bodies and judiciaries to be committed to eliminating the worst forms of child labour. He stated that if any member's culture or law promoted the existence of the worst forms of child labour then they had the task of ensuring that it was changed.

405. The Government member of Chile, speaking on behalf of the Government members of Argentina and Brazil, supported the adoption of the Convention and quoted the Secretary-General who had noted the historical contribution of this Convention. He stated that they were disappointed that, despite their efforts, there had not been greater emphasis on education in the Convention. He referred to Article 32 of the United Nations Convention on the Rights of the Child and welcomed the reference in the Recommendation to adopting appropriate measures to improve the educational infrastructure and the training of teachers. He hoped the instruments would be effective in their aims and would be ratified by as many member States as possible.

406. The Government member of the Russian Federation stated that the new instruments belonged among the core standards of the ILO and were major instruments for the protection of human rights. He noted that the weakest point was the inclusion of the provision on children in armed conflict.

407. The Government representative of South Africa considered that the new Convention was a meaningful, realistic and balanced text, which accommodated all views and opinions without compromising its basic object of prohibiting and taking immediate action for the elimination of the worst forms of child labour. The Convention would strengthen and reinforce the principle of tripartism and social dialogue, which was necessary for the campaign against the worst forms of child labour. He believed that the compromise text regarding child soldiers would have some impact in removing children from armed hostilities but he would have preferred stronger language since thousands of children were forced to volunteer owing to poverty and economic necessity. He urged governments to assist the work on an optional protocol to the United Nations Convention on the Rights of the Child on the involvement of children in armed conflicts. He reiterated that new instruments supplemented Convention No. 138, which remained the fundamental instrument on the total abolition of child labour. The Convention was one of the core ILO Conventions that came within the scope of the ILO Declaration on Fundamental Principles and Rights at Work and its Follow-up. He reiterated the importance of technical cooperation, within the framework of the IPEC programme.

408. The Government member of Bolivia supported the new instruments, but stated that the issue of the age to which the provisions of the Convention applied might lead to difficulties, as national traditions and economies differed on the age at which an individual ceased to be considered a child. He considered that a clearer distinction should have been drawn between hazardous work and the exploitation of children in slavery and similar practices, in prostitution and pornography, and in illicit activities, in which the perpetrators were the criminals but the children were the victims.

409. The Government member of France stated her Government's satisfaction but felt that there remained some issues of concern, notably that of child soldiers, which had been only partially addressed. She concluded by stating that this Convention should be one of the core ILO standards which came within the scope of the ILO's Declaration on Fundamental Principles and Rights at Work and its Follow-up.

410. The Government member of Belgium supported the statement of France and stated that this Convention should be seen as a lever to the ratification and implementation of Convention No. 138, and called on members to promote its ratification and implementation.

411. The Government member of Venezuela stated that whilst he welcomed the new Convention he regretted that some basic principles had not been included. He agreed with the Government member of Chile that the exclusion of a reference to the systematic denial of access to basic education in the definition of the worst forms of child labour was a particular shortcoming. He noted that, while areas such as prostitution, slavery and trafficking, and involvement in illicit activities were, on the whole, already legislated against, the definition of hazardous work was not: He concluded that for action against the worst forms of child labour to be implemented effectively, workers' and employers' organizations would have to be consulted.

412. The Government member of Morocco endorsed the statement of the Government member of Ethiopia speaking on behalf of the members of the African Group on the Committee. He welcomed, in particular, the commitment expressed with regard to international cooperation and/or assistance for national efforts aimed at eliminating the worst forms of child labour, but stated that this should not be conducted in such a way that it interfered with national efforts.

413. The Government member of Italy supported the statement of the Government member of the Netherlands on behalf of the members of the IMEC Group on the Committee. He said that he would have preferred to have seen the Committee move further forward on the issue of child soldiers but was happy that the United Nations Working Groups' work on an optional protocol to the United Nations Convention on the Rights of the Child on involvement of children in armed conflicts was continuing to address this issue. He concluded by appealing for universal ratification.

414. The Government member of Cuba supported the adoption of the Convention and Recommendation. However she had reservations about the manner in which the issue of children in armed conflict was addressed, as she considered that all involvement of children in armed conflicts should have been banned. However, work on an optional protocol to the United Nations Convention on the Rights of the Child on involvement of children in armed conflict would continue to strive towards this end. She commented that the involvement of children in the worst forms of child labour was a problem affecting every country, regardless of the level of development. Whilst poverty was not the only causal factor for this, there was a direct relationship between poverty and the worst forms of child labour. Support through international assistance and cooperation was necessary, and, together with national action, would help overcome the difficulties of the elimination of the worst forms of child labour.

415. The Government member of Algeria stated that adoption of a new Convention and Recommendation on the worst forms of child labour was coming at a very difficult time in her country and great efforts would be required to implement the provisions of the Convention. In particular, there was a great

need for technical cooperation and her Government regretted that, in this context, not enough emphasis had been placed on this subject.

416. The Government member of Lebanon expressed that the term "child" as indicating a person who is under the age of 18 is not in consistency with the terms used in the Lebanese Labour Code whereby a person between the ages of 14 and 18 is called adolescent and children under the age of 14 are prohibited to work. The Government member of Lebanon also stated that the provisions of point 4 of the Recommendation should have been a subparagraph of Article 3 of the Convention as was the case with Article 3, paragraph 3, of Convention No. 138.

She also expressed her opinion that reference to relevant international standards in Article 4 of the Convention was not welcomed since Conventions are initially independent. Such reference could be made in the Preamble which has actually recognized relevant international labour standards. She thanked the Legal Adviser for his legal opinion and considered that they should be the basis for future interpretations. On point 15(d) she stated that bilateral agreements should be signed if extradition was to be considered, and wondered whether the questions of extra-territoriality or double conviction could be raised in this respect. She raised concern on the linkage between the Convention and the Recommendation as stated in the Preamble of the Recommendation: "in conjunction". She further noted that it would have been preferable had the Convention defined the scope for its application to avoid future misinterpretations.

417. The Government member of Paraguay, speaking on behalf of the countries of MERCOSUR (Argentina, Brazil, Paraguay and Uruguay) commented that the Ministers of Labour for these countries had, on 8 June 1999, signed a Declaration to strengthen their Governments' commitment to the elimination of the worst forms of child labour.

418. The Government member of Rwanda expressed his Government's support for a new Convention. Its full implementation required the full involvement of social partners, and in this context there was an important role to be played by NGOs as they were often in the best possible position to reach those children involved in the worst forms of child labour. NGOs should therefore be involved in all measures targeting the worst forms of child labour.

419. The Government member of Egypt referred to his previous concluding intervention and the need for efforts at all levels aimed at the elimination of all forms of child labour through the eradication of poverty. He stated that this Convention did not include domestic work, nor did it cover the issue of denial of access to education. He strongly supported the new Convention and believed that it complemented Convention No. 138. Its ratification should not weaken the resolve of member States to ratify the minimum age Convention. He reaffirmed Egypt's commitment to ban the worst forms of child labour.

420. Before it was adopted, the Reporter presented the report of the Committee's work which synthesized the discussion and contained the text of the draft Convention and Recommendation. She introduced it as a comprehensive account of the Committee's work which historians and legal experts would be able to use to understand the context within which the Convention was developed.

421. The Reporter pointed out that the Drafting Committee had considered questions which the Committee had referred to it and had made some drafting changes to the proposed Convention and Recommendation. Most of these were linguistic or stylistic, or were intended to align the English and French versions of the text.

422. The first change was in Article 7, paragraph 2(b), where the text was edited to clarify the reference to the removal of children from the worst forms of child labour and for their rehabilitation and social reintegration. Among the drafting changes to align the French and English texts, the Drafting Committee felt that the reference to "de toute urgence" in Article 1 should also be at the end of the sentence as in the English text; that the complete French phrase of "the worst forms of child labour", that is "les pire formes de travail des enfants", should be used; and in Article 7, paragraph 1, it was felt that "par l'établissement et l'application de sanctions pénales" better captured the meaning of the English text which read "including the provision and application of penal sanctions".

423. In the Recommendation, the Drafting Committee was concerned about both the use and translation of "the girl child" in Paragraph 2(b)(ii). Members were conscious that the term "girl child" had a narrower interpretation in the United Nations parlance than what was intended by the Committee in the context of the new draft instruments. It was clear in English that it applied to all girls under the age of 18, but the French translation might have implied a younger age. The Drafting Committee therefore translated "the girl child" into French to read "aux enfants de sexe féminin" which was considered to be accurate to the intention of the Committee.

424. In Paragraph 14, the Drafting Committee had qualified the word "remedies" to read "criminal, civil or administrative remedies" because it became clear that without such qualification, the interpretation could be different in different legal systems. The Drafting Committee had also redrafted Paragraph 15(k) which was a little longer than the amended text proposed but expressed more clearly the intentions of the Committee.

425. The Chairperson thanked the members of the Committee for their cooperation, constructive spirit and seriousness of purpose. He expressed great satisfaction and joy for the work carried out and underscored the fact that the Committee had reached a full consensus on the adoption of the instruments.

426. The report of the Committee and the proposed Convention and

Recommendation concerning the prohibition and immediate action for the elimination of the worst forms of child labour are submitted for consideration.

Geneva, 14 June 1999.

(Signed) A. Atsain,
Chairperson.

M. Niven,
Reporter.

1. The modifications were as follows:

(a) 3 June: 232 members (99 Governments entitled to vote with 1,378 votes each, 53 Employer members with 2,574 votes each and 78 Worker members with 1,749 votes each);

(b) 4 June: 205 members (106 Governments entitled to vote with 22 votes each, 53 Employer members with 44 votes each and 44 Worker members with 53 votes each);

(c) 5 June: 192 members (105 Governments entitled to vote with 1,763 votes each, 43 Employer members with 4,305 votes each and 41 Worker members with 4,515 votes each);

(d) 7 June: 192 members (106 Governments entitled to vote with 1,763 votes each, 43 Employer members with 4,346 votes each and 41 Worker members with 4,558 votes each);

(e) 8 June: 186 members (108 Governments entitled to vote with 119 votes each, 42 Employer members with 306 votes each and 34 Worker members with 378 votes each);

(f) 9 June: 179 members (110 Governments entitled to vote with 111 votes each, 37 Employer members with 330 votes each and 30 Worker members with 407 votes each);

(g) 10 June: 179 members (111 Governments entitled to vote with 532 votes each, 38 Employer members with 1,554 votes each and 28 Worker members with 2,109 votes each);

(h) 11 June: 174 members (111 Governments entitled to vote with 300 votes each, 36 Employer members with 925 votes each and 25 Worker members with 1,332 votes each);

(i) 14 June: 173 members (111 Governments entitled to vote with 175 votes each, 35 Employer members with 555 votes each and 25 Worker members with 777 votes each).

A. Proposed Convention Concerning the Prohibition and Immediate Action for the Elimination of the Worst Forms of Child Labour

The General Conference of the International Labour Organization,

Having been convened at Geneva by the Governing Body of the International Labour Office, and having met in its 87th Session on 1 June 1999, and

Considering the need to adopt new instruments for the prohibition and elimination of the worst forms of child labour, as the main priority for national and international action, including international cooperation and assistance, to complement the Convention and Recommendation concerning minimum age for admission to employment, 1973, which remain fundamental instruments on child labour, and

Considering that the effective elimination of the worst forms of child labour requires immediate and comprehensive action, taking into account the importance of free basic education and the need to remove the children concerned from all such work and to provide for their rehabilitation and social integration while addressing the needs of their families, and

Recalling the resolution concerning the elimination of child labour adopted by the International Labour Conference at its 83rd Session in 1996, and

Recognizing that child labour is to a great extent caused by poverty and that the long-term solution lies in sustained economic growth leading to social progress, in particular poverty alleviation and universal education, and

Recalling the Convention on the Rights of the Child adopted by the United Nations General Assembly on 20 November 1989, and

Recalling the ILO Declaration on Fundamental Principles and Rights at Work and its Follow-up, adopted by the International Labour Conference at its 86th Session in 1998, and

Recalling that some of the worst forms of child labour are covered by other international instruments, in particular the Forced Labour Convention, 1930, and the United Nations Supplementary Convention on the Abolition of Slavery, the Slave Trade, and Institutions and Practices Similar to Slavery, 1956, and

Having decided upon the adoption of certain proposals with regard to child labour, which is the fourth item on the agenda of the session, and

Having determined that these proposals shall take the form of an international Convention;

adopts this ... day of June of the year one thousand nine hundred and ninety-nine the following Convention, which may be cited as the Worst Forms of Child Labour Convention, 1999.

Article 1

Each Member which ratifies this Convention shall take immediate and effective measures to secure the prohibition and elimination of the worst forms of child labour as a matter of urgency.

Article 2

For the purposes of this Convention, the term "child" shall apply to all persons under the age of 18.

Article 3

For the purposes of this Convention, the expression "the worst forms of child labour" comprises:

(a) all forms of slavery or practices similar to slavery, such as the sale and trafficking of children, debt bondage and serfdom and forced or compulsory labour, including forced or compulsory recruitment of children for use in armed conflict;

(b) the use, procuring or offering of a child for prostitution, for the production of pornography or for pornographic performances;

(c) the use, procuring or offering of a child for illicit activities, in particular for the production and trafficking of drugs as defined in the relevant international treaties;

(d) work which, by its nature or the circumstances in which it is carried out, is likely to harm the health, safety or morals of children.

Article 4

1. The types of work referred to under Article 3(d) shall be determined by national laws or regulations or by the competent authority, after consultation with the organizations of employers and workers concerned, taking into consideration relevant international standards, in particular Paragraphs 3 and 4 of the Worst Forms of Child Labour Recommendation, 1999.

2. The competent authority, after consultation with the organizations of employers and workers concerned, shall identify where the types of work so determined exist.

3. The list of the types of work determined under paragraph 1 of this Article shall be periodically examined and revised as necessary, in consultation with the organizations of employers and workers concerned.

Article 5

Each Member shall, after consultation with employers' and workers' organizations, establish or designate appropriate mechanisms to monitor the implementation of the provisions giving effect to this Convention.

Article 6

1. Each Member shall design and implement programmes of action to eliminate as a priority the worst forms of child labour.

2. Such programmes of action shall be designed and implemented in consultation with relevant government institutions and employers' and workers' organizations, taking into consideration the views of other concerned groups as appropriate.

Article 7

1. Each Member shall take all necessary measures to ensure the effective implementation and enforcement of the provisions giving effect to this Convention including the provision and application of penal sanctions or, as appropriate, other sanctions.

2. Each Member shall, taking into account the importance of education in eliminating child labour, take effective and time-bound measures to:

(a) prevent the engagement of children in the worst forms of child labour;

(b) provide the necessary and appropriate direct assistance for the removal of children from the worst forms of child labour and for their rehabilitation and social integration;

(c) ensure access to free basic education, and, wherever possible and appropriate, vocational training, for all children removed from the worst forms of child labour;

(d) identify and reach out to children at special risk; and

(e) take account of the special situation of girls.

3. Each Member shall designate the competent authority responsible for the implementation of the provisions giving effect to this Convention.

Article 8

Members shall take appropriate steps to assist one another in giving effect to the provisions of this Convention through enhanced international cooperation and/or assistance including support for social and economic development, poverty eradication programmes and universal education.

B. Proposed Recommendation Concerning the Prohibition and Immediate Action for the Elimination of the Worst Forms of Child Labour

The General Conference of the International Labour Organization,

Having been convened at Geneva by the Governing Body of the International Labour Office, and having met in its 87th Session on 1 June 1999, and

Having adopted the Worst Forms of Child Labour Convention, 1999, and

Having decided upon the adoption of certain proposals with regard to child labour, which is the fourth item on the agenda of the session, and

Having determined that these proposals shall take the form of a Recommendation supplementing the Worst Forms of Child Labour Convention, 1999;

adopts this ... day of June of the year one thousand nine hundred and ninety-nine the following Recommendation, which may be cited as the Worst Forms of Child Labour Recommendation, 1999.

1. The provisions of this Recommendation supplement those of the Worst Forms of Child Labour Convention, 1999 (hereafter referred to as "the Convention"), and should be applied in conjunction with them.

I. Programmes of Action

2. The programmes of action referred to in Article 6 of the Convention should be designed and implemented as a matter of urgency, in consultation with relevant government institutions and employers' and workers' organizations, taking into consideration the views of the children directly affected by the worst forms of child labour, their families and, as appropriate, other concerned groups committed to the aims of the Convention and this Recommendation. Such programmes should aim at, inter alia:

(a) identifying and denouncing the worst forms of child labour;

(b) preventing the engagement of children in or removing them from the worst forms of child labour, protecting them from reprisals and providing for their rehabilitation and social integration through measures which address their educational, physical and psychological needs;

(c) giving special attention to:

(i) younger children;

(ii) the girl child;

(iii) the problem of hidden work situations, in which girls are at special risk;

(iv) other groups of children with special vulnerabilities or needs;

(d) identifying, reaching out to and working with communities where children are at special risk;

(e) informing, sensitizing and mobilizing public opinion and concerned groups, including children and their families.

II. Hazardous Work

3. In determining the types of work referred to under Article 3(d) of the Convention, and in identifying where they exist, consideration should be given, inter alia, to:

(a) work which exposes children to physical, psychological or sexual abuse;

(b) work underground, under water, at dangerous heights or in confined spaces;

(c) work with dangerous machinery, equipment and tools, or which involves the manual handling or transport of heavy loads;

(d) work in an unhealthy environment which may, for example, expose children to hazardous substances, agents or processes, or to temperatures, noise levels, or vibrations damaging to their health;

(e) work under particularly difficult conditions such as work for long hours or during the night or work where the child is unreasonably confined to the premises of the employer.

4. For the types of work referred to under Article 3(d) of the Convention and Paragraph 3 above, national laws or regulations or the competent authority could, after consultation with the workers' and employers' organizations concerned, authorize employment or work as from the age of 16 on condition that the health, safety and morals of the children concerned are fully protected, and that the children have received adequate specific instruction or vocational training in the relevant branch of activity.

III. Implementation

5. (1) Detailed information and statistical data on the nature and extent of child labour should be compiled and kept up to date to serve as a basis for determining priorities for national action for the abolition of child labour, in particular for the prohibition and elimination of its worst forms as a matter of urgency.

(2) As far as possible, such information and statistical data should include data disaggregated by sex, age group, occupation, branch of economic activity, status in employment, school attendance and geographical location. The importance of an effective system of birth registration, including the issuing of birth certificates, should be taken into account.

(3) Relevant data concerning violations of national provisions for the prohibition and elimination of the worst forms of child labour should be compiled and kept up to date.

6. The compilation and processing of the information and data referred to in Paragraph 5 above should be carried out with due regard for the right to privacy.

7. The information compiled under Paragraph 5 above should be communicated to the International Labour Office on a regular basis.

8. Members should establish or designate appropriate national mechanisms to monitor the implementation of national provisions for the prohibition and elimination of the worst forms of child labour after consultation with employers' and workers' organizations.

9. Members should ensure that the competent authorities which have responsibilities for implementing national provisions for the prohibition and elimination of the worst forms of child labour cooperate with each other and coordinate their activities.

10. National laws or regulations or the competent authority should determine the persons to be held responsible in the event of non-compliance with national provisions for the prohibition and elimination of the worst forms of child labour.

11. Members should, in so far as it is compatible with national law, cooperate with international efforts aimed at the prohibition and elimination of the worst forms of child labour as a matter of urgency by:

(a) gathering and exchanging information concerning criminal offences, including those involving international networks;
(b) detecting and prosecuting those involved in the sale and trafficking of children, or in the use, procuring or offering of children for illicit activities, for prostitution, for the production of pornography or for pornographic performances;
(c) registering perpetrators of such offences.

12. Members should provide that the following worst forms of child labour are criminal offences:

(a) all forms of slavery or practices similar to slavery, such as the sale and trafficking of children, debt bondage and serfdom and forced or compulsory labour, including forced or compulsory recruitment of children for use in armed conflict;
(b) the use, procuring or offering of a child for prostitution, for the production of pornography or for pornographic performances; and
(c) the use, procuring or offering of a child for illicit activities, in particular for the production and trafficking of drugs as defined in the relevant international treaties, or for activities which involve the unlawful carrying or use of firearms or other weapons.

13. Members should ensure that penalties including, where appropriate, criminal penalties are applied for violations of the national provisions for the prohibition and elimination of any type of work referred to in Article 3(d) of the Convention.

14. Members should also provide as a matter of urgency for other criminal, civil or administrative remedies, where appropriate, to ensure the effective enforcement of national provisions for the prohibition and elimination of the worst forms of child labour, such as special supervision of enterprises which have used the worst forms of child labour, and, in cases of persistent violation, consideration of temporary or permanent revoking of permits to operate.

15. Other measures aimed at the prohibition and elimination of the worst forms of child labour might include the following:

(a) informing, sensitizing and mobilizing the general public, including national and local political leaders, parliamentarians and the judiciary;

(b) involving and training employers' and workers' organizations and civic organizations;

(c) providing appropriate training for the government officials concerned, especially inspectors and law enforcement officials, and for other relevant professionals;

(d) providing for the prosecution in their own country of the Member's nationals who commit offences under its national provisions for the prohibition and immediate elimination of the worst forms of child labour even when these offences are committed in another country;

(e) simplifying legal and administrative procedures and ensuring that they are appropriate and prompt;

(f) encouraging the development of policies by undertakings to promote the aims of the Convention;

(g) monitoring and giving publicity to best practices on the elimination of child labour;

(h) giving publicity to legal or other provisions on child labour in the different languages or dialects;

(i) establishing special complaints procedures and making provisions to protect from discrimination and reprisals those who legitimately expose violations of the provisions of the Convention, as well as establishing helplines or points of contact and ombudspersons;

(j) adopting appropriate measures to improve the educational infrastructure and the training of teachers to meet the needs of boys and girls;

(k) as far as possible taking into account, in national programmes of action, the need for job creation and vocational training for the parents and adults in the families of children working in the conditions covered by the Convention, and the need for sensitizing parents on the problem of children working in such conditions.

16. Enhanced international cooperation and/or assistance among Members for the prohibition and effective elimination of the worst forms of child labour should complement national efforts and may, as appropriate, be developed and implemented in consultation with employers' and workers' organizations. Such international cooperation and/or assistance should include:

(a) mobilizing resources for national or international programmes;

(b) mutual legal assistance;

(c) technical assistance including the exchange of information;

(d) support for social and economic development, poverty eradication programmes and universal education.

REPORT IV (2 B): CHILD LABOUR

Fourth Item on the Agenda

International Labour Office Geneva

87th Session Geneva, June 1999

Introduction

The first discussion of the question of child labour took place at the 86th Session (1998) of the International Labour Conference (ILC). Following that discussion, and in accordance with article 39 of the Standing Orders of the Conference, the International Labour Office prepared and communicated to the governments of members States a report containing a proposed Convention and a proposed Recommendation concerning the prohibition and immediate elimination of the worst forms of child labour, based on the conclusions adopted by the Conference at its 86th Session.

Governments were invited to send any amendments or comments they might wish to make so as to reach the Office by 30 November 1998 at the latest, or to inform it, by the same date, whether they considered that the proposed texts constituted a satisfactory basis for discussion by the Conference at its 87th Session (1999).

At the time of drawing up this report, the Office had received replies from the governments of the following 83 members States: Argentina, Australia, Austria, Bahrain, Bangladesh, Belarus, Belgium, Benin, Bolivia, Botswana, Brazil, Bulgaria, Canada, Cape Verde, Chile, China, Colombia, Croatia, Cyprus, Czech Republic, Denmark, Ecuador, Egypt, El Salvador, Estonia, Ethiopia, Finland, France, Germany, Greece, Haiti, Hungary, India, Indonesia, Ireland, Italy, Japan, Jordan, Kenya, Republic of Korea, Kuwait, Latvia, Lebanon, Madagascar, Malaysia, Mali, Mauritius, Mexico, Morocco, Myanmar, Netherlands, New Zealand, Norway, Pakistan, Peru, Poland, Portugal, Qatar, Romania, Saudi Arabia, Senegal, Slovakia, South Africa, Spain, Sri Lanka, Sudan, Sweden, Switzerland, Syrian Arab Republic, United Republic of Tanzania, Thailand, Togo, Tunisia, Turkey, Uganda, Ukraine, United Arab Emirates, United Kingdom, United States, Venezuela, Yemen, Zambia, Zimbabwe and the Holy See.

In accordance with article 39, paragraph 6, of the Standing Orders of the Conference, governments were requested to consult the most representative organizations of employers and workers before finalizing their replies and to indicate which organizations were consulted.

The governments of the following 49 member States (Bangladesh, Belarus, Belgium, Benin, Brazil, Bulgaria, Canada, Chile, China, Croatia, Cyprus, Czech Republic, Denmark, Egypt, El Salvador, Estonia, Finland, France, Germany, Greece, Hungary, Indonesia, Ireland, Italy, Japan, Jordan, Kenya, Republic of Korea, Latvia, Mauritius, Myanmar, Netherlands, New Zealand, Norway, Portugal, Slovakia, South Africa, Spain, Sweden, Switzerland, Syrian Arab Republic, United Republic of Tanzania, Togo, Turkey, United Arab Emirates, United Kingdom, United States, Venezuela, Zimbabwe) stated that the most representative organizations of employers and workers had been consulted.

In the case of the following 37 member States the replies of employers' and workers' organizations were incorporated into those of the government, were appended or were communicated directly to the Office: Bangladesh, Belarus, Belgium, Brazil, Bulgaria, Canada, Chile, Croatia, Czech Republic, Denmark, Egypt, Estonia, Finland, France, Germany, Greece, Hungary, Indonesia, Ireland, Italy, Japan, Jordan, Kenya, Republic of Korea, Netherlands, New Zealand, Norway, Portugal, South Africa, Spain, Sweden, Switzerland, Syrian Arab Republic, Turkey, United States, Venezuela, Zimbabwe.

The United Nations Committee on the Rights of the Child formulated comments during its 20th Session.

To ensure that the texts in English and French of the proposed Convention and the proposed Recommendation concerning the prohibition and immediate elimination of the worst forms of child labour are in the hands of governments within the time-limit laid down in article 39, paragraph 7, of the Standing Orders of the Conference, Report IV (2) is published in two volumes. The present bilingual volume (Report IV (2 B)) contains the English and French versions of the proposed texts, amended in the light of the observations made by governments and by employers' and workers' organizations and for the reasons set out in the Office commentaries. In addition, some slight changes were made, where appropriate, in the wording of the texts, mainly to ensure full convergence between the two versions of the proposed instruments. If the Conference so decides, these texts will serve as a basis for the second discussion, at the 87th Session (1999), of the question of child labour.

PROPOSED TEXT

The following are the English versions of (A) the proposed Convention concerning the prohibition and immediate elimination of the worst forms of child labour, and (B) the proposed Recommendation concerning the prohibition and immediate elimination of the worst forms of child labour, which are submitted as a basis for discussion of the fourth item on the agenda of the 87th Session of the Conference.

A. Proposed Convention Concerning the Prohibition and Immediate Elimination of the Worst Forms of Child Labour

The General Conference of the International Labour Organization,

Having been convened at Geneva by the Governing Body of the International Labour Office, and having met in its 87th Session on 1 June 1999, and

Considering the need to adopt new instruments for the prohibition and effective elimination of the worst forms of child labour, as the main priority for national and international action, to complement the Convention and Recommendation concerning Minimum Age for Admission to Employment, 1973, which remain the fundamental instruments with a view to achieving the total abolition of child labour, and

Considering that the effective elimination of the worst forms of child labour requires immediate and comprehensive action, taking into account the importance of basic education and the need to remove the concerned children from work and to provide for their rehabilitation and social reintegration, and

Recalling the Convention on the Rights of the Child adopted by the United Nations General Assembly on 20 November 1989, and

Recalling that some of the worst forms of child labour are covered by other international instruments, in particular the Forced Labour Convention, 1930, and the United Nations Supplementary Convention on the Abolition of Slavery, the Slave Trade, and Institutions and Practices Similar to Slavery, 1956, and

Recalling the relevant provisions of the Labour Inspection Convention, 1947, and the Human Resources Development Convention and Recommendation, 1975, and

Recalling the Declaration on Equality of Opportunity and Treatment for Women Workers, adopted by the International Labour Conference in 1975, as well as the Copenhagen Declaration on Social Development and the Programme of Action of the World Summit for Social Development, 1995, and the Beijing Declaration and Platform for Action of the Fourth World Conference on Women, 1995, and

Having decided upon the adoption of certain proposals with regard to child labour, which is the fourth item on the agenda of the session, and

Having determined that these proposals shall take the form of an international Convention;

adopts this day of June of the year one thousand nine hundred and ninety-nine the following Convention, which may be cited as the Immediate Abolition of the Worst Forms of Child Labour Convention, 1999.

Article 1

Each Member which ratifies this Convention shall take measures to secure the prohibition and immediate elimination of the worst forms of child labour.

Article 2

For the purposes of this Convention, the term "child" shall apply to all persons under the age of 18.

Article 3

For the purposes of this Convention, the expression "the worst forms of child labour" comprises:

(a) all forms of slavery or practices similar to slavery, such as the sale and trafficking of children, forced or compulsory labour, debt bondage and serfdom;

(b) the use, procuring or offering of a child for prostitution, for the production of pornography or for pornographic performances;

(c) the use, procuring or offering of a child for illicit activities, in particular for the production and trafficking of drugs as defined in the relevant international treaties;

(d) work which, by its nature or the circumstances in which it is carried out, is likely to jeopardize the health, safety or morals of children.

Article 4

1. The types of work referred to under Article 3 (d) shall be determined by national laws or regulations or by the competent authority, after consultation with the organizations of employers and workers concerned, taking into account relevant international standards.

2. The competent authority, after consultation with the organizations of employers and workers concerned, shall identify where the types of work so determined exist.

3. The list of the types of work determined under paragraph 1 of this Article shall be periodically examined and revised as necessary, after consultation with the organizations of employers and workers concerned.

Article 5

Each Member shall establish or designate appropriate mechanisms to monitor the implementation of the provisions giving effect to this Convention.

Article 6

1. Each Member shall design and implement programmes of action to eliminate as a priority the worst forms of child labour.

2. Such programmes of action shall be designed and implemented in consultation with relevant government institutions and employers' and workers' organizations.

Article 7

1. Each Member shall take all necessary measures to ensure the effective implementation and enforcement of the provisions giving effect to this Convention including the provision and application of penal sanctions or, as appropriate, other sanctions.

2. Each Member shall, taking into account the importance of education in eliminating child labour, take effective and time-bound measures to:

(a) prevent children from engaging in the worst forms of child labour;

(b) provide the necessary and appropriate direct assistance for their removal from work, rehabilitation and social reintegration through, inter alia, access to free basic education;

(c) identify and reach out to children at special risk; and

(d) take account of the special situation of girls.

3. Each Member shall designate the competent authority responsible for the implementation of the provisions giving effect to this Convention.

Article 8

Members shall take steps, as appropriate, to assist one another in giving effect to the provisions of this Convention through international cooperation or assistance.

B. Proposed Recommendation Concerning the Prohibition and Immediate Elimination of the Worst Forms of Child Labour

The General Conference of the International Labour Organization,

Having been convened at Geneva by the Governing Body of the International Labour Office, and having met in its 87th Session on 1 June 1999, and

Having adopted the Immediate Abolition of the Worst Forms of Child Labour Convention, 1999, and

Having decided upon the adoption of certain proposals with regard to child labour, which is the fourth item on the agenda of the session, and

Having determined that these proposals shall take the form of a Recommendation supplementing the Immediate Abolition of the Worst Forms of Child Labour Convention, 1999;

adopts this day of June of the year one thousand nine hundred and ninety-nine the following Recommendation, which may be cited as the Immediate Abolition of the Worst Forms of Child Labour Recommendation, 1999.

1. The provisions of this Recommendation supplement those of the Immediate Abolition of the Worst Forms of Child Labour Convention, 1999 (hereafter referred to as "the Convention"), and should be applied in conjunction with them.

I. Programmes of action

2. The programmes of action referred to in Article 6 of the Convention should be designed and implemented in consultation with relevant government institutions, employers' and workers' organizations and, as appropriate, other concerned groups. They should aim at, inter alia:

(a) identifying and denouncing the worst forms of child labour;

(b) preventing children from engaging in or removing them from the worst forms of child labour, protecting them from reprisals and providing for their rehabilitation and social reintegration through measures which address their educational, physical, emotional and psychological needs;

(c) giving special attention to:

(i) younger children;

(ii) the problem of hidden work situations, in which girls are at special risk;

(iii) other groups of children with special vulnerabilities or needs;

(d) identifying and reaching out to communities where children are at special risk;

(e) informing, sensitizing and mobilizing public opinion and concerned groups, including children and their families.

II. Hazardous Work

3. In determining the types of work referred to under Article 3(d) of the Convention, and in identifying where they exist, consideration should be given, as a minimum, to:

(a) work which exposes children to physical, emotional or sexual abuse;

(b) work underground, under water, at dangerous heights or in confined spaces;

(c) work with dangerous machinery, equipment and tools, or which involves the manual handling or transport of heavy loads;

(d) work in an unhealthy environment which may, for example, expose children to hazardous substances, agents or processes, or to temperatures, noise levels, or vibrations damaging to their health;

(e) work under particularly difficult conditions such as work for long hours or during the night or work which does not allow for the possibility of returning home each day.

III. Implementation

4. (1) Detailed information and statistical data on the nature and extent of child labour should be compiled and kept up to date to serve as a basis for determining priorities for national action for the abolition of child labour, in particular for the prohibition and immediate elimination of its worst forms.

(2) As far as possible, such information and statistical data should include data disaggregated by sex, age group, occupation, branch of economic activity and status in employment.

(3) Relevant data concerning violations of national provisions for the prohibition and immediate elimination of the worst forms of child labour should be compiled and kept up to date.

5. The compilation and processing of the information and data referred to in Paragraph 4 above should be carried out with due regard for the right to privacy.

6. The information compiled under Paragraph 4 should be communicated to the International Labour Office on a regular basis.

7. Members should establish or designate appropriate national mechanisms to monitor the implementation of national provisions for the prohibition and immediate elimination of the worst forms of child labour after consultation with employers' and workers' organizations and, as appropriate, other concerned groups.

8. Members should ensure that the competent authorities which have responsibilities for implementing national provisions for the prohibition and immediate elimination of the worst forms of child labour cooperate with each other and coordinate their activities.

9. National laws or regulations or the competent authority should determine the persons to be held responsible in the event of non-compliance with national provisions for the prohibition and immediate elimination of the worst forms of child labour.

10. Members should, in so far as it is compatible with national law, cooperate with international efforts aimed at the prohibition and immediate elimination of the worst forms of child labour by:

(a) gathering and exchanging information concerning criminal offences, including those involving international networks;

(b) detecting and prosecuting those involved in the sale and trafficking of children, or in the use, procuring or offering of children for illicit activities, for prostitution, for the production of pornography or for pornographic performances;

(c) registering perpetrators of such offences.

11. Members should provide that the following worst forms of child labour are criminal offences:

(a) all forms of slavery or practices similar to slavery, such as the sale and trafficking of children, forced or compulsory labour, debt bondage and serfdom;

(b) the use, procuring or offering of a child for prostitution, for the production of pornography or for pornographic performances; and

(c) the use, procuring or offering of a child for illicit activities, in particular for the production and trafficking of drugs as defined in the relevant international treaties.

12. Members should ensure that penalties including, where appropriate, criminal penalties are applied for violations of the national provisions for the prohibition and immediate elimination of any type of work referred to in Article 3(d) of the Convention.

13. Members should also provide for other remedies, where appropriate, to ensure the effective enforcement of national provisions for the prohibition and immediate elimination of the worst forms of child labour.

14. Other measures aimed at the prohibition and immediate elimination of the worst forms of child labour might include the following:

(a) informing and sensitizing the general public, including national and local political leaders, parliamentarians and the judiciary;

(b) involving and training employers' and workers' organizations and civic organizations;

(c) providing appropriate training for concerned government officials, especially inspectors and law enforcement officials, and for other relevant professionals;

(d) providing for the prosecution in their own country of the Members' nationals who commit offences under national provisions for the prohibition and immediate elimination of the worst forms of child labour even when these offences are committed in another country;

(e) simplifying legal and administrative procedures and ensuring that they are appropriate and prompt;

(f) giving publicity to best practices on child labour;

(g) giving publicity to legal or other provisions on child labour in the different languages or dialects;

(h) establishing special complaints procedures and making provisions to protect those who legitimately expose violations of the provisions of the Convention from discrimination and reprisals, as well as establishing help lines or points of contact and ombudspersons.

15. International cooperation or assistance among Members for the prohibition and immediate elimination of the worst forms of child labour should include:

(a) mobilizing resources for national or international programmes;

(b) mutual legal assistance;

(c) technical assistance including the exchange of information.

8

Select National Laws on Child Labour

U.S. DEPARTMENT OF LABOUR: BUREAU OF INTERNATIONAL LABOUR AFFAIRS

Introduction

This report on the laws of Australia governing exploitative child labor has been prepared pursuant to section 2102(c)(9) of the Trade Act of 2002 ("Trade Act") (Pub. L. No. 107-210). Section 2102(c)(9) provides that the President shall:

> with respect to any trade agreement which the President seeks to implement under trade authorities procedures, submit to the Congress a report describing the extent to which the country or countries that are parties to the agreement have in effect laws governing exploitative child labor.

The President, by Executive Order 13277 (67 Fed. Reg. 70305), assigned his responsibilities under section 2102(c)(9) of the Trade Act to the Secretary of Labor, and provided that they be carried out in consultation with the Secretary of State and the United States Trade Representative. The Secretary of Labor subsequently provided that such responsibilities would be carried out by the Secretary of State, the United States Trade Representative and the Secretary of Labor. (67 Fed. Reg. 77812). For information on the incidence and nature of child labor in Australia and government efforts to eliminate the worst forms of child labor, please see the U.S. Department of Labor's"Australia: Labor Rights Report."

Exploitative Child Labor

There is no universally accepted definition of the term "exploitative child labor." Under article 2(3) of the International Labor Organization (ILO) Convention 138, Minimum Age for Admission to Employment, the minimum age of admission into employment or work in any occupation "shall not be less than the age of completion of compulsory schooling and, in any case, shall not be less than 15."

Countries whose economy and educational facilities are insufficiently developed may initially specify a minimum legal working age of 14 when ratifying the convention. Additionally, under article 7(1), "National laws or regulations may permit the employment or work of persons 13 to 15 years of age on light work which is – (a) not likely to be harmful to their health ordevelopment; and (b) not such as to prejudice their attendance at school, their participation in vocational orientation or training programmes approved by the competent authority or their capacity to benefit from the instruction received." Countries that have specified a minimum legal working age of 14 may permit the employment or work of persons 12 to 14 years of age on light work as defined in article 7(1). Examples of such light work may include work in a family business, on a family farm, after school, or in legitimate apprenticeship opportunities that is not hazardous and that does not affect a child's attendance at school.

While there is no universal definition for exploitative child labor, the ILO has defined the "worst forms" of child labor in ILO Convention 182, Worst Forms of Child Labor. Under article 3 of ILO Convention 182, "the term the worst forms of child labour comprises" 3

(a) all forms of slavery or practices similar to slavery, such as the sale and trafficking of children, debt bondage and serfdom and forced or compulsory labour, including forced or compulsory recruitment of children for use in armed conflict;

(b) the use, procuring or offering of a child for prostitution, for the production of pornography or for pornographic performances;

(c) the use, procuring or offering of a child for illicit activities in particular for the production and trafficking of drugs as defined in the relevant international treaties;

(d) work which, by its nature or the circumstances in which it is carried out, is likely to harm the health, safety or morals of children.

According to Convention 182, the types of work referred to under article 3(d) "shall be determined by national laws or regulations or by the competent authority..." Article 2 of the convention states that "the term child shall apply to all persons under the age of 18."

This report relies on information obtained from the Department of State, the U.S. Embassy in Australia, and other U.S. Government reports. It also relies on a wide variety of reports and materials originating from Australia, international organizations, and non-governmental organizations (NGOs), as well as consultations held by Department of Labor officials with Australian government officials, representatives of worker and employment organizations, and NGOs pursuant to section 2102(c)(7) of the Trade Act.2 The report also makes use of information submitted in response to a Department request for public comment published in the Federal Register.

Child Labor Laws and Enforcement

While there is no federal legislation in Australia setting a minimum age for employment,4states and territories regulate the employment of children through laws setting minimumages for leaving compulsory education, claiming unemployment benefits, and entering into certain occupations. Additionally, many certified collective bargaining agreements and awards by the Australian Industrial Relations Commission (AIRC) and State Industrial Relations Commissions (IRC) regulate various aspects of the employment of children and young people. State laws place responsibilities on employers regarding occupational health and safety for young people.6In 2001 and 2003, laws enacted in the States of Victoria and New South Wales strengthened protections for children in the workplace, and Victoria increased fines for child labor abuses.

There are no federal laws explicitly prohibiting forced or bonded labor. However, conditions amounting to slavery carry a penalty of up to 25 years imprisonment under the Criminal Code Amendment (Slavery and Sexual Servitude) Act of 1999.9Under this Act, forcing or intending to force a child under 18 years to provide sexual services or having knowledge of such activity warrants a penalty of 19 years imprisonment. The Crimes (Child Sex Tourism) Amendment Act of 1994 provides for a penalty of 17 years imprisonment for Australians who travel abroad for the purpose of sexual exploitation of a child under 16 years. The Migration Act punishes smuggling of human beings, including trafficking in persons, with up to 20 years imprisonment. Sexual servitude, slavery, people smuggling, and child sex tourism offenses have been included as serious offenses in the Proceeds of Crime Act of 2002, which allows for the forfeiture of assets of the guilty party.

State and territory-level agencies overseeing education monitor and enforce compulsory education laws. The federal Department of Family and Community Services plays a consultative role in monitoring children's rights in Australia. The Australian Broadcasting Authority investigates complaints of Internet-based child pornography. Specialized task forces have been set up at the state level to be used in criminal prosecutions involving child victims. The Department of Immigration and Multicultural Affairs and the Australian Federal Police have jurisdiction in trafficking matters. Enforcement of legislation concerning education and employments rests mainly with individual states and territories.

The Government of Australia has not ratified ILO Convention 182 on the Worst Forms of Child Labor or ILO Convention 138 on the Minimum Age for Admission to Employment. On October 8, 2003, the Government of Australia tabled ILO Convention 182 and an accompanying National Interest Analysis at a meeting of an Australian parliamentary committee, signaling an intent to ratify. However, the Analysis statement recommended the postponement of ratification until all state and territory laws complied with the treaty's obligations. Four states were in the process of amending legislation to come into compliance with the obligations of Convention 182.

LABOR RIGHTS AND CHILD LABOR LAWS IN AUSTRALIA

Submitted by the American Federation of Labor and Congress of Industrial Organizations September 2, 2003

I. Introduction

The AFL-CIO appreciates this opportunity to comment on Australia's labor laws and its compliance with the core labor standards, including standards on child labor. While Australia is a developed country with a relatively high standard of living and a vibrant, independent labor movement, it also has an imbalanced, inadequate system of labor laws that fails to fully protect workers' core rights. Like the U.S., Australia has a federal legal system with various laws covering labor issues at the national and sub-national levels. But Australia's federal labor laws are far from comprehensive, leaving significant gaps in legal guarantees for workers' rights that are filled only partially, if at all, by the labor laws of Australia's states and territories and by common law.

It is vital that any free trade agreement (FTA) between the U.S. and Australia address these deficiencies in Australia's labor laws. The kind of workers' rights provisions contained in the Chile and Singapore FTAs are insufficient to ensure that core labor standards will actually be respected in Australia, and must not serve as the model for the U.S. - Australia FTA. The Chile and Singapore FTAs only require governments to enforce the labor laws they have, no matter how inadequate those laws may be. In addition, the FTAs allow governments to specify which set of laws, at which level of government, they are committing to enforce.

The U.S., for example, has only committed itself to enforce its federal labor laws and regulations under the Chile and Singapore FTAs. If Australia made a similar decision, and only committed to enforce the federal labor laws it has on the books, it would leave a broad range of core workers' rights completely unprotected under the FTA. There are, for example, no federal laws in Australia prohibiting forced labor, setting a minimum age for employment, or prohibiting forced or bonded labor by children. In addition, the federal laws that do exist on labor relations have been criticized by the U.S. State Department, the International Confederation of Free Trade Unions (ICFTU), and the International Labor Organization (ILO) for failing to fully protect workers' freedom of association and their right to organize and bargain collectively.

It is imperative that the Department of Labor develop a comprehensive analysis of Australia's labor laws early enough to inform the content of the FTA negotiations now taking place. The administration should not conclude its FTA negotiations until it has a full understanding of the problems in Australia's labor laws and has developed FTA provisions that will address these problems. To truly protect workers' rights in the U.S. and Australia, FTA negotiators should follow the principles outlined in the attached joint statement between the AFL-CIO and the Australian Council of Trade Unions (ACTU), which states:

> The FTA must include meaningful and enforceable commitments to the core workers' rights outlined in the International Labour Organisation (ILO) 1998 Declaration on Fundamental Principles and Rights at Work. These obligations must be in the core of the agreement, and be subject to the same enforcement mechanisms as the agreement's commercial provisions.

Absent a binding obligation to meet the ILO core labor standards, the proposed FTA will only allow the serious flaws in Australia's labor law system to continue to go unremedied, to the detriment of both American and Australian workers.

II. Freedom of Association and the Right to Organize and Bargain Collectively

Australia's laws contain a number of onerous restrictions on workers' right to freedom of association and their right to organize and bargain collectively. Many of these restrictions were created by the 1996 Federal Workplace Relations Act (WRA), which constituted a major restructuring of Australia's labor laws and has been criticized repeatedly by the ILO, the U.S. State Department, and the ICFTU. The fairly recent enactment of the WRA shows that problems with workers' rights in Australia are not the result of insufficient enforcement resources or the inheritance of outdated labor legislation from another era - they are the result oF a conscious and recent decision in the Australian government to restrict the fundamental rights of workers. Many Australian states and territories have labor laws with defects similar to those in the federal law.

A. Freedom to Choose a Union

The WRA allows employers to choose a union to bargain with before it has even employed any workers, through "greenfield" agreements. These agreements can last for up to three years. effectively denying workers the right to choose their own bargaining representative for that length of time. The ILO criticized this provision in 1998 and again in 2000, and requested that the Australian government review and amend the WRA to eliminate this problem. According to the ICFTU, the WRA also makes it much harder for unions to get into workplaces to organize workers, further depriving workers of their ability to freely join the union of their choosing.

In addition, the WRA undermines the ability of a majority-supported union to represent all of the members in a bargaining unit by abolishing closed shops and union demarcations. These provisions deprive majority-supported unions of the ability to reach closed-shop agreements or use demarcation tools to maintain bargaining power on behalf of their members, and could foster the proliferation of small, competing unions within the workplace. The State Department calls these provisions "the primary curb on union power" in the WRA.

B. Anti-Union Discrimination

The WRA provides workers only partial protection from anti-union discrimination, in violation of ILO Convention 98. The Act gives regulators wide latitude to exclude whole categories of workers - including contract workers, casual workers, or workers paid above a specified salary -from the Act's most comprehensive protections against dismissal based on trade union activities. These excluded workers may enjoy some more limited protections against anti-union discrimination in other sections of the Act, but these protections fall short of those required by the ILO.

For example, an excluded worker participating in an industrial action regarding the negotiation of a single-employer collective bargaining agreement can be protected from employer discrimination, but the same excluded worker would not be protected if the industrial action she were involved in was related to a multi-employer agreement. In addition, a non-excluded worker enjoys protection against employer discrimination if he refuses to bargain an individual contract with the employer outside of the collective bargaining agreement. An excluded worker does not appear to enjoy the same protection. The ILO recommended in 1998 and 2000 that the government amend the WRA to ensure that all workers are covered by the Act's more comprehensive protections against anti-union discrimination.

Finally, the ICFTU and State Department both note that the Act imposes new limits on redress and compensation claims by employees that have been targeted by employers for their union activities.

C. Collective Bargaining

The WRA law allows employers to conclude individual "Australian Workplace Agreements" (AWAs) with their employees, and privileges these agreements over collective bargaining agreements. AWAs are less regulated than collective agreements and easier to file, yet they can cover all of the conditions of employment and are fully enforceable. The AWAs take primacy over federal awards and over any subsequent collective agreement in the workplace. This creates an incentive for employers to conclude AWAs with their workers in order to avoid being bound by a collective agreement, and the ICFTU reports that employers are using the law to undermine collective bargaining. In 2000, the ILO found that theses AWA provisions "do not promote collective bargaining as required under Article 4 of [ILO] Convention [98]," and recommended amendments to the WRA to bring Australia into compliance with international standards on the right to bargain collectively.

While AWAs are supposed to meet working condition standards comparable to those in then-sectors, the content of AWAs is in fact confidential, making it very difficult for unions to ensure that this requirement is met. The ICFTU reports that Australian Bureau of Statistics figures show most AWA workers being paid $100 - $193 (Australian dollars) less a week than workers doing similar work under collective bargaining agreements. The State Department reports that 290,029 AWAs have been approved since the new labour law came into effect in 1997.

In addition, the WRA privileges bargaining at the enterprise and workplace level over industrial and sectoral bargaining arrangements. This preference is written directly into the WRA. which gives priority to single-business agreements over multiple-business agreements. In fact, a multiple-business agreement can only be certified if it is found to be in the "public interest." and the Industrial Relations Commission must consider whether matters covered by the agreement would be more appropriately dealt with at the enterprise level. The ILO, noting that the level of bargaining should be determined by the parties themselves and not by the government, requested that the Australian government amend the legislation to bring it into compliance with ILO Convention 98 in 1998 and again in 2000.

Australian law also impermissibly restricts the subjects of collective negotiation by not allowing parties to bargain over strike pay. The ICFTU has criticized this provision, and in 1998 and 2000 the ILO recommended amendments to this provision in order to bring Australia up to international standards on the right to bargain collectively.

D. The Right to Strike

In Australia, a worker can be subject to common law court claims and onerous personal damages for strike activities unless Australian law explicitly protects those activities. The WRA only protects some categories of strike activity, thus penalizing workers engaging in other industrial actions and undermining workers' right to strike as it the ILO has defined it. Workers striking over a multi-employer agreement, strike pay, demarcation issues, or economic and social interests outside of the direct employer-employee relationship enjoy no protection from common law liability. This lack of protection effectively limits the permissible subjects of strike activity. a violation of workers' rights under ILO Conventions 87 and 98. In 2003. the ILO recommended Australia fix this violation by amending its laws on the right to strike.

In addition, Australia's Crimes Act forbids strikes in services that are declared by the government to be "prejudicing or threatening trade or commerce." Boycotts that obstruct government delivery of services or the transport of goods or persons in international trade are also prohibited. The WRA also allows the Industrial Relations Commission to suspend a strike that threatens to cause significant damage to the economy. These prohibitions go far beyond the limited exception to the right to strike for essential services recognized by the ILO, and the ILO recommended amending these provisions in 2003. These provisions, by protecting employers engaged in international trade from legal industrial actions, undermine Australian workers' right to strike for better wages and working conditions in precisely those sectors where American workers will face more direct competition under the proposed U.S. - Australia FTA.

III. Child Labour and Forced Labour

There are no federal laws in Australia prohibiting forced labour, setting a minimum age for employment, or prohibiting forced or bonded labour by children. Australia has not ratified ILO Convention 138 establishing a Minimum Age for Employment, nor Con \ention 182 on the worst forms of child labour. While technical discussions are continuing between the Federal Government and the State and Territory Governments, there is no timetable for ratification of either of these Conventions. In terms of the issues covered in ILO C. 182, the Australian Government has refused to make any commitments to ensuring effective collection, monitoring and analysis of data related to the "worst forms of child labour."

A. Involvement in Prostitution/Pornography

Adequate and reliable data related to the size and scale of the commercial exploitation of children in Australia is not regarded as a priority by any state or federal government.

However, the following overview of the data currently available will provide some indication of the seriousness of the situation:

* The Australian Institute of Criminology research *"using a variety of different figures and sources resulted in an estimate of approximately 400 - 450 children across Australia believed to be engaged in commercial or quasi-commercial sexual activity during a typical 24 hour period."*
* Child Wise surveyed 451 agencies. Of those, 258 agencies were aware of incidences of young people engaging in commercial sexual activities, reporting 3,100 young people confirmed or believed to be participating. This is in addition to 600 cases reported in the pilot study undertaken in Melbourne. A disturbing finding was that a few agencies reported children in the 10 - 12 years and under 10 years of age categories engaging in commercial sexual activities.
* A further note on indicative data is to be found in the 1999 Queensland Criminal Justice Commission study on *Reported Sexual Offences* in *Queensland*. This found that *"on average approximately 6,500 sexual offences were reported to the Queensland Police Service annually between the years 1996 - 1998"*\ with *"the majority of reported offences committed against children younger than 16 years of age (58%)*

B. Harmful Work

Again, the Australian government has ignored the problem of inadequate data related to children and harmful or dangerous work.

While the exposure of children to dangerous work is not a new problem, recent reports indicate that the situation has not improved and perhaps is becoming more serious:

The Australian Bureau of Statistics, *Work -Related Injuries, Report, September 2000.* indicated that in the year ending September 2000:

- a total of 29,000 people 15-19 years old experienced work-related injury (a rate of 39.5 per 1,000 persons working).
- 14,200 of these did not have leave entitlements.

The NOHSC report, *Work-related aspects of patient presentations to general practitioners in Australia: Analysis of the first two years of BEACH data.* December 2001. reports:

- 21,000 work-related problems of persons under 15.
- 374,000 work-related problems of persons aged 15 to 24.

The NOHSC *Compendium of Workers' Compensation statistics Australia 2000-2001* indicates that 6,943 new compensation cases were reported that year for persons under 20 years.

In New South Wales (NSW), "*at least four people under 18 are killed at workplaces and farms each year, 377 suffer permanent injury, and more than 1,300 suffer temporary' disabilities, according to WorkCover NSW statistics in the report. Every 13 days, a child on an Australian farm dies an accidental death, and one in every four tractor deaths is a child under 16.* "(Sydeny Morning Herald. 4/11/2000)

In Victorian workplaces some 998 workers under 18 years were injured; "*Among the injuries sustained by Victoria's teenage workforce last year were 18 amputations and 134 fractures. Worksafe statistics revealed 60 teenagers suffered severe bruises or crush injuries, 22 had burns, 175 suffered cuts, 381 reported sprains and strains from work, and 26 had foreign-bod\ injuries to their eyes, ears and noses. The figures are slightly up on 977 in 2000". (The Herald Sun,* 25/1/02).

C. Sweatshops

Recent research in Australia indicates that "*the number of outworkers employed in the clothing industry increased ten-fold over the past ten years ... there were about 330,000 sweatshop workers in Australia". (Daily Telegraph,* 12/4/01)

Recent reports provide an insight into the use of children in outwork (home work):

(i) "*Children as young as eight are working up to 18 hours a day alongside their parents in Sydney 'sweatshops' making fashion garments ... young children are working past mid night, after school, and during holidays and weekends to help terrified parents meet impossible deadlines". (Sydnes Morning Herald, 31/3/95)*

(ii) *"An estimated 70,000 Australian children as voting as eight have been caught in the shift to outworking in the garment industry ... one store measures and 'fits' children for heavy industrial sewing machines destined for outworkers sweatshops". (Insight Special Report: Rag 'Trade Entraps Migrant Families. The* Age, 27/10/98)

(iii) *"Sweatshop Anger: Children as young as nine are being exploited by unscrupulous clothing manufacturers in background sweatshops in Whitehorse".*

(Whitehorse Gazette. 2 I /3/01)

D. Armed Conflict

While it had been a long standing practice not to send defense force members under the age of 18 years to areas of hostility, a report by the Australian national Audit found that at least four under-18-year-olds had been sent to East Timor during the crisis *(Herald Sun,* 25/3/02). The Audit Report noted that, *"Personnel tracking was so inadequate that at least four soldiers under the age of 18 served in areas of hostility despite directives that this should not happen and was a contravention of the UN Rights of the Child Treaty"* (Sydney Morning Herald, 18/4/03).

There have been some reports of abuse of child labour among ethnic communities and in clothing sweatshops in Sydney and Melbourne over the past few years. According to the State Department, though the Australian government committed to study the need for laws on these matters, no action has yet been taken.

IV. Conclusion

The State Department, the ICFTU, and the ILO have all criticized Australian labour laws for falling short of the international core labour standards. Australia has refused to amend its laws to comply with these standards, despite repeated ILO recommendations that it do so. In fact. Australia's labour laws seem to be deteriorating rather than improving over time, given that some of the most often-criticized portions of its labour law went into effect just six years ago. The FTA now being negotiated between the U.S. and Australia must require full compliance with the ILO core labour standards, and must make that obligation fully enforceable. Given the restrictions on workers' rights contained in Australia's federal law, the gaps in federal law not filled by Australia's states and territories, and the ability of the Australian government to further weaken protections for workers' rights in the future just as it did in 1996, a mere obligation to enforce existing law will simply not be sufficient to ensure that workers' fundamental rights will he respected under the proposed FTA.

U.S. CHILD LABOUR CHRONOLOGY

1904- The National Child Labour Committee, the first effective lobbying group for reforming child labour conditions, is established in the United States.

1906- Senator Albert Beveridge introduces the first bill in the U. S. Congress to regulate child labour.

1912- The first federal agency devoted expressly to the welfare of children, the U. S. Children's Bureau, is founded.

1916- The U. S. Congress passes and President Woodrow Wilson signs the Keating-Owens Act, the first federal legislation regulating child labour.

1917- In Hammer v. Dagenhart, the U. S. Supreme Court declares the Keating-Owens Act unconstitutional.

1919- The International Labour Organization adopts the Convention Fixing the Minimum Age for Admission of Children to Industrial Employment and the Convention Concerning the Night Work of Young Persons Employed in Industry, which establish minimum employment ages for children in specific industries and places of employment on an international level. Lower minimum ages for child workers in Japan and India are included in both conventions.

1919- The Child Welfare League of America is chartered. 1922 The Young Workers International and the International Union of Socialist Youth Organizations proclaim the Declaration of the Rights of the Adolescent, a set of guidelines for the employment of youth and adolescents, with specific restrictions proposed for the workday, prohibitions on work during preschool and compulsory school age, compulsory medical examinations for young persons prior to employment and reform of the apprenticeship system.

1922- International Council of Women issues its Children's Charter, a declaration based on initial resolutions by Women's Councils in Italy and the United States calling for the development of a charter embodying minimum rights of children in all countries. The Children's Charter includes seven sections: prenatal care, care of mothers and children up to school age, children of school age, children in employment, delinquent children, children's state departments, and international conferences.

1924- The U. S. Congress submits a child labour amendment to the individual states for ratification following signature by President Calvin Coolidge. This amendment would have given Congress the power to pass Federal child labour legislation.

1930- Delegates to the White House Conference on Child Health and Protection prepare the Children's Charter, a set of 19 principles that summarized the recommendations of the conference deliberations and reports. Under the guidance of President Herbert Hoover, the Children's Charter contained key principles in the areas of education, child labour, vocational training, recreation, family welfare, health, growth and development, disabled children, and related areas, including the Bill of Rights for the Handicapped Child.

1933- U.S. First Lady Eleanor Roosevelt actively campaigns for child labour laws.

1933- The National Recovery Act includes a prohibition on labour by children under the age of 16.

1936- The Walsh-Healy Act is signed into law, becoming the first legally binding federal legislation to prevent the use of child labour in companies with federal contracts.

1937- 28 states had ratified the proposed federal child labour amendment submitted by Congress to the states in 1924. This total remained 8 states short of ratification.

1938- The Fair Labour Standards Act is signed into law by President Franklin Delano Roosevelt, prohibiting the interstate shipment of goods made in firms that employ children under the age of 16, or children under the age of 18 in hazardous occupations.

1941- The U. S. Supreme Court upholds the provisions of the Fair Labour Standards Act concerning child labour prohibitions in the case of United States v. Darby.

1943- Child labour laws are relaxed to allow teenagers to work in wartime factories; by 1944, 2.9 million teenagers are employed in such work.

1950- Participants in the Mid-Century Conference on Children and Youth prepare the Pledge to Children, a 19 paragraph set of commitments by adults to children. Continuing the tradition of earlier U. S. public declarations about child welfare, the Pledge to Children contains commitments by adults to children in the areas of promoting education, strengthening family life, safeguarding civil equality and nondiscrimination, improving workplace conditions, enhancing democratic citizenship and institutions, and advocating the development of the child's individual talents and potential.

FEDERAL CHILD LABOUR LAWS IN U.S.A.

Federal child labour laws are stringently regulated in the USA, but it wasn't always so. Children worked long hours in appalling conditions until these laws were passed.

Child labour is stringently regulated in the United States. Children under the age of fourteen do not work. Some eleven-year-olds may work if their parents own a farm, but not for very many hours per day.

The federal government passed laws specifying the hours that children of appropriate age may work: Children can't work during school hours. During the school year, work hours can't exceed three hours per day, or eighteen hours per week. This seems reasonable to Americans, but it wasn't always that way. It isn't normal now for many children in third world countries.

In the late seventeen hundreds and the mid-eighteen hundreds, power-driven machines replaced hand labour. Since these machines produced quickly, factories started to appear everywhere. More factories meant that companies needed to hire more employees to fill jobs and work the machines.

Immigrants worked cheaply, and then companies realized that it was even less expensive to hire the immigrant's children. There weren't enough adults willing to work in the factories, and they could pay the children much lower wages, which meant more money for the company. Children as young as the age of seven worked for cheap wages, just so that their families could afford to survive.

Girls would often work in the factories while the boys of these poor families would go to school. That way, the boys could get an education and perhaps a good job when they grew up. But many boys couldn't go to school, and the conditions in the factories were appalling.

One company in Massachusetts put a barbwire fence around their glass factory to keep the young children inside. Children carried loads of hot glass all night inside the factory. Deaths often occurred because the children were exhausted from overwork.

Those children working in mines had even worse conditions to contend with. They were chained and harnessed like horses to a mine cart, and sometimes they crawled to pull the heavy vehicle through narrow spaces.

The mines were hot, so they worked half-naked and they emerged at the end of their shift black with dirt, wet, and exhausted. They grew up with a hump on their backs, and they inhaled so much mine dust that it congested their lungs and made them unable to breathe. They often died early in life of black lung and other diseases, because of the hazardous conditions that they worked in.

A great number of people were appalled at the conditions that children worked in, and about the hours per day that they put in at their jobs. They said that child labour was wrong, and these people campaigned for reforms.

In the United States, numerous organizations worked to eliminate child labour, including the National Child Labour Commitee, lauched in 1904 by social workers.

Public support came when journalists exposed the horrible conditions children worked in.

Eventually, cities and states set forth guidelines limiting the number of hours that children could work. In 1916, President Wilson passed the Keating-Owen Act through Congress. This banned articles produced by child labour from interstate commerce. A 1918 Supreme Court ruling declared it unconstitutional.

It was not until 1938, when the Fair Labour Standards Act was passed, did any attempt at child labour legislation succeed. This requires employers to pay child labourers the minimum wage. It also limits the age of child labourer to age 18 if the occupation in hazardous. Gradually conditions improved, but child labour has still not been wiped out.

Children in the rural U.S. and Mexico work alongside their parents on farms. Their salary depends on how much that they can do each day. The average wage of a child labourer in Mexico is between two and three dollars a day. They generally work about twelve hours each day.

Children of poor families in Pakistan are often apprenticed at the age of seven: This means that their parents receive money for them to go to work for as long as fourteen hours each day. They live at their jobs, sometimes crowded in with other children, four and five to a tiny room. They are often underfed, mistreated, and in poor health.

Many countries that have child labour laws do not enforce them. Charitable organizations have begun to strenuously campaign to improve the lives of children around the world. They publish the names of companies that use goods made by child labour, and ask that consumers boycott these companies.

Many children around the world work lengthy hours in horrifying conditions, and these organizations are bringing this situation into the spotlight. They want child labour to cease.

THE PROBLEM

Although child labour had been subject to regulation in New Jersey and many other states beginning in the first decade of the 20th Century, the scope of government regulation and subsequent enforcement of child labour laws varied tremendously.

Non-governmental organizations such as the National Child Labour Committee and the Consumers' League of New Jersey, monitored the conditios of work for children and actively lobbied to improve the regulation of child labour. Conversely, opponents of child labour regulation, including agricultural and manufacturing interests and advocates of minimal government regulation of the economy, lobbied equally hard to restrict child labour regulation.

During the period 1920-1935, a number of reports were prepared concerning the conditions of child labour in New Jersey. These reports were authored by non-governmental organizations, bureaus of state and federal governments, and educational institutions. In one case (Document 3), the case studies of children in street work were done in selected New Jersey cities along with cities in other U.S. states by the U.S. Children's Bureau, an agency of the U.S. Department of Labour.

THE STRUGGLE FOR REFORM

In 1924, the Congress submitted to the states for ratification an amendment to the U.S. Constitution that would enable the Congress to regulate child labour. Despite support from Republican president Calvin Coolidge (1923-1928) and Herbert Hoover (1929-1932), by the beginning of the New Deal (1932) the amendment had not achieved ratification by the necessary three-fourths of the states.

Despite the slow process of garnering support for the national child labour amendment, individual states continued to refine their child labour laws in response to problems faced by children. In New Jersey, four problems were identified that led non-government organizations to agitate for reform of the state's child labour laws.

- — no regulation of agricultural child workers, particularly those who migrated periodically to different workplaces
- — workplace hazards and protecting children from participation in dangerous or high risk occupations
- — participation by children in street work, which fell outside the scope of the state's existing labour regulation (examples included peddlers, newspaper vendors and carriers)
- — the minimum age for employment, which was 14 provided 8th grade had been completed or 15 after the 6th grade or training for one grade beyond the 5th grade; this was a lower minimum age than in some states and higher than in some others.

The 1930's saw continuing efforts to ratify the 1924 federal child labour amendment, while other measures were proposed at both the federal and state levels to address the problems noted above, particularly as the effects of the Great Depression spread nationwide.

Task: Read the following scenario. Then use the sources provided here, as well as others in this module in THE PROBLEM section, to complete your report to the Governor of New Jersey concerning child labour.

Scenario

It is 1939. The problems facing children during the 7th year of FDR's New

Deal remain significant, and no more so than in the area of child labour. You have been commissioned by the Governor of New Jersey to prepare a 500 word essay about the problems facing child workers and how the state of New Jersey could address them - possibly through legislation or other means.

In your 500 word essay, you should:

1. Describe the problems facing child workers
2. Discuss pros/cons of the impact of the Federal Fair Labour Standards Act (passed in 1938) on child labour in New Jersey and
3. Propose solutions for at least two of the four problems noted here: migrant workers, workplace hazards, street workers and the minimum age for employment.

Be certain to consider all sides of the issue as you write. The Governor relies on your expert advice and looks forward to receiving your recommendations

CHILD LABOUR REGULATIONS, ORDERS AND STATEMENTS OF INTERPRETATION

Child Labour Violations—Civil Money Penalties

This document revises the child labour regulations in order to implement two amendments of the Fair Labour Standards Act's child labour standards—the Compactors and Balers Safety Standards Modernization Act, (August 6, 1996) (The Compactor and Baler Act); and the Drive for Teen Employment Act, (October 31, 1998). This document also revises procedural regulations dealing with administrative hearings and appeals of civil money penalties.

The Compactor and Baler Act sets conditions which permit 16- and 17-year-old workers to load, but not operate or unload, certain scrap paper balers and paper box compactors. The Act also specifies that civil money penalties may be assessed for violations of these conditions. This document also revises the regulation to implement the provisions of this Act. The Drive for Teen Employment Act prohibits minors under 17 years of age from driving automobiles and trucks on public roadways on the job, and establishes the conditions and criteria under which 17-year-olds may drive automobiles and trucks on public roadways on the job. The regulation is also revised to implement the provisions of this Act.

A regulation concerning government-issued Certificates of Age is also being revised. Prior to this Final Rule, the regulation required that the employer return the certificate to the issuing agency when the employee left employment, except that a certificate issued for employment in agriculture may be given to the named minor at termination of employment and a certificate issued to an 18- or 19- year-old shall be given to the named worker at termination of employment. This revision modifies the regulation to direct the employer to give the certificates to the employees when their employment ends.

Further, the Department is revising the regulation regarding the types of cooking and cooking-related duties that 14- and 15-year-olds may perform. The Department is updating the regulation to modify a long-standing Department of Labour (DOL) interpretation of this child labour standard.

Finally, this document revises certain other provisions which proscribe certain hazardous employment for 16- and 17-year-olds. Prior to this revision, the regulation prohibited these minors from working in roofing operations. The Department has revised the regulation to also prohibit all work on or about roofs. In addition, the Department has revised the regulation to update the definition of the terms explosives and articles containing explosive components in the prohibition on employment of minors in establishments which manufacture or store explosives.

DATES: Effective Dates: This rule is effective February 14, 2005. The incorporation by reference of American National Standards Institute standards in the regulations is approved by the Director of the Federal Register as of February 14, 2005. FOR FURTHER INFORMATION CONTACT: Arthur M. Kerschner, Jr., Office of Enforcement Policy, Child Labour and Special Employment Team, Wage and Hour Division, Employment Standards Administration, U.S. Department of Labour, Room S-3510, 200 Constitution Avenue, NW., Washington, DC 20210; telephone: (202) 693-0072 (this is not a toll free number). Copies of this final rule may be obtained in alternative formats (Large Print, Braille, Audio Tape or Disc), upon request, by calling (202) 693-0023. TTY/TDD callers may dial toll-free 1-877-889-5627 to obtain information or request materials in alternative formats. Questions of interpretation and/or enforcement of final regulations issued by this agency or referenced in this notice may be directed to the nearest Wage and Hour Division District Office. Locate the nearest office by calling the Wage and Hour Division's toll-free help line at 1-866-4USWAGE (1-866-487-9243) between 8 a.m. and 5 p.m. in your local time zone, or log onto the Wage and Hour Division's website for a nationwide listing of Wage and Hour District and Area Offices at: http://frwebgate.access.gpo.gov/cgi-bin leaving.cgi?from =leavingFR.html&log=linklog&to=http://www.dol.gov/esa/contacts/whd/america2.htm.

SUPPLEMENTARY INFORMATION

I. Background

The child labour provisions of the Fair Labour Standards Act (FLSA) establish a minimum age of 16 years for employment in nonagricultural occupations, but the Secretary of Labour is authorized to provide by regulation for 14- and 15-year-olds to work in suitable occupations other than manufacturing or mining, and during periods and under conditions that will not interfere with their schooling or health and well-being. The FLSA provisions permit 16- and 17-year-olds to work in the nonagricultural sector, without hours or time limitations, except in certain occupations found and declared by the Secretary to be particularly hazardous, or detrimental to the health or well-being of such workers.

The regulations for 14- and 15-year-olds are known as Child Labour Regulation No. 3 (Reg. 3) and are contained in subpart C of part 570 (29 CFR 570.31-.38). Reg. 3 limits the hours and times of day that such minors may work, and identifies occupations that are either permitted or prohibited for such minors. Under Reg. 3, 14- and 15-year-olds may work in certain occupations in retail, food service, and gasoline service establishments, but are not to work in certain other occupations (including all occupations found by the Secretary to be particularly hazardous for 16- and 17-year-olds). Reg. 3, originally promulgated in 1939, was revised to reflect the 1961 amendments to the FLSA which extended the Act's coverage to include enterprises engaged in commerce or the production of goods for commerce. Because of the statutory amendments, the FLSA's child labour protections became applicable to additional areas of employment for young workers in retail, food service, and gasoline service establishments.

The regulations concerning nonagricultural hazardous occupations are contained in subpart E of 29 CFR part 570 (29 CFR 570.50-.68). These Hazardous Occupations Orders (HOs) apply either on an industry basis, specifying the occupations in the industry that are prohibited, or on an occupational basis, irrespective of the industry in which performed. The seventeen HOs were adopted individually during the period of 1939 through 1963.

Because of changes in the workplace, the introduction of new processes and technologies, the emergence of new types of businesses where young workers may find employment opportunities, the existence of differing Federal and State standards, and divergent views on how best to correlate school and work experiences, the Department has long been reviewing the criteria for permissible child labour employment. In this review, the [[Page 75383]] Department published a Proposed Rule in 1982, a Final Rule in 1991, both an Advance Notice of Proposed Rulemaking and a Proposed Rule in 1994, a Final Rule in 1995, and a Notice of Proposed Rulemaking in 1999.

On July 16, 1982, a Proposed Rule was published in the Federal Register (47 FR 31254) which proposed to revise several elements of Reg. 3, including the permissible hours and times of employment for 14- and 15-year-olds and the types of cooking operations those minors would be permitted to perform. The Proposed Rule generated considerable public interest and controversy, most having to do with the expansion of the hours and times of work for this age group.

The Department subsequently suspended the proposal from further consideration and no final rule was implemented (50 FR 17434, April 29, 1985; DOL's Semiannual Regulatory Agenda). The Department continued to receive communications from the public suggesting that certain changes should be made to the child labour regulations on a number of issues. In 1987, the Department established a Child Labour Advisory Committee (CLAC) composed of 21 members representing employers, education, labour, child guidance professionals, civic groups, child advocacy groups, State officials and safety groups. The mission of the CLAC was to give advice and guidance in developing possible proposals to change existing standards. After reviewing a number of issues, the CLAC proposed making certain changes to the child labour regulations. The Department considered the CLAC's suggestions, as well as suggestions received from the public as noted above. A Proposed Rule was published in October 1990, proposing changes to three HOs (55 FR 42612). In December 1991, the Department promulgated a Final Rule which revised the three HOs (56 FR 58626).

The Department continued to review the child labour regulations and, in an effort to accumulate data concerning all aspects of the provisions, published both a Notice of Proposed Rulemaking (NPRM) (59 FR 25164) and an Advance Notice of Proposed Rulemaking (ANPRM) (59 FR 25167) on May 13, 1994.

The NPRM proposed to exempt 14- and 15-year-olds from Reg. 3 hours standards when employed under certain restrictions as sports attendants for professional sports teams, to standardize the Reg. 3 process for issuing occupational variances for Work Experience and Career Exploration Program (WECEP) participants, to remove an outdated exemption for enrollees in certain work training programs, and to revise the process by which HOs are promulgated. A Final Rule on these issues was published April 17, 1995 (60 FR 19336).

The 1994 ANPRM requested public comment on several specific topics as well as all aspects of the child labour provisions. Several individuals and organizations submitted comments. The National Institute for Occupational Safety and Health (NIOSH) provided the Department with epidemiological data on a number of issues related to both Reg. 3 and the HOs. NIOSH also provided the Department with statistics regarding occupational injuries and made several recommendations. A number of child guidance professionals, educators, unions, employer associations and child labour advocates also commented and made various recommendations.

Twice in the last eight years, Congress has amended the child labour provisions of the FLSA. The Compactors and Balers Safety Standards Modernization Act, Public Law 104-174 (Compactor and Baler Act), was signed by the President on August 6, 1996. This legislation adds a section 13(c)(5) to the FLSA, permitting minors 16 and 17 years of age to load, but not operate or unload, certain scrap paper balers and paper box compactors if certain requirements are met. The Drive for Teen Employment Act, Public Law 105-334, was signed by the President on October 31, 1998. This legislation adds a section 13(c)(6) to the FLSA, prohibiting minors under 17 years of age from driving automobiles and trucks on public roadways on the job and establishing the conditions and criteria for 17-year-olds to drive automobiles and trucks on public roadways on the job.

The Department published a Notice of Proposed Rulemaking in the Federal Register on November 30, 1999 (64 FR 67130), inviting comments until January 31, 2000, on revisions of regulations to implement the recent legislation and to update certain regulatory standards. The Compactor and Baler Act affects the HO 12 standards (Occupations involved in the operation of paper-products machines) (29 CFR 570.63) and certain other related regulations; amendments of those regulations were proposed. The Drive for Teen Employment Act affects the HO 2 standards (Occupations of motor-vehicle driver and outside helper) (29 CFR 570.52); an amendment of that regulation was proposed. As a result of its ongoing review of the child labour provisions, the Department also proposed changes to HO 1 (Occupations in or about plants or establishments manufacturing or storing explosives or articles containing explosive components) (29 CFR 570.51), HO 16 (Occupations in roofing operations) (29 CFR 570.67), the Reg. 3 limitations on cooking (29 CFR 570.34), and 29 CFR 570.6(b)(1) which deals with the disposition of a Certificate of Age when the named individual's employment ends.

II. Summary of Comments

A total of 16 comments were received in response to the notice— from trade and professional associations, advocacy organizations, private consultants, an employer, a State department of labour, a State department of education, and one Federal agency (the National Institute for Occupational Safety and Health (NIOSH)). The sole employer responding restricted his comments to recommending changes to Hazardous Occupations Order No. 8 (Occupations involved in the operations of power-driven metal forming, punching, and shearing machines), a subject not raised by the Proposed Rule. The New Jersey Department of Labour limited its comments to commending the Secretary's concern for the safety of minors and advising her that the proposed rule would in no way impede in the enforcement of New Jersey's child labour laws. A consultant with the Ohio Department of Education reported that a committee of teachers of Career Based Intervention Programs agreed with all the proposals with the assumption that the Department would continue to grant variances to WECEP participants as it has done in the past.

In July of 2002, NIOSH disseminated its report entitled National Institute for Occupational Safety and Health Recommendations to the U.S. Department of Labour for Changes to Hazardous Orders. The report, which makes many recommendations, also repeats the comments NIOSH submitted in response to the NPRM which are discussed later in this document. Since receiving the NIOSH report, the Department has been conducting a detailed review and has met with various stakeholders to evaluate and prioritize each recommendation for possible regulatory action consistent with the established national policy of balancing the benefits to employment opportunities for youth with the necessary and most effective safety protections.

A. Certificates of Age (29 CFR 570.5-.27)

Section 3(l) of the FLSA provides an affirmative defense against the citation of child labour violations for employers who "have on file an unexpired [[Page 75384]] certificate issued and held pursuant to regulations of the Secretary of Labour certifying that such [employee] is above the oppressive child labour age" (29 U.S.C. 203(l)). The use of such certificates is not mandatory under the FLSA. The Department's regulations, at 29 CFR 570.5-.27, set out the procedures for application, issuance, retention and disposition of certificates of age. The regulations authorize the issuance of certificates by most of the States as well as by the Wage and Hour Division. Most certificates are, in fact, requested from and issued by the States.

Section 570.6(b), prior to this Final Rule, directed the employer to return the certificate to the issuing authority when the named worker's employment terminated, except that a certificate issued for employment in agriculture could be given to the worker and a certificate issued to an 18- or 19-year-old was to be given to the worker. The Department proposed to revise Sec. 570.6(b) to specify that the worker's certificate issued by DOL be given to him/her when employment ends, regardless of the worker's age or type of employment. The youth could then provide the certificate to any future employer(s). This regulatory amendment, suggested by the Office of Management and Budget, would preclude unneeded repetition of the certification process and reduce paperwork burdens on employers.

The Department received two comments on this proposal. A consultant with the Ohio Department of Education's Career Based Intervention Programs commented that when the responsibility of providing the age certificate to the new employer is delegated to the minor, the certificate may not actually get to the new employer in many cases. The Department believes that young workers will be cooperative with prospective employers in providing employment-related information. The National Grocers Association (NGA) recommended that the proposal be expanded to include certificates issued by State governments as well. Although the Department encourages States to adopt similar rules regarding the disposition of age certificates, it is left to the individual States to establish rules regarding the disposition of the certificates they issue. This portion of the proposal is adopted as a Final Rule.

B. Reg. 3 Occupations: Cooking (29 CFR 570.34)

Reg. 3 established restrictions on the type of cooking and cooking- related work which 14- and 15-year-olds may perform as employees of retail, food service, and gasoline service establishments. At Sec. 570.34(b)(5), the regulation prohibits these minors from "cooking (except at soda fountains, lunch counters, snack bars, or cafeteria serving counters) and baking." Under Sec. 570.34(a)(7), however, 14- and 15-year-olds are permitted to perform "kitchen work and other work involved in preparing and serving food and beverages, including the operation of machines and devices used in the performance of such work, such as but not limited to, dish-washers, toasters, dumbwaiters, popcorn poppers, milkshake blenders, and coffee grinders."

These regulatory standards were added to Reg. 3 after the 1961 FLSA amendments which extended the FLSA's coverage to include certain enterprises engaged in commerce or in the production of goods for commerce. The Act's child labour provisions became applicable to additional areas of employment in retail, food service, and gasoline service establishments. The regulations were the Department's response to the challenge of identifying those food preparation activities which 14- and 15-year-olds could safely perform without interfering with their schooling, health or well-being.

In establishing these standards, the Department recognized that some forms of cooking were not appropriate for persons under 16 years of age. Lifting large containers of hot materials, working over a hot stove for long periods of time, cooking over an open flame or with equipment that utilize extremely high temperatures, and operating pressure cookers were all considered too dangerous for young workers. On the other hand, preparing an occasional hamburger or grilled cheese sandwich or performing simple cooking functions like those which minors safely might do in their own homes did not seem to place young workers at risk. The Department determined that the type of cooking performed at a snack bar or soda fountain, where the worker would not only take the customer's order but also prepare and serve the light fare, did not pose serious risks to the minor's health or well-being. The work was not strenuous, did not require continuous cooking at a stove or range, and did not require the minor to use complicated or dangerous equipment.

The Department's promulgation and interpretation of the Reg. 3 standards were based, to some extent, upon a factor common to snack bars and soda fountains—namely, that the cooking performed in such food service operations was performed "in plain view" of the customer. This factor, in and of itself, did not make the activity safer, but it did tend to limit the scope of the cooking to activities that were relatively free of risk. By limiting cooking work to soda fountains and snack bars, Reg. 3 barred the "heavy duty" and more strenuous types of cooking performed in full-service restaurants, while permitting other, less strenuous types of "light" cooking. Over a period of time in the 1960's, the Department developed an "in plain view" interpretation of the regulation, making the Reg. 3 standard dependent upon whether the 14- and 15-year-olds are performing their cooking duties within the customers' sight. Under this interpretation, cooking performed "in plain view" would be permissible even if the minor was not working at a traditional soda fountain or snack bar, and cooking performed out of plain view (i.e., in the kitchen or behind a partition) would not be permissible.

The snack bars and soda fountains upon which the Reg. 3 standards were established have been largely, if not entirely, replaced by different kinds of quick-service restaurants (also referred to as fast food establishments) that evolved during the decades of the 1970's, 1980's and 1990's. In recognition of the changing nature of the retail food service industry, the Wage and Hour Division examined quick- service restaurants in 1977 and conducted a survey of quick-service restaurants in 1979 to determine what, if any, changes were needed in the cooking prohibitions. Interested parties, including major quick- service restaurant chains, organized labour, and child labour advocates, were consulted.

In 1982, the Department published a Proposed Rule (47 FR 31254) which would have revised several elements of Reg. 3, including the permissible hours and times of employment for 14- and 15-year-olds and the types of cooking operations they would be allowed to perform. Under the proposal, all cooking would have been permitted except: cooking with hot oils at temperatures over 140 [deg]F; cooking over an open flame; and cooking involving the use of pressure cookers without proper safety valves. The "in plain view" interpretation would no longer have been applied. The Proposed Rule generated considerable public interest and controversy, most having to do with the expansion of the hours and times of employment standards. The Department subsequently suspended the proposal from further consideration and no final rule was implemented (50 FR 17434, April 29, 1985; DOL's Semiannual Regulatory Agenda). [[Page 75385]]

The Department continued to receive communications from the public suggesting that certain changes should be made to the regulations concerning cooking. A general consensus seemed to develop that the "in plain view" interpretation no longer served as an important safety standard as it did in the 1960's, because the activities involved were no longer limited to "light" cooking. Further, the general view appeared to be that the interpretation did not provide sufficient guidance to employers, parents, and working teens. The proscription of tasks mainly on the basis of place of performance complicated the regulation and led to confusion. For example, in one quick-service restaurant, 14- and 15-year-olds may perform most cooking jobs because all cooking is performed in the plain view of the customers; but at another food service establishment, those minors would not be able to perform the identical functions because all cooking is done in a closed kitchen away from the customer's view. Complications may also exist within a single establishment when some cooking equipment is placed so customers may view the cooking operation and additional pieces of the same equipment are placed outside of the customer's line of sight.

The Department recognized the need to review and update the Reg. 3 standards. New generations of cooking devices have been introduced since the cooking regulation was published in the 1960s, including microwaves, automatic cooking machines and systems, and computerized equipment and systems. Any proposed changes to the cooking prohibitions—to take into account all of these changes in the food service industry—must carefully consider the safety risks to young workers.

In an effort to accumulate data concerning all aspects of the child labour provisions, the Department in 1994 published an Advance Notice of Proposed Rulemaking (ANPRM) (59 FR 25167). The ANPRM requested public comment on many aspects of the child labour provisions, specifically including the Reg. 3 cooking standards. The Department received numerous and diverse comments on this matter.

The Department carefully considered all the comments and materials received, and reviewed the Reg. 3 standards, to develop the Proposed Rule which was published on November 30, 1999. Recognizing the delicate balance between the value of jobs that provide positive, formative experiences and the negative effects that the wrong type of jobs can have on the health and well-being of young workers, the Department preliminarily concluded that the regulations should be revised so that 14- and 15-year-olds may perform a limited number of cooking activities—i.e., only those that are safe and appropriate for their age group. The Department believed that this regulatory revision could be accomplished without negatively impacting employment opportunities for young workers.

The Department proposed to eliminate the "in plain view" interpretation and establish standards for cooking duties which it believed to be safe and appropriate for these minors regardless of where the cooking is performed within the food service establishment. The proposed standards would prohibit 14- and 15-year-olds from any cooking except cooking with electric or gas grilles which does not involve cooking over an open flame, and using deep fat fryers which are equipped with and utilize, during the frying process, devices which automatically raise and lower the "baskets," but not pressurized fryers. The proposal also would permit 14- and 15-year-olds to clean, maintain (including the changing, cleaning, and disposing of oil or grease and oil or grease filters) and repair cooking devices (other than power-driven equipment) when the surfaces of the equipment or liquids do not exceed a temperature of 140 [deg]F. The proposal would, thus, prohibit 14- and 15-year-olds from performing any of the following duties when the minor would be exposed to or working with liquid or equipment surfaces which exceed a temperature of 140 [deg]F: cleaning equipment such as grilles, deep fat fryers, and steam tables; removing grease filters; filtering grease or oil; and lifting, moving or carrying receptacles or containers of hot grease or oil. This ban on carrying or working with hot oil would apply regardless of the type of oil. The Department proposed to continue the current interpretation of Reg. 3 as banning 14- and 15-year-olds from using such equipment as rotisseries, pressurized equipment including fryolators, and cooking devices that operate at extremely high temperatures such as "Neico broilers."

The Department also proposed to continue its long-standing interpretation of the regulation as permitting these minors to operate microwave ovens that are used only to warm prepared food and do not have the capacity to warm above 140 [deg]F, and to use, dispense, and serve food from warmers, steam tables, and other warming devices (even if the temperatures exceed 140 [deg]F). Further, the proposal preserved the current Reg. 3 provision allowing these minors to perform kitchen work and other work to prepare and serve food and beverages, including operating certain machines used in performing such work. Additionally, the Department proposed to continue the ban on all baking activities by those under 16 years of age. These minors would still be prohibited from performing all jobs that are part of the baking process, such as weighing and mixing ingredients; placing or assembling products in pans or on trays; operating ovens, including convection ovens, microwave ovens (except those used for warming food as described above), pizza ovens, and automatic feeding ovens; removing items from ovens; placing items on cooling trays; and finishing baked products. This ban on baking tasks exists because of the dangers to young workers in activities such as lifting heavy bags of ingredients, filling hot pans, moving hot pans and trays into and out of ovens, emptying hot pans and trays, having clothing or fingers entangled in conveyors or other mechanisms, and operating power-driven equipment. Although the proposal continued the ban on all baking activities by those under 16 years of age, the Department requested evidence regarding whether certain activities would be safe for 14- and 15-year- olds to perform in the baking process in retail establishments, and if so, whether consideration should be given to modifying the ban on the baking process performed in retail establishments by 14- and 15-year- olds. Specifically, the Department sought evidence and comments on whether such youths should be permitted to perform certain prescribed activities such as measuring and weighing ingredients and finishing baked goods, provided that operation of power-driven equipment is not performed. As a result of recommendations submitted by NIOSH in response to the 1994 ANPRM, the Department also sought evidence and comments as to whether, if the Department does amend the rules to allow certain baking activities to be performed, there should be a weight limit, such as 10 pounds, for jobs requiring lifting by 14- and 15-year olds.

Finally, the proposal preserved the current Reg. 3 process whereby State agencies operating approved Work Experience and Career Exploration Programs (WECEPs) (in which students are closely supervised and receive safety instruction) may seek variances from the Department to authorize students to cook and to perform certain jobs that would otherwise be banned. [[Page 75386]]

Ten comments were received in response to these proposals. The commenters were unanimous in supporting the elimination of the "in plain view" standard, although they disagreed concerning the standards which had been proposed to replace it. NIOSH recommended that the "in plain view" interpretation be withdrawn; this position was endorsed by the American Federation of Labour and Congress of Industrial Relations (AFL-CIO), the United Food and Commercial Workers International Union (UFCW), and the Child Labour Coalition of the National Consumers League (CLC). However, each of these commenters took issue with particular aspects of the proposed standards. NIOSH noted that, when it had commented on the Department's 1994 ANPRM, it had "recommended that all cooking and working in proximity to cooking appliances should be a prohibited activity for youths under 16 years of age, regardless of whether the cooking was within 'plain view' of the customer." But in commenting on the Proposed Rule, NIOSH endorsed the elimination of the "in plain view" standard while supporting some of the proposals concerning permissible activities in food service employment. NIOSH stated that it "appreciates and concurs with DOL's intent [in the Proposed Rule] to permit 14- and 15-year-olds to conduct safe and appropriate work activities, including those associated with cooking, while prohibiting them from performing more hazardous activities." The NIOSH comment included copies of several reports and publications concerning occupational injuries including injuries in food service establishments. The National Restaurant Association (Association), the National Child Labour Committee (NCLC), and the National Council of Chain Restaurants (Council) commented that the "in plain view" standard is no longer appropriate and should be eliminated. The Association approved of the " 'common sense' approach" taken in the Proposed Rule, and stated that "[t]he current interpretation is a product of a bygone era and is not practical in most restaurant settings. * * * the Association supports the proposal to eliminate the 'in plain view' interpretation while allowing limited cooking and cleaning of cooking devices." The Council pointed out that "the restaurant industry provides a tremendous number of entry level positions that are often the ideal 'first' jobs for teenage individuals seeking part-time employment, but who otherwise have little or no job skills to offer employers. * * * any expansion of the child labour restrictions in a manner that is not directly necessary to the safety and well-being of teenage employees will only serve to eliminate entry level job opportunities for young individuals that otherwise may have little experience to offer employers."

The commenters expressed differing views with regard to the proposal to allow 14- and 15-year-olds to cook with electric and gas grills that do not involve cooking over an open flame and with deep fryers which are equipped with and utilize devices which automatically raise and lower the baskets.

Several commenters opposed the proposal. NIOSH stated that cooking appliances, such as grills and deep fryers, are associated with serious occupational burns among youth caused not only by cooking but also by the worker coming into contact with hot surfaces or hot grease as a result of slipping, or falling, or being in close enough proximity to food that is "popping" as it cooks. NIOSH also commented that limiting the use of fryers to only those which automatically raise and lower cooking baskets may reduce the risk of injuries, but the limitation would not prevent all burn injuries associated with fryers. The CLC, the AFL-CIO, and the UFCW cited data provided by NIOSH and expressed concerns about the risks associated with the high temperatures at which grills and fryers operate. With regard to the use of deep fat fryers equipped with devices that automatically raise and lower the baskets, the UFCW questioned whether such devices are effective in assuring safety; and the NCLC opposed allowing youths to cook with such fryers because of the unreliability of such equipment and a concern that supervisors of young workers would assign them to operate equipment even though it did not comply with the restriction. A Dallas based labour consultant recommended that the Department heed the NIOSH and CLC recommendations.

The National Restaurant Association supported the proposal to allow 14- and 15-year-olds to cook with gas and electric grills that do not involve cooking over an open flame; the Association did not comment concerning the proposal pertaining to the use of deep fryers. The National Council of Chain Restaurants supported the proposal regarding cooking with gas and electric grills, and noted its assumption that the proposal would allow these employees to operate "automated broilers" which cook chicken, hamburgers, and other foods without exposure to an open flame. The Council recommended that the proposal regarding deep fryers be modified, to permit these employees to cook with all fryers including those not equipped with devices that automatically raise and lower the baskets. The Council stated that such devices do not add to operator safety and that "the job of using a deep fryer is just as safe for the operator regardless of whether the basket is lowered and raised automatically or manually." The NCLC commented that, absent any contrary-indicating injury data, it would appear that permitting the use of electric and gas grills that do not include an open flame may not contribute to a rise in teen occupational injuries; the NCLC stated that should such data exist, promulgating this portion of the proposal should be delayed until NIOSH could generate a study of teen occupational injuries resulting from the use of such grills.

Only one commenter—NIOSH—addressed the proposal to continue the Department's long-standing positions on several additional matters: permitting 14- and 15-year-olds to operate microwave ovens that are used only to warm prepared food and do not have the capacity to warm above 140 [deg]F; permitting such minors to use, dispense, and serve food from warmers, steam tables, and other warming devices (even if the temperatures exceed 140 [deg]F); permitting them to perform kitchen work and other work to prepare and serve food and beverages; and banning them from using such equipment as rotisseries, pressurized equipment including fryolators, and cooking devices that operate at extremely high temperatures such as "Neico broilers." On all of these matters, NIOSH concurred with the Department's proposal.

The commenters expressed contradictory views with regard to the proposal to allow 14- and 15-year-old workers to clean kitchen equipment (not otherwise prohibited), remove oil or grease filters, pour oil or grease through filters, and move receptacles containing hot grease or hot oil, but only when the equipment, surfaces, containers and liquids do not exceed a temperature of 140 [deg]F. NIOSH did not oppose minors performing the named tasks, but did object to establishing 140 [deg]F as the maximum temperature. Noting that the Department had proposed this temperature because it had been established as the minimum temperature at which a first-degree burn can occur, NIOSH objected to the Department allowing youths performing [[Page 75387]] these clean-up tasks to be exposed to a temperature sufficient to cause first-degree burns. The AFL-CIO, the UFCW, and the CLC expressed similar concerns. Neither NIOSH nor any of the other commenters suggested a temperature which, in their opinion, would be an acceptable standard for the equipment or materials with which these youths would be performing clean-up tasks. The AFL-CIO, the UFCW, and the CLC along with the NCLC questioned the practicality of the proposal. These commenters expressed doubt that the minors, their employers, and enforcement officials would be able to determine when and if the equipment, oil, or grease had cooled to the permissible temperature of 140 [deg]F, and the CLC inquired whether the Department could enforce the standard "short of a reported injury which indicates non- compliance." The UFCW and the AFL-CIO expressed further concern about the lack of training provided to adolescents in the quick-service restaurant industry, as reported in a 1999 study by NIOSH.

The Education Development Center, Inc. (EDC) of Newton, Massachusetts, took no position on the matter but submitted data and incident reports from the Massachusetts Department of Public Health regarding occupational injuries in restaurants and retail bakeries. The EDC expressed the view that this information "underscores the problem of burn injuries among teen workers." Included in the information was a reference to training materials prepared by the Educational Foundation of the National Restaurant Association for its members, Aware; Employee and Customer Safety. Manager's Manual, Preventing Burns, 1997 (Inventory Code MG 525, ISBN: 1-883904-62-5. National Safety Council Inventory Code: 15865-0600), which identified 100 [deg]F as the appropriate temperature for oil or grease to be handled by workers (adults or minors) for disposal.

The National Restaurant Association supported the proposal concerning clean-up tasks, including the standard of a maximum allowable temperature of 140 [deg]F for equipment and materials to be handled by youths in such tasks. The National Council of Chain Restaurants did not directly address the proposal concerning permissible clean-up tasks and the maximum allowable temperature.

The Department received some general comments, but no detailed information, in response to the Proposed Rule's request for data and comments on baking activities. NIOSH and the UFCW recommended that the Reg. 3 ban on all baking activities be maintained. The only comment concerning a possible weight limitation came from the UFCW, which recommended against establishing weight limitations on lifting by minors, because a standard would be difficult to enforce and would not work in practice. The Council of Chain Restaurants recommended that the Department give consideration to relaxing the across-the-board prohibition on baking when such functions are performed in a retail restaurant setting, stating that such activities are "generally extremely safe" for employees, including 14- and 15-year-olds. The National Restaurant Association, while not addressing the issue of identifying potentially permissible baking activities, offered to conduct a survey of its membership to gather more detailed information for the Department's consideration.

The Department has given careful consideration to all the views and recommendations presented in the comments, and has examined all the materials and authorities that were provided and/or cited by the commenters. Based on this thorough evaluation, the Department has concluded that the Proposed Rule concerning Reg. 3 cooking restrictions will be made final with certain limited modifications as described below.

With regard to the elimination of the "in plain view" interpretation, the Department has concluded that the proposed standard should be adopted to replace the "soda fountains, lunch counters, snack bars" regulatory language which had been the basis of that interpretation. The Final Rule permits 14- and 15-year-olds to perform only cooking tasks using electric or gas grills which do not have open flames, and using deep fryers which are equipped with and utilize devices that automatically lower and raise the baskets. This standard allows all 14- and 15-year-olds to perform the kinds of cooking tasks that many such workers have, for decades, been permitted to perform under the "lunch counter" regulatory language (provided that these tasks were performed "in plain view" of the customers). The Department, therefore, does not view this standard as substantially altering the nature of the Reg. 3 restriction, or as increasing the exposure of individual youngsters to possible harm in their food service establishment work sites. The standard provides more consistency in protecting young workers' health and well-being, by specifying the allowable cooking tasks without regard to the manner in which work sites may be arranged by different employers (i.e., the existence of a wall or a pass-though partition, which may vary from worksite to worksite, will have no effect on whether a cooking task is allowable). The standard provides more consistency for employers' child labour compliance efforts and business operations, since all employers will be held to the same rule on allowable cooking tasks regardless of the appearance or arrangement of their worksites. The standard assures the health and well-being of young workers by limiting their cooking tasks to specific types of equipment (i.e., no open flames, no manually-operated deep fryer baskets), but leaves opportunities for employment in the food service establishments which have been—and will continue to be—extremely important "first job" experiences for many thousands of young workers. The Department is sensitive to the concerns of commenters who recommended that 14- and 15-year-olds should no longer be permitted to perform any cooking duties whatsoever, due to the possibilities of accidents in the workplace. But the Department believes that such a rule would be unnecessarily broad and that it would be an unwarranted barrier to the personal development of youths that benefit in many ways from positive, healthful work experiences in food service establishments. The Department considers the Final Rule— severely restricting the types of cooking duties that may be performed by such minors—to be appropriate.

The Department seeks to forestall any confusion which might arise from the comment of the Council of Chain Restaurants concerning this portion of the Proposed Rule. The Council indicated that it viewed the proposal to allow youths to cook with "no open flame" electric and gas grills as permitting these workers to use a number of automated broilers which are used to broil chicken, beef, and hamburgers as well as toast bread and buns. The Department cautions that the proposal did not alter the Department's long-standing position that cooking with such broilers is prohibited. That position is expressly stated in the Final Rule to prevent misunderstanding, as further discussed below. The Council also recommended that 14- and 15-year-old employees be permitted to cook with all deep fryers, including those not equipped with devices that automatically raise and lower the baskets. The Council stated that "the job of using a deep fryer is just as safe for the operator regardless of whether the basket is lowered and raised automatically or manually." The Department considers both the use of [[Page 75388]] baskets and the automatic basket device to be important safety features because they significantly restrict the young workers' likelihood of contact with the hot oil or grease in the fryer. Therefore, the Department cautions that 14- and 15-year-olds may not use deep fryers that do not use baskets to contain the food product during frying, nor may they use fryers that require the operator to manually lower or raise the baskets. To assure that employers are fully informed, the Final Rule expressly requires that deep fryers must utilize automatic baskets in order for such employees to cook with them.

In connection with the proposal to continue several long-standing Departmental positions concerning cooking and cooking-related activities, the Department has concluded that the positions should be continued in the Final Rule. As explained in the NPRM Preamble, these positions ban 14- and 15-year-olds from using equipment such as rotisseries, fryolators and "Neico broilers," and permit them to use certain microwave ovens, to use and serve foods from certain warming devices, and to perform various food preparation and kitchen work. The only commenter that addressed these positions—NIOSH—specifically endorsed each of them. No commenter objected to any of the positions. In light of the comment record, as well as the Department's enforcement experience, we believe that it is appropriate to maintain all of these positions. In addition, we believe that the text of Reg. 3 should be modified to add clear statements of two of these standards that have, heretofore, been interpretations of the existing regulatory provisions. Having all of these standards expressly included in the regulation will provide better guidance for employers and greater protections for young workers. Consequently, the Final Rule contains all of these long- established departmental standards.

With regard to the proposal that 14- and 15-year-olds be permitted to perform certain clean-up functions on equipment and materials at a temperature no higher than 140 [deg]F, the Department has concluded— after review of the comments—that a modification in the maximum allowable temperature is appropriate.

While the commenters did not object to the tasks that would be permitted, most of the commenters objected to the maximum allowable temperature of 140 [deg]F, the temperature at which a minor would be exposed to a first-degree burn. Upon careful consideration, the Department concurs with the views of the commenters and has concluded that the regulation should set a temperature standard which would substantially alleviate the potential for these young employees receiving even a superficial burn when performing the authorized cleaning, filtering and disposal activities. None of the commenters suggested an alternative to the proposed maximum allowable temperature. Therefore, the Department has looked to available data and industry publications in order to identify the appropriate maximum allowable temperature of 100 [deg]F.

The Department has reviewed the data presented in a 1990 article entitled Recommended Maximum Temperatures for Touchable Surfaces (Applied Ergonomics 1990, 21.1, 69-73), in which the author, H. Siekman, demonstrates that there can be no single "maximum temperature for touchable surfaces" below which burns can be avoided. The maximum safe temperature varies with both the materials from which the surface is made and the amount of time the skin stays in contact with the hot surface. The article notes that the maximum safe touchable temperature is attained at 140 [deg]F when contact is made for a period of 3-4 seconds with a smooth, uncoated metal surface or with water. The maximum safe touchable temperature for these two same surfaces is reached at 149 [deg]F when the contact lasts no more than one second. Although the author did not determine the maximum safe touchable temperature for oil or grease, the Occupational Safety and Health Administration's Office of Occupational Medicine has advised us that similar burns will occur from contact with oil or water when the temperature and length of the exposures are the same for each liquid.

The Department has considered the safety guidelines for the food service industry, published by the Educational Foundation of the National Restaurant Association—Aware: Employee and Customer Safety. Manager's Manual, Preventing Burns, 1997 (Inventory Code MG 525, ISBN: 1-883904-62-5. National Safety Council Inventory Code: 15865-0600). These safety guidelines recommend that the oil from deep fryers be cooled to 100 [deg]F prior to disposal (without differentiating when an adult or a minor employee performs such tasks).

The Department has concluded that a maximum allowable temperature of 100 [deg]F—for equipment surfaces as well as for oil and grease— will significantly diminish the possibility of young workers suffering burns while cleaning equipment and surfaces or while filtering and disposing of cooking oil and grease.

The Department recognizes that compliance with this standard will require vigilance by employers, whose managers and supervisors must assure that equipment and materials have cooled to 100 [deg]F or less, before young workers are allowed to undertake any clean-up tasks such as washing the machines or removing or filtering the oil or grease. This supervision may be exercised through the use of thermometers, and through the imposition of cool-down waiting periods during which the equipment is out of use while the temperature falls. The Department's enforcement of this standard will use the investigative methods which have consistently been used in the child labour program. As with other child labour restrictions, the investigator would, of course, consider a violation to be self-evident where there is an injury to a young worker as a result of the specified activities (e.g., worker's hand burned by oil that the worker was filtering or removing). As with other restrictions, the investigator would also identify violations through observations at the worksite and through interviews with workers (both adults and minors) and supervisors, to obtain information concerning the tasks performed by youths.

The ban on cleaning grilles that exceed a temperature of 100 [deg]F would not prohibit 14- and 15-year-olds from performing the normal grill "maintenance" that an employee routinely does during the actual cooking process involving the use of water and a spatula to scrape away and remove food particles and grease from the surface of the grill.

With regard to the Reg. 3 prohibition on all baking activities by 14- and 15-year-olds, the Department has concluded that no regulatory modification will be undertaken at the present time. The comments addressing this point were general statements of positions, either opposed to any change in the existing regulation or in favor of a relaxation of the existing prohibition. No specific information was submitted. The National Restaurant Association offered to conduct a survey of its members to obtain information and requested an extension of the comment period for this purpose, but the Department concluded that it would not be appropriate to further delay the rule making procedure to provide time for this activity. The Department would welcome any survey information that the Association may provide. The matter of the Reg. 3 prohibition on [[Page 75389]] baking activities may be considered in future rule making. The Proposed Rule did not contain provisions dealing with the training of young workers. However, several commenters expressed concerns that young workers fail to receive on-the-job training that is crucial to protecting their health and well-being. The Department recognizes the important roles that occupational safety education and training—in the home, in the classroom, and on-the-job—play in helping teens experience positive work experiences and in reducing injuries to all workers. The Department encourages all those who can positively impact the health and well-being of young workers to expand their efforts in this important area of safety instruction.

C. Explosives and Articles Containing Explosive Materials (HO 1) (29 CFR 570.51)

Hazardous Occupations Order No. 1, originally issued in 1939, greatly restricts the employment of minors in any establishment which manufactures or stores explosives or articles containing explosive components (e.g., plants that manufacture dynamite, fireworks, or gunpowder). HO 1 also prohibits minors from handling and transporting primers and blasting caps.

The regulation's definition of the crucial terms "explosives and articles containing explosive components" has become, in part, obsolete. The definition states that these terms "mean and include ammunition, black powder, blasting caps, fireworks, high explosives, primers, smokeless powder, and all goods classified and defined as explosives by the Interstate Commerce Commission in regulations for the transportation of explosives and other dangerous substances by common carriers * * * issued pursuant to the [Interstate Commerce Act] * * * ". Congress abolished the Interstate Commerce Commission in 1995. The HO 1 incorporation of ICC regulatory standards is, therefore, no longer feasible and the Department proposed to revise the definition to eliminate this ICC reference.

The Department considers it essential that the HO 1 definition of "explosives and explosive components" be as complete, clear, and user-friendly as possible, so as to best serve the FLSA's purpose of protecting young workers from hazards. Therefore, while preparing to delete the incorporation of ICC standards, the Department sought an alternate source of expertise in the identification of explosives and explosive components. After careful consideration, the Department concluded that the appropriate source of expertise is the Bureau of Alcohol, Tobacco, Firearms, and Explosives, Department of Justice (ATF). Prior to the enactment of the Homeland Security Act of 2002, the ATF was part of the Department of Treasury and was named the Bureau of Alcohol, Tobacco and Firearms. Under statutory and regulatory mandates (18 U.S.C. 841(d); 27 CFR 55.23), the Director of ATF must revise and publish at least annually in the Federal Register a list of explosives covered by the U.S. Code Title 18 provisions concerning importation, manufacture, distribution and storage of explosive materials. The ATF list, which covers explosives, blasting agents and detonators, is intended to include any and all mixtures containing any of the materials on the list. At the time of the publication of the Proposed Rule, the most recent ATF list had been published in the Federal Register on May 1, 1998 (63 FR 24207). The most recent list was published in the Federal Register on March 31, 2004 (69 FR 16958). The Department proposed to revise the HO 1 definition of "explosives and articles containing explosive components" to include the materials identified in the 1998 ATF list, and have it appear in an appendix to the HO 1 subsection of the regulations. The Department pointed out that, by comparing this alphabetical list of materials to the product information for materials that are used or stored at the work site (e.g., the list of contents found on the product package), employers and other parties could readily determine whether any product or material is an explosive or contains explosive components, so as to be within the HO 1 prohibition.

Only two comments were received on this proposal. NIOSH recommended that, as the ATF list is to be updated in the Federal Register annually, the Department should reference the "current" list rather than incorporate the 1998 list into the regulations. NIOSH also recommended that the Department retain the more general terminology (e.g., ammunition, fireworks, primers and smokeless powders) within the text of HO 1 as these terms are not contained in the List of Explosive Materials. The CLC supported the Department's referencing of the ATF list of explosives but expressed a concern about the Department's "enforcement of HO 1 protection when it comes to minors being employed in the U. S. military."

The Department has carefully considered these comments and consulted with the ATF. The ATF has advised that the Department's proposed definition of explosives and articles containing explosive components is incomplete as it does not contain all the explosives listed in 18 U.S.C. 841(c)-(f). The ATF noted that the proposed definition, should, but does not, "encompass any chemical compound, mixture or device, the primary or common purpose of which is to function by explosion" as per 18 U.S.C. 841(d). The ATF also reminded the Department that its annual list of explosive materials is not all- inclusive and the fact that an explosive material is not on the list does not mean that it falls outside of the coverage of the law if it otherwise meets the statutory definitions in 18 U.S.C. 841. The ATF also recommended, as did NIOSH, that the Department not publish the annual list of explosives as an appendix of HO 1 but incorporate the list in the HO by reference so as to ensure that the list is current and to avoid the need for additional rulemaking each time the list is revised. The ATF also recommended that the regulation refer the public to the website where ATF publishes the list.

As explained above, the Department's intention in the Proposed Rule was to provide the most complete, clear and user friendly regulation possible, through the incorporation of the ATF list into the regulation (as a complete, alphabetical list in Appendix A) rather than a mere cross-reference to the ATF publication. Upon reconsideration, the Department agrees with NIOSH and the ATF that these goals can be better achieved by incorporating the ATF list of explosive materials into the rule by reference and by providing the public with information as to how to obtain the most current list. Accordingly, the HO 1 Appendix presented in the Proposed Rule has been omitted.

The Department also agrees that greater clarity can be brought to the definition of explosives and articles containing explosive component by adopting ATF's recommendations to expand that definition to include "any chemical compound, mixture, or device the primary or common purpose of which is to function by explosion" and incorporate the statement, as contained on the ATF list of explosive materials, that the list is updated annually and not intended to be all-inclusive. The Department believes that these changes serve to clarify the proposed definition and are of such a nature that they can be incorporated into the final rule without additional public comment. Accordingly, the Department adopts the proposal as a Final Rule with the modifications listed above. The Department notes that, while the Proposed Rule contained a detailed list [[Page 75390]] of particular materials in the Appendix, it did not propose to remove the more general terminology of ammunition, black powder, blasting caps, fireworks, high explosives, primers, and smokeless powder from the HO 1 definition of the terms explosives and articles containing explosive components. Therefore, the NIOSH concern about the regulatory definition is accommodated through the adoption of the rule, as proposed.

In response to the comments of the CLC concerning minors in military service, the Department notes that the jurisdiction of the FLSA—including its child labour provisions—does not extend to members of the United States' armed forces.

D. Driving on Public Roads or Highways (HO 2) (29 CFR 570.52)

Hazardous Occupations Order No. 2, originally issued in 1940, generally prohibits minors under 18 years of age from employment in the occupations of motor-vehicle driver and outside helper on any public road or highway; in or about any mine, logging or sawmilling operations; or in any excavation covered by HO 17 (which includes excavation in trenches, building construction, or tunnels; 29 CFR 570.68). The occupational dangers specifically identified by the original HO 2 included the high degree of accident risk for persons of any age in these occupations, the fact that 16- and 17-year-old drivers experience a proportionately larger number of fatal accidents than older drivers, and the fact that States placed numerous restrictions on employees who perform as drivers and driver helpers.

HO 2 contains two limited exemptions to the prohibition on minors driving on public roads and highways: "incidental and occasional" driving under certain restrictions; and school bus drivers for a limited period under certain restrictions. The history of these two exemptions was discussed in the Proposed Rule. The exemptions are discussed separately below.

1. "Incidental and occasional driving" (Sec. 570.52(b)(1)).

HO 2 provides a limited exemption (Sec. 570.52(b)(1)) permitting 16- and 17-year-olds to drive automobiles and trucks on public roads and highways on an "incidental and occasional" basis when all the following criteria are met:

The automobile or truck being driven does not exceed 6,000 pounds gross vehicle weight;

The driving is restricted to daylight hours;

The minor holds a State driver's license valid for the type of driving involved in the job performed and has completed a State-approved driver education course; and

The vehicle is equipped with a seat belt or similar restraining device for the driver and for each helper, and the employer has instructed each minor that such belts or other devices must be used.

The limited exemption is not applicable to any occupation of motor- vehicle driver that involves towing a vehicle.

The term "incidental and occasional"—while not defined in the regulations—was for many years interpreted by the Department to mean only driving that involves emergency-type situations or that happens at rare intervals. Thus, the Department enforced the exemption as not including driving which, even if only infrequent or sporadic, is an integral part of the job. The Department's interpretation excluded from the exemption any situations where a minor's employment requires routine and regular driving, such as to deliver auto parts, make pizza deliveries, or run errands.

The Department reviewed HO 2 in 1984 and concluded, based upon data involving vehicle-related injuries and fatalities, that HO 2 should be retained in its current form. The Department found that 16-year-olds were involved in a disproportionate share of accidents and tended to be responsible for fatal accidents more often than other drivers. Seventeen-year-old drivers were the next most likely to be involved in such accidents. Teenagers accounted for 8 percent of the population at the time but sustained 17 percent of fatal injuries in automobile accidents.

In 1987, concerned that some of the child labour regulations needed updating, the Department created the Child Labour Advisory Committee (CLAC), a committee whose mandate was to consider, among other things, the appropriate scope of "incidental and occasional" driving in the HO 2 exemption. In 1989, after careful consideration of HO 2, the CLAC recommended clarification of the term "incidental and occasional" driving. The committee's recommendation, discussed below, was later adopted with modifications and issued by the Department as interpretative guidance.

In 1994, in its continuing effort to review its child labour regulations, the Department published an Advance Notice of Proposed Rulemaking (59 FR 25167) seeking the views of the public on possible changes in the child labour regulations, including the Hazardous Occupations Orders. Although HO 2 was not specifically mentioned in the ANPRM, the Department received comments from various groups with differing views of HO 2. For example, the National Automobile Dealers Association (NADA), individual automobile dealerships, and florists requested more flexibility in the Department's interpretation of "incidental and occasional" driving and urged a change in HO 2 to permit minors to spend more time driving on the job. Child advocacy groups, on the other hand, sought to further limit, or to abolish completely, job-related teenage driving. The Child Labour Coalition, for example, supported a definition of "incidental and occasional" which permitted emergency-situation driving only. The Washington State Child Labour Advisory Committee recommended a complete ban on teenagers driving on-the-job.

As a result of comments received in response to the ANPRM, the Department decided to review HO 2. In 1995, in order to clarify the appropriate scope of "incidental and occasional" driving until further rulemaking could be completed, the Wage and Hour Division adopted the Child Labour Advisory Committee's 1989 recommended interpretation. Under this Departmental interpretation of the regulatory language, driving was deemed incidental if it was limited to no more than 20% of the minor's work in any workday and did not exceed 5% of the minor's worktime in any workweek when performed. Driving was deemed occasional if the minor drove on average no more than once in a workweek and no more than four times in a calendar month. A "single episode" of driving meant an occurrence when the employee was working and operated a motor vehicle on behalf of the employer. Although the Child Labour Advisory Committee also recommended that the HO 2 exception should be permitted only for 17-year-olds, the Department did not address this point because it was considered too substantive to be adopted without rulemaking.

The Drive for Teen Employment Act (Pub. L. 105-334) was signed by the President on October 31, 1998. The Act amended the FLSA by adding a new subsection 13(c)(6). This provision prohibits employees under 17 years of age from performing any on-the-job driving of automobiles and trucks on public roadways. It permits 17-year-old employees to drive automobiles and trucks on public roadways only if such driving meets all of the following conditions:

"(A) Such driving is restricted to daylight hours; [[Page 75391]]

"(B) The employee holds a State license valid for the type of driving involved in the job performed and has no records of any moving violation at the time of hire;

"(C) The employee has successfully completed a State approved driver education course;

"(D) The automobile or truck is equipped with a seat belt for the driver and any passengers and the employee's employer has instructed the employee that the seat belts must be used when driving the automobile or truck;

"(E) The automobile or truck does not exceed 6,000 pounds of gross vehicle weight; "(F) Such driving does not include—

"(i) The towing of vehicles;

"(ii) Route deliveries or route sales;

"(iii) The transportation for hire of property, goods, or passengers;

"(iv) Urgent, time-sensitive deliveries;

"(v) More than two trips away from the primary place of employment in any single day for the purpose of delivering goods of the employee's employer or to a customer (other than urgent, time-sensitive deliveries);

"(vi) More than two trips away from the primary place of employment in any single day for the purpose of transporting passengers (other than employees of the employer);

"(vii) Transporting more than three passengers (including employees of the employer); or

"(viii) Driving beyond a 30 mile radius from the employee's place of employment; and

"(G) Such driving is only occasional and incidental to the employee's employment.

"For purposes of subparagraph (G), the term "occasional and incidental" is no more than one-third of an employee's worktime in any workday and no more than 20 percent of an employee's worktime in any workweek."

While the Drive for Teen Employment Act affected the HO 2 exemption for "occasional and incidental" driving, the Act did not affect any other parts of HO 2, which continue to apply as it has since the regulation's promulgation. The HO restrictions apply to driving on public roadways and have no effect on driving of motor vehicles by 16- and 17-year-old employees when performed exclusively on private property (except in or about any mine, logging or sawmilling operations, or any excavation covered by HO 17). The HO 2 prohibition against the employment of 16- and 17-year-olds driving motor vehicles on public roads other than cars and trucks—such as truck-tractors, trailers, semitrailers, and motorcycles—remains the same. The HO 2 prohibition concerning the towing of any vehicle (whether such vehicle is motorized or non-motorized) also remains the same. The HO 2 prohibition concerning the employment of 16- and 17-year-olds as "outside helpers" on motor vehicles is unchanged. The Act also leaves unchanged the applicability of HO 2 regardless of the registration or ownership of the vehicle being driven by the minor. Further, the Act has no effect on the relationship between the FLSA, HO 2, and State laws. Many States have laws setting standards for child labour and teen drivers. When both Federal and State laws apply, the law setting the more stringent standard must be observed.

The Department proposed to revise HO 2 to incorporate the provisions of the Drive for Teen Employment Act and to provide guidance regarding what constitutes "urgent, time-sensitive deliveries." The Department stated its view that such deliveries—prohibited by the Act—would include trips which, because of such factors as customer satisfaction, the rapid deterioration of the quality or change in temperature of the product, and/or economic incentives, are subject to timelines, schedules, and/or turn-around times which might impel the driver to hurry in the completion of the delivery. Such trips would include, but are not limited to, the delivery of pizzas and prepared foods to the customer; the delivery of materials under a deadline (such as deposits to a bank at closing); and the shuttling of passengers to and from transportation depots to meet transport schedules. "Urgent, time-sensitive deliveries" would not depend on the delivery's points of origin and termination, and would include the delivery of people and things to the employer's place of business as well as from that business to some other location.

The Department noted that the employer bears the burden of proving compliance with several conditions contained in the Drive for Teen Employment Act that must be met before a 17-year-old employee may drive automobiles and trucks on public roadways in his/her job performance. These conditions include: the employee must have a State license valid for the type of driving being performed; the employee must have successfully completed a State approved driver education course; and the employee must have no records of any moving violations at the time of hire. The Department did not propose to require that employers create or maintain any records with regard to compliance with the Drive for Teen Employment Act. The Department observed that, in order to better protect themselves against unwitting violations of HO 2, employers may wish to obtain, at the time of hire, sufficient documentation from 17-year-old employees who will be expected to drive on-the-job. This documentation could include such things as an age certificate issued in accordance with the child labour regulations (29 CFR 570.5-.27), photocopies of the minor's driver license and his/her certificate of completion or diploma issued by the State approved driver education course, and correspondence from State or local authorities and/or the minor's insurance company verifying that the minor has no records of moving violations.

The Department also noted that the Drive for Teen Employment Act limits the type and extent of driving a 17-year-old may perform on-the- job. The Department did not propose to require that employers create or maintain any records with regard to compliance with these provisions of the Act. The Department observed, however, that in order to better protect themselves against unwitting violations of these restrictions, employers may wish to maintain logs to keep track of on-the-job driving performed by 17-year-old employees. These logs could identify the driver and show such things as the starting and stopping times of each trip, the destination of each trip, the purpose of each trip, the number of miles driven, the vehicle driven, and the number of passengers riding in the vehicle.

Four comments were received on the proposal to revise HO 2.

NIOSH concurred with the Department's proposal to incorporate the provisions of the Drive for Teen Employment Act in HO 2 and supported the proposed standard regarding "urgent and time-sensitive deliveries." Though agreeing that requiring employers to create new systems of records to document compliance with the revised HO 2 would be unnecessarily prescriptive, NIOSH expressed the view that the proposed guidance to employers—concerning possible records and driving log information—would be helpful to them in their efforts to comply with the law. NIOSH recommended that these suggestions and guidance should be retained in the final rule.

The NCLC stated that it was "disturbed by the extension of commercial driving activities permitted for seventeen year olds" but did support the requirements that these drivers be properly licensed and have no record of moving violations. The NCLC expressed concern as to the enforceability of the proposed regulation, and stated that the [[Page 75392]] Department might be able to monitor and enforce compliance if the Department's suggestions (concerning employer documentation of the licensing and driving history of 17-year-olds, as well as logs concerning the nature and extent of their driving) were made requirements.

A Dallas-based labour consultant echoed the sentiments of the NCLC and stated that the proposal—suggesting, but not requiring, possible records—gave an incentive for the employer not to keep any records. He recommended that the rule should require that adequate records be maintained "so that when an investigator checks for compliance it is all documented." He also suggested that the rule should include a requirement that 17-year-old drivers maintain safe driving records while employed.

The National Automobile Dealers Association (NADA) commented on three aspects of the proposal. First, NADA objected to the NPRM Preamble statement that "the employer bears the burden of proving compliance" with the Drive for Teen Employment Act; NADA suggested that the statement should be that "employers are responsible for complying with the Act and with HO 2." Further, NADA objected to the NPRM Preamble's "list[ing] gratuitously a host of detailed recordkeeping 'suggestions.' " NADA recommended that these suggestions be deleted "so as to avoid any conflict with the Act's intent or with Paperwork Reduction and Regulatory Flexibility Acts requirements." Finally, NADA objected to the proposed definition of urgent, time sensitive deliveries. While acknowledging that "employers should not require employee drivers, least of all teenagers, to drive under time restraints that may result in speeding or otherwise compromise safety," NADA stated that that the proposed definition "can be read to restrict an employer's ability to see that work responsibilities are completed in a timely manner and without inappropriate delay." NADA observed that "[t]he fact is, younger workers often require extra oversight regarding their work timeliness. Consequently, the * * * definition should * * * distinguish between deliveries that are prohibited because they necessarily call for haste or undue speed and those that evidence responsible work habits." NADA did not suggest alternative language.

The Department has fully considered these comments.

With regard to the employer's obligation to assure compliance, and the NPRM Preamble suggestions as to methods by which the employer may meet that obligation, the Department has concluded that the rule will be issued as proposed and that the compliance suggestions (which were not proposed for inclusion in the regulation) will not be withdrawn.

As pointed out by NADA, the employer bears the burden of complying with the Drive for Teen Employment Act. An employer can permit a 17- year-old employee to drive on public roads or highways in the course of his/her job duties only through the "incidental and occasional driving" exemption incorporated into the FLSA by the Drive for Teen Employment Act. If the Department conducts an investigation, it will follow its normal investigation procedures to determine if the employer complied with child labour requirements, including the restrictions on driving. If the Department finds a violation, it will be the employer's burden—as it is for all statutory and regulatory exemptions—to establish that it did not violate the driving restrictions. It is well settled that an employer seeking to avail itself of any exemption to FLSA provisions must be able to prove satisfaction of all the requirements of that exemption. See e.g., Arnold v. Ben Kanowsky, 361 U.S. 388, 392 ; reh. denied, 362 U.S. 945 (1947); Donovan v. United Video, Inc., 725 F.2d 577, 580-81 (10th Cir. 1984). The employer may carry this burden of proof through documents or records of its own choice; the Department does not impose any particular requirements as to documentation. However, we consider it to be appropriate to offer assistance to employers who seek to comply with the FLSA and HO 2. Therefore, the Department has made suggestions of several easy-to-use methods that employers may wish to follow—which include obtaining and/ or photocopying documentation concerning such things as the age, licensing and driving history of the 17-year-old, and the maintaining of certain logs concerning on-the-job driving. These suggested methods are purely voluntary, despite the recommendations of some commenters that these records be made mandatory. No employer will be penalized for not having the materials identified in the suggestions. Since the Department is not imposing any recordkeeping burdens on employers through this compliance assistance, there is no conflict with the intent of the Drive for Teen Employment Act, or with the requirements of the Paperwork Reduction Act and Regulatory Flexibility Act.

With regard to the definition of urgent, time-sensitive deliveries, the Department has concluded that the rule will be issued as proposed. The definition encompasses the types of on-the-job driving that are likely to involve 17-year-old employees in hurried and therefore hazardous work activity. The Department concurs with NADA's comment that "young workers often require extra oversight regarding their work timeliness" and believes that this need for oversight is a natural result of their youth and inexperience in the world of work. The Department recognizes that, on a day-to-day basis, employers of young workers provide training in important work habits such as timeliness, productive use of worktime, attention to details, and responsiveness to instructions. Employers can better protect the health and well-being of their young workers by taking their need for extra oversight into account during all aspects of their employment. An employer's oversight should include assuring that adequate time is provided for the young worker's safe completion of tasks, and assuring that appropriate instructions are given to the worker in a clear and effective manner. Employers should be aware that if a young driver is not given enough time to complete a trip without hurrying, or if he/she is given instructions which imply a requirement for hurried action, an on-the- job trip that would not normally fall within the definition of an urgent, time-sensitive delivery would become one.

The Department is confident that employers of 17-year-old drivers will recognize the needs of their young workers, and will exercise appropriate oversight in developing work skills while assuring compliance with the Drive for Teen Employment Act. The Department has considered the suggestion of one commenter that the rule should include a requirement that 17-year-old drivers maintain safe driving records while employed. However, we have concluded that the Drive for Teen Employment Act does not authorize the imposition of such a requirement. The statute speaks only of the young driver having "no records of any moving violation at the time of hire." 2. School Bus Drivers (Sec. 570.52(b)(2))

Hazardous Occupations Order No. 2 provides a limited exemption for driving on public roads and highways by certain youths employed as school bus drivers (Sec. 570.52(b)(2)). This exemption has been included in HO 2 for decades, but was revised to its present form in 1991. The Department conducted a review of the school bus driver exemption in 1990, and gave particular attention to the views of the Child Labour Advisory Committee (discussed above). A Proposed Rule was [[Page 75393]] published in 1990, addressing this exemption along with some other issues concerning other HOs (55 FR 42812). A Final Rule was issued in 1991 (56 FR 58626), revising the school bus drivers exemption to permit employment of young workers as school bus drivers only through the 1995-1996 school year, for certain schools that were already employing young drivers under authorizations previously issued by the Department.

The Department proposed to delete from HO 2 the now-expired school bus driver exemption. The exemption was available only to certain "grandfathered" school districts and, by the explicit language of the regulation, expired with the 1995-1996 school year. The Department saw no justification for a revival of the exemption, since our records reflect that this exemption was last used by a school district in the 1994-1995 school year, one year before the exemption's last available school term under the regulation.

No comments were received concerning this proposal. The proposed deletion of this HO 2 provision is implemented in the Final Rule.

E. Scrap Paper Balers and Paper Box Compactors (HO 12) (29 CFR 570.63)

Hazardous Occupations Order No. 12 generally prohibits minors under 18 years of age from working in occupations involving the operation of paper-products machines. The HO prohibits the loading, operation and unloading of scrap paper balers, including paper box balers and compacting machines, and other power-driven machines used in the remanufacture or conversion of paper or pulp into a finished product. When HO 12 was promulgated in 1954, the dangers specifically associated with the operation of scrap paper balers involved being caught in the plungers during the compression process and suffering strains and other injuries while moving the compressed bales.

The Department has consistently interpreted HO 12 to apply to any establishments that use such paper-products machines, including retail stores. The Department has long interpreted the regulation as applying to paper box compactors (which generally perform the same function, utilize the same processes of compacting, and present the same dangers as scrap paper balers) although paper box compactors are not specifically named in the HO. The Department has also interpreted the prohibitions of HO 12 as applying to equipment used exclusively to process paper products, even though machines used to process other materials, in addition to paper products, share the identical machine designs, operation methods, and potential risks.

As a result of reports the Department received in the 1980s of injuries to minors employed in retail stores involving paper balers, in 1990-91 the Wage and Hour Division conducted a review of HO 12 as it applied to grocery stores and other retail operations. Through a Proposed Rule (55 FR 42812), followed by a Final Rule (56 FR 58626), HO 12 was amended in December 1991. The regulation was clarified as applying where the baled paper products were recycled, as well as where they were disposed of as trash. Further, the regulation's prohibition on "operation" was clarified as not including the stacking of materials in areas adjacent to the machine. Finally, the regulation was revised to explicitly state that HO 12 applied to all establishments that used such machines, consistent with long-established Departmental interpretation.

The Department published an Advance Notice of Proposed Rulemaking in

1994 (59 FR 25167), seeking the public's views on possible changes in the child labour regulations, including the Hazardous Occupations Orders. Although HO 12 was not specifically mentioned in the ANPRM, the Department received comments from representatives of the grocery industry asserting that recent technological changes have rendered certain new balers and compactors safe for minors to load. The Food and Allied Service Trades Department, AFL-CIO, opposed any relaxation of the prohibitions contained in HO 12. The Child Labour Coalition also opposed any relaxation of HO 12 and suggested that it should be expanded to include all compactors.

The Compactor and Baler Act was signed by the President on August 6, 1996 (Pub. L. 104-174). This legislation amends the FLSA by adding a new subsection 13(c)(5) to permit 16- and 17-year-olds to load, but not operate or unload, scrap paper balers and paper box compactors only if all of the following conditions are met:

"(A) [The loading involves] * * * scrap paper balers and paper box compactors—

"(i) That are safe for 16- and 17-year-old employees loading the [machines]; and

"(ii) That cannot be operated while being loaded.

"(B) For purposes of subparagraph (A), scrap paper balers and paper box compactors shall be considered safe for 16- and 17-year-old employees to load only if:

"(i) (I) The scrap paper balers and paper box compactors meet the American National Standard Institute's Standard ANSI Z245.5-1990 for scrap paper balers and Standard ANSI Z245.2-1992 for paper box compactors; or

"(II) The scrap paper balers and paper box compactors meet an applicable standard that is adopted by the American National Standards Institute after the date of enactment of this paragraph and that is certified by the Secretary to be at least as protective of the safety of minors as the standard described in subclause

"(ii) The scrap paper balers and paper box compactors include an on-off switch incorporating a key-lock or other system and the control of the system is maintained in the custody of employees who are 18 years of age or older;

"(iii) The on-off switch of the scrap paper balers and paper box compactors is maintained in an off position when the scrap paper balers and paper box compactors are not in operation; and

"(iv) The employer of 16- and 17-year-old employees provides notice, and posts a notice, on the scrap paper balers and paper box compactors stating that:

"(I) The scrap paper balers and paper box compactors meet the applicable standard described in clause (i);

"(II) 16- and 17-year-old employees may only load the scrap paper balers and paper box compactors; and

"(III) Any employee under the age of 18 may not operate or unload the scrap paper balers and paper box compactors."

The NPRM stated that the Compactor and Baler Act required that all employers subject to the FLSA submit a report to the Secretary of Labour when an employee under 18 years of age died or suffered an injury requiring medical treatment (other than first aid) as a result of contact with a scrap paper baler or a paper box compactor during the loading, operation, or unloading of the equipment (Sec. 13(c)(5)(C)). This reporting obligation, which expired on August 6, 1998, required that the report be submitted within ten days of the occurrence of the injury or death. Only one report, involving the serious injury of a minor in Cass County, Texas, was received by the Department during the mandatory reporting period.

The NPRM also explained that the Compactor and Baler Act modified section 16(e) of the FLSA—concerning civil money penalties—to specify that such penalties may be assessed for violations of the new subsection 13(c)(5) as well as other child labour provisions. The Act did not modify the amount of the penalty under section 16(e), which [[Page 75394]] at that time was a maximum of $10,000 per violation for each minor who was the subject of the violation.

The Department proposed to amend HO 12 to incorporate the provisions of the Compactor and Baler Act. The NPRM specified that the regulation's prohibition on 16- and 17-year-olds operating and unloading compactors and balers would not be changed, and the regulation would specify that these minors may load machines only in accordance with the standards set by the Act. The Department noted that employers bear the burden of proving compliance with these standards:

(1) The equipment must meet the ANSI standards imposed by the Act. The NPRM recognized that Congress explicitly applied certain industry standards for the determination of which balers and/or compactors are safe for minors to load: American National Standards Institute's (ANSI) Standard ANSI Z245.5-1990 for scrap paper balers or Standard ANSI Z245.2-1992 for paper box compactors. ANSI is a national organization that coordinates the development of voluntary, consensus standards in a wide range of areas, including product and worker safety. Congress has used ANSI standards in other contexts as expressions of the best available technology in the safety area. For example, the Occupational Safety and Health Act of 1970 directed the Department of Labour to adopt the then-existing ANSI standards, rather than delay any activity until the agency

promulgated particular occupational safety and health standards (see section 6(a) of the Occupational Safety and Health Act, 29 U.S.C. Sec. 655(a)). The ANSI standards for scrap paper balers and paper box compactors govern the manufacture and modification of the equipment, the operation and maintenance of the equipment, and employee training. Because these ANSI standards are copyright-protected, the NPRM stated that the Department cannot include them in the regulations or reproduce them for distribution to the public. Copies of the applicable ANSI standards are available for inspection at the Office of the Federal Register, 800 North Capitol Street, NW., Suite 700, Washington, DC, 20408, at the Occupational Safety and Health Administration Docket Office at Room N2625, U.S. Department of Labour, 200 Constitution Avenue, NW., Washington, D.C., 20210, and at any of the OSHA regional offices. Copies of these standards are available for purchase at the American National Standards Institute, 11 West 42nd Street, New York, New York 10036. The Department proposed that the employer will be required to make an initial determination of whether its machine(s) meet the ANSI standards, and that the Wage and Hour Division may make a final determination in any investigation concerning minors' work with the machines.

The Department's proposal incorporated only the two ANSI standards specified in the Compactor and Baler Act. However, the Department recognized that the Act also provides that any new standard(s) adopted by ANSI would be sufficient for the determination of safety of the balers and compactors if the Secretary of Labour certifies the new standards to be at least as protective of the safety of minors as Standard ANSI Z245.5-1990 for scrap paper balers or Standard ANSI Z245.2-1992 for paper box compactors. The NPRM explained that the Department was aware that ANSI has adopted newer standards for scrap paper balers (Standard ANSI Z245.5-1997) and for paper box compactors (Standard ANSI Z245.2-1997). When the NPRM was issued, the Department was in the process of reviewing these standards to determine if they are at least as protective of the safety of minors as those standards cited in the Compactor and Baler Act. A preliminary review indicated the new standards are as protective as those cited in the Act, and the NPRM noted that the Department was considering whether to include the new standards along with the older standards when the final rule was promulgated. The public was invited to provide comment on whether Standard ANSI Z245.5-1997 is as protective of the safety of minors as Standard ANSI-S245.5-1990, and whether Standard ANSI Z245.2-1997 is as protective of the safety of minors as Standard ANSI Z245.2-1992.

(2) Notice is provided and posted on each piece of equipment. The Compactor and Baler Act requires that, before any 16- or 17-year-olds may load materials into scrap paper balers and paper box compactors, the employer must provide notice and post a notice on each piece of equipment stating that the machine meets the applicable ANSI standard, that 16- and 17-year-olds may only load the equipment, and that no employee under age 18 may operate or unload such

equipment. The Department proposed that the employer meet this statutory requirement by posting a permanent notice—containing the necessary information—in a place on the machine that is prominent and easily visible to any persons loading, operating, or unloading it. The Department proposed no specific form of notice but proposed specific language taken from the statutory requirements to be included in the notice.

(3) The equipment must have certain controls and locks. The Compactor and Baler Act requires that the equipment must include an on- off switch incorporating a key-lock or other system, that the control of the system must be maintained in the custody of employees who are 18 years of age or older, and that the on-off switch must be maintained in an off position when the equipment is not in operation. The Department proposed to include these explicit requirements in the regulation.

The Department also proposed to include in the regulation a specific identification of paper box compactors among the types of equipment subject to HO 12. The NPRM explained that this addition was required by the legislation, which explicitly includes paper box compactors. In addition, the NPRM stated, this regulatory change would communicate the Department's long held position that HO 12 also applies to paper box compactors which perform the same function, operate in a similar manner, and present the same risks as scrap paper balers, which are explicitly listed in the current regulation.

In addition to the regulatory changes necessitated by the Compactor and Baler Act, the Department proposed to modify HO 12 and its title to include scrap paper balers and paper box compactors that are used to process other materials in addition to paper products. In the past, HO 12 has prohibited minors from loading, operating, and unloading only those scrap paper balers and paper box compactors that are used exclusively to process paper products.

The proposed rule also would amend the regulations in part 579 concerning civil money penalties, to implement the Compactor and Baler Act's explicit authorization for penalties not to exceed $10,000 for each employee who was the subject of a violation of new subsection 13(c)(5) of the FLSA.

The Department received six comments on this proposal—from NIOSH, the Food Marketing Institute (FMI), the Council, the NCLC, the CLC, and the National Grocers Association (NGA). None of the commenters opposed the proposal to incorporate the provisions of the Compactor and Baler Act into the regulation. However, the commenters differed with regard to some of the particulars of the proposed regulation, as discussed by topic below. Notice to be posted on machine. Opinions differed as to the wording of the notices that must be posted on balers and compactors that 16- and 17- [[Page 75395]] year-olds would be authorized to load, but not operate or unload.

The Department proposed that the exact language appearing in the statute be required on all notices in order to eliminate confusion and provide employers with clear guidance. The Department also believed that minors, who change jobs frequently, would receive greater overall protection if the posting language were consistent among all employers.

The NCLC commented that, while it had opposed and continues to oppose the Compactor and Baler Act, it realized that the Department must implement the provisions of the statute. In that context, the NCLC stated that it supported "the clear and stringent proposed revisions" to HO 12. The CLC also supported the Department's proposal but recommended that the notice should also include language prohibiting any minor from placing his or her hands, arms, or legs into the machine at any time.

Both the NGA and the FMI objected to the Department's proposal to adopt, for the required notice, the language exactly as it appears in the statute. Both organizations recommended that the Department not adopt the verbatim statutory language for the notice but, instead, allow employers to use the notice "stickers" which these organizations have developed for their industry. The NGA stated that, along with the FMI, it had undertaken an educational compliance program to inform retailers and wholesalers of how to comply with the new law. This program included the developing and marketing of notice stickers, copies of which were provided to the Department along with their comments. The organizations asserted that these stickers were in compliance with the posting requirements of the Compactor and Baler Act. The FMI also stated that it worked closely with ANSI experts to ensure that the stickers were consistent with industry safety standards and would effectively attract the attention of employees approaching or intending to use the machines. The FMI and the NGA pointed out that adoption of the proposed rule would render their stickers unusable.

After carefully considering the comments, the Department agrees that accepting only those notices which reflect the exact wording of the Compactor and Baler Act would be overly prescriptive. The Department believes that the intent of the Compactor and Baler Act will be satisfied if each notice: (1) Contains an accurate statement that the baler or compactor to be loaded by the minor meets the applicable ANSI standard named in section 13(c)(5)(B)(i)(I) of the FLSA or meets a more recent ANSI standard which the Secretary has certified to be at least as protective of the safety of minors as the standard described in section 13(c)(5)(B)(i)(I); (2) cites the specific ANSI standard, including the year of issuance, that the employer is providing notice that the equipment meets; (3) includes a clear statement that 16- and 17-year-olds may only load the scrap paper balers and paper box compactors; and, (4) includes a clear statement that no employee under the age of 18 may operate or unload the scrap paper balers and paper box compactors.

The Department has examined the sample notices—stickers—provided by both the NGA and the FMI. We note that these stickers do not clearly identify the applicable ANSI standard as required by the Compactor and Baler Act. ANSI includes, in the caption or title of each of its standards, both a "series identifier" and a year of issuance, so as to eliminate confusion between different editions of standards that apply to the same type of machinery. Congress recognized this precision of ANSI nomenclature when, in adopting the Compactor and Baler Act, it specifically required that balers meet Standard ANSI Z245.5-1990 and compactors meet Standard ANSI Z245.2-1992. ANSI has issued a succession of standards in the Z245.5 series for balers: Standard ANSI Z245.5- 1982; revised and replaced by Standard ANSI Z245.5-1990 (approved December 12, 1989); revised and replaced by Standard ANSI Z245.5-1997. ANSI does not always adopt the same series identifier when revising and replacing standards for a type of machinery. The standard specified in the Act for compactors—Standard ANSI Z245.2-1992—replaced Standard ANSI Z245.1-1984. The sample notices submitted by the FMI and the NGA do not include the year the ANSI standard was issued, but merely reference the series identifier number. The Department considers this notice to be inadequate. We are concerned that an employer who utilizes a baler that is over 20 years old—but which meets the antiquated Standard ANSI Z245.5-1982—would be under the mistaken impression that after applying the sticker provided by the FMI or NGA, he/she could legally allow 16- and 17-year-old employees to load that equipment. We are also concerned about employers who might apply this sticker, and mistakenly assume themselves to be in compliance with the law by relying on a new ANSI standard which had not been certified by the Department as providing at least the same levels of protection to young workers as those specifically named in the Compactor and Baler Act. It is imperative that all notices posted in accordance with the Compactor and Baler Act cite both the series identifier and year of issuance for the ANSI standard, so that employers, their supervisory staff, and their young workers are fully informed, as Congress intended them to be.

The Department would consider the NGA and FMI stickers to constitute acceptable notices if they are modified to state explicitly the full caption of the ANSI standard (both the series identifier and the year of issuance). This modification may, of course, be made by printing all future stickers with the full, accurate information as to the specific applicable standard. But existing stickers may also be modified by making hand-written insertions of the additional information that is necessary to identify the specific standard. Such insertions must be written legibly, in indelible ink, and in the same size of lettering as the ANSI standard identifiers already printed on the sticker.

The NGA and the FMI have also provided copies of stickers they have developed to be placed on equipment that does not meet the requirements of the Compactor and Baler Act and, therefore, cannot be loaded, operated or unloaded by any employee who is less than 18 years of age. These stickers, which are not required by the Act and the use of which is completely voluntary, alert employees that they may not load, operate or unload the equipment unless they are 18 years of age or older. The Department appreciates these efforts by the NGA and the FMI and encourages all employers to adopt similar signage when applicable, as part of their efforts to reduce occupational injuries to young workers and increase compliance with the child labour provisions.

Making the determination that the equipment meets the ANSI standard named in the Compactor and Baler Act or a more recent ANSI standard the Secretary has certified as being at least as protective of the safety of minors. The FMI objected to the Department proposal that the employer will be required to make an initial determination of whether its machine(s) meet the ANSI standards, and that the Wage and Hour Division may make a final determination in any investigation concerning minors' work with the machines. The FMI asserted that the Compactor and Baler Act does not support this proposal, and suggested [[Page 75396]] that a machine's satisfaction of ANSI standards should be established by the reasonable assurances of the machine's manufacturer coupled with maintenance records. The FMI expressed concern that the employer should not be required to maintain any records beyond these assurances and maintenance records.

The Department considers the proposed provision to be necessary to achieve the clear intent of the Act, which is to allow minors to load machines (despite the HO 12 prohibition) only if such machines meet the ANSI standards specified in the statutory and regulatory exemption. The employer which has its young employees loading these machines can lawfully do so only pursuant to this exemption. As discussed above with respect to the HO 2 "incidental and occasional driving" regulation, the employer must be able to prove its satisfaction of all the requirements of this, or any other, FLSA exemption. The employer cannot know whether its operation is in compliance with the exemption (i.e., cannot know whether its minor employees are permitted to load a particular machine) unless and until it determines that the machine meets the applicable ANSI standard. While the information mentioned by FMI would, of course, be important, the employer should also consider other pertinent information, such as equipment modifications, performance of scheduled maintenance, and equipment malfunctions. The Department does not, and will not, prescribe that any particular documentation or records be created by the employer.

As part of an investigation authorized by section 11(a) of the FLSA, the Wage and Hour Administrator may make a determination as to whether the equipment meets the ANSI standard cited on the notice posted by the employer on the machine; such a determination may be essential to an investigative finding of whether the employer has violated the regulation. The employer, of course, may request administrative review where the Administrator determines that minors are working in violation of the regulation because the machine they are using does not meet the ANSI standard. Upon reflection, the Department recognizes that the phrase "final determination" in the Proposed Rule may be confusing, in that the Administrator's investigative determination would be subject to review and, if appropriate, to revision in the administrative adjudicatory process. Therefore, the Department has concluded that the regulation should not state that the Administrator's investigative determination is "final."

After carefully considering the FMI comment, the Department has concluded that the proposed provision is necessary and appropriate under the FLSA and the Compactor and Baler Act. The proposed provision—with the word "final" deleted—is included in the Final Rule.

The Secretary's review of the more recent ANSI standards. The Compactor and Baler Act applies specific ANSI standards, issued by the organization in 1990 (balers) and 1992 (compactors). However, the Act also provides that any new standard(s) adopted by ANSI would also be sufficient for the determination of safety of the balers and compactors, if the Secretary of Labour certifies the new standard(s) to be at least as protective of the safety of minors as the two standards specified in the Act. In the NPRM, the Department stated that it was reviewing two new ANSI standards, and invited the public to comment on whether those standards should be certified by the Secretary.

Only one commenter, NIOSH, directly addressed the newer ANSI standards, supporting their incorporation into the regulation "as they are as protective as previous standards cited in the Compactor and Baler Act." The CLC cautioned the Department to review thoroughly new ANSI standards for their effectiveness in protecting working minors, and to revise the regulation to reflect improved safety protection standards as they are introduced. The Department agrees with the CLC, concerning the importance of careful consideration of new safety standards. The Department's review of the new ANSI standards agrees with NIOSH's findings. The Secretary, in promulgating this Final Rule, hereby certifies that Standard ANSI Z245.5-1997 is as protective of the safety of minors as Standard ANSI-S245.5-1990 and that Standard ANSI Z245.2-1997 is as protective of the safety of minors as Standard ANSI Z245.2-1992. Accordingly, these newer standards are included in the Final Rule.

Revising HO 12 to include scrap paper balers and paper box compactors that are used to process other materials in addition to paper products. The Department proposed to modify HO 12 to include scrap paper balers and paper box compactors that are used to process other materials in addition to paper products. As explained in the NPRM, HO 12 has, in the past, prohibited minors from loading, operating, and unloading only those scrap paper balers and paper box compactors that are used exclusively to process paper products.

The FMI and the NGA objected to this proposal as being unauthorized, stating that the Compactor and Baler Act addresses only machinery used for paper products. These commenters, along with the Council, also stated that the Department had provided no basis or evidence for the expansion of HO 12.

NIOSH supported this proposal, stating "[r]eview of surveillance and investigation data demonstrate that baling and compacting equipment are associated with deaths and injuries of workers, that these deaths are associated with uncontrolled hazardous energy and inadequate machine guards, and that deaths and injuries result from machines that process non-paper materials (e.g., aluminum cans, plastic, foam, and rubber) as well as paper materials." NIOSH reported that data covering the period of October 1, 1996 through December 31, 1999, reflects that balers and compactors were responsible for an estimated 2,625 injury reports nationwide. Almost half of the injuries occurred while working in either a retail or grocery store, with 24% occurring in manufacturing. NIOSH also reported that at least 29 occupational fatalities involving paper balers and compactors occurred between 1992 and 1997.

In making the proposal to modify HO 12, and in considering the comments on the proposal, the Department has given careful thought to the Secretary's long-standing and important statutory duty to ban unsafe working conditions for minors. The FLSA, at section 3(l), gives the Secretary the authority and responsibility to identify and declare those occupations which are "particularly hazardous for the employment of children * * * or detrimental to their health or well-being." In meeting this statutory duty, the Secretary has promulgated the seventeen Hazardous Occupations Orders, including HO 12 on balers and compactors. The Secretary need not and should not wait for additional legislation when making determinations concerning the safety and well- being of working youth.

Since its inception, HO 12 has prohibited minors from loading, operating and unloading balers and compactors that are used exclusively to process paper products. In proposing to expand the scope of the regulation, the Department recognized that the existing, narrow prohibition ignores the fact that these machines are used to compress materials in addition to paper without any changes in design or procedures for loading, operating and unloading. Such other materials which may be processed [[Page 75397]] by scrap paper balers and paper box compactors include, but are not limited to, plastics, rubber, food waste, foam rubber and aluminum cans. The risks which these machines present to minor employees remain the same, regardless of the materials being processed. The information provided by NIOSH demonstrates that injuries and deaths continue to occur in the loading, operation and unloading of these machines, whether or not they are used exclusively for paper products. Further, the Department's enforcement experience shows that these machines are, indeed, "particularly hazardous" to load, operate or unload. For example, in recent years the Wage and Hour Administrator has investigated cases involving a 16-year-old who was killed operating a compactor, a 17-year-old whose arm was crushed while operating a compactor, and a 15-year-old who suffered a serious injury to his hand while operating a paper baler.

The Department does not believe that its revision of the scope of HO 12 required a new legislative authorization through the enactment of the Compactor and Baler Act. The Department's authority with regard to all of the Hazardous Occupations Orders is based on long-standing FLSA provisions. However, we note that the proposed expansion of HO 12 to include machines used for materials in addition to paper products is, in fact, supported by the definitions of both balers and compactors contained in the ANSI Standards which Congress adopted in the Compactor and Baler Act. Standard Z245.5-1990, for balers, identifies the materials which may be processed by the machines: "Primary materials includ[ing] natural and synthetic fibers and their by-products;" "Waste paper (newsprint, corrugated containers, and the like), trim scrap, mill broke, metals (other than ferrous scrap), and textiles* * *" Standard Z245.2-1992, for compactors, identifies the "refuse" which may be processed: "Any type of solid waste (except human wastes), including garbage, rubbish, ashes, incinerator residues, street cleanings, plant trimmings, and residential, commercial, and industrial solid wastes, including recyclable materials." Further, the Department takes the position that the lack of reports from employers pursuant to the Compactor and Baler Act is not a factor in this revision of HO 12; the Department's enforcement experience and the data provided by NIOSH are ample information as to the "particular hazards" of these machines. We note, however, that the one report submitted by an employer pursuant to the Act involved an incident in which a 17-year-old had both his legs amputated in a baler machine at a recycling center. At the time of his injury, the machine was crushing cardboard, but the machine was the only baler at the center and, therefore, was also used for processing other materials, including plastic.

Accordingly, the Secretary has determined that occupations involving the loading, operating and unloading of scrap paper balers and paper box compactors that process other materials in addition to paper are particularly hazardous for minors between 16 and 18 years of age. The proposed modification of HO 12 is included in the Final Rule. The Department notes that after the issuance of this Final Rule, there will still be one class of balers and compactors that falls outside of the scope of HO 12—those machines that process everything and anything but paper products. These machines share similar designs and operating procedures with those compactors and balers that process only paper products or process other materials in addition to paper products. The Secretary has not made a determination that occupations involving the loading, operating and unloading of balers and compactors that do not process paper are particularly hazardous to the health and well-being of youths between 16 and 18 years of age. The Department will continue to review this matter and may consider future rulemaking to further revise HO 12.

In addition, two minor editorial modifications to the existing regulation have been made in the Final Rule. The word "also" in the last sentence of section

570.63(b)(2) (ii) which is part of the definition of the term paper products machine was moved to avoid any confusion over what types of machines are subject to the HO. The word "of" in section 570.63(b) (3) that defines the term scrap paper baler has been replaced with the word "or" to comport with the language in the ANSI standard.

Proposal to amend the regulations in part 579 concerning civil money penalties. In the 1999 NPRM, the Department proposed to amend the regulations in sections 579.1 and 579.5 to implement the Compactor and Baler Act's explicit authorization for civil money penalties not to exceed $10,000 for each employee who was the subject of a violation of new subsection 13(c)(5) of the FLSA. No comments were received on this proposal. After publication of the 1999 NPRM, but prior to the publication of this Final Rule, the Department published a different Final Rule in accordance with the Federal Civil Penalties Inflation Adjustment Act of 1990, as amended by the Debt Collection Improvement Act of 1996 (66 FR 63501, December 7, 2001). That regulatory action not only increased the maximum amount of the civil money penalty that may be assessed under the FLSA for a child labour violation to $11,000, but also implemented the Compactor and Baler Act's authorization for civil money penalties. As the Compactor and Baler Act's authorization for civil money penalties has already been incorporated into section 579.5, that proposed change need not be included in this Final Rule. The corresponding proposed changes to section 579.1, however, are included in this Final Rule.

The Final Rule includes both the Federal Civil Penalties Inflation Adjustment Act change in the maximum amount of the penalty and the change specified in the Proposed Rule.

F. Work in Roofing Occupations (HO 16) (29 CFR 570.67)

Hazardous Occupations Order No. 16 covers "occupations in roofing operations." It bans all occupations in roofing, but not all work on roofs. Roofing operations, as defined by the regulation, include most roofing activities and related occupations whether performed at elevations or at ground level. Not included are other tasks performed on or near roofs such as the installation, repair and maintenance of roofing sheathing, television and microwave antennas, air conditioning equipment, and gutters and downspouts.

The Department has received inquiries questioning why employees under 18 years of age may perform any work on a roof. Available data, such as that provided by NIOSH and the Massachusetts State Department of Health, indicates that working at heights is a major contributor to injuries and deaths of young workers.

The Department's 1994 Advance Notice of Proposed Rulemaking (59 FR 25167) raised the issue of minors working at heights. The ANPRM requested comments regarding a ban on all work performed by minors on roofs. The ANPRM also requested information as to whether such a prohibition should be a generic restriction or one limited to a particular industry or industries. Finally, the ANPRM sought information regarding exemptions from HO 16 for apprentices and student learners.

The Department received a number of comments on this issue, the vast majority of which supported the prohibition of roofing work and all work [[Page 75398]] on a roof. Many supported a complete prohibition against minors working above a certain elevation, often specified as 6 to 10 feet. The comments came from a variety of sources, including industry organizations, child advocates, and State and Federal agencies.

The single ANPRM commenter not in favor of prohibiting all work on a roof was the Associated Builders and Contractors, Inc. (ABC), which opposed a ban on 16- and 17-year-olds working at heights. ABC commented that a ban would jeopardize valuable career-advancing opportunities and that proper supervision, safety instructions, and training are sufficient to reduce or alleviate any heightened risk of injury without sacrificing the benefit of work experience.

After considering all of the information obtained in response to the ANPRM, the Department proposed to amend HO 16 to expand the ban from all roofing occupations to include all work performed on or about a roof. This ban would include, but not be limited to, occupations on or in close proximity to roofs such as the installation, repair, and maintenance of gutters and downspouts, installation of sheathing, roof trusses or roof bases, television antennas, air conditioners, exhaust and ventilating equipment, heating equipment, and similar appliances attached to roofs. The Department also proposed that the exemption for apprentices and student-learners employed under the conditions prescribed in 29 CFR 570.50(b) and (c) would continue to apply under HO 16. The Department stated its view that the additional supervision and training required by the exemption, coupled with the limited exposures provided by the exemption, will help to reduce safety risks to 16- and 17-year-olds working on roofs.

Four comments were received concerning this proposal. NIOSH supported broadening the scope of HO 16, as proposed.

NIOSH reported that the roofer occupation is among the occupations at highest risk of fatal work-related injury among workers of all ages. NIOSH stated that work on and around roofs is associated with falls from heights and contact with electrical energy, and that these two causes of injury together accounted for 18% of work-related injury deaths of 16- and 17-year-olds in the 1980's. Further, NIOSH reported that hazards are associated with workers using roofs as a means of access or support for other work at heights. As an example of such hazards, NIOSH discussed the death of a 17-year-old window washer who plunged 15 floors to his death due to the failure of the rigging he had attached to the roof of the building.

ABC--which had been the only ANPRM commenter that did not favor prohibiting all work on a roof—commented that it believed its previous concerns had been substantially addressed through the proposed regulation's preservation of the exceptions for apprentices and student-learners.

The NCLC and the CLC opposed the proposal as not having gone far enough. These commenters recommended that the regulation should prohibit minors working at elevations "in any and every capacity" whether on roofs, hanging out windows, or working on ladders, scaffolds, or other elevated surfaces. The CLC suggested that the prohibition should apply to work at elevations above 6 feet.

The Department has carefully considered the comments and available data, as well as our own enforcement experience. Based on this information, the Department has concluded that the dangers cited in the report supporting the promulgation of HO 16 still persist for youths working not only in roofing occupations but also on or about roofs. The main danger for such youths is from falls which may occur in any work performed on or about a roof. This danger was demonstrated by three recent incidents investigated by the Wage and Hour Administrator. Two minors (one in Pennsylvania and one in Alabama) fell to their deaths while employed in the installation of roofing trusses (part of building construction, but not a roofing occupation under the current regulation). A third minor, 16 years of age, died in July of 2002 in Arizona after falling from a roof while assisting in the maintenance of an air conditioning unit (again, work on a roof but not a roofing occupation under the current regulation). The danger of falls was also demonstrated in the incident cited by NIOSH: death of a window washer who worked on the roof of the building to attach and then enter the rigging which failed and caused his fall. Additional dangers in work on or about a roof include exposure to electricity, as discussed by NIOSH and as demonstrated in a case recently investigated by the Wage and Hour Administrator in which a 17-year-old was killed when the pipes he was hoisting to a roof (for assembly there into clothing racks) came into contact with overhead power lines.

The Department notes that the regulatory phrase on or about a roof is not limited to circumstances where the minor employee is standing or working on the roof itself. The prohibition extends to standing or working on a ladder or scaffold at or near the roof, working on the installation of roof trusses or joists which will support the roof, as well as working from or being transported to or from the roof in mechanical devices such as hoists. Thus, for example, a minor is prohibited from working on a scaffold (as well as on the roof itself) to install roof flashing or gutters. To avoid the possibility of confusion as to the scope of this prohibition, the proposed definition of the term on or about a roof has been modified in the Final Rule, to clarify that the term includes work "upon or in close proximity to a roof" and to clarify that the installation of trusses or joists is included in the "construction of the base of roofs" within the meaning of this definition.

The Department ·s carefully considered the views of commenters who suggested that the regulation should ban all work at an elevation, such as at a height of six feet. While we recognize that there may be some risk of accidents whenever workers are performing tasks above ground level, we have concluded, based on available data, that all such work by minors cannot be declared to be particularly hazardous. Therefore, we believe that such an across-the-board prohibition would be unwarranted, at the present time, and would deny minors many safe and promising employment opportunities such as library assistants climbing low ladders to retrieve or replace books, or retail stock clerks retrieving or restoring merchandise to shelving, or lifeguards mounting their stands at poolside. This matter may be further addressed in a future rule making, if appropriate. The Department has concluded that occupations involving working on or about roofs, as well as all occupations in roofing operations, are particularly hazardous for minors between 16 and 18 years of age, and accordingly adopts the proposal as a Final Rule with the modifications discussed above.

G. Miscellaneous Matters

The Department has also made minor, nonsubstantive, changes to the regulations that are not discussed above. The 1999 NPRM proposed that the section headings contained in Subparts B and C of 29 CFR Part 570 and in 29 CFR Part 579 be presented as questions. It was believed such a format would more clearly identify the contents of each section. Upon further review, the Department has determined that headings consisting of a few words, or a short phrase, will be more useful to [[Page 75399]] the reader. Accordingly, the question format has not been adopted and the section headings will now consist of a few words or a short phrase. Also, as mentioned earlier, the 1999 NPRM proposed to revise 29 CFR Part 579.5 to incorporate the civil money penalty provisions of the Compactor and Baler Act. This revision was accomplished by a separate Final Rule published by the Department (66 FR 63501, December 7, 2001) and therefore does not need to be included in this Final Rule. Furthermore, the Department has concluded that four numbered subsections of the existing regulation on civil money penalties are obsolete—three "reserved" (Sec. Sec. 579.6-.8) and one dealing with the implementation of the1990 FLSA amendment which increased the child labour civil money penalty to $10,000 (Sec. 579.9). The Final Rule removes these subsections from the regulation. In addition, the Department is also revising 29 CFR Part 579.3(a)(5) to remove a no longer appropriate reference to 29 CFR Part 545. Part 545, which was titled Homeworkers in Industries in Puerto Rico, was removed by the Department in 1990 as a result of the 1989 amendments to the FLSA (55 FR 12114, March 30, 1990). Finally, in keeping with current guidance provided by the Federal Register, we have restructured the definitions in 29 CFR 570.63 and 570.67 to reflect an alphabetical sequence.

III. Changes to Procedural Regulations (29 CFR Part 580)

The Department has determined that the procedural regulations— dealing with administrative hearings and appeals of civil money penalties—require updating to make it clear that the administrative procedures are a prerequisite to judicial review and to identify the Department's Administrative Review Board as the entity to which appeals from Administrative Law Judge decisions are taken. The Final Rule makes the necessary changes in Part 580 procedural regulations. Because these revisions pertain to rules of agency procedure or practice, notice of proposed rulemaking and public comment procedures are not required for these revisions pursuant to Section 553(b)(3)(A) of the Administrative Procedure Act, 5 U.S.C. 553(b)(3)(A). Therefore, these procedural amendments are being adopted as a final rule without prior notice and comment.

IV. Paperwork Reduction Act

Federal Certificate of Age

Title: Form WH-14, Application for Federal Certificate of Age.

Summary: Section 3(l) of the Fair Labour Standards Act (FLSA), 29 U.S.C. 203(l), provides, in part, that an employer may protect against unwitting employment of "oppressive child labour" (as defined in section 3(l)) by having on file a certificate issued pursuant to DOL regulations, certifying that the named person meets the FLSA minimum age requirements for employment.

Section 11(c) of the FLSA, 29 U.S.C. 211(c), requires that all employers covered by the Act make, keep and preserve records of wages, hours and other conditions and practices of employment with respect to their employees. The employer is to maintain the records for such period of time and make such reports as prescribed by regulations issued by the Secretary of Labour.

Regulations, at 29 CFR Part 570, subpart B, set forth the requirements for obtaining certificates of age from the Department. The regulations provide that State-issued age, employment or working certificates, which substantially meet the Federal regulatory requirements for certificates of age, are an acceptable alternative to obtaining a Federal certificate of age. The regulations contain a list of States that may issue such acceptable certificates. Since age certificates are issued by most States, these are widely used as proof of age for FLSA child labour purposes.

Federal certificates of age are issued by the Department upon request by the youth and the prospective employer. Form WH-14 is the DOL application form. As a practical matter, it is used in those States where no State certificates are issued or State certificates do not meet the Federal regulatory requirements. The Wage and Hour Division reviews each WH-14 application and the accompanying proof of age, which is identified in the regulation as sufficient to establish the young applicant's age and thus to achieve the intended purpose of the statutory provision (i.e., to afford the employer an affirmative defense against unwitting violations of the child labour provisions). As appropriate, a Federal certificate of age is issued and forwarded to the employer (if the youth is under 18 years of age) or to the youth (if he/she is 18 or 19 years of age). The supporting evidence of age is returned to the applicant(s). The 18- or 19-year-old presents the certificate to his/her employer upon entering employment.

The employer is required to keep the certificate on file for the duration of the youth's employment, in order to achieve the intended purpose of the FLSA provision (i.e., to protect the employer in situations where compliance with the child labour standards is questioned). The estimated average employment period is 6 months. When a youth under 18 years of age leaves employment, the employer was directed, prior to this revision of the regulation, to return the certificate to the office that issued it, except that a certificate for employment in agriculture might be given to the youth; any subsequent certificate of age requested for that youth could be issued without additional proof of age. A certificate of age issued for a youth 18 or 19 years of age was to be given by the employer to the youth upon his/ her leaving employment.

Need: In August 1998, the Office of Management and Budget (OMB), in its review and approval of the Form WH-14 under the Paperwork Reduction Act, approved this information collection (OMB No. 1215-0083). OMB's approval was contingent upon DOL's agreement to eliminate the requirement for an employer to return the certificate to the issuing official in certain circumstances. The Department, as agreed with OMB, has revised the regulation at Sec. 570.6(b)(1) to direct employers to give to each employee, upon termination of employment, any Federal age certificate issued in his/her name. This would occur regardless of the age of the employee and regardless of the type of employment (i.e., agriculture or nonagriculture). This regulatory provision will enable young workers to provide future employer(s) with a properly issued age certificate without having to make another application to a government official. The Department has also revised the statement at the end of Sec. 570.6(b)(2) to reflect the new OMB control number.

Respondents and frequency of response: It is estimated that 10 such WH-14 applications will be submitted annually.

Estimated total annual burden: It is estimated that each such application will take approximately ten minutes to complete for a total annual burden of one and two-thirds hours (10 applications x 10 minutes per application = 1.667 hours). The filing of a Federal Certificate of Age is estimated to take one-half minute per document for a total annual burden of .083 hours (10 Federal Certificates of Age x .5 minutes = .083 hours).

Total Annual Reporting and Recordkeeping Burden = 1.75 Hours.

Employees and employers of any of a wide variety of businesses, from small farms or retail stores to large manufacturing plants, may request Federal certificates of age. Absent specific wage data regarding applicants, respondent costs are estimated utilizing the average hourly rate of non-supervisory workers on non-farm payrolls of $15.38 for 2003 (Monthly Labour Review, U.S. Department of Labour, Bureau of Labour Statistics). Total annual respondent costs are estimated at $26.92 ($15.38 x 1.75 hours).

Total estimated annual postage and envelope costs for transmitting these applications are $4.00 (10 reports x $.37 postage + $.03 per envelope).

Total Annual Respondent Costs for FORM WH-14, Application for Federal Certificated of Age—$30.92 ($26.92 + $4.00). No comments were received from the public regarding this burden. Two comments were received on the substantive aspects of the regulatory proposal concerning age certificates and these are discussed earlier in this document.

No changes have been made in this Final Rule which affect the information collection and recordkeeping requirements and estimated burdens previously submitted to OMB and discussed in the proposed rule.

V. Executive Order 12866

This rule is being treated as a "significant regulatory action" within the meaning of Executive Order 12866, because of its importance to the public and the Department's priorities. Therefore, the Office of Management and Budget has reviewed the rule. However, because this rule is not "economically significant" as defined in section 3(f)(1) of EO 12866, it does not require a full economic impact analysis under section 6(a)(3)(C) of the Order. In addition, this rule imposes no new information collection, recordkeeping, or reporting requirements subject to the Paperwork Reduction Act of 1995 (44 U.S.C. 3501, et seq.).

It is well established that several characteristics of youth place adolescent workers at increased risk of injury and death. Lack of experience in the work place and in assessing risks, and developmental factors—physical, cognitive, and psychological—all contribute to the higher rates of occupational injuries and deaths experienced by young workers. The Census of Fatal Occupational Injuries, U.S. Department of Labour, Bureau of Labour Statistics, reported that during the years of 1992-1997, 15-year-olds actually experience an occupational fatality rate per 100,000 fulltime equivalents that is greater than the average for all workers. A NIOSH report also showed that the fatality rate for adolescents aged 16 and 17 was 5.1 per 100,000 full-time equivalent workers for the 10-year period 1980-89 [Castillo et al. 1994], while the rate for adults aged 18 and older was 6.1. As NIOSH stated, "[t]his relatively small difference in rates is cause for concern because youths under age 18 are employed less frequently in especially hazardous jobs." Special Hazard Review: Child Labour Research Needs. Recommendations from the NIOSH Child Labour Working Team, Ch. 2, August 1997. NIOSH also estimates that youth work injuries exceed 200,000 each year, and of that number,

77,000 are serious enough to warrant treatment in hospital emergency rooms. The NIOSH statistics show that, despite the fact that workers aged 15 through 17 are generally restricted from performing in hazardous occupations such as mining, motor-vehicle driving, logging, sawmilling and construction, they have a higher rate of injuries requiring emergency room treatment than any other age group except 18- and 19-year-olds (who are not restricted from performing such work). NIOSH Recommendations to the U. S. Department of Labour for Changes to Hazardous Orders, p. 8, May 2002. The economic and social costs associated with the deaths and serious injuries of young workers are substantial.

The Department considers the issuance of this rule as an important and necessary step in its ongoing review of the criteria for permissible child labour employment, a review which strives to balance the potential benefits of transitional, staged employment opportunities for youth with the necessary protections for their education, health and safety. Because youth often overcome the effects of those characteristics that initially place them at increased risk of injury and death in the workplace only through the maturation process, it is believed that requiring older workers to perform those tasks that present greater risks to younger workers actually eliminates injuries and deaths " rather than delaying them or transferring them to the older workers.

This rule revises the child labour regulations in response to two statutory amendments enacted by the Congress that altered two of the child labour hazardous occupation orders: HO 12, affecting activities involving certain scrap paper balers and paper box compactors; and HO 2, affecting the operation of motor vehicles. The economic impact of these statutory provisions is expected to be minimal. The Department believes that only a few minors employed in such occupations would be affected by these revisions. In addition, any costs that might result from using older employees to perform the prohibited tasks would be more than offset by reduced health and productivity costs resulting from accidents and injuries to minors on the job. The additional changes are also expected to have little or no direct cost impact. The changes affecting the types of cooking and related food preparation activities that 14- and 15-year olds may perform in food service establishments (Reg. 3 Occupations) are primarily clarifications of existing provisions. Changes to HO 16 to prohibit youth under age 18 from performing all work on roofs and an update of definitions for the term "explosives" in HO 1 that prohibits minors working where "explosives" are made or stored are expected to affect few minors. A change in the regulation on government-issued certificates of age intended to reduce paperwork when a minor's employment ends would reduce the cost impact of the existing regulation.

In addition, the information required to be disclosed or posted on machines covered by the Baler and Compactor Act does not impose new burdens under the Paperwork Reduction Act because the information to be disclosed is originally supplied by the Federal government under the statute and these regulations (see

5 CFR 1320.3(c)(2)). The Department believes that any new costs incurred by employers to comply with the notice requirements would be de minimis. The Department estimates that the largest group of employers that will qualify for and take advantage of this limited exemption are grocery stores and food service establishments, of which only approximately 20% of the grocery stores (3,395) and 1% of the eating and drinking establishments (2,003) are covered by the FLSA, have balers or compactors which meet the ANSI standards named in the Compactor and Baler Act, and employ 16- and 17- year-old minors who they wish to utilize to load the balers or compactors, for a total of 5,398 affected employers.

Compliance with the notice requirements can be achieved by purchasing or creating a notice with all required information and affixing it to the baler or compactor. Once the notice is affixed and assuming all the equipment continues to meet the required ANSI Standard, the requirement is permanently satisfied and need only be repeated if the notice [[Page 75401]] is damaged or destroyed. Some employers may purchase the required notice. Some employers may create their own notice. Some employers have only one baler or compactor; others have several, possibly at multiple locations. Considering these various situations, we estimate that it will take an average of 4 minutes per employer to satisfy the notice requirement for a total, one-time burden of 360 hours. Absent specific wage data regarding the employees who will satisfy these notice requirements, respondent costs are estimated utilizing the average hourly rate of nonsupervisory workers of $10.04 in the retail trade for 2002 (Monthly Labour Review, U.S. Department of Labour, Bureau of Labour Statistics). The total additional costs associated with the notice requirement are estimated at $3,614.40 ($10.04 x 360 hours).

The Department also believes that this rule will not reduce the overall number of safe, positive and legal employment opportunities available to young workers. The rule overall modifies certain existing restrictions under two of the HOs and Reg. 3 occupations, expands restrictions under one HO, reduces paperwork burden involving age certificates, and makes other technical, clarifying changes. Although a small number of employers may be required to hire an older worker to perform the prohibited tasks, we believe that any resulting costs directly incurred would be minimal. Rules that limit permissible job activities for working youth to those that are safe do not, by themselves, impose significant added costs on employers, in our view. In fact, ensuring that permissible job opportunities for working youth are safe and healthy and not detrimental to their education, as required by the statute, produces many positive benefits in addition to fewer occupational injuries and deaths, including reduced health and productivity costs that employers may otherwise incur because of higher accident and injury rates to young and inexperienced workers. In any event, the direct, incremental costs imposed by this rule are expected to be minimal. Collectively, they will not have an annual effect on the economy of $100 million or more or adversely affect in a material way the economy or its individual sectors, productivity, jobs, the environment, public health or safety, or State, local, or tribal governments or communities. Therefore, this rule is not "economically significant" and no regulatory impact analysis has been prepared.

VI. Small Business Regulatory Enforcement Fairness Act

The Department has similarly concluded that this rule is not a "major rule" requiring approval by the Congress under the Small Business Regulatory Enforcement Fairness Act of 1996 (5 U.S.C. 801 et seq.). It will not likely result in (1) an annual effect on the economy of $100 million or more; (2) a major increase in costs or prices for consumers, individual industries, Federal, State or local government agencies, or geographic regions; or (3) significant adverse effects on competition, employment, investment, productivity, innovation, or on the ability of U.S.-based enterprises to compete with foreign-based enterprises in domestic or export markets.

VII. Regulatory Flexibility Act and Executive Order 13272

This rule is not expected to have a significant economic impact on a substantial number of small entities. Two provisions (driving and paper balers) are specifically required by statutory amendments enacted by Congress. It is anticipated that the other provisions would have little or no cost impact on any small entities. The amendment to the provisions concerning the circumstances when 14- and 15-year-olds are permitted to cook is primarily a clarification of the existing provision. We believe that the prohibition against work on a roof and the revision to the paper baler and box compactor provisions would affect few minors, and therefore few small businesses. Although a small number of employers would be required to use an older employee to perform the prohibited tasks, we believe that any resulting costs directly incurred would be minimal. Indeed, we believe that the child labour regulations, by fostering safer work environments for working youth, would reduce health and productivity costs to employers, including covered small businesses, resulting from accidents and injuries to minors on the job. Thus, given the nature of the changes proposed by the rule, and for the reasons discussed above, we do not believe the rule will have a significant economic impact on a substantial number of small entities. The Department has certified to this effect to the Chief Counsel for Advocacy of the U.S. Small Business Administration. Therefore, no Regulatory Flexibility Analysis is required.

VIII. Unfunded Mandates Reform Act of 1995

Title II of the Unfunded Mandates Reform Act of 1995 (2 U.S.C. 1531 et seq.) directs agencies to assess the effects of Federal regulatory actions on State, local, and tribal governments, and the private sector, "...(other than to the extent that such regulations incorporate requirements specifically set forth in law)." For purposes of the Unfunded Mandates Reform Act, and as noted above, this rule does not include any Federal mandate that may result in increased annual expenditures in excess of $100 million by State, local or tribal governments in the aggregate, or by the private sector. Moreover, two of the changes constitute "regulations [that] incorporate requirements specifically set forth in law" (i.e., amendments to HO 2 and HO 12).

IX. Effects on Families

This rule has been assessed under section 654 of the Treasury and General Government Appropriations Act, 1999, for its effect on family well-being and the undersigned hereby certifies that the rule will not adversely affect the well-being of families.

X. Executive Order 13045, Protection of Children

Executive Order No. 13045, dated April 23, 1997 (62 FR 19885), applies to any rule that (1) is determined to be "economically significant" as defined in Executive Order No. 12866, and (2) concerns an environmental health or safety risk that the promulgating agency has reason to believe may have a disproportionate effect on children. This action is not subject to Executive Order No. 13045 because it is not economically significant as defined in Executive Order No. 12866. In addition, although this rule impacts the youth employment provisions of the FLSA and the employment of adolescents and young adults, it does not impact the environmental health or safety risks of children.

XI. Executive Order 13132, Federalism

The Department has reviewed this rule in accordance with Executive Order 13132 regarding federalism, and has determined that it does not have "federalism implications." The rule does not "have substantial direct effects on the States, on the relationship between the national government and the States, or on the distribution of power and responsibilities among the various levels of government."
[[Page 75402]]

XII. Executive Order 13175, Indian Tribal Governments

This rule was reviewed under the terms of E.O. 13175 and determined not to have "tribal implications." The rule does not have "substantial direct effects on one or more Indian tribes, on the relationship between the Federal government and the Indian tribes, or on the distribution of power and responsibilities between the Federal government and the Indian tribes." As a result, no tribal summary impact statement has been prepared.

XIII. Executive Order 12630, Constitutionally Protected Property Rights

This rule is not subject to E.O. 12630 because it does not involve implementation of a policy "that has takings implications" or that could impose limitations on private property use.

XIV. Executive Order 12988, Civil Justice Reform Analysis

This final rule was drafted and reviewed in accordance with E.O. 12988 and will not unduly burden the Federal court system. The rule was: (1) Reviewed to eliminate drafting errors and ambiguities; (2) written to minimize litigation; and (3) written to provide a clear legal standard for affected conduct, and to promote burden reduction.

XV. Executive Order 13211, Energy Supply

This rule is not subject to E.O. 13211. It will not have a significant adverse effect on the supply, distribution, or use of energy.

XVI. Environmental Impact Assessment

The Department has reviewed this rule in accordance with the requirements of the National Environmental Policy Act (NEPA) of 1969 942 U.S.C. 1500) and the Department's NEPA procedures (29 CFR part 11). The rule will not have a significant impact on the quality of the human environment, and, thus, the Department has not conducted an environmental assessment or an environmental impact statement.

List of Subjects

29 CFR Part 570 Child labour,

Child labour occupations, Employment, Government, Incorporation by reference, Intergovernmental relations, Investigations, Labour, Law enforcement, Minimum age.

29 CFR Part 579

Child labour, Law enforcement, Penalties.

29 CFR Part 580

Administrative practice and procedure, Child labour, Employment, Labour, Law enforcement, Penalties.

Signed at Washington, DC on the 7th day of December, 2004. Victoria A. Lipnic, Assistant Secretary for Employment Standards. Alfred B. Robinson, Jr., Acting Administrator, Wage and Hour Division. 0

For the reasons set forth above, title 29, parts 570, 579, and 580, of the Code of Federal Regulations are amended as set forth below.

PART 570—CHILD LABOUR REGULATIONS, ORDERS AND STATEMENTS OF INTERPRETATION

Subpart B—[Amended]

0 1.-2. The authority citation for part 570 Subpart B is revised to read as follows:

Authority: 29 U.S.C. 203(l), 211, 212.

0 3. In Sec. 570.5, the section heading is revised to read as follows:

Sec. 570.5 Certificates of age and their effect.

0 4. In Sec.

570.6, the section heading, paragraph

(b)(1) and the parenthetical statement following paragraph (b)(2) are revised to read as follows: Sec. 570.6 Contents and disposition of certificates of age. ***

(b)(1) We will send a certificate of age for a minor under 18 years of age to the prospective employer of the minor. That employer must keep the certificate on file at the minor's workplace. When the minor terminates employment, the employer must give the certificate to the minor. The minor may then present the previously issued certificate to future employers as proof of age as described in Sec. 570.5.

(2) * * *

(The information collection requirements contained in paragraph (a) were approved by the Office of Management and Budget under control number 1215-0083.)

0 5. In

Sec. 570.7, the section heading is revised to read as follows:

Sec. 570.7 Documentary evidence required for issuance of a certificate of age.

0 6.

In Sec. 570.8, the section heading is revised to read as follows:

Sec. 570.8 Issuance of a Federal certificate of age.

0 7.

In Sec. 570.9, the section heading is revised to read as follows:

Sec. 570.9 States in which State certificates of age are accepted.

0 8.

In Sec. 570.10, the section heading is revised to read as follows:

Sec. 570.10 Rules for certificates of age in the State of Alaska and the Territory of Guam.

0 9.

In Sec. 570.11, the section heading is revised to read as follows:

Sec. 570.11 Continued acceptability of certificates of age.

0 10.

In Sec. 570.12, the section heading is revised to read as follows:

Sec. 570.12 Revoked certificates of age.

0 11.

In Sec. 570.25, the section heading is revised to read as follows:

Sec. 570.25 Effect on laws other than the Federal child labour standards.

0 12.

In Sec. 570.27, the section heading is revised to read as follows:

Sec. 570.27 Revision of subpart B.

Subpart C—[Amended]

0 13.

The authority citation for part 570 Subpart C is revised to read as follows: Authority: 29 U.S.C. 203(l), 212.

0 14.

In Sec. 570.31, the section heading is revised to read as follows:

Sec. 570.31 Secretary's determinations concerning the employment of minors 14 and 15 years of age.

0 15.

In Sec. 570.32, the section heading is revised to read as follows:

Sec. 570.32 Effect of subpart

C.

0 16.

In Sec. 570.33, the section heading is revised to read as follows:

Sec. 570.33 Prohibited occupations for minors 14 and 15 years of age.

0 17.

In Sec. 570.34, the section heading and paragraphs (a)(7) and

(b)(5) are revised to read as follows:

Sec. 570.34 Occupations minors 14 and 15 years of age are permitted to perform in retail, food service, and gasoline service establishments.

(a) * * *

(7) Kitchen work and other work involved in preparing and serving food and beverages, including operating machines and devices used in performing such work. Examples of permitted machines and devices include, but are not limited to, dishwashers, toasters, dumbwaiters, popcorn poppers, milk shake blenders, coffee grinders, automatic coffee [[Page 75403]] machines, devices used to maintain the temperature of prepared foods (such as warmers,

steam tables, and heat lamps), and microwave ovens that are used only to warm prepared food and do not have the capacity to warm above 140 [deg]F. Minors are permitted to clean kitchen equipment (not otherwise prohibited), remove oil or grease filters, pour oil or grease through filters, and move receptacles containing hot grease or hot oil, but only when the equipment, surfaces, containers and liquids do not exceed a temperature of 100 [deg]F; * * * * *

(b) * * *

(5) Baking and cooking are prohibited except:

(i) Cooking is permitted with electric or gas grilles which does not involve cooking over an open flame (Note: this provision does not authorize cooking with equipment such as rotisseries, broilers, pressurized equipment including fryolators, and cooking devices that operate at extremely high temperatures such as "Neico broilers"); and

(ii) Cooking is permitted with deep fryers that are equipped with and utilize a device which automatically lowers the baskets into the hot oil or grease and automatically raises the baskets from the hot oil or grease; * * * *

* 0 18.

In Sec. 570.35, the section heading is revised to read as follows:

Sec. 570.35 Hours of work and conditions of employment permitted for minors 14 and 15 years of age.

0 19.

In Sec. 570.35a, the section heading is revised to read as follows:

Sec. 570.35a Work experience and career exploration program.

0 20.

In Sec. 570.36, the section heading is revised to read as follows:

Sec. 570.36 Effect of a certificate of age under this subpart.

0 21.

In Sec. 570.37, the section heading is revised to read as follows:

Sec. 570.37 Effect of this subpart on other laws.

0 22.

In Sec. 570.38, the section heading is revised to read as follows:

Sec. 570.38 Revision of subpart C. Subpart E—[Amended]

0 23.

The authority citation for part 570 subpart E is revised to read as follows: Authority: 29 U.S.C. 203(l), 212, 213(c).

0 24.

In Sec. 570.51, paragraph (b) (2) is revised to read as follows:

Sec. 570.51 Occupations in or about plants or establishments manufacturing or storing explosives or articles containing explosive components (Order 1).

* * * * * (b)

(2) The terms explosives and articles containing explosive components mean and include ammunition, black powder, blasting caps, fireworks, high explosives, primers, smokeless powder, and explosives and explosive materials as defined in 18 U.S.C. 841(c)-(f) and the implementing regulations at 27 CFR part 555. The terms include any chemical compound, mixture, or device, the primary or common purpose of which is to function by explosion, as well as all goods identified in the most recent list of explosive materials published by the Bureau of Alcohol, Tobacco, Firearms, and Explosives, Department of Justice. This list is not intended to be all-inclusive and is updated and published annually in the Federal Register pursuant to 18 U.S.C. 841(d). A copy of the most recent version of the list may be found through the Bureau of Alcohol, Tobacco, Firearms, and Explosives' Web site at http://frwebgate.access.gpo.gov/cgi-bin/leaving.cgi?from=leavingFR.html &log=linklog&to=http://www.atf.gov . * * * * *

0 25.

In Sec. 570.52, paragraph (b) is revised and new paragraphs (c)(5) and (c)(6) are added to read as follows:

Sec. 570.52 Occupations of motor-vehicle driver and outside helper (Order 2). * * * * *

(b) Exemption—Incidental and occasional driving by 17-year-olds. Minors who are at least 17 years of age may drive automobiles and trucks on public roadways when all the following criteria are met:

(1) The automobile or truck does not exceed 6,000 pounds gross vehicle weight, and the vehicle is equipped with a seat belt or similar restraining device for the driver and for any passengers and the employer has instructed the employee that such belts or other devices must be used;

(2) The driving is restricted to daylight hours;

(3) The minor holds a State license valid for the type of driving involved in the job performed and has no records of any moving violations at the time of hire;

(4) The minor has successfully completed a State-approved driver

education course;

(5) The driving does not involve: the towing of vehicles; route deliveries or route sales; the transportation for hire of property, goods, or passengers; urgent, time-sensitive deliveries; or the transporting at any one time of more than three passengers, including the employees of the employer;

(6) The driving performed by the minor does not involve more than two trips away from the primary place of employment in any single day for the purpose of delivering goods of the minor's employer to a customer (except urgent, time-sensitive deliveries which are completely banned in paragraph (b)(5) of this section;

(7) The driving performed by the minor does not involve more than two trips away from the primary place of employment in any single day for the purpose of transporting passengers (other than the employees of the employer);

(8) The driving takes place within a thirty (30) mile radius of the minor's place of employment; and,

(9) The driving is only occasional and incidental to the employee's employment.

(c) * * *

(5) The term occasional and incidental means no more than one-third of an employee's worktime in any workday and no more than 20 percent of an employee's worktime in any workweek.

(6) The term urgent, time-sensitive deliveries means trips which, because of such factors as customer satisfaction, the rapid deterioration of the quality or change in temperature of the product, and/or economic incentives, are subject to time-lines, schedules, and/ or turn-around times which might impel the driver to hurry in the completion of the delivery. Prohibited trips would include, but are not limited to, the delivery of pizzas and prepared foods to the customer; the delivery of materials under a deadline (such as deposits to a bank at closing); and the shuttling of passengers to and from transportation depots to meet transport schedules. Urgent, time-sensitive deliveries would not depend on the delivery's points of origin and termination, and would include the delivery of people and things to the employer's place of business as well as from that business to some other location.

0 26.

In Sec. 570.63, the section heading and paragraphs (a)(1)(i), (b) and (c) are revised to read as follows:

Sec. 570.63 Occupations involved in the operation of paper-products machines, scrap paper balers, and paper box compactors (Order 12).

(a) * * *

(1) * * *

(i) Arm-type wire stitcher or stapler, circular or band saw, corner cutter or mitering machine, corrugating and single-or-double facing machine, [[Page 75404]] envelope die-cutting press, guillotine paper cutter or shear, horizontal bar scorer, laminating or combining machine, sheeting machine, scrap paper baler, paper box compactor, or vertical slotter. * * * * *

(b) Definitions.

Applicable ANSI Standard means the American National Standard Institute's Standard ANSI Z245.5-1990 ("American National Standard for Refuse Collection, Processing, and Disposal—Baling Equipment—Safety Requirements") for scrap paper balers or the American National Standard Institute's Standard ANSI Z245.2-1992 ("American National Standard for Refuse Collection, Processing, and Disposal Equipment— Stationary Compactors—Safety Requirements") for paper box compactors. Additional applicable standards are the American National Standard Institute's Standard ANSI Z245.5-1997 ("American National Standard for Equipment Technology and Operations for Wastes and Recyclable Materials—Baling Equipment—Safety Requirements") for scrap paper balers or the American National Standard Institute's Standard ANSI Z245.2-1997 ("American National Standard for Equipment Technology and Operations for Wastes and Recyclable Materials—Stationary Compactors— Safety Requirements") for paper box compactors, which the Secretary has certified to be at least as protective of the safety of minors as Standard ANSI Z245.5-1990 for scrap paper balers or ANSI Z245.2-1992 for paper box compactors. The ANSI standards for scrap paper balers and paper box compactors govern the manufacture and modification of the equipment, the operation and maintenance of the equipment, and employee training. These ANSI standards are incorporated by reference in this paragraph and have the same force and effect as other standards in this part. Only the mandatory provisions (i.e., provisions containing the word "shall" or other mandatory language) of these standards are adopted as standards under this part. These standards are incorporated by reference as they exist on the date of the approval; if any changes are made in these standards which the Secretary finds to be as protective of the safety of minors as the current standards, the Secretary will publish a Notice of the change of standards in the Federal Register. These incorporations by reference were approved by the Director of the Federal Register in accordance with 5 U.S.C. 552(a) and 1 CFR part 51. Copies of these standards are available for purchase from the American National Standards Institute (ANSI), 23 West 43rd St., Fourth Floor, New York, NY, 10036. In addition, these standards are available for inspection at the National Archives and Records

Administration (NARA) and at the Occupational Safety and Health Administration's Docket Office, Room N2625, U.S. Department of Labour, 200 Constitution Avenue, NW., Washington, DC, 20210, or any of its regional offices. For information on the availability of this material at NARA, call 202-741-6030, or go to: http://frwebgate.access.gpo.gov/cgi-bin/leaving.cgi?from=leavingFR.html&log=linklog&to=http://www.archives.gov/federal_register/code_of_federal_regulations/ibr_locations.html .

Operating or assisting to operate means all work which involves starting or stopping a machine covered by this section, placing materials into or removing materials from a machine, including clearing a machine of jammed paper or cardboard, or any other work directly involved in operating the machine. The term does not include the stacking of materials by an employee in an area nearby or adjacent to the machine where such employee does not place the materials into the machine.

Paper box compactor means a powered machine that remains stationary during operation, used to compact refuse, including paper boxes, into a detachable or integral container or into a transfer vehicle. Paper products machine means:

(1) All power-driven machines used in—

(i) Remanufacturing or converting paper or pulp into a finished product, including preparing such materials for recycling; or

(ii) Preparing such materials for disposal.

(2) The term applies to such machines whether they are used in establishments that manufacture converted paper or pulp products, or in any other type of manufacturing or nonmanufacturing establishment. The term also applies to those machines which, in addition to paper products, process other material for disposal.

Scrap paper baler means a powered machine used to compress paper and possibly other solid waste, with or without binding, to a density or form that will support handling and transportation as a material unit without requiring a disposable or reusable container.

(c) Exemptions.

(1) Sixteen- and 17-year-olds minors may load materials into, but not operate or unload, those scrap paper balers and paper box compactors that are safe for 16- and 17-year-old employees to load and cannot be operated while being loaded. For the purpose of this exemption, a scrap paper baler or a paper box compactor is considered to be safe for 16- and 17-year-old to load only if all of the following conditions are met:

(i) The scrap paper baler or paper box compactor meets the applicable ANSI standard (the employer must initially determine if the equipment meets the applicable ANSI standard, and the Administrator or his/her designee may make a determination when conducting an investigation of the employer);

(ii) The scrap paper baler or paper box compactor includes an on- off switch incorporating a key-lock or other system and the control of the system is maintained in the custody of employees who are 18 years of age or older;

(iii) The on-off switch of the scrap paper baler or paper box compactor is maintained in an off position when the machine is not in operation; and

(iv) The employer posts a notice on the scrap paper baler or paper box compactor (in a prominent position and easily visible to any person loading, operating, or unloading the machine) that includes and conveys all of the following information:

(A) That the scrap paper baler or compactor meets the industry safety standard applicable to the machine, as specified in paragraph (b)(5) of this section. The notice shall completely identify the appropriate ANSI standard.

(B) That sixteen- and 17-year-old employees may only load the scrap paper baler or paper box compactor.

(C) That no employee under the age of 18 may operate or unload the scrap paper baler or paper box compactor.

(2) This section shall not apply to the employment of apprentices or student-learners under the conditions prescribed in Sec. 570.50 (b) and (c).

0 27.

In Sec. 570.67 the section heading and paragraphs (a) and (b) are revised to read as follows:

Sec. 570.67 Occupations in roofing operations and on or about a roof (Order 16).

(a) Finding and declaration of fact. All occupations in roofing operations and all occupations on or about a roof are particularly hazardous for the employment of minors between 16 and 18 years of age or detrimental to their health.

(b) Definitions. On or about a roof includes all work performed upon or in close proximity to a roof, including carpentry and metal work, alterations, additions, maintenance and repair, including painting and coating of existing roofs; the construction of the sheathing or base of roofs (wood or metal), including roof [[Page 75405]] trusses or joists; gutter and downspout work; the installation and servicing of television and communication equipment such as cable and satellite dishes; the installation and servicing of heating, ventilation and air conditioning equipment or similar appliances attached to roofs; and any similar work that is required to be performed on or about roofs.

Roofing operations means all work performed in connection with the installation of roofs, including related metal work such as flashing, and applying weatherproofing materials and substances (such as waterproof membranes, tar, slag or pitch, asphalt prepared paper, tile, composite roofing materials, slate, metal, translucent materials, and shingles of asbestos, asphalt, wood or other materials) to roofs of buildings or other structures. The term also includes all jobs on the ground related to roofing operations such as roofing labourer, roofing helper, materials handler and tending a tar heater. * * * * *

PART 579—CHILD LABOUR VIOLATIONS—CIVIL MONEY PENALTIES

0 28.-29.

The authority citation for part 579 is revised to read as follows: Authority:

29 U.S.C. 203(l), 211, 212, 213(c), 216; Reorg. Plan No. 6 of 1950, 64 Stat. 1263, 5 U.S.C. App; secs. 25, 29, 88 Stat. 72, 76; Secretary of Labour's Order No. 4-2001, 66 FR 29656; 104 Stat. 890 (28 U.S.C. 2461 note), as amended by 110 Stat. 1321-373 and 112 Stat. 3293.

0 30.

In Sec. 579.1, the section heading and paragraphs (a) introductory text, (a)(1), (a)(6) and (c) are revised to read as follows:

Sec. 579.1 Purpose and scope.

(a) Section 16(e), added to the Fair Labour Standards Act of 1938, as amended, by the Fair Labour Standards Amendments of 1974, and as further amended by the Fair Labour Standards Amendments of 1989, the Omnibus Budget Reconciliation Act of 1990, and the Compactors and Balers Safety Standards Modernization Act of 1996, provides that—

(1) Any person who violates the provisions of section 12 relating to child labour, section 13(c)(5), or any regulation issued under those sections shall be subject to a civil penalty of not to exceed $11,000 for each employee who was the subject of such a violation. * * * * *

(6) Except for civil money penalties collected for violations of sections 12 and 13(c)(5), sums collected as penalties pursuant to this section shall be applied toward reimbursement of the costs of determining the violations and assessing and collecting such penalties in accordance with the provision of section 2 of an Act entitled "An Act to authorize the Department of Labour to make special statistical studies upon payment of the cost thereof, and for other

purposes" (29 U.S.C. 9a). * * * * *

(c) This part explains our procedures for issuing a notice of civil penalty to an employer that has violated section 12 or section 13(c)(5) of the Act, or any regulation issued under those sections; describes the types of violations for which we may impose a penalty and the factors we will consider in assessing the amount of the penalty; outlines the procedure for a person charged with violations to file an exception to the determination that the violations occurred; and summarizes the methods we will follow for collecting and recovering the penalty.

0 31.

In Sec. 579.3, the section heading and paragraph (a)(5) are revised to read as follows: Sec. 579.3 Violations for which child labour civil money penalties may be assessed. (a) * * * (5) The failure by an employer employing any minor for whom records must be kept under any provision of part 516 of this title to maintain and preserve, as required by such provision, such records concerning the date of the minor's birth and concerning the proof of the minor's age as specified therein; and * * * * *

0 32.

In Sec. 579.5, the section heading is revised to read as follows:

Sec. 579.5 Determining the amount of the penalty and assessing the penalty.

Sec. Sec. 579.6 through 579.8 [Removed]

0 33.

Sections 579.6 through 579.8 are removed.

PART 580—CIVIL MONEY PENALTIES—PROCEDURES FOR ASSESSING AND CONTESTING PENALTIES

0 34.-35.

The authority citation for part 580 is revised to read as follows:

Authority: 29 U.S.C. 9a, 203, 209, 211, 212, 213(c), 216; Reorg. Plan No. 6 of 1950, 64 Stat. 1263, 5 U.S.C. App; secs. 25, 29, 88 Stat. 72, 76; Secretary of Labour's Order No. 4-2001, 66 FR 29656; 5 U.S.C. 500, 503, 551, 559; 103 Stat. 938.

0 36. Section 580.5 is revised to read as follows:

Sec. 580.5 Finality of notice.

If the person charged with violations does not, within 15 days after receipt of the notice, take exception to the determination that the violation or violations for which the penalty is imposed occurred, the administrative determination by the Administrator of the amount of such penalty shall be deemed final and not subject to administrative or judicial review. Upon the determination becoming final in such a manner, collection and recovery of the penalty shall be instituted pursuant to Sec. 580.18.

0 37.

In Sec. 580.6, paragraph (a) is revised to read as follows:

Sec. 580.6 Exception to determination of penalty and request for hearing.

(a) Any person desiring to take exception to the determination of penalty, or to seek judicial review, shall request an administrative hearing pursuant to this part. The exception shall be in writing to the official who issued the determination at the Wage and Hour Division address appearing on the determination notice, and must be received no later than 15 days after the date of receipt of the notice referred to in Sec. 580.3. No additional time shall be added where service of the determination of penalties or of the exception thereto is made by mail. If such a request for an administrative hearing is timely filed, the Administrator's determination shall be inoperative unless and until the case is dismissed or the Administrative Law Judge issues a decision affirming the determination. * * * * *

0 38.

Section 580.13 is revised to read as follows: Sec. 580.13 Procedures for appeals to the Administrative Review Board.

(a) Any party desiring review of a decision of the Administrative Law Judge, including judicial review, must file a petition for review with the Department's Administrative Review Board (Board). To be effective, such petition must be received by the Board within 30 days of the date of the decision of the Administrative Law Judge. Copies of the appeal shall be served on all parties and on the Chief Administrative Law Judge. If such a petition for review is timely filed, the decision of the Administrative Law Judge shall be inoperative unless and until the Board dismisses the appeal or issues a decision affirming the decision of the Administrative Law Judge.

(b) All documents submitted to the Board shall be filed with the Administrative Review Board, Room S- [[Page 75406]] 4309, U.S. Department of Labour, Washington, DC 20210. An original and two copies of all documents must be filed.

(c) Documents are not deemed filed with the Board until actually received by the Board, either on or before the due date. No additional time shall be added where service of a document requiring action within a prescribed time was made by mail.

(d) A copy of each document filed with the Board shall be served upon all other parties involved in the proceeding. Such service shall be by personal delivery or by mail. Service by mail is deemed effected at the time of mailing to the last known address of the party. Sec. 580.14 [Removed and Reserved]

0 39.

Section 580.14 is removed and reserved.

0 40.

Section 580.16 is revised to read as follows: Sec. 580.16

Final decision of the Administrative Review Board. The Board's final decision shall be served upon all parties and the Chief Administrative Law Judge, in person or by mail to the last known address.

0 41. In Sec. 580.18, paragraph

(a) is revised to read as follows: Sec. 580.18 Collection and recovery of penalty.

(a) When the determination of the amount of any civil money penalty provided for in this part becomes final under Sec. 580.5 in accordance with the administrative assessment thereof, or pursuant to the decision and order of an Administrative Law Judge in an administrative proceeding as provided in Sec. 580.12, or the decision of the Board pursuant to Sec. 580.16, the amount of the penalty as thus determined is immediately due and payable to the U.S. Department of Labour. The person against whom such penalty has been assessed or imposed shall promptly remit the amount thereof, as finally determined. The payment shall be by certified check or by money order, made payable to the order of the Wage and Hour Division, and shall be delivered or mailed to the District Office of the Wage and Hour Division which issued and served the original notice of the penalty.

CHILD LABOUR LAWS IN U.S.: A CARE STUDY OF SOUTH DAKOTA

Most teenagers would probably yell and scream if anyone called them a child, but when it comes to employment, that's how the law views anyone under 18.

The laws aren't there to prevent young people from getting a job; in fact the laws recognize that many young people want to work. The main reason for child labour laws is to protect young people from hazardous jobs, and to make sure employers aren't asking them to work long hours, especially during the school year.

Child labour laws are broken down into three age groups:

16 and 17-year-olds

14 and 15-year-olds

Under 14

16 and 17 Year Olds

The only job restrictions for 16- and 17-year-olds are hazardous occupations. Jobs in this category include:

Working with explosives and radioactive materials.

Mining of any kind.

Logging and saw milling.

Manufacturing brick, tile or similar products.

Excavation, wrecking, demolition and salvage work.

Operating power-driven bakery machines, including dough mixers used in pizza restaurants.

Operating power-driven woodworking machines, including circular band saws and table saws.

Operating power-driven metal forming, punching or shearing machines.

Operating power-driven paper product machines, including paper balers.

Operating or riding on power-driven hoisting apparatus, including non-automatic elevators, fork lifts and cranes, and work that involves riding on a manlift or unattended freight elevator.

All jobs in roofing operations, except work on gutters and downspouts, or installing air conditioners or ventilation equipment.

Most jobs involved in slaughtering and meatpacking, and all jobs involved with operating meat slicing or processing machines.

Driving and/or delivery work (As of October 31, 1998, 16-year-olds are no longer permitted to perform on-the-job driving. The minimum age to drive on public roadways as part of employment is now 17. Seventeen-year-olds are not prevented from occasionally using a vehicle to run an errand for an employer. They may do so only during daylight hours, they must have completed a driver's education course, and they must wear seat belts). Exemptions are provided in some of the hazardous occupations for apprentices and students in vocational education programs.

14 and 15 Year-Olds

Youth in this age group may work in various jobs outside school hours, but the types of jobs open to them are more restricted than 16- and 17-year-olds. Workers under 16 cannot use ladders or scaffolds, or work from windows sills washing outside windows. They cannot work in freezers or meat coolers or in meat preparation, except packaging it away from the prohibited areas. They may not operate most power-driven machinery. They may not load or unload goods from trucks, railroad cars or conveyors. They also may not work in warehouses or on construction sites.

The following types of employment are generally open to 14- and 15-year-olds:

They can perform office and clerical work.

They can cashier, sell, model, produce artwork and work in advertising departments.

They can bag and carry out customers orders.

They can price, mark and tag merchandise, as well as assemble, pack and shelve.

They can perform grounds maintenance and clean-up work, including the use of a vacuum cleaner or floor waxer, but not a power driven mower or cutter.

They can wait on tables and work in kitchens including the use of dishwashers, toasters, popcorn poppers and blenders. They can also prepare salads and other food, but only at lunch counters or diners where the work can be SP :. from the counter.

They can work at service stations pumping gasoline or oil, washing or vacuuming cars and providing other courtesy services.

They can perform errand and delivery work by foot, bicycle or using public transportation.

Under Age 14

Fourteen is the minimum age for employment outside of school hours, but there are some jobs open to those in the under 14 age group. They may work for their parents as long as it's not one of the hazardous occupations described in this article. They may also perform "independent contractor" services such as newspaper delivery. household cleaning, babysitting, snow shoveling or yard work. Exempt work also includes performing in theatrical, motion picture or broadcast productions.

Limitations on Hours Worked

The law limits the number of hours that children under 16 are allowed to work. They may not work during school hours except as part of a Work Experience or Career Exploration program. They may not work before 7:00 a.m. or after 7:00 p.m., except during the summer months when the evening hour is extended to 9:00 p.m. They may not work more than three hours a day on a school day and no more than 18 hours a week during a school week. They may not work more than eight hours a day on non-school days or more than 40 hours a week in non-school weeks.

Agricultural Employment is Different

A different set of laws applies to work performed on farms and ranches. Generally speaking, there are no restrictions on agricultural employment for anyone 16 or older.

Fourteen and 15-year-olds can work on a farm or ranch outside of schools hours, as long as the job doesn't involve any hazardous work. Jobs considered hazardous would involve:

Operating a tractor of over *20* PTO horsepower.

Operating any harvesting or hay cutting equipment or feed grinders.

Working around bulls, boars, stud horses, sows with suckling pigs or cows with newborn calves.

Working inside grain storage bins, silos within two weeks after silage has been added, or in manure pits.

Applying ag chemicals or anhydrous ammonia, or handling or using a blasting agent.

There are a couple exceptions to these laws. The prohibition does not apply to youths employed on farms owned or operated by their parents. In addition, a 14- or 15-year-old may perform some hazardous farm work if they are enrolled in a vocational agricultural program, if there is a written training agreement with the employer and the student is closely supervised. They may also operate machinery if they have completed a 4-H or other approved tractor or machine operation program.

There are some other exceptions to the agricultural employment laws. Youths 12 and 13 years old may work outside school hours on a farm with their parent's consent. In addition, local youth 10 and 11 years old may work outside school hours to hand harvest crops such as fruits and vegetables.

Youths of any age may work at any time in any job on a farm owned or operated by their parents

Minimum Wage for Children

The federal minimum wage is $5.15 per hour.

Summary

There are many regulations affecting the employment of children, and there are also a number of exceptions. Anyone who has a question about whether a particular job can be performed by someone under 18 should contact the South Dakota Division of Labour and Management at (605) 773-3682.

The federal minimum wage for covered nonexempt employees is $5.15 per hour. The federal minimum wage provisions are contained in the Fair Labour Standards Act (FLSA). Many states also have minimum wage laws. Where an employee is subject to both the state and federal minimum wage laws, the employee is entitled to the higher of the two minimum wages.

Various minimum wage exceptions apply under specific circumstances to workers with disabilities, full-time students, youth under age 20 in their first 90 consecutive calendar days of employment, tipped employees and student-learners.

The Fair Labour Standards Act (FLSA) sets 14 as the minimum age for most non-agricultural work. However, at any age, youth may deliver newspapers; perform in radio, television, movie, or theatrical productions; work in businesses owned by their parents (except in mining, manufacturing or hazardous jobs); and perform babysitting or perform minor chores around a private home. Also, at any age, youth may be employed as homeworkers to gather evergreens and make evergreen wreaths.

Many states have enacted child labour laws, some of which may have a minimum age for employment which is higher than the FLSA. Where both the FLSA and state child labour laws apply, the higher minimum standard must be obeyed.

The federal minimum wage is $5.15 per hour. However, a special minimum wage of $4.25 per hour applies to employees under the age of 20 during their first 90 consecutive calendar days of employment with an employer. After 90 days, the Fair Labour Standards Act (FLSA) requires employers to pay the full federal minimum wage.

Other programs that allow for payment of less than the full federal minimum wage apply to workers with disabilities, full-time students, and student-learners employed pursuant to sub-minimum wage certificates. These programs are not limited to the employment of young workers.

Under the Fair Labour Standards Act (FLSA), the minimum age for employment in non-agricultural employment is 14. Hours worked by 14- and 15-year-olds are limited to:

- Non-school hours;
- 3 hours in a school day;
- 18 hours in a school week;
- 8 hours on a non-school day;
- 40 hours on a non-school week; and
- hours between 7 a.m. and 7 p.m. (except from June 1 through Labour Day, when evening hours are extended to 9 p.m.)

Youth 14 and 15 years old enrolled in an approved Work Experience and Career Exploration Program (WECEP) may be employed for up to 23 hours in school weeks and 3 hours on school days (including during school hours).

The FLSA does not limit the number of hours or times of day for workers 16 years and older.

Many states have enacted child labour laws as well. In situations where both the FLSA child labour provisions and state child labour laws apply, the higher minimum standard must be obeyed.

Regulations governing youth employment in non-agricultural jobs differ somewhat from those pertaining to agricultural employment. In non-agricultural work, the permissible jobs, by age, are as follows:

1. Workers 18 years or older may perform any job, whether hazardous or not;
2. Workers 16 and 17 years old may perform any non-hazardous jobs; and
3. Workers 14 and 15 years old may work outside school hours in various non-manufacturing, non-mining, non-hazardous jobs

Fourteen is the minimum age for most non-agricultural work. However, at any age, youth may deliver newspapers; perform in radio, television, movie, or theatrical productions; work in businesses owned by their parents (except in mining, manufacturing or on hazardous jobs); perform babysitting or perform minor chores around a private home. Also, at any age, youth may be employed as homeworkers to gather evergreens and make evergreen wreaths.

Different Age Requirements Apply to the Employment of Youth in Agriculture

Must a youth have a work permit to work?

The Fair Labour Standards Act (FLSA) does not require that youth get work permits or working papers to get a job. Some states do require work permits prior to getting a job. School counselors may be able to advise if a work permit is needed before getting a job.

9

Towards Elimination of Child Labour

Social Entrepreneurship—Educational Campaign.—Education a fundamental human right, is an essential component for social development and a perquisite for the prevalence of social justice that has been treated as a mere charity.

Out of 800 million illiterate adults across the globe in 2002, 70% live in nine countries belonging mostly to sub-Saharan Africa and East and South Asia, out of which India has 34% of the total illiterate population of the world India is home to more than a third of illiterate people in nine of the world's most populous countries.

The fundamental right to education is denied to millions despite the fact that having a fully educated society will end economic exploitation of children and break the cycle or poverty. National Coalition for Education (NCE) seeks to bring synergy in policy and planning dealing the three basic issues affecting the future of children across national regional and global level through strong lobbying and advocacy work. Triangular paradigm; Read More.

In India National Coalition for Education (NCE) has been pro-actively involved in their efforts to safeguard the rights of children and, to work towards achieving education for all.

(*a*) "**Quality Education for All—Make it Happen Now**".—A clear message has been sent across the world to end the worldwide crisis on education. Today, 103.5 million children are not attending school unable to learn to their fit potential. 800 million adults have already in their lives pass by without being to read or write. The fundamental right to education is denied to millions describe the fact that having a fully educated ?? will end economic exploitation children and break the cycle of poverty.

Child labour is a critical obstacle in the path of children's development and society's sustainable development. Children who must spend the most important stage of their lives striving merely to survive are denied the opportunity to develop to their full potential. Many of the world's 246 million child labourers are denied their fundamental rights, including the right to education. Discovering and learning to your fullest potential during childhood determine what opportunities will be available not only to the individual but also to the generations to follow. A fully educated society is assured of breaking the cycle of poverty.

In October, 1999, on the eve of the World Education Forum, a coalition of civil society organisations joined forces to launch Global Campaign for Education." The GCE was by Action Aid, Education International, Oxfam International and the Global March Against Child Labour, and currently represents developmental NGOs and teachers unions in more than 100 countries. The Global March's Education Campaign collaborates closely with the GCE to take action for increasing resources for education and ensuring that education as key to ending child labour, remains high on the political agenda among the Governments of developing and donor countries.

We firmly believe that providing free, quality and compulsory education lies within the states responsibilities. At the International level, our lobbying extends to various arms of UNESCO, the World Bank, IMF, G-8 and other agencies responsible for meeting developmental needs. At the National level, our partners which include teachers educators civil society leaders and child activists, continue to lead activities to demand their rights to education. The GCE partners are committed to mobilising civil society and stakeholders in ensuring that the Governments fulfill their promises to provide free, quality and compulsory education for all by the year 2015.

(*b*) **The Campaign demands**:

* Free and compulsory, quality public basic education for all children and a second chance for adults who have missed out.
* Increased provision of quality early childhood education and care
* Increased public expenditure on education to at least, 6% of GNP, and new resources, through aid and debt relief, for the poorest countries; and an end to child labour
* Democratic participation of, and accountability to civil society, including teachers and their unions, in decision making on education at all levels
* Reform of International Monetary Fund and World Bank Structural Adjustment polices to ensure that they support, rather than undermine, free, quality public basic education
* Fair and regular salaries for teachers, properly equipped classrooms and a supply of quality text books

* Inclusive and non-discriminatory provision of services for all
* A global action plan for basic education to mobilise political will and new resources in

(2) Social Enterpreneurship—School Campaign.—Aiming to involve the students and teaching community on the sensitive issue of child illiteracy and child labour, competitions are organized in schools and colleges. Essay writing, debate painting and skits focusing child labour and illiteracy issues are conducted. The teaching community also supports the cause and provides permission to hold the events in the premises. Prizes are distributed to the winners as a token of appreciation of their concern for the less fortunate children.

* Essay writing and painting competitions on child labour theme were held at Guru Nanak Public School, Delhi on 11 August. The principal helped the SACCS/BBA activists to organize the events in her school and also promised all possible help for future campaigns also. 15 Students participated in the essay writing and 20 in painting competitions.
* Two more competitions were organized on the 3rd and 11th Sept. 2000. The children came up with excellent ideas in painting and the essays also conveyed their deep anguish over the sufferings of working children. Prizes were distributed to the successful candidates.
* On the 31st July 2000, a debate was organized on the legal aspect of child exploitation in Lady Irwin School Delhi. The teachers moderated the programme. Sixteen students participated, in the event. The debate brought out some of the loopholes in the law. Most of the students were of the view that there should not be any provision to employ children whether the that there should not be any provision to employ children whether the occupation is hazardous or otherwise. Education and recreation should be the first and last benchmark of any child. The girl students excelled in the competition. The prize distribution event was held on 5th Sept. 2000.
* On the occasion of the Independence Day (15th August) SACCS/BBA organised essay writing and painting competition at the Government Boys Senior Secondary School, Janakpuri, Delhi. 15 Students participated in the painting and 18 in essay competitions. The students also created some articles out of Jute, a fibrous material.
* On the 15th August 2000 all the schools run by SACCS/BBA in Delhi celebrated the Independence day. 210 Children participated in a rally organised on this occasion. The children shouting slogans against child exploitation and illiteracy marched in the town area of Faridabad (near Delhi).

* Meditation programmes were organised in September, 2000 in schools run by SACCS/BBA in Delhi to improve the power of concentration. 30 Students participated.

* On 2nd October, 2000, the children of Mukti Ashram were taken to Rajghat, the place where the remains of the father of the nation Mahatma Gandhi is kept. The children rendered devotional songs. The children also rendered speeches on the life of Mahatma and the freedom struggle. They also indicated that though the nation got its independence, yet there are thousands of slaves still living in this free country.

Social Entrepreneurship—Fair play campaign.—In post partition India around the year 1950, the after independent India and constitution came into force, the sports goods industry started. Today the industry is worth 600 crores and the goods are exported to Britain, USA, Netherlands, Germany, France, etc. In all, 318 sports items are produced. All the activities are centered around Meerut (Western U.P.) and Jalandhar (Punjab). What is peculiar to the sports good industry is the fact that the tiny fingers of the children are, extensively used for the production of sports items like the cricket balls, footballs, shuttle corks etc. All the children are brought through middlemen.

The Fair Play Campaign in the sporting goods industry initiated by SACCS/ BBA is a bench mark amongst the several campaigns that it has successfully run over the years.

(*a*) **The main objectives of Fair Play Campaign are :—**

* Identification of critical instances of child labour; these children, along with their mothers will constitute the critical target group (CTG).

* Negotiating with employer/contractors whether the task performed by the child can be assigned to an adult of the same family e.g. the mother; providing a monetary incentive e.g. salary of the mother may initially be paid by the project.

* Setting up of sewing cooperatives for income augmentation of CTG mothers; flextime provisions, memberships conditional to project coordinator's certification that children have ceased working .

* Setting up of cooperative store for sale of sewing coop products.

* Facilitating admission of older children into vocational training schools.

* Allied activities including teacher training, community awareness, networking advocacy consumer education, policy level lobbying local government functionary-sensitisation etc.

The overall experience of running the two schools under the Fairplay

Campaign for SACCS/BBA has been enriching. The common myth that the children of the poor do not have the privilege of education was dispelled due to the existence of these schools. Some of them did not know the basics of reading and writing and alphabets too. The change was miraculous to the parents who sent their children to stitch balls and make cricket bats a few months ago, were chanting slogans STOP CHILD LABOUR. The children were in the range of 13-14 years and some of them were total orphans. Besides conventional education they were also taught the basics of daily hygiene and cleanliness.

In the village of Jewari it was found that there was large scale unawareness. It was not felt necessary in this village to impart education to all the children. However, due to the school being run by SACCS/BBA, the village has made considerable progress on the education front. Success has been achieved because parents were convinced about the usefulness of education.

(*b*) **Major Achievements**

1. Reduced the number of child labour in sports goods industry.
2. Increased school participation.
3. Sensitisation and mobilisation of the community on the issue of child labour in sports tools industry.
4. Involvement of other players on the issue of child labour in the sports goods industry like ILO/IPEC, FICCI, UNICEF and SCF etc.
5. Community participation.
6. Awareness among the manufacturers/exporters/middleman and masses.
7. Promotion of IGP such as stitching and making button holes.
8. Reduced the number of household industrial activity.
9. Improvement in the adult wage system.
10. Improvement in the working condition of the womens.
11. Introduced community work culture.
12. There has been enormous pressure on the industry and due to that they have started their own monitoring system to make their products free of child labour.
13. Due to the sensitisation of the foreign buyers the women are made to work in the shade in order to make the buyers realise that the product is made by the adults.

14. The industry owners have started their own rehabilitation and education programme for the children.

Social Entrepreneurship—Firecrackers.—(*a*) **Some Heart-Rending facts.**—Pyrotechnics or the commonly known fireworks have become an inseparable part of festivities not only in India but all over the world. India produces roughly Rs. 250 crores worth of firecrackers annually. Despite the erratic fluctuation in the market prices this commodity sells like hot-cake during almost all national festivities including marriages, victory celebrations and other occasions of revelry. Of these, Diwali is one festival which accounts for the highest consumption in our country.

For a person with a bent of mind towards the social cause and possessing a humane heart, the under mentioned points on the dark reality of the dazzling fireworks would provide food for thought.

1. The effulgent, colorful and deafening crackers come out of the tiny hands of over one and half lakh children compelled to toil day and night in suffocating worksheds anticipating death or mutilation due to the explosive nature of the material they handle.
2. The matches and fireworks industries of Sivakasi, Virudh Nagar, Sattur districts of Tamil Nadu State are holding more than a lakh of children crushing the very enjoyable span of their childhood. Besides Agra, Jhansi, Lucknow, Kanpur, Etawah, Varansi districts of Uttar Pradesh; Jaipur, Bikaner, Udaipur of Rajasthan; Bhopal, Indore, Raipur of Madhya Pradesh; Rohtak, Bhiwani of Haryana, Howrah 24 Pargans of West Bengal also account for child employment in thousands in this extremely hazardous industry. Even places unknown earlier for firecrackers have been reported of having illegal firecrackers units. 100 child labourers were rescued last year from 15 such illegal firecrackes units in the town of Gwalior, Madhya Pradesh.
3. The production pace gets accelerated during September-October to meet the enormous demand during Diwali. To cope up with the target, thousands of children are employed on casual basis.
4. A large number of accidents occurring in units located in remote areas go unreported.
5. The raw material for firecrackers are highly explosive in nature. A speck of slackness could mean instant death or crippling. Besides due to constant exposure to chemicals like sulphur, potash, phosphorous, chlorate etc. the children contract deadly infections of lung, skin kidney and eyes.
6. Matches and fireworks industry being highly hazardous, the law provides for imprisonment from 3 months to years and a fine upto

Rs. 20,000. But, thanks to the various law-enforcing agencies, this legal instrument has remained a paper tiger till date. Leave alone the imprisonment, till date the maximum penalty imposed for violation of this law is a paltry Rs. 200/-.

7. The revelations of both governmental and non-governmental studies on this subject agree that these units keep flouting the norms and provisions of Explosive Act, Factory Act and Labour Laws. Yet there is a mushrooming of such units all over the country are run without registration of license.

(*b*) **Some of the worst accidents of recent past** :

* Recently, on 15th September, 2005, an explosion in a firecrackers unit killed 36 people including 10 children and others were seriously injured in Patna, Bihar.
* On 20th September, 1996, an explosion in firecrackers unit killed 6 people and seriously injured one women in village Tikra, 6 km away from Kanpur City.
* On 12th September, 1996, a devastating blast occurred in a fireworks unit in Sivakasi in Kamarajar District of Tamil Nadu, Killin nine labourers and severely injuring eight workers.
* On 26th August, 1996, a powerful explosion in a fireworks factory in Prakash Nagar, a residential area of Agra City, Uttar Pradesh, claimed 3 lives including two child labourers. Three child labourers were seriously injured.
* On 11 September, 1995, an explosion in a fire-cracker unit in a village Baghnan of Howrah District, West Bengal claimed 17 lives of children and severely burnt 140 child and adults workers. The youngest among the deceased was 10 years old.
* On 24 May, 1995, another blast in a unit on the outskirts of Rohtak Town (Haryana) took away 30 innocent lives (23 as per Government figures), The majority of them were bonded children hailing from Sivakasi, Tamil Nadu.
* 4th October, 1994 witnesses another shocking explosion in a cracker factory in Jhansi, U.P. which claimed 70 lives (45 as per the Government version) of the child workers. The accident was so grave that the limbs of the victims were found thrown over a radius of the kilometer from the site.

(*c*) **How can we tackle the menace?**—

* "Charity begins at home". Let us not buy crackers and educate our

children about the darker side of this illuminating object. In its place, provide your children with colourful candles attractive toys etc. The children might be obstinate in the beginning. But certainly they will watch the point with our perserverance and commitment.

* Spread the message among your friends, relatives and well-wishers. Try to arrange an informal family get-together of theses persons, well ahead of Diwali and explain the plight of the children engaged in the industry. Try to convince them and the children on the wasteful extravaganza, the environmental pollution risk of accidents and dangers to lives and property involved in lighting fireworks.

* If you happen to be a teacher, or doctor, or people's representative social worker or a village head your responsibility naturally assumes greater dimension. Try to educate the children, parents and others taking few hours off your schedule. You are doing a world of good to those lakhs of children for whom Diwali or Dusshera does not convey anything special than a killing routine at work.

* Social workers can organize wall-writing distribution of handbills, personal contact of head-masters/head-mistresses etc. The children will easily get influenced through their teacher. If possible the teachers can arrange a rally in their area to highlight the issue.

* During the festivities of Diwali, Dussehra and other religious functions, cultural programmes like street drama, audio-visual programmes etc. can be organized.

* Contact press/media and get them involved in highlighting the issue, Press statements be issued converting the entire gamut of the campaign. Launch a signature campaign in support of boycott of fireworks involving prominent personalities of the area.

* If you are running a school or a center a take out procession of children and others to speed the message in the school and the neighborhood.

* Just a couple of days before Diwali, organise a public gathering of like-minded persons to demonstrate symbolic boycott of crackers by immersing them in water.

(5) Social Entrepreneurship—Childnet.—Childnet International's mission is to work in partnership with others around the world to help make the Internet a great and safe place for children.

In all its work Childnet seeks to take a balanced approach. On this website you can read about the way we have sought to promote the positive and highlight the creative and inspiring ways children and young people are using the medium for good. You can also read about the ways we have responded to the negative aspects and dangers for children.

Childnet works in 3 main areas of Access, Awareness, Protection & Policy.

Access and promoting quality content.—Helping children and young people to use the net constructively, showcase quality content and enable others to use our resources and develop new projects.

Awareness and advice.—Helping children and young people acquire new "net literacy" skills and giving advice to industry, organisations, parents, teachers and carers about Internet and mobile safety.

Protection and policy.—Working with others to help protect children from being exploited in the online environments provided by new technologies as well as seeking to initiate and respond to policy changes.

(6) Rugmark logo for carpets.—It is only recently that India in a process of liberalisation, envolves a policy of promoting more export and import of consumer products. One of the main reasons is money, as it brings much foreign exchange and maximises the profit by the Government and industrialists.

Among the many lucrative export products, one is the carpet. The carpet industry is spinning an annual foreign exchange of Rs. 1500 crores (approx., U.S. $ 500 million) which is coming from the main carpet importing countries as the United States of America, Germany, England and other European countries. The harsh truth why this is a profitable industry, however is because of its cheap labour force spinning the partners ; namely children under the age of 14 years being severely exploited in this industry.

Instead of having a healthy joyous childhood with the basics of primary education, these children are lured into he darkness of the carpet loom units. Chained to the laws of the employer the bonded child labour is too young and mute to raise his voice and just obeys his master. Separated from their parents, without nutritious food and breaks these children work for 14-16 hours in poorly ventilated workspaces, regularly beaten up because they work not hard enough or ask for their parents. The nimble fingers spin the carpets without seeing daylight without seeing any payment.

As these carpets are exported, the South Asian Coalition on Child Servitude (SACCS) launched a big Consumers Awareness Campaign in European countries and United States about the inhuman malpractices in the carpet industry. Consumers in these countries were ignorant of how the carpet actually are made. As the consumers and others got deeply concerned about child labour in carpet making, the result was big drop in the import of these carpets. Public pressure of Germany and other European countries on the issue of child labour in India and other Asian countries is rapidly increasing. The U.S. Senators even moved a bill to ban all the products made by children entering into the U.S.

SACCS has the determination to eradicate this form of modern slavery *i.e.*, debt bondage and child labour in the carpet industry but is not against the export of carpets of carpet industry. It wants child labour to be replaced with adult labour and advocates affixing labels after scientific and independent inspection & monitoring.

For the last three years SACCS worked out the idea of labelling carpets which are not made by children. This label called the RUGMARK guarantees the buyer/consumer that the carpet is manufactured without childlabour. Together with representatives of carpet industry, Indo-German Export Promotion Programme (IGEP - a trade promotion organisation), UNICEF, Carpet manufacturers (who do not employ children), NGOs etc. a system was developed and named RUGMARK (RMF). This foundation acts as an international, independent, legal. Professional and non-commercial certification and monitoring system to guarantee after random checks at carpet looms by professional experts that not a single child is working in these units. If all the certification criteria officials are fulfilled by the carpet manufacturers/exporters and loom owners and the inspections carried out by the RUGMARK officials indicate absence of child labour, then the carpet manufacturer/exporter is licensed by the RMF to use the RUGMARK logo for his carpets.

Let the RUGMARK be a model and trend-setter for other products also where child labour constituent exists. Because compared to carpet industry in which more than 300,000 children are employed there are other industries also which totally account for about 67 million child labour.

(a) The Long Road to the "Rug Mark Foundation".—Confusion exists around the initiative of RUGMARK. Was it imposed on India by western countries or was it an initiative of India itself ? What is the exact of SACCS in this initiative ? Many more questions and nerve-racking apprehensions can only be answered by presenting candid information covering all aspects. The RUGMARK initiatives was under immense stress and attracted both positive & negative criticism from carpet manufacturers/exporters and main carpet importers. The reason could be lack of right knowledge of aims and objectives of the RUGMARK Foundation and the circumstances that compelled to conceive on a labelling system.

(b) Crusade against Child Servitude.—The crusade against Bonded Labour and Child servitude in carpet industry was launched in 1983 and Mr. Kailash Satyarthi has been the spirit and nerve center of this movement. During the struggle it was felt that children were the worst victims of this scourge because the burden of slavery fell on them right from birth for no fault of theirs. They are the most vulnerable physically and mentally. They can be intimidated easily. Moreover in servitude the relationship equation of employer and the employed is reduced to that of master and slave. The master has complete control over the physical, mental and intellectual attributes of the slave. The slave has to implicity carry out the orders of the master without question. The master can abuse, insult, rape, torture and physically liquidate the slave. There is no union to raise the voice against exploitation, injustice and crushing of human rights.

The phenomenon of child servitude is almost similar in the South Asian countries. Against such a backdrop, a coalition of like minded NGOs of South Asian countries came into being to pie out this menace throw concerted efforts pooling and sharing their resources, experience and expertise.

Mirzapur-Varanasi-Bhadohi areas of Uttar Pradesh have already acquired the dubious distinction of the biggest child labour belt accounting for about 300,000 children in carpet manufacture. Thought he Government and the industry were unanimous in declaring that there are no child labour in the industry, SACCS and its associates had been freeing thousands of child slaves thro direct interventions, raids and seeking help of High Courts and Supreme Court. Till date more than 50,000 have been got freed from various economic sectors of which over 15,000 alone is from carpet industry. Only recently, the Government and the industry have acknowledged the presence of Child labour in the carpet sector as a result of the campaigns initiated by SACCS and like-minded NGOs.

(c) Lack of Political & Administrative will.—One of the paramount causes for the perpetuation of child labour is the total absence of political will to change this menace. There are many legal instruments *i.e.*, Child Labour Acts, Factory Act etc. that categorically prohibit employment of children in any factory and/or hazardous industry. But the tragedy is that the law enforcing agencies are corrupt and apathetic, in turn, helping and child employers to carry on with their unlawful business. Though "Child Labour (Prohibition & Regulation) Act 1986", specifies carpet weaving as a hazardous industry, many employers engage children under the garb of family trade, posing as relatives of the children. The Child Labour Act has anomalies of this kind, which allow the child employers to circumvent the law. It is reality that till date no child employer has been punished for the violation this law, though, SACCS itself has liberated hundreds of children.

Child Labour still exists in the carpet industry, because the local bureaucracy is hand in glove with the carpet trade and on several occasions, have virtually placed hurdles in the rescue operation initiated by NGOs. The Government even attempts to justify child labour on the grounds of poverty, family labour and learning a trade.

(d) Consumers Awareness Campaign.—Having received no support from the Government at the national level, ACCS launched a carpet consumer awareness campaign in Germany-major importer of Indian carpets in 1990 with the help of trade unions, human rights organisations and consumer groups. Soon the campaign spread out to Holland, Sweden, England etc. in Europe besides United States of America. The impact was terrific and the carpet exports to these countries dropped considerably sending waves of panic among the manufactures and exporters. This also played a catalyst role in expanding the network of organisations supporting the consumer movement. Special mention needs to be made here about organisations like, Bread for the World, Terre Des Hommes, Miserior, German Trade Unions etc. who kept up the momentum of the campaign and till date they are vigorously pursuing the goals. Also in U.S.A. : Asian American Free Labour Institute, Child Labour Coalition, International Labour Rights Education and Research Fund, National Consumer League, in U.K. : Christian Aid, Anti-Slavery International, in the Netherlands : India Committee of Netherlands, in Belgium : India Workgroup, Brussles, International Confederation of Free Trade Unions (ICFTU), Brussels, in Sweden : Radda Barnen, BLLF Sweden, in New Zealand : Asian Pacific Workers Solidarity Link (APWSL) etc. played a very crucial role in spreading the message across the masses.

The German importers also applied pressure of Indian carpet exporters to remove child labour from their industry or face boycott. Besides, the Government of Germany also too up the issue of child labour with the Indian counterpart. Meanwhile, the Senate of U.S.A. witnessed the introduction of a bill initiated by Senator Tom Harkin and Congressman George Brown an others seeking ban on imports of all products made by children. The European and German Parliaments are also contemplating to legislate on the same lines.

SACCS never advocated for the total boycott of goods. It suggested the buyers to look for products made by adults. Its contention was why children are made to labour destroying their health, growth the childhood when millions of adults are jobless ? Removing child labour means opening up of millions of job opportunities for adults. The children should be sent to schools instead of workplaces, books and toys should be in their hands and not sharp and dangerous working tools.

(e) The Concept of labeling system.—The decline in carpet exports compelled some of the major manufactures and exports who are associates of the All India Carpet Manufactures Association (AICMA) and the Carpet Export Promotion Council (CEPC) to seek a dialogue with SACCS to settle the problem. A series of meetings followed and finally on 17 December 1991, the AICMA declared that by March 1992 all the child labourers would be sent back to their homes and adults would be employed in their place with decent wages and facilities. Another salient event was about 50 carpet manufacturers broke away from AICMA and formed a separate association called Carpet Manufacturers Association without Child Labour (CMAWCL) pledging not to use child labour in their units. It is pertinent to mention here that this group has been very co-operative and helpful for the formulation of the Label system whereas AICMA and some of the big exporters backed out of the deliberations mid-way under the impression that the Tom Harkin Bill will not become a law or it might get delayed. They also did not take any effective steps to remove children as promised, on the contrary the influx of children was ascending.

In the meanwhile, SACCS continued its efforts to develop further the labelling and monitoring system of carpets made by children. It kept on demanding before the United Nations Human Rights Commission (Sub Group on contemporary Form of Slavery), Geneva that needful steps be taken to ban traded on child made goods and also adopt a labelling system to facilitate the consumer to confirm that a particular product is not child made. In 1991, UNHRC welcomed the demand of SACCS are recommended it in its report as under :

1991/119. Recommends that products such as carpets whose manufacture is liable to involve child labour should bear a special mark guaranteeing that they have not been produced by children. In this context consumers should be alerted so that they will demand products bearing such a mark.

(f) Working Committee on Rugmark Initiative.—For SACCS the recommendations of the UNHRC was one of the factors for a green light of mooting the idea of formulation of an independent international agency comprising representatives of NGOs (engaged in the area of child labour), carpet manufactures, importers, exporters (pledged to deal with carpets free of child labour), international organisation like UNICEF etc. which has the authority to certify the carpets made free of child labour and affix a label to that effect.

SACCS emphasised that this monitoring & labeling system as mentioned above should be independent, non-commercial, professional and international. Because the very important question that arose among the consumers with reference to carpet labels was "Who could fix the labels ? to make it credible and reliable, who would inspect the carpet loom units"?

The consumers will have no faith if the labels for the carpets are fixed by manufacturers and exporters themselves. Similarly, they cannot place faith on a label issued by a government agency. NGOs too are not in position to carry out extensive inspections and conduct processing of labeling. Also, SACCS disagreed with the clause in the Tom Harkin bill that self certification by importers that the carpets are free of child labour, will make the carpets eligible for import. When Mr. Kailash Satyarthi pointed out this flaw, the Senator complied and amended the bill.

As reliability, credibility and international authenticity of a monitoring a labelling agency was such an important matter, SACCS discussed on this thoroughly in a working committee attended by many an international organisation, legal experts and professionals. In the succeeding meetings of the working committee held during 1991-1994, some concrete steps were initiated in collaboration with Indo-German Export Promotion Programme (IGEP), other NGOs, carpet manufacturers/exporters, CMACWCL and importers.

IGEP not only agreed to participate in formulation of such an agency but also took responsibility to frame a professional system for inspection and labeling consistent with international standards and requirements. The system was named "RUGMARK Foundation (RMF) and the label RUGMARK".

Some major carpet exporters did not want to participate in the RUGMARK Foundation as they were afraid that the latter would jeopardise their interests. IGEP who took lead in the process of formulation of RMF wanted the whole thing to be completed before the end of 1993. One of the reasons of this was that the famous DOMOTEX fair held in Germany where some of the finest carpets with RUGMARK logo could be presented. According to IGEP, the RUGMARK initiative would loose its credibility among the traders and the public if the introduction of the logo were delayed any further.

(g) The RUGMARK Foundation.—Finally, after prolonged debates and dialectic processes of working committee, RUGMARK Foundation (RMF) was formally got registered on 5 September, 1994 as a private limited company under Section 25 of the Indian Companies Act of 1956.

A Board of Directors was constituted with the representatives of carpet manufacturers and exporters in India, representatives of NGOs, Indo-German Export Promotion Programme (IGEP) and UNICEF.

The RMF is a non-commercial, independent, international and professional body with legal power to verify, inspect, monitor and subsequently affix a trade mark label, that is RUGMARK logo to the carpets which are not made by children. The RUGMARK label provides that importers & consumers a visual guarantee that these carpets are manufactured without child labour.

The certification system, inspection criteria and labeling system are shaped and calculated in a way that requirements can simply by fulfilled by the carpet manufacturers exporters and loom owners. Cost for the inspection of the loom units and the certification has been minimised to bearable level to the carpet trade.

The RUGMARK will go a long way in helping the carpet industry from facing any import ban. The close and trusting co-operation of NGO's international development agencies, carpet importers and IGEP with the Indian carpet manufacturers reduces child abuse in this industry to a large extent.

RM, hopefully, will contribute towards rise in the exports of carpets made free of child labour and assure a regular inflow of the badly needed foreign exchange into India. Also it will be instrumental in eradicating child labour in the carpet industry, provided employment to adults, reverse the negative image that is presently projected on Indian carpets abroad.

(h) In short.—In short the RUGMARK label will bear a computerised code number indicating the details about exporter, manufacturer, loom owner, registration number of the loom, the weavers etc. Any carpet manufacturer/ exporter who voluntarily agrees to produce carpets free of child labour can apply for critical inspections and issues of licence from RMF.

Finally RMF decides on the right to use the RUGMARK logo. It examines all applicants for membership in detail according to all the RMF, requirements and inspection modalities.

The brief history of RMF will hopefully give a better understanding as to how the RMF was development and why it was so important that it is legally formalized. Export of carpets can continue but not on the heavy cost of running future generations as adults can no enter the vacant jobs in the carpet industry.

Main concern of SACCS is the rehabilitation of the freed as more carpet manufacturers to let their carpets be manufactured by adults and not children. The RM will involve itself narrowly in programmes for rehabilitation.

(i) Main Objectives of RUGMARK Foundation.—The Foundation has been established with the following salient objectives in view :

* To provide a non-commercial, independent, professional and internationally credible monitoring and certification mechanism for carpets made free of child labour.
* To initiate conducive steps that would child labour employed by individuals, firms and companies engaged in carpet manufacture. Also to encourage adult employment with reasonable wages & facilities.
* To help promote trade prospects (thro consumer education) to firms and establishments who are genuine in their commitment to use only adult labour and abide by the RUGMARK criteria.

(j) Follow-up of Rehabilitation & Education.—Now the most often repeated question that has cropped up is "what will be the fate of freed children numbering in thousands and how will they be rehabilitated ?" Though the onus of rehabilitation of freed children is of the Governments, yet the problem, has been envisaged to be tackled as under :

* Campaign partners in Germany *viz.* : BFW, TDH and MISERIOR have jointly pooled a fund on a modest scale to facilitate the local NGOs to

open up rehabilitation and educational programmes for freed carpet children.

* RUGMARK Foundation has setup a sub-committee to carry out follow-up of rehabilitation thro' local NGOs.
* Follow-up of rehabilitation of about 300,000 children (thro' NGOs) who would be freed from the carpet industries. The primary responsibility of rehabilitation is of the Government.
* Massive awareness campaigns thro NGOs for the admission of children in local schools, pressurizing the Government to open up new schools.
* According to necessity opening up of non-formal education centres and health centres in acute backward areas.
* To draw up projects for the improvement of social conditions in Indian carpet industry in close co-operation with international NGOs, international developmental agencies like UNICEF, ILO in collaboration with carpet trade.

(k) Result Envisaged.—Total elimination of child labour from carpet industry and employment to unemployed adults.

* Uninterrupted pace of trade and export of carpets.
* Education and proper rehabilitation of freed children.
* With the induction of adults the productivity of carpet industry will improve.
* By ensuring full time employment to parents and adult family members the economic conditions of the family will improve.

(l) Certification Criteria.—RUGMARK Foundation has laid down norms and rules for the issue of licence and labels to manufacturers and exporters of carpets. A licensee is a person or a firm authorised by the foundation to use its logo and labels on the carpets produced free of child labour.

The cardinal criterion is that the manufacturer/exporters should employ only adult labour for the manufacture of his product. His workplaces will be liable for inspections at any time. He/the firm will apply to RUGMARK Foundation along with the fees for issue of license. Once the foundation is satisfied that the applicant has fulfilled all the required conditions after inspections and scrutiny, a license agreement is made out and this would hold legally. After obtaining the license the manufacturer/exporter is free to use the RUGMARK label in his carpets. There would be regular and frequent inspection to ensure that he does not use child labour.

The certification criteria covers :

* That the applicant is a *bona fide* dealer, manufacturer or exporter of carpets.

* That the applicant agrees to remove child labour if any from his production unit from the date of application.

* That the applicant has furnished an updated list of all the looms, loom owners, and other allied workplaces related carpet manufacturing. The loom units should have been registered with Carpet Export Promotion Council.

* That the applicant shall certify about the correctness of the list and intimate.

* The Foundation in the event of any change. Updating should be done every 6 months to facilitate the inspection team.

* That the applicant shall certify that the carpets submitted for inspection are not produced by children (under 14 years of age). In case of dispute on the age of the employee the decision of the Chief Medical Officer of the area will prevail.

Apart from the above, the applicant desirous of RUGMARK licence shall fulfill the following conditions :

* Submit a signed declaration that he will not pay less than the official minimum wages to the loom owners. In turn, the loom owner will submit an affidavit to the applicant indicating :

  (a) No child labour is employed in his workplaces.

  (b) All the employees are being paid as per minimum wages declared by the Government.

When the above mentioned criteria have been fulfilled and after receiving satisfactory inspection reports from the Foundation Inspection, RUGMARK will enter into a licence agreement with the applicant, granting the right to use the logo of the Foundation.

(m) Inspection Modalities.—The credibility of the whole exercise of the labeling system very much depends on the clarity and precision of inspection and hence the Inspectors should not only be professionals but committed to ensure the production of child labour free carpets. This calls for integrity and character of high order.

In addition, the NGOs attached to the Foundation also carry out random inspections to plug any plausible loopholes. The lists of looms furnished by the carpet manufacturer/exporter should be accorded due confidentiality and the lists should be used only for inspections. The Foundation along with the inspection report within a stipulated period.

The parameters governing the loom inspections cover :

* Name of loom owner.
* Location of the loom/unit.
* Evidence such as Registration of the loom with CEPC
* No of looms.
* Name(s), age, sex of the person(s) working in the unit.
* In case of family child labour evidence of attendance record.
* Order and other references & description of carpet (s) produced.
* Name(s) of the agent (s), firm (s), exporters (s) to which the carpets are supplied.
* Weaving charges per sq. metre/yard received by the loom owner for his carpets.
* Every loom unit will be marked by a number with RUGMARK code number for clear identification.

The inspection parameters at the exporter's place govern :

* Details of the source of the carpet(s) with serial number of RUGMARK.
* Packing list the RUGMARK serial number for each carpet.
* Weaving charges paid per sq. metre/yard by the exporter.
* Details of the importer, if identifiable.
* Checks to ensure the RUGMARK labelled carpets are not mixed with carpets of other sources.
* Checks to ensure that same serial numbers are not used again.
  > The Inspections would be carried out as per the methodology laid down by RUGMARK Foundation from time to time.

  > The findings of the inspections will be recorded and documented in a database which is constantly updated and cane by verified at any time.

  > The documentation of the inspection finding must be clear and categorical to facilitate easy tracing back of any loom unit of a particular carpet at any given time.

  > The inspection will continue even after the issue of licence to a manufacturer/exporter and violation of the terms and conditions of the agreement would tantamount to cancellation of licence and termination of using RUGMARK labels.

> Every carpet will be assigned an internal Rugmark code number in the date base to identify the following sources.

> The actual exporter.

> The loom owner/loom unit.

> Actual loom thro which produced.

> Description of the carpet.

For example : 1234 - 5678 - 9123 - 45 will indicate :

1234-Exporter, 5678 Loom owner/unit, 9123 actual loom, 45 about carpet.

(n) Conclusion.—RUGMARK -the smiling carpet logo-serves as a model and forerunner and would certainly expand its ambit from carpets of other child made goods like matches & fireworks, glass & bangles, brassware, precious gems/stones, handlooms, beedis and various items. It is a model for other South Asian countries like Pakistan, Nepal, Bangladesh, Sri Lanka etc. where millions of children are languishing in servitude in different economic sectors. This is a humble beginning and RUGMARK has miles to go to achieve its aims and objectives. It is certainly a Herculean task but not impossible is socially committed souls support and stand by for the noble cause of eradication of child servitude and restoration of the rights of the child.

Zari Campaign

(a) Background.—It was somewhere during the Moughal period that the art of Embroidery came to India. Since then it has become major part of the Indian fashion Industry. Ladies suits with embroidery on it have always remained the first choice amongst the women of this country. Delhi, Mumbai U.P., Haryana, Punjab, Karnataka etc. are some important places where this art is flourishing. Over the period of time with its rising demands, India has become a major exporter of embroidery made products to US, UK Germany France, Australia and some gulf country. The annual export of this industry is around Rs. 300 Crores.

(b) Why Children.—Besides being paid low wages, children can be monitored and exploited easily. Also children tend to remain with the master weavers for longer periods than adults. The reasons being trotted out to just the employment of children are that "they learn a skill" and that "their fingers are nimble enough to make small, intricate designs faster than adults." Some parents, particularly from communities that are traditionally not weavers, believe that their children will learn a skill if they are sent to a "task master" at a tender. age. But studies have proved that these beliefs are wrong.

(c) Child labour in Zari Industry.—India has the largest number of working children in the world. It is estimated that 60 to 115 million children are working in India. Most or all of these children are working under some form of compulsion, whether from their parents, from the expectations attached to their caste, or from simple economic necessity. At least fifteen million of them, however, are workings as virtual slaves. These are the bonded child laborers of India.

"Bonded child labour" refers to the phenomenon of children working in From (can be written as phenomenon of working children from) picking rags, building bricks, working in the domestic households, rolling *beedi* Cigarette) leaves, manufacturing firecrackers to weaving carpet in looms and in *zari* (embroidery) manufacturing units. Conservative reports suggest that there are about 1 lakh child labourers in embroidery and zari sweatshops in Delhi and nearly the same numbers in Mumbai and elsewhere.

(d) Appeal to Fashion Designer

Sub : Serious concern about fashion Industry and the use of child labour

Dear Sir/Madam

Greetings from Bachpan Bachao Andolan!

14 years old Saimul was working for the last 6 years in on of the raided Zari units. Youngest among 4 siblings, Saimul was trafficked from West Bengal by an agent along with his brother to Delhi. For 6 years he did not meet his parents. For working tirelessly from 9 a.m. in the morning to 1 a.m. past midnight, Saimul's earning was a paltry Rs. 600 a year. The plight of young children slaving in dilapidated ill-lit, ill-ventilated and cramped rooms sewing expensive brocaded zari saris and suits with their fragile hands is not unknown to Bachpan Bachao Andolan.

Over the last year, Bachpan Bachao Andolan has in collaboration with the labour department, police and other NGOs, rescued over 1200 child labourers from the illegal embroidery and Zari. Sweatshops scattered in New Delhi. We have made safe repatriation and are working hard for follow-up on rehabilitation for these children.

It is most appalling that Zari units which take contracts from fashion houses are involved in exploitation and employment of children, a gross violation of a child's basic human right, albeit in third parties processes. For an organisation that has for years tried to comply with labour standards and international conventions, this is absolutely deplorable.

There are about 1 lakh child labourers in embroidery and zari sweatshops in Delhi and nearly the same numbers in Mumbai and elsewhere. Rough estimates show that there might be 5000-7000 embroidery units functioning in Delhi, with each unit employing around 25-30 children. Most of the children working in embroidery and zari workshops are trafficked from Bihar, Jharkhand and West Bengal. The children, who had been rescued through our raid and rescue operations, reported that they got as little as Rs. 20-30 a month and worked for more than 12-14 hours in small crowded rooms with poor lighting and ventilation. As a result many had eye problems/infections and skin allergies.

As architect of the first social labelling initiative "Rugmark" child labour free rugs, Bachpan Bachao Andolan and its partners led the first international consumer awareness campaign, particularly in Europe and USA. The first social labelling on any child labour free product, Rugmark, is a concrete example our strategy in tapping the consumers consciousness and in promoting ethical trading practices by corporate and industry., Formation of Rugmark and the subsequent awareness campaign led to the release of thousands of child and bonded labourers from carpet weaving. Now Rugmark is successfully functioning in India, Nepal and Pakistan as well as in Germany, USA, UK and Canada.

Bachpan Bachao Andolan is also part of the office Task Force on Labour by Delhi Government constituting various administrative agencies and civil society organisations, which has been initiated to check child labour (with focus on child labour in embroidery and zari industry), bonded labour and the application of labour laws and conventions in Delhi. On behalf of the Bachpan Bachao Andolan, we urge you to take serious note of the menace of child labour and ensure that there is no illegal child labour engaged in promotion of goods and products made by your fashion house. We would also highly recommend you to initiate an initial research and monitoring exercise on this issue a ensure that all goods that are produced by you are "child labour free" goods.

We hope and look forward to your prompt and urgent cooperation on the concern of child labour and help Bachpan Bachao Andolan in building a better future for thousands of children engaged in Zari Units of Delhi.

In solidarity,

R.S. Chaurasia

General Secretary

(c) Zari Campaign by Bachpan Bachao Andolan.—In 2003, BBA first came across the problem of child labour working in the zari (embroidery) factories in the centre of power, the capital-New Delhi. A basic survey was conducted in potential areas the research was conducted by some professionals who during there course of visit to the identified areas found 5000-7000 embroidery units functioning in Delhi, with each unit employing around 25-30 children. Moreover, most of the children working in these embroidery nits are working as slaves or bonded labour with salaries ranging from nothing at all to rupees 300 per month.

Zari workers are split into shagirds (apprentices), karigars and owners. Most of the young boys are shagirds. In addition to doing some basic embroidery, a shagird does the cleaning and washing of clothes and some cooking for the unit. For this he is paid about Rs. 50 a month. Eventually he becomes a karigar.

Most of the embroidery work is carried out for the big export houses for clothes, handicrafts, etc., to be exported all-over the world. It is critical to identify the links with the export house that buy these embroidered products and to study the wage and production system used by them to know and understand the demand and supply routes.

The first ever raid was conducted in a zari factory in New Delhi and 7 children were rescued in September 2003. It is most appalling that Zari units which take contracts from fashion houses are involved in exploitation and employment of children, a gross violation of a child's basic human right, albeit in third parties processes. For an organisation that has for years tried to comply with labour standards and international conventions, this was absolutely deplorable.

The initial raid led to a series of complaints being filed by the BBA with the Sub-Divisional Magistrate (who has the constitutional power to release the children) and also with he local Labour Commissioner's office. The second raid was organized in June 2004 releasing 17children from Govindpuri extension in south Delhi. This raid exposed the sordid tale or children working in dismal conditions of Zari units.

Hari (name changed to protect identity), a 8-years-old boy originally from Bihar, was forced to work for 12-13 hours everyday in 10 feet by 10 feet basement for no salary. When the lock of his factory was broken by the BBA activists and the labour department officials (he was rescued on 5th June, 2004 along with 11 other children of the same fate), he was shaven from head to toe and was working wearing only underwear. When asked why he was like that he said that it was because of the unbearable heat (New Delhi's average temp, in June is more than 42'c) and there was no fan or any other means of escaping the heat.

The story of exploitation and abuse in the heart of the nation did little to wake up the govt. However, after months of regular follow up, the local govt. finally yielded and the series of raids were conducted by Bachpan Bachao Andolan, Government departments and other NGOs in Delhi and Mumbai. These raids resulted in rescuing 1805 children from Zari industry from September 2004 to June 6, 2006.

CHILD RIGHTS

The United Nations Convention on the Rights of the Child (CRC) — the most expansive international treaty that protects children's rights in 191 participating countries — awaits ratification by the United States. Its consideration by the Senate Foreign Relations Committee has been delayed for more than ten years due to procedural and political barriers.

Families and Governments Protecting Children Together

The Convention calls for governments to respect the responsibilities, rights and duties of parents to provide direction and guidance for the development of their children. In addition, it calls on governments to develop policies conducive to family and community environments that will allow children to grow up in an atmosphere of happiness, love and understanding.

The Convention sets forth basic norms and standards that individual nations agree to pursue on behalf of their children. The CRC's internationally recognized norms include:

- Protection from violence, abuse and abduction
- Protection from hazardous employment and exploitation
- Adequate nutrition
- Free compulsory primary education
- Adequate health care
- Equal treatment regardless of gender, race or cultural background

How the Convention Helps Children

The treaty protects children around the world in a variety of ways:

- In Rwanda, children have been moved out of adult detention centers where they had been held for alleged war offenses, and have been transferred to special juvenile institutions where they were allotted lawyers to defend them.
- In Belgium and Germany, laws inspired by the Convention extended the national jurisdiction in cases of child prostitution and pornography.
- In Romania, adoption laws were amended, magistrates were trained for juvenile delinquency and child abuse cases and reforms were made to the child protection system.
- In Viet Nam, the Ministry of Justice is working with UNICEF and non-governmental organizations to review the judicial process for juveniles, as well as to train judges, police and other legal professionals on how to apply the Convention.
- El Salvador, Peru and Bolivia have all enacted new justice codes for children.

Take Action Now

Individuals and organizations in the U.S. that support the treaty must make a considerable effort to educate their Members of Congress about the need for ratification of the CRC.

In addition, individuals can organize informational meetings and distribute materials about the CRC; organize a letter-writing campaign to U.S. Senators in support of the CRC; work with local churches, schools and community groups to create grassroots support; and contact local newspapers with letters to the editor and op-eds in support of the CRC.

Organizations can help by educating their staff and members about the Convention; discussing the CRC in newsletters and membership magazines; sending informational mailings to members; including the CRC as an issue at annual meetings; getting field offices involved; and officially endorsing U.S. ratification of the Convention.

Advancing the Campaign Against Child Labour: Efforts at the Country Level identifies 33 countries in which the problem is present and documents the laws, policies and programs adopted by those countries to combat abusive child labour. The countries profiled in the report reflect various levels of economic development and a wide range of efforts to address the problem of child labour.

The report also includes information on the economically active population, unemployment rates, education, and government expenditures on the military, health and education in each country. The bureau's International Child Labour Program collected data from a wide variety of sources, including the State Department, U.S. embassies and consulates, foreign governments, nongovernmental organizations and international agencies. In addition, bureau staff conducted field visits to many of the countries covered in the report.

UNICEF demands urgent action to end hazardous child labour.

"Hazardous child labour is a betrayal of every child's rights as a human being and is an offense against our civilization," says UNICEF in The State of the World's Children 1997.

The report, by UNICEF's Executive Director, Carol Bellamy, stresses the progress the world has made in protecting children and ensuring their rights. But it also highlights exploitative child labour as one of the worst abuses of those rights and confronts the myth that such practices have been eliminated from the industrialized world.

The State of the World's Children 1997 explains the profound shift in the world's thinking about children and their rights that has taken place in the past 50 years and is embodied in the Convention on the Rights of the Child. The Convention — now the most widely ratified human rights agreement in history — legally obligates ratifying countries to protect children's rights and to ensure that children's best interests are taken into account when actions are undertaken for them.

One of those rights is to be protected from exploitative or hazardous labour. The report surveys the extent of the problem worldwide, while exposing four of the commonly held myths about child labour. It includes a positive investigation of key actions to be taken to eliminate hazardous child labour, from providing free and compulsory primary education to implementing and enforcing legislation, from empowering the poor to mobilizing society and adopting corporate codes of conduct.

As usual, the publication contains statistical tables of health, nutrition, demographic, economic and other indicators — including child mortality rates, immunization levels, school enrolment and safe water access — to offer a detailed profile of children's lives around the world. (These are available in the full-text pdf version.)

A future without child labour is within our grasp.

Significant progress is being made in global efforts to end child labour, but much remains still to be done - progress should not lead to complacency. A strong and sustained global effort is still required. The ILO has a central leadership role to play in the promotion of a more cohesive and coherent worldwide movement that is mobilized around attainable targets.

This second Global Report on child labour under the Declaration on Fundamental Principles and Rights at Work, offers for the first time a truly dynamic picture. The new global estimates presented in Part I allow the ILO to assess global and regional trends. A remarkable picture emerges. In 2004 there were 218 million children trapped in child labour of which 126 million were in hazardous work. Though the participation of girls in child labour and hazardous work is on a par with boys in the youngest age group (5-11 years), boys predominate very considerably at older ages in both categories.

However, the number of child labourers globally fell by 11 per cent over the last four years whilst those engaged in hazardous work decreased by 26 per cent. For the age group of 5-14 years the decline in hazardous work was even steeper - by 33 per cent. The global picture that emerges is that child work is declining, and the more harmful the work and the more vulnerable the children involved, the faster the decline.

Latin America and the Caribbean are making the greatest progress - the number of children in work has fallen by two-thirds over the last four years with just 5 per cent of children now engaged in work. Least progress has been made in sub-Saharan Africa where population growth, HIV/AIDS infection and child labour remain alarmingly high.

An important part of the positive trends set out here has been related to ILO standards. There are encouraging advances in ratifications in many parts of the world, and while ratification of Conventions Nos. 138 and 182 is only a first step, many ratifications have been accompanied by concrete action against child labour.

Political commitment through the adoption of coherent policies in the areas of poverty reduction, basic education and human rights, is central to the progress made by countries, both past and present, in combating child labour. Economic growth alone will not eliminate child labour, though clearly it is important. Policy choices matter, and those which open gateways of opportunity for poor people, are central to efforts aimed at eliminating child labour. The report presents country examples from East Asia, including China, and from Brazil to illustrate that in addition to poverty reduction, the decision to focus on mass education in particular is an important prerequisite for moving countries to the transition point in tackling child labour.

Around a century ago, the extensive use of child labour ended in the first industrial nations due to a mix of interventions that helped transfer children from the workplace to the schoolroom. Economic growth, improvements in the adult labour market, changes in technology, decline in fertility rates, the availability of decent schools, changing cultural patterns, and legal instruments and their enforcement worked together to create a virtuous cycle. The report goes on to examine how a society can be "tipped" from one where there is a high prevalence of child labour, to one where the right of children not to work becomes fully recognized and the social norm.

This distilled wisdom concerning how to put an end to child labour has become part of the ILO's policy framework and is embodied in its core standards on child labour. In fact, as this report makes plain, our knowledge of the dynamics of child labour is profound. What has become clearer over the years is that responding to child labour requires making the right policy choices, and not simply having the right technical tools. And it requires the central involvement of employers' and workers' organizations in the spirit of social dialogue.

In many cases these choices have to be made within the context of crisis and insecurity, exemplified by the tsunami of 2004 and the earthquake in Pakistan in 2005, as well as by the man-made disasters of conflict and economic crisis. Children are often the most affected by crises, and are at increased risk of entering child labour, in particular its worst forms.

Global reports provide an important opportunity to reflect on progress over the last four years. International Programme on the Elimination of Child Labour (IPEC) is the leading international programme dedicated to child labour elimination and the largest programme of its kind within the ILO. Since its establishment in 1992, IPEC has spent $350 million with annual expenditure running at $50-60 million. Since 2002 IPEC's projects and programmes have reached around 5 million children.

In taking stock of the last four years there is much to be proud of. IPEC has continued to gain support from the donor community and has been at the forefront of the worldwide movement against child labour. New frameworks and technical tools have been put at the disposal of member States, in particular support to Time-Bound Programmes (TBPs) aimed at assisting countries to implement Convention No. 182 on the Worst Forms of Child Labour. Important contributions to research and data collection have been made, not least in illuminating global and regional trends set out in Part I of the report. There have been important breakthroughs by IPEC in advocacy, tackling the worst forms of child labour, child labour monitoring, developing a learning culture through knowledge management, and in mainstreaming child labour within the Decent Work Agenda.

Set against these considerable accomplishments, the report highlights important challenges. Agriculture and child domestic work have been relatively neglected for action against child labour at national and international levels. Furthermore, there is a need to craft political strategies that seize opportunities to mobilize constituencies for combating child labour utilizing multiple entry points. The report concludes that greater national ownership, supported by employers' and workers' organizations, and backed up by a more vibrant worldwide movement, can create the environment in which technical tools and frameworks are put to optimum use and child labour action taken to national scale to have real impact.

Of particular concern is how to position child labour concerns within the Millennium Development Goals (MDGs), and the Poverty Reduction Strategies linked to them. Though child labour is not an explicit target, action will have to be taken against child labour to reach many of the MDG targets, especially those related to education. The report draws attention to the increasing recognition of this connection at the national and international levels, though much still needs to be done.

Perhaps the greatest progress has been made in recognizing the link between child labour elimination and Education for All (EFA). Since 2002, an interagency group combining ILO, UNESCO, UNICEF, the World Bank, and the Global March Against Child labour has met annually, which has led to the establishment of a Global Task Group at the Beijing EFA High Level Meeting in November 2005. The report also highlights the extent to which HIV/AIDS is transforming our view of child labour and achieving EFA, and how IPEC is developing models of response to HIV/AIDS. In many ways education can be viewed as a "social vaccine" against the pandemic.

Youth employment has a prominent place in the MDGs and is also, through a life-cycle approach, intimately linked to the Decent Work Agenda. This report suggests ways in which a better connection can be made between youth employment and child labour concerns using both the Youth Employment Network (YEN) and the ILC Resolution on youth employment adopted in 2005.

Sub-Saharan Africa remains the greatest challenge to the development community, as the region least on track to reach the MDGs. The region also has the highest incidence of working children and has made the least progress, due in part to its staggering population growth, where the population doubles every generation. This report examines a number of possible entry points whereby child labour elimination can be strategically placed in the follow-up to the G8 agenda set out at the Gleneagles Summit in July 2005 and IPEC's role in helping the region face this crisis.

The need to strengthen and widen the worldwide movement against child labour is a major theme. A growing set of global actors has emerged over the last decade, including other UN-system agencies. Donors have been central to putting child labour on the international agenda. The role of employers' and workers' organizations of course remains central to child labour elimination efforts, and the report provides examples of important initiatives taken by them over the last four years. It also examines the challenge presented by the growth of the informal economy where much of the world's child labour, particularly its worst forms, is to be found. It also provides examples of how employers and trade unions are broadening their partnerships with other civil society actors, for example through sector alliances in industries such as sporting goods and agriculture.

There is a growing consensus that children should be viewed as active partners in the worldwide movement against child labour. The first global report reflected this and this second report explores the meaning of children's participation and the strategies that have been adopted to ensure that this goes beyond tokenism.

One of the by-products of a more vigorous and pluralistic worldwide movement over the last decade has been a growing diversity concerning basic concepts, causation and responses. This has not always been in support of ILO policy and there were points during the last decade where the worldwide movement appeared polarized. The adoption of Convention No. 182 in 1999 did much to accommodate diversity within unity but residual disagreements on strategy remain among the international agencies, and with some elements of the international NGO community. That said, the worldwide movement is stronger than a decade ago, though part of the momentum generated at the end of the 1990s appears to have stalled. The report outlines several steps that need to be taken at all levels, in particular by the ILO, towards revitalizing and strengthening the global effort against child labour.

Findly, the report proposes that the ILO and its member States continue to pursue the goal of the effective abolition of child labour committing themselves to the elimination of all the worst forms of child labour by 2016, and that they put in place appropriate time-bound measures by the end of 2008. In pursuit of these targets, over the next four years the ILO will strengthen its efforts to develop coherent and comprehensive approaches to abolishing child labour. The proposed action plan rests on three pillars: supporting national responses to child labour, in particular through effective mainstreaming in national development and policy frameworks; deepening and strengthening the worldwide movement; and promoting further integration of child labour concerns within overall ILO priorities regarding Decent Work as a global goal. This more focused and strategic approach to global leadership will help ensure that the ILO will make a more effective contribution to making child labour history.

Child labour is more than a children's issue. The world community has consistently called for an end to the persistent exploitation of children. We in India, at the Global March Against Child Labour a NGO, have demonstrated our capacity to mobilise world-wide efforts and support to protect and promote the rights of millions of children.

The Global March is not just only about eliminating child labour. If one were to follow a service delivery model, perhaps it would be meaningful to talk of numbers—the number of children that get out of a child-labour status every year. The Global March seeks to eliminate child labour by questioning, attacking and changing the very systems that compel children to work at the global, regional and national levels.

Without changing these systems and without attacking them at their very roots, the existing numbers will decline but there will be new entrants to the child labour force almost daily. This underscores the importance of addressing the root causes of child labour and the poor quality and access to education within a broader poverty alleviation strategy.

Talking about international commitment, the UN Convention on the Rights of the Child (CRC), which is unanimously ratified by almost all countries, brings together civil and political as well as economic, social and cultural rights of children in one instrument. Article 32 on protecting children from exploitative and harmful work is applicable to all children in all situations.

ILO Convention 138 on the Minimum Age of Employment calls for the elimination of child labour up to age of the completion of compulsory education and Convention 182 (1999) on the Worst Forms of Child Labour calls for immediate elimination of child labour in the worst forms such as children who are forced into bondage and slavery, hazardous occupations, armed conflict, trafficking and illegal activities.

The World Education Forum held in Dakar, Senegal, in April 2000 adopted six major goals for education, covering the attainment of Universal Primary Education (UPE) and gender equality, improving literacy and educational quality and increasing life-skills and expanding early childhood education programmes. These are to be achieved within 15 years ending 2015.

In September 2000, 189 heads of state and governments made a passionate commitment to meet the Millennium Development goals that include eradicating extreme poverty and hunger, achieving universal primary education, promoting gender equality and empowering women, reducing child mortality, improving maternal health, combating HIV/AIDS, malaria and other diseases, ensuring environmental sustainability, and developing a global partnership for development.

During September 1999, the World Bank group and the IMF came out with the initiative of nationally-owned participatory poverty reduction strategies to provide the basis of all World Bank and IMF concessional lending and for debt relief. This approach, building on the principles of the Comprehensive Development Framework, will be reflected in the development of Poverty Reduction Strategy Papers by country authorities. There is the Fast Track Initiative by the World Bank following this.

All these recent developments provide a favourable climate for realising the rights of children. But in spite of this the latest estimate on global magnitude of child labour during May 2002 found that 246 million children – one in every six children aged 5-17 — is involved in child labour; One in every eight children in the world – some 179 million children aged 5-17 – is still exposed to the worst forms of child labour, which endangers the child's physical, mental or moral well being. Of these 111 million are under 15 years of age and of these 8.4 million children are caught in unconditional worst forms of child labour including slavery, trafficking, debt bondage and other forms of forced labour, forced recruitment for armed conflict, prostitution, pornography and other illicit activities.

The three key processes affecting the future of the world, in particular our children, are the elimination of child labour, education For all and poverty alleviation.

It has been witnessed that in poor countries the affects of poverty and unemployment are dramatic. The child's very right to survival may be threatened by the parents' unemployment.

In addition to suffering severe economic hardships, families are disintegrating. The outcome includes increased child labour, rising drop-out rates and even juvenile delinquency. These issues are not fully captured in the poverty alleviation strategies.

The education sector has a great potential to contribute to the prevention and elimination of child labour, which should be an integral part of education policies worldwide. In addition to preventing child labour, the education sector can provide special measures to reintegrate children withdrawn from hazardous work into schools. Still, policies that focus exclusively on the education system without accounting for the economic environment of households and the general state of the labour market will not be sufficient to reduce child labour and achieve education for all over long run.

An anti-poverty, child-friendly strategy must pay greater attention to converge with other policies on education and the elimination of child labour. Education For All and the elimination of child labour should find a prominent focus in poverty alleviation programmes.

A multi-dimensional approach consisting of awareness building and consciousness raising, community participation, alternative and viable social economic rehabilitation, and enforcement of national and international legal instruments in relation to children and other similar plans is needed for linking the elimination of child labour with the overall poverty alleviation and education strategies. There is need for a synergy in policy planning and programmes that addresses these three vital issues that affect the lives of millions of children for a sustainable development.

The focus will also be to promote a better cooperation and understanding between policy planners, children and advocacy groups working on children's behalf. We adults have a commitment to provide all children of this world with an environment for their full and harmonious development to lead a life in the spirit of peace, dignity, tolerance, freedom, equality and solidarity.

As consumers in affluent countries, we are appalled at the thought that the fruits and vegetables we eat, the soccer balls we buy for our kids and the carpets we put in our homes might be the products of child labour. Strong international human rights conventions are therefore in place to outlaw the practice. But deep-set cultural traditions and delicate local economies do not lend themselves to interference and, reinforced by the demographic distortions created by HIV/AIDS, child labour shows no sign of becoming history.

There is no universally accepted, precise definition of child labour. The issue is differentiated by reference to the age of a child, the potential impairment of health, physical development and education, and engagement in the "worst forms of child labour" such as trafficking, and illegal or hazardous activities.

More than 10 per cent of the world's 2.2 billion children are engaged in child labour, the majority of them working in agriculture, often wit. hazardous chemicals or machinery. About 10 million are trapped in slavery, trafficking, prostitution, and armed conflict.

The problem of child labour is very substantially located in the developing world where poor parents send their children to work for reasons of economic expediency, unable or sometimes unwilling to perceive the long term value of education for the family's prospects. In this way poverty and child labour are mutually reinforcing and often passed on from generation to generation.

This supply of child labour is accommodated by the demand of employers for a cheap and flexible workforce, including small-scale family enterprises that cannot afford adult paid labour. The absence of regulations together with weak law enforcement often allows the practice to flourish. And it is a mistake to think of globalisation as a force for improvement in labour standards. Although large-scale manufacturing export industries may not directly rely on child labour, the backward linkages to these industries through subcontracting to labour-intensive segments of the product may be less compliant. For example, India's sporting goods industry has strong backward linkages to suppliers of components using child labour.

HIV/AIDS

The HIV/AIDS pandemic has regenerated the supply side of the child labour equation. Households where adult members suffer prolonged periods of illness with HIV and related conditions suffer dramatic cuts in income and forced sales of assets. To make up for these economic losses, children may be withdrawn from school and put to work.

Africa in particular has in the last decade seen a dramatic rise in the new phenomenon of child-headed households, brought on by HIV/AIDS mortality. It is estimated that over 7% of Zambian households are without any adult member; headed instead by a boy or a girl aged 14 or under. An estimated 10% of all children orphaned by HIV/AIDS in Africa are heads of households and caring for siblings.

Several African governments have instituted reductions in, or elimination of, school fees for orphaned children. However, little has been done to implement and strengthen programs, policies or legislation to reduce the risk of AIDS orphans being drawn into hazardous forms of work.

Gender

Millions of girl children are put to work in unacceptable circumstances. The worst form of exploitation of girls - commercial sexual exploitation or child prostitution - is being fought in part by extra-territoriality laws that permit prosecution of citizens who sexually abuse children in another country. For example nationals from many European countries and the US can now be charged at home for engaging a child prostitute in Thailand. By contrast, other forms of exploitation affecting girls have not been highlighted. Indeed, because girls are often employed inside private houses rather than in factories or in public, their exploitation tends to have been invisible, making them even more vulnerable. Unvalued as human beings, girls are often treated as objects to be used and abused for domestic labour or for sex.

Girls who escape work outside the home may instead be kept away from school in order to work for their own families. Despite the large number of girls who are in employment, parents and employers in many societies still consider that the most appropriate place of work for them is at home.

The latest ILO Convention on Worst Forms of Child Labour lays special emphasis on the plight of the girl child and, by making a pointed reference to her problems, it urges nations to take a closer look at the not so visible circumstances of her work

Children's Rights

In 1989, the United Nations General Assembly adopted the Convention on the Rights of the Child (CRC) that singly enshrines the full range of rights of children necessary to their survival, development, and protection in society. Because of the connection between child rights and survival and development, virtually all of the Convention's articles apply to the distressing effects of child labour. In particular, Article 32 recognises the right of children to be protected from work that threatens their health, education, or moral development. This almost universally ratified human rights framework, together with the 1999 ILO Convention for the Elimination of the Worst Forms of Child Labour, provides a consistent paradigm and solid foundation for tackling child labour.

Universally recognised children's rights however are far from a sufficient means of combating child labour. Although almost every country has laws prohibiting the employment of children below a certain age, the legislation often exempts certain sectors - often the very sectors where the highest numbers of working children are found. In other countries, the penalties for violating child labour laws are inadequate. And probably the most common obstacle to adequate legal protection for children is the fact that legislation is not enforced.

Compulsory and accessible education reinforces child labour legislation. Every full-time student is one less full-time child worker. Many developing countries have adopted compulsory education laws but have not created the conditions in which schooling is a viable option for all children. For example, schools may be inaccessible or the cost of attending school is prohibitive.

The effective abolition of child labour remains one of the most urgent challenges of the present times and should be a universal goal.

Consumer Pressures

The concentrated use of child labour in certain highly visible industries has, in some cases, attracted intense media attention and ultimately successful public campaigns for governments to legislate to phase out the use of child labour. There is increasing consensus that, to be effective, such targeted programs need to do more than remove children from work. Removal alone, without ensuring children's access to education and other services, could have harmful consequences for children and their families. Myriad other social programs aimed at poverty alleviation, health and nutrition, and income generation and employment creation for adults, can also help reduce and prevent child labour. Such programs, which address underlying social and economic conditions that contribute to child labour, are often long-term efforts that do not produce immediate results.

Trade sanctions have been frequently used as a tool to combat child labour. The effectiveness of trade sanctions is however highly questionable in their priority for political demonstration that "something is being done" ahead of addressing the root causes of child labour. Child exploitation is not foremost a trade issue, and the eradication of abuse cannot be accomplished through the trading system.

Another "solution" driven by external pressures is the voluntary labelling of goods judged to be at risk of production involving child labour. Ethical labelling systems in general have difficulty in establishing necessary credibility, and products sourced from developing countries are no exception. Controversy can arise on the question of loss of family income and viability of the producers in the face of cultural change imposed from outside.

Effective solutions to child labour must be based on the reduction of chronic poverty through broad-based economic and social development, with a strong emphasis on human resource development. Multifaceted and complex, managing the child labour issue requires a wide-arranging multi-dimensional and multi-institutional approach.

Child labour is a challenging issue, one which raises difficult questions and does not have a clear-cut solution. However, it is important that an organisation such as Christian Aid that works in places where child labour is all too common, has a position on the problem. This policy briefing sets out Christian Aid's approach to child labour. It aims to inform the practice of staff and partners, as well as other interested partners.

Christian Aid is committed to supporting efforts to protect and promote the rights of children, as part of our commitment to the poor and marginalised. There are an estimated 250 million working children worldwide, many of whom are denied the right to an education and the the chance to have a proper childhood. Of particular concern to Christian Aid are those children who work in highly dangerous and exploitative conditions - conditions which damage their health and long-term physical and mental development.

Christian Aid and Child Labour

Over the last decade, child labour has received increasing attention from many different organisations, including human rights groups, development agencies, governments, trade unions, UN agencies and the private sector. Christian Aid was one of the first international development non-governmental organisations (NGOs) to campaign against child labour. We now work in collaboration with such agencies as part of a global movement to protect children from hazardous and exploitative labour. A central part of Christian Aid's approach is our belief that the elimination of child labour cannot be tackled in isolation, but needs to be part of a broader strategy of eradicating poverty and injustice

Christian Aid began supporting campaigns against child labour in India. Since 1989 we have supported the South Asia Coalition Against Child Servitude (SACCS) who have led a campaign to rescue children from bonded labour in India. More recently we have supported a number of initiatives against child labour, including the Global March Against Child Labour, the Rugmark initiative which sought to eliminate child labour from the carpet industry in South Asia, and the campaign against the use of children in the manufacture of footballs in India. These campaigns have all played an important role in raising the problem of child labour among the general public, the media and governments. Of particular note is the central role that the Global March Against Child Labour played in getting the International Labour Organisation to adopt the convention on The Worst Forms of Child Labour (no.182) in 1999.

Although the experiences of our partners in India have dominated our campaigning work on child labour, we also support a wide range of partners in other countries who promote children's rights. This includes a campaign against child prostitution, pornography and trafficking in South East Asia, protecting street and working children in Latin America, and campaigning for children's rights in South Africa. Such examples of the work of Christian Aid partners on promoting children's rights are expanded upon in the text boxes.

We recognise that the reasons children work are complex, diverse and context-specific. In each context there is a unique range of factors that have denied children their basic rights. Consequently there are no simple, universal solutions to removing children from exploitative and dangerous types of work. It is therefore essential that thorough research and analysis is carried out before intervening, and Christian Aid will expect partners to have done this before we support their efforts to protect children from exploitation. Unless the reasons children work are understood, any solutions may, at best, be of little help and, at worst, make the situation even more harmful to children.

Passage House was established in Recife, Northeast Brazil, in 1989 and has been supported by Christian Aid since 1992. Initially it focused on girls who lived in the streets and squares of Recife's city centre, providing them with food, health and education. In 1994, it shifted its focus to social and educational work with vulnerable children and teenagers from Recife's outlying communities, from which many of the street children originate.

There are two parts to its social and education programme. The first is called the 'Centre for Restoration of Identity' and focuses on girls in high social risk categories who either live on the streets or in the communities. The second part stems from the first and includes the 'Centre for Skills Training for Employment', for young men and women between 14 and 20 years, and the 'Centre for Capacity-building and Assistance to the Communities'. Passage House also uses the media, publications and promoted events to raise awareness about these children, their rights, and the causes of their predicament.

While Christian Aid recognises there are no universal solutions to combating child labour, we believe any solution must be based on promoting the rights of the child. The Convention on the Rights of the Child (CRC) was passed by the UN in 1989 and provides an international legal framework for the promotion and protection of children's rights. It has been ratified by all but two countries in the world and has been instrumental in making governments more aware of their obligations towards children. The CRC sets out a clear vision for children's rights that has inspired many organisations to adopt a much more child-centred approach to working with children.

The CRC is based on four fundamental principles:

- there must be no discrimination of any kind against any child, such as on grounds of gender, ethnicity, caste, religion or race.
- the best interests of the child must be the primary consideration in all decisions affecting children.
- the survival and development of the child must be ensured; every child has the inherent right to life and to education.
- the views of the child must be taken into account in any decisions that affect him/her, the views of the child being given due weight in accordance with the age and maturity of the child.

Any action affecting children must be based on these principles. Although these principles are open to interpretation, they do set out a basic framework for protecting children's rights.

The CRC also explicitly addresses the issue of child labour in Article 32:

> States parties recognise the right of the child to be protected from economic exploitation and from performing any work that is likely to be hazardous or to interfere with the child's education, or to be harmful

to the child's health and physical, mental, spiritual, moral or social development.

This is expanded in Article 34 against sexual exploitation, in Article 35 on the sale, trafficking and abduction of children, and in Article 36 which states that 'State parties shall protect the child against all other forms of exploitation prejudicial to any aspects of the child's welfare'. The CRC is not against all forms of child work but focuses on those which are damaging to children.

South African children have grown up in a deeply divided society. The majority of black children face conditions of extreme deprivation with poor and overcrowded housing, lack of recreational facilities and an education system generally seen as hampering development rather than stimulating it.

Molo Songololo, along with other human rights organisations, has done a great deal to put the issue of children's rights on the agenda of the South African Government. Molo Songololo is a magazine and community project for children aged between 6 and 15 in the Western Cape. It was set up in 1980 under the trusteeship of the Cape Churches Urban Trust and works primarily in the townships and squatter camps of the Cape Town area. Christian Aid has supported Molo Songololo since 1987. Although small, it has had a great influence in the Western Cape and beyond. South Africa's constitution has a clause enshrining children's rights and Molo staff feel that they have played a part in ensuring this came about. They organised a conference for children to discuss their rights in 1992, which raised the profile of the issues considerably. More recently, Molo Songololo has focused on the sexual exploitation of children and in 2000 published the report, 'The Trafficking of Children for Purposes of Sexual Exploitation - South Africa'.

In relation to child labour, the International Labour Organisation (ILO) has also passed two international human rights conventions in order to protect children from harmful forms of child labour. A third ILO Convention, no. 29 on forced labour that was adopted by the ILO in 1930, is also relevant in relation to the specific case of bonded child labour.

The Minimum Age Convention (no. 138) was adopted by the ILO in 1973. The main requirement of this convention is that states ratifying it must establish a minimum age for children to work. This covers all forms of economic activity, not just waged employment, although work on small family farms, domestic work in the household and educational work are excluded. The minimum age must be higher than the age that children are required to be in school, but the convention states that this should be no lower than 15 years. Provision is made for a temporary minimum age of 14 years in under-developed countries. However, the convention sets 18 years as the minimum age for hazardous work, while allowing light, part-time work at 13 years, or 12 years in under-developed countries.

There are some limitations with Convention 138 in relation to relevance and enforcement. Most child labour takes place on small family farms or within the household - which are exempt from the convention - or in the informal sector where enforcement is very difficult. In these contexts, the application of a minimum age may seem rather arbitrary. A further problem of enforcement in some contexts is establishing the exact age of a child. Convention 138 reflects the ILO's focus on the formal labour market in which its concern is as much to safeguard reasonable employment opportunities for adults as to protect children. It is thus a particularly important convention in the context of industrialisation and the growth of formal employment, although is less useful in relation to the employment of children in rural areas and informal sectors.

A new ILO Convention has recently been adopted that is much more focused on protecting children. Convention 182 Concerning the Prohibition and Immediate Action For the Elimination of the Worst Forms of Child Labour was passed by the ILO in 1999. This is more specific than the CRC and ILO Convention 138, and has also brought a new urgency to combating the worst forms of child labour, an urgency which is lacking in the CRC.

Convention 182 identifies the following as the worst forms of child labour, the ones which require immediate action (Article 3):

- all forms of slavery or practices similar to slavery such as the sale and trafficking of children, debt bondage and serfdom and forced or compulsory recruitment of children for use in armed conflict;
- prostitution or pornography;
- illicit activities;
- work which . . . will harm health, safety or morals of children.

In the accompanying Recommendation (No. 190) to the Convention, those states which have ratified the Convention are asked to consider the following as hazardous to children:

- work which exposes children to physical, psychological or sexual abuse;
- work underground, under water, at dangerous heights or in confined spaces;
- work with dangerous machinery, equipment and tools, or which involves manual handling or transport of heavy loads;
- work in an unhealthy environment which may, for example, expose children to hazardous substances, agents or processes, or to temperatures, noise levels, or vibrations damaging to their health;
- work under particularly difficult conditions such as work for long

hours or during the night or work where the child is unreasonably confined to the premises of the employer.

These international conventions - the CRC and ILO Conventions 138 and 182 - provide clear obligations to states about eliminating exploitative child labour. In particular, ILO Convention 182 provides more clarity about what actually constitutes the worst forms of child labour, while the CRC provides the fundamental principles that must be applied if children's rights are to be respected. Together they provide a strong legal framework for protecting children from the worst forms of child labour. States that ratify these conventions are subject to inspection and monitoring procedures administered by UN bodies and can be held accountable to international law for failure to implement the requirements set out in the conventions.

On 17 January 1998 the largest ever social movement to help exploited children was launched in the Philippines. The Global March Against Child Labour travelled over 80,000 kilometres mobilising millions of people from all parts of society and areas of the world. They joined together shouting slogans, waving banners and collecting signatures, footprints and thumbprints. School children and trade unions, child labourers and heads of state, all united to show their determination to end child labour and give these children back their childhood. On 17 June when the world's governments, employers and workers unanimously adopted the Convention on the Worst Forms of Child Labour 1999, it was a long awaited and well deserved moment of celebration for the whole Global March movement. The Global March was initiated by the long-term Christian Aid partner, the South Asia Coalition Against Child Servitude (SACCS), based in Delhi. Christian Aid has been one of the major international funders of the Global March.

Christian Aid recognises that, in order to promote the rights of children not to be economically exploited, it is necessary to understand firstly the reasons why children enter such forms of work. Child labour is a complex issue requiring careful analysis.

It is widely recognised that poverty is the most fundamental cause of child labour. Most of the worst cases of child labour involve children from poor families in developing countries. To eliminate child labour in the long term it is therefore necessary to break the cycle of poverty that underlies much child labour. For example, children of former child labourers often end up as child labourers themselves. Many child labourers grow up illiterate, unskilled and with serious health problems. As a consequence, many of them are unable to support their own families in adulthood, so their own children may get drawn into work to support the family.

Yet poverty is not the only explanation and other factors play a significant role. Social differentiation within societies - gender, class, ethnicity and caste -

can all is be critical in influencing which children are most vulnerable to exploitation. Family structures, cultural values and attitudes towards education are also important factors. Children in urban settings are often vulnerable to different forms of exploitation to those in rural communities.

Also, within the same community, some children may be at more risk than others. For example, children from single-parent households may be under more pressure to work than those in which both parents are present, and children from large families more likely to work than those from smaller families. Even within the same household older children may be under more pressure to work than younger children, and girls expected to work more than their brothers.

Cristian Aid supports the Convention on the Rights of the Child as applicable to all children throughout the world. But while child rights are universal, Christian Aid also recognises that different societies have different notions of childhood. For many societies, the modern, western idea that childhood should be a time for education and play is quite alien. Many see work as a central part of childhood and as a means by which children learn the skills they need in adult life. This is the reality in many of the societies in which Christian Aid partners work. This implies that measures which seek to remove children from exploitative labour need to recognise the importance of work in many societies to both adults and the children themselves. Unless alternative forms of work are found that are not exploitative and detrimental to their education, children are likely to return to exploitative forms of child labour.

One of the key principles of the CRC - children's participation in decisions that affect them - is vital in understanding the causes of child labour. If children are to benefit from initiatives to remove them from harmful work places, or improve the conditions within which they work, such initiatives must be based on children's perceptions of work and on what changes they would like to see. This may throw up challenging and discomforting views: many studies have found that children want to continue to work, usually because they or their families are dependent on their income, but also because they may find school of little value. When asked, children often say they prefer to work in a factory or workshop for money rather than at home, where they may be subject to abuse and receive no money for their work. And while no child is likely to say that they want to continue working in a harmful environment, many may feel they have no alternative because of the lack of other income-generating activities. Children from poor households may think that not working is simply not a real option, so continue to undertake harmful work if they have no other options. This presents very real challenges for organisations such as Christian Aid and our partners who support children's rights.

Christian Aid recognises that not all work is harmful to children. Work has, under certain circumstances, the potential to bring many positive benefits to children. Work can be an integral part of the child's development, teaching them skills which will be of great benefit later in life. For many poor households, children can make a valuable contribution to family income. Work can also help teach children to develop a sense of responsibility to others. Yet work can also have extremely negative effects on children. This is a major concern for Christian Aid.

A distinction is sometimes made between child 'work' and child 'labour'; while the former is work carried out by children which is not harmful to them, the latter refers to exploitative forms of work. However, in many situations it is very difficult to define precisely which types of work are harmful to a child and which are not. Take, for example, children in rural communities who assist their families in agricultural work. Assisting parents in agricultural tasks is essential if children are to learn to farm themselves later. In many places the demand for extra labour at certain points in the agricultural calendar mean that families are dependent on children at these times. The issue is one of degree: help with planting or harvesting at certain points in the year, or light daily tasks such as milking are activities which need not be detrimental to children's development, and may bring many positive benefits to the child. Yet heavy manual work, or working such long hours that the child has neither the time nor energy to attend school or to play, are potentially damaging.

In addition to the tasks undertaken, the working conditions must also be taken into consideration. For example, many children in India are employed in the manufacture of beedis, a local cigarette. The actual work of rolling a cigarette is a light task, but when a child has to make beedis for long hours, crouched on the floor with poor light and ventilation, and with an abusive employer, such work is likely to be physically and emotionally harmful. Similarly, helping with domestic tasks such as cooking and cleaning becomes harmful when, for example, the child is working very long hours so that schooling suffers, or if the child works in a household where they are subject to physical or sexual abuse.

It is more helpful to think of child labour as a continuum; at one end there are the most harmful and dangerous types of work done by children; at the other end there are types of work that are neither exploitative nor detrimental to children. In between there are types of work that are not in themselves necessarily harmful but can be so under certain conditions. Christian Aid believes that some tasks undertaken by children are without question extremely harmful to them and steps must immediately be taken to end such practices. We believe that any type of work that is hazardous to a child can never be in the 'child's best interest'. We will therefore focus our support on programmes that target the elimination of the worst forms of child labour, as defined in ILO Convention 182 and its Recommendation 190, (see above).

There are other, less harmful types of child labour - such as working as a waiter in a tea shop or as a street vendor - which are not covered in ILO Convention 182. Tackling these is not generally a priority, added to which we recognise that removing children from the work place in such situations is not always in their best interests. For this reason we will support partners who promote the rights of working children through working to improve the conditions in which they work, and providing them with schooling which meets the special needs of working children.

ECPAT (End Child Prostitution, Child Pornography and the Trafficking of Children for Sexual Purposes. International was set up in Bangkok in 1991 to campaign against child prostitution in Asian tourism. It now has a wider remit to campaign against child prostitution, child pornography and the trafficking of children for sexual purposes. The ECPAT network now consists of groups and individuals in over 50 countries. Christian Aid has supported ECPAT International since its formation and played a major role in setting up and funding ECPAT UK. ECPAT International has three major activities:

1. The principal task is to monitor the implementation by states of the Agenda for Action, agreed by the consensus of 122 governments at the World Congress against the Commercial Sexual Exploitation of Children in 1996. The results of the monitoring are used to make the Agenda more widely understood and implemented and to share good practices with a wide audience.
2. ECPAT has a number of activities and projects which increase the capacity of NGOs to ensure the implementation of the Agenda for Action.
3. ECPAT also has a number of specialist international projects all of which contribute to the monitoring process and promote the implementation for the Agenda for Action. These projects are: preventing child sex tourism, preventing child pornography on the internet, and promoting law enforcement and best legal practices.

Christian Aid welcomes the ratification of ILO Convention 182 by many governments, and, through our partners, will campaign for more governments to follow suit. We will also support partners who monitor governments' implementation of the convention, particularly by the introduction of national legislation which outlaw the worst forms of child labour.

However, while introducing new legislation is essential in establishing a legal framework for combating child labour, it is not in itself enough. The enforcement of legislation to prohibit child labour must protect children. The danger is that legislation can end up penalising or criminalising them, leaving them even more vulnerable to abuse. If children are to be removed from the work place, then alternative sources of livelihood for them and their families must be found. Otherwise children may need to seek alternative sources of work. Often this is in the informal economy where regulation by the state is more difficult and where working conditions are often far worse than in the formal sector.

Strategies for taking action against child labour can only be developed once the causes of child labour in each context are understood. Over the last decade many well-meaning initiatives to remove children from the workplace have failed because little analysis was made of why children were engaged in such exploitative forms of work. Talking with children about their needs, fears, hopes and desires is also essential for identifying effective strategies.

Nevertheless, in some situations there is a potential conflict between the views of the child on the one hand and the protection and development of the child on the other. This is particularly the case with young children who may be unaware of the hazardous nature of their work, or the long-term impact of such work on their health, such as working with toxic chemicals. The CRC states that the weight given to the child's view depends on age and maturity. In such situations it is still important that the views of the child be heard, but adults will need to judge what is in the best interests of the child when it comes to devising strategies for action.

Child labour also has an impact on the adult labour market. Children can be more easily exploited than adults and may be prepared to work for less money. Not only does this deny work opportunities to adults, but can lead to a lowering of the general rates of pay in the sectors in which children work. This can keep poor families in poverty if it means adult family members have no access to secure forms of employment or livelihood. Tackling child labour through improving employment opportunities and conditions for adults is a long-term measure that we support. However, Christian Aid believes that child protection and child development must take precedence over concerns about the impact of child labour on the adult labour market.

The complexity of the problem of child labour needs addressing at different levels. High profile campaigns such as the Global March Against Child Labour and ECPAT have played a critical role in changing international law and raising global awareness of the problem of child labour. These campaigns have taken uncompromising positions in lobbying governments to introduce strong legislation to protect children from exploitation. Christian Aid will continue to support such campaigns. Changing international and national legislation to provide greater protection to children is essential if the worst forms of child labour are to be eliminated. Christian Aid shares the long term mission of the Global March Against Child Labour, 'to mobilise worldwide efforts to protect and promote the rights of all children, especially the right to receive a free, meaningful education and to be free from economic exploitation and from performing any work that is likely to be damaging to the child's physical, mental, spiritual, moral or social development'.

While it is essential that governments implement tough measures to make this vision a future reality, Christian Aid also recognises the importance of supporting civil society organisations working on more localised, grassroots initiatives that directly support working children. Such initiatives involve seeking alternative sources of income, and providing education and health care for working children. Sometimes the approach requires efforts to improve the conditions within which children work. While it is essential to protect children who undertake tasks that are not in themselves harmful, but where the conditions are harmful, removing them from the work place may not always be the best way of helping. A more realistic means of protecting children in the short term may be to improve working conditions by reducing children's hours, to establish a better environment at the work place and to ensure that employers follow agreed codes of conduct in their treatment of children.

In some contexts there are good reasons to take a stronger approach against child labour. There may be extreme cases, notably bonded child labour or enslavement, where immediate action must be taken to remove children from the work place. In India, for example, Christian Aid's partners have taken an uncompromising stand against bonded child labour and physically rescued children from bonded labour camps. Although recognising that bonded labour is rooted in the Indian caste system and poverty, partners argue that taking a more liberal, gradualist approach to child labour in this context is to accept the status quo in which millions of children, especially from lower caste or 'dalit' families, work in conditions similar to slavery. Yet removing children is not enough; they need support to rehabilitate them back into their communities, or education and alternative sources of livelihood. Rescuing children should always only be part of a broader, long-term programme of tackling the causes of bonded labour and enslavement.

Another SACCS initiative supported by Christian Aid is Mukti Ashram. Mukti Ashram provides rehabilitation and training for approximately 300 children a year who have been freed from labour in the carpet industry. So far the children involved are almost all boys, but SACCS plans to provide for girls in the future. Mukti Ashram enables children to recover from their experience of child labour and to provide them with an education and skills for the future.

Christian Aid believes that there are many valid approaches to combating child labour, and that different strategies are needed at different levels and in different contexts. Christian Aid's main priority, above all, is to support effective action that brings about genuine, long-term improvements to the lives of children. We believe partners need to carefully monitor and evaluate the situation of children who have been the subject of efforts to combat child labour, in order to assess the long-term impact of such efforts. This will also facilitate institutional learning within Christian Aid and its partners about how best to tackle the problem of child labour.

The Support Centre for Working Children (CANTC) is supported by the Community Movement of Matagalpa (MCM), which has been a Christian Aid partner since 1992. CANTC is based in the city of Matagalpa. CANTC provides educational and recreational activities for 82 working children, mainly drawn from one of the city markets, which also serves as a bus station. The children are aged between 8 and 15 and all work in the informal sector doing such jobs as shoe-shining or selling items such as newspapers, water or food. Most of their earnings are given to their mothers to boost family income.

The working children are taught new skills at CANTC, such as typing or sewing, but are also taught about the importance of rest and play as well as work. Education is an important part of the project and one of the conditions for attending the centre is that the child must also go to school. They are also offered support for their schooling at the centre, such as literacy training, or a place to do their homework if adequate conditions do not exist at home.

Christian Aid recognises that different approaches are needed in relation to child labour, but believes that the following steps should be taken in all the countries in which Christian Aid works:

- Christian Aid believes that the worst forms of child labour must be eradicated. This requires urgent action by governments, UN agencies, trade unions, NGOs and the private sector. Nonetheless such forms of child labour must be eliminated responsibly. Governments should commit themselves to time-bound plans of action which should include the provision of education and rehabilitation for the children and better employment opportunities for their parents. There must be no new recruitment of children into these worst forms of child labour.
- More specifically, Christian Aid seeks immediate action by governments to ratify and implement the new Convention on the Worst Forms of Child Labour. Christian Aid will continue to work with partners and others to put pressure on governments to ratify the Convention. In those countries in which we work that have already ratified the Convention, Christian Aid will support partners in the monitoring of implementation of the Convention.
- In situations in which children are engaged in work that is not categorised as among the worst forms of child labour, a more gradual approach is recommended. As an interim measure, partners should seek to make improvements in the conditions under which children are working, rather than remove them from employment. The effect of such work on children must be carefully monitored, however, to ensure that no harm comes to children from such work. In the long term, Christian Aid believes that the governments should work progressively to enforcing

ILO Convention 138 on the minimum age, but that this should be part of a general programme to eradicate poverty and promote education.

- The provision of free, universal good quality and compulsory education is of critical importance for eradicating child labour in the long term. However in the short term education must also be available for working children. Education provision should be of good quality, relevant and flexible. Governments must commit the necessary resources to this, and implement a time-bound programme for its introduction.
- The adoption of comprehensive national legislation on child labour and education is a key factor in securing the elimination of child labour. Such legislation must conform to international standards, must encompass all children, including those working in the informal sector, and must take into account specific gender needs. Government policy must be coherent, with departments working together rather than in isolation. Strong measures need to be implemented for ensuring full compliance with such laws. Furthermore, civil society must be allowed to monitor the implementation of legislation by government bodies.
- Finally, given our commitment to promote ethical trading practices in Britain and Ireland, Christian Aid will continue to support campaigns against the international trade in products that have been manufactured or produced using child labour. Public awareness raising can play an effective role in putting consumer pressure on British and Irish importers and retailers to take an ethical and responsible approach towards child labour. Products should not be sold in Britain and Ireland that have been made in breach of international conventions and national legislation on the employment of children. However any resulting action to eliminate child labour in production must be accompanied by effective rehabilitation and education programmes. Although the involvement of child labour in the production of exports for international trade is a small proportion of the overall problem of child labour, nonetheless Christian Aid believes that it is entirely unethical for British and Irish businesses to profit from child labour.

'EU-India Summit should focus on urgent issues of child labour and education'. The campaign 'Stop Child Labour- School is the best place to work' calls on the European Union (EU) to raise the issues of child labour and right to education at the EU-India Summit on October 13th. Tomorrow, on October 10th, the new Indian regulation prohibiting domestic child labour and work in restaurants, hotels, bars etc. comes into force. While applauding this, 'Stop Child Labour' is concerned about the rehabilitation and education of the children freed from these types of work. The EU itself can and should also contribute to eradicating child labour ánd implementing the right to education in India.

In a letter to the Finish Prime Minister Matti Vanhanen, acting president of the EU, the campaign 'Stop Child Labour' raises five points. First, the EU is urged to bring up the issue of rehabilitation and education of children banned from work after October 10th. As the EU is already supporting primary education in India (200 million over 2002-2008), it should support the transition from 'work to school' via the existing or new to be developed programmes. Secondly, 'Stop Child Labour' also urges the European Union to reach an agreement with India on monitoring and rehabilitation of child labour in the operations and supply chain of EU-based companies. Such an agreement should also include other labour rights.

Thirdly, the European Union should strongly encourage fast and effective implementation of India's 86th Constitutional Amendment of 2002 which made education a right of every child. However, an Education Bill which translates this fundamental right into practice is still to be presented to Parliament and even then the Bill still has to be implemented. The result is that more than 100 million children between the ages of 6 and 14 are not in school on an average day.

More than three out of four countries have now ratified both ILO Conventions 138 (Minimum Age for Employment) and 182 (Worst Forms of Child Labour). India has not signed either of these Conventions. In line with recommendation of the European Parliament which calls on India to ratify both Conventions, 'Stop Child Labour' asks the EU to convey this call to India at the Summit.

A fifth and related point to be raised at the Summit is the relation between ILO Convention 138 which says that a child is not allowed to work until it is 15 (or 14 if a developing country so decides) and the fact that the Millennium Development Goals aim only at five years of education. This gap between the legal working age and the provision of education should be closed. 'Stop Child Labour' therefore urges the EU and India to aim at 'every child in a free and full-time school until he/she is at least 15 by 2015'.

Child labour is a worldwide problem which, according to ILO's latest Global Report on the issue, still affects the lives of 218 million children. India has the largest number of working children in the world: 13 million children according to official Indian statistics, but unofficial estimates claim between 60 and more than 100 million. The Indian Child labour (Prohibition and Regulation) Act prohibits child labour in a limited number of occupations and processes that are considered hazardous. Domestic labour and work in hotels, restaurants, bars etc. have now been added to that list. In other occupations, e.g. agriculture, child labour is limited to 6 hours a day (although not enforced). There is no legal limit to the work a child can do at home, even if this home-work is part of an industrial subcontracting chain.

India's child labour laws are failing India is coming under increasing pressure to take action over massive human rights abuses against child workers and indentured labourers.

Investigations show that it has more child labourers than any other country - and that millions of adult labourers still work in near slave like conditions - despite laws being passed to stop it.

For example, government-owned land is leased out for quarrying to private contractors - who are meant to have signed up to India's state of the art labour laws.

But the men working the sites have no safety gear at all, no helmets, shoes, masks, and claim that they are being paid only half of what they had been promised.

Ram Yadav was until a few years ago a bonded labourer, condemned to work off a debt run up by his parents.

He was freed because a charity went to court on his behalf.

Now he goes round checking on conditions of other workers.

"I'm telling you, the laws are there for you, but the politicians and the mine owners get together to make sure you have to work under conditions which are no better than for animals," he says.

No serious safety equipment could be seen anywhere through the quarries.

The finger of blame is firmly pointed at vested interests - including those in government - who are making money out of it - and therefore there is no political will to stop it.

India has world standard labour legislation, but in practice it has more slave and abused labourers than any other country.

The whole system is riddled with corruption, with politicians and contractors benefiting from it.

Amazingly VK Sharma, in the office of the local labour commission, agreed to the accusation.

The allegation of government neglect in this issue becomes more stark at a near-by care centre for children who recently were victims of abusive labour.

They are aged between 10 and 15, and are now learning how to play again and going through special trauma counselling.

The centre is run - not by the government, but by a charity, which often has to go to the courts to get a child freed from work.

Kailash Satyarthi of South Asian Coalition Against Child Labour said: "We see a massive abuse of human rights and labour rights in government contracted works. But the greyest area is the implementation of law"

Evidence for this was clear when you consider the case of Sada Abhindar was making bricks near a police station.

The police saw him everyday but did nothing.

And until recently Surita Rania was working to pay off her father's loan.

She gathers firewood and breaks up quarry stones.

But when she got things wrong, they hit her hands with a metal rod.

In this vast country there are many more like Surita and Sada - lone children unprotected by the law.

It's estimated that there are 12.5 million children working in India. Most are sent away from rural areas to the cities, by poor parents and families desperate to bolster their incomes. But the Indian government has just announced that it is changing the law on child labour - outlawing children under the age of 14 from working in domestic and hotel work.

Kinds continue working as ban on child labour startys in India. Ten-year-old Sonu sits forlornly on a plastic chair in a ramshackle street food stall in New Delhi, taking a break after serving customers tea.

A ban on child labour in households, restaurants, hotels and resorts came into effect in India on Tuesday but nothing has changed for the tired-looking boy, dressed in scruffy blue jeans and a faded green shirt.

Sonu, whose father also works in a food stall, says he'd rather be in school.

'But what to do? This is necessary,' said the boy, reality teaching him an early and harsh lesson in life.

Sonu comes from a poor family from a New Delhi slum and is one of the millions of children who work in roadside food stalls or in the homes of India's upper and middle-class.

Officials hope the new ban, which will apply to children under 14, will protect underage workers from psychological and sexual abuse as well as from strenuous working conditions.

On the eve of the ban, Prime Minister Manmohan Singh warned of 'firm action' against violators but appealed to Indians to give up the practice voluntarily.

Under the country's existing Child Labour (Prohibition and Regulation) Act of 1986, children under 14 are already banned from working in industries deemed 'hazardous' such as fireworks, matchstick-making, auto workshops or carpet weaving.

Activists say they have their doubts about how authorities will implement the new ban, given their past record.

'This ban on child domestic labour is a welcome step, but changes on paper are not enough,' Zama Coursen-Neff of New York-based Human Rights Watch said in a statement.

Less than five km (three miles) from India's labour ministry, 10-year-old Shehzad is covered with grime and dust as he uses a foot pump to inflate a tyre tube of a scooter belonging to a policeman, who watches him impassively.

Shehzad does not know children have been banned for a decade from working in workshops but says it does not make a difference.

'I can't go to school as my father can't afford to buy books for me,' the son of a rickshaw-puller said.

The new ban for children in food stalls and working in homes is aimed at providing legal protection to millions more children. Those found violating the law could face up to two years' jail and a maximum fine of 20,000 rupees ($435) or both.

The labour ministry says there are 12 million children under 14 years old working in India – the largest such group in the world – but activists say the number could be five times higher.

Dozens of former child laborers demonstrated outside the ministry.

'It's the right of every child: bread, play, study and love,' they shouted at a rally organised by the Bachpan Bachao Andolan (Save the Childhood Movement or BBA).

The United Nations said stopping children working was just a first step, and urged the government to set up counselling support for freed children, provide shelters and ensure that they are welcomed back in their families.

'This declaration of political will needs to be concretised in the forms of safety nets for the children who will be freed,' said Victoria Rialp, UNICEF's child protection chief in India.

Authorities say results from the new ban will not come overnight as many Indians do not see the age-old practice of employing children from impoverished families as a crime.

Activists say the new ban will expose the problems faced by child servants – whose living and working conditions are not exposed to public scrutiny – including sexual exploitation.

'These children are very vulnerable. Their employment is an invisible form of slavery,' BBA's Kailash Satyarthi said.

Child labour ban is not effective in helping kids. Child labour seems so categorically wrong that it's difficult and almost inappropriate to criticize a law banning it.

But a ban against child labour that was announced in India earlier this week merits criticism.

On Tuesday, the Indian government passed legislation banning the employment of children younger than 14 from working in restaurants, tea shops, hotels and spas or as maids in domestic service.

Children within this age range make up about 3.6 percent of the labour force in India, according to the Indian Embassy's Web site. About 13 million children work in India, and some estimates put the number much higher. About 256,000 of those work in cafes and hotels or as domestic servants.

The ban on labour for these 256,000 children, which is aimed at taking them out of the labour force and putting them in school, leaves one very big question – will they be able to survive without work?

The Associated Press spoke to children in New Delhi earlier this week, and it seems the answer to that question is no.

"As it is, I barely make enough to survive," 12-year-old Dinesh Kumar told The Associated Press. "This will be a bad blow. I don't really know what I'll do."

Kumar, who has been working at odd jobs since he moved to New Delhi three years ago, is one of the hundreds of thousands of children in India whose lives depend on their ability to work.

Rama Chandran, a 13-year-old, said he sends his family the money he earns from working at an eatery in New Delhi.

"If I didn't send money home, they would starve," he told The Associated Press.

Though it is heartbreaking that the situation in India dictates that children must work to survive and that they are responsible for supporting parents, grandparents and siblings, taking away the option of working will only make life for these children more difficult.

If enforced, the ban will push children into other sectors or into underground labour, where they will continue to work anyway. If the ban is sufficiently enforced, these children will simply go on working but will be doing so illegally.

Though Indian Prime Minister Manmohan Singh said firm action would be taken against anyone violating the new law, India's history of child labour bans suggests child labour is not likely to cease as a result of the new legislation.

India already has a ban against children working in hazardous industries, including factories that produce incense sticks, firecrackers and carpets, but the law has been ignored and tens of thousands of children continue to work in those jobs.

Only now they are working illegally. Based on the situation for those working illegally in the U.S., who usually work for less than minimum wage, children in India are likely to see a decline in wages.

This editorial could not conclude without again emphasizing that child labour is terrible and that it is sad to think about children having to work each day rather than attend school. But a ban on child labour is not the way to approach the problem. It is a superficial way to address a very deep and complicated problem, and it likely won't fix anything.

The problem of child labour in India is rooted in myriad complex causes, primarily desperate poverty, and the problem can only really be addressed by dealing with the economic problems that have allowed child labour to flourish.

Before the Indian government tells these children they can't work, they must first set in place some sort of safety net for them, so when they find themselves out of the workforce, they will not also find themselves out on the streets.

International Programme on the Elimination of Child Labour (IPEC)

- established in 1998
- main objectives:
  - collect and disseminate quantitative and qualitative data on child labour
  - create a basis for child labour data analysis to be used in formulating interventions
  - establish a database on child labour in individual countries and in the ILO
  - develop methodologies and standard indicators of child labour to enable comparability of data across countries
- actively involved in over 50 countries from all major world regions

- main donors:
  - — Canada
  - — Denmark
  - — France
  - — Italy
  - — Netherlands
  - — Norway
  - — Portugal
  - — Sweden
  - — USA
- key instruments:
  - — *National Child Labour Surveys*
    - 45 national surveys carried out
    - sample size of 5,000 to 120,000 households
    - designed and implemented in collaboration with national institutions, and in some cases other UN agencies and international financial institutions
    - national capacity-building involved
  - — *Rapid assessments*
    - 90 rapid assessments completed
    - focus on worst forms of child labour
  - — *Baseline surveys*
    - 90 baseline surveys completed
    - identify target groups and establish information to monitor and evaluate large IPEC projects in specific sectors or geographical areas
  - — *Establishment surveys*
    - examine demand-side issues
  - — *School surveys*
    - study relationship between child labour and schooling
    - include interviews with teachers and education administration
  - — *Street children surveys*
    - provide insight into informal or hidden economic activities
- features of all SIMPOC surveys:
  - — a broad age range of children (5-17) covered
  - — both parents and children as respondents, which allows for comparability of information

  - detailed industry/occupation information
  - information on working hours and health effects
  - information on related relevant indicators, such as community variables, adult labour force activity and parents' education
- gender-sensitive analysis of data. All surveys include disagreggation by sex and capture data on gender-sensitive areas, such as
  - household chores
  - commercial sexual exploitation
  - hazardous agriculture
  - armed conflict
- In 2002, SIMPOC lauched new global estimates on child labour, based on an improved methodology compared to older estimates. These included
  - children in economic activites
  - children in hazardous activities
  - children in the Wost Forms of Child Labour

A Call for Universal Ratification

In the last two years, hundreds of thousands of children throughout the world have taken part in the Global March to ban child labour. Many reached the ILO in Geneva holding hands with adults who cared enough to join their quest in this 'impossible dream'. These girls and boys organized and advocated for themselves and on behalf of millions who could not be present. How can we not listen to them?

We have it within our power to bring an end to the worst forms of child labour that are stunting the lives of millions of girls and boys. We have the resources – not just material, but also spiritual, political and organizational. We must use them fully.

How can we not do everything in our power to free each child on this planet from this scourge? How can we fail to free ourselves from our person-al and professional blinkers that prevent us from seeing abuse and injustice? Moral indifference is not possible.

A lot has been said about solidarity among generations. This is clearly a key form of solidarity of adults with children.

Child labour is not jobs for kids. It is neither valuable work experience nor apprenticeship combined with schooling that enhances a child's pre-sent and future prospects. Child labour – in its worst forms – is abuse of power. It is adults exploiting the young, naive, innocent, weak, vulnerable and insecure for personal profit; although so many valuable efforts are going on, we have not yet mustered enough courage and imagination to really go beyond chipping at the margins and actually stop it.

These children sense our actions and inactions, even if we don't hear them speak. Intuitively, they know that creating and ratifying this Convention is the easy part. The tougher part is finding ladders for them to climb out of the deep pits of violence and discrimination they live in.

The Statistical Information and Monitoring Programme on Child Labour (SIMPOC)

SIMPOC is the statistics and monitoring unit of the ILO's International Programme on the Elimination of Child Labour (IPEC). SIMPOC provides technical assistance to ILO member States to generate reliable, comparable and comprehensive data on child labour in all its forms. The assistance includes developing and implementing child labour surveys as well as enhancing capacity in ILO member States to collect, process, disseminate and analyse data on child labour on a regular and sustainable basis. New techniques for investigating the more hidden forms of child labour have also been developed. The data and qualitative information generated by the various SIMPOC instruments form essential inputs to child labour policies and programmes. Further, their availability promotes research and raises awareness of the problem of child labour. The data and studies are made accessible through various publications and a data repository on the SIMPOC website.

History of SIMPOC

SIMPOC was launched in 1998 in response to the growing need for more comprehensive statistics on child labour. The programme built on the work undertaken by the ILO Bureau of Statistics from 1992-97 on the development of statistical methodologies for collecting data on child labour. Over the last few years SIMPOC has further refined the quantitative methods and survey questionnaires used in national child labour surveys and vastly extended their coverage. The programme now operates in all major world regions. SIMPOC has also collaborated with UNICEF on the development of a new qualitative approach, the Rapid Assessment Methodology (RA) with a view to gathering information on the less visible forms not easily captured by national child labour surveys.

Legal and Policy Framework

The legal and policy framework for all ILO work on child labour is provided in two fundamental ILO Conventions: The Minimum Age Convention, 1973 (No. 138) and the Worst Forms of Child Labour Convention, 1999 (No. 182). With the rapid rise in the number of ratifications of Convention No. 182, the demand for SIMPOC technical support has increased strongly. For countries that have ratified this Convention, data collection is one of the necessary first steps in fulfilling the Convention's provisions to withdraw and rehabilitate victims of child labour and prevent other children from becoming victims.

Methods of Data Collection

Six basic methods have been applied to generate child labour statistics and information: (a) National Child Labour Surveys (NCLS); (b) the Rapid Assessment Methodology (RA); (c) Baseline Surveys; (d) Establishment-based Surveys; (e) Street Children Surveys; and (f) School-based Surveys. These child labour survey methodologies, however, are not mutually exclusive; instead they can be applied in a combined and complimentary way.

National Child Labour Surveys

These are household-based national sample surveys whose target respondents are parents or guardians and children living in the same household. The surveys are carried out as stand-alone surveys or as modules attached to other national household-based surveys such as labour force surveys. The statistics and information generated from these surveys cover both economic and non-economic activities (such as household chores) of children, demographic and social characteristics of household members, working hours, nature of tasks, health and safety issues including injuries at work and perceptions of parents about children's work. With regard to the worst forms of child labour, the national surveys usually capture information on jobs targeted by Convention No. 182 as "hazardous work". To capture the more hidden and illicit forms of child labour, SIMPOC mainly relies on other methodologies such as the Rapid Assessment.

Rapid Assessments

In response to the lack of data and information on the worst forms of child labour, the ILO and UNICEF jointly developed the Rapid Assessment (RA) methodology. The RA is a method of gathering descriptive information on hidden or illicit forms of child labour quickly and in a limited geographical area. It is often used at the first stage of programme planning. While more qualitative and less scientific in approach than household-based surveys, the RA is considerably easier, less costly, and faster to implement. The method has proven very useful for obtaining detailed knowledge of the working conditions and life circumstances of children who are the victims of the worst forms of child labour. In general, the RA methodology is not designed to extrapolate figures or make generalizations outside the scope of the interviewed respondents.

Baseline Surveys

Baseline surveys are aimed at the precise identification of specific child labour populations and their characteristics, as well as the determinants and consequences of child labour in specific sectors. They are closely linked to action programmes in terms of identifying target groups and monitoring their withdrawal from work over time. Baseline surveys combine both quantitative and qualitative techniques. The methods used are usually a mix of sample survey and participatory approaches, such as community-level inquiries, household and employer surveys, street children inquiries, school surveys, and RAs.

Establishment-Based Surveys

Establishment surveys seek out and query employers of children, and where possible, the child workers themselves. The establishments are often selected from a list derived from a National Child Labour Survey. Establishment-based surveys cover issues such as working hours and conditions, benefits and injuries of children as compared with adults. They also obtain information on the reasons employers hire children and the recruitment methods used.

Street Children Surveys

Street children surveys target two main categories of children: (a) those who live and work on the streets and by definition do not have any other place of residence; and (b) those who work on the streets but normally reside with their parents or guardians. While category (b) can be captured through the household surveys, category (a) cannot. The approach relies on randomly interviewing children and, if possible, their employers and/or clients, using questions similar to those in the National Child Labour Surveys.

School-Based Surveys

School-based surveys are intended to obtain further information concerning children who have been identified as working via the household surveys. The purpose is to determine the impact of work on performance and attendance in school as well as the children's attitudes to studying in general. The surveys include interviews with teachers and school management allowing for comparisons of working children and non-working children in school. The surveys also attempt to assess some of the school-related factors that may influence a child to work, such as the quality of the school and the children's perception of the relevance of their education.

Gender Mainstreaming

Child labour involves different working conditions, terms of payment, and risks for boys and girls. Gender is one of the relevant social variables permitting more accurate assessment of the problem of child labour. Since 1998, SIMPOC has encouraged and included in its mandate the need for accurate quantitative and qualitative data on child labour that is gender-sensitive. Collecting such data is now an institutional norm for all SIMPOC-supported surveys.

Criteria for Obtaining SIMPOC Technical Assistance

The following criteria are often used to determine priorities in selecting countries for SIMPOC technical assistance:

- The country is an IPEC-participating country; that is, it has signed a Memorandum of Understanding with IPEC and has ratified ILO Convention No. 182 on the worst forms of child labour;
- The country has an active programme to combat child labour and a favourable institutional infrastructure for conducting surveys. SIMPOC now gives greater consideration to countries that have embarked on the new initiative of preparing Time-Bound Programmes, a set of tightly integrated and coordinated policies and programmes to prevent and eliminate a country's worst forms of child labour within a defined period of time.
- Government commitment, implying a willingness both to assign adequately qualified national personnel to the programme and to provide appropriate budgetary resources;
- Non-IPEC-participating countries that request SIMPOC's assistance to conduct child labour surveys and have sufficient in-country capacity to carry them out are also considered.

SIMPOC Partners

SIMPOC's implementing partners are generally national statistics offices; ministries of labour or other government agencies responsible for children's welfare; research and academic institutions; employers' and workers' organizations and NGOs. SIMPOC collaborates closely with other international organizations, notably UNICEF and the World Bank, to create synergies among existing data-collecting initiatives.

TABLE 1
List of countries with SIMPOC activities

Albania	Ghana	Pakistan
Argentina	Guatemala	Panama
Bangladesh	Honduras	Philippines
Belize	India	Portugal
Bolivia	Indonesia	Romania
Brazil	Italy	Russia
Bulgaria	Jamaica	Senegal
Burkina Faso	Jordan	South Africa

Cambodia	Kenya	Sri Lanka
Chile	Lebanon	Tanzania
Colombia	Madagascar	Thailand
Costa Rica	Malawi	Turkey
Cote d'Ivoire	Mali	Uganda
Dominican Republic	Mongolia	Ukraine
Ecuador	Morocco	Vietnam
El Salvador	Namibia	West Bank & Gaza Strip
Estonia	Nepal	Yemen
Ethiopia	Nicaragua	Zambia
Georgia	Nigeria	Zimbabwe

International Programme on the Elimination of Child Labour: IPEC

SIMPOC's experience in over 35 countries across the globe has resulted in a robust collection of questionnaires serving multiple needs. This includes questionnaires for collecting both quantitative and qualitative data and for a number of different forms of child labour. For countries committed to developing a national child labour survey with relatively advanced data collection and processing capacities, a very comprehensive questionnaire encompassing more than one hundred questions is on offer; for other countries a core questionnaire has been elaborated, allowing for the collection of essential child labour data within a relatively short time. And for organizations or research institutions conducting baseline surveys or rapid assessments questionnaires have been developed and tested for various worst forms of child labour.

Guides and Indicators

In keeping with SIMPOC's goals of collecting high quality data and information on child labour issues, a number of "How to" guides have been produced. The guides cover topics of survey methodology, data processing and data analysis. Model questionnaires are also available as well as child labour indicators. Additional detailed manuals on data analysis and data dissemination continue to be prepared.

CAMPAIGN AGAINST CHILD LABOUR (CACL)[1]

Organisation aims and activities: CACL consists of a network of over 5400 anti-child labour groups spread over 12 states in India. CACL is committed to the eradication of child labour through building public opinion, investigation of abuse/expoitation, advocacy, lobbying and monitoring of national and international developments.

1. C/o PECUC, House No. VII-H-26, Sailashree Vihar, Bhubaneswar, 751021, Orissa, India

Further Details

Operational level: National

Works with age groups: Children 0 - 18

Organisation type: NGO national child rights coalition]

Organisation mandate: Lobby governments and the United Nations, Provide training or education on child rights, Research child rights, Undertake legal casework on behalf of children, Work in partnership with organisations, Work with media and press

Areas of expertise: Child labour and working children, Children and citizenship, Children and education, Children and the media, Children in conflict with the law, Children working and living on the street, Individual cases of violations, Reporting to and monitoring the CRC, Sexual exploitation of children

Countries in which this organisation works: India

Other Organisations Based in India

- A.P. Alliance for Child Rights
- Abyudaya Yuvajana Sangam
- Action for People Through the Promotion of the Arts
- Action on Disability and Development (ADD) - India
- Andhra Pradesh Urban and Rural Social Development Society
- Animators for Rural Multipurpose Development Society
- Anusha Mahila Mandali
- Aravind Children's Hospital
- ARISE - Agency of Research on Integration Services and Empowerment
- Arunodhaya - Centre for Street Children
- Asian Center for Human Rights
- Asian Indigenous & Tribal Peoples Network
- Association For Integrated Development Of Women
- Association For Integrated Medical Services Of India
- Association for Promoting Social Action
- Association for Welfare Activities and Rural Education
- Awake Friends Trust
- Bal Niketan Singh
- Bal Sahyog

- Bangalore Onlyavara Seva Coota
- Bharat Integrated Social Welfare Agency
- Bharat Vikas Parishad
- Bharathiar Makkal Nalvalvu Sangam
- Bhavani Mahila Mandali
- Bonded Labour Liberation Front
- Books for Change
- Butterflies - Programme for Street and Working Children
- Care for Orphans Rehabilitation and Educational Society
- Centre for Child and the Law
- Centre for Community Health Research
- Centre for Coordination of Voluntary Works and Research
- Centre for Health Education and Nutrition Awareness
- Centre for Organisation, Research & Education
- Centre for Rural Education and Development
- Centre for Rural Education and Development Action
- Centre for Rural Education Research and Development Association
- Centre for Social Research
- Centre of Concern for Child Labour
- Child In Need Institute
- Child Labour Action Network
- Child Relief and You
- Child Rights Trust
- Childline India Foundation
- Children in Domestic Work
- Children's Rights in Goa
- Childright - India
- CHOLAI - Action for Child Labour
- Christian Workers Movement
- Citron Education Trust
- City Montessori School, Lucknow
- Committee for Legal Aid to the Poor

- Community Development Centre
- Concerned for Working Children
- Council for Socio Economic Benevolent Action
- Crescent Educational Society
- CRY - Child Relief and You
- Cuddapah District Grama Seva Samithi
- Cuddapah District Khadi Grama Bhyudaya Samtha
- Divya Disha
- Durga Mahila Sangham
- Dynamic Action for Rural Education
- ECPAT - Calcutta
- Educational Trust Of India
- Farmer's Development Agency
- Forum for Child Rights
- Foundation for Legal Aid, Environment & Social Action
- Free the Children - India
- Fulmonidevi Memorial Public Library
- Gania Unnayan Committee
- Global March Against Child Labour
- Good Shepherd Social, Educational and Economic Development Trust
- Goodwill Social Work Centre
- GRACE
- Grace Action India
- Grace Vision Centre
- Grama Pengal Munnetra Sangam Society
- Green Planet
- Hamara Club
- HAQ Centre for Child Rights
- India Alliance for Child Rights
- Indian Committee of Youth Organisations
- Indian Council for Child Welfare - Tamil Nadu
- Indian Social Service Institute

- Indira Gandhi Integral Education Centre
- Indira Nahila Mandali
- Institute for Development Exchange
- Institute of Social Sciences
- Integrated Village Development Centre
- Jana Chetana
- Janakalyan Samity
- Janavikas Society
- Krityanand UNESCO Club
- Kwality (Karnataka Welfare Society)
- LearningChannel.org
- Liberal Assocation for Movement of People
- Love Humanity International
- Loyola Organisation for Rural Development Society
- Madhar Nala Thondu Niruvanam
- Madhavi Social Development Organisation for the Weaker Sections
- Madurai Non Formal Education Centre
- Mahila Rural Development Youth Society
- Mahita
- Manav Kalyan Sansthan
- Meljol
- Mountain Children's Foundation
- Movement for Alternatives and Youth Awareness - Maya
- Mythri Sarva Scva Samithi
- Nanban, Centre for Street and Working Children
- National Coalition on Children in Armed Conflict INDIA
- National Educational Minorities Society
- National Institute Of Public Cooperation And Child Development
- National Integrated Rural Development Agency
- NGO Forum for Combating Sexual Exploitation
- Nishtha Centre for the Development of Women and Children
- Organization for Socio-Economic Development

- Our Lady Of Charity Of The Good Shepherd
- Paraspara Trust
- Peace Trust (Child Rights Coordination Committee)
- People's Action in Development
- People's Association for Rural Development
- People's Association for Rural Women Development Trust
- People's Organisation for Rural Health, Education and Economic Development
- Plan International - India
- Power Healee Trust
- Prathidhwani Srota Sangha
- Research Academy for Rural Enrichment
- Rural Development Society - Andhra Pradesh
- Rural Development Society - Tamil Nadu
- Rural Economic and Education Development Society
- Rural Education Centre for Development
- Rural Health Development Centre
- Rural Integrated Development Organisation
- Rural Organisation for Social Education
- Rural Organisation for Social Emancipation
- Rural Uplift Centre
- Russ Foundation
- SACCS - South Asia Coalition on Child Servitude
- SACRED - Society For Agricultural, Cultural And Rural Educational Development
- SAI Education Society
- Salaam Baalak Trust
- Sambhav Social Service Organisation
- Sanctuary of Living Springs
- Sankalp
- Sanlaap
- SANYOG
- SARTHI

- Sarvodaya Gram Sevak Sangh
- Search Years
- Sebama Foundation
- Shabnam Resources
- Shanti Educational Society
- SKCV Children's Trust
- Social Aid Improvement and Mass Action
- Social Education and Environmental Development
- Society for Community Development Project
- Socio Legal Information Centre (Child Rights Initiative)
- Socio-legal Aid Research and Training Centre
- Sradhanjali Charitable Trust
- Sree Sakthi Mahila Mandali
- Sri Sevasadan
- Strides Society
- Tamilnadu Primary School Improvement Campaign
- Tear Fund India Committee on Relief and Rehabilitation Service
- Tulir Centre for the Prevention and Healing of Child Sexual Abuse
- Unity Charitable Trust
- Upliftment of Democratic Village Improvement Society
- Valarchi India Trust
- Valley Commonwealth Public School
- Vidya Bharati Sansthan
- Vimochana Devadasi Punarvasati Sangh
- Visakha Rural Development Society
- Vivekananda Adibasi Kalyan Samity
- VOC Rural Development Centre
- VV Giri National Labour Institute
- Women Activities for Voluntary Empowerment
- Women and Child Development Society
- Women Hope Foundation - India
- Women's Organisation for Rural Development

- Working Group on the Convention on the Rights of the Child
- World Vision India
- Yanadi Education Society
- Youth Council for Development Alternatives
- Youth for Unity and Voluntary Action
- Youth for Unity and Voluntary Action - Regional Office

Organisations working in similar fields:

- Accion por los Ninos
- ACTIVE
- African Child Association
- African Child Policy Forum
- African Commission on Human and People's Rights
- Anita Home
- Association Défis - Jeunes pour le Développement
- Association for Promoting Social Action
- Autre Vie
- Bangladesh Coalition for Child Rights
- Bangladesh Mohila Unnayan Sanghstha
- Bangladesh Shishu Adhikar Forum
- Bharat Integrated Social Welfare Agency
- Centre for Women's Studies - University of Nijmegen
- Centre pour la Promotion des Droits de l'Enfant et de la Femme
- Centro Internazionale Studi Famiglia
- Centros Comunitarios de Aprendizaje
- Child Labour Action Network
- Child Legal Aid Centre
- Child Protection Alliance
- Child Rights Advisory Documentation and Legal Centre
- Child Rights Information and Documentation Centre
- Child Rights Information Network
- Child Rights Trust
- Childline India Foundation

- Children Concern Organisation
- Children in Adversity Consultation website
- Children's Human Rights Centre of Albania
- Children's Rights Alliance for England
- Children's Rights in Goa
- ChildRight
- Christian Children's Fund - Geneva Office
- Commissioner for Human Rights, Council of Europe
- Consortium for Street Children
- Coordination des ONG pour les Droits de l'Enfant
- Defence for Children International
- Defence for Children International - Costa Rica
- Defence for Children International - Nigeria
- Defence for Children International - Sierra Leone
- Division of Childhood and Adolescence, Department of Health, Canada
- Enfants et Développement
- Forum for Rehabilitation and Integrated Development Approach by the Youth
- Fundacion Paniamor
- Human Rights - First the Child
- Human Rights Information and Documentation Center
- Integrated Regional Information Networks - IRIN
- International Center for Child and Youth Studies
- Jonathan's Child Care Center Sierra Leone
- Kanifing East Youth Development Society
- Korean Foster Care Association
- La Lumière
- Lembaga Advokasi Anak Indonesia
- Maison des Droits de l'Enfant
- National Centre For Playwork Education - North East
- New Life Foundation of Bangladesh
- NGO Group for the Convention on the Rights of the Child

- NGO/UNICEF Regional Network for Children in Central and Eastern Europe, Commonwealth of Independent States and Baltic States
- Northern Ireland Commissioner for Children and Young People
- Nous les Enfants
- Office of the Commissioner for Chidren
- Ombudsman for Children - Norway
- ONG Espoir pour les enfants
- Organisation for the Protection of Children's Rights
- People's Action in Development
- Plan International - India
- Relief Society of Tigray
- Resources Aimed at the Prevention of Child Abuse and Neglect
- Samundra Devi UNESCO CLUB/ Nepal
- Sanlaap
- SARTHI
- Save the Children New Zealand
- Save the Children Norway - Cambodia Office
- Save the Children Sweden - Guatemala Office
- Save the Children Sweden - Nicaragua Office
- Save the Children UK
- Save the Children UK - DRC Office
- Save the Children UK - Office for South and Central Asia Region
- Save the Children UK - Sierra Leone Office
- Sindh Journalists Network for Children
- Society for the Empowerment of People
- Society for the Protection for the Rights of the Child
- Spanish Committee for UNICEF
- Tanzania Movement for and with Children
- UNICEF - Belgique
- UNICEF - Bhutan
- UNICEF - Colombia
- UNICEF - Cuba country office

- UNICEF - East and Southern Africa Regional Office - Regional Emergency Support Unit
- UNICEF - Gambia
- UNICEF - Georgia
- UNICEF - Malaysia
- UNICEF Innocenti Research Centre
- UNICEF Pacific
- UNICEF Podgorica
- UNICEF Togo
- World Vision - Japan
- Zimbabwe Council for the Welfare of Children

Child Workers in Asia (CWA)[1]

Organisation aims and activities: CWA focuses on working children and is involved in network support and development with NGO partners. It organises workshops and seminars, develops publicity materials, undertakes studies on child workers, supports fundraising activities of partners, supports international initiatives such as the Global March Against Child Labour, disseminating information.

Further Details

Child Workers in Asia work to end child labour exploitation, strengthen and build solidarity among NGOs, facilitate information and experience sharing among NGOs, regional advocacy

Operational level: Regional

Works with age groups : Children 0 - 18

Organisation type: NGO national child rights coalition

Organisation mandate: Lobby governments and the United Nations

Areas of expertise: Child labour and working children, Reporting to and monitoring the CRC, Rights based programming

Countries in which this organisation works: Bangladesh, Cambodia, India, Indonesia, Maldives, Nepal, Pakistan, Sri Lanka, Thailand

Other organisations Based in Thailand

- All Burma Federation of Students Unions Foreign Affairs Committee
- Burmese Relief Centre
- Centre for the Protection of Children's Rights Foundation

1. 120/16 Soi Sukhumvit 23 Klongtoey-Nua, Wattana Bangkok 10110

- Child Rights Asianet
- Children in Asia
- Christian Children's Fund Foundation in Thailand
- Christian Children's Fund Foundation of Thailand
- Development And Education Program For Daughters And Communities
- Duang Prateep Foundation
- ECPAT - International Secretariat
- Forum-Asia
- Fountain Of Life Centre - Good Shepherd Sisters
- Karen Human Rights Group
- National Coalition Government of the Union of Burma-Human Rights Documentation Unit
- National Council for Child and Youth Development
- Plan Asia Regional Office
- Plan International, Asia Regional Office
- Project OutReach - Thailand
- Regional Working Group on Child Labour
- Save the Children Sweden - South East Asia Pacific Regional Office
- UNICEF East Asia and the Pacific Regional Office
- UNICEF Thailand
- Working Group on Children
- World Vision Foundation of Thailand

BUTTERFLIES - PROGRAMME FOR STREET AND WORKING CHILDREN[1]

Organisation type: NGO - non governmental organisation

Areas of expertise: Child labour and working children, Children and education, Children working and living on the street

Countries in which this organisation works: India

Other Organisations Based in India

- A.P. Alliance for Child Rights
- Abyudaya Yuvajana Sangam
- Action for People Through the Promotion of the Arts

---

1. 2U 4 Green Park Extension, 1st Floor New Delhi 110016, India

- Action on Disability and Development (ADD) - India
- Andhra Pradesh Urban and Rural Social Development Society
- Animators for Rural Multipurpose Development Society
- Anusha Mahila Mandali
- Aravind Children's Hospital
- ARISE - Agency of Research on Integration Services and Empowerment
- Arunodhaya - Centre for Street Children
- Asian Center for Human Rights
- Asian Indigenous & Tribal Peoples Network
- Association For Integrated Development Of Women
- Association For Integrated Medical Services Of India
- Association for Promoting Social Action
- Association for Welfare Activities and Rural Education
- Awake Friends Trust
- Bal Niketan Singh
- Bal Sahyog
- Bangalore Onlyavara Seva Coota
- Bharat Integrated Social Welfare Agency
- Bharat Vikas Parishad
- Bharathiar Makkal Nalvalvu Sangam
- Bhavani Mahila Mandali
- Bonded Labour Liberation Front
- Books for Change
- Campaign Against Child Labour
- Care for Orphans Rehabilitation and Educational Society
- Centre for Child and the Law
- Centre for Community Health Research
- Centre for Coordination of Voluntary Works and Research
- Centre for Health Education and Nutrition Awareness
- Centre for Organisation, Research & Education
- Centre for Rural Education and Development
- Centre for Rural Education and Development Action

- Centre for Rural Education Research and Development Association
- Centre for Social Research
- Centre of Concern for Child Labour
- Child In Need Institute
- Child Labour Action Network
- Child Relief and You
- Child Rights Trust
- Childline India Foundation
- Children in Domestic Work
- Children's Rights in Goa
- Childright - India
- CHOLAI - Action for Child Labour
- Christian Workers Movement
- Citron Education Trust
- City Montessori School, Lucknow
- Committee for Legal Aid to the Poor
- Community Development Centre
- Concerned for Working Children
- Council for Socio Economic Benevolent Action
- Crescent Educational Society
- CRY - Child Relief and You
- Cuddapah District Grama Seva Samithi
- Cuddapah District Khadi Grama Bhyudaya Samtha
- Divya Disha
- Durga Mahila Sangham
- Dynamic Action for Rural Education
- ECPAT - Calcutta
- Educational Trust Of India
- Farmer's Development Agency
- Forum for Child Rights
- Foundation for Legal Aid, Environment & Social Action
- Free the Children - India

- Fulmonidevi Memorial Public Library
- Gania Unnayan Committee
- Global March Against Child Labour
- Good Shepherd Social, Educational and Economic Development Trust
- Goodwill Social Work Centre
- GRACE
- Grace Action India
- Grace Vision Centre
- Grama Pengal Munnetra Sangam Society
- Green Planet
- Hamara Club
- HAQ Centre for Child Rights
- India Alliance for Child Rights
- Indian Committee of Youth Organisations
- Indian Council for Child Welfare - Tamil Nadu
- Indian Social Service Institute
- Indira Gandhi Integral Education Centre
- Indira Nahila Mandali
- Institute for Development Exchange
- Institute of Social Sciences
- Integrated Village Development Centre
- Jana Chetana
- Janakalyan Samity
- Janavikas Society
- Krityanand UNESCO Club
- Kwality (Karnataka Welfare Society)
- LearningChannel.org
- Liberal Assocation for Movement of People
- Love Humanity International
- Loyola Organisation for Rural Development Society
- Madhar Nala Thondu Niruvanam
- Madhavi Social Development Organisation for the Weaker Sections

- Madurai Non Formal Education Centre
- Mahila Rural Development Youth Society
- Mahita
- Manav Kalyan Sansthan
- Meljol
- Mountain Children's Foundation
- Movement for Alternatives and Youth Awareness - Maya
- Mythri Sarva Scva Samithi
- Nanban, Centre for Street and Working Children
- National Coalition on Children in Armed Conflict INDIA
- National Educational Minorities Society
- National Institute Of Public Cooperation And Child Development
- National Integrated Rural Development Agency
- NGO Forum for Combating Sexual Exploitation
- Nishtha Centre for the Development of Women and Children
- Organization for Socio-Economic Development
- Our Lady Of Charity Of The Good Shepherd
- Paraspara Trust
- Peace Trust (Child Rights Coordination Committee)
- People's Action in Development
- People's Association for Rural Development
- People's Association for Rural Women Development Trust
- People's Organisation for Rural Health, Education and Economic Development
- Plan International - India
- Power Healee Trust
- Prathidhwani Srota Sangha
- Research Academy for Rural Enrichment
- Rural Development Society - Andhra Pradesh
- Rural Development Society - Tamil Nadu
- Rural Economic and Education Development Society
- Rural Education Centre for Development

- Rural Health Development Centre
- Rural Integrated Development Organisation
- Rural Organisation for Social Education
- Rural Organisation for Social Emancipation
- Rural Uplift Centre
- Russ Foundation
- SACCS - South Asia Coalition on Child Servitude
- SACRED - Society For Agricultural, Cultural And Rural Educational Development
- SAI Education Society
- Salaam Baalak Trust
- Sambhav Social Service Organisation
- Sanctuary of Living Springs
- Sankalp
- Sanlaap
- SANYOG
- SARTHI
- Sarvodaya Gram Sevak Sangh
- Search Years
- Sebama Foundation
- Shabnam Resources
- Shanti Educational Society
- SKCV Children's Trust
- Social Aid Improvement and Mass Action
- Social Education and Environmental Development
- Society for Community Development Project
- Socio Legal Information Centre (Child Rights Initiative)
- Socio-legal Aid Research and Training Centre
- Sradhanjali Charitable Trust
- Sree Sakthi Mahila Mandali
- Sri Sevasadan
- Strides Society

- Tamilnadu Primary School Improvement Campaign
- Tear Fund India Committee on Relief and Rehabilitation Service
- Tulir Centre for the Prevention and Healing of Child Sexual Abuse
- Unity Charitable Trust
- Upliftment of Democratic Village Improvement Society
- Valarchi India Trust
- Valley Commonwealth Public School
- Vidya Bharati Sansthan
- Vimochana Devadasi Punarvasati Sangh
- Visakha Rural Development Society
- Vivekananda Adibasi Kalyan Samity
- VOC Rural Development Centre
- VV Giri National Labour Institute
- Women Activities for Voluntary Empowerment
- Women and Child Development Society
- Women Hope Foundation - India
- Women's Organisation for Rural Development
- Working Group on the Convention on the Rights of the Child
- World Vision India
- Yanadi Education Society
- Youth Council for Development Alternatives
- Youth for Unity and Voluntary Action
- Youth for Unity and Voluntary Action - Regional Office

WORLD BANK GROUP - GLOBAL CHILD LABOUR PROGRAMME[1]

1818 H. St. NW, Washington DC 20008 20433

Organisation aims and activities: The World Bank's Global Child Labour Programme (programme) was created in May 1998 and is housed in the Bank's Social Protection Unit and Human Development Network. The Programme is the focal point for Bank-wide child labour/ related issues and activities, projects and policy.

1. 1818 H. St. NW, Washington DC 20008 20433

Operational level: International

Organisation type: NGO - non governmental organisation

Areas of expertise: Child labour and working children

Other Organisations Based in United States

- Adventist Development And Relief Agency
- Advocacy Project
- Advocates for Children and Families
- AECF Annie E Casey Foundation
- African Child Care Association, Inc
- Another Look
- Antarctica University
- Arkansas Democrat-Gazette
- Better Care Network
- CARE USA
- Casa Alianza - Covenant House Latin America
- Catholics For a Free Choice
- Center for Defence Information
- Center for Reproductive Law and Policy
- Centre for Media Education
- Chadwick Center for Children and Families
- Child Centered Millennium Project
- Child Rights Caucus for the UN General Assembly Special Session on Children
- Child Rights International Research Institute
- Child to Child International
- Child Violence Identification and Prevention
- Child Welfare League of America
- Childhope International
- Children and Violence Caucus for the 2001 United Nations General Assembly Special Session on Children
- Children in Armed Conflict Caucus for the 2001 UN General Assembly Special Session on Children

- Children Internationally Abducted of America
- Children Vaccine Programme
- Children's Forum 21
- Children's Pressline
- Children's Vaccine Program
- Christian Children's Fund - Liason Office
- Christian Children's Fund - USA
- Coalition Against Trafficking In Women - USA
- Coalition of Cuban-American Women
- Code of Conduct for the Protection of Children from Sexual Exploitation in Travel and Tourism
- Community Information and Epidemiological Technology
- Congregation of Our Lady of Charity of the Good Shepherd
- Council for Professional Recognition
- Council on Foreign Relations
- Develop Africa Inc.
- Dreams Can Be Foundation
- EarthAction International
- ECPAT - USA
- End Physical Punishment of Children - USA
- Environment and Health Caucus for the UN General Assembly Special Session on Children 2001
- Espoir pour les Enfants
- Francois-Xavier Bagnoud Center for Health and Human Rights
- Girls Educational and Mentoring Services
- Global Action Network
- Global Fund for Children
- Global Youth Connect
- Haitian Street Kids, Inc.
- Hariri Foundation
- Harrington Park Press
- Human Rights Advocates Natural Heritage Institute

- Human Rights Educational Initiative
- Human Rights in China
- Human Rights Watch
- Human Rights Watch, Children's Rights Division
- Injustice Studies
- Institute for Families in Society
- Institute of Child Development
- Institute of Human Rights, Emory University
- Institute on Family and Neighbourhood Life
- Inter-American Commission on Human Rights
- International Campaign for Tibet
- International Child Art Foundation
- International Coalition for Genital Integrity
- International Families
- International Foundation for Children's Education
- International League for Human Rights
- International NGO Task Group on Legal and Institutional Matters
- International Rescue Committee - USA
- International Social Services - USA
- International Society for Prevention of Child Abuse and Neglect
- Jubilee Campaign - USA
- Juvenile Law Center
- Kabissa
- Kosova Action Network
- La Leche League International
- Madre, Inc.
- Medical Mission Sisters
- Minnesota Advocates for Human Rights
- National Coalition for Haitian Rights
- National Coalition to Abolish the Death Penalty
- National Committee for the Rights of the Child USA

- National Council of Churches of Christ USA
- National Council on Child Abuse and Family Violence
- National Education Association
- National Spiritual Assembly of the Baha'is of the United States
- Natural Heritage Institute
- New School University
- NGO Committee on UNICEF
- NGO Working Group on Girls
- Office of the Special Representative of the Secretary-General for Children and Armed Conflict
- Pangaea
- Peaceways- Young General Assembly Secretariat
- Perhaps...Kids Meeting Kids
- Program on Forced Migration and Health, Columbia University
- Project Grads for Teen Mothers
- Rainbows of Hope
- Randolph Macon College
- Rehabilitation International
- Results
- RUGMARK Foundation
- Save the Children USA
- Special Representative for Children and Armed Conflict
- Sports for Hunger/Hunger Resource Centre
- Stop Child Poverty
- Student Campaign for Child Survival
- Task Force on Children's Nutritional Rights
- Temple of Understanding
- Tibet Justice Center
- Try-Again Homes, Inc.
- UN - United Nations
- UN Enable, Division for Social Policy and Development, Focal Point on

Disability

- UN Foundation
- UN High Commissioner for Human Rights - New York
- UN OHCHR - Committee on the Elimination of All Forms of Discrimination Against Women
- UN Security Council
- UNICEF
- UNICEF - Division of Evaluation Policy & Planning
- UNICEF - Nicaragua
- UNICEF Library
- Unitarian Universalist Association
- United Church of Christ Justice and Witness Ministries
- United Nations - Division for the Advancement of Women
- United Nations Population Fund
- United States Fund for UNICEF
- University of Colorado - Children, Youth and Environments
- University of Iowa - Center for Human Rights
- US Campaign to Ban Landmines
- US Coalition for Child Survival
- Watchlist on Children and Armed Conflict
- Winrock International
- Witness
- Women's Commission for Refugee Women and Children
- Working Group on Girls Caucus
- World Bank Group
- World Coalition for Indigenous Children and Youth
- World Organisation for Early Childhood Education - USA
- World Vision International - USA
- World Vision Relief and Devolopment
- Youth Advocate Program International
- Zonta International

UNDERSTANDING CHILDREN'S WORK (UCW)[1]

Organisation aims and activities: As part of broader efforts to develop effective and long-term solutions to child labour UCW's goals are: improve child labour research, data collection and data analysis; Enhance capacity for child labour data collection and research, especially at the local and national levels; and improve impact assessments of interventions against child labour.

Organisation type: Other

Organisation mandate: Work in partnership with organisations

Areas of expertise: Child labour and working children

Countries in which this organisation works: El Salvador, Guatemala, Morocco, Nepal, Yemen

Other Organisations Based in Italy

- Associazione Amici dei Bambini
- Associazione Italiana Amici di Raoul Follereau
- Centro Internazionale Studi Famiglia
- Coordination for Child Rights
- ECPAT - Italy
- Food and Agricultural Organisation of the United Nations
- Gruppo di Lavoro per la Convenzione sui diritti del fanciullo
- Gruppo di Lavoro per la Convenzione sui diritti dell'infanzia e dell'adolescenza
- Inter Press Service - News Agency
- International Federation of Business and Professional Women - Italy
- International Federation of Educative Communities - Italy
- International Inner Wheel
- International Secretariat for Child Friendly Cities
- International Union of Anthropological and Ethnological Sciences
- Istituto Degli Innocenti di Firenze
- Italian Coordination of Public and Private Services Against Child Abuse
- Mondo e Missione
- NAT's Bologna

1. Innocenti Research Centre Piazza Annunziata 12, 50122, Florence

- National Association of Children's Residential Homes
- Organismo do Voluntarito per la Cooperazione Internazionale la Nostra Famiglia
- Save the Children Italia
- Telefono Azzurro - Italy
- Terre des hommes - Italy
- UNICEF Innocenti Research Centre
- United Nations Interregional Crime and Justice Research Institute

INSTITUTE FOR RESEARCH ON WORKING CHILDREN (IREWOC)[1]

Organisation aims and activities: IREWOC's goal is to generate more research on child labour, and to raise awareness and motivate action around this complex issue. The focus is on children living in adverse conditions and research is usually based on intensive fieldwork with a child's perspective.

Further details: IREWOC studies the changing approach to child labour and the impact of the process of globalisation on changes in the condition of children. This is done by means of education, research, publications and conferences.

Operational level: International

Works with age groups: Children 0 - 18

Organisation type: Academic institution

Organisation mandate: Provide training or education on child rights, Research child rights, Work in partnership with organisations

Areas of expertise: Child labour and working children, Children and citizenship, Children and education, Children working and living on the street

Other Organisations Based in Netherlands

- Bernard van Leer Foundation
- Canadian Council of Natural Mothers
- Centre for Women's Studies - University of Nijmegen
- Child Helpline International
- Children's Rights Consultancy International
- ChildRight

1. Cruquiusweg 68-70, 1019AH Amsterdam, Netherlands

- Childright Worldwide
- Defence for Children International - Netherlands
- Dutch National Youth Council
- Dutch NGO Coalition for Children's Rights
- ECPAT - Netherlands
- European Journalism Centre
- European Network for School Age Childcare - Netherlands
- Human Rights Education Associates
- INDRA - Institute for Development Research Amsterdam, University of Amsterdam
- Institute for Development Research Amsterdam
- Institute for Society and Politics
- Institute of Social Studies
- International Advocates for Children
- International Center for Child and Youth Studies
- International Child Development Initiatives
- International Commission of Jurists: Dutch section
- International Foster Care Organisation
- International Institute for the Urban Environment
- Jubilee Campaign - Netherlands
- Kluwer Academic Publishers
- Plan International - Netherlands
- Save the Children Netherlands
- Terre des Hommes - Netherlands
- War Child Netherlands
- Watoto Wa Amani (Children For Peace)
- Young in Prison

Organisations Working in Similar Fields

- 4 Nations Child Policy Network
- Adeeba Women and Children Resource Centre
- Adult Education for Development
- African Child Association

- African Child Policy Forum
- African Commission on Human and People's Rights
- African Network for the Prevention and Protection Against Child Abuse and Neglect - Liberia Chapter
- Agência de Notícias dos Direitos da Infância
- Agyapomaa Societal Needs International
- Anita Home
- Asociación Cristiana de Jóvenes de Bogotá
- Association Appui a la Rue
- Association Communautaire Pour la Promotion et la Protection des Droits de l'Homme
- Association Défis - Jeunes pour le Développement
- Association for Promoting Social Action
- Association for Welfare Activities and Rural Education
- Association Intervida
- Association Mondiale Pour l'Ecole Instrument de Paix
- Autre Vie
- Azerbaijan Young Lawyers' Union
- Bangladesh Coalition for Child Rights
- Bangladesh Mohila Unnayan Sanghstha
- Bangladesh Shishu Adhikar Forum
- Bernard van Leer Foundation
- Bharat Integrated Social Welfare Agency
- Cambridge Female Education Trust
- Campaign Against Child Labour
- Canadian International Development Agency
- CARE USA
- Catholic Action for Street Children
- Catholic Relief Services
- Center for Children's Rights

- Centre for Development Communication
- Centre for Rural Education Research and Development Association
- Centre for Women and Children's Rights
- Centre for Women's Studies - University of Nijmegen
- Centro Internazionale Studi Famiglia
- Cherish the Kids Liberia
- Child Mirror Liberia Incorporated
- Child Protection Alliance
- Child Restoration Outreach
- Child Rights Information and Documentation Centre
- Child Rights Information Network
- Child Rights Trust
- Child-to-Child Trust
- Childline India Foundation
- Children Concern Organisation
- Children of the Andes
- Children's Human Rights Centre of Albania
- Children's Rights in Goa
- Children's Rights Network
- ChildRight
- Concern for Children and Environment - Nepal
- Consortium for Street Children
- Coordination des ONG pour les Droits de l'Enfant
- Council for Socio Economic Benevolent Action
- Crescent Educational Society
- Cultural Movement for Human Development
- Defence for Children International
- Defence for Children International - Costa Rica
- Developmental Action Without Borders

- Dogodogo Centre Street Children Trust
- Dynamic Action for Rural Education
- Educational Trust Of India
- Egyptian Coalition on the Rights of the Child
- Espoir pour les Enfants
- European Network of Masters on Children's Rights
- Femme Action
- Forum for Rehabilitation and Integrated Development Approach by the Youth
- Fundación Comparte
- Fundacion Paniamor
- Fundacion Rafael Pombo
- Ghana Working and Children's Protection Association
- Global Movement for Children
- Gorfotepur Gram Progress Sangstha
- Hamara Club
- Hope for Children UK
- Human Rights - First the Child
- Idara Aaghosh Lahore
- Institute of Human Development and Training
- Institute of Neglected Oppressed Children's Environmental Networking and Training
- Integrated Regional Information Networks - IRIN
- Integrated Social Development Effort (ISDE) Bangladesh
- International Catholic Child Bureau - Switzerland
- International Center for Child and Youth Studies
- International Child Development Initiatives
- International Federation Terre des Hommes - International Secretariat
- International NGO Training and Research Centre
- Janakalyan Samity

- Jonathan's Child Care Center Sierra Leone
- Kanifing East Youth Development Society
- Kindernothilfe
- La Lumière
- Lembaga Advokasi Anak Indonesia
- Liberal Assocation for Movement of People
- Lixbey Environmental Foundation
- Mahila Rural Development Youth Society
- Maison des Droits de l'Enfant
- Maji Mazuri Children's Center
- Materi Chechni
- Mathare Youth Sports Association
- Mercy Foundation International
- Mythri Sarva Scva Samithi
- National Centre for Human Rights
- National Centre For Playwork Education - North East
- National Child Protection Authority
- National Institute Of Public Cooperation And Child Development
- National Integrated Rural Development Agency
- National Movement of Street Boys and Girls
- New Life Foundation of Bangladesh
- NGO/UNICEF Regional Network for Children in Central and Eastern Europe, Commonwealth of Independent States and Baltic States
- Northern Ireland Commissioner for Children and Young People
- Nous les Enfants
- ONG Espoir pour les enfants
- PAK Environment Education Society
- Pakistan International Peace & Human Rights Organization
- Pakistan Labour Federation
- Pan African Congress Movement for Humanity

- Paraspara Trust
- Peacelinks
- People's Action in Development
- Philippine National Red Cross
- Philippine Resource Network on Child Protection
- Plan International - HQ
- Plan International - India
- Plan International - Indonesia
- Power Healee Trust
- Project OutReach - Thailand
- Questscope
- Regional Working Group on Child Labour
- Samundra Devi UNESCO CLUB/ Nepal
- Sanlaap
- SARTHI
- Save the Children New Zealand
- Save the Children Norway
- Save the Children Norway - Cambodia Office
- Save the Children Sweden
- Save the Children Sweden - Guatemala Office
- Save the Children Sweden - Nicaragua Office
- Save the Children Sweden - South East Asia Pacific Regional Office
- Save the Children UK
- Save the Children UK - Bangladesh Office
- Save the Children UK - DRC Office
- Save the Children UK - Office for South and Central Asia Region
- Save the Children UK - Sierra Leone Office
- Save the Children UK - Uzbekistan Office
- Save the Children UK - Zimbabwe

- Shabnam Resources
- SIMA Community Based Organisation
- SKCV Children's Trust
- Social Welfare Advancement Brilliant Association
- Society for the Protection for the Rights of the Child
- Socio-legal Aid Research and Training Centre
- Somali Child Protection and Development
- SOS Enfants en Detresse
- Spanish Committee for UNICEF
- Terre des Hommes - Germany
- UNICEF
- UNICEF - Belgique
- UNICEF - Belgrade
- UNICEF - Bhutan
- UNICEF - Cuba country office
- UNICEF - East and Southern Africa Regional Office - Regional Emergency Support Unit
- UNICEF - Gambia
- UNICEF - Georgia
- UNICEF - Kenya
- UNICEF - Malaysia
- UNICEF Podgorica
- UNICEF Togo
- UNICEF Turkey
- Winrock International
- World Vision - Canada
- World Vision - Japan
- World Vision - UK
- World Vision Foundation of Thailand
- World Vision International - International Liaison Office

- World Vision International - USA
- Y Care International
- Youth Cultural and Information Centre

V.V. GIRI NATIONAL LABOUR INSTITUTE

V.V. Giri National Labour Institute is a premier national institution involved with research, training, education, publication and consultancy on labour related issues. The Institute, established in 1974, is an autonomous body of the Ministry of Labour, Government of India. The Institute was renamed in 1995 in honour of the late President of India, **Shri V.V. Giri.**

The Institute is dedicated through its core activities:

- To address the issues of transformation of the world of work in a global economy
- To project labour issues as a core concern of policy making
- To empower the social actors with capacities to meet the challenge of change
- To highlight the role of labour in shaping of modern India
- To preserve and disseminate information on labour matters

INSTITUTE'S MANDATE

The Memorandum of Association spells out clearly a wide range of activities which are essential to fulfill the objectives of the Institute. It mandates the Institute:

- To undertake, aid, promote and coordinate research on its own and in collaboration with other agencies, both national and international;
- To undertake and assist in organising training and educational programmes, seminars and workshops;
- To analyse specific problems encountered in the planning and implementation of labour and allied programmes and to suggest remedial measures;
- To establish and maintain library and information services;
- To establish wings for:
  - Education, training and orientation;
  - Research, including action research;
  - Consultancy; and

- Publication and other such activities as may be necessary for achieving the objectives of the society.
- To collaborate with other institutions and agencies in India and abroad which have similar objectives.

INSTITUTE'S STRUCTURE

The General Council, the apex governing body of the Institute, with Union Labour Minister as its President lays down the broad policy parameters for the functioning of the Institute.

The Executive Council with Secretary (Labour) as Chairman, monitors and guides the activities of the Institute. Both the General Council and the Executive Council are tripartite in nature and consists of members representing the government, trade union federations, employers' associations and also eminent scholars and practitioners in the field of labour.

Director of the Institute is the Principal Executive and is responsible for management and administration of its affairs. Director is aided in the day to day functioning by a faculty consisting of 15 professionals representing a wide range of disciplines and support by administrative staff.

10

INDIAN LEGAL REGIME

1. THE CHILD LABOUR (PROHIBITION AND REGULATION) ACT, 1986

(61 OF 1986)

STATEMENT OF OBJECTS AND REASONS

There are a number of Acts which prohibit the employment of children below 14 years and 15 years in certain specified employments. However, there is no procedure laid down in any law for deciding in which employments occupations or processes the employment of children should be banned. There is also no law to regulate the working conditions of children in most of the employments where they are not prohibited from working and are working under exploitative conditions.

2. This Bill intends to—

(*i*) ban the employment of children, *i.e.* those who have not completed their fourteenth year, in specified occupations and processes;

(*ii*) lay down a procedure to decide modifications to the Schedule of banned occupations or processes;

(*iii*) regulate the conditions of work of children in employments where they are not prohibited from working;

(*iv*) lay down enhanced penalties for employment of children in violation of the provisions of this Act, and their Acts which forbid the employment of children;

(*v*) to obtain uniformity in the definition of "child" in the related laws.

3. The Bill seeks to achieve the above objects.—Gaz. of Ind. 22.8.1986, Pt. II, Section 2 Ext. p. 9 (No. 40).

THE CHILD LABOUR (PROHIBITION AND REGULATION) ACT, 1986

(61 OF 1986)

[23*rd December*, 1986]

An Act to prohibit the engagement of children in certain employments and to regulate the conditions of work of children in certain other employments.

Be it enacted by Parliament in the Thirty-seventh Year of the Republic of India as follows :—

PART I
PRELIMINARY

1. Short title, extent and commencement.—(1) This Act may be called the Child Labour (Prohibition and Regulation) Act, 1986.

(2) It extends to the whole of India.

(3) The provisions of this act, other than Part III, shall come into force at once, and Part III shall come into force on such date as the Central Government may, by notification[1] in the Official Gazette, appoint, and different dates may be appointed for different States and for different classes of establishments.[2]

2. Definitions.—In this Act, unless the context otherwise requires,—

(*i*) "*appropriate Government*" means in relation to an establishment under the control of the Central Government or a railway administration or a major port or a mine or oilfield, the Central Government, and in all other cases, the State Government;

(*ii*) "*child*" means a person who has not completed his fourteenth year of age;

(*iii*) "*day*" means a period of twenty-four hours beginning at mid-night;

(*iv*) "*establishment*" includes a shop, commercial establishment, workshop, farm, residential hotel, restaurant, eating house, theatre or other place of public amusement or entertainment;

(*v*) "*family*" in relation to an occupier, means the individual the wife or husband, as the case may be of such individual and their children, brother or sister of such individual;

(*vi*) "*occupier*" in relation to an establishment or a workshop, means the person who has the ultimate control over the affairs of the establishment or workshop;

(*vii*) "*port authority*" means any authority administering a port;

(*viii*) "*prescribed*" means prescribed by rules made under Section 18;

(*ix*) "*week*" means a period of seven days beginning at mid-night on Saturday night or such other night as may be approved in writing for a particular area by the Inspector;

(*x*) "*workshop*" means any premises (including the precincts thereof) wherein any industrial process is carried on, but does not include any

1. 26.5.1993 appointed on which Part III comes into force—*See* Gaz. of Ind. 26.5.1993, Pt. II-S, 3(ii) Ext. p. 2 (No. 303).

2. For notification applying the provisions of Pt. III to the establishments where the under mentioned process are carried on.

1. Zari making and embroidery	—Delhi and Uttar Pradesh
2. Precious stone polishing	—Gujarat and Rajasthan
3. State and slate pencil manufacturing	—Madhya Pradesh nd Andhra Pradesh

—*See* Gaz. of Ind. 3.8.1987 Pt II Section 3(ii), Ext. p. 2 (No. 396).

premises to which the provisions of Section 67 of the Factories Act, 1948, for the time being apply.

COMMENTS

Child Labour—No prohibition under workmen and Compensation Act.—In the instant case , compensation was awarded to boy of 13 for injury while working in handwriting machine. Submission of appellant that boy of 13 could not have been appointed under the Child Labour Act, whereby contested the award. Held that no specific provision in the Workmen's Compensation Act, prohibiting children being employed.—*New India Assurance Co. Ltd.* v. *Rachaiah Baraiah Ganachari*, (2001) III LLJ (Suppl) 254 (Kant).

Child—As envisaged for purposes of Section 2(ii)—In the instant case, the revisionist was accused of employing child labour in violation of Section 3 of the Act. However, there was no certificate or any other document showing age of alleged. But, trial and appellate Courts blindly accepted age stated by the Enforcement Officer without any basis. Held that it cannot be said he was a child as defined in Section 2(ii).—*Subhash Chandra Jaiswal* v. *State of U.P.*, 2002 All LJ 28 : (2002) IV LLJ (Suppl) 59 (All).

Fine for employing child labour.—In the instant case the employer imposed fine of Rs. 20,000/- for employing child labour. However, there was no evidence nor any finding on record that child employee is below 14 years of age, thus impugned order set aside as bad in law.—*Raj Kumar Tiwari* v. *State*, (2003) IV LLJ 1045 (MP).

Offence of employing child—Proof.—In the instant case there was allegation of employing child below 14 years of age. Burden to prove person was below 14 years being on prosecution not discharged. Thus, conviction and sentence set aside.—*Ram Chander* v. *State of U.P.*, 2002 (92) FLR 213 : (2002) I LLJ 907 (All).

Child labour—Directions and guidelines.—In the instant case Labour Inspector, labelled petitioners employees "offending employers" and said employers to pay Rs. 20,000 compensation per child no employed. But, no show cause notice, and no opportunity given. Before labelling petitioners employers "*offending employers*" and demanding compensation, show cause notice should have been issued and reasonable opportunity of being heard given which was not done.—*Sooryanarayana Shetty P.* v. *State of Karnataka*, (2000) III LLJ (Suppl) 123 (Kant).

Child—As per Section 2(ii).—In the instant case, where right hand of the boy who was thirteen years old was stuck while working on the harvesting machine, he could be termed as `child' on defined in Section 2 (ii) as on the date of the accident.—(2000) 88 FLR 488 : ILR (2000) Kant 4743.

Child—Determination of age.—In the instant case, Labour Enforcement Officer stated that child labour who was found working was aged about 11 years. Neither any documents nor any medical certificate regarding age of child was produced. These the blind acceptance of said age by trial Court and appellate Court was improper. In absence of improper as certainment of age, such labour cannot be farmed as "child" as defined in Section 2(ii) of the Act. Hence, the accused employer could not be convicted for offence under the Act.—2002 Cr LJ 1223.

PART II

PROHIBITION OF EMPLOYMENT OF CHILDREN IN CERTAIN OCCUPATIONS AND PROCESSES

3. Prohibition of employment of children in certain occupations and processes.—No child shall be employed or permmitted to work in any of the occupations set forth in Part A of the Schedule or in any workshop wherein any of the processes set forth in Part B of the Schedule is carried on :

Provided that nothing in his section shall apply to any workshop wherein any process is carried on by the occupier with the aid of his family or to any school established by, or receiving assistance or recognition from Government.

COMMENTS

Imposition of penalty.—Where the age of child labour was not found to be below 14 years imposition of penalty of Rs. 20,000/- on the petitioner. for employing him would be improper.—2003 Lab IC 2000 : (2003) 3 MPLJ 318.

Taking problem of child labour.—In the instant case the Apex Court issued directions to State Governments regarding fulfillment of legislative intendment behind enactment. Further held that offending employer to pay compensation of Rs. 20,000/- for every child employed—*M.C. Mehta* v. *State of Tamil Nadu.*

Implication of Workmen's Compensation Act.—In view of Section 3 in the absence of any specific prohibition under the Workmen's Compensation Act, 1923, it can be said that child can be employed to carry out the work provided such work does not came under the Part A and B of the Scheduled of the Act.—(2001) 88 Fac LR 488 : ILR (2000) Kant 4743.

Fresh notices if without holding fresh survey.—In the instant case notices were issued for violation of provision of the Act, were quashed holding survey conducted as ırregular. Therefore, held that issuance of fresh notices on basis of same survey without holding fresh survey would be illegal.—2000 All LJ 575 : (2000) I UPLBEC 530.

Prosecution for violation of Section 3.—In the instant case according to the firm the workers entered into an agreement with firm and took raw material for *bidi* making to their respective houses with an understanding that they themselves would make *bidis* and then supply is to the firm. Therefore, the firm could not be prosecuted for violation of Section 3 if workers took assistance of children at home and made *bidis* and supplied them to the firm.—(2003) 2 Lab LJ 645 : (2003) 2 MPHT 1 (Chh).

Regulating condition of work.—The object of the Act is to prohibit child labour in certain occupation and processes and to permit it in certain others while regulating conditions of work. But there is exception in favour of work carried on by occupier with aid of family or in school receiving assistance or recognition from Government. Then, the impugned notice, not having considered subsequent order of the Supreme Court, quashed.—*Choota Bhai Munnu Bhai and Co.* v. *State of U.P.*, 1999 (82) FLR 269.

Penalty it without finding as to age of child.—Where the order imposing penalty of Rs. 20,000 on the petitioner for employing a child labour without recording a finding that whether child was below 14 years in liable to be set aside.—2003 Lab IC 2000 : (2003) 3 MPLJ 318.

Legality of imposing penalty.—In the instance case, the Assistant Labour Commissioner directed the petitioners to make payment of Rs. 20,000/- per child labour and release them. More no opportunity of hearing was given to the petitioner and show cause notice was also given. Held that order as such passed was in accordance with law laid down by the Supreme Court in 1996 (6) SCC 746, is valid.—(2003) Lab LJ 626 (630) : (2003) 2 MPLJ 572.

Order calling upon to pay penalty held proper.—In the instant case there was allegations that petitioner engaged Child Labourers for digging work. Submission of petitioner that he was not engaged in constructions of houses but sale thereof. However, construction of houses allegedly to be entrusted to contractors who had engaged said child labourers. However, there was failure on past of petitioner to mention contractors petitioner in reply filed to show cause notice described himself "Raj Homes Pvt. Ltd. Builders and Colonizers", found enough to show that petitioner was engaged in construction of houses. Denial in after thought to avoid liability. Moreover show cause notice was issued pursuant to spot inspection by Inspector visited spot and found children engaged in construction work. Then, the order calling upon petitioner to pay Rs. 20,000/- to each child passed after taking into consideration reply of petitioner held proper.—2003 Lab IC (NOC) 237 : (2003) 4 MPLJ 458 (DB).

Child if engaged in cashew nut descaling and processing.—Where any child is found employed in respect of process of cashew nut descaling and processing them apart from the penal provision contained in the Act, employer concerned would also come within the ambit of the directions of the Supreme Court with regard to payment of Rs. 20,000/- in respect of each child no employed.—(2003) 3 Lab LJ 123.

4. Power to amend the Schedule.—The Central Government, after giving by notification in the Official Gazette, not less than three months notice of its intention so to do, may by like notification, add any occupation or process to the Schedule and thereupon the Schedule shall be deemed to have been amended accordingly.

5. Child Labour Technical Advisory Committee.—(1) The Central Government may, by notification in the Official Gazette, constitute an advisory committee to be called the Child Labour Technical Advisory Committee (hereafter in this section referred to as the Committee) to advise the Central Government for the purpose of addition of occupations and processes to the Schedule.

(2) The Committee shall consist of a Chairman and such other members not exceeding ten, as may be appointed by the Central Government.

(3) The Committee shall meet as often as it may consider necessary and shall have power to regulate its own procedure.

(4) The Committee may if it deems it necessary so to do constitute one or more sub-committees and may appoint to any such sub-committee, whether generally or for the consideration of any particular matter, any person who is not a member of the Committee.

(5) The term of office of the manner of filling casual vacancies in the office of and the allowances, if any, payable to the Chairman and other members of the Committee, and the conditions and restrictions subject to which the Committee may appoint any person who is not a member of the Committee as a member of any of its sub-committees shall be such as may be prescribed.

PART III

REGULATION OF CONDITIONS OF WORKS OF CHILDREN

6. Application of Part.—The provisions of this Part shall apply to an establishment or a pass of establishment in which none of the occupations or processes referred to in Section 3 is carried on.

7. Hours and period of work.—(1) No child shall be required or permitted to work in any establishment in excess of such number of hours as may be prescribed for such establishment or class of establishments.

(2) The period of work on each day shall be so fixed that no period shall exceed three hours and that no child shall work for more than three hours before he has had an interval for rest for at least one hour.

(3) The period of work, of a child shall be so arranged that inclusive of his interval for rest, under sub-section (2), it shall not be spread over more than six hours, including the time spent in waiting for work on any day.

(4) No child shall be permitted or required to work between 7 p.m. and 8 a.m.

(5) No child shall be required to permitted to work overtime.

(6) No child shall be required or permitted to work in any establishment on any day on which he has already been working in another establishment.

8. Weekly holidays.—Every child employed in an establishment shall be allowed in each week a holiday of one whole day, which day shall be specified by the occupier in a notice permanently exhibited in a conspicuous place in the establishment and the day so specified shall not be altered by the occupier more than once in three months.

9. Notice to Inspector.—(1) Every occupier in relation to an establishment in which a could was employed or permitted to work immediately before the date of commencement of the Act in relation to such establishment shall within a period of thirty days from such commencement, send to the Inspector within whose local limits the establishment is situated, a written notice containing the following particulars, namely :—

(*a*) the name and situation of the establishment;

(*b*) the name of the person in actual management of the establishment;

(*c*) the address to which communications relating to the establishment should be sent; and

(*d*) the nature of the occupation or process carried on in the establishment.

(2) Every occupier, in relation to an establishment who employees, or permits to work, any child after the date of commencement of this Act in relation to such establishment, shall within a period of thirty days, from the date of such employee,t send to the Inspector within whose local limits the establishment is situated a written notice containing the particulars as are mentioned in sub-section (1).

Explanation.—For the purposes of sub-sections (1) and (2), "date of commencement of this Act, in relation to an establishment" means the date of bringing into force of this Act in relation to such establishment.

(3) Nothing in Sections 7, 8 and 9 shall apply to any establishment wherein any process is carried on by the occupier with the aid of his family or to any school established by or receiving assistance or recognition from, Government.

10. Disputes as to age.—If any question arises between an Inspector and an occupier as to the age of any child who is employed or is permitted to work by him in an establishment, the question shall in the absence of a certificate as to the age of such child granted by the prescribed medical authority, be referred by the Inspector for decision to the prescribed medical authority.

COMMENTS

Dispute as to age—Determination.—In the instant case, the Labour Enforcement Officer stated that child labour who was found working was aged about 11 years. However, neither any document nor any medical Certificate regarding age of child was produced. Held that in absence of proper ascertainment of age, such labourer could not be farmed as "child" as defined in Section 2(ii). Accused employee thus could not be convicted for offence under the Act.—2002 Cri LJ 1233 : 2002 All LJ 28.

Implication of Section 10.—The civil liability of paying compensation has nothing to do with the criminal prosecution under the Act and both can continue simultaneously. If the age of the child is disputed by employer and the challenge in made to the age mentioned in the inspection report, the reference has to be made to the prescribed medical Authority by the Inspector himself. The failure to make reference in accordance with the provision of Section 10 would render the action of realisation of compensation as invalid. Section 10 which deals with the determination of the age, in case of dispute regarding the age of child has to be taken assistance of even in the matter where civil liability is to be fastened upon the employer/occupier.—(2000) 2 UPLBEC 1426 (All).

11. Maintenance of register.—There shall be maintained by every occupier in respect of children employed or permitted to work in any establishment a register to be available for suspection by an Inspector at all times during working hours or when work is being carried on an any such establishment showing—

(*a*) the name and date of birth of every child so employed or permitted to work;

(*b*) hours and periods of work of any such child and the intervals of rest to which he is entitled;

(*c*) the nature of work of any such child; and

(*d*) such other particulars as may be prescribed.

12. Display of notice containing abstract of Sections 3 and 14.—Every railway administration every port authority and every occupier shall cause to be displayed in a conspicuous and accessible place at every station on its railway or within the limits of a port or at the place of work, as the case may be, a notice in the local language and in the English language containing an abstract of Sections 3 and 14.

13. Health and safety.—(1) The appropriate Government may, by notification in the Official Gazette make rules for the health and safety of the children employed or permitted to work in any establishment or class of establishments.

(2) Without prejudice to the generality of the foregoing provisions, the said rules may provide for all or any of the following matters, namely :—

(*a*) cleanliness in the place of work and its freedom from nuisance;

(*b*) disposal of wastes and effluents;

(*c*) ventilation and temperature.

(*d*) dust and fume;

(*e*) artificial humiotification;

(*f*) lighting;

(*g*) drinking water;

(*h*) latrine and urinals;

(*i*) spittoons;

(*j*) fencing of machinery;

(*k*) work at or near machinery in motion;

(*l*) employment of children on dangerous machines;

(*m*) instructions training and supervision in relation to employment of children on dangerous machines;

(*n*) device for cutting off power;

(*o*) self-acting machines;

(*p*) easing of new machinery;

(*q*) floor stairs and means of access;

(*r*) pits, sumps, openings in floors etc.;

(*s*) executive weights;

(*t*) protection of eyes;

(*u*) explosive or inflammable dust, gas, etc.;

(*v*) precautions in case of fire;

(*w*) maintenance of buildings; and

(*x*) safety of buildings and machinery.

PART IV

MISCELLANEOUS

14. Penalty.—(1) Whoever, employs any child or permits any child to work in contravention of the provisions of Section 3 shall be punishable with imprisonment for a term which shall not be less than three months but which may extend to one year or with fine which shall not be less than ten thousand rupees but which may extend to twenty thousand rupees or with both.

(2) Whoever having been convicted of an offence under Section 3, commits a like offence afterwards he shall be punishable with imprisonment for a term which shall not be less than six months but which may extend to two years.

(3) Whoever—

(*a*) fails to give notice as required by Section 9, or

(*b*) fails to maintain a register as required by Section 11 or make any false entry in any such register; or

(*c*) fails to display a notice containing an abstract of Section 3 and this section as required by Section 12; or

(*d*) fails to comply with or contravenes any other provisions of this Act or the rules made thereunder,

shall be punishable with simple imprisonment which may extend to one month or with fine which may extend to ten thousand rupees or with both.

COMMENTS

Offence of employing Child Labour.—In the instant case children below 14 years of age found employed by the Assistant Inspector. However, the opinion of doctor that they were below 14 years. But accused petitioner could not prove that children were below 14 years; held that the conviction is legal since prosecution had proved its case beyond doubt.—*Bhageerathan N.* v. *State*, (1999) I LLJ 840 (Mad).

Proof and prosecution.—Prosecution under Section 14 quashed for served reasons among with one reason cognisance of offence allegedly committed by petitioner. More no the firm was not employee in child labour in question. It was not at workshop of accused that child labour found to work no proof that child below 14 years.—*Hemendra Bhai* v. *State of Chhattisgarh*, 2003 (97) FLR 402 : (2003) II LLJ 645 (Chhat).

Offence under 67 of Factories Act if established.—An offence under Section 67 of the Factories Act, if established, minimum penalty prescribed under Section 14(1) of the Child Labour (Prohibition and Regulation) Act, to be imposed.—*State of Gujarat* v. *Bhupendra Kumar Jagjivandas Patel*, (2001) II LLJ 1517 (Guj) : 2001 LIC 2352.

Penalty under Section 14(1).—In a case where the employee had accepted the commission of offence of employing young children under Section 67 of the Factories Act, penalty prescribed under Section 14(1) of the Act has to be imposed.—2001 Lab IC 2352.

Reduction of sentence.—It was established that the applicant had engaged a child aged about 12 years as a 'labour' in his carpet factory, held that him conviction under Section 14(1) was proper. Since long time had elapsed from date of incident and the applicant had already served a sentence, of 20 days, sentence of imprisonment was reduced to one month rigorous imprisonment and payment of fine of Rs. 3,000.—(2001) 43 All Cri C 498.

Legality of order to pay compensation.—The order to pay Rs. 20,000 to each of four child labourers, held proper and not liable to challenge.—*Raj Homes (Pvt.) Ltd.* v. *State of M.P.*, (2004) I LLJ 690 (MP).

Order to pay.—On factor, it has been held, that show cause notice and order to pay Rs. 20,000 per child labour, valid ad proper.—*Raj Homes (Pvt.) Ltd.* v. *State of M.P.*, 2003 LIC 2210 : 2003 III CLR 247 : (2003) III LLJ 626 (MP).

Payment of compensation—Legality.—In the instant case petitioner engaged child labour, and respondent straight away asked to pay compensation. However, no opportunity was given to explain ; held, that order as such was illegal ad invalid.—*Panch Ram Barat* v. *State of M.P.*, 2001 (81) FLR 1106 : (2001) II LLJ 841 (MP).

Violation of Statutory provisions.—In the instant case, demand notice for depositing amount on account of engaging *child labour*, however, no opportunity given to petitioner to object and explain, since it was violative of provisions of the Act, notice as such was quashed.—*Bhaiyalal Shukla* v. *State of M.P.*, (2000) I LLJ 640 (MP) : 1999 LLR 1189 : 2000 (1) Cur LR 219.

Child labour engaged—Finding of fact—Interference with.—In the instant case finding of fact by the concerned authority that the child labour was engaged ; finding as such was based on evidence ; the interference with declined in the writ petition.—*Om Prakash* v. *Assistant Labour Consumer*, (2002) 95 FLR 217 : (2003) 1 LLJ 100 (All).

Bar as to realisation of compensation.—The civil liability to pay compensation of Rs. 20,000 per child as per decision in AIR 1997 SC 699, arises due to violation of fundamental rights. More so conviction of employer under Act is not a precondition for enforcing civil liability. The Court observed that the substantive punishment of imprisonment with or without fine under Section 14 of the Act, would not bar civil action for realisation of compensation.—1998 All LJ 2502 : (1998) 2 All CJ 1371.

Failure to prove age of child—Effect of.—Regarding prosecution for employing child labour, burden of proof that child in below 14 years of age is on the prosecution and such burden can of be shifted on employer. So for as prosecution failed to prove age of child as required by the Act, accused cannot be compelled to fill up lacuna of prosecution. Thus, conviction of accused as such liable to be set aside.—2002 All LJ 96 : 2000 Cri LJ 1253.

Opportunity of hearing of not given.—It has been held that the order calling upon the employer to pay Rs. 20,000 in respect of each child employed without giving opportunity of being heard would be improper.—(2002) 3 Lab LJ 123 : (2000) 5 Kant LJ 570.

Improper imposition of penalty.—For employing a child labour, imposition of penalty of Rs. 20,000 as the employer even without recording a finding that child was below 14 years would be improper.—2003 Lab IC 2000 : (2003) 3 MPLJ 318.

Absence of proper ascertainment of age—No conviction.—In the extent case the Labour Enforcement Officer stated that the child labour who was found working was aged about 11 years. Neither any documents nor any medical certificate regarding age of child war produced. Then, is absence of proper ascertainment of age, such labourer cannot be formed as 'child' as defined under Section 2(ii). Held that the accused employer hence cannot be convicted for offence under the Act. 2002 Cri LJ 1223 : 2002 All LJ 28

Direction to State Government.—The Supreme Court issued directions to the State Government, regarding fulfillment of legislative intendment of the enactment whereby offending employer to pay compensation of Rs. 20,000 for every child employed.—AIR 1997 SC 699 : 1997 Lab IC 563 : (2003) 4 MPLJ 458 (DB).

15. Modified application of certain laws in relation to penalties.—(1) Where any person is found guilty and convicted of contravention of any of the provisions mentioned in sub-section (2), he shall be liable to penalties as provided in sub-sections (1) and (2) of Section 14 of this Act and not under the Acts in which those provisions are contained.

(2) The provisions referred to in sub-section (1) are the provisions mentioned below:—

(*a*) Section 67 of the Factories Act, 1948 ;

(*b*) Section 40 of the Mines Act, 1952 ;

(*c*) Section 109 of the Merchant Shipping Act, 1958 ; and

(*d*) Section 21 of the Motor Transport Workers Act, 1961.

16. Procedure relating to offences.—(1) Any person, police officer or Inspector may file a complaint of the commission of an offence under this Act in any Court of competent jurisdiction.

(2) Every certificate as to the age of a child which has been granted by a prescribed medical authority shall, for the purposes of this Act, be conclusive evidence as to the age of the child to whom it relates.

(3) No Court inferior to that of a Metropolitan Magistrate or a Magistrate of the first class call try any offence under this Act.

COMMENT

Observance of Section 14.—Before the employer is labelled as an offending employer containing the provisions of the Act and before he is consequently asked to pay Rs. 20,000 in respect of each child, the least that could be expected was a show-cause notice and an opportunity of being heard. Thus the order passed without giving opportunity of hearing held illegal.—(2002) 3 Lab LJ 123 : (2000) 5 Kant LJ 570.

17. Appointment of Inspectors.—The appropriate Government may appoint Inspectors for the purposes of securing compliance with the provisions of this Act and any Inspector so appointed shall be deemed to be a public servant within the meaning of the Indian Penal Code.

COMMENT

Inspectors to receive compliance of Act.—Where the concerned employer engaging child labour asked by the Inspectors to deposit Rs. 20,000 per child in the Child Labour Rehabilitation-cum-Welfare Fund, held that the impugned action to be violative of principle of natural justice in that no opportunity of hearing before recording a finding, afforded.—*Bhagwandas* v. *State of M.P.*, (2000) III LLJ (Suppl) 661 (MP).

18. Power to make rules.—(1) The appropriate Government may, by notification in the official Gazette and subject to the condition of previous publication, make rules[1] for carrying into effect the provisions of this Act.

(2) In particular and without prejudice to the generality of the foregoing power, such rules may provide for all or any of the following matters, namely :—

(*a*) the term of office of the manner of filing casual vacancies of, and the allowances payable to, the Chairman and members of the Child Labour Technical Advisory Committee and the conditions and restrictions subject to which a non-member may be appointed to a sub-committee under sub-section (5) of Section 5;

(*b*) number of hours for which a child may be required or permitted to work under sub-section (1) of Section 7;

(*c*) grant of certificates of age in respect of young persons in employment or seeking employment the medial authorities which may issue such certificate, the form of such certificate, the charges which may be made thereunder and the manner in which such certificate may be issued :

Provided that no charge shall be made for the issue of any such certificate if the application is accompanied by evidence of age deemed satisfactory by the authority concerned;

(*d*) the other particulars which a register maintained under Section 11 should contain.

19. Rules and notifications to be laid before Parliament or State Legislature.—(1) Every rule made under this Act by the Central Government and every notification issued under Section 4, shall be laid as soon as may be after it is made or issued,

---

1. For Child Labour (Prohibition and Regulation) Rules, 1988—*See* Gaz. of Ind. 10.8.1988, Pt. II Section 3(i), Ext. P. 4 (No. 429).

before each House of Parliament while it is in session for a total period of thirty days which may be comprised in one session or in two or more successive sessions and if, before the expiry of the session immediately following the session or the successive sessions aforesaid, both Houses agree in making any modification in the rule or notification or both Houses agree that the rule or notification should not be made or issued, the rule or notification shall thereafter have effect only in such modified form or be of no effect, as the case may be so, however, that any such modification or annulment shall be without prejudice to the validity of anything previously done under that rule or notification.

(2) Every rule made by a State Government under this Act shall be laid as soon as may be after it is made, before the legislature of the State.

20. Certain other provisions of law not barred.—Subject to the provisions contained under Section 15 the provisions of this Act and the rules made thereunder shall be in addition to, cannot in derogation of the provisions of the Factories Act, 1948, the Plantations Labour Act, 1951 and the Mines Act, 1952.

21. Power to remove difficulties.—(1) If any difficulty arises in giving effect to the provisions of this Act, the Central Government may by order published in the Official Gazette, make such provisions not inconsistent with the provisions of this Act as appear to it to be necessary or expedient for removal of the difficulty :

Provided that no such order shall be made after the expiry of period of three years from the date on which this Act receives the assent of the President.

(2) Every order made under this section shall, as soon as may be after it is made, be laid before this House of Parliament.

22. Repeal and savings.—(1) The Employment of Children Act, 1938 is hereby repealed.

(2) Notwithstanding such repeals, anything done or any action taken or purported to have been done or taken under the Act so repealed shall, in so far as it is not inconsistent with the provisions of this Act, be deemed to have been done or taken under the corresponding provisions of this Act.

23. Amendment of Act, 11 of 1948.—[*Repealed by the Repealing and Amending Act, 2001 (30 of 2001), Section 2, First Schedule (3.9.2001).*]

24. Amendment of Act 69 of 1951.—[*Repealed by the Repealing and Amending Act, 2001 (30 of 2001), Section 2, First Schedule (3.9.2001).*]

25. Amendment of Act 44 of 1958.—[*Repealed by the Repealing and Amending Act, 2001 (30 of 2001), Section 2, First Schedule (3.9.2001).*]

26. Amendment of Act 27 of 1961.—[*Repealed by the Repealing and Amending Act, 2001 (30 of 2001), Section 2, First Schedule (3.9.2001).*]

THE SCHEDULE

(See Section 3)

PART A

Occupations

Any occupation connected with—

(1) Transport of passengers, goods of mail by railway;

(2) Cinder picking clearing of an as pit or building operation in the railway premises;

(3) Work in a catering establishment at a railway station involving the movement of a vendor or any other employee of the establishment from one platform to another or into or out of a moving train.

(4) Work relating to the construction of a railway station or with any other work where such work is done in close proximity to or between the railway lines;

(5) A port authority within the limits of any port.

[1][(6) Work relating to selling of crackers and fire works in shops with temporary licences].

[2][(7) Abattoirs/Slaughter Houses].

[3][(8) Automobile workshops and garages;

(9) Foundries;

(10) Handling of toxic or infilammable substances or explosives;

(11) Handloom and power loom industry;

(12) Mines (underground and under water) and collieries;

(13) Plastic units and fibreglass workshops.]

PART B

Processes

(1) Bidi-making.

[4][(2) Carpet-weaving including preparatory and incidental process thereof.]

(3) Cement manufacture, including bagging of cement.

[5][(4) Cloth printing dyeing and weaving including processes preparatory and incidental thereto.]

(5) Manufacture of matches explosives and fire-works.

(6) Mica-cutting and splitting.

(7) Shellac manufacture.

---

1. Inserted vide S.O. 404(E)/1989—*See* Gaz. of Ind. 5.6.1989 Pt. II S. 3(ii), Ext. p. 2 (No. of 315).
2. Inserted vide S.O. 263(E)/1994—*See* Gaz. of Ind. 29.3.1994, Pt. II S. 3(ii), Ext. p. 2 (No. 149).
3. Inserted vide S.O. 36(E)/1999—*See* Gaz. of Ind. 27.1.1999, Pt. II S. 3(ii), Ext. p. 2.
4. Substituted vide S.O. 36(E)/1999—*See* Gaz. of Ind. 27.1.1999, Pt. II S. 3(ii), Ext. p. 3.
5. Substituted vide S.O. 36(E)/1999—*See* Gaz. of Ind. 27.1.1999, Pt. II S. 3(ii), Ext. p. 3.

(8) Soap manufacture.

(9) Training.

(10) Wool-cleaning.

[1][(11) Building and Construct on Industry including processing and polishing of granite stones.]

[2][(12) Manufacture of slate, pencils (including packing).

(13) Manufacture of product from agate.

(14) Manufacturing Processes using toxic metals and substances such as lead mercury, manganese, chromium, cadmium, benzene, pesticides and asbestos].

[3][(15) Hazardous processes as defined in Section 2(cb) and dangerous operations as notified in rules made under Section 87 of the Factories Act, 1948 (63 of 1948).

(16) Printing as defined in Section 2(k)(iv) of the Factories Act, 1948 (63 of 1948).

(17) Cashew and Cashewnut descaling and processing.

(18) Soldering processes in electronic industries].

[4][(19) Aggarbatti manufacturing.

(20) Automobile repairs and maintenance including processes incidental thereto namely welding lather work dent beating and painting.

(21) Brick Kilns and Roof tiles, units.

(22) Cotton ginning and processing and production of hosiery goods.

(23) Detergent manufacturing.

(24) Fabrication workshops (ferrous and non-ferrous).

(25) Gem cutting and polishing.

(26) Handling of chromite and manganese ores.

(27) Jute textile manufacture and coir making.

(28) Lime Kilns and Manufacture of Lime.

(29) Lock making.

(30) Manufacturing process having exposure to lead such as primary and secondary semlting welding and cutting of lead-painted metal constructions welding of galvanized or zinc silicate polyvinyl chloride, mixing (by hand) of crystal glass mass, sanding or scrapping of lead paint, burning of lead in enamelling worships. lead mining plumbing, cable, making wire patenting lead casting type founding in printing ships. Store type setting assembling of cars, shot making and lead glass blowing.

1. Substituted vide S.O. 397(E)/2001—*See* Gaz. of Ind. 10.5.2001, Pt. II S. 3(ii), Ext. p. 2.
2. Inserted vide S.O. 404(E)/1989—*See* Gaz. of Ind. 5.6.1989 Pt. II S. 3(ii), Ext. p. 2 (No. of 315).
3. Inserted vide S.O. 263(E)/1994—*See* Gaz. of Ind. 29.3.1994, Pt. II S. 3(ii), Ext. p. 2 (No. 149).
4. Inserted vide S.O. 36(E)/1999—*See* Gaz. of Ind. 27.1.1999, Pt. II S. 3(ii), Ext. p. 3.

(31) Manufacture of cement pipes, cement products and other related work.

(32) Manufacturing of glass, glass ware including bangles, fluorescent tubes, bulbs and other similar glass products.

(33) Manufacturing of dyes and dye stuff.

(34) Manufacturing or handling of pesticides and insecticides.

(35) Manufacturing or processing and handling of corrosive and toxic substances, metal cleaning and photo engraving and soldering processes in electronic industry.

(36) Manufacturing of turning coal and coal briquettes.

(37) Manufacturing of sports goods involving exposure to synthetic materials chemicals and leather.

(38) Moulding and processing of fibreglass and plastic.

(39) Oil expelling and refinery.

(40) Paper making.

(41) Potteries and ceramic industry.

(42) Polishing, moulding, cutting, welding and manufacture of brass goods in all forms.

(43) Processes in agriculture where tractor, threshing and harvesting machines are used and chaff cutting.

(44) Saw mill—all processes.

(45) Sericulture processing.

(46) Skinning, dying and processes or manufacturing or leather and leather products.

(47) Stone breaking and stone crushing.

(48) Tobacco processing including manufacturing of tobacco, tobacco paste and handling of tobacco in any form.

(49) Tyre making, repairing, re-treating and graphic benefication.

(50) Utensils making polishing and metal buffing.

(51) Zari making (all processes).]

[1][(52) Electroplating;

(53) Graphite powdering and incidental processing.

(54) Grinding of glazing of metals;

(55) Diamond cutting and polishing;

(56) Extraction of slate from mines;

(57) Rag picking and scavenging.]

— — — — —

1. Inserted vide S.O. 397(E)/2001—*See* Gaz. of Ind. 10.5.2001, Pt. II S. 3(ii), Ext. p. 2.

2. THE CHILDREN (PLEADING OF LABOUR) ACT, 1933

(2 of 1933)

STATEMENT OF OBJECTS AND REASONS

The Royal Commission on Labour found evidence in such widely separate area as Amritsar Ahemadabad and Madars of the practice of pleading child labour—that is, the taking of advance by parents for guardians on agreement written or oral, pledging the labour of their children. In some cases, the children so pledged were subject to particularly non-satisfactory working conditions. The commission considered that the State would be justified in adopting strong measure to eradicate the civil the civil and the Bill seeks to do so by imposing penalties on persons knowingly employing children whose labour has been pledged.

THE CHILDREN (PLEADING OF LABOUR) ACT, 1933

(2 of 1933)

[24*th February*, 1933]

An Act to prohibit the pledging of the labour of children.

Whereas it is expedient to prohibit the making of agreements to pledge the labour of children, and the employment of children, whose labour has been pledged. It is hereby enacted as follows :—

1. Short title and extent.—(1) This Act may be called the Children (Pleading of Labour) Act, 1933.

[1][(2) It extends to the whole of India [2][***]

(3) This section and Sections 2 and 3 shall come into force at once, and the remaining sections of this Act shall come into force on the first day of July 1933.

2. Definition.—(1) In this Act, unless there is anything repugnant in the subject or context—

> *"an agreement to pledge the labour of a child"* means an agreement written or oral express or implied whereby the parent or guardian of a child in return for any payment or benefit received or to be received by him, undertakes to cause or allow the services of the child to be utilised in any employment :
>
> Provided that an agreement made without detriment to a child, and not made in consideration of any benefit other than reasonable wages to be paid for the child's services and terminable at not more than a week's notice, is not an agreement within the meaning of this definition.

Note—This Act has been extended to the new Provinces and Merged States by the Merged States (Laws) Act, 1949 (59 of 1949), Section 3 (1.1.1950) and to the Union Territories

1. Subs. for sub-section (2) by A.I.O., 1950.
2. The words accept the State of Jammu and Kashmir has been omitted by Act 51 of 1970.

of Manipur, Tripura and Vindhya Pradesh by the Union Territories (Laws) Act, 1950 (30 of 1950), Section 3 (16.4.1950). Manipur and Tripura are full-fledged States now (*See* Act 81 of 1971) but Vindhya Pradesh now forms part of the State of Madhya Pradesh—*See* Act 37 of 1956, Section 9(1)(e) (1.11.1956).

This Act has been extended to States Merged in the States of (1) Bombay (see Bombay Act 4 of 1950) and (2) Punjab (see Punjab Act 5 of 1950). It has been made applicable to the State of Jammu and Kashmir by Act 51 of 1970.

It has now been extended to the Union Territories of—

(1) Dadra and Nagar Haveli by Reg. 6 of 1963 (1.7.1965);

(2) Pondicheryy by Reg. 7 of 1963 (1.10.1963).

(3) Laccadive, Minicoy and Amindivi Islands by Regn. 2 of 1970 Section 2(a).

These Islands are now known as Lakshadweep Islands.

"*Child*" means person who is under the age of fifteen years; and

"*guardian*" includes any person having legal custody of or control over a child.

3. Agreement contrary to the Act to be void.—An agreement to pledge the labour of a child shall be void.

4. Penalty for parent or guardian making agreement to pledge the labour of a child.—Whoever being the parent or guardian of a child, makes an agreement to pledge the labour of that child, shall be punished with fine which may extend to fifty rupees.

5. Penalty for making with a parent or guardian an agreement to pledge the labour of a child.—Whoever, makes with the parent or guardian of a child an agreement whereby such parent or guardian pledges the labour of the child shall be punished with fine which may extend to two hundred rupees.

6. Penalty for employing a child whose labour has been pledged.—Whoever, knowing or having reason to believe that an agreement has been made to pledge the labour of a child, in furtherance of such agreement employees such child, or permits such child to be employed in any premises or place under his control, shall be punished with fine which may extend to two hundred rupees.

------

3. THE CHILDREN ACT, 1960

(60 of 1960)

STATEMENT OF OBJECTS AND REASONS

"Children are the most vulnerable group in any population and in need of the greatest social care. On account of their vulnerability and dependence they can be exploited, ill-treated and directed into undesirable channels by anti-social elements in the community. The State has the duty of according proper care and protection to children at all times, as it is on their physical and mental well being that the future of the nation depends. With increased industrialisation and urbanisation. The State needs to be even more alert and vigilant in this respect. This Bill provides for the care, protection, maintenance welfare, training, education and rehabilitation of neglected or delinquent children and for the trial of delinquent children in the Union Territories for which the Central Government has direct responsibility.

It should also be remembered that the children often become delinquent by force of circumstances and not by choice. By improving the unfavourable environment and giving suitable training, it is possible to reform his anti-social attitudes and to mould him into a responsible citizen. Measures for juvenile delinquents should, therefore, aim at rehabilitation rather than punishment. The programmes proposed to be undertaken under this bill are meant to be of a positive character.

At present the Bombay Children Act, 1924 is in force in Delhi. It was considered whether a replacement of this out-moded Act by the Bombay Children Act, 1948 would not achieve the aims and objects referred to above. It was found that the Bombay Children Act, 1948 or any other State Act for that matter would not fully meet the needs of the Union Territories. As such the present Bill which takes into account the Special needs of the Union Territories has been prepared".—Gaz. of Ind. 1959 Ext, Pt. II—Sec. 2 p. 1487.

Act 15 of 1978.—The Children Act, 1960, provides for the care protection maintenance, welfare training education and rehabilitation of neglected or delinquent children and for the trial of delinquent children in the Union Territories. Experience gained in the implementation of the Act has brought to light certain inadequacies and weakness. It is proposed to amend the Act to make good the inadequacies. The amendments proposed are as follows :—

(i) It is proposed to provide that children's Court constituted under the Act should be assisted by at least two qualified social workers one of whom should be a woman.

(ii) Under the Act, Child Welfare Boards are expected to deal with neglected children, while delinquent children are referred to the children's Court. Very often, it is found that reported cases of delinquents are in fact cases of negligence. The converse may also, on occasions be true. It is, therefore, proposed to make provisions enabling mutual transfer of cases between a Child Welfare Board and a children's Court.

(iii) The functions of the children's homes and special schools are sought to be widened with a view to ensuring the development of the personality of the child.

(iv) It is proposed to empower the Administrator of a Union territory to provide for a comprehensive programme of after care for completing the process of care and treatment of children under the Act.

(v) The ban imposed on the appearance of legal practitioners before the children's Courts is proposed to be removed.

2. The other amendments proposed are minor and consequential in nature.—Gaz. of Ind. 14.12.1977 pt. II, Section 2, Ext. p. 862.

Cognate Laws

Employment of Children Act, 26 of 1938.

Reformatory Schools Act, 8 of 1897.

Women and Children's Institutions (Licensing) Act, 105 of 1956.

Assam Children Act, 12 of 1971.

Bihar Children Act, Presi. Act 10 of 1970.

Bombay Children Act, 71 of 1948.

Haryana Children Act, 10 of 1974.

H.P. Children Act, 21 of 1979.

J&K Children Act, 20 of 1970.

Karnataka Children Act, 19 of 1964.

Kerala Children Act, 3 of 1973.

Manipur Children Act (1 of 1979).

Punjab Children Act, 39 of 1949.

Rajasthan Children Act, 16 of 1970.

Tamil Nadu Children Act, 4 of 1920.

U.P. Children Act, 1 of 1952.

W.B. Children Act, 30 of 1952.

Probation of Offenders Act, 20 of 1958.

Child Labour (Prohibition and Regulation) Act, 61 of 1986.

THE CHILDREN ACT, 1960
(60 of 1960)[1]

[26*th December*, 1960]

An Act to provide for the care, protection, maintenance, welfare, training education and rehabilitation of neglected or delinquent children and for the trial of delinquent children in the Union Territories.

Be it enacted by Parliament in the Eleventh Year of the Republic of India as follows :—

CHAPTER I
PRELIMINARY

1. Short title, extent and commencement.—(1) This Act may be called the Children Act, 1960.

(2) It extends[2] to all Union Territories.

(3) It shall come into force in any Union Territory on such date[3] as the Administrator may, by notification in the Official Gazette, appooint and different dates may be appointed for different areas thereof.

2. Definitions.—In this Act, unless the context otherwise requires,—

(a) "*Administrator*" means the administrator of a Union Territory, whether called a Lieutenant Governor, a Chief Commissioner or by any other name :

(b) "*beging*" means—

(i) soliciting or receiving alms in a public place or entering on any private premises for the purpose of soliciting or receiving alms, whether under the pretence of singing, dancing fortune-telling, performing tricks or selling articles or otherwise.

(ii) exposing or exhibiting with the object of obtaining or extorting alms any sore, wound, injury, deformity or disease, whether of himself or of any other person or of an animal;

(iii) allowing oneself to be used as an exhibit for the purpose of soliciting or receiving alms;

(c) "*Board*" means a Child Welfare Board constituted under Section 4;

(d) "*brothel*", "*prostitute*", "*prostitution*" and "*public place*" shall have the meaning respectively assigned to them in the Suppression of Immoral Traffic in Women and Girls Act, 1956;

---

1. *See* Gazette of India Extra Part II, Sec. 2 Page 57, dated 22.8.1960.
2. The Act has been extended to—Goa, Daman and Diue see Regn. 12 of 1962 Dadra and Nagar Haveli see Regn. 6 of 1963 as amended by Regn. 2 of 1965 (1.7.1965). Pondicherry) : see Regn. 7 of 1963 (1.10.1963).
3. The Act was enforced in Himachal Pradesh by Notifn. No. 9-21/60. Wel (2.10.1962); See H.P. Gazette, 29.9.1962, Pt. 1p. 565. Himachal Pradesh is now a State—See Act 53 of 1970, Section 3 w.e.f. 25.1.1971 and in Goa from 1.1.1964—See Goa Gaz. 18.12.1963. S.I. No. 50, p. 430.

(e) "*child*" means a boy who has not attained the age of sixteen years or a girl who has not attained the age of eighteen years;

(f) "*children's court*" means a Court constituted under Section 5;

(g) "*children's home*" means an institution established or certified by the Administrator under Section 9 as a children's home;

(h) "*competent authority*" means in relation to neglected children, a Board constituted under Section 4 and in relation to delinquent children a children's Court constituted under Section 5, and where no such Board or children's Court has been constituted, includes any Court empowered under sub-section (2) of Section 7 to exercise the powers conferred on a Board or children's Court;

(i) "*dangerous drug*" shall have the meaning assigned to it in the Dangerous Drugs Act, 1930;

(j) "*delinquent child*" means a child who has been found to have committed an offence;

[1][(jj) "*fit person*" or "*fit institution*" means any person or institution (not being a police station or jail) found fit by the competent authority to receive and take care of a child entrusted to his or its care and protection on he terms and conditions specified by the competent authority;]

(k) "*guardian*" in relation to a child, includes any person who in the opinion of the competent authority having cognizance of any proceedings in relation to a child, has, for the time being, the actual charge of, or control over that child;

(l) "*neglected child*" means a child who—

(i) is found begging; or

(ii) is found without having any home or settled place of abode or any ostensible means of subsistence or is found destitute, whether he is an orphan or not; or

(iii) has a parent or guardian who is unfit [or unable] to exercise or does not exercise proper care and control over the child; or

(iv) lives in a brothel or with a prostitute or frequently goes to any place used for the purpose of prostitution, or is found to associate with any prostitute or any other person who leads an immoral, drunken or depraved life;

(*m*) "*observation home*" means any institution or place established or recognised by the Administrator under Section 11 as an observation home;

(*n*) "*offence*" means an offence punishable under any law for the time being in force;

---

1. Clause (jj), clause (nn) and word "or unable" in clause (1) (iii), inserted by the Children (Amendment) Act, (15 of 1978), Section 3 (1.10.1978 in Delhi; 1.3.1979 in Goa, Daman and Diu and 6.12.1978 in Pondicherry).

[1][(*nn*) *"place of safety"* means any place or institution (not being a police station or jail), the person in charge of which is willing temporarily to receive and take care of a child and which in the opinion of the competent authority may be a place of safety for the child;]

(*o*) *"prescribed"* means prescribed by rules made under this Act;

(*p*) *"Probation Officer"* means an officer appointed as a Probation Officer under this Act or under the Probation of Offenders Act, 1958;

(*q*) *"special school"* means an institution established or certified by the Administrator under Section 10;

(*r*) *"supervision"* in relation to a child placed under the care of any parent, guardian or other [2][fit person or fit institution] under this Act means the supervision of that child by a Probation Officer for the purpose of ensuring that the child is property looked after and that the conditions imposed by the competent authority are complied with;

(*s*) all words and expressions used but not defined in this Act and defined in the [3][Code of Criminal Procedure, 1973] shall have the meanings assigned to them in that Code.

COMMENTS

Child under Section 2(e)—Where the appellant was less than 16 years at the time he first appeared before the Trial Court, held that he was a child within meaning of the term under clause (e) of Section 2 of the Act—*Raghbir* v. *State of Haryana*, AIR 1981 SC 2037 : 1981 Cri LJ 1997.

3. Continuation of Inquiry of respect of child who had ceased to be child.—Where an inquiry has been initiated against a child and during the course of such inquiry the child ceases to be such, then notwithstanding anything contained in this Act or in any other law for the time being in force, the inquiry may be continued and orders may be made in respect of such person as if such person had continued to be a child.

CHAPTER II

COMPETENT AUTHORITIES AND INSTITUTIONS FOR CHILDREN

4. Child Welfare Boards.—(1) The Administrator may by notification in the Official Gazette constitute for any area specified in the notification, one or more Child Welfare Boards for exercising the powers and discharging the duties conferred or imposed on such Board in relation to neglected children under this Act.

(2) A Board shall consist of a Chairman and such other members as the Administrator thinks fit to appoint, of whom not less than one shall be a woman;

---

1. Clause (jj), clause (nn) and word "or unable" in clause (1) (iii), inserted by the Children (Amendment) Act, (15 of 1978), Section 3 (1.10.1978 in Delhi; 1.3.1979 in Goa, Daman and Diu and 6.12.1978 in Pondicherry).
2. Substituted for the words "fit person", ibid.
3. Substituted for the words "Code of Criminal Procedure, 1898", ibid S. 2.

and every such member shall be vested with the powers a Magistrate under the [1][Code of Criminal Procedure, 1973].

(3) The Board shall function as a Bench of Magistrates and shall have the powers conferred by the [2][Code of Criminal Procedure, 1973, on a Metropolitan Magistrate, or as the case may be a Judicial Magistrate of the first class.]

5. Children's Courts.—(1) Notwithstanding anything contained in the [3][Code of Criminal Procedure, 1973], the Administrator may, by notification in the Official Gazette, constitute for any area specified in the notification one or more children's Courts for exercising the powers and discharging the duties conferred or imposed on such Court in relation to delinquent children under this Act.

[4][(2) A children ; Court shall consist of such number of Metropolitan Magistrates or Judicial Magistrates of the first class, as the case may be, forming a Bench as the Administrator thinks fit to appoint, of whom one shall be designated as the principal magistrate ; and every such Bench shall have the powers conferred by the Code of Criminal Procedure, 1973, on a Metropolitan Magistrate or, as the case may be, a judicial Magistrate of the first class.

(3) Every children's Court shall be assisted by a panel of two honorary social workers possessing such qualifications as may be prescribed, of whom at least one shall be a woman, and such panel shall be appointed by the Administrator.]

COMMENTS

Reformatory vision.—The principle underlying there laws that if children or adolescents found to be guilty of offences by Criminal Courts were in lieu of ordinary sentence of imprisonment kept in a special form of detention in a place other than a prison, of which the purpose was to develop mentally, physically, and movable all inmates by giving them necessary training, there was every likelihood of such persons being reformed and accepted by society as person who had no inalienation to commit crimes in future.—*State of U.P.* v. *Vallabhapuram Ravi*, AIR 1985 SC 870 : 1984 Cri LJ 1511.

Children—Trial of.—The trial of children must take place in the Juvenile Court's and not in the regular Courts.—*Sheela Barse* v. *Union of India*, AIR 1986 SC 1773 : 1986 Cri LJ 1736.

Conflicting provisions.—The Haryana Children Act come into force on 1.3.1974, while the Criminal Procedure Code, 1973 Come into force on 1.4.1974. If there be any conflict between any provisions of the Act and the Code, in view of the Article 24(1) of the Constitution of India, the provisions of the Code will be void to be extent of repugnancey.—*Raghbir* v. *State of Haryana*, AIR 1987 SC 2037 : 1981 Cri LJ 1497.

Trial of offence.—This section carves out a clear exception to the provisions of the trial of an offence under any special or local law for the time being in force or any Special

---

1. Substituted for the words, "Code of Criminal Procedure, 1898" by the Children (Amendment) Act (15 of 1978) Section 4 (1.10.1978) in Delhi; 1.3.1979 in Goa, Daman and Diu and 6.12.1978 in Pondicherry).
2. Substituted for the words "Code of Criminal Procedure, 1898, on a Magistrate of the first Class". ibid.
3. Substituted for original sub-secretion (2) by the Children (Amendment) Act (15 of 1978), Section 5 (1.10.1978) in Delhi 1.3.1979 in Goa, Daman Diu and 6.12.1978 in Pondicherry).
4. Substituted for the words "Code of Criminal Procedure, 1898" ibid, Section 2.

Jurisdiction or power conferred or any special form or procedure prescribed by any other law for the time being in force.—*Rohtas* v. *State of Haryana and others*, AIR 1979 SC 1839 : (1979) Cri LJ 1365.

6. Procedure, etc., in relation to Boards and Children's Courts.—(1) In the event of any difference of opinion among the members of a Board or among the magistrates of a Children's Court the opinion of the majority shall prevail, but where there is no such majority, the opinion of the chairman or of the [1][principal magistrate] as the case may be, shall prevail.

(2) A Board or Children's Court may act notwithstanding the absence of any member of the Board or, as the case may be, any magistrate of the Children's Court, and no order made by the board or Children's Court shall be invalid by reason only of the absence of any member or magistrate, as the case may be, during any stage of the proceeding.

(3) No person shall be appointed as a member of the Board or as a magistrate in the Children's Court unless he has, in the opinion of the Administrator, special knowledge of child psychology and child welfare.

7. Power of Board and Children's Court.—(1) Where a Board or a Children's Court has been constituted for any area, such Board or Court shall, notwithstanding anything contained in any other law for the time being in force but save as otherwise expressly provided in this Act, have power to deal exclusively with all proceedings under this Act relating to neglected children or delinquent children, as the case may be.

[2][Provided that a Board or a children's Court may, if it is of opinion that it is necessary so as do having to the circumstances of the case, transfer any proceedings to any children's Court or Board, as the case may be :

Provided further that where there is any difference of opinion between a Board and children's Court regarding the transfer of any proceedings under the first proviso, it shall be referred to the Chief Metropolitan Magistrate or, as the case may be, the Chief Judicial Magistrate for decision, and in a case where the District Magistrate is functioning as a Board or a children's court, such difference of opinion shall be referred to the Court of Session, and the decision of the Chief Metropolitan Magistrate or Chief Judicial Magistrate or, as the case may be, the Court of Session on such reference shall be final.]

(2) Where no Board or Children's Court has been constituted for any area, the powers conferred on the Board or the Children's Court by or under this Act shall be exercised in that area, only by the following namely:—

(*a*) the district magistrate ; or

(*b*) the sub-divisional magistrate ; or

---

1. Substituted for words, "Senior Magistrate", by the Children (Amendment) Act (15 of 1978), Section 6 (1.10.1978) in Delhi ; 1.3.1979 in Goa, Daman and Diu and 6.12.1978 in Pondicherry).
2. Added by the Children (Amendment) Act (15 of 1978), Section 7 (1.10.1978), Delhi 1.3.1979 in Goa, Daman and Diu and 6.12.1978 in Pondicherry).

[1][(*c*) any Metropolitan Magistrate or Judicial Magistrate of the first class as the case may be.]

(3) The powers conferred on the Board or Children's Court by or under this Act may also be exercised by the High Court and the Court of Session, when the proceeding comes before them in appeal, revision or otherwise.

8. Procedure to be followed by a magistrate not empowered under the Act.—(1) When any magistrate not empowered to exercise the powers of a Board or a Children's Court under this Act is of opinion that a person brought before him under any of the provisions of this Act (otherwise than for the purpose of giving evidence) is a child, he shall record such opinion and forward the child and the record of the proceeding to the competent authority having jurisdiction over the proceeding.

(2) The competent authority to which the proceeding is forwarded under sub-section (1) shall hold the inquiry as if the child had originally been brought before it.

9. Children's homes.—(1) The Administrator may establish and maintain as many children's homes as may be necessary for the reception of neglected children under this Act.

(2) Where the Administrator is of opinion that any institution other than an institution established under sub-section (1) is fit for the reception of the neglected children to be sent there under this Act, he may certify such institution as a children's home for the purposes of this Act.

(3) Every, children's home to which a neglected child is sent under this Act shall not only provide the child with accommodation, maintenance and facilities for education, but also provide him with facilities for the development of his character and abilities and give him necessary training for protecting himself against moral danger or exploitation and shall also perform such other functions as may be prescribed [2][to ensure all round growth and development of his personality.]

(4) The Administrator may, by rules made under this Act, provide for the management of children's homes [3][including the standard and the nature of services to be maintained by them] and the circumstances under which, and the manner in which, the certificate of a children's home may be granted or withdrawn.

10. Special schools.—(1) The Administrator may establish and maintain as may special schools as may be necessary for the reception of a delinquent children under this Act.

(2) Where the Administrator is of opinion that any institution other than an institution established under sub-section (1) is fit for the reception of the delinquent children to be sent there under this Act, he may certify such institution as a special school for the purposes of this Act.

---

1. Substituted for the sub-section (e), ibid.
2. Added by the Children (Amendment) Act (15 of 1978), Section 8 (1.10.1978 in Delhi ; 1.3.1979 in Goa, Daman and Diu and 6.12.1978 in Pondicherry.
3. Inserted, ibid.

(3) Every special school to which a delinquent child is sent under this Act shall not only provide the child with accommodation, maintenance and facilities for education but also provide him with facilities for the development of his character and abilities and give him necessary training for his reformation and shall also perform such other functions as may be prescribed to ensure all round growth and development of his personality.

(4) The Administrator may, by rules made under this Act, provide for the management of special schools [1][including he standards and the nature of services to be maintained by them] and the circumstances under which, and the manner in which, the certificate of a special school may be granted or withdrawn.

11. Observation homes.—The Administrator may establish and maintain as many observation homes as may be necessary for the temporary reception of children during the pendency of any inquiry regarding them under this Act.

(2) Where the Administrator is of opinion that any institution other than an institution established under sub-section (1) is fit for the temporary reception of children during the pendency of any inquiry regarding them under this Act, he may recognise such institution as an observation home for the purposes of this Act.

(3) Every observation home to which a child is sent under this Act shall not only provide the child with accommodation, maintenance and facilities for medical examination and treatment, but also provide him with facilities for useful occupation.

(4) The Administrator may, by rules made under this Act, provide for the management of observation homes [2][including the standards and nature of services to be maintained by them] and the circumstances under which, an the manner in which, an institution may be recognised as an observation home or the recognition may be withdrawn.

[3][**12. After care organisations.**—The Administrator may, by rules made under this Act, provide.

(*a*) for the establishment or recognition of after-care organisations and the powers that may be exercised by them for effectively carrying out their functions under this Act :

(*b*) for a scheme of after-care programme to be followed by such after-care organisations for the purpose of taking care of children after they leave children's homes or special schools and for the purpose of enabling them to lead an honest, industrious and useful life ;

(*c*) for the preparation and submission of a report by the probation officer

---

1. Added by the Children (Amendment) Act (15 of 1978), Section 9 (1.10.1978 in Delhi, 1.3.1979 in Goa, Daman and Diu and 6.12.1978 in Pondicherry).
2. Inserted, Ibid.
3. Inserted by the Children (Amendment) Act (15 of 1978), Section 10 (1.10.1978 in Delhi ; 1.3.1979 in Goa, Daman and Diu and 6.12.1978 in Pondicherry).

in respect of each child prior to his discharge from a children's home or special school, as the case may be, regarding the necessity and nature of after-care of such child, the period of such after-care, supervision thereof and for the submission of a report by the probation officer on the progress of each such child;

(*d*) for the standards and the nature of services to be maintained by such after-care organisations ;

(*e*) for such other matter as may be necessary for the purpose of effectively carrying out the scheme of after-care programme of children.]

CHAPTER III
NEGLECTED CHILDREN

13. Production of neglected children before Boards.—(1) If any police officer or any other person authorised by the Administrator in this behalf, by general or special order, is of opinion that a person is apparently a neglected child, such police officer or other person may take charge of that person for bringing him before a Board.

(2) When information is given to an officer-in-charge of the police station about any neglected child found within the limits of such station, he shall enter in a book to be kept for the purpose the substance of such information and take such action thereon as he deems fit and if such officer does not propose to take charge of the child, he shall forward a copy of the entry made to the Board.

(3) Every child taken charge of under sub-section (1) shall be brought before the Board within a period of twenty-four hours of such charge taken excluding the time necessary for the journey from the place where the child had been taken charge of to the Board.

(4) Every child taken charge of under sub-section (1) shall, unless he is kept with his parent or guardian, be sent to an observation home (but not to a police station or jail) until he can be brought before a Board.

14. Special procedure to be followed when neglected child has parent.—(1) If a person, who, in the opinion of the police officer or the authorised person, is a neglected child, has a parent or guardian who has the actual charge of, or control over, the child, the police officer or the authorised person may, instead of taking charge of the child, make a report to the Board for initiating an inquiry regarding that child.

(2) On receipt of a report under sub-section (1), the Board may call upon the parent or guardian to produce the child before it and to show cause why the child should not be dealt with as a neglected child under the provisions of this Act and if it appears to the Board that the child is likely to be removed from its jurisdiction or to be concealed, it may immediately order his removal (if necessary by issuing a

search warrant for the immediate production of the child) to an observation home [1][or a place of safety.]

15. Inquiry by Board regarding neglected children.—(1) When a person alleged to be a neglected child is produced before a Board, it shall examine the police officer or the authorised person who brought the child or made the report and record the substance of such examination and hold the inquiry in the prescribed manner and may make such orders in relation to the sold as it may deem fit.

(2) Where a Board is satisfied on inquiry that a child is a neglected child and that it is expedient so to deal with him, the Board may make an order directing the child to be sent to a children's home for the period until he ceases to be a child :

Provided that the Board may, for reasons to be recorded, extend the period of such stay, but in no case the period of stay shall extend beyond the time when the child attains the age of eighteen years, in the case of a boy, or twenty years, in the case of a girl :

Provided further that the Board may, if it is satisfied that having regard to the circumstances of the case it is expedient so to do, for reasons to be recorded, reduce the period of stay to such period as it thinks fit.

(3) During the pendency of any inquiry regarding a child, the child shall, unless he is kept with his parent or guardian, be sent to an observation home [2][or a place of safety] for such period as may be specified in the order of the Board :

Provided that no child shall be kept with his parent or guardian if, in the opinion of the Board, such parent or guardian is unfit or unable to exercise or does not exercise proper care of control over the child.

16. Power to commit neglected child to suitable custody.—(1) If the Board so thinks fit, it may, instead of making an order under sub-section (2) of Section 15 for sending the child to a children's home, make an order placing the child under the care of a parent, guardian or other fit person, on such parent, guardian or fit person executing a bond with or without surety to be responsible for the good behaviour and well-being of the child and for the observance of such conditions as the Board may think fit to impose.

(2) At the time of making an order under sub-section (1) or at any time subsequently, the Board may, in addition, make an order that the child be placed under supervision for any period not exceeding three years in the first instance.

(3) Notwithstanding anything contained in sub-section (1) or sub-section (2), if at any time it appears to the Board, on receiving a report from the probation officer or otherwise, that there has been a breach of any of the conditions imposed by it in respect of the child, it may, after making such inquiry as it deems fit, order the child to be sent to a children's home.

---

1. Inserted by the Children (Amendment) Act (15 of 1978), Section 12 (1.10.1078 in Delhi, 1.3.1979 in Goa Daman and Diu and 6.12.1978 in Pondicherry).
2. Inserted by the Children (Amendment) Act (15 of 1978), Section 13 (1.10.1978 in Delhi : 1.3.1979 in Goa, Daman and Diu and 6.12.1978 in Pondicherry).

17. Uncontrollable children.—Where a parent or guardian of a child complains to the Board that he is not able to exercise proper care and control over the child and the Board is satisfied on inquiry that proceedings under this Act should be initiated regarding the child, it may send the child to an observation home [1][or a place of safety] and make such further inquiry as it may deem fit and the provisions of Section 15 and Section 16 shall, as far as may be, apply to such proceedings.

CHAPTER IV

DELINQUENT CHILDREN

18. Bail and custody of children.—(1) When any person accused of a bailable or non bailable offence and apparently a child is arrested or detained or appears or is brought before a Children's Court, such person shall, notwithstanding anything contained in the Code of Criminal Procedure, 1973 or in any other law for the time being in force, be released on bail with or without surety but he shall not be so released if there appear reasonable grounds for beleving that the release is likely to bring him into association with any reputed criminal or expect him to moral danger or that his release would defeat the ends of justice.

(2) When such person having been arrested is not released on bail under sub-section (1) by the officer-in-charge of the police station, such officer shall cause him to be kept in an observation home [2][or a place of safety] in the prescribed manner (but not in a police station or jail until he can be brought before Children's Court.

(3) When such person is not released on bail under sub-section (1) by the Children's Court, it shall, instead of committing him to prison, make an order sending him to an observation home [3][or a place of safety] for such period during the pendency of the inquiry regarding him as may be specified in the order.

COMMENTS

Effect of failure to prove age.—Where the petitioner have led no evidence and have failed to prove that either of them was under the age of 16 years on the date of the occurrence and therefore entitled to the benefit of the U.P. Children Act.—*Hawaldar Singh* v. *State of U.P.*, 1984 All LJ 6.

Applicability of Act.—In the instant case the child was of sixteen years at the time of occurrence ; the Court observed that the relevant date for the applicability of the Act is the date on which the offence taken place and not the date of the trial.—*Umesh Chandra* v. *State of Rajasthan*, AIR 1982 SC 1057 : 1982 Cri LJ 994.

Detention of children.—It has been observed under the age of 16 years' is not to be sent to jail, but should be detained in children home or other place of safety.—*Munna* v. *State of U.P.*, AIR 1982 SC 806 : 1982 Cri LJ 620.

19. Information to parent or guardian or probation officer.—Where a child is arrested, the officer-in-charge of the police station to which the child is brought shall, as soon as may be after the arrest, inform—

---

1. Inserted by the Children (Amendment) Act (15 of 1978), Section 12 (1.10.1978 in Delhi ; 1.3.1979 in Goa, Daman and Diu and 6.12.1978 in Pondicherry).
2. Inserted by the Children (Amendment) Act (15 of 1978), Section 12 (1.10.1978 in Delhi, 1.3.1979 in Goa, Daman and Diu and 6.12.1978 in Pondicherry).
3. Substituted for the words "Code of Criminal Procedure, 1898", ibid, Section 2.

(*a*) the parent or guardian of the child, if he can be found of such arrest and direct him to be present at the Children's Court before which the child will appear; and

(*b*) the probation-officer of such arrest in order to enable him to obtain information regarding the antecedents and family history of the child and other material circumstances likely to be of assistance to the Children's Court for making inquiry.

20. Inquiry by Children's Court regarding delinquent children.—Where a child having been charged with an offence appears or, is produced before a Children's Court, the Children's Court shall hold the inquiry in accordance with the provisions of Section 39 and may subject to the provisions of this Act, make such order in relation to the child as it deems fit.

21. Orders that may be passed regarding delinquent children.—(1) Where a Children's Court is satisfied on inquiry that a child has committed an offence, then, notwithstanding anything to be contrary contained in any other law for the time being in force, the Children's Court may, if it so thinks fit,—

(*a*) allow the child to go home after advice or admonition ;

(*b*) direct the child to be released on probation of good conduct and placed under the care of any parent, guardian or other fit person on such parent, guardian or other fit person executing a bond, with or without surety as that Court may require for the good behaviour and well-being of the child for any period not exceeding three years:

(*c*) make an order directing the child to be sent to a special school—

(*i*) in the case of a boy over fourteen years of age or of a girl over sixteen years of age, for a period of not less than three years ;

(*ii*) in the case of any other child, for the period until he ceases to be a child :

Provided that the Children's Court may, if it is satisfied that having regard to the nature of the offence and the circumstances of the case it is expedient so to do, for reasons to be recorded, reduce the period of stay to such period as it thinks fit :

Provided further that the Children's Court may, for reasons to be recorded extend the period of such stay, but in no case the period of stay shall extend beyond the time when the child attains the age of eighteen years, in the case of a boy, or twenty years, in the case of a girl ;

(*d*) order the child to pay a fine if he is over fourteen years of age and earns money :

(2) Where an order under clause (b) or clause (d) of sub-section (1) is made, the Children's Court may, if it is of opinion that in the interests of the child and of the public it is expedient so to do, in addition make an order that the delinquent child shall remain under the supervision of a probation officer named in the order during

such period nor exceeding three years as may be specified therein, and may in such supervision order impose such conditions as it deems necessary for the due supervision of the delinquent child :

Provided that if at any time afterwards it appears to the Children's Court on receiving a report from the probation officer or otherwise that the delinquent child has not been of good behaviour during the period of supervision, it may, after making such inquiry as it deems fit, order the delinquent child to be sent to a special school.

(3) The Children's Court making a supervision order under sub-section (2) shall explain to the child and the parent, guardian or other fit person, as the case may be, under whose care the child has been placed, the terms and conditions of the order and shall forthwith furnish one copy of the supervision order to the child, the parent, guardian or other fit person, as the case may be, the sureties, if any, and the probation officer.

(4) In determining the special school, or any person to whose custody a child is to be committed or entrusted under this Act, the Court shall pay due regard to the religious denomination of the child to ensure that religious instruction contrary to the religious persuasion of the child is not imparted to him.

22. Orders that may not be passed against delinquent children.—(1) Notwithstanding anything to the contrary contained in any other law for the time being in force, no delinquent child shall be sentenced to death or imprisonment or committed to prison in default of payment of fine, or in default of furnishing security :

Provided that where a child who has attained the age of fourteen years has committed an offence and the Children's Court is satisfied that the offence committed is of so serious a nature or that his conduct and behaviour have been such that it would not be in his interest or in the interest of other children in a special school to sent him to such special school and that done of the other measures provided under this Act is suitable or sufficient, the Children's Court may order the delinquent child to be kept in safe custody in such place and manner as it thinks fit and shall report the case for the orders of the Administrator.

(2) On receipt of a report from a Children's Court under sub-section (1), the Administrator may make such arrangement in respect of the child as he deems proper and may order such delinquent child to be detained at such place and on such conditions as he thinks fit :

Provided that the period of detention so ordered shall not exceed the maximum period of imprisonment to which the child could have been sentenced for the offence committed.

23. Proceeding under Chapter VIII of the Criminal Procedure Code not competent against child.—Notwithstanding anything to the contrary contained in the [1][Code of Criminal Procedure 1973] no proceedings shall be instituted and no order shall be passed against a child under Chapter VIII of the said Code.

---

1. Substituted for the words and figures, "Code of Criminal Procedure, 1898" by the Children (Amendment) Act (15 of 1978), Section 2 (1.10.1078 in Delhi ; 1.3.1979 in Goa, Daman and Diu and 6.12.1978 in Pondicherry).

24. No joint trial of child and person not a child.—(1) Notwithstanding anything contained in [1][Section 223 of the Code of Criminal Procedure, 1973), or in any other law for the time being in force no child shall be charged with or tried for, any offence together with a person who is not a child.

(2) If a child is accused of an offence for which under [2][Section 223 of the Code of Criminal Procedure, 1973), or in any other law for the time being in force, such child and any person who is not a child would, but for the prohibition contained in sub-section (1), have been charged and tried together, the Court taking cognizance of that offence shall direct separate trials of the child and the other person.

25. Removal of disqualification attaching to conviction.—Notwithstanding anything contained in any other law, a child who has committed an offence and has been dealt with under the provisions of this act shall not suffer disqualification, if any, attaching to a conviction of an offence under such law.

26. Special provision in respect of pending cases.—Notwithstanding anything contained in this Act, all proceedings in respect of a child pending in any Court in any area on the date on which this Act comes into force in that area, shall be continued in that Court as if this Act has not been passed and if the Court finds that the child has committed an offence, it shall reason such finding and, instead of passing any sentence in respect of the child, forward the child to the Children's Court which shall pass orders in respect of that child in accordance with the provisions of this Act as if it had borne satisfied on inquiry under this Act that the child the committed the offence.

CHAPTER V

PROCEDURE OF COMPETENT AUTHORITIES GENERALLY AND APPEALS AND REVISION FROM ORDERS OF SUCH COURTS

27. Sittings etc. of Boards and children's Courts.—(1) A Board or a children Court shall hold its sittings at such place, on such day and in such manner as may be prescribe.

(2) A Magistrate empowered to exercise the powers of a Board, or, as the case may be, Children's Court under sub-section (2) of Section 7 shall, while holding any inquiry regarding a child under this Act, as far as practicable, sit in a building or room different from that which the ordinary sittings of civil and criminal Courts are held, or on different days or time different from those at which the ordinary sittings of such Courts are held.

28. Persons who may be present before competent authority.—(1) Save as provide in this Act, no person shall be present at any sitting of a competent authority, except—

---

1. Substituted for the words "Section 239 of the Code of Criminal Procedure, 1898 by the Children (Amendment) Act 15 of 1978), Section 14 (1.10.1978 in Delhi; 1.3.1979 in Goa, Daman and Diu and 6.12.1978 in Pondicherry).
2. Substituted for the words "Section 239 of the Code of Criminal Procedure, 1898 by the Children (Amendment) Act 15 of 1978), Section 14 (1.10.1978 in Delhi; 1.3.1979 in Goa, Daman and Diu and 6.12.1978 in Pondicherry).

(*a*) any officer of the competent authority, or

(*b*) the parties to the inquiry before the competent authority, the parent or guardian of the child and other persons directly concerned in the inquiry including police officer [1][and legal practitioners]; and

(*c*) such other persons as the competent authority may permit to be present.

(2) Notwithstanding anything contianed in sub-section (1), if at any stage during the inquiry, a competent authority considers it to be expedient in the interest of the child or on grounds of decency or morality that any person including the police officers, legal practitioner the parent guardian or the child himself should withdraw, the competent authority may give such direction and if any person refuses to comply with such direction, the competent authority may have him removed and may, for this purpose cause to be used such force as may be necessary.

[2][(3) No legal practitioner shall be entitled to appear, before a Board in any case proceedings before it except with the special permission of that Board.]

29. Attendance, of parent or guardian of child.—Any competent authority before which a child is brought under any of the provisions of this Act, may, whenever it so thinks to required any parent or guardian having the actual charge of, or control over the child to be present at any proceeding in respect of the child.

30. Dispensing with attendance of child.—If, at any stage during the course of inquiry, a competent authority is satisfied that the attendance of the child is not essential the purpose of the inquiry, the competent authority may dispense with his attendance and proceed with the inquiry in the absence of the child.

31. Committal to approved place of child suffering from dangerous disease and its future disposal.—(1) When a child who has been brought before a competent authority under this act is found to be suffering from a disease requiring prolonged medical treatment or physical or mental complaint that will respond to treatment, the competent authority may send the child to any place recognized to be an approved place in accordance with the rules made under this Act for such period as it may think necessary for the required treatment.

(2) Where a child is found to be suffering from leprosy or is of unsound mind, he shall be dealt with under the provisions of the Lepers Act, 1898, or the Indian Lunacy Act, 1912 as the case may be.

(3) Where a competent authority has taken action under sub-section (1) in the case of a child suffering from an infectious or contagious disease, the competent authority before restoring the said child to his partner in marriage, if there, has bene such, or to the guardian, as the case may be, shall where it is satisfied that such action will be in the interest of the said child call upon his partner in marriage or the guardian, as the case may be, to satisfy the Court by submitting to medical examination that such partner of guardian will not re-infect the child in respect of whom the order has been passed.

---

1. Inserted by the Children (Amendment) Act, 15 of 1978), Section 15 (1.10.1978 in Delhi, 1.3.1979 in Daman and Diu and 6.12.1978 in Pondicherry).
2. Substituted, ibid.

32. Presumption and determination of age.—(1) Where it appears to a competent authority that a person brought before it under any of the provisions of this act (otherwise than for the purpose of giving evidence) is a child the competent authority shall make due inquiry as to the age of that person and for that purpose shall take such evidence as may be necessary and shall record a finding whether the person is a child or not, stating his age as nearly as may be.

(2) No order of a competent authority shall be deemed to have become invalid merely by any subsequent proof that the person in respect of whom the order has been made is not a child, and he age recorded by the competent authority to be the age of the person so brought before it shall for the purposes of this Act, be deemed to be the true age of that person.

33. Circumstances to be taken into consideration in making orders under the Act.—In making any order in respect of a child under this Act, a competent authority shall take into consideration the following circumstances, namely :—

(*a*) the age of the child;

(*b*) the circumstances in which the child is living;

(*c*) the reports made by the probation officer;

(*d*) the religious persuasion of the child;

(*e*) such other circumstances as may, in the opinion of the competent authority, require to be taken into consideration in the interest of the child :

Provided that in the case of delinquent child, the above circumstances shall be taken into consideration after the Children's Court has recorded a finding against the child that he has committed the offence :

Provided further that if no report of the probation officer is received within ten weeks of his being informed under Section 19, it shall be open to the Children's Court to proceed without it.

34. Sending a child outside jurisdiction.—In the case of a neglected or delinquent child whose ordinary place of residence lies outside the jurisdiction of the competent authority before which he is brought the competent authority may if satisfied after due inquiry that it is expedient so to do, send the child back to a relative or other person who is fit and willing to receive him at his ordinary place of residence and exercise proper care and control over him, notwithstanding that such place of residence is outside the jurisdiction of the competent authority, and the competent authority exercising jurisdiction over the place to which the child is sent in respect of any matter arising subsequently have the same powers in relation to the child as if the original order had bene passed by itself.

35. Reports to be treated as confidential.—The report of the probation officer or any circumstance considered by the competent authority under Section 33 shall be treated a confidential :

Provided that the competent authority may, if it so thinks fit, communicate the substance thereof to the child or his parent or guardian and may give such child, parent or guardian an opportunity of producing such evidence as may be relevant to the matter stated in the report.

36. Prohibition of publication of names, etc. of children involved in any proceedings under the Act.—(1) No report in any newspaper, magazine or news sheet of any inquiry regarding a child under this act shall disclose the name, address or school or any other particular calculated to lead to the identification of the child, nor shall any picture of any such child be published :

Provided that for reasons to be recorded in writing the authority holding the inquiry may permit such disclosure if in its opinion such disclosure is in the interest of the child.

(2) Any person contravening the provisions of sub-section (1) shall be punishable will fine which may extend to one thousand rupees.

37. Appeals.—(1) Subject to the provisions of this section any person aggrieved by an order made by a competent authority under this Act may within thirty days from the date of such order prefer an appeal to the Court of Session :

Provided that the Court of Session may entertain the appeal after the expiry of the said period of thirty days if it is satisfied that the appellant was prevented by sufficient cause from filing the appeal in time.

(2) No appeal shall lie from—

(*a*) any order of acquittal by the Children's Court in respect of a child alleged to have committed an offence, or

(*b*) any order made by a Board in respect of a finding that a person is not a neglected child.

(3) No second appeal shall lie from any order of the Court of Session passed in appeal under this section.

38. Revision.—The High Court may, at any time, either of its own motion or on an application received in this behalf, call for the record of any proceeding in which any competent authority or Court of Session passed an order for the purpose of satisfying itself as to the authority or Court of Session passed an order for the purpose of satisfying itself as to the legality or propriety of any such order and may pass such order in relation thereto as it thinks fit :

Provided that the High Court shall not pass an order under this section prejudicial to any person without giving him a reasonable opportunity of being heard.

39. Procedure in inquiries, appeals and revision proceedings.—(1) Save as otherwise expressly provided by this Act, a competent authority while holding any inquiry under any of the provisions of this Act, shall follow such procedure as may be prescribed and subject thereto, shall follow, as far as may be, the procedure laid down in the [1][Code of Criminal Procedure, 1973] for trial in summons cases.

(2) Save as otherwise expressly provided by or under this Act, the procedure to be followed in hearing appeal, or revision proceedings under this Actshall be, as far as practicable, in accordance with the provisions of the [1][Code of Criminal Procedure, 1973]

40. Power to amend orders.—(1) Without prejudice to the provisions for appeal and revision under this act, any competent authority may, either on its own motion or on an application received in this behalf amend any order as to the institution to which a child is to be sent or as to the person under whose care or supervision a child is to be placed under this Act.

(2) Clerical mistakes in orders passed by a competent authority or errors arising therein from any accidental slip or omission may, at any time be corrected by the competent authority either on its own motion or on an application received in this behalf.

CHAPTER VI

SPECIAL OFFENCES IN RESPECT OF CHILDREN

41. Punishment for cruelty to child.—(1) Whoever, having the actual charge of or control over a child assaults abandons exposes or wilfully neglects the child or causes or procures him to be assaulted, abandoned expressed or neglected in a manner likely to cause such child unnecessary mental and physical suffering shall be punishable with imprisonment for a term which may extend to six months or with fine or with both.

(2) No Court shall take cognizance of an offence punishable under sub-section (1) unless the complaint is filed with the previous sanction of the Administrator or an officer authorised by him in this behalf.

42. Employment of children for begging.—(1) Whoever, employees or uses any child for the purposes of begging or causes any child to beg shall be punishable with imprisonment for a term which may extend to one year, or with fine or with both.

(2) Whoever, having the actual charge of, or control over a child abets the commission of the offence punishable under sub-section (1), shall be punishable with imprisonment for a term which may extend to one year, or with fine or with both.

(3) The offence punishable under this section shall be cognizable.

43. Penalty for giving intoxicating liquor or dangerous drug to a child.—Whoever, gives, or causes to be given to any child any intoxicating liquor in a public place or nay dangerous drug except upon the order of a duly qualified medical practitioner or in case of sickness or other urgent cause, shall be punishable with fine which may extend to two hundred rupees.

---

1. Substituted for the words and figures" Code of Criminal Procedure, 1898" by the Children (Amendment) Act (15 of 1978), Section 2 (1.10.1078 in Delhi ; 1.3.1978 in Goa, Daman and Diu and 6.12.1978 in Pondicherry).

44. Exploitation of child employees.—Whoever ostensibly procures a child for the purpose of any employment and withholds the earnings of the child or uses such earnings for his own purposes shall be punishable with fine which may extend to one thousand rupees.

CHAPTER VII

MISCELLANEOUS

45. Power of Administrator to discharge and transfer children.—(1) The Administrator may notwithstanding anything contained in this Act, at any time, order a neglected or delinquent child to be discharged from the children's home or special school either absolutely or on such conditions as he may think fit to impose.

(2) The Administrator may notwithstanding anything contained in this Act, order—

(*a*) a neglected child to be transferred from one children's home to another;

(*b*) a delinquent child to be transferred from one special school to another or from a special school to a borstal school where such school exists or from a special school to a children's home;

(*c*) a child who has bene released on licence which has been revoked or forfeited, to be send to the special school or children's home from which he was released or to any other children's home or special school or borstal school :

Provided that the total period of the stay of the child in a children's home or a special school shall not be increased by such transfer.

(3) The Administrator may, notwithstanding anything contained in this Act, at any time, discharge a child from the care of any person under whom he was placed under this Act either absolutely or on such conditions as the Administrator may think fit to impose.

STATE AMENDMENT

Himachal Pradesh—For the words The Administrator wherever occurring substitute the words the Government of Himachal Pradesh and for the word he substitute the word if.—H.P.A.L.O. 1973 (w.e.f. 25.1.1971).

46. Transfers between children's homes, etc., under the Act, and children's homes, etc. of like nature in different parts of India.—(1) The Administrator of a Union territory may direct any neglected child or delinquent child to be transferred from any children's home or special school within a the Union territory to any other children's home special school or institution of a like nature in another State with the consent of the Government of that State.

(2) The Administrator of a Union territory may, by general or special order, provide for the reception in a children's home or special school within the Union Territory of a neglected child or delinquent child detained in a children's home or special school or institution of a like nature in any other State where the Government of that State makes an order for such transfer, and upon such transfer the provisions of this Act, shall apply to such child as if he had been originally ordered to be sent to such children's home or special school under this Act.

STATE AMENDMENT

Himachal Pradesh—In its application to the State of Himachal Pradesh, in Section 46, in sub-sections (1) and (2) for the words Union Territory substitute the word State, and in sub-section (1), for the words the Administrator of the Union Territory, substitute the words "the Government of Himachal Pradesh". *Vide* H.P.A.L.O. 1973 (w.e.f. 25.1.1971).

47. Transfer of children of unsound mind or suffering from leprosy.—(1) Where it appears to the Administrator that any child kept in a special school or children's home in pursuance of this Act is suffering from leprosy or is of unsound mind, the Administrator may order his removal to a leper asylum or mental hospital or other place of safe custody for being kept there for the remainder of the term or which he has to be kept in custody under the orders of the competent authority or for such further period as may be certified by a medical officer to be necessary for the proper treatment of the child.

(2) Where it appears to the Administrator that the child is cured of leprosy or of unsoundness of mind, he may if the child is still liable to be kept in custody, order the person take charge of the child to send him to the special school or children's home from which he may removed or if the child is no longer liable to be kept in custody, order him to be discharged.

STATE AMENDMENT

Himachal Pradesh—For the words The Administrator wherever occurring substitute the words the Government of Himachal Pradesh.—H.P.A.L.O. 1973 (w.e.f. 25.1.1971).

48. Placing out on licence.—(1) When a child is kept in a children's home or special school the Administrator may, if he so thinks fit, release the child from the children's home or special school and grant him a written licence for such period and on such conditions as may be specified in the licence permitting him to live with, or under the supervision of, any responsible person named in the licence willing to receive and take charge of him with a view to educate him and train him for some useful trade or calling.

(2) Any licence so granted under sub-section (1) shall be in force for the period specified in the licence or until revoked or forfeited by the breach of any of the conditions on which it was granted.

(3) The Administrator may, at any time, by order in writing revoke any such licence and order the child to return to the children's home or special school from which he was released or to any other children's home or special school and shall do so at the desire of the person with whom or under whose supervision the child has been permitted to live in accordance with a licence granted under sub-section (1).

(4) When a licence has been revoked or forfeited and the child refuses or fails to return to the special school or children's home to which he was directed so to return, the Administrator may if necessary, cause him to be taken charge of and to be taken back to the special school or children's home :

(5) The time during which a child is absent from a special school or children's home in pursuance of a licence granted under this section shall be deemed to be

part of the time for which he is liable to be kept in custody in the special school or children's home :

Provided that when a child has failed to return to the special school or children's home on the licence being revoked or forfeited, the time which elapses after his failure so to return shall be excluded in computing the time during which he is liable to be kept in custody.

49. Provision in respect of escaped children.—Notwithstanding anything to the contrary contained in any other law for the time being in force, any police officer may take charge without warrant of a child who has escaped from a special school or a children's home or from the care of a person under whom he was placed under this Act and shall send the child back to the special school or the children's home or that person, as the case may be; and no proceeding shall be instituted in respect of the child by reason of such escape but the special school, children's home or the person may, after giving the information to the competent authority which passed the order in respect of the child, take such steps against the child as may be deemed necessary.

50. Contribution by parents.—(1) The competent authority which makes an order for sending a neglected child or a delinquent child to a children's home, or a special school or placing the child under the care of a fit person may make an order requiring the parents or other person liable to maintain the child to contribute to his maintenance, if able to do so, in the prescribed manner.

(2) The competent authority before making any order under sub-section (1) shall inquire into the circumstances of the parent or other person liable to maintain the child and shall record evidence, if any, in the presence of the parent or such other person, as the case may be.

(3) The person liable to maintain a child shall, for the purposes of sub-section (1), include in the case of illegitimacy, his putative father :

Provided that where the child is illegitimate, his maintenance has been made under [1][Section 125 of the Code of Criminal Procedure, 1973], the competent authority shall not ordinarily make an order for contribution against the putative father but may order the whole or any part of the sums accruing due under the said order for maintenance to be paid to such person as may be named by the competent authority and such shall be paid by him towards the maintenance of the child.

(4) Any order made under this section may be enforced in the same manner as an order under [2][Section 125 of the Code of Criminal Procedure, 1973].

51. Control of custodian over child.—Any person in whose custody a child is placed in pursuance of this Act shall, while the order is in force, have the like control

1. Substituted for the words and figures "Section 488 of the Code of Criminal Procedure, 1898" by the Children (Amendment) Act (15 of 1978), Section 16 (1.10.1078 in Delhi ; 1.3.1979 in Goa, Daman and Diu and 6.12.1978 in Pondicherry).
2. Substituted for the words and figures "Section 488 of the Code of Criminal Procedure, 1898" by the Children (Amendment) Act (15 of 1978), Section 16 (1.10.1078 in Delhi ; 1.3.1979 in Goa, Daman and Diu and 6.12.1978 in Pondicherry).

over the child as he would have if he were his parent and shall be responsible for his maintenance, and the child shall continue in his custody for the period stated by the competent authority notwithstanding that the is claimed by his parent or any other person :

Provided that no child while in such custody shall be married except with the permission of the competent authority.

52. Delinquent child undergoing sentence at commencement of the Act.—In any area in which this Act is brought into force, the Administrator may, direct that a deliquent child who is undergoing any sentence of imprisonment at the commencement of this Act shall, in lieu of undergoing such sentence, be sent to a special school or be kept in safe custody in such place and manner as the Administrator thinks fit for the remainder of the period of the sentence, and the provisions of this Act, shall apply to the child as if he had been ordered by a children's Court to be sent to such special school or as the case may be, ordered to be detained under sub-section (2) of Section 22.

53. Appointment of officers.—(1) The Administrator may appoint as many probation officers, officers for the inspection of special schools children's homes, observation homes or after-care organisations and such other officers as he may deem necessary for carrying out the purposes of this Act.

(2) It shall be the duty of the probation officer—

(*a*) to inquire, in accordance with the direction of a competent authority, into the antecedents and family history of any child accused of an offence with a view to assist the authority in making the inquiry;

(*b*) to visit neglected and delinquent children at such intervals as the probation officer may think fit;

(*c*) to report to the competent authority as to the behaviour of any neglected or delinquent child.

(*d*) to advise and assist neglected or delinquent children and if necessary, endeavour to find them suitable employment;

(*e*) where a neglected or delinquent child is placed under the care of any person on certain conditions to see whether such conditions are being complied with; and

(*f*) to perform such other duties as may be prescribed.

(3) Any officer empowered in this behalf by the Administrator may enter any special school, children's home observation home or after care organisation and make a complete inspection thereof in all its departments and of all papers, registers and accounts relating thereto and shall submit the report of such inspection to the Administrator.

54. Officers appointed under the Act to be public servants.—Probation officers and other officers appointed in pursuance of this Act shall be deemed to be public servants within the meaning of Section 21 of the Indian Penal Code.

55. Procedure in respect of bonds.—The provisions of [1][Chapter XXXIII of the Code of Criminal Procedure, 1973], shall as far as may be apply to bonds taken under this Act.

56. Delegation of powers.—The Administrator may by general or special order, direct that any power exercisable by him under this Act shall in such circumstances and under such conditions if any as may be specified in the order be exercisable also by an officer subordinate to the Administrator.

57. Protection of action taken in good faith.—No suit or other legal proceeding shall lie against the Administrator or any probation officer or other officer appointed under this Act in respect of anything which is in good faith done or intended to be done in pursuance of this Act or of any rules or orders made thereunder.

58. Act 8 of 1897 and certain provisions of Act 2 of 1974 not to apply.—(1) The Reformatory Schools Act, 1897, and [2][Section 27 of the Code of Criminal Procedure, 1973], shall cease to apply to any area in which this Act has been brought into force.

(2) The Women's and Children's Institutions (Licensing) Act, 1956 shall not apply to any Children's home special school or observation home established and maintained under this Act.

59. Power to make rules.[3]—(1) The Administrator may, by notification in the Official Gazette, make rules to carry out the purposes of this Act.

(2) In particular and without prejudice to the generality of the foregoing power such rules may provide for all or any of the following matters namely :—

(*a*) the places at which the days on which, the time at which and the manner in which a competent authority may hold its sitting;

(*b*) the procedure to be followed by a competent authority in holding inquiries under this Act; and the mode of the dealing with children suffering from dangerous diseases or mental complaints;

(*c*) the circumstances in which and the conditions subject to which, an institution may be certified as a special school or a children's home or recognised as an observation home, and the certification or recognition withdrawn;

(*d*) the internal management of special schools, children's home and observation homes, [4][and the standards and the nature of services to be maintained by them;]

---

1. Substituted for the words and figures" Chapter XLII of the Code of Criminal Procedure, 1898" by the Children (Amendment) Act (15 of 1978), Section 17 (1.10.1078 in Delhi ; 1.3.1979 in Goa, Daman and Diu and 6.12.1978 in Pondicherry).

2. Substituted for the words and figures and letter Section 29-B and Section 399 of the Code of Criminal Procedure, 1898" by the Children (Amendment) Act (15 of 1978), Section 18 (1.10.1078 in Delhi ; 1.3.1979 in Goa, Daman and Diu and 6.12.1978 in Pondicherry).

3. For Pondicherry Children Rules 56—See Pondi Gaz. Ext. dated 3.12.1966, Fro Manipur Children Rules 1962—See Manipur Gaz. Ext. dated 20.6.1962.

4. Added by the Children (Amendment) Act (15 of 1978 Section 19 (1.10.1978 in Delhi, 1.3.1979 in Goa, Daman and Diu and 6.12.1978 in Pondicherry).

(*e*) the functions sand responsibilities of special schools children's homes and observation homes;

(*f*) the inspection of special schools children's home observation homes and after care organisations;

(*g*) the establishment management and functions of after care organisations the circumstances in which and the conditions subject to which an institution may be recognised as an after care organisation [1][and such other matters as are referred to in Section 12;]

(*h*) the qualifications and duties of probation officers;

(*i*) the recruitment and training of persons appointed to carry out the purposes of this Act and the terms and conditions of their service;

(*j*) the conditions subject to which a girl who is a neglected or delinquent child may be escorted from one place to another and the manner in which a child may be sent outside the jurisdiction of a competent authority;

(*k*) the manner in which contribution for the maintenance of a child may be ordered to be paid by a parent or guardian.

(*l*) the conditions under which a child may be placed out on licence and the form and condition of such licence;

(*m*) the conditions subject to which children may be placed under the care of any parent, guardian or other [2][fit person or fit institution] under this act and the obligations of such [3][persons or institutions] towards the children so placed;

(*n*) any other matter which has to be, or may be, prescribed.

[4][(3) Every rule made under this section shall be laid, as soon as may be after it is made, before each House of Parliament while it is in session for a total period of thirty days which may be comprised in one session or in two or more successive sessions, and if, before the expiry of the session immediately following the session or the successive sessions, aforesaid, both Houses agree in making any modification in the rule or both Houses agree that the rule should not be made the rule shall thereafter have effect only in such modified form or be of no effect as the case may be; so, however, that any such modification or annulment shall be without prejudice to the validity of anything previously done under that rule.

60. Repeal and savings.—If immediately before the date on which this Act comes into force in any area, there is in force in that area, any law corresponding to this Act, that law shall stand repealed on the said date :

---

1. Added by the Children (Amendment) Act (15 of 1978), Section 19 (1.10.1078 in Delhi ; 1.3.1979 in Goa, Daman and Diu and 6.12.1978 in Pondicherry).
2. Substituted for the words, "fit person, and the word persons ibid.
3. Substituted for the words "fit person" and the word persons ibid.
4. Substituted for original sub-section (3), ibid.

Provided that the repeal shall not affect;—

(*a*) the previous operation of any law so repealed or anything duly done or suffered thereunder; or

(*b*) any right privilege, obligation or liability acquired, accrued or incurred under any law so repealed; or

(*c*) any penalty forfeiture or punishment incurred in respect of any offence committed against any law so repealed; or

(*d*) any investigation legal proceedings or remedy in respect of any such right, privilege, obligation liability penalty forfeiture or punishment as aforesaid;

and any such investigation legal proceedings or remedy may be instituted continued or enforced and any such penalty, forfeiture or punishment may be imposed as if this Act had not been passed.

———————

4. THE COMMISSIONS FOR PROTECTION OF CHILD RIGHTS ACT, 2005

(Act No. 4 of 2006)[1]

[20*th January*, 2006].

An Act to provide for the Constitution of a National Commission and State Commissions for Protection of Child Rights and Children's Courts for providing speedy trial of offences against children or of violation of child rights and for matters connected therewith or incident thereto.

Whereas India participated in the United Nations (UN) General Assembly Summit in 1990, which adopted a Declaration on Survival, Protection and Development of Children;

And whereas India has also acceded to the Convention on the Rights of the Child (CRC) on the 11th December, 1992;

And whereas CRC is an international treaty that makes it incumbent upon the signatory States to take all necessary steps to protect children's rights enumerated in the Convention :

And whereas in order to ensure protection of rights of children one of the recent initiatives that the Government have taken for children is the adoption of National Charter for Children, 2003;

And whereas the UN General Assembly Special Session on Children held in May, 2002 adopted an Outcome Document titled, A World Fit for Children containing the goals objectives strategies and activities to be undertaken by the member countries for the current decade;

And whereas it is expedient to enact a law relating to children to give effect to the polices adopted by the Government in this regard, standards prescribed in the CRC, and all other relevant international instruments :

Be it enacted by Parliament in the Fifty-sixth Year of the Republic of India as follows :—

CHAPTER I

PRELIMINARY

1. Short title, extent and commencement.—This Act may be called the Commissions for Protection of Child Rights Act, 2005.

(2) It extends to the whole of India except the State of Jammu and Kashmir.

(3) It shall come into force on such date as the Central Government may, by notification in the Official Gazette appoint.

2. Definitions.—In this Act, unless the context otherwise requires,—

(*a*) "*Chairperson*" means the Chairperson of the Commission or of the State Commission as the case may be;

---

1. Received the assent of the President on 20th January, 2006.

(*b*) "*child rights*" includes the children's right adopted in the United Nations convention on the Rights of the Child on the 20th November, 1989 and ratified by the Government of India on the 11th December, 1992;

(*c*). "*Commission*" means the National Commission for Protection of Child Rights constituted under Section 3;

(*d*) "*Member*" means a Member of the Commission or of the State Commission, as the case may be, and includes the Chairperson;

(*e*) "*notification*" means a notification published in the Official Gazette;

(*f*) "*prescribed*" means prescribed by rules made under this Act;

(*g*) "*State Commission*" means a State Commission for Protection of Child Rights constituted under Section 17.

CHAPTER II

THE NATIONAL COMMISSION FOR PROTECTION OF CHILD RIGHTS

3. Constitution of National Commission for Protection of Child Rights.—(1) The Central Government shall by notification, constitute a body to be known as the National Commission for Protection of Child Rights to exercise the powers conferred on and to perform the functions assigned to it, under this Act.

(2) The Commission shall consist of the following Members, namely :—

(*a*) a Chairperson who is a person or eminence and has done outstanding work for promoting the welfare of children; and

(*b*) six Members out of which at least two shall be women, from the following fields, to be appointed by the Central Government from amongst persons of eminence, ability integrity, standing and experience in,—

(*i*) education;

(*ii*) child health, care, welfare or child development;

(*iii*) juvenile justice or care of neglected or marginalized children or children with disabilities;

(*iv*) elimination of child labour or children in distress;

(*v*) child psychology or sociology; and

(*vi*) law relating to children.

(3) The office of the Commission shall be at Delhi.

4. Appointment of Chairperson and Members.—The Central Government shall by notification, appoint the Chairperson and other Members :

Provided that the Chairperson shall be appointed on the recommendation of a three member Selection Committee constituted by the Central Government under the Chairmanship of the [1][Minister in-charge of the Ministry or the Department of Women and Child Development].

---

1. Subs. by Act 4 of 2007, Section 2 (w.e.f. 29.12.2006) for "Minister in-charge of the Ministry of Human Resource Development.

5. Term of Office and conditions of service of Chairperson and Members.—(1) The Chairperson and every Member shall hold office as such for a term of three years from the date on which he assumes office :

Provided that no Chairperson or a Member shall hold the office for more than two terms :

Provided further that no Chairperson or any other Member shall hold office as such after he has attained—

(*a*) in the case of the Chairperson, the age of sixty-five years; and

(*b*) in the case of a Member, the age of sixty years.

(2) The Chairperson or a Member may, by writing under his hand addressed to the Central Government, resign his office at any time.

6. Salary and allowances, or Chairperson and Members.—The salary and allowances payable to, and other terms and conditions of service of, the Chairperson and Members, shall be such, as may be, prescribed by the Central Government :

Provided that neither the salary and allowances nor the other terms and conditions of service of the Chairperson or a Member, as the case may be shall be varied to his disadvantage after his appointment.

7. Removal from office.—(1) Subjects to the provisions of sub-section (2), the Chairperson may be removed from his office by an order of the Central Government on the ground of proved misbehaivour or incapacity.

(2) Notwithstanding anything contained in sub-section (1), the Central Government may by order remove from office the Chairperson or any other Member, if the Chairperson, or as the case may be, such other Member,—

(*a*) is adjudged an insolvent; or

(*b*) engages during his term of office in any paid employment outside the duties of his office; or

(*c*) refuses to act or becomes incapable of acting; or

(*d*) is of unsound mind and stands so declared by a competent Court; or

(*e*) has so abused his office as to render his continuance in office detrimental to the public interest; or

(*f*) is convicted and sentenced to imprisonment for an offence which in the opinion of the Central Government involves moral turpitude; or

(*g*) is without obtaining leave of absence from the Commission, absent from three consecutive meetings of the Commission.

(3) No person shall be removed under this section until that person has been given an opportunity of being heard in the matter.

8. Vacation of office by Chairperson or Member.—(1) If the Chairperson or, as the case may be, a Member,—

(*a*) becomes subject to any of the disqualifications mentioned in Section 7; or (*b*) tenders his resignation under sub-section (2) of Section 5,

his seat shall thereupon become vacant.

(2) If a casual vacancy occurs in the office of the Chairperson or a Member, whether by reason of his death, resignation or otherwise, such vacancy shall be filed within a period of ninety days by making afresh appointment in accordance with the provisions of Section 4 and the person so appointed shall hold office for the remainder of the term of office for which the Chairperson or a Member, as the case may be, in whose place he is so appointed would have held that office.

9. Vacancies, etc. not to invalidate proceedings of Commission.—No act or proceeding of the Commission shall be invalid merely be reason of—

(*a*) any vacancy in or any defect in the constitution of the Commission; or

(*b*) any defect in the appointment of a person as the Chairperson or a Member; or

(*c*) any irregularity in the procedure of the Commission not affecting the merits of the case.

10. Procedure for transaction of business.—(1) The Commission shall meet regularly at its office at such time as the Chairperson thinks fit, but three months shall not intervene between its last and the next meeting;

(2) All decisions at a meeting shall be taken by majority :

Provided that in the case of equality of votes, the Chairperson, or in his absence the person presiding shall have and exercise a second or casting vote.

(3) If for any reason, the Chairperson, is unable to attend the meeting of the Commission, any member chosen by the Members present from amongst themselves at the meeting shall preside.

(4) The Commission shall observe such rules of procedure in the transaction of its business at a meeting, including the quorum at such meeting, as may be prescribed by the Central Government.

(5) All orders and decisions of the Commission shall be authenticated by the Member Secretary or any other officer of the Commission duly authorised by Member-Secretary in this behalf.

11. Member-Secretary, officers and other employee of Commission.—(1) The Central Government shall, by notification appoint an officer not below the rank of the Joint Secretary or the Additional Secretary to the Government of India as a Member-Secretary of the Commission and shall make available to the Commission, such other officers and employees as may be necessary for the efficient performance of its functions.

(2) The Member-Secretary shall be responsible fore the proper administration of the affairs of the Chairperson and its day-to-day management and shall exercise and discharge such other powers and perform such other duties as may be prescribed by the Central Government.

(3) The salary and allowances payable to and the other terms and conditions of

service of the Member-Secretary, other officers and employees appointed for the purpose of the Commission shall be such as may be prescribed by the Central Government.

12. Salaries and allowances to be paid out of grants.—The salaries an allowances payable to the Chairperson and Members and the administrative expenses, including salaries allowances and pensions payable to the Member-Secretary other officers and employees referred to in Section 11, shall be paid out of th grants referred to in sub-section (1) of Section 27.

CHAPTER III

FUNCTIONS AND POWERS OF THE COMMISSION

13. Functions of Commission.—(1) The Commission shall perform or any of the following functions namely :—

(*a*) examine and review the safeguards provided by or under any law for the time being in force for the protection of child rights and recommend measures for their effective implementation;

(*b*) present to the Central Government, annually and a such other intervals as the Commission may deem fit, reports, upon the working of those safeguards;

(*c*) inquire into violation of child rights and recommend initiation of proceedings in such case;

(*d*) examine all factors that inhibit the enjoyment of rights of children affected by terrorism, communal violence, riots natural disaster, domestic violence, HIV/AIDS, trafficking maltreatment, torture and exploitation, pornography and prostitution and recommend appropriate remedial measures;

(*e*) look into the matters relating to children in need of special care and protection including children in distress, marginalized and disadvantaged children, children in conflict with law, juveniles children without family and children of prisoners and recommend appropriate remedial measures;

(*f*) study treaties and other international instruments and undertake periodical review of existing polices programmes and other activities on child rights and make recommendations for their effective implementation in the best interest of children;

(*g*) undertake and promote research in the filed of child rights;

(*h*) spread child rights literacy among various sections of the society and promote awareness of the safeguards available for protection of these rights through publications the media, seminars and other available means;

(*i*) inspect of cause to be inspected any juvenile custodial home or any other place of residence or institution meant for children, under the control of the Central Government or any State Government or any other authority, including any institution run by a social organisation; where children are detained or lodged for the purpose of treatment reformation or protection and take up with these authorities for remedial action, if found necessary;

(*j*) inquiry into complaints and take *suo motu* notice of matters relating to,—

(*i*) deprivation and violation of child rights;

(*ii*) non-implementation of laws providing for protection and development of children;

(*iii*) non-compliance of policy decisions, guidelines or instructions aimed at mitigating hardships to and ensuring welfare of the children and to provide relief to such children.

or take up the issues arising out of such matters with appropriate authorities; and

(*k*) such other functions as it may consider necessary for the promotion of child rights and any other matter incidental to the above functions.

(2) The Commission shall not inquire into any matter which is pending before a State Commission or any other Commission duly constituted under any law for the time being in force.

14. Powers relating to inquiries.—(1) The complainant shall, while inquiring into any matter referred to in clause (j) of sub-section (1) of Section 13 have all the powers of a civil Court trying a suit under the Code of Civil Procedure, 1908 (5 of 1908) and, in particular, in respect of the following matters, namely :—

(*a*) summoning and enforcing the attendance of any person and examining him on oath;

(*b*) discovery and production of any document;

(*c*) receiving evidence on affidavits;

(*d*) requisitioning any public record or copy thereof from any Court or office; and

(*e*) issuing commissions for the examination of witnesses or documents.

(2) The Commission shall have the power to forward any case to a Magistrate having jurisdiction to try the same and the Magistrate to whom any such case is forwarded shall proceed to hear the complaint against the accused as if the case has been forwarded to him under Section 346 of the Code of Criminal Procedure, 1973 (2 of 1974).

15. Steps after inquiry.—The Commission may take any of the following steps upon the completion of an inquiry held under this Act namely :—

(*i*) where the inquiry discloses the Commission of violation of child rights of a serious nature of contravention of provisions of an law for the time being in force it may recommend to the concerned Government or authority the initiation of proceeding for prosecution or such other action as the Commission may deem fit against the concerned person or persons;

(*ii*) approach the Supreme Court or the High Court concerned for such directions, order or writs as that Court may deem necessary;

(*iii*) recommend to the concerned Government or authority for the grant of such interim relief to the victim or the members of the family as the Commission may consider necessary.

16. Annual and special reports of Commission.—(1) The Commission shall submit an annual report to the Central Government and to the State Government concerned and may at any time submit special reports on a matter which, in its opinion, is of such urgency or impotence that it should not be deferred till submission of the annual report.

(2) The Central Government and the State Government concerned, as the case may be, shall cause the annual and special reports of the Commission to be laid before each House of Parliament or the State Legislature respectively, as the case may be along with a memorandum of action taken or proposed to be taken on the recommendations of the Commission and the reasons for non-acceptance of the recommendations, if any, within a period of one year from the date of receipt of such report.

(3) The annual report shall be prepared in such form, manner and contain such details as may be prescribed by the Central Government.

CHAPTER IV

STATE COMMISSIONS FOR PROTECTION OF CHILD RIGHTS

17. Constitution of State Commission for Protection of Child Rights.—(1) A State Government may constitute a body to be known as the .... (name of the State) Commission for Protection of Child Rights to exercise the powers conferred upon, and to perform the functions assigned to, a State Commission under this chapter.

(2) The State Commission shall consist of the following Members namely :—

(*a*) a Chairperson who is a person of eminence and has done outstanding work for promoting the welfare of children; and

(*b*) six Members out of which a least two shall be women, from the following fields, to be appointed by the State Government from amongst persons of eminence, ability, integrity, standing and experience in,—

(*i*) education;

(*ii*) child health, care welfare or child development;

(*iii*) juvenile justice or care of neglected or marginalized children or children with disabilities;

(*iv*) elimination of child labour or children in distress;

(*v*) child psychology or sociology; and

(*vi*) laws relating to children.

(3) The headquarters of the State Commission shall be at such place as the State Government may, by notification, specify.

18. Appointment of Chairperson and other Members.—The State Government shall, by notification appoint the Chairperson and other Members :

Provided that the Chairperson shall be appointed on the recommendation of a three Member Selection Committee constituted by the State Government under the Chairmanship or the Minister-in-charge of the Department dealing with children.

19. Term of office and conditions of service of Chairperson and Members.—(1) The Chairperson and every Member shall hold office as such for a term of three years from the date on which he assumes office :

Provided that no Chairperson or a Member shall hold the office for more than two terms :

Provided further that no Chairperson or any other Member shall hold office as such after he has attained—

(*a*) in the case of a Chairperson, the age of sixty-five years; and

(*b*) in the case of a Member, the age of sixty years.

(2) The Chairperson or a Member may, by writing under his hand addressed to the State Government, resign his office at any time.

20. Salary allowances of Chairperson and Members.—The salaries and alliances payable to, and other terms and conditions of service of the Chairperson and Members shall be such as may be prescribed by the State Government :

Provided that neither the salary and allowances nor the other terms and conditions of service or the Chairperson or a Member, as the case may be, shall be varied to his disadvantage after his appointment.

21. Secretary, officers and other employees of the State Commission.—(1) The State Government shall, by notification appoint an officer not below the rank of the Secretary to the State Government as the Secretary of the State Commission and shall make available to the State Commission such other officers and employees as may be necessary for the efficient performance of its functions.

(2) The Secretary shall be responsible for the proper administration of the affairs of the State Commission and its day-to-day management and shall exercise and discharge such other powers and perform such other duties as may be prescribed by the State Government.

(3) The salary and allowances payable to, and the other terms and condition of service of the Secretary, other officers and employees, appointed for the purpose of the State Commission shall be such as may be prescribed by the State Government.

22. Salaries and allowances to be paid out of grants.—The salaries and allowances payable to the Chairperson and Members and the administrative expenses, including salaries, allowances and pensions payable to the Secretary, other officers and employees referred to in Section 21, shall be paid out of the grants referred to in sub-section (1) of Section 28.

23. Annual and special reports of State Commission.—(1) The State Commission shall submit an annual report to the State Government and may at any time submit special reports on any matter which, in its opinion, is of such urgency or importance that it should not be deferred till submission of the annual report.

(2) The State Government shall cause all the reports referred to in sub-section (1) to be laid before each Houses of State Legislature, where it consists of two Houses, or where such Legislature consists of one House, before that House along with a memorandum explaining the action taken or proposed to be taken on the recommendation relating to the State and the reasons for the non-acceptance, if any, of any of such recommendations.

(3) The annual report shall be prepared in such form, manner and contain such details as may be prescribed by the State Government.

24. Application of certain provisions relating to National Commission for Protection of Child Rights to State Commission.—The provisions of Sections 7, 8, 9, 10, sub-section (1) of Section 13 and Sections 14 and 15 shall apply to a State Commission and shall have effect, subject to the following modifications namely :—

(*a*) references to "Commission" shall be construed as references to State Commission;

(*b*) reference to "Central Government" shall be construed as references to State Government; and

(*c*) reference to "Member-Secretary" shall be construed as references to "secretary".

CHAPTER V

CHILDREN'S COURTS

25. Children's Court.—For the purpose of providing speedy trial of offences against children or of violation of child rights, the State Government may, with the concurrence of the Chief Justice of the High Court, by notification specify at least a Court in the State or specify for each district a Court of Session to be a Children's Court to try the said offences :

Provided that nothing in this section shall apply if—

(*a*) a Court of Session is already specified as a special Court; or

(*b*) a special Court is already constituted.

for such offences under any other law for the time being in force.

26. Special Public Prosecutor.—For every Children's Court, the State Government shall, by notification specify a Public Prosecutor or appoint an advocate who has been in practice as an advocate for not less than seven years, as a Special Public Prosecutor for the purpose of conducting cases in that Court.

CHAPTER VI

FINANCE, ACCOUNTS AND AUDIT

27. Grants by Central Government.—(1) The Central Government shall after due appropriation made by Parliament by law in this behalf pay to the Commission by way of grants such sums of money as the Central Government may think fit for being utilised for the purposes of this Act.

(2) The Commission may spend such sums of money as it thinks fit for performing the functions under this Act, and such sums shall be treated as expenditure payable out of the grants referred to in sub-section (1).

28. Grants of State Government.—(1) The State Government shall, after due appropriation made by Legislature by law in this behalf pay to the State Commission by way of grants such sums of money as the State Government may think fit for being utilised for the purposes of this Act.

(2) The State Commission may spend such sums of money as it thinks fit for performing the functions under Chapter III of this Act, and such sums shall be treated as expenditure payable out of the grants referred to in sub-section (1).

29. Accounts and audit of Commission.—The Commission shall maintain proper accounts and other relevant records and prepare an annual statement of accounts in such form as may be prescribed by the Central Government in consultation with the Comptroller and Auditor-General of India.

(2) The accounts of the Commission shall be audited by the Comptroller and Auditor-General at such intervals as may be specified by him and any expenditure incurred in connection with such audit shall be payable by the Commission to the Comptroller and Auditor-General.

(3) The Comptroller and Auditor-General and any person appointed by him in connection with he audit of the accounts of the commission under this Act shall have the same rights and privileges and the authority in connection with such audit as the Comptroller and Auditor General generally has in connection with the audit of Government accounts and, in particular shall have the right to demand the production of books, accounts, connection vouchers and other documents and papers and to inspect any of the offices of the Commission.

(4) The accounts of the Commission of as certified by the Comptroller and Auditor-General or any other person appointed by him in this behalf, together with the audit report thereon shall be forwarded annually to the Central Government by the Commission and the Central Government shall cause the audit report to be laid, as soon as may be after it is received, before each House of Parliament.

30. Accounts and audit of State Commission.—(1) The State Commission shall maintain proper accounts and other relevant records an prepare an annual statement of accounts in such form as may be prescribed by the State Government in consultation with the Comptroller and Auditor-General of India.

(2) The accounts of the State Commission shall be audited by the Comptroller and Auditor-General at such intervals as may be specified by his and any expenditure incurred in connection with such audit shall be payable by the State Commission to the Comptroller to the Comptroller and Auditor-General.

(3) The Comptroller and Auditor-General and any person appointed him in connection with th audit of the accounts of the State Commission under this Act

shall, have the same rights and privileges and the authority connection with such audit as the Comptroller and Auditor-General general has in connection with the audit of Government accounts and, in particular, shall have the right to demand the production of books accounts connected vouchers and other documents and papers and to inspect any of the offices of the State Commission.

(4) The accounts of the State Commission as certified by the Comptroller and Auditor-General or any other person appointed by him in this behalf, together with the audit report thereon shall be forwarded annually to the State Government by the State Commission and the State Government shall cause the audit report to be laid, as soon as may be after it is received, before the State Legislature.

CHAPTER VII

MISCELLANEOUS

31. Protection of action taken in good faith.—No suit, prosecution or other legal proceeding shall lie against the Central Government, the State Government the Commission the State Commission, or any Member thereof or any person acting under the direction either of the Central Government, State Government, Commission or the State Commission, in respect of anything which is in good faith done or intended to be done in pursuance of this Act or of any rules made thereunder or in respect of the publication by or under the authority of the Central Government, State Government, Commission or the State Commission of any report or paper.

32. Chairperson, Members and other officers to be public servant.—Every Member of the Commission, State Commission and every officer appointed in the Commission or the State Commission to exercise functions under this Act shall be deemed to be a public servant within the meaning of Section 21 of the Indian Penal Code (45 of 1860).

33. Directions by Central Government.—(1) In the discharge of its functions under this Act, the Commission shall be guided by such directions on questions of policy relating to national purposes as may be given to it by the Central Government.

(2) If any dispute arises between the Central Government and the Commission as to whether a question is or in not a question of policy relating to national purposes, the decision of the Central Government thereon shall be final.

34. Returns or information.—The Commission shall furnish to the Central Government such returns or other information with respect to its activities as the Central Government may, from time to time, require.

35. Power of Central Government to make rules.—(1) The Central Government may, by notification make rules to carry out the provisions of this Act.

(2) In particular, and without prejudice to the generality of the foregoing power, such rules, may provide for all or any of the following matters, namely :—

(*a*) terms and conditions of service of the Chairperson and Members of the Commission and their salaries and allowances under Section 6;

(*b*) the procedure to be followed by the Commission in the transaction of its business of a meeting under sub-section (4) of Section 10 ;

(*c*) the powers and duties which may be exercised and performed by the Member-Secretary of the Commission under sub-section (2) of Section 11 ;

(*d*) the salary and allowances and other terms and conditions of service of officers and other employees of the Commission under sub-section (3) of Section 11 ; and

(*e*) form of the statement of accounts and other records to be prepared by the Commission under sub-section (1) of Section 29.

(3) Every rule made under this Act shall be laid, as soon as may be after it is made, before each House of Parliament, while it is in session for a total period of thirty days which may be comprised in one session or in two or more successive sessions, and if, before the expiry of the session immediately following the session or the successive sessions aforesaid, both Houses agree in making any modification in the rule or both Houses agree that the rule should not be made, the rule shall thereafter have effect only in such modified form or be of no effect, as the case may be ; so, however, that any such modification or annulment shall be without prejudice to the validity of anything previously done under that rule.

36. Power of State Government to make rules.—The State Government may, by notification, make rules to carry out the provisions of this Act.

(2) In particular, and without prejudice to the generality of the foregoing power, such rules may provide for all or any of the following matters, namely:—

(*a*) terms and conditions of service of the Chairperson and Members of the State Commission and their salaries and allowances under Section 20 ;

(*b*) the procedure to be followed by the State Commission in the transaction of its business at a meeting under sub-section (4) of Section 10 read with Section 24 ;

(*c*) the powers and duties which may be exercised and performed by the Secretary of the State Commission under sub-section (2) of Section 21 ;

(*d*) the salary and allowances and other terms and conditions of service of officers and other employees of the State Commission under sub-section (3) of Section 21 ; and

(*e*) form of the statement of accounts and other records to be prepared by the State Commission under sub-section (1) of Section 30.

(3) Every rule made by the State Government under this section shall be laid, as soon as may be after it is made, before each House of the State Legislature where it consists of two Houses, or where such State Legislature consists of one House, before that House.

37. Power to remove difficulties.—(1) If any difficulty arises in giving effect to the provisions of this Act, the Central Government may, by order published in the Official Gazette, make such provisions, not inconsistent with the provisions of this Act, as may appear to be necessary for removing the difficulty :

Provided that no order shall be made under this section after the expiry of the period of two years from the date of commencement of this Act.

(2) Every order made under this section shall be laid, as soon as may be after it is made, before each House of Parliament.

———

5. THE PROTECTION OF HUMAN RIGHTS ACT, 1993[1]

(Act No. 10 of 1994)

[As Amended by Act 43 of 2006]

[*8th January*, 1994]

An Act to provide for the Constitution of a National Human Rights Commission, State Human Rights Commissions in States and Human Rights Courts for better protection of human rights and for matters connected therewith or incidental thereto.

Be it enacted by Parliament in the Forty-fourth Year of the Republic of India as follows :—

CHAPTER I

PRELIMINARY

1. Short title, extent and commencement.—(1) This Act may be called the Protection of Human Rights Act, 1993.

(2) It extends to the whole of India :

Provided that it shall apply to the State of Jammu and Kashmir only in so far as it pertains to the matters relatable to any of the entries enumerated in List I or List III in the Seventh Schedule to the Constitution as applicable to that State.

(3) It shall be deemed to have come into force on the 28th day of September, 1993.

2. Definitions.—(1) In this Act, unless the context otherwise requires:—

(*a*) *"armed forces"* means the naval, military and air forces and includes any other armed forces of the Union ;

(*b*) *"Chair person"* means the Chairperson of the Commission, or of the State Commission as the case may be ;

(*c*) *"Commission"* means the National Human Rights Commission constituted under Section 3 ;

(*d*) *"human rights"* means the rights relating to life, liberty, equality and dignity of the individual guaranteed by the Constitution or embodied in the International Covenants and enforceable by courts in India ;

(*e*) *"Human Rights Court"* means the Human Rights Court specified under Section 30 ;

[2][(*f*) *"International Covenants"* means the International Covenants on Civil and Political Rights and the International Covenants on Economic, Social and Cultural Rights adopted by the General Assembly of the United Nations on the 16th December, 1966 and such other Covenant

1. Gazette of India Part II Section 1, dated 10.1.1994.
2. Cl. (f), subs. by Act 43 of 2006, Section 2(a).

or Convention adopted by the General Assembly of the United Nations as the Central Government may, by notification, specify;]

[1][(*g*) *"Member"* means a Member of the Commission or of the State Commission, as the case may be;]

(*h*) *"National Commission for Minorities"* means the National Commission for Minorities constituted under Section 3 of the National Commission for Minorities Act, 1992 (19 of 1992) ;

[2][(*i*) *"National Commission for the Scheduled Castes"* means, the National Commission for the Scheduled Castes referred to in Article 338 of the Constitution ;

(*i-a*) *"National Commission for the Scheduled Tribes"* means the National Commission for the Scheduled Tribes referred to in Article 338-A of the Constitution;]

(*j*) *"National Commission for Women"* means the National Commission for Women constituted under Section 3 of the National Commission of Women Act, 1990 (20 of 1990) ;

(*k*) *"notification"* means a notification published in the Official Gazette ;

(*l*) *"prescribed"* means prescribed by rules made under this Act ;

(*m*) *"public servant"* shall have the meaning assigned to it in Section 21 of the Indian Penal Code (45 of 1860) ;

(*n*) *"State Commission"* means a State Human Rights Commission constituted under Section 21.

(2) Any reference in this Act to a law, which is not in force in the State of Jammu and Kashmir shall, in relation to that State, be construed as a reference to a corresponding law, if any, in force in that State.

CHAPTER II

THE NATIONAL HUMAN RIGHTS COMMISSION

3. Constitution of a National Human Rights Commission.—(1) The Central Government shall constitute a body to be known as the National Human Rights Commission to exercise the powers conferred upon, and to perform the functions assigned to it under this Act.

(2) The Commission shall consist of—

(*a*) a Chairperson who has been a Chief Justice of the Supreme Court ;

(*b*) one Member who is, or has been, a Chief Justice of the Supreme Court ;

(*c*) one Member who is, or has been, the Chief Justice of a High Court ;

(*d*) two Members to be appointed from amongst persons having knowledge of, or practical experience in, matters relating to human rights.

---

1. Cl. (g), subs. by Act 43 of 2006, Section 2(b).
2. Cl. (i), subs. by Act 43 of 2006, Section 2(c).

(3) The Chairperson of the National Commission for Minorities, [1][the National Commission for the Scheduled Castes, the National Commission for the Scheduled Tribes] and the National Commission for Women shall be deemed to be Members of the Commission for the discharge of functions specified in clauses (b) to (j) of Section 12.

(4) There shall be a Secretary-General who shall be the Chief Executive Officer of the Commission and shall exercise such powers and discharge such functions of the Commission [2][(except judicial functions and the power to make regulations under Section 40-B) as may be delegated to him by the Commissioner or the Chairperson, as the case may be].

(5) The headquarters of the Commission shall be at Delhi and the Commission, may, with the previous approval of the Central Government, establish offices at other places in India.

4. Appointment of Chairperson and other Members.—(1) The Chairperson and [3][The Members] shall be appointed by the President by warrant under his hand and seal :

Provided that every appointment under this sub-section shall be made after obtaining the recommendations of a Committee consisting of—

(*a*)	the Prime Minister	—Chairperson ;
(*b*)	the Speaker of the House of the Peoples	—Member ;
(*c*)	Minister-in-charge of the Ministry of Home Affairs in the Government of India	—Member
(*d*)	Leader of the Opposition in the House of the People	—Member ;
(*e*)	Leader of the Opposition in the Council of States	—Member ;
(*f*)	Deputy Chairman of the Council of States	—Member.

Provided further that no sitting Judge of the Supreme Court or sitting Chief Justice of a High Court shall be appointed except after consultation with the Chief Justice of India.

(2) No appointment of Chairperson or a Member shall be invalid merely by reason of any [4][vacancy of any member in the Committee referred to in the first proviso to sub-section (1)].

[5][**5. Resignation and removal of Chairperson and Members.**—(1) The Chairperson or any Member may, by notice in writing under his hand addressed to the President of India, resign his office.

(2) Subject to the provisions of sub-section (3), the Chairperson or any Member shall only be removed from his office by order of the President of India on the

1. Subs. by Act 43 of 2006, Section 3(a).
2. Subs. by Act 43 of 2006, Section 3(b).
3. Subs. by Act 43 of 2006, Section 4(a).
4. Subs. by Act 43 of 2006, Section 4(b).
5. Subs. by Act 43 of 2006, Section 5.

ground of proved misbehaviour or incapacity after the Supreme Court, on reference being made to it by the President, has, on inquiry held in accordance with the procedure prescribed in that behalf by the Supreme Court, reported that the Chairperson or the other Member, as the case may be, ought on any such ground to be removed.

(3) Notwithstanding anything in sub-section (2), the President, may, by order remove from office the Chairperson or any Member if the Chairperson or such Member , as the case may be,—

(*a*) is adjudged in insolvent ; or

(*b*) engages during his term of office in any paid employment outside the duties of his office ; or

(*c*) is unfit to continue in office by reason of infirmity of mind or body ; or

(*d*) is of unsound mind and stands so declared by a competent Court, or

(*e*) is convicted and sentenced to imprisonment for an offence which in the opinion of the President involves moral turpitude.]

[1][**[6. Term of office of Chairperson and Member.**—(1) A person appointed as Chairperson shall hold office for a term of five years from the date on which he enters upon his office or until he attains the age of seventy years whichever is earlier.

(2) A person appointed as a Member shall hold office for a term of five years from the date on which he enters upon his office and shall be eligible for re-appointment for another term of five years :

Provided that no Member shall hold office after he has attained the age of seventy years.

(3) On ceasing to hold office, a Chairperson or a Member shall be ineligible for further employment under the Government of India or under the Government of any State.]

7. Member to act as Chairperson or to discharge his functions in certain circumstances.—(1) In the event of the occurrence of any vacancy in the office of the Chairperson by reason of his death, resignation or otherwise, the President, may by notification, authorise one of the Members to act as the Chairperson until the appointment of a new Chairperson to fill such vacancy.

(2) When the Chairperson is unable to discharge his functions owing to absence on leave or otherwise, such one of the Members as the President, may, by notification, authorise in this behalf, shall discharge the functions of the Chairperson until the date on which the Chairperson resumes his duties.

[2][**8. Terms and conditions of service of Chairperson and Members.**—The salaries and allowances payable to and other terms and conditions of service of the Chairperson and Member shall be such as may be prescribed.

Provided that neither the salary and allowances nor the other terms and

1. Section 6, Subs. by Act 43 of 2006, Section 6.
2. Subs. by Act 43 of 2006, Section 7.

conditions of service of the Chairperson or a Member shall be varied to his disadvantage after his appointment.]

9. Vacancies, etc. not to invalidate the proceedings of the Commission.—No act or proceedings of the Commission shall be questioned or shall be invalidated merely on the ground of existence of any vacancy or defect in the Constitution of the Commission.

10. Procedure to be regulated by the Commission.—(1) The Commission shall meet at such time and place as the Chairperson may think fit.

[1][(2) Subject to the provisions of this Act and the rules made thereunder, the Commission shall have the power to lay down by regulations its own procedure.]

(3) All orders and decisions of the Commission shall be authenticated by the Secretary-General or any other officer of the Commission duly authorised by the Chairperson in this behalf.

11. Officers and other staff of the Commission.—(1) The Central Government shall make available to the Commission—

(*a*) an officer of the rank of the Secretary to the Government of India who shall be the Secretary-General of the Commission ; and

(*b*) such police and investigative staff under an officer not below the rank of a Director-General of Police and such other officers and staff as may be necessary for the efficient performance of the functions of the Commission.

(2) Subject to such rules as may be made by the Central Government in this behalf, the Commission may appoint such other administrative, technical and scientific staff as it may consider necessary.

(3) The salaries, allowances and conditions of service of the officers and other staff appointed under sub-section (2) shall be such as may be prescribed.

CHAPTER III

FUNCTION AND POWERS OF THE COMMISSION

12. Functions of the Commission.—The Commission shall perform all or any of the following functions, namely:—

(*a*) inquire, *suo motu* or on a petition presented to it by a victim or any person on his behalf, [2][or on a direction or order of any Court] into complaint of—

(*i*) violation of human rights or abatement thereof ; or

(*ii*) negligence in the prevention of such violation, by a public servant ;

(*b*) intervene in any proceedings involving any allegation of violation of human rights pending before a Court with the approval of such Court ;

[3][(*c*) visit, notwithstanding anything contained in any other law for the time

1. Sub-section (2), subs. by Act 43 of 2006, Section 8.
2. Ins. by Act 43 of 2006, Section 9(a).
3. Clause (c), subs. by Act 43 of 2006, Section 9(b).

being in force, any jail or other institution under the control of the State Government, where persons are detained or lodged or purposes of treatment, reformation or protection, for the study of the living conditions of the inmates thereof and make recommendations thereon to the Government.]

(*d*) review the safeguards provided by or under the Constitution or any law for the time being in force for the protection of human rights and recommend measures for their effective implementation :

(*e*) review the factors, including acts of terrorism, that inhibit the enjoyment of human rights and recommend appropriate remedial measures ;

(*f*) study treaties and other international instruments on human rights and make recommendations for their effective implementation ;

(*g*) undertake and promote research in the field of human rights ;

(*h*) spread human rights literacy among various sections of society and promote awareness of the safeguards available for the protection of these rights through publications, the media, seminars and other available means ;

(*i*) encourage the efforts of non-Governmental organisations and institutions working in the field of human rights ;

(*j*) such other functions as it may consider necessary for the promotion of human rights.

13. Power relating to inquiries.—(1) The Commission shall, while inquiring into complaints under this Act, have all the powers of a civil Court trying a suit under the Code of Civil Procedure, 1908 (5 of 1908), and in particular in respect of the following matters namely:—

(*a*) summoning and enforcing the attendance of witnesses and examining them on oath ;

(*b*) discovery and production of any document ;

(*c*) receiving evidence on affidavits ;

(*d*) requisitioning any public record or copy thereof from any Court or office ;

(*e*) issuing commissions for the examination of witnesses or documents ;

(*f*) any other matter which may be prescribed.

(2) The Commission shall have power to require any person, subject to any privilege which may be claimed by that person under any law for the time being in force, to furnish information on such points or matters as, in the opinion of the Commission may be useful for, or relevant to the subject-matter of the inquiry and any person so required shall be deemed to be legally bound to furnish such information within the meaning of Section 176 and Section 177 of the Indian Penal Code (45 of 1860).

(3) The Commission or any other officer, not below the rank of a Gazetted

Officer, specially authorised in this behalf by the Commission, may, enter any building or place where the Commission has reason to believe that any document relating to the subject-matter of the inquiry may be found, and may seize any such document or take extracts or copies therefrom subject to the provisions of Section 100 of the Code of Criminal Procedure, 1973 (2 of 1974), in so far as it may be applicable.

(4) The Commission shall be deemed to be a civil Court and when any offence as is described in Section 175, Section 178, Section 179, Section 180 or Section 228 of the Indian Penal Code (45 of 1860) is committed in the view on presence of the Commission, the Commission, may, after recording the facts constituting the offence and the statement of the accused as provided for in the Code of Criminal Procedure, 1973 (2 of 1974) forward the case to a Magistrate having jurisdiction to try the same and the Magistrate to whom any such case is forwarded shall, proceed to hear the complaint against the accused as if the case has been forwarded to him under Section 346 of the Code of Criminal Procedure, 1973.

(5) Every proceeding before the Commission shall be deemed to be a judicial proceeding within the meaning of Sections 193 and 228 and for the purposes of Section 196, of the Indian Penal Code (45 of 1860), and the Commission shall be deemed to be a civil Court for all the purposes of Section 195 and Chapter XXVI of the Code of Criminal Procedure, 1973 (2 of 1974) ;

[1][(6) Where the Commission considers it necessary or expedient so to do, a may, by order, transfer any complaint filed or pending before it to the State Commission of the State from which the complaint arises, for disposal in accordance with the provisions of this Act :

Provided that no such complaint shall be transferred unless the same is one respecting which the State Commission has jurisdiction to entertain the same.

(7) Every complaint transferred under sub-section (6) shall be dealt with and disposed of by the State Government as if it were a complaint initially filed before it.]

14. Investigation.—(1) The Commission, may, for the purpose of conducting any investigation pertaining to the inquiry, utilise the services of any officer or investigation agency of the Central Government or any State Government with the concurrence of the Central Government or the State Government, as the case may be.

(2) For the purpose of investigating into any matter pertaining to the inquiry, any officer or agency whose services are utilised under sub-section (1), may, subject to the direction and control of the Commission,—

(*a*) summon and enforce the attendance of any person and examine him ;

(*b*) require the discovery and production of any document ; and

(*c*) requisition any public record or copy thereof from any office.

(3) The provisions of Section 15 shall apply in relation to any statement mode

1. Sub-sections (6) and (7), ins. by Act 43 of 2006, Section 10.

by a person before any officer or agency whose services are utilised under sub-section (1) as they apply in relation to any statement made by a person in the course of giving evidence before the Commission.

(4) The officer or agency whose services are utilised under sub-section (1) shall investigate into any matter pertaining to the inquiry and submit a report thereon to the Commission within such period as may be specified by the Commission in this behalf.

(5) The Commission shall satisfy itself about the correctness of the facts stated and the conclusion, if any, arrived at in the report submitted to it under sub-section (4) and for this purpose the Commission may make such inquiry (including the examination of the person or persons who conducted or assisted in the investigation) as it thinks fit.

15. Statement made by persons to the Commission.—No statement made by a person in the course of giving evidence before the Commission shall subject him to, or be used against him in, any civil or criminal proceeding except a prosecution for giving false evidence by such statement :

Provided that the statement—

(*a*) is made in reply to the question which he is required by the Commission to answer ; or

(*b*) is relevant to the subject-matter of the inquiry.

16. Persons likely to be prejudicially affected to be heard.—If, at any stage of the inquiry, the Commission—

(*a*) considers it necessary to inquire into the conduct of any person ; or

(*b*) is of the opinion that the reputation of any person is likely to be prejudicially affected by the inquiry,

it shall give to the person a reasonable opportunity of being heard in the inquiry and to produce evidence in his defence :

Provided that nothing in this section shall apply where the credit of a witness is being impeached.

CHAPTER IV

PROCEDURE

17. Inquiry into complaints.—The Commission while inquiring into the complaints of violation of human rights, may—

(*i*) call for information or report from the Central Government or any State Government or any other authority or organisation subordinate thereto within such time as may be specified by it :

Provided that—

(*a*) if the information or report is not received within the time stipulated by the Commission, it may proceed to inquiry into the complaint on its own ;

(b) if, on receipt of information or report, the Commission is satisfied either that no further inquiry is required or that the required action has been initiated or taken by the concerned Government or authority, it may not proceed with the complaint and inform the complainant accordingly ;

(ii) without prejudice to anything contained in clause (i), if it considers necessary, having regard to the nature of the complaint, initiate an inquiry.

[1][**18. Steps during and after inquiry.**—The Commission, may, take any of the following steps during or upon the completion of an inquiry held under this Act, namely:—

(a) where the inquiry discloses the commission of violation of human rights or negligence in the prevention of violation of human rights or abatement thereof by a public servant, it may recommend to the concerned Government or authority—

(i) to make payment of compensation or damages to the complainant or to the victim or the members of his family as the Commission may consider necessary ;

(ii) to initiate proceedings for prosecution or such other suitable action as the Commissioner may deem fit against the concerned person or persons ;

(iii) to take such further action as it may think fit ;

(b) approach the Supreme Court or the High Court concerned for such directions, orders or writs as that Court may deem necessary ;

(c) recommend to the concerned Government or authority at any stage of the inquiry for the grant of such immediate interim relief to the victim or the members of his family as the Commission may consider necessary ;

(d) subject to the provisions of clause (e), provide a copy of the inquiry report to the petitioner or his representative ;

(e) the Commission shall send a copy of its inquiry report together with its recommendations to the concerned Government or authority and the concerned Government or authority shall, within a period of one month, or such further time as the Commission may allow forward its comments on the report, including the action taken or proposed to be taken thereon, to the Commission ;

(f) the Commission shall publish its inquiry report together with the comments of the concerned Government or authority, if any, and the action taken or proposed to be taken by the concerned Government or authority on the recommendations of the Commission.]

---

1. Section 18, subs. by Act 43 of 2006, Section 11.

19. Procedure with respect to armed forces.—(1) Notwithstanding anything contained in this Act, while dealing with complaints of violation of human rights by members of the armed forces, the Commission shall adopt the following procedure, namely:—

(*a*) it may, either on its own motion or on receipt of a petition, seek a report from the Central Government ;

(*b*) after the receipt of the report, it may, either not proceed with the complaint or, as the case may be, make its recommendations to that Government.

(2) The Central Government shall inform the Commission of the action taken on the recommendations within three months or such further time as the Commission may allow.

(3) The Commission shall publish its report together with its recommendations made to the Central Government and the action taken by that Government on such recommendations.

(4) The Commission shall provide a copy of the report published under sub-section (3) to the petitioner or his representative.

20. Annual and special reports of the Commission.—(1) The Commission shall submit an annual, report to the Central Government and to the State Government concerned and, may, at any time submit special reports on any matter which, in its opinion, is of such urgency or importance that it should not be deferred till submission of the annual report.

(2) The Central Government and the State Government, as the case may be, shall cause the annual and special reports of the Commission to be laid before each House of Parliament or the State Legislature, respectively, as the case may be, along with a memorandum of action taken or proposed to be taken on the recommendations of the Commission and the reasons for non-acceptance of the recommendations, if any.

CHAPTER V

STATE HUMAN RIGHTS COMMISSIONS

21. Constitution of State Human Rights Commissions.—(1) A State Government, may constitute a body to be known as the.... (name of the State) Human Rights Commission to exercise the powers conferred upon, and to perform the functions assigned to, a State Commission under this Chapter.

[1][(2) The State Commission on shall, with effect from such date as the State Government may by notification specify, consist of—

(*a*) A Chairperson who has been a Chief Justice of a High Court ;

(*b*) One Member who is, or has been, a Judge of a High Court or District

---

1. Sub-section (2), subs. by Act 43 of 2006, Section 12(a).

Judge in the State with a minimum of seven years experience as District Judge ;

(*c*) One Member to be appointed from among persons having knowledge of or practical experience in matters relating to human rights.]

(3) There shall be a Secretary who shall be the Chief Executive Officer of the State Commission and shall exercise such powers and discharge such functions of the State Commission as it may delegate to him.

(4) The headquarters of the State Commission shall be at such place as the State Government, may, by notification, specify.

(5) A State Commission may inquire into violation of human rights only in respect of matters relatable to any of the entries enumerated in List II and List III in the Seventh Schedule to the Constitution :

Provided that in any such matter is already being inquired into by the Commission or any other Commission duly constituted under any law for the time being in force, the State Commission shall not inquire into the said matter :

Provided further that in relation to the Jammu and Kashmir Human Rights Commission, this sub-section shall have effect as if that for the words and figures "Last II and List III in the Seventh Schedule to the Constitution", the words and figures "List III in the Seventh Schedule to the Constitution as applicable to the State of Jammu and Kashmir and, in respect of matters in relation to which the Legislature of that State has power to make laws" had been substituted.

[1][(6) Two or more State Governments may, with the consent of a Chairperson or Member of a State Commission, appoint such Chairperson or, as the case may be, such Member of another State Commission simultaneously if such Chairperson or Member consents to such appointment :

Provided that every appointment made under this sub-section shall be made after obtaining the recommendations of the Committee referred to in sub-section (1) of Section 22 in respect of the State for which a common Chairperson or Member, or both, as the case may be, is to be appointed.]

22. Appointment of Chairperson and [2][Members] of State Commission.—(1) The Chairperson and [3][Members] shall be appointed by the Governor by warrant under this hand and seal :

Provided that every appointment under this sub-section shall be made after obtaining the recommendation of a Committee consisting of,—

(*a*) the Chief Minister —Chairperson ;

(*b*) Speaker of the Legislative Assembly —Member ;

(*c*) Minister-in-charge of the Department of Home in that State —Member ;

1. Ins. by Act 43 of 2006, Section 12(b).
2. Subs. by Act 43 of 2006, Section 13(a).
3. Subs. by Act 43 of 2006, Section 13(a).

(*d*) Leader of the Opposition in the Legislative Assembly—Member ;

Provided further that when there is a Legislative Council in a State, the Chairman of that Council and the Leader of the Opposition in that Council shall also be members of the Committee :

Provided also that no sitting Judge of a High Court or a sitting District Judge shall be appointed except after consultation with the Chief Justice of the High Court of the concerned State.

(2) No appointment of a Chairperson or a Member of the State Commission shall be invalid merely by reason of [1][any vacancy of any Member in the Committee referred to in sub-section (1)].

23. [2]**[Resignations and Removal of Chairperson or a Member of the State Commission.]**—[3][(1) The Chairperson or a Member of a State Commission may, by notice in writing under his hand addressed to the Governor, resign his office.

(1-A) Subject to the provisions of sub-section (2), the Chairperson or any Member of the State Commission shall only be removed from his office by order of the President on the ground of proved misbehaviour or incapacity after the Supreme Court, on a reference being made to it by the President, has, on inquiry held in accordance with the procedure prescribed in that behalf by the Supreme Court, reported that the Chairperson or such Member, as the case may be, ought on any such ground to be removed.]

(2) Notwithstanding anything in [4][sub-section (1A)], the President, may, by order remove from office the Chairperson or any [5][Member] if the Chairperson or such [6][Member] as the case may be,—

(*a*) is adjudged an insolvent ; or

(*b*) engages during his term of office in any paid employment outside the duties of his office, or

(*c*) is unit to continue in office by reason of infirmity of mind or body ; or

(*d*) is of unsound mind and stands so declared by a competent Court ; or

(*e*) is convicted and sentenced to imprisonment for an offence which in the opinion of the President involves moral turpitude :

[7]**[24. Term of office of Chairperson and Members of the State Commission.**—(1) A person appointed as Chairperson shall hold office for a term of five years from the date on which he enters upon his office or until he actions the age of seventy years, whichever is earlier.

(2) A person appointed as a Member shall hold office for a term of five years

1. Subs. by Act 43 of 2006, Section 13(c).
2. Subs. by Act 43 of 2006, Section 14(a).
3. Subs. by Act 43 of 2006, Section 14(b).
4. Subs. by Act 43 of 2006, Section 14(c)(a).
5. Subs. by Act 43 of 2006, Section 14(c)(b).
6. Subs. by Act 43 of 2006, Section 14(c)(b).
7. Subs. by Act 43 of 2006, Section 15.

from the date on which he enters upon his office and shall be eligible for re-appointment for another term of five years :

Provided that no Member shall hold office after he has attained the age of seventy years.

(3) On ceasing to hold office, a Chairperson or a Member shall be ineligible for further employment under the Government of a State or under the Government of India.

25. Members to act as Chairperson or to discharge his functions in certain circumstances.—(1) In the event of the occurrence of any vacancy in the office of the Chairperson by reason of his death, resignation or otherwise, the Governor, may, by notification, authorise one of the Members to act as the Chairperson until the appointment of a new Chairperson to fill such vacancy.

(2) When the Chairperson is unable to discharge his functions owing to absence on leave or otherwise, such one of the Members as the Governor, may by notification, authorise in this behalf, shall discharge the functions of the Chairperson until the date on which the Chairperson resumes his duties.

[1][**26. Terms and conditions of service of Chairperson and Members of State Commissions.**—The salaries and allowances payable to, and other terms and convictions of service of, the Chairperson and Members shall be such as may be prescribed by the State Government :

Provided that neither the salary and allowances nor the other terms and conditions of service of the Chairperson or a Member shall be varied to his disadvantage after his appointment.]

27. Officers and others staff of the State Commission.—(1) The State Government shall make available to the Commission—

(*a*) an officer not below the rank of a secretary to the State Government who shall be the Secretary of the State Commission ; and

(*b*) such police and investigative staff under an officer not below the rank of an Inspector-General of Police and such other officers and staff as may be necessary for the efficient performance of the function of the State Commission.

(2) Subject to such rules as may be made by the State Government in this behalf, the State Commission, may, appoint such other administrative, technical and scientific staff as it may consider necessary.

(3) The salaries, allowances and conditions of service of the officers and other staff appointed under sub-section (2) shall be such as may be prescribed by the State Government.

28. Annual and special reports of State Commission.—(1) The State Commission shall submit an annual report to the State Government, and, may, at any time submit special reports on any matter which in its opinion, is of such urgency or importance that it should not be deferred till submission of the annual report.

1. Subs. by Act 43 of 2006, Section 16.

(2) the State Government shall cause the annual and special reports of the State Commission to be laid before each House of State Legislature where it consists of two Houses, or where such Legislature consists of one House, before that House along with a memorandum of action taken or proposed to be taken on the recommendations of the State Commission and the reasons for non-acceptance of the recommendations, if any.

29. Application of certain provisions relating to National Human Rights Commission to State Commission.—The provisions of Sections 9, 10, 12, 13, 14, 15, 16, 17 and 18 shall apply to a State Commission and shall have effect, subject to the following modifications, namely:—

(*a*) references to "Commission" shall be construed as references to "State Commission" ;

(*b*) in Section 10, in sub-section (3), for the words "Secretary-General", the word "Secretary" shall be substituted ;

(*c*) in Section 12, clause (f) shall be omitted ;

(*d*) in Section 17, in clause (i), the words "Central Government or any" shall be omitted.

CHAPTER VI

HUMAN RIGHTS COURTS

30. Human Rights Courts.—For the purpose of providing for speedy trial of offences arising out of violation of human rights, the State Government, may, with the concurrence of the Chief Justice of the High Court, by notification, specify for each district a Court of Session to be a Human Rights Court to try the said offences :

Provided that nothing in this section shall apply if—

(*a*) a Court of Session is already specified as a special Court ; or

(*b*) a special Court is already constituted ;

for such offences under any other law for the time being in force.

31. Special Public Prosecutor.—For every Human Rights Court, the State Government shall, by notification, specify a Public Prosecutor or appoint an advocate who has been in practice as an advocate for not less than seven years, as a Special Public Prosecutor for the purpose of conducting cases in that Court.

CHAPTER VII

FINANCE, ACCOUNTS AND AUDIT

32. Grants by the Central Government.—(1) The Central Government shall, after due appropriation made by Parliament by law in this behalf, pay to the Commission by way of grants such sums of money as the Central Government may think fit for being utilised for the purposes of this Act.

(2) The Commission, may, spend such sums as it thinks fit for performing the functions under this Act, and such sums shall be treated as expenditure payable out of the grants referred to in sub-section (1).

33. Grants by the State Government.—(1) The State Government shall, after due appropriation made by Legislature by law in this behalf, pay to the State Commission by way of grants such sums of money as the State Government may think fit for being utilised for the purposes of this Act.

(2) The State Commission may spend such sums as it thinks fit for performing the functions under Chapter V, and such sums shall be treated as expenditure payable out of the grants referred to in sub-section (1).

34. Accounts and audit.—(1) The Commission shall maintain proper accounts and other relevant records and prepare an annual statement of accounts in such form as may be prescribed by the Central Government in consultation with the Comptroller and Auditor-General of India;

(2) The accounts of the Commission shall be audited by the Comptroller and Auditor-General at such intervals as may be specified by him and any expenditure incurred in connection with such audit shall be payable by the Commission to the Comptroller and Auditor-General.

(3) The Comptroller and Auditor-General and any person appointed by him in connection with the audit of the accounts of the Commission under this Act shall have the same rights and privileges and the authority in connection with such audit as the Comptroller and Auditor-General generally has in connection with the audit of Government accounts and, in particular, shall have the right to demand the production of books, accounts, connected vouchers and other documents and papers and to inspect any of the offices of the Commission.

(4) The accounts of the Commission as certified by the Comptroller and Auditor-General or any other person appointed by him in this behalf, together with the audit report thereon shall be forwarded annually to the Central Government by the Commission and the Central Government shall cause the audit report to be laid, as soon as may be, after it is received, before each House of Parliament.

35. Accounts and audit of State Commission.—(1) The State Commission shall maintain proper and other relevant records and prepare an annual statement of accounts in such form as may be prescribed by the State Government in consultation with the Comptroller and Auditor-General of India.

(2) The accounts of the State Commission shall be audited by the Comptroller and Auditor-General at such intervals as may be specified by him and any expenditure incurred in connection with such audit shall be payable by the State Commission to the Comptroller and Auditor-General.

(3) The Comptroller and Auditor-General and any person appointed by him in connection with the audit of the accounts of the State Commission under this Act shall have the same rights and privileges and the authority in connection with such audit as the Comptroller and Auditor-General generally has in connection with the audit of Government accounts and, in particular, shall have the right to demand the production of books, accounts connected vouchers and other documents and papers and to inspect any of the offices of the State Commission.

(4) The accounts of the State Commission as certified by the Comptroller and Auditor-General or any other person appointed by him in this behalf, together with the audit report thereon, shall be forwarded annually to the State Government by the State Commission and the State Government shall cause the audit report to be laid, as soon as may be, after it is received, before the State Legislature.

CHAPTER VIII

MISCELLANEOUS

36. Matters not subject to jurisdiction of the Commission.—(1) The Commission shall not inquire into any matter which is pending before a State Commission on any other Commission duly constituted under any law for the time being in force.

(2) The Commission or the State Commission shall not inquire into any matter after the expiry of one year from the date on which the act constituting violation of human rights is alleged to have been committed.

37. Constitution of special investigation terms.—Notwithstanding anything contained in any other law for the time being in force, where the Government considers it necessary so to do, it may constitute one or more special investigation teams, consisting of such police officers as it thinks necessary for purposes of investigation and prosecution of offences arising out of violations of human rights.

38. Protection of action taken in good faith.—No suit or other legal proceeding shall lie against the Central Government, State Government Commission the State Commission or any Member thereof or any person acting under the direction either of the Central Government. State Government Commission or the State Commission in respect of anything which is in good faith done or intended to be done in pursuance of this Act or of any rules or any order made thereunder or in respect of the publication by or under the authority of the Central Government, State Government Commission or the State Commission of any report, paper or proceedings.

39. Members and officers to be public servants.—Every Member of Commission, State Commission and every officer appointed or authorised the Commission or the State Commission to exercise functions under this shall be deemed to be a public servant within the meaning of Section 21 of Indian Penal Code (45 of 1860).

40. Power of Central Government to make rules.—(1) The Central Government may by notification make rules to carry out the provision of this Act.

(2) In particular and without prejudice to the generality of the foregoing power such rules may provide for all or any of the following matter namely :—

(*a*) the salaries and allowances and other terms and condition service of the [1][Chairperson and Members) under Section 8;

(*b*) the conditions subject to which other administrative, technical and

1. Subs. by Act 43 of 2006, Sec. 17.

scientific staff may be appointed by the Commission and salaries and allowances of officers and other staff under sub-section (3) of Section 11;

(*c*) any other power of a civil Court required to be prescribed of clause (f) of sub-section (1) of Section 13;

(*d*) the form in which the annual statement of accounts is to be passed by the Commission under sub-section (1) of Section 34;

(*e*) any other matter which has to be or may be, prescribed.

(3) Every rule made under this Act shall be laid, as soon as may be, it is made, before each House of Parliament, while it is in session, for a period of thirty days which may be comprised in one session or in the more successive sessions and if, before the expiry of the session immed following the session or the successive sessions aforesaid both Houses in making any modification in the rule or both Houses agree that the should not be made, the rule shall thereafter have effect only in such more form or be of no effect, as the case may be, so, however, that any modification or annulment shall be without prejudice to the valid anything previously done under that rule.

[1][**40-A. Power to make rules retrospectively.**—The power to make under Clause (b) of sub-section (2) of Section 40 shall include the power make such rules or any of them retrospectively from a date not earlier the date on which this Act received the assent of the President, but not retrospective effect shall be given to any such rule so as to prejudicially the interest of any person to whom such rule may be applicable.]

[2][**40-B. Power of Commission to make regulations.**—(1) Subject provision of this Act and the rules made thereunder, the Commission with the previous approval of the Central Government, by notification regulations to carry out the provisions of this Act.

(2) In particular and without prejudice to the generality of the for power such regulations may provide for all or any of the following matter namely :—

(*a*) the procedure to be followed by the Commission under sub-section (2) of Section 10;

(*b*) the returns and statistics to be furnished by the State Commission;

(*c*) any other matter which has to be, or may be, specified by regulations.

(3) Every regulation made by the Commission under this Act shall be laid, as soon as may be, it is made, before each House of Parliament, while it is in session, for a total period of thirty days which may be comprised in one session or in the more successive sessions and if, before the expiry of the session or the successive sessions aforesaid both Houses agree in making any modification in the regulation

1. Inserted by Act 49 of 2000, Sec. 2 (w.e.f. 11.12.2000).
2. Ins. by Act 43 of 2006, Sec. 18.

or both Houses agree that the regulation should not be made, the regulation shall thereafter have effect only in such modified form or be of no effect, as the case may be, so, however, that any such modification or annulment shall be without prejudice to the validity anything previously done under that regulation.

41. Power of State Government to make rules.—(1) The State Government may, by notification make rules to carry out the provisions of this Act.

(2) In particular and without prejudice to the generality of the foregoing power, such rules may provide for all or any of the following mattes, namely :—

(*a*) the salaries and allowances and other terms and condition of service of the Members under Section 26;

(*b*) the conditions subject to which other administrative, technical and scientific staff may be appointed by the State Commission and salaries and allowances of officers and other staff under sub-section (3) of Section 27;

(*c*) the form in which the annual statement of accounts is to be prepared under sub-section (1) of Section 35.

(3) Every rule made by the State Government under this section shall be laid as soon as may, be after it is made, before each House of the State Legislature, where it consists of two Houses or where such Legislature consists of one House, before that House.

42. Power to remove difficulties.—(1) If any difficulty arises in giving effect to the provisions of this Act, the Central Government may by order published in the Official Gazette make such provisions not inconsistent with the provisions of this Act as appear to it to be necessary or expedient for removing the difficulty :

Provided that no such order shall be made after expiry of the period of two years from the date of commencement of this Act.

(2) Every order made under this section shall, as soon as may be, after it is made by laid before each House of Parliament.

43. Repeal and savings.—(1) The Protection of Human Rights Ordinance, 1993 (Order XXX of 1993) is hereby repealed.

(2) Notwithstanding such repeal, anything done or nay action taken under the said ordinance, shall be deemed to have been done or taken under the corresponding provisions of this Act.

——————

APPENDIX 1

THE JUVENILE JUSTICE (CARE AND PROTECTION OF CHILDREN) ACT, 2000

(56 OF 2000)

[30th December, 2000]

An Act to consolidate and amend the law relating to juveniles in conflict with law and children in need of care and protection, by providing for proper care, protection and treatment by catering to their development needs, and by adopting a child-friendly approach in the adjudication and disposition of matters in the best interest of children and for their ultimate rehabilitation through various institutions established under this enactment.

WHEREAS the Constitution has, in several provisions, including clause (3) of article 15, clauses (*e*) and (*f*) of article 39, articles 45 and 47, impose on the State a primary responsibility of ensuring that all the needs of children are met and that their basic human rights are fully protected;

AND WHEREAS, the General Assembly of the United Nations has adopted the Convention on the Rights of the Child on the 20th November, 1989;

AND WHEREAS, the Convention on the Rights of the Child has prescribed a set of standards to be adhered to by all State parties in securing the best interests of the child;

AND WHEREAS, the Convention on the Rights of the Child emphasises social reintegration of child victims, to the extent possible, without resorting to judicial proceedings;

AND WHEREAS, the Government of India has ratified the Convention on the 11th December, 1992.

AND WHEREAS, it is expedient to re-enact the existing law relating to juveniles bearing in mind the standards prescribed in the Convention on the Rights of the Child, the United Nations Standard Minimum Rules for the Administration of Juvenile Justice, 1985 (the Beijing rules), the United Nations Rules for the Protection of Juveniles Deprived of their Liberty (1990), and all other relevant international instruments.

BE it enacted by Parliament in the Fifty-first Year of the Republic of India as follows:

CHAPTER I
PRELIMINARY

1. Short title, extent and commencement.—(1) This Act may be called the Juvenile Justice (Care and Protection of Children) Act, 2000.

(2) it extends to the Whole of India except the State of Jammu and Kashmir.

(3) It shall come into force on such date as the Central Government may, by notification in the Official Gazette, appoint.

2. Definitions.—In this Act, unless the context otherwise requires,—

(*a*) "*advisory board*" means a Central or a state advisory board or a district and city level advisory board, as the case may be, constituted under section 62;

(*b*) "*begging*" means—

(*i*) soliciting or receiving alms in a public place or entering into any private premises for the purpose of soliciting or receiving alms, whether under any pretence;

(*ii*) exposing or exhibiting with the object of obtaining or extorting alms, any sore, wound, injury, deformity or disease, whether of himself or of any other person or of an animal;

(*c*) "*Board*" means a Juvenile Justice Board constituted under section 4;

(*d*) "child in need of care and protection" means a child —

(*i*) who is found without any home or settled place or abode and without any ostensible means of subsistence,

(*ii*) who resides with a person (whether a guardian of the child or not) and such person—

(*a*) has threatened to kill or injure the child and there is a reasonable likelihood of the threat being carried out, or

(*b*) has killed, abused or neglected some other child or children and there is a reasonable likelihood of the child in question being killed, abused or neglected by that person,

(*iii*) who is mentally or physically challenged or ill children or children suffering from terminal diseases or incurable diseases having no one to support or look after,

(*iv*) who has a parent or guardian and such parent or guardian is unfit or incapacitated to exercise control over the child,

(*v*) who does not have parent and no one is willing to take care of or whose parents have abandoned him or who is missing and run away child and whose parents cannot be found after reasonable injury,

(*vi*) who is being or is likely to be grossly abused, tortured or exploited for the purpose of sexual abuse or illegal acts,

(vii) who is found vulnerable and is likely to be inducted into drug abuse or trafficking,

(viii) who is being or is likely to be abused for unconscionable gains,

(ix) who is victim of any armed conflict, civil commotion or natural calamity;

(e) *"children's home"* means an institution established by a State Government or by voluntary organisation and certified by that Government under section 34;

(f) *"Committee"* means a Child Welfare Committee constituted under section 29;

(g) *"competent authority"* means in relation to children in need of care and protection a Committee and in relation to juveniles in conflict with law a Board;

(h) *"fit institution"* means a governmental or a registered non-governmental organisation or a voluntary organisation prepared to own the responsibility of a child and such organisation is found fit by the competent authority;

(i) *"fit person"* means a person, being a social worker or any other person, who is prepared to own the responsibiliy of a child and is found fit by the competent authority to receive and take care of the child;

(j) *"guardian"*, in relation to a child, means his natural guardian or any other person having the actual charge or control over the child and recognised by the competent authority as a guardian in course of proceedings before that authority;

(k) *"juvenile"* or *"child"* means a person who has not completed eighteenth year of age;

(l) *"juvenile in conflict with law"* means a juvenile who is alleged to have committed an offence;

(m) *"local authority"* means Panchayats at the village and Zila Parishad at the district level and shall also include a Municipal Committee or Corporation or a Cantonment Board or such other body legally entitled to function as local authority by the Government;

(n) *"narcotic drug"* and "psychotropic substance" shall have the meanings respectively assigned to them in the Narcotic Drugs and Psychotropic Substances Act, 1985 (61 of 1985);

(o) *"observation home"* means a home established by a State Government or by a voluntary organisation and certified by that State Government under section 8 as an observation home for the juvenile in conflict with law;

(p) *"offence"* means an offence punishable under any law for the time being in force;

(*q*) "*place of safety*" means any place or institution (not being a police lock-up or jail), the person incharge of which is willing temporarily to receive and take care of the juvenile and which, in the opinion of the competent authority, may be a place of safety for the juvenile;

(*r*) "*prescribed*" means prescribed by rules made under this act;

(*s*) "*Probation officer*" means an officer appointed by the State Government as a probation officer under the Probation of Offenders Act, 1958 (20 of 1958);

(*t*) "*public place*" shall have the meaning assigned to it in the Immoral Traffic (Prevention) Act, 1956 (104 of 1956);

(*u*) "*shelter home*" means a home or a drop-in-centre set up under section 37;

(*v*) "*special home*" means an institution established by a State Government or by a voluntary organisation and certified by that Government under section 9;

(*w*) "*special juvenile police unit*" means a unit of the police force of a State designated for handling of juveniles or children under section 63;

(*x*) "*State Government*", in relation to a Union territory, means the Administrator of that Union territory appointed by the President under article 239 of the Constitution;

all words and expressions used but not defined in this Act and defined in the Code of Criminal Procedure, 1973 (2 of 1974), shall have the meanings respectively assigned to them in that code.

3. Continuation of Inquiry in respect of juvenile who has ceased to be a juvenile.—Where an inquiry has been initiated against a juvenile in conflict with law or a child in need of care and protection and during the course of such inquiry the juvenile or the child ceases to be such, then, notwithstanding anything contained in this Act or in any other law for the time being in force, the inquiry may be continued and orders may be made in respect of such person as if such person had continued to be a juvenile or a child.

CHAPTER II

JUVENILE IN CONFLICT WITH LAW

4. Juvenile Justice Board.—(1) Notwithstanding anything contained in the Code of Criminal Procedure, 1973 (2 of 1974), the State Government may, by notification in the Official Gazette, constitute for a district or a group of districts specified in the notification, one or more Juvenile Justice Boards for exercising the powers and discharging the duties conferred or imposed on such Boards in relation to juveniles in conflict with law under this act.

(2) A Board shall consist of a Metropolitan Magistrate or a Judicial Magistrate of the first class, as the case may be, and two social workers of whom at least one shall be a woman, forming a Bench and every such Bench shall have the powers conferred by the Code of Criminal Procedure, 1973 (2 of 1974), on a Metropolitan Magistrate or, as the case may be, a Judicial Magistrate of the first class and the Magistrate on the Board shall be designated as the principal Magistrate.

(3) No Magistrate shall be appointed as a member of the Board unless he has special knowledge or training in child psychology or child welfare and no social worker shall be appointed as a member of the Board unless he has been actively involved in health, education, or welfare activities pertaining to children for at least seven years.

(4) The term of office of the members of the Board and the manner in which such member may resign shall be such as may be prescribed.

(5) The appointment of any member of the Board may be terminated after holding inquiry, by the State Government, if —

(*i*) he has been found guilty of misuse of power vested under this act,

(*ii*) he has been convicted of an offence involving moral turpitude, and such conviction has not been reversed or he has not been granted full pardon in respect of such offence,

(*iii*) he fails to attend the proceedings of the Board foe consecutive three months without any valid reason or he fails to attend less than three-fourth of the sittings in a year.

COMMENTS

The State Government has been authorised to constitute for a district or a group of districts one or more Juvenile Boards for exercising the powers and discharging the duties, conferred or imposed on such Boards in relation to Juveniles in conflict with the law under this act. The Board shall consist of a Metropolitan Magistrate or a Judicial Magistrate of the first class, as the case may be, and two social workers of whom at least one shall be a woman.

5. Procedure, etc. in relation to Board.—(1) The Board shall meet at such times and shall, observe such rules of procedure in regard to the transaction of business at its meetings, as may be prescribed.

(2) A child in conflict with law may be produced before an individual member of the Board, when the Board is not sitting.

(3) A Board may act notwithstanding the absence of any member of the Board, and no order made by the Board shall be invalid by reason only of the absence of any member during any stage of proceedings:

Provided that there shall be at least two members including the principal Magistrate present at the time of final disposal of the case.

(4) In the event of any difference of opinion among the members of the Board in the interim or final disposition, the opinion of the majority shall prevail,

but where there is no such majority, the opinion of the principal Magistrate, shall prevail.

COMMENTS

A child in conflict with law can be produced before an individual member of the Board, when the Board is not sitting.

6. Powers of Juvenile Justice Board.—(1) Where a Board has been constituted for any district or a group of districts, such Board shall, notwithstanding anything contained in any other law for the time being in force but save as otherwise expressly provided in this Act, have power to deal exclusively with all proceedings under this Act, relating to juvenile in conflict with law.

(2) The powers conferred on the Board by or under this Act may also be exercised by the High Court and the Court of Session, when the proceedings comes before them in appeal, revision or otherwise.

7. Procedure to be followed by a Magistrate not empowered under the Act.—(1) When any Magistrate not empowered to exercise the powers of a Board under this Act is of the opinion that a person brought before him under any of the provisions of this Act (other than for the purpose of giving evidence), is a juvenile or the child, he shall without any delay record such opinion and forward the juvenile or the child, and the record of the proceeding to the competent authority having jurisdiction over the proceeding.

(2) The competent authority to which the proceeding is forwarded under sub-section (1) shall hold the inquiry as if the juvenile or the child had originally been brought before it.

8. Observation homes.—(1) Any State Government may establish and maintain either by itself or under an agreement with voluntary organisations, observation homes in every district or a group of districts, as may be required for the temporary reception of any juvenile in conflict with law during the pendency of any inquiry regarding them under this Act.

(2) Where the State Government is of opinion that any institution other than a home established or maintained under sub-section (1), is fit for the temporary reception of juvenile in conflict with law during the pendency of any inquiry regarding them under this Act, it may certify such substitution as an observation home for purposes of this Act.

(3) The State Government may, by rules made under this Act, provide for the management of observation homes, including the standards and various types of services to be provided by them for rehabilitation and social integration of a juvenile, and the circumstances under which, and the manner in which, the certification of an observation home may be granted or withdrawn.

(4) Every juvenile who is not placed under the charge of parent or guardian and is sent to an observation home shall be initially kept in a reception unit of the observation home for preliminary inquiries, care and classification for juveniles

according to his age group, such as seven to twelve years, twelve to sixteen years and sixteen to eighteen years, giving due considerations to physical and mental status and degree of the offence committed, for further induction into observation home.

COMMENTS

State Governments have been empowered to establish and maintain either by themselves or under an agreement with voluntary organisations, observation homes in every district or a group of districts as may be required for the temporary reception of any juvenile in conflict with law during the pendency of any inquiry regarding them. State Governments have also been empowered to certify any institution, other than a home established or maintained by themselves or under an agreement with voluntary organisations, as an observation home for this purposes of this Act.

9. Special Homes.—(1) Any State Government may establish and maintain either by itself or under an agreement with voluntary organisations, special homes in every district or a group of districts, as may be required for reception and rehabilitation of juvenile in conflict with law under this Act.

(2) Where the State Government is of opinion that any institution other than a home established or maintained under sub-section (1), is fit for the reception of juvenile in conflict with law to be sent there under this Act, it may certify such institution as a special home for the purposes of this Act.

(3) The State Government may, by rules made under this Act, provide for the management of special homes, including the standards and various types of services to be provided by them which are necessary for re-socialisation of a juvenile, and the circumstances under which and the manner in which, the certification of a special home may be granted or withdrawn.

(4) The rules made under sub-section (3) may also provide for the classification and separation of juvenile in conflict with law on the basis of age and the nature of offences committed by them and his mental and physical status.

COMMENTS

State Governments have been empowered to establish and maintain, either by themselves or under an agreement with voluntary organisations, special homes in every district or a group of districts for the reception and rehabilitation of juvenile in conflict with law. State Governments have also been empowered to certify any institution, other than a home established or maintained by themselves or under an agreement with voluntary organisations, that it is fit for the reception of juvenile in conflict with law.

10. Apprehension of juvenile in conflict with law.—(1) As soon as a juvenile in conflict with law is apprehended by police, he shall be placed under the charge of the special juvenile police unit or the designated police officer who shall immediately report the matter to a member of the Board.

(2) The State Government may make rules consistent with this Act,—

(*i*) to provide for persons through whom (including registered voluntary organisations) any juvenile in conflict with law may be produced before the Board;

(*ii*) to provide the manner in which such juvenile may be sent to an observation home.

COMMENTS

When a juvenile in conflict with law is apprehended by police, he has to be placed under the charge of the special juvenile police unit or the designated police officer who shall immediately report the matter to a member of the Board.

11. Control of custodian over juvenile.—Any person in whose charge a juvenile is placed in pursuance of this Act shall, while the order is in force have the control over the juvenile as he would have if he were his parents, and shall be responsible for his maintenance, and the juvenile shall continue in his charge for the period stated by competent authority, notwithstanding that he is claimed by his parents or any other person.

COMMENTS

When any juvenile is placed in the charge of a person he shall have the control over the juvenile as he would have if he were his parents, and shall be responsible for his maintenance and the juvenile shall continue in his charge for the period stated by the competent authority.

12. Bail of juvenile.—(1) When any person accused of a bailable or non-bailable offence, and apparently a juvenile, is arrested or detained or appears or is brought before a Board, such person shall, notwithstanding anything contained in the Code of Criminal Procedure, 1973 (2 of 1974) or in any other law for the time being in force, be released on bail with or without surety but he shall not be so released if there appear reasonable grounds for believing that the release is likely to bring him into association with any known criminal or expose him to moral, physical or psychological danger or that his release would defeat the ends of justice.

(2) When such person having been arrested is not released on bail under sub-section (1) by the officer incharge of the police station, such officer shall cause him to be kept only in an observation home in the prescribed manner until he can brought before a Board.

(3) When such person is not released on bail under sub-section (1) by the Board it shall, instead of committing him to prison, make an order sending him to an observation home or a place of safety for such period during the pendency of the inquiry regarding him as may be specified in the order.

13. Information to parent, guardian or probation officer.—Where a juvenile is arrested, the officer incharge of the police station or the special juvenile police unit to which the juvenile is brought shall, as soon as may be after the arrest, inform—

(*a*) the parent or guardian of the juvenile , if he can be found, of such arrest and direct him to be present at the Board before which the juvenile will appear; and

(*b*) the probation officer of such arrest to enable him to obtain information regarding the antecedents and family background of the juvenile and other material circumstances likely to be of assistance to the Board for making the inquiry.

COMMENTS

When any juvenile is arrested, the officer in charge of the police station or the special juvenile police unit to which the juvenile is brought, as soon as may be after the arrest, has to inform the parent or guardian of the juvenile about his arrest and direct him to be present at the Board before which the juvenile will appear and he has also to inform the probation officer of such arrest to enable him to obtain information regarding the antecedents and family background of the juvenile.

14. Inquiry by Board regarding juvenile.—Where a juvenile having been charged with the offence is produced before a Board, the Board shall hold the inquiry in accordance with the provisions of this Act and may make such order in relation to the juvenile as it deems fit:

Provided that an inquiry under this section shall be completed within a period of four months from the date of its commencement, unless the period is extended by the Board having regard to the circumstances of the case and in special cases after recording the reasons in writing for such extension.

15. Order that may be passed regarding juvenile.—(1) Where a Board is satisfied on inquiry that a juvenile has committed an offence, then notwithstanding anything to the contrary contained in any other law for the time being in force, the Board may, if it thinks so fit,—

(*a*) allow the juvenile to go home after advice or admonition following appropriate inquiry against and counselling to the parent or the guardian and the juvenile;

(*b*) direct the juvenile to participate in group counselling and similar activities;

(*c*) order the juvenile to perform community service;

(*d*) order the parent of the juvenile or the juvenile himself to pay a fine, if he is over fourteen years of age and earns money;

(*e*) direct the juvenile to be released on probation of good conduct and placed under the care of any parent, guardian or other fit person, on such parent, guardian or other fit person executing a bond, with or without surety, as the Board may require, for the good behaviour and well-being of the juvenile for any period not exceeding three years;

(*f*) direct the juvenile to be released on probation of good conduct and placed under the care of any fit institution for the good behaviour and well-being of the juvenile for any period not exceeding three years;

(*g*) make an order directing the juvenile to be sent to a special home,—

(*i*) in the case of juvenile, over seventeen years but less than eighteen years of age for a period of not less than two years;

(*ii*) in case of any other juvenile for the period until he ceases to be a juvenile:

Provided that the Board may, if it is satisfied that having regard to the nature of the offence and the circumstances of the case it is expedient so to do, for reasons to be recorded, reduce the period of stay to such period as it thinks fit.

The Board shall obtain the social investigation report on juvenile either through a probation officer or a recognised voluntary organisation or otherwise, and shall take into consideration the findings of such report before passing an order.

Where an order under clause (*d*), clause (*e*) or clause (*f*) of sub-section (1) is made, the Board may, if it is of opinion that in the interests of the juvenile and of the public, it is expedient so to do, in addition make an order that the juvenile in conflict with law shall remain under the supervision of a probation officer named in the order during such period, not exceeding three years as may be specified therein, and may in such supervision order impose such conditions as it deems necessary for the due supervision of the juvenile in conflict with law:

Provided that if at any time afterwards it appears to the Board on receiving a report from the probation officer or otherwise, that the juvenile in conflict with law has not been of good behaviour during the period of supervision or that the fit institution under whose care the juvenile was placed is no longer able or willing to ensure the good behaviour and well-being of the juvenile it may, after making such inquiry as it deems fit, order the juvenile in conflict with law to be sent to a special home.

The Board shall while making a supervision order under sub-section (3), explain to the juvenile and the parent, guardian or other fit person or fit institution, as the case may be, under whose care the juvenile has been placed, the terms and conditions of the order shall forthwith furnish one copy of the supervision order to the juvenile, the parent, guardian or other fit person or fit institution, as the case may be, the sureties, if any, and the probation officer.

16. Order that may not be passed against juvenile.—(1) Notwithstanding anything to the contrary contained in any other law for the time being in force, no juvenile in conflict with law shall be sentenced to death or life imprisonment, or committed to prison in default of payment of fine or in default of furnishing security:

Provided that where a juvenile who has attained the age of sixteen years has committed an offence and the Board is satisfied that the offence committed is of so serious in nature or that his conduct and behaviour have been such that it would not be in his interest or in the interest of other juvenile in a special home to send him to such special home and that none of the other measures provided under this Act is suitable or sufficient, the Board may order the juvenile in conflict with law to be kept in such place of safety and in such manner as it thinks fit and shall report the case for the order of the State Government.

(2) On receipt of a report from a Board under sub-section (1), the State Government may make such arrangement in respect of the juvenile as it deems proper and may order such juvenile to be kept under protective custody at such place and on such conditions as it thinks fit:

Provided that the period of detention so ordered shall not exceed the maximum period of imprisonment to which the juvenile could have been sentenced for the offence committed.

17. Proceeding under Chapter VIII of the Code of Criminal Procedure not component against juvenile.—Notwithstanding anything to the contrary contained in the Code of Criminal Procedure, 1973 (2 of 1974) no proceeding shall be instituted and no order shall be passed against the juvenile under Chapter VIII of the said Code.

18. No joint proceeding of juvenile and person not a juvenile.—(1) Notwithstanding anything contained in section 223 of the Code of Criminal Procedure, 1973 (2 of 1974) or in any other law for the time being in force, no juvenile shall be charged with or tried for any offence together with a person who is not a juvenile.

(2) If a juvenile is accused of an offence for which under section 223 of the Code of Criminal Procedure, 1973 (2 of 1974) or any other law for the time being in force, such juvenile and any person who is not a juvenile would, but for the prohibition contained in sub-section (1), have been charged and tried together, the Board taking cognizance of that offence shall direct separate trials of the juvenile and the other person.

COMMENTS

No juvenile can be charged with or tried for any offence together with a person who is not a juvenile.

19. Removal of disqualification attaching to conviction.—(1) Notwithstanding anything contained in any other law, a juvenile who has committed an offence and has been dealt with under the provisions of this Act shall not suffer disqualification, if any, attaching to a conviction of an offence under such law.

(2) The Board shall make an order directing that the relevant records of such conviction shall be removed after the expiry of the period of appeal or a reasonable period as prescribed under the rules, as the case may be.

20. Special provision in respect of pending cases.—Notwithstanding anything contained in this Act, all proceedings in respect of a juvenile pending in any court in any area on the date on which this Act comes into force in that area, shall be continued in that court as if this Act had not been passed and if the court finds that the juvenile has committed an offence, it shall record such finding and instead of passing any sentence in respect of the juvenile, forward the juvenile to the Board which shall pass orders in respect of that juvenile in accordance with the provisions of this Act as if it had been satisfied on inquiry under this Act that a juvenile has committed the offence.

21. Prohibition of publication of name, etc., of juvenile involved in any proceeding under the Act.—(1) No report in any newspaper, magazine, news-sheet or visual media of any inquiry regarding a juvenile in conflict with law under this Act shall disclose the name, address or school or any other particulars calculated to lead to the identification of the juvenile nor shall any picture of any such juvenile be published:

Provided that for reasons to be recorded in writing the authority holding the inquiry may permit such disclosure, if in its opinion such disclosure is in interest of the juvenile.

(2) Any person contravening the provisions of sub-section (1) shall be punishable with fine, which may extend to one thousand rupees.

COMMENTS

Newspapers, magazines, news-sheet or visual media have been prohibited to disclose the name, address or school or any other particulars calculated to lead to the identification of the juvenile in conflict with law nor they can publish any picture of such juvenile. Any person who contravenes this provision shall be punishable with fine upto one thousand rupees.

22. Provision in respect of escaped juvenile.—Notwithstanding anything to the contrary contained in any other law for the time being in force, any police officer may take charge without warrant of a juvenile in conflict with law who has escaped from a special home or an observation home or from the care of a person under whom he was placed under this Act, and shall be sent back to the special home or the observation home or that person, as the case may be; and no proceeding shall be instituted in respect of the juvenile by reason of such escape, but the special home, or the observation home or the person may, after giving the information to the Board which passed the order in respect of the juvenile, take such steps in respect of the juvenile as may be deemed necessary under the provisions of this Act.

23. Punishment for cruelty to juvenile or child.—Whoever, having the actual charge of, or control over, a juvenile or the child, assaults, abandons, exposes or wilfully neglects the juvenile or causes or procures him to be assaulted, abandoned, exposed or neglected in a manner likely to cause such juvenile or the child unnecessary mental or physical suffering shall be punishable with imprisonment for a team which may extend to six months, or fine, or with both.

COMMENTS

If any person having the actual charge of, or control over, a juvenile or the child, assaults, abandons, exposes or wilfully neglects the juvenile or causes or procures him to be assaulted, abandoned, exposed or neglected in any manner likely to cause such juvenile or the child unnecessary mental or physical suffering, he shall be punishable with imprisonment upto six months, or fine, or with both.

24. Employment of juvenile or child for begging.-(1) Whoever employs or uses any juvenile or the child for the purpose or causes any juvenile to beg shall be punishable with imprisonment for a term which may extend to three years and shall also be liable to fine.

(2) Whoever, having the actual charge of, or control over, a juvenile or the child abets the commission of the offence punishable under sub-section (1), shall be punishable with imprisonment for a term which may extend to one year and shall also be liable to fine.

25. Penalty for giving intoxicating liquor or narcotic drug or psychotropic substance to juvenile or child.—Whoever gives, or causes to be given, to any juvenile or the child any intoxicating liquor in a public place or any narcotic drug or psychotropic substance except upon the order of duly qualified medical practitioner or in case of sickness shall be punishable with imprisonment for a term which may extend to three years and shall be liable to fine.

26. Exploitation of juvenile or child employee.—Whoever ostensibly procures a juvenile or the child for the purpose of any hazardous employment keeps him in bondage and withholds his earnings or uses such earning for his own purposes shall be punishable with imprisonment for a term which may extend to three years and shall be liable to fine.

27. Special offences.—The offences punishable under sections 23, 24, 25 and 26 shall be cognizable.

28. Alternative punishment.—Where an act or omission constitute an offence punishable under this Act and also under any other Central or State Act, then, notwithstanding anything contained in any law for the time being in force, the offender found guilty of such offences shall be liable to punishment only under such Act as provides for punishment which is greater in degree.

CHAPTER III

CHILD IN NEED OF CARE AND PROTECTION

29. Child Welfare Committee.—(1) The State Government may, by notification in Official Gazette, constitute for every district or group of districts, specified in the notification, one or more Child Welfare Committees for exercising the powers and discharge the duties conferred on such Committees in relation to child in need of care and protection under this Act.

(2) The Committee shall consist of a Chairperson and four other members as the State Government may think fit to appoint, of whom at least one shall be a woman and another, an expert on matters concerning children.

(3) The qualifications of the Chairperson and the members, and the tenure for which they may be appointed shall be such as may be prescribed.

(4) The appointment of any member of the Committee may be terminated, after holding inquiry, by the State Government, if—

(*i*) he has been found guilty of misuse of power vested under this Act;

(*ii*) he has been convicted of an offence involving moral turpitude, and such conviction has not been reversed or he has not been granted full pardon in respect of such offence;

(*iii*) he fails to attend the proceedings of the Committee for consecutive three months without any valid reason or he fails to attend less than three-fourth of the sittings in a year.

(5) The Committee shall function as a Bench of Magistrates and shall have the powers conferred by the Code of Criminal Procedure, 1973 (2 of 1974) on a Metropolitan Magistrate or, as the case may be, a Judicial Magistrate of the first class.

COMMENTS

State Governments have been empowered to constitute for every district or group of districts one or more Child Welfare Committees for exercising the powers and discharge the duties in relation to child in need of care and protection under the Act. The Committee shall consist of a Chairperson and four other members, of whom at least one shall be a woman and another an expert on matters concerning children.

30. Procedure, etc., in relation to Committee.—(1) The Committee shall meet at such times and shall observe such rules of procedure in regard to the transaction of business at its meetings, as may be prescribed.

(2) A child in need of care and protection may be produced before an individual member for being placed in safe custody or otherwise when the Committee is not in session.

(3) In the event of any difference of opinion among the members of the Committee at the time of any interim decision, the opinion of the majority shall prevail but where there is no such majority the opinion of the Chairperson shall prevail.

(4) Subject to the provisions of sub-section (1), the Committee may act, notwithstanding the absence of any member of the Committee, and no order made by the Committee shall be invalid by reason only of the absence of any member during any stage of the proceeding.

31. Powers of Committee.—(1) The Committee shall have the final authority to dispose of cases for the care, protection, treatment, development and rehabilitation of the children as well as to provide for their basic needs and protection of human rights.

(2) Where a Committee has been constituted for any area, such Committee shall, notwithstanding anything contained in any other law for the time being in force but save as otherwise expressly provided in this Act, have the power to deal exclusively with all proceedings under this Act relating to children in need of care and protection.

32. Production before Committee.—(1) Any child in need of care and protection may be produced before the Committee by one of the following persons:—

(*i*) any police officer or special juvenile police unit or a designated police officer;

(*ii*) any public servant;

(*iii*) childline, a registered voluntary organisation or by such other voluntary organisation or an agency as may be recognised by the State Government;

(*iv*) any social worker or a public spirited citizen authorised by the State Government; or

(*v*) by the child himself.

(2) The State Government may make rules consistent with this Act to provide for the manner of making the report to the police and to the Committee and the manner of sending and entrusting the child to children's home pending the inquiry.

33. Inquiry.—(1) On receipt of a report under section 32, the Committee or any police officer or special juvenile police unit or the designated police officer shall hold an inquiry in the prescribed manner and the Committee, on its own or on the report from any person or agency as mentioned in sub-section (1) of section 32, may pass an order to send the child to the children's home for speedy inquiry by a social worker or child welfare officer.

(2) The inquiry under this section shall be completed within four months of the receipt of the order or within such shorter period as may be fixed by the Committee: Provided that the time for the submission of the inquiry report may be extended by such period as the Committee may, having regard to the circumstances and for the reasons recorded in writing, determine.

(3) After the completion of the inquiry if the Committee is of the opinion that the said child has no family or ostensible support, it may allow the child to remain in the children's home or shelter home till suitable rehabilitation is found for him or till he attains the age of eighteen years.

34. Children's homes.—(1) The State Government may establish and maintain either by itself or in association with voluntary organisations, children's homes, in every district or group of districts, as the case may be, for the reception of child in need of care and protection during the pendency of any inquiry and subsequently for their care, treatment, education, training, development and rehabilitation.

(2) The State Government may, by rules made under this Act, provide for the management of children's homes including the standards and the nature of services to be provided by them, and the circumstances under which, and the manner in which, the certification of a children's home or recognition to a voluntary organisation may be granted or withdrawn.

COMMENTS

State Governments have been empowered to establish and maintain either by themselves or in association with the voluntary organisations, children's homes in every district or a group of districts for the reception of child in need of care and protection during the pendency of any inquiry and subsequently for their care, treatment, education, training, development and rehabilitation.

35. Inspection.—(1) The State Government may appoint inspection committees for the children's homes (hereinafter referred to as the inspection committees) for the State, a district and city, as the case may be, for such period and for such purposes as may be prescribed.

(2) The inspection committee of a State, district or of a city shall consist of such number of representatives from the State Government, Local Authority, Committee, voluntary organisations and such other medical experts and social workers as may be prescribed.

36. Social auditing.—The Central Government or State Government may monitor and evaluate the functioning of the children's homes at such period and through such persons and institutions as may be specified by that Government.

37. Shelter homes.—(1) The State Government may recognise, reputed and capable voluntary organisations and provide them assistance to set up and administer as many shelter homes for juveniles or children as may be required.

(2) The shelter homes referred in sub-section.—(1) shall function as drop-in-centres for the children in the need of urgent support who have been brought to such homes through such persons as are referred to in sub-section (1) of section 32.

(3) As far as possible, the shelter homes shall have such facilities as may be prescribed by the rules.

COMMENTS

State Governments have been empowered to recognise reputed and capable voluntary organisations and provide them assistance to set up and administer shelter homes for juveniles or children. These shelter homes shall function as drop-in-centres for the children in the need of urgent support.

38. Transfer.—(1) If during the inquiry it is found that the child hails from the place outside the jurisdiction of the Committee, the Committee shall order the transfer of the child to the competent authority having jurisdiction over the place of residence of the child.

(2) Such juvenile or the child shall be escorted by the staff of the home in which he is lodged originally.

(3) The State Government may make rules to provide for the travelling allowance to be paid to the child.

39. Restoration.—(1) Restoration of and protection to a child shall be the prime objective of any children's home or the shelter home.

(2) The children's home or a shelter home, as the case may be, shall take such steps as are considered necessary for the restoration of and protection to a child deprived of his family environment temporarily or permanently where such child is under the care and protection of a children's home or a shelter home, as the case may be.

(3) The Committee shall have the powers to restore any child in need of care and protection to his parent, guardian, fit person or fit institution, as the case may be, and give them suitable directions.

Explanation.—For the purposes of this section "restoration of child" means restoration to—

(*a*) parents;

(*b*) adopted parents;

(*c*) foster parents.

CHAPTER IV

REHABILITATION AND SOCIAL REINTEGRATION

40. Process of rehabilitation and social reintegration.—The rehabilitation and social reintegration of a child shall begin during the stay of the child in a children's home or special home and the rehabilitation and social reintegration of children shall be carried out alternatively by (*i*) adoption, (*ii*) foster care, (*iii*) sponsorship, and (*iv*) sending the child to an after-care organisation.

41. Adoption.—(1) The primary responsibility for providing care and protection to children shall be that of his family.

(2) Adoption shall be resorted to for the rehabilitation of such children as are orphaned, abandoned, neglected and abused through institutional and non-institutional methods.

(3) In keeping with the provisions of the various guidelines for adoption issued from time to time by the State Government, the Board shall be empowered to give children in adoption and carry out such investigations as are required or giving children in adoption in accordance with the guidelines issued by the State Government from time to time in this regard.

(4) The children's homes or the State Government run institutions for orphans shall be recognised as an adoption agencies both for scrutiny and placement of

such children for adoption in accordance with the guidelines issued under sub-section (3).

(5) No child shall be offered for adoption—

(*i*) until two members of the Committee declare the child legally free for placement in the case of abandoned children,

(*ii*) till the two months period for reconsideration by the parent is over in the case of surrendered children, and

(*iii*) without his consent in the case of a child who can understand and express his consent.

(6) The Board may allow a child to be given in adoption-

(*i*) to a single parent, and

(*ii*) to parents to adopt a child of same sex irrespective of the number of living biological sons or daughters.

42. Foster care.—(1) The foster care may be used for temporary placement of those infants who are ultimately to be given for adoption.

(2) In foster care, the child may be placed in another family for a short or extended period of time, depending upon the circumstances where the child's own parent usually visit regularly and eventually after the rehabilitation, where the children may return to their own homes.

(3) The State Government may make rules for the purposes of carrying out the scheme of foster care programme of children.

43. Sponsorship.—(1) The sponsorship programme may provide supplementary support to families, to children's homes and to special homes to meet medical, nutritional, educational and other needs of the children with a view to improving their quality of life.

(2) The State Government may make rules for the purposes of carrying out various schemes of sponsorship of children, such as individual to individual sponsorship, group sponsorship or community sponsorship.

44. After-care organisation.—The State Government may, by rules made under this Act, provide—

(*a*) for the establishment or recognition of after-care organisations and the functions that may be performed by them under this Act;

(*b*) for a scheme of after-care programme to be followed by such after-care organisations for the purpose of taking care of juveniles or the children after they leave special homes, children homes and for the purpose of enabling them to lead an honest, industrious and useful life;

(*c*) for the preparation or submission of a report by the probation officer or any other officer appointed by that Government in respect of each juvenile or the child prior to his discharge from a special home, children's home, regarding the necessity and nature of after-care of such juvenile or of a child, the period of such after-care, supervision thereof and for the submission of report by the probation officer or any other officer appointed for the purpose, on the progress of each juvenile or the child;

(*d*) for the standards and the nature of services to be maintained by such after care organisations;

(*e*) for such other matters as may be necessary for the purpose of carrying out the scheme of after-care programme for the juvenile or the child:

Provided that any rule made under this section shall not provide for such juvenile or child to stay in the after-care organisation for more than three years:

Provided further that a juvenile or child over seventeen years of age but less than eighteen years of age would stay in the after-care organisation till he attains the age of twenty years.

45. Linkages and co-ordination.—The State Government may make rules to ensure effective linkages between various governmental, non-governmental, corporate and other community agencies for facilitating the rehabilitation and social reintegration of the child.

CHAPTER V

MISCELLANEOUS

46. Attendance of parent or guardian of juvenile or child.—Any competent authority before which a juvenile or the child is brought under any of the provisions of this Act, may, whenever it so thinks fit, require any parent or guardian having the actual charge of or control over the juvenile or the child to be present at any proceeding in respect of the juvenile or the child.

47. Dispensing with attendance of juvenile or child.—If, at any stage during the course of an inquiry, a competent authority is satisfied that the attendance of the juvenile or the child is not essential for the purpose of inquiry, the competent authority may dispense with his attendance and proceed with the inquiry in the absence of the juvenile or the child.

48. Committal to approved place of juvenile or child suffering from dangerous diseases and his future disposal.—(1) When a juvenile or the child who has been brought before a competent authority under this Act, is found to be suffering from a disease requiring prolonged medical treatment or physical or mental complaint that will respond to treatment, the competent authority may send the juvenile or the child to any place recognised to be an approved place in accordance with the rules made under this Act for such period as it may think necessary for the required treatment.

(2) Where a juvenile or the child is found to be suffering from leprosy, sexually transmitted disease, Hepatitis B, open cases of Tuberculosis and such other diseases or is of unsound mind, he shall be dealt with separately through various specialised referral services or under the relevant laws as such.

49. Presumption and determination of age.—(1) Where it appears to a competent authority that person brought before it under any of the provisions of this Act (otherwise than for the purpose of giving evidence) is a juvenile or the child, the competent authority shall make due inquiry so as to the age of that person and for that purpose shall take such evidence as may be necessary (but not an affidavit) and shall record a finding whether the person is a juvenile or the child or not, stating his age as nearly as may be.

(2) No order of a competent authority shall be deemed to have become invalid merely by any subsequent proof that the person in respect of whom the order has been made is not a juvenile or the child, and the age recorded by the competent authority to be the age of person so brought before it, shall for the purpose of this Act, be deemed to be the true age of that person.

50. Sending a juvenile or child outside jurisdiction.—In the case of a juvenile or the child, whose ordinary place of residence lies outside the jurisdiction of the competent authority before which he is brought, the competent authority may, if satisfied after due inquiry that it is expedient so to do, send the juvenile or the child back to a relative or other person who is fit and willing to receive him at his ordinary place of residence and exercise proper care and control over him, notwithstanding that such place of residence is outside the jurisdiction of the competent authority; and the competent authority exercising jurisdiction over the place to which the juvenile or the child is sent shall in respect of any matter arising subsequently have the same powers in relation to the juvenile or the child as if the original order had been passed by itself.

51. Reports to be treated as confidential.—The report of the probation officer or social worker considered by the competent authority shall be treated as confidential:

Provided that the competent authority may, if it so thinks fit, communicate the substance thereof to the juvenile or the child or his parent or guardian and may give such juvenile or the child, parent or guardian an opportunity of producing such evidence as may be relevant to the matter stated in the report.

52. Appeals.—(1) Subject to the provisions of this section, any person aggrieved by an order made by a competent authority under this Act may, within thirty days from the date of such order, prefer an appeal to the Court of Session:

Provided that the Court of Session may entertain the appeal after the expiry of the said period of thirty days if it is satisfied that the appellant was prevented by sufficient cause from filing the appeal in time.

(2) No appeal shall lie from—

(*a*) any order of acquittal made by the Board in respect of a juvenile alleged to have committed an offence; or

(*b*) any order made by a Committee in respect of a finding that a person is not a neglected juvenile.

(3) No second appeal shall lie from any order of the Court of Session passed in appeal under this section.

53. Revision.—The High Court may, at any time, either of its own motion or on an application received in this behalf, call for the record of any proceeding in which any competent authority or Court of Session has passed an order for the purpose of satisfying itself as to the legality or propriety of any such order and may pass such order in relation thereto as it thinks fit:

Provided that the High Court shall not pass an order under this section prejudicial to any person without giving him a reasonable opportunity of being heard.

54. Procedure in inquiries, appeals and revision proceedings.—(1) Save as otherwise expressly provided by this Act, a competent authority while holding any inquiry under any of the provisions of this Act, shall follow such procedure as may be prescribed and subject thereto, shall follow, as far as may be, the procedure laid down in the Code of Criminal Procedure, 1973 (2 of 1974) for trials in summons cases.

(2) Save as otherwise expressly provided by or under this Act, the procedure to be followed in hearing appeals or revision proceedings under this Act shall be, as far as practicable, in accordance with the provisions of the Code of Criminal Procedure, 1973 (2 of 1974).

55. Power to amend orders.—(1) Without prejudice to the provisions for appeal and revision under this Act, any competent authority may, on an application received in this behalf, amend any order as to the institution to which a juvenile or the child is to be sent or as to the person under whose care or supervision a juvenile or the child is to be placed under this Act:

Provided that there shall be at least two members and the parties or its defence present during the course of hearing for passing an amendment in relation to any of its order.

(2) Clerical mistakes in orders passed by a competent authority or errors arising therein from any accidental slip or omission may, at any time, be corrected by the competent authority either on its own motion or on an application received in this behalf.

56. Power of competent authority to discharge and transfer juvenile or child.—The competent authority or the local authority may, notwithstanding anything contained in this Act, at any time, order a child in need of care and protection or a juvenile in conflict with law to be discharged or transferred from one children's home or special home to another, as the case may be, keeping in view the best interest of the child or the juvenile, and his natural place of stay, either absolutely or on such conditions as it may think fit to impose:

Provided that the total period of stay of the juvenile or the child in a children's home or a special home or a fit institution or under a fit person shall not be increased by such transfer.

57. Transfer between children's homes, under the Act, and juvenile homes, of like nature in different parts of India.—The State Government or the local authority may direct any child or the juvenile to be transferred from any children's home or special home outside the State to any other children's home, special home or institution of a like nature with the prior intimation to the local Committee or the Board, as the case may be, and such order shall be deemed to be operative for the competent authority of the area to which the child or the juvenile is sent.

58. Transfer of juvenile or child of unsound mind or suffering from leprosy or addicted to drugs.—Where it appears to the competent authority that any juvenile or the child kept in a special home or a children's home or shelter home or in an institution in pursuance of this Act, is suffering from leprosy or is of unsound mind or is addicted to any narcotic drug or psychotropic substance, the competent authority may order his removal to a leper asylum or mental hospital or treatment centre for drug addicts or to a place of safety for being kept there for such period not exceeding the period for which he is required to be kept under the order of the competent authority or for such further period as may be certified by the medical officer necessary for the proper treatment of the juvenile or the child.

COMMENTS

If any juvenile or the child kept in a special home or children's home or shelter home or in an institution, is suffering from leprosy or is of unsound mind or is addicted to any narcotic drug or psychotropic substance, the competent authority can order his removal to a leper asylum or mental hospital or treatment centre for drug addicts or to a place of safety for being kept there.

59. Release and absence of juvenile or child on placement.—(1) When a juvenile or the child is kept in a children's home or special home and on a report of a probation officer or social worker or of Government or a voluntary organisation, as the case may be, the competent authority may consider, the release of such juvenile or the child permitting him to live with his parent or guardian or under the supervision of any authorised person named in the order, willing to receive and take charge of the juvenile or the child to educate and train him for some useful trade or calling or to look after him for rehabilitation.

(2) The competent authority may also permit leave of absence to any juvenile or the child, to allow him, on special occasions like examination, marriage of relatives, death of kith and kin or the accident or serious illness of parent or any emergency of like nature, to go on leave under supervision, for maximum seven days, excluding the time taken in journey.

(3) Where a permission has been revoked or forfeited and the juvenile or the child refuses or fails to return to the home concerned or juvenile to which he was directed so to return, the Board may, if necessary, cause him to be taken charge of and to be taken back to the concerned home.

(4) The time during which a juvenile or the child is absent from a concerned home in pursuance of such permission granted under this section shall be deemed to be part of the time foe which he is liable to be kept in the special home:

Provided that when a juvenile has failed to return to the special home on the permission being revoked or forfeited, the time which lapses after his failure so to return shall be excluded in computing the time during which he is liable to be kept in the institution.

60. Contribution by parents.—(1) The competent authority which makes an order for sending a juvenile or the child to a children's home or to a special home or placing the juvenile under the care of a fit person or fit institution may make an order requiring the parent or other person liable to maintain the juvenile or the child to contribute to his maintenance, if able to do so, in the prescribed manner according to income.

(2) The competent authority may direct, if necessary, the payment to be made to poor parent or guardian by the Superintendent or the Project Manager of the home to pay such expenses for the journey of the inmate or parent or guardian or both, from the home to his ordinary place of residence at the time of sending the juvenile as may be prescribed.

61. Fund.—(1) The State Government or local authority may create a Fund under such name as it thinks fit for the welfare and rehabilitation of the juvenile or the child dealt with under this Act.

(2) There shall be credited to the Fund such voluntary donations, contributions or subscriptions as may be made by any individual or organisation.

(3) The Fund created under sub-section (1) shall be administered by the State advisory board in such manner and for such purposes as may be prescribed.

COMMENTS

State Governments or local authorities have been empowered to create Funds for the welfare and rehabilitation of the juvenile or the child. Such funds may be created with voluntary donations, contributions or subscriptions as may be made by any individual or organisation. Such funds are to be administered by the State Advisory Boards.

62. Central, State, district and city advisory boards.—(1) The Central Government or a State Government may constitute a Central or State Advisory board, as the case may be, to advise that Government on matter relating to the establishment and maintenance of the homes, mobilisation of resources, provision of facilities for education, training and rehabilitation of child in need of care and protection and juvenile in conflict with law and co-ordination among the various official and non-official agencies concerned.

(2) The Central or State advisory board shall consist of such persons as the Central Government or the State Government, as the case may be, may think fit

and shall include eminent social workers, representatives of voluntary organisations in the field of the child welfare corporate sector, academicians, medical professionals and the concerned Department of the State Government.

(3) The district or city level inspection committee constituted under section 35 of this Act shall also function as the district or city advisory board.

63. Special juvenile police unit.—(1) In order to enable the police officers who frequently or exclusively deal with juveniles or are primarily engaged in the prevention of juvenile crime or handling of the juveniles or children under this Act to perform their functions more effectively, they shall be specially instructed and trained.

(2) In every police station at least one officer with aptitude and appropriate training and orientation may be designated as the 'juvenile or the child welfare officer' who will handle the juvenile or the child in co-ordination with the police.

(3) Special juvenile police unit, of which all police officers designated as above, to handle juveniles or children will be members, may be created in every district and city to co-ordinate and to upgrade the police treatment of the juveniles and the children.

64. Juvenile in conflict with law undergoing sentence at commencement of this Act.—In any area in which this Act is brought into force, the State Government or the local authority may direct that a juvenile in conflict with law who is undergoing any sentence of imprisonment at the commencement of this Act, shall, in lieu of undergoing such sentence, be sent to a special home or kept in fit institution in such manner as the State Government or the local authority thinks fit for the remainder of the period of the sentence; and the provisions of this Act shall apply to the juvenile as if he had been ordered by the Board to be sent to such special home or institution or, as the case may be, ordered to be kept under protective care under sub-section (2) of section 16 of this Act.

65. Procedure in respect of bonds.—Provisions of Chapter XXXIII of the Code of Criminal Procedure, 1973 (2 of 1974) shall, as far as nay be, apply to bonds taken under this Act.

66. Delegation of powers.—The State Government may, by the general order, direct that any power exercisable by it under this Act shall, in such circumstances and under such conditions, if any, as may be prescribed in the order, be exercisable also by an officer subordinate to that Government or the local authority.

67. Protection of action taken in good faith.—No suit or legal proceedings shall lie against the State Government or voluntary organisation running the home or any officer and the staff appointed in pursuance of this Act in respect of anything which is in good faith done or intended to be done in pursuance of this Act or of any rules or order made thereunder.

68. Power to make rules.—(1) The State Government may, by notification in the Official Gazette, make rules to carry out the purposes of this Act.

(2) In particular, and without prejudice to the generality of the foregoing powers, such rules may provide for all or any of the following matters, namely:—

(*i*) the term of office of the members of the Board, and the manner in which such member may resign under sub-section (4) of section (4);

(*ii*) the time of the meetings of the Board and the rules of procedure in regard to the transaction of business at its meeting under sub-section (1) of section 5;

(*iii*) the management of observation homes including the standards and various types of services to be provided by them and the circumstances in which and the manner in which, the certification of the observation home may be granted or withdrawn and such other matters as are referred to in section 8;

(*iv*) the management of special home including the standards and various types of services to be provided by them and the circumstances in which and the manner in which, the certification of the special home may be granted or withdrawn and such other matters as are referred to in section 9;

(*v*) persons by whom any juvenile in conflict with law may be produced before the Board and the manner of sending such juvenile to an observation home under sub-section (2) of section 10;

(*vi*) matters relating to removal of disqualifications attaching to conviction of a juvenile under section 19;

(*vii*) the qualifications of the Chairperson and members, and the tenure for which they may be appointed under sub-section (3) of section 29;

(*viii*) the time of the meetings of the Committee and the rules of procedure in regard to the transaction of business at its meeting under sub-section (1) of section 30;

(*ix*) the manner of making the report to the police and to the Committee and the manner of sending and entrusting the child to children's home pending the inquiry under sub-section (2) of section 32;

(*x*) the management of children's homes including the standards and nature of services to be provided by them, and the manner in which certification of a children's home or recognition to a voluntary organisation may be granted or withdrawn under sub-section (2) of section 34;

(*xi*) appointment of inspection committees for children's homes, their tenure and purposes for which inspection committees may be appointed and such other matters as are referred to in section 35;

(*xii*) facilities to be provided by the shelter homes under sub-section (3) of section 37;

(*xiii*) for carrying out the scheme of foster care programme of children under sub-section (3) of section 42;

(*xiv*) for carrying out various schemes of sponsorship of children under sub-section (2) of section 43;

(*xv*) matters relating to after-care organisation under section 44;

(*xvi*) for ensuring effective linkages between various agencies for facilitating rehabilitation and social integration of the child under section 45;

(*xvii*) the purposes and the manner in which the Fund shall be administered under sub-section (3) of section 61;

(*xviii*) any other matter which is required to be or may be, prescribed.

(3) Every rule made by a State Government under this Act shall be laid, as soon as may be after it is made, before the Legislature of that State.

69. Repeal and savings.—(1) The Juvenile Justice Act, 1986 (53 of 1986) is hereby repealed.

(2) Notwithstanding such repeal, anything done or any action taken under the said Act shall be deemed to have been done or taken under the corresponding provisions of this Act.

70. Power to remove difficulties.—(1) If any difficulty arises in giving effect to the provisions of this Act, the Central Government may, by order, not inconsistent with the provisions of this Act, remove the difficulty:

Provided that no such order shall be made after the expiry of the period of two years from the commencement of this Act.

(2) However, order made under the section shall be laid, as soon as may be after it is made, before each House of Parliament.

— — — — —

APPENDIX 2

THE JUVENILE JUSTICE (CARE AND PROTECTION OF CHILDREN) AMENDMENT ACT, 2006

No. 33 of 2006

[22nd August, 2006.]

An Act to amend the Juvenile Justice (Care and Protection of Children) Act, 2000.

Be it enacted by Parliament in the Fifty-seventh Year of the Republic of India as follows:—

1. Short title.—This Act may be called the Juvenile Justice (Care and Protection of Children) Amendment Act, 2006.

2. Amendment of long title.—In the Juvenile Justice (Care and Protection of Children) Act, 2000 (hereinafter referred to as the principal Act), in the long title, for the words "through various institutions established under this enactment", the words "and for matters connected therewith or incidental thereto" shall be substituted.

3. Amendment of section 1.—In section 1 of the principal Act,—

(*i*) in the marginal heading, for the words "and commencement", the words, "commencement and application" shall be substituted;

(*ii*) after sub-section (3), the following sub-section shall be inserted, namely:—

"(4) Notwithstanding anything contained in any other law for the time being in force, the provisions of this Act shall apply to all cases involving detention, prosecution, penalty or sentence of imprisonment of juveniles in conflict with law under such other law."

4. Amendment of section 2.—In section 2 of the principal Act,—

(*i*) after clause (*a*), the following clause shall be inserted, namely:—

'(*aa*) "adoption" means the process through which the adopted child is permanently separated from his biological parents and become the legitimate child of his adoptive parents with all the rights, privileges and responsibilities that are attached to the relationship;';

(*ii*) in clause (*d*),—

(*I*) after sub-clause (*i*), the following sub-clause shall be inserted, namely:—

"(*ia*) who is found begging, or who is either a street child or a working child,";

(*II*) in sub-clause (*v*), after the word 'abandoned', the words 'or surrendered' shall be inserted;

(*iii*) in clause (*h*), for the words "competent authority", the words "State Government on the recommendation of the competent authority" shall be substituted;

(*iv*) for clause (*l*), the following clause shall be substituted, namely:—

'(*l*) "juvenile in conflict with law" means a juvenile who is alleged to have committed an offence and has not completed eighteenth year of age as on the date of commission of such offence;';

(*v*) clause (*m*) shall be omitted.

5. Omission of certain expressions.—Throughout the principal Act, the words "local authority", "or local authority" and "or the local authority", wherever they occur, shall be omitted.

6. Amendment of section 4.—In section 4 of the principal Act, in sub-section (1), for the words "by notification in the Official Gazette, constitute for a district or a group of districts specified in the notification", the words "within a period of one year from the date of commencement of the Juvenile Justice (Care and Protection of Children) Amendment Act, 2006, by notification in the Official Gazette, constitute for every district" shall be substituted.

7. Amendment of section 6.—In section 6 of the principal Act, in sub-section (1), the words "or a group of districts" shall be omitted.

8. Insertion of new section 7A.—After section 7 of the principal Act, the following section shall be inserted, namely:—

"7A.Procedure to be followed when claim of juvenility is raised before any court.—(1) Whenever a claim of juvenility is raised before any court or a court is of the opinion that an accused person was a juvenile on the date of commission of the offence, the court shall make an inquiry, take such evidence as may be necessary (but not an affidavit) so as to determine the age of such person, and shall record a finding whether the person is a juvenile or a child or not, stating his age as nearly as may be:

Provided that a claim of juvenility may be raised before any court and it shall be recognised at any stage, even after final disposal of the case, and such claim shall be determined in terms of the provisions contained in this Act and the rules made thereunder, even if the juvenile has ceased to be so on or before the date of commencement of this Act.

(2) If the court finds a person to be a juvenile on the date of commission

of the offence under sub-section (1), it shall forward the juvenile to the Board for passing appropriate order, and the sentence if any, passed by a court shall be deemed to have no effect."

9. Amendment of section 10.—In section 10 of the principal Act, for sub-section (1), the following sub-section shall be substituted, namely:—

"(1) As soon as a juvenile in conflict with law is apprehended by police, he shall be placed under the charge of the special juvenile police unit or the designated police officer, who shall produce the juvenile before the Board without any loss of time but within a period of twenty-four hours of his apprehension excluding the time necessary for the journey, from the place where the juvenile was apprehended, to the Board:

Provided that in no case, a juvenile in conflict with law shall be placed in a police lockup or lodged in a jail.".

10. Amendment of section 12.—In section 12 of the principal Act, in sub-section (1), after the words "with or without surety", the words "or placed under the supervision of a Probation Officer or under the care of any fit institution or fit person" shall be inserted.

11. Amendment of section 14.—Section 14 of the principal Act shall be renumbered as sub-section (1) thereof, and after sub-section (1) as so renumbered, the following subsection shall be inserted, namely:—

"(2) The Chief Judicial Magistrate or the Chief Metropolitan Magistrate shall review the pendency of cases of the Board at every six months, and shall direct the Board to increase the frequency of its sittings or may cause the constitution of additional Boards."

12. Amendment of section 15.—In section 15 of the principal Act, in sub-section (1), for clause (*g*), the following clause shall be substituted, namely:—

"(*g*) make an order directing the juvenile to be sent to a special home for a period of three years:

Provided that the Board may, if it is satisfied that having regard to the nature of the offence and the circumstances of the case, it is expedient so to do, for reasons to be recorded, reduce the period of stay to such period as it thinks fit.".

13. Amendment of section 16.—In section 16 of the principal Act,—

(i) in sub-section (1), for the words "or life imprisonment", the words "or imprisonment for any term which may extend to imprisonment for life" shall be substituted;

(ii) in sub-section (2), for the proviso, the following proviso shall be substituted, namely:—

"Provided that the period of detention so ordered shall not exceed in any case the maximum period provided under section 15 of this Act.".

14. Amendment of section 20.—In section 20 of the principal Act, the following proviso and Explanation shall be inserted, namely:—

"Provided that the Board may, for any adequate and special reason to be mentioned in the order, review the case and pass appropriate order in the interest of such juvenile.

Explanation.—In all pending cases including trial, revision, appeal or any other criminal proceedings in respect of a juvenile in conflict with law, in any court, the determination of juvenility of such a juvenile shall be in terms of clause (*l*) of section 2, even if the juvenile ceases to be so on or before the date of commencement of this Act and the provisions of this Act shall apply as if the said provisions had been in force, for all purposes and at all material times when the alleged offence was committed.".

15. Substitution of new section for section 21.—For section 21 of the principal Act, the following section shall be substituted, namely:—

"21. Prohibition of publication of name, etc., of juvenile in conflict with law or child in need of care and protection involved in any proceeding under the Act.—(1) No report in any newspaper, magazine, news-sheet or visual media of any inquiry regarding a juvenile in conflict with law or a child in need of care and protection under this Act shall disclose the name, address or school or any other particulars calculated to lead to the identification of the juvenile or child nor shall any picture of any such juvenile or child be published:

Provided that for reasons to be recorded in writing, the authority holding the inquiry may permit such disclosure, if in its opinion such disclosure is in the interest of the juvenile or the child.

(2) Any person who contravenes the provisions of sub-section (1), shall be liable to a penalty which may extend to twenty-five thousand rupees.".

16. Amendment of section 29.—In section 29 of the principal Act, in sub-section (1), for the words "by notification in Official Gazette, constitute for every district, or group of districts specified in the notification", the words "within a period of one year from the date of commencement of the Juvenile Justice (Care and Protection of Children) Amendment Act, 2006, by notification in the Official Gazette, constitute for every district" shall be substituted.

17. Amendment of section 32.—In section 32 of the principal Act,—

(a) in sub-section (1),—

(i) in clause (*iv*), the words "authorised by the State Government" shall be omitted;

(ii) the following proviso shall be inserted at the end, namely:—

"Provided that the child shall be produced before the Committee without any loss of time but within a period of twenty-four hours excluding the time necessary for the journey.";

(*b*) in sub-section (2), the words "to the police and" shall be omitted.

18. Amendment of section 33.—In section 33 of the principal Act,—

(*a*) in sub-section (1), the words "or any police officer or special juvenile police unit or the designated police officer" shall be omitted;

(*b*) for sub-section (3), the following sub-sections shall be substituted, namely:—

"(3) The State Government shall review the pendency of cases of the Committee at every six months, and shall direct the Committee to increase the frequency of its sittings or may cause the constitution of additional Committees.

(4) After the completion of the inquiry, if, the Committee is of the opinion that the said child has no family or ostensible support or is in continued need of care and protection, it may allow the child to remain in the children's home or shelter home till suitable rehabilitation is found for him or till he attains the age of eighteen years."

19. Amendment of section 34.—In section 34 of the principal Act, after sub-section (2), the following sub-section shall be inserted, namely:—

"(3) Without prejudice to anything contained in any other law for the time being in force, all institutions, whether State Government run or those run by voluntary organisations for children in need of care and protection shall, within a period of six months from the date of commencement of the Juvenile Justice (Care and Protection of Children) Amendment Act, 2006, be registered under this Act in such manner as may be prescribed."

20. Amendment of section 39.—In section 39 of the principal Act, for the Explanation, the following Explanation shall be substituted, namely:—

'*Explanation.*— For the purposes of this section "restoration of and protection of a child" means restoration to—

(*a*) parents;

(*b*) adopted parents;

(*c*) foster parents;

(*d*) guardian;

(*e*) fit person;

(*f*) fit institution.'.

21. Amendment of section 39.—In section 41 of the principal Act,—

(*i*) for sub-sections (2), (3) and (4), the following sub-sections shall be substituted, namely:—

"(2) Adoption shall be resorted to for the rehabilitation of the children who are orphan, abandoned or surrendered through such mechanism as may be prescribed.

(3) In keeping with the provisions of the various guidelines for adoption issued from time to time, by the State Government, or the Central Adoption Resource Agency and notified by the Central Government, children may be given in adoption by a court after satisfying itself regarding the investigations having been carried out, as are required for giving such children in adoption.

(4) The State Government shall recognise one or more of its institutions or voluntary organisations in each district as specialised adoption agencies in such manner as may be prescribed for the placement of orphan, abandoned or surrendered children for adoption in accordance with the guidelines notified under sub-section (3):

Provided that the children's homes and the institutions run by the State Government or a voluntary organisation for children in need of care and protection, who are orphan, abandoned or surrendered, shall ensure that these children are declared free for adoption by the Committee and all such cases shall be referred to the adoption agency in that district for placement of such children in adoption in accordance with the guidelines notified under sub-section (3).";

(*ii*) for sub-section (6), the following sub-section shall be substituted, namely:—

"(6) The court may allow a child to be given in adoption—

(*a*) to a person irrespective of marital status; or

(*b*) to parents to adopt a child of same sex irrespective of the number of living biological sons or daughters; or

(*c*) to childless couples.".

22. Substitution of new section for section 57.—For section 57 of the principal Act, the following section shall be substituted, namely:—

"57. Transfer between children's homes under the act, and juvenile homes of like nature in different parts of India. The State Government may direct any child or the juvenile to be transferred from any children's home or special home within the State to any other children's home, special home or institution of a like nature or to such institutions outside the State in consultation with the concerned State Government and with the prior intimation to the Committee or the Board, as the case may be, and such order shall be deemed to be operative for the competent authority of the area to which the child or the juvenile is sent.".

23. Amendment of section 59.—In section 59 of the principal Act, in sub-section (2), for the words "for maximum seven days", the words "for a period generally not exceeding seven days" shall be substituted.

24. Insertion of new section 62A.—After section 62 of the principal Act, the following section shall be inserted, namely:—

"62A.Constitution of Child Protection Unit responsible for implementation of the Act.—Every State Government shall constitute a Child Protection Unit for the State and, such Units for every District, consisting of such officers and other employees as may be appointed by that Government, to take up matters relating to children in need of care and protection and juveniles in conflict with law with a view to ensure the implementation of this Act including the establishment and maintenance of homes, notification of competent authorities in relation to these children and their rehabilitation and co-ordination with various official and non-official agencies concerned."

25. Amendment of section 64.—In section 64 of the principal Act,—

(*i*) for the words "may direct", the words "shall direct" shall be substituted;

(*ii*) the following proviso and Explanation shall be inserted, namely:—

"Provided that the State Government, or as the case may be the Board, may, for any adequate and special reason to be recorded in writing, review the case of a juvenile in conflict with law undergoing a sentence of imprisonment, who has ceased to be so on or before the commencement of this Act, and pass appropriate order in the interest of such juvenile.

Explanation.—In all cases where a juvenile in conflict with law is undergoing a sentence of imprisonment at any stage on the date of commencement of this Act, his case including the issue of juvenility, shall be deemed to be decided in terms of clause (*l*) of section 2 and other provisions contained in this Act and the rules made thereunder, irrespective of the fact that he ceases to be a juvenile on or before such date and accordingly he shall be sent to the special home or a fit institution, as the case may be, for the remainder of the period of the sentence but such sentence shall not in any case exceed the maximum period provided in section 15 of this Act."

26. Amendment of section 68.—In section 68 of the principal Act,—

(*a*) in sub-section (1), the following proviso shall be inserted, namely:—

"Provided that the Central Government may, frame model rules in respect of all or any of the matters with respect to which the State Government may make rules under this section, and where any such model rules have been framed in respect of any such matter, they shall apply to the State until the rules in respect of that matter is made by the State Government and while making any such rules, so far as is practicable, they conform to such model rules.";

(*b*) in sub-section (2),—

(*i*) in clause (*x*), after the words, letter and brackets "sub-section (2)", the following words, letter and brackets shall be inserted, namely:—

"and the manner of registration of institutions under sub-section (3)";

(*ii*) after clause (*xii*), the following clause shall be inserted, namely:—

"(*xiia*) rehabilitation mechanism to be resorted to in adoption under sub-section (2), notification of guidelines under sub-section (3) and the manner of recognition of specialised adoption agencies under sub-section (4) of section 41;";

(*c*) sub-section (3) shall be re-numbered as sub-section (4) thereof, and before sub-section (4) as so re-numbered, the following sub-section shall be inserted namely:—

"(3) Every rule made by the Central Government under this Act shall be laid, as soon as may be after it is made, before each House of Parliament, while it is in session, for a total period of thirty days which may be comprised in one session or in two or more successive sessions, and if, before the expiry of the session immediately following the session or the successive sessions aforesaid, both Houses agree in making any modification in the rule or both Houses agree that the rule should not be made, the rule shall thereafter have effect only in such modified form or be of no effect, as the case may be; so, however, that any such modification or annulment shall be without prejudice to the validity of anything previously done under that rule.".

— — — — —

Bibliography

Agnelli, S., (1986) *Street Children: A Growing Urban Tragedy*. London: Weidenfeld and Nicolson.

Alexy, Robert, "Individual Rights and Collective Goods," in Carlos Nino, ed., *Rights* (New York: New York University Press, 1992)

Anti-Slavery International (1991) *Children in Bondage: Slaves of the Subcontinent*. London: Anti-Slavery Society.

Anti-Slavery International (1997) *Child Domestic Workers: A Handbook for Research and Action*. London: Anti-Slavery Society.

Applbaum, Arthur Isak. "Are Violations of Rights Ever Right?" *Ethics* vol.108 no.2 (1998): 340-366.

Arnedt, Hannah, *On Revolution* (Harmondsworth: Penguin, 1973)

Arnold, C. "Analyses of Rights," in E. Kamenka and A. E.-S. Tay (eds.), *Human Rights* (London: Edward Arnold, 1978): 74-86

Austin, John. *Lectures on Jurisprudence; or, The Philosophy of Positive Law.* (ed.) Robert Campbell 4 London: J. Murray, 1879.

Baker, Judith. *Group Rights*. Toronto: University of Toronto Press, 1994.

Balton, David A. (1990) The Convention on the Rights of the Child: Prospects for International Enforcement. *Human Rights Quarterly* 12(1):120-130.

Bandman, Bertram (1999) *Children's Right to Freedom, Care, and Enlightenment*. New York: Garland Publishing.

Banerjee, S. (1979) *Child Labor in India*. London: The Anti-Slavery Society.

Banerjee, S. (1980) *Child Labor in Thailand*. London: The Anti-Slavery Society.

Becker, Lawrence, "The Moral Basis of Property Rights," in J. Roland Pennock and John W. Chapman (eds.) *Nomos XXII: Property* (New York: New York University Press, 1980): 187-220.

Becker, Lawrence, "Three Types of Rights," *Georgia Law Review* 13 (1980): 1197-1220.

Becker, Lawrence. "Individual Rights," In *And Justice For All: New Essays on*

Individual Rights and Public Policy (ed.) Tom Regan and Donald Van De Veer New Jersey: Rowman and Littlefield, 1982.

Becker, Lawrence. *Property Rights: Philosophic Foundations.* London: Routledge and Kegan Paul, 1977.

Bedau, Hugo Adam, "Anarchical Fallacies": Bentham's Attack on Human Rights, *Human Rights Quarterly* 22.1 (2000) 261-279

Bedau, Hugo. "The Right to Life." *Monist* 52 (1968): 550-572.

Benditt, Theodore M., *Rights* (Totowa, N.J.: Rowman & Littlefield, 1982)

Benn, Stanley & Peters, R.S. *Social Principles and the Democratic State.* London: Allen and Unwin, 1959.

Bentham, Jeremy, "Anarchical Fallacies," in *II The Works of Jeremy Bentham*, Bowring, ed., (Edinburgh: William Tait, 1843), extracted in Waldron, *Nonsense upon Stilts: Bentham, Burke and Marx on the Rights of Man*

Black, M. (1996) *Children in War.* Reading: Children's Aid Project.

Brandt, Richard B. "The Concept of a Moral Right and Its Function." *Journal of Philosophy* 80 (1983): 29-45.

Brandt, Richard B. "Utilitarianism and Moral Rights." *Canadian Journal of Philosophy* 14 (1984): 1-20.

Brandt, Richard B. *Ethical Theory: The Problems of Normative and Critical Ethics.* Englewood Cliffs: Prentice Hall, 1959.

Bread for the World Institute on Hunger and Development.(1995) *Hunger 1995: Causes of Hunger Fifth Annual Report on the State of World Hunger,* Marc J. Cohen, ed. Silver Spring, Maryland: Bread for the World Institute on Hunger and Development.

Brett, R. And M. McCallin (1996) *Children: The Invisible Soldiers.* Stockholm Vaxjo. Raddo Barnet (Swedish Save the Children).

Brown Jr., Stuart M. "Inalienable Rights." *Philosophical Review* 64 (1955): 192-211.

Brownlie, Ian, ed., *Basic Documents on Human Rights*, 3d ed. (Oxford: Clarendon, 1992)

Buchanan, Allen. "What's So Special About Rights?" *Social Philosophy and Politics* 2 (1984): 61-83.

Burke, Edmund, *Reflections on the Revolution in France* (Harmondsworth: Penguin, 1969)

Byrne, I. (1998) *The Human Rights of Street and Working Children.* London: Intermediate Technology Publications.

Calabresi, G. & Melamed, A.D., "Property Rules, Liability Rules and Inalienability: One View of the Cathedral," 85 *Harvard Law Review* ___ (1972)

Campbell, Tom. *Human Rights: From Rhetoric to Reality*. New York: Blackwell , 1986.

Campbell, Tom. *The Left and Rights: A Conceptual Analysis of the Idea of Socialist Rights*. London: Routledge and Kegan Paul, 1983.

Charvet, John, "A Critique of Human Rights," in Pennock & Chapman, eds., *Human Rights*

Childrens Rights International (1990) *Children Without Childhood: Violations of Children's Rights in Guatemala*. Washington, D.C.: Childrens Rights International.

Cohen, Carl, "Why Racial Preference Is Illegal and Immoral," 67 *Commentary* 40-52 (June, 1979)

Cohen, Cynthia Price and Howard A. Davidson, eds. (1990) *Children's Rights in America: United Nations Conventions on the Rights of the Child Compared with United States Law*. Washington, D.C.: American Bar Association Center for Children in the Law and Defense for Children International.

Cole, S. (1980) *Working Kids on Working*. New York: Lothrop, Lee, and Shepard.

Colson, Elizabeth (1995) War and Domestic Violence. *Cultural Survival Quarterly* 19(1):35-38.

Cooper, John M., "Justice and Rights in Aristotle's *Politics*," 49 *Review of Metaphysics* 859-72 (1996)

Corbin, Arthur L. "Legal Analysis and Terminology." *Yale Law Journal* (1920): 163-173.

Cranston, Maurice William. "Human Rights: A Reply to Prof. Raphael," In *Political Theory and the Rights of Man* (ed.) D.D. Raphael London: MacMillian Press, 1967.

Cranston, Maurice William. *What Are Human Rights*? New York: Basic Books, 1962.

Crawford, James, ed., *The Rights of Peoples* (Oxford: Clarendon, 1992)

Cultural Survival Quarterly (2000) *Rethinking Childhood: Perspectives on Children's Rights*. Cambridge, Massachusetts: Cultural Survival, Inc.

Cutter, Susan (1995) The Forgotten Casualties: Women, Children, and Environmental Change. *Global Environmental Change: Human and Policy Dimensions* 5(3):181-194.

Decew, Judith Wagner. "Moral Rights: Conflicts and Valid Claims." *Philosophical Studies* 54 (1988): 63-86

DeGrazia, David, *Taking Animals Seriously: Mental Life and Moral Status* (Cambridge UP 1996)

Demsetz, Harold, "Toward a Theory of Property Rights," 57 *American Economic Review: Proceedings and Papers* ___ (1967)

Djeddah, C. And P.M. Shah (1996) *The Impact of Armed Conflict on Children: A Threat to Public Health.* Geneva: World Health Organization.

Dodge, C. (1987) *War, Violence, and Children in Uganda.* Oxford: Oxford University Press.

Donnelly, Jack. *The Concept of Human Rights.* New York: St. Martin's Press, 1985.

Dover, K.J., *Greek Popular Morality in the Time of Plato and Aristotle* (Berkeley: University of California Press, 1974)

Downie, R.S. "The Right to Criticize." *Journal of Philosophy* 44 (1969): 116-126.

Dworkin, Ronald . *Taking Rights Seriously* (Harvard, 1977)

Dworkin, Ronald, "Baake's Case: Are Quotas Unfair?" in Dworkin, *A Matter of Principle* 293-303 (Cambridge, Mass.: Harvard, 1985)

Dworkin, Ronald, "Do We Have a Right to Die?" in Ronald Dworkin, *Freedom's Law* 130-46 (Cambridge, Mass.: Harvard, 1996)

Dworkin, Ronald, *Life's Dominion: An Argument about Abortion, Euthanasia, and Individual Freedom* (New York: Knopf, 1993)

Dworkin, Ronald. "Rights as Trumps," collected in Waldron, ed., *Theories of Rights,*

Edmonds, Beverly C. And William R. Fernekes (1996) *Children's Rights: A Handbook.* Santa Barbara, California: ABC Clio.

Eliot, Robert, "Moral Autonomy, Self-Determination and Animal Rights," 70 *Monist* 83-97 (1987)

Elshtain, Jean Bethke. "The dignity of the human person and the idea of human rights: four inquiries." 14 J.L. & Relig. 53-65 (1999-2000).

Ennew, Judith (1986) *The Sexual Exploitation of Children.* Cambridge: Polity Press.

Ennew, Judith (1994) *Street and Working Children: A Guide to Planning.* Development Manual 4. London: Save the Children UK.

Fay, Thomas. "Maritain on Rights and Natural Law." *Thomist* vol.55 no.3 (1991): 439-___

Feinberg, Joel, *Rights, Justice, and the Bounds of Liberty: Essays in Social Philosophy* Princeton: Princeton University Press, 1980

Feinberg, Joel, *The Problem of Abortion* (Belmont, Calif.: Wadsworth, 1973)

Feinberg, Joel. "Comments on Richard Wasserstrom's Rights, Human Rights, and Racial Discrimination'." *Journal of Philosophy* 61 (1964): 641-644.

Feinberg, Joel. "Duties, Rights, and Claims," *American Philosophical Quarterly* 3 (1966): 137-144.

Feinberg, Joel. "Human Duties and Animal Rights." *Etyka* 18 (1980): 11-83.

Feinberg, Joel. "In Defense of Moral Rights: Their Constitutional Relevance" In *Freedom and Fulfillment*, Princeton: Princeton University Press, 1992.

Feinberg, Joel. "Is There a Right to be Born?" in Feinberg, *Rights, Justice, and the Bounds of Liberty*

Feinberg, Joel. "The Moral and Legal Responsibility of the Bad Samaritan." *Criminal Justice Ethics* 3 (1984): 56-68.

Feinberg, Joel. "The Nature and Value of Rights." *Journal of Value Inquiry* 4 (1970): 263-267.

Feinberg, Joel. "The Rights of Animals and Unborn Generations," In *Rights, Justice, and the Bounds of Liberty: Essays in Social Philosophy* Princeton: Princeton University Press, 1980.

Feinberg, Joel. "Voluntary Euthenasia and the Inalienable Right to Life." *Philosophy and Public Affairs* 7 (1978): 93-123.

Feinberg, Joel. *Social Philosophy*. Englewood Cliffs: Prentice-Hall, 1973.

Finnis, John, "The Rights and Wrongs of Abortion: A Reply to Judith Thomson," 2 *Philosophy & Public Affairs* 92 (1978)

Finnis, John. *Natural Law and Natural Rights*. Oxford: Clarendon Press, 1980

Fitch, Frederick B. "A Revision of Hohfeld's Theory of Legal Concepts.". *Logique et Analyse* 10 (1967): 269-276.

Flathman, Richard. *The Practice of Rights*. New York: Cambridge University Press, 1976

Food and Agriculture Organization of the United Nations (1996) *Report on the Study on the Nutritional Impact of Armed Conflict on Children*. Rome: Food and Agriculture Organization of the United Nations.

Fozzard, S. (1995) *Surviving Violence: A Recovery Program for Children and Families*. Geneva: International Catholic child Bureau.

Francione, Gary L., *Rain without Thunder: The Ideology of the Animal Rights Movement* (Philadelphia: Temple University Press, 1996)

Frankena, William K. "Natural and Inalienable Rights." *Philosophical Review* 64 (1955): 212-232.

Franklin, B., ed. (1986) *The Rights of Children*. Oxford: Basil Blackwell.

Freeden, Michael, *Rights* (Open University Press, 1991).

Freeman, Michael (1997) *The Moral Status of Children: Essays on the Rights of the Child*. The Hague, the Netherlands: Martinus Nijhof Publishers.

Frey, Raymond G. *Interests and Rights: The Case Against Animals*. Oxford: Oxford University Press, 1980.

Frey, Raymond G. *Utility and Rights*. Minneapolis: University of Minnesota Press, 1984.

Fried, Charles, "Distributive Justice," 1 *Social Policy and Philosophy* 52 (1983)

Fried, Charles, "Rights and Health Care—Beyond Equity and Efficiency," *New England J. Med.* 293 (31 July 1975)

Fried, Charles. *Right and Wrong*. Cambridge: Harvard University Press, 1978.

Friere, Paulo (1985) *Pedagogy of the Oppressed*. London: Pelican.

Fyfe, Alec (1985) *All Work and No Play: Child Labor Today*. London: Trade Unions Congress.

Fyfe, Alec (1989) *Child Labor*. Cambridge: Policy Press.

Galston, William A. "On the Alleged Right to do Wrong: A Response to Waldron." *Ethics* 93 (1983): 320-324

George, Robert P., *Making Men Moral* [esp. ch. 4, contra Waldron's "Right to Do Wrong"] (Oxford, 1993)

Gewirth, Alan, "Are There Any Absolute Rights?," collected in Waldron, ed., *Theories of Rights*

Gewirth, Alan. "Why Rights are Indispensable," *Mind* 95 (1986): 329-344.

Gewirth, Alan. *Human Rights: Essays on Justification and Applications*. Chicago: University of Chicago Press, 1982.

Gibbard, Allan. "Utility and Human Rights." *Social Philosophy and Policy* 1 (1984):92-
———

Gilligan, Carol, *In a Different Voice* (Cambridge, Mass.: Harvard University Press, 1982)

Glendon, Mary Ann. *Rights Talk: The Impoverishment of Political Discourse*. New York: Free Press, 1991.

Godwin, William, *Enquiry Concerning Political Justice*, K. Codell Carter, ed. (Oxford: Clarendon, 1971)

Golding, Martin P., "Aristotelean Ethics and Natural Rights: a Critique," 18 *Reason Papers* 71-77 (1993)

Golding, Martin P., "Community and Rights," 9 *Bulletin of the Australian Society of Legal Philosophy* 185-96 (1985)

Golding, Martin P., "From Prudence to Rights: A Critique," J.R. Pennock & J.W. Chapman, eds., *Human Rights* 165-74 (New York, 1981)

Golding, Martin P., "Justice and Rights: A Study in Relationship," in E. Shelp, ed., *Justice and Health Care* 23-36 (Dordrecht, 1981)

Golding, Martin P., "Obligations to Future Generations," 56 *The Monist* 85-99 (1972)

Golding, Martin P., "The Concept of Rights: A Historical Sketch," in E. Bandman & B. Bandman, eds., *Bioethics and Human Rights* 44-50 (Boston, 1978)

Golding, Martin P., "The Presuppositions of Rights Discourse," *A.R.S.P.*, 1988, 135-39

Golding, Martin P., "The Primacy of Welfare Rights." *Social Philosophy and Policy* 1 (1984): 119-136.

Golding, Martin P., "The Significance of Rights Discourse," 18 *Philosophical Topics* 53-64 (1990)

Golding, Martin P., "Towards a Theory of Human Rights." *The Monist* 52 (1968): 521-549.

Goodwill-Gill, C. And I. Cohn (1994) *Child Soldiers: The Role of Children in Armed Conflicts*. Oxford: Clarendon Press.

Greaney, Vincent (1985) *Children - Needs and Rights*. New York: Irvington Publishers.

Green, T.H., *Lectures on the Principles of Political Obligation* (Oxford: Clarendon, 1882)

Griffin, James, "Towards a Substantive Theory of Rights," in Frey, ed., *Utility and Rights*

Grimke, A.E. *Appeal to the Christian Women of the South* (New York, Arno Press, 1969)

Gross, Beatrice and Ronald Gross, eds. (1977) *The Children's Rights Movement*. New York: Doubleday (Anchor Books).

Grotius, Hugo. *On the Law of War and Peace,* Francis W. Kelsey, trans. (Oxford: Clarendon, 1925)

Gutmann, Amy, "Communitarian Critics of Liberalisam," 14 *Philosophy & Public Affairs* ___ (1985)

Haksar, Vinit. "The Nature of Rights." *Archiv fuer Rechts- und Soziaphilosophie* 64 (1978): 183-204.

Halpin, Andrew. "Rights and Reasons: A Response to Harel," *Oxford Journal of Legal Studies* 18, no. 3 (Fall 1998): 485-___

Halpin, Andrew. *Rights and Law—Analysis and Theory*, Hart Publishing, 1997.

Hampson, F.J. (1990) *Legal Protection Afforded to Children Under International Humanitarian Law*. Colchester: University of Essex.

Hardin, Garrett, "The Tragedy of the Commons," in Ackerman, ed., *Economic Foundations of Property Law*

Hardin, Russell, "The Utilitarian Logic of Liberalism," 97 *Ethics* 47-74(1986)

Hardwig, John, "Should Women Think in Terms of Rights?" 94 *Ethics* 441-___ (1984)

Hare, R.M., *Moral Thinking: Its Methods, Levels, and Point* (Oxford: Clarendon, 1981)

Harel, Alon, "Revisionist Theories of Rights: An Unwelcome Defense," 11 *Canadian Journal of Law & Jurisprudence* 227-44 (1998)

Harel, Alon, "What Demands Are Rights? An Investigation into the Relation between Rights and Reasons," 17 *Oxford Journal of Legal Studies* 101-___ (1997)

Harre, R. and D.N. Robinson, "On the Primacy of Duties," *Philosophy* 70 (1995): 513-532.

Hart, H.L.A. "Are There Any Natural Rights?" *Philosophical Review* 64 (1955): 175-191, collected in *Theories of Rights*, Waldron, ed.

Hart, H.L.A. "Bentham on Legal Rights," in *Essays on Bentham*

Hart, H.L.A. "Definition and Theory in Jurisprudence." *Law Quarterly Review* 70 (1954): 49-60, collected in *Essays in Jurisprudence and Philosophy* (q.v.)

Hart, H.L.A. "Legal and Moral Obligation," in *Essays in Moral Philosophy* (ed.) A.I. Melden Seattle: University of Washington Press, 1966.

Hart, H.L.A. "The Asciption of Responsibility and Rights." *Proceedings, Aristotelian Society* 49 (1949): 171-194

Hart, H.L.A. *Essays in Jurisprudence and Philosophy*. New York: Clarendon Press, 1983.

Hart, H.L.A. *Essays on Bentham: Studies in Jurisprudence and Political Theory*. Oxford: Clarendon Press, 1982.

Hart, H.L.A., "Between Utility and Rights," in Hart, *Essays in Jurisprudence and Philosophy*

Hartney, Michael, "Some Confusions Concerning Collective Rights," 4 *Canadian Journal of Law and Jurisprudence* 293-314 (1991)

Henkin, Louis, "International Human Rights as 'Rights'," in Pennock & Chapman, *Human Rights*

Hill, Thomas, *Autonomy and Self-Respect* esp. 4-18, 19-24 (Cambridge: Cambridge University Press, 1991)

Hinman, Lawrence N., *Ethics: A Pluralistic Approach to Moral Theory*, 2d ed. (New York: Harcourt, Brace, 1997) (bibliographic essay)

Hitchcock, Robert K. (2002) Globalization, Child Labor, and Children's Rights. *Nebraska Report*, April, 2002, pp. 8, 11. Lincoln, Nebraska: Nebraskans for Peace.

Hobbes, Thomas. *Leviathan*, Richard Tuck, ed. (Cambridge, 1996)

Hodgin, Rachel, Peter Hewell, and UNICEF (1998) *Implementation Handbook for the Convention on the Rights of the Child*. New York: United Nations Childrens Fund.

Hohfeld, Wesley Newcomb, *Fundamental Legal Conceptions as Applied in Judicial Reasoning* (New Haven: Yale University Press, 1919) collecting 23 *Yale Law Journal* 16 (1913) and 26 *Yale Law Journal* 710 (1917)

Holt, J. (1975) *Escape from Childhood*. London: Pelican.

Honore, Tony, "Rights and the Rightless," in *Making Law Bind* (Oxford: Oxford University Press, 1987)

Hudson, Stephen D. & Husak, Douglas N. "Legal Rights: How Useful in Hohfeldian Analysis?" *Philosophical Studies* 37 (1980): 45-53

Human Rights and Equal Opportunity Commission (1997) *Bring Them Home: Separation of Aboriginal and Torres Strait Islander Children from Their Families*. Canberra, Australia: Human Rights and Equal Opportunity Commission.

Human Rights Watch (1997) *The Scars of Death: Children Abducted by the Lord's Resistance Army in Uganda*. New York: Human Rights Watch.

Human Rights Watch (2000) *Fingers to the Bone: United States Failure to Protect Child Farm Workers*. New York: Human Rights Watch.

Human Rights Watch Children's Project (1996) *Children in Combat*. New York: Human Rights Watch.

Hurka, T., "Why Value Autonomy?" 13 Social Theory and Practice 361-82 (1987)

Husak, Donald. "Why There are No Human Rights," in Smith and Blocker, ed. *Applied Social and Political Philosophy*, Prentice Hall, 1994.

Ignatieff, Michael, *The Needs of Strangers* (London: Chatto & Windus, 1984)

Ingram, Attracta. *A Political Theory of Rights*. (Oxford: Clarendon, 1994)

International Labor Organization (1999) *International Labor Organization Convention Concerning the Prohibition and Immediate Action for the Elimination of the Worst Forms of Child Labor*. Geneva: International Labor Organization.

International Save the Children Alliance (1996) *Promoting Psychological Well-being among Children Affected by Armed Conflict and Displacement: Principles and Approaches*. Geneva: International Save the Children Alliance.

Irwin, T.H., "The Good of Each, the Good of All," *Times Literary Supplement* 26 (Aug. 16, 1996) (reviewing Fred D. Miller, Jr., *Nature, Justice, and Rights in Aristotle's "Politics"*)

Jacobs, Lesley A., "The Enabling Model of Rights," 41 Political Studies ___ (1993)

Jacobs, Lesley A., *Rights and Deprivation* (Oxford: Clarendon, 1993)

James, J. And A. Prout, eds. (1990) *Constructing and Reconstructing Childhood*. Philadelphia: Fulmer Press.

Jeffries, Allison, ed. *Women's Voices, Women's Rights: Oxford Amnesty Lectures 1996* (Westview Press, 1998).

Jones, Peter, *Rights* (Macmillan, 1994)

Kadjar-Hamouda, E. (1996) *An End to Silence: A Preliminary Study on Sexual Violence, Abuse, and Exploitation of Children Affected by Armed Conflicts*. Geneva: International Federation Terre des Hommes and Group for the Convention on the Rights of the Child.

Kagan, Shelly, *Normative Ethics* (Boulder, Colo.: Westview, 1998)

Kagan, Shelly, *The Limits of Morality* (Oxford: Clarendon, 1989)

Kamenka, Eugene & Tay, Alice Erh-Soon. *Human Rights*. London: Edward Arnold, 1978.

Kamm, F.M. *Morality, Morality, Vol. II: Rights, Duties and Status*,

Kamm, F.M., "Harming, Not Aiding, and Positive Rights," 15 Philosophy & Public Affairs ___ (1986)

Kanger, Stig & Kanger, Helle. "Rights and Parliamentarism" *Theoria* 32 (1966): 85-115.

Kateb, George, "Democratic Individuality and the Claims of Politics," 12 *Political Theory* ___ (1984)

Kateb, George, "Democratic Individuality and the Meaning of Rights," in Nancy L. Rosenblum, *Liberalism and the Moral Life* 183-206 (Cambridge, Mass.: Harvard University Press, 1989)

Kavka, Gregory S., "Disability and the Right to Work," 9 *Social Philosophy & Policy* ___ (1992)

Kempadoo, Kamala and Jo Doezema, eds. (1998) *Global Sex Workers; Rights, Resistance, and Redefinition*. New York: Routledge.

Kent, George (1995) *Children in the International Political Economy*. Roundmills, Hampshire: Macmillan Press and New York, New York: St. Martin's Press.

Kielburger, Craig and Kevin Major (1998) *Free the Children: A Young Man's Personal Crusade Against Child Labor*. New York: HarperCollins.

Kilbride, Philip, Collette Suda, and Enos Njeru, eds. (2001) *Street Children in Kenya: Voices of Children in Search of a Childhood*. Westport, Connecticut: Praeger.

Kilkelly, Ursula (2001) The Best of Both Worlds for Children's Rights? Interpreting the European Convention on Human Rights in the Light of the UN Convention on the Rights of the Child. *Human Rights Quarterly* 23(2):308-326.

Kramer, Matthew H., Simmonds, N.E., & Steiner, Hillel, *A Debate Over Rights* (Oxford, 1998)

Kuflik, Arthur, "The Utilitarian Logic of Inalienable Rights," 97 *Ethics* 75-87 (1986)

Kymlicka, Will, ed., *The Rights of Minority Cultures* (Oxford: Oxford University Press, 1995)

Kymlicka, Will, *Liberalism, Community, and Culture* 135-61 (Oxford: Clarendon Press, 1989)

Kymlicka, Will, *Multicultural Citizenship: A Liberal Theory of Minority Rights* (Oxford: Oxford University Press, 1996)

Ladenson, Robert F. "Two Kinds of Rights." *Journal of Value Inquiry* 13 (1979): 161-___

Larmore, Charles, "The Moral Basis of Political Liberalism," 96 *Journal of Philosophy* 599-625 (1999)

Lemos, Ramon M. *Rights, Goods, and Democracy*. Newark: University of Delaware Press, 1986.

Leveque, Roger J.R. (1999) *Sexual Abuse of Children: A Human Rights Perspective*. Bloomington: Indiana University Press.

Lindahl, Lars: Position and Change: A Study in Law and Logic, D. Reidel Publishing Company, Dordrecht, 1977.

[Rikard Levin: "Contains a good, informal survey of the British analytical view on rights."]

Locke, John. *The Second Treatise on Civil Government*, Peter Laslett, ed., (Mentor, 1960)

Lomasky, Loren E. *Persons, Rights, and the Moral Community*. Oxford: Oxford University Press, 1987.

Louden, R.B., "Rights Infatuation and the Impoverishment of Moral Theory," 17 *Journal of Value Inquiry* ___ (1983)

Lund, William R. "Politics, Virtue, and the Right To Do Wrong: Assessing the Communitarian Critique of Rights." *Journal of Social Philosophy* vol. 28 no. 3 (1997): 134-___

Lyons, David, "Human Rights and the General Welfare," 6 *Philosophy & Public Affairs* 113-29 (1977)

Lyons, David, "Utility and Rights," collected in Waldron, ed., *Theories of Rights*

Lyons, David. "Rights, Claims, and Beneficiaries." *American Philosophical Quarterly* 6 (1969): 173-185

Lyons, David. "The Correlativity of Rights and Duties." *Nous* 4 (1970): 45-57.

Lyons, David. *Rights, Welfare, and Mill's Moral Theory*. Oxford: University of Oxford Press, 1994.

MacCormick, Neil, "Children's Rights: A Test Case for Theories of Rights," in MacCormick, *Legal Right and Social Democracy*

MacCormick, Neil. "Rights in Legislation," in *Law, Morality, and Society: Essays in Honor of H.L.A. Hart* (eds.) Hacker and Raz Oxford: Clarendon Press, 1979.

MacCormick, Neil. *H.L.A. Hart*. Stanford: Stanford University Press, 1981

MacCormick, Neil. *Legal Right and Social Democracy: Essays in Legal and Poltitical Philosophy*. New York: Clarendon Press, 1982.

Machan, Tibor, "Some Recent Work oin Human Rights Theory," 17 *American Philosophical Quarterly* 103-16 (1980)

Machan, Tibor, *Individuals and Their Rights* (LaSalle, Ill.: Open Court, 1989)

Machel, Graca (1996) *The Impact of Armed Conflict on Children*. New York: United Nations.

Macintyre, Alasdair, *After Virtue* (Notre dame: Notre dame University Press, 1981)

Mackie, J. L., "Can There Be a Right-Based Moral Theory?," collected in Waldron, ed., *Theories of Rights*

Macpherson, C. B., *The Political Theory of Possessive Individualism: Hobbes to Locke* (Oxford: Oxford University Press, 1964)

Malm, H.M., "Killing, Letting Die, and Simple Conflicts," 18 *Philosophy & Public Affairs* ___ (1989)

Mantaphor, Withit and United Nations Center for Human Rights (1996) *Sexual Exploitation of Children*. New York: United Nations.

Marcuse, Herbert, "Repressive Tolerance," in Wolff, R.P., Moore, B., & Marcuse, H., *A Critique of Pure Tolerance* (Boston: Beacon Press, 1971)

Maritain, Jacques, *The Rights of Man* (London, 1944)

Marks., Stephen P., "Emerging Human Rights: A New Generation for the 1980s?," 33 *Rutgers Law Review* 435-52 (1981)

Marshall, Geoffrey. "Rights, Options, and Entitlements," in *Oxford Essays in Jurisprudence 2nd series* (ed.) A.W.B. Simpson Oxford: Clarendon Press, 1978.

Martin, C.B.. "Rules and Powers," *Nous*, 1998 n 12 supp. 283

Martin, Rex & Nickel, James W. "Recent Work on the Concept of Rights." *American Philosophical Quarterly* 17 (1980): 165-180

Martin, Rex. "Human Rights and Civil Rights." *Philosophical Studies* 37 (1980): 391-???.

Martin, Rex. *A System of Rights*. Oxford: Oxford University Press, 1993.

Marx, Karl, "On the Jewish Question," collected in David McLellan, ed., *Karl Marx: Early Texts* (Oxford: Blackwell, 1972)

Mautner, Thomas, "Pufendorf and the Correlativity Theory of Rights," in Sten Lindstrom & Wlodzimierz Rabinowicz, eds., *In So Many Words* 37-57 (Uppsala, 1989)

Mayo, Bernard (?). "Human Rights.", *Proceedings, Aristotelian Society*. 34 (1965)

McCallin, M. (1996) *The Psychological Well-being of Refugee Children: Research, Practice, and Policy Issues*. Geneva: International Catholic Child Bureau.

McCloskey, H.J. "Moral Rights and Animals." *Inquiry* 22 (1979): 23-54.

McCloskey, H.J. "Rights - Some Conceptual Issues." *Australian Journal of Philosophy* 54 (1976): 99-115.

McCloskey, H.J. "The Right to Life." *Mind* 84 (1975): 403-425.

McCloskey, H.J., "Rights," 15 *Philosophical Quarterly* 115-27 (1965)

McConnell, Terrance. "The Nature and Basis of Inalienable Rights." *Law and Philosophy* 3 (1984): 25-60.

McKechnie, J. And S. Hobbs (1998) *Working Children: Reconsidering the Debate*. Amsterdam: International Working Group on Child Labor.

Melden, A. I., *Rights and Persons*. (Berkeley: University of California Press, 1980)

Melden, A. I., *Rights in Moral Lives: A Historical-Philosophical Essay*. Berkeley: University of California Press, 1988.

Meyer, Michael J., & Parent, W.W., eds., *The Constitution of Rights: Human Dignity and American Values* (Ithaca, N.Y.: Cornell University Press, 1992)

Meyers, Diana T. *Inalienable Rights: A Defense*. New York: Columbia University Press, 1985.

Miller, Fred D., Jr., "Aristotle and the Origins of Natural Rights," 49 *Review of Metaphysics* 873-907 (1996)

Miller, Fred D., Jr., *Nature, Justice, and Rights in Aristotle's Politics*. New York: Clarendon Press, 1995. (with bibliography)

Milne, A.J.M. *Human Rights and Human Diversity: An Essay in the Philosophy of Human Rights*. Albany: Suny Press, 1986.

Minority Rights Group International (1997) *War: The Impact on Minority and Indigenous Children*: London: Minority Rights Group International.

Mitsis, Philip, "The Stoic Origin of Natural Rights" from Ierodiakonou, ed., *Topics in Stoic Philosophy* 153-77 (Oxford: Oxfrod U.P.,1999)

Monshipouri, Mahmood (2001) Human Rights and Child Labor in South Asia. Paper presented at the Conference on "Global Human Rights and Diversity:

Area Expressions," University of Nebraska-Lincoln, Lincoln, Nebraska, October 12-13, 2001.

Montague, Phillip. "Regarding Absolute Rights." *Philosophical Studies* 46 (1984): 1 -18.

Montague, Phillip. "Rights and Duties of Compensation." *Philosophy and Public Affairs* 13 (1984): 79-88.

Montague, Phillip. "The Nature of Rights: Some Logical Considerations." *Nous* 19 (1985): 365-377.

Montague, Phillip. "Two Concepts of Rights." *Philosophy and Public Affairs* 9 (1980): 372-384.

Montague, Phillip. "When Rights are Permissibly Infringed." *Philosophical Studies* 53 (1988): 347-366.

Moore, Wayne D. *Constitutional Rights and Powers of the People*. Princeton, N.J.: Princeton University Press, 1996.

Myers, Mary (1994) Women and Children First: Introducing a Gender Strategy Into Disaster Preparedness. *Focus on Gender* 2 (1): 14-16.

Nagel, Thomas. "Personal Rights and Public Space." *Philosophy and Public Affairs* vol.24 no.2 (1995): 83-107.

National Research Council and Institute of Medicine (1998) *Protecting Youth at Work: Health, Safety, and Development of Working Children and Adolescents in the United States*. Washington, D.C.: National Academy Press.

Neilsen, Kai, "Skepticism and Human Rights," 52 *Monist* ___ (1968)

Nelson, William, "Special Rights, General Rights, and Social Justice," 3 *Philosophy & Public Affairs* ___ (1974)

Nelson, William. "On the Alleged Importance of Moral Rights." *Ratio* 18 (1976): 145-155

Nickel, James W. "Are Human Rights Utopian?" *Philosophy and Public Affairs* 11 (1982): 246-264.

Nickel, James W. "Dworkin on the Nature and Consequences of Rights." *Georgia Law Review* 11 (1977): 1115-1142.

Nickel, James W. *Making Sense of Human Rights: Philosophical Reflections on the Universal Declaration of Human Rights*. Berkeley: University of California Press, 1987.

Nielsen, Kai. "Scepticism and Human Rights." *Monist* 52 (1968): 573-594.

Nono, Carlos, *The Ethics of Human Rights* (Oxford: Clarendon Press, 1991)

Nozick, Robert, *Anarchy, State and Utopia* (Basic, 1974)

O'Neill, Onora, "Children's Rights and Children's Lives," 98 *Ethics* 445-63 (1988)

Paine, Thomas, *Rights of Man*, H. Collins, ed. (Harmondsworth: Penguin, 1969)

Parfit, Derek, *Reasons and Persons* (Oxford, 1984)

Peffer, Rodney, "A Defense of Rights to Well-Being," 8 *Philosophy & Public Affairs* 65-87 (1978)

Pennock, J. Roland. *Human Rights: Nomos XXIII* NewYork: New York University Press, 1981.

Perry, Michael J. *The Idea of Human-Rights: Four Inquires* New York: Oxford University Press, 1998.

Perry, Thomas D. "A Paradigm of Philosophy: Hohfeld on Legal Rights." *American Philosophical Quarterly* 14 (1977): 41-50.

Perry, Thomas D. "Reply in Defense of Hohfeld." *Philosophical Studies* 37 (1980): 203-209.

Pettit, Philip, "Rights, Constraints, and Trumps," 47 Analysis 8-13 (1987)

Plamenatz, J. "Rights, Part I." *Aristotelian Society* 24 (1950): 72-82.

Porter, Jean. "From natural law to human rights: or, why rights talk matters." 14 J.L. & Relig. 77-96 (1999-2000).

Purdy, Laura M. (1992) *In Their Best Interest? The Case Against Equal Rights for Children*. Ithaca, New York: Cornell University Press.

Rachels, James, "Do Animals Have a Right to Life?," in H.B. Miller & W.H. Williams, *Ethics and Animals* (Clifton, N.J.: Humana Press, 1983)

Rachels, James, "Why Do Animals Have a Right to Liberty?," in Regan & Singer, eds., *Animal Rights and Human Obligations*

Radin, Max. "A Restatement of Hohfeld." *Harvard Law Review* 51 (1938): 1141-1164.

Raffaelli, Marcela and R.W. Larson, eds. (1999) *Homeless and Working Children Around the World: Exploring Developmental Issues*. San Francisco: Jossey-Bass.

Rainbolt, George, "Rights as Normative Constraints on Others," 53 *Philosophy and Phenomenological Research* ___ (1993)

Raoul Wallenberg Institute of Human Rights and Humanitarian Law (1991) *Children of War: Report from the Conference on Children and War*. Stockholm: Raoul Wallenberg Institute of Human Rights and Humanitarian Law.

Raphael, D.D. "Human Rights, Part I." *Aristotelian Society* 39 (1965): 205-218.

Raphael, D.D. "The Rights of Man and the Rights of the Citizen," In *Political Theory and the Rights of Man* (ed.) Raphael London: MacMillan, 1967.

Rawls, John, "The Law of Peoples," in Stephen Shute & Susan Hurley, eds., *On Human Rights: The Oxford Amnesty Lectures* 41-82, 220-30 (New York: Basic Books, 1993)

Rawls, John, *A Theory of Justice* (Cambridge, Mass., 1971)

Raz, Joseph, "Right-Based Moralities," in Waldron, ed., *Theories of Rights.*

Raz, Joseph. "Hart on Moral Rights and Legal Duties," 4 *Oxford Journal of Legal Studies* 126 (1984)

Raz, Joseph. "On the Nature of Rights." *Mind* 93 (1984): 194-214.

Raz, Joseph. "Prof. Dworkin's Theory of Rights," *Political Studies* 26 (1978): 123-
___

Raz, Joseph. *The Morality of Freedom* Oxford: Oxford University Press, 1986.

Regan, Tom & Singer, Peter, eds., *Animal Rights and Human Obligations* (Englewood Cliffs, N.J.: Prentice Hall, 1976)

Regan, Tom, *The Case for Animal Rights* (Berkeley: University of California Press, 1983)

Reich, Charles, "The New Property," 73 *Yale Law Journal* ___ (1964)

Richard, B.A. "Inalienable Rights: Recent Criticism and Old Doctrine." *Philosophy and Phenomenological Research* 29 (1969): 391-404.

Rigterink, Roger J. *Warning: The Surgeon Moralist Has Determined that Claims of Rights Can be Detrimental to Everyone's Interests.* Bloomington: Indiana University Press, 1992.

Ritchie, D. G., *Natural Rights: A Criticism of Some Political and Ethical Conceptions* (London: Muirhead, 1952)

Robinson, R.E. "The Logic of Rights." *University of Toronto Law Journal* 33 (1983): 267-278

Rodgers, G. And G. Standing, eds. (1981) *Child Work, Poverty, and Underdevelopment.* Geneva: International Labor Organization.

Rodham, Hilary (1974) Children Under the Law. In *The Rights of Children. Harvard Educational Review, Reprint Series,* No. 9:1-28.

Rorty, Richard, "Post-modernist Bourgeois Liberalism," 80 *Journal of Philosophy* ___ (1983)

Rosenblatt, R. (1984) *Children of War.* New York: Anchor Press.

Roshwald, Mordecai. "The Concept of Human Rights." *Philosophy and Phenomenological Research* 19 (1959): 354-379.

Ross, Alf: Tûtû. Harvard Law Review 70(March):812-825, 1957. [Rikard Levin: "Introduces the idea to view concepts like "property" ("property right") as an "intermediary concept"; if certain conditions are fulfilled then x possesses y, and this fact in its turn has a set of consequences."]

Rousseau, Jean-Jacques. *The Basic Political Writings,* Donald A. Cress, trans. (Indianapolis: Hackett, 1987)

Rowlands, Mark. *Animal Rights: A Philosophical Defence* (New York: St. Martin's Press, 1998).

Sadasivam, Bharati (1997) The Impact of Structural Adjustment on Women: A Governance and Human Rights Agenda. *Human Rights Quarterly* 19(3):630-665.

Salmond, John William, *Jurisprudence, or, The Theory of the Law.* London: Stevens and Haynes, 1902.

Sandel, Michael J., "The Procedural Republic and the Unencumbered Self, " 12 *Political Theory* ___ (1984)

Sandel, Michael J., *Liberalism and the Limits of Justice* (Cambridge, 1982)

Sapir, Debarati Guha (1993) Natural and Man-Made Disasters: The Vulnerability of Women-Headed Households and Children Without Families. *World Health Statistics Quarterly* 46: 227-233.

Sarat, Austin & Kearnes, Thomas R., *Legal Rights: Historical and Philosophical Perspectives* (Michigan 1996)

Sarat, Austin & Kearns, Thomas R. *Identities, Politics, and Rights.* Ann Arbor: University of Michigan Press, 1995

Sass, Herbert Ravenel, "Mixed Schools and Mixed Blood," 198 *Atlantic Monthly* 45-49 (Nov., 1956)

Scanlon, T.M. "Rights, Goals, and Fairness." *Erkenntnis* 11 (1977): 81-95, collected in Waldron, ed., *Theories of Rights*

Schauer, Frederick, *Free Speech: A Philospohical Inquiry* 89-92 (Cambridge: Cambridge University Press, 1982)

Scheffler, Samuel, "Natural Rights, Equality, and the Minimal State," 6 *Canadian Journal of Philosophy* 59-76 (1976)

Schiller, Marvin. "Are There Any Inalienable Rights?" *Ethics* 79 (1969): 309-315.

Schneewind, J.B., *Sidgwick's Ethics and Victorian Moral Philosophy* (Oxford: Clarendon, 1977)

Schneewind, J.B., *The Invention of Autonomy: A History of Modern Moral Philosophy* (Cambridge: Cambridge University Press, 1998)

Schofield, Malcolm, "Sharing in the Constitution," 49 *Review of Metaphysics* 831-58 (1996)

Schorsch, A. (1979) *Images of Childhood: An Illustrated Social History*. New York: Main Street Press.

Schwartzman, Helen B. (2001) *Children and Anthropology: Perspectives for the 21st Century*. Westport, Connecticut: Praeger.

Searight, S. (1980) *Child Labor in Spain*. London: Anti-Slavery Society.

Sen, Amartya. "Rights and Agency," *Philosophy and Public Affairs* 11 (1982): 3.-39

Sen, Amartya. *Development as Freedom*, esp. ch. 10 (Knopf, 1999)

Sen, Amartya. *Human Rights and Asian Values* (Carnegie Council on Ethics and International Affairs, 1997)

Sen, Amatya & Williams, Bernard, *Utilitarianism and Beyond* (Cambridge 1980)

Sereny, G. (1984) *The Invisible Children: A Study of Child Prostitution*. London: Andre Deutsch.

Shafer-Landau, Russ. "Specifying Absolute Rights." 37 *Arizona Law Review* 209-25 (1995)

Shah, P. And N. Cantwell, eds. (1985) *Child Labor: A Threat to Health and Development*. Geneva: Defence for Children International (DCI).

Shapiro, Ian, *The Evolution of Rights in Political Theory* (Cambridge: Cambridge University Press, 1986)

Shue, Henry. *Basic Rights: Subsistence, Affluence, and U.S. Foreign Policy*. Princeton: Princeton University Press, 1996

Sidgwick, Henry, *Methods of Ethics* (7th ed., Indianapolis: Hackett, 1981)

Silverstein, Helena, *Unleashing Rights* (Ann Arbor: University of Michigan Press, 1996)

Singer, Marcus G. "The Basis of Rights and Duties." *Philosophical Studies* 23 (1972): 48-57.

Singer, Peter, *Animal Liberation* (Random House, 1975)

Slack, Alison (1988) Female Circumcision: A Critical Appraisal. *Human Rights Quarterly* 19(4):440-488.

Smart, J.J.C. & Williams, Bernard, *Utilitarianism: For and Against* (Cambridge 1973)

Smith, M.B.E., "Rights and Responsibilities." *Criminal Justice Ethics* vol.15 no.1 (1996): ???.

Smith, Tara. "Rights, Wrongs, and Aristotelian Egoism: Illuminating the Rights/ Care Dichotomy." *Journal of Social Philosophy*. Fall 1998 v 29 n 2, p. 5.

Soyinka, Wole, "Every Dictator's Nightmare," *New York Times Magazine* 90-92 (April 18, 1999)

Spector, Horacio, *Autonomy and Rights* (Oxford: Oxford University Press, 1992)

Stalker, Peter, ed. (1995) *States of Disarray: The Social Effects of Globalization*. London: United Nations Research Institute for Social Development.

Steinbock, Bonnie & Norcross, Alastair, eds., *Killing and Letting Die*, 2d ed. (New York: Fordham University Press, 1994)

Steiner, Hillel, *An Essay on Rights* (Blackwell, 1994)

Steiner, Hillel. "The Structure of a Set of Compossible Rights." *Journal of Philosophy* 74 (1977): 767-775.

Stoljar, Samuel. *An Analysis of Rights*. New York: St. Martin Press, 1984.

Stone, Christopher D. "Should Trees Have Standing?—Toward Legal Rights for Natural Objects," 45 *S. Cal. L. Rev.* 450 (1972)

Strauss, Leo, *The Political Philosophy of Hobbes* (Oxford: Oxford University Press, 1936)

Sumner, L.W. *The Moral Foundation of Rights*. (New York: Oxford University Press, 1989)

Tay, Alice Ehr-Soon, "Marxism, Socialism, and Human Rights," in E. Kamenka & Tay, A. E.-S., *Human Rights*

Taylor, Charles. "Atomism," in Kontos, Alkis, ed., *Powers, Possessions, and Freedom* (Toronto: University of Toronto Press, 1979)

Thompson, Judith Jarvis, *The Realm of Rights* (Harvard, 1990)

Thompson, Judith Jarvis. *Rights, Restitution, and Risk*. Cambridge: Harvard University Press, 1986.

Tierney, Brian, "Marsilius on Rights," Journal of the History of Ideas 52:1, pp 3-17

Tierney, Brian, "Tuck on Rights: Some Medieval Problems," 4 *History of Political Thought* 429-41 (1983)

Tierney, Brian, "Villey, Ockham and the Origin of Individual Rights," in John Witte, Jr., & Frank Alexander, The Weightier Matters of Law 1-31 (Atlanta, 1988)

Trakman, Leon, and Gatien, Sean, *Rights and Responsibilities* (Toronto: University of Toronto Press, 1999)

Tribe, Laurence H., *Abortion: The Clash of Absolutes* (New York: W.W. Norton, 1992)

Trubek, David M., "Economic, Social and Cultural Rights in the Third World: Human Rights Law and Human Needs Programs, " in Meron, Theodore, ed., *Human Rights in International Law* (Oxford: Clarendon, 1984)

Tuck, Richard. *Natural Rights Theories: Their Origin and Development*. New York: Cambridge University Press, 1982.

Tushnet, Mark. "An Essay on Rights." *Texas Law Review* 62 (1984): 1363-1403

Unger, Peter, *Living High and Letting Die: Our Illusion of Innocence* (Oxford, 1996)

United Nations (1989) *Convention on the Rights of the Child*. New York: United Nations.

United Nations Center for Human Rights (1996) *The Impact of Armed Conflict on Children: A Survey of Existing Standards and their Relevance and Adequacy*. Geneva: United Nations Center for Human Rights.

United Nations Childrens Fund (various) *The State of the World's Children*. Oxford: Oxford University Press.

United Nations Childrens Fund and World Vision (1998) *Where Is My Home? Children in War*. Kampala, Uganda: Creda Communications.

United Nations High Commissioner for Refugees (1994) *Refugee Children: Guidelines on Protection and Care*. Geneva: UNHCR.

United Nations High Commissioner for Refugees (1995) *Sexual Violence against Refugees: Guidelines on Prevention and Response*. Geneva: UNHCR.

Van De Veer. "Are Human Rights Inalienable?" *Philosophical Studies* 37 (1980): 165-176.

Van Heer, N. (1982) Child Labor and the Development of Capitalist Agriculture in Ghana. *Development and Change* 13:499-514.

Vardin, Patricia A., ed. And Irene N. Brody, eds. (1979) *Children's Rights: A Contemporary Perspective*. New York: Teachers College, Columbia University.

Varner, Gary E. *In Nature's Interests?: Interests, Animal Rights, and Environmental Ethics*. New York: Oxford University Press, 1998.

Villey, Michel, "L'Idee du droit subjectif et les systemes juridiques romains," *Revue historique de droit*, series 4 (1946)

Vincent, R.J., "The Idea of Rights in International Ethics," Terry Nardin & David Mapel, eds., *Traditions of International Ethics* (Cambridge: Cambridge University Press, 1992)

Waldron, Jeremy, "Can Communal Goods Be Human Rights?," in Waldron, *Liberal Rights*.

Waldron, Jeremy, "Galston on Rights," 93 *Ethics* 325-27 (1983)

Waldron, Jeremy, "Mill and the Value of Moral Distress," 35 *Political Studies* ___ (1987)

Waldron, Jeremy, "Theoretical Foundations of Liberalism," collected in Waldron, *Liberal Rights*

Waldron, Jeremy, "When Justice Replaces Affection: The Need for Rights," collected in Waldron, *Liberal Rights*

Waldron, Jeremy, *Liberal Rights: Collected Papers 1981-91* (Cambridge, 1993)

Waldron, Jeremy, *The Right to Private Property* (Oxford, 1988)

Waldron, Jeremy. "Rights in Conflict." *Ethics* 99 (1989): 503-519, collected in Waldron, *Liberal Rights*

Waldron, Jeremy. *Nonsense Upon Stilts: Bentham, Burke, and Marx on the Rights of Man* (London: Methuen, 1987)

Waldron, Jeremy. *Theories of Rights* (Oxford,1984)

Walker, Samuel. *The Rights Revolution: Rights and Community in Modern America.* New York: Oxford University Press, 1998.

Walzer, Michael, *Spheres of Justice* (New York: Basic, 1983)

Wasserstrom, Richard, "The University and the Case for Preferential Treatment," 13 *American Philosophical Quarterly* 165-70 (1976)

Wasserstrom, Richard. "Rights, Human Rights, and Racial Discrimination." *Journal of Philosophy* 61 (1964): 628-640

Wedberg, Anders: Some Problems in the Logical Analysis of Legal Science. Theoria 17:246-275, 1951. [Rikard Levin: "Discusses ideas and problems connecting to those of Ross."]

Weinreb, Lloyd, L., *Oedipus at Fenway Park: What Rights Are and Why There Are Any* (Cambridge, Mass.: Harvard University Press, 1994)

Wellman, Carl, "A New Conception of Human Rights, " in Kamenka & Tay, *Human Rights*

Wellman, Carl, *Real Rights* 105-36 (New York: Oxford University Press, 1995)

Wellman, Carl. *A Theory of Rights: Persons Under Laws, Institutions, and Morals.* : Totowa Rowman and Allanheld, 1985.

Wellman, Carl. *An Approach to Rights: Studies in the Philosophy of Law and Morals.* Dordecht: Kluwer Academic Publishers, 1997.

Wellman, Carl. *The Proliferation of Rights: Moral Progress or Empty Rhetoric?* (Boulder, Colo.:Westview, 1998) (contains bibliographic essays)

Wellman, Carl. *Welfare Rights.* Totowa: Rowan Littlefield, 1982.

Wellman, Christopher, "On Conflicts Between Rights," *Law and Philosophy* 14, nos. 3-4 (November 1995): 271-295.

Westen, Peter. "Comment on Montague's 'Rights and Duties of Compensation'." *Philosophy and Public Affairs* 14 (1985): 385-389.

White, Alan R. *Rights.* Oxford: Clarendon Press, 1984

White, B., ed. (1982) *Child Workers*. Special Issue of *Development and Change*, Vol. 13, No. 4. London: Sage Publications.

Williams, Bernard, "A Critique of Utilitarianism," in B. Williams & A. Sen, eds., *Utilitarianism: For and Against* (Cambridge 1973)

Williams, Wendy W., "Equality's Riddle: Pregnancy and the Equal Treatment/ Special Treatment Debate," 13 *New York University Review of Law and Social Change* 325-80 (1985)

Wise, Steven M. *Rattling the Cage: Toward Legal Rights for Animals*. New York: Perseus, 2000

Wolgast, Elizabeth H., *Equality and the Rights of Women* (Ithaca: Cornell University Press, 1980)

Woods, D., ed. (1990) *Child Soldiers: The Recruitment of Children in Armed Conflicts 1975-1989*. Eureka Springs, Arkansas: Center on War and the Child.

Wright, R. George. "Michael Perry, Peter Singer, and Quasimodo: persons with disabilities and the nature of rights." 14 J.L. & Relig. 113-159 (1999-2000).

Wringe, C.A. *Children's Rights: A Philosophical Study*. Boston: Routledge and K. Paul, 1981.

Wringe, Colin A. (1981) *Children's Rights: A Philosophical Study*. London and Boston: Routledge and Kegan Paul.

Young, Richard A. *Is God a Vegetarian?: Christianity, Vegetarianism, and Animal Rights* (Chicago: Open Court, 1999).

Young, Robert. "Dispensing with Moral Rights." *Political Theory* 6 (1978): 63.

INDEX

N

P

R

S

T

U

W